PA3465 .A2 2007

Broken laughter : se
fragments of Greek
2007.

MW01119811

BROKEN LAUGHTER

Broken Laughter

Select Fragments of Greek Comedy

Edited with Introduction, Commentary, and Translation
S. DOUGLAS OLSON

OXFORD
UNIVERSITY PRESS

OXFORD
UNIVERSITY PRESS

Great Clarendon Street, Oxford OX2 6DP

Oxford University Press is a department of the University of Oxford.
It furthers the University's objective of excellence in research, scholarship,
and education by publishing worldwide in

Oxford New York

Auckland Cape Town Dar es Salaam Hong Kong Karachi
Kuala Lumpur Madrid Melbourne Mexico City Nairobi
New Delhi Shanghai Taipei Toronto

With offices in

Argentina Austria Brazil Chile Czech Republic France Greece
Guatemala Hungary Italy Japan Poland Portugal Singapore
South Korea Switzerland Thailand Turkey Ukraine Vietnam

Oxford is a registered trade mark of Oxford University Press
in the UK and in certain other countries

Published in the United States
by Oxford University Press Inc., New York

British Library Cataloguing in Publication Data
Data available

Library of Congress Cataloging in Publication Data
Data available

Typeset by RefineCatch Limited, Bungay, Suffolk
Printed in Great Britain
on acid-free paper by
Biddles Ltd., King's Lynn, Norfolk

ISBN 978–0–19–928785–7

1 3 5 7 9 10 8 6 4 2

For my beloved friend Alex Sens
(cf. Ar. *Pax* 765–74)

Preface

This volume is intended to make a substantial collection of Greek comic fragments accessible to readers who might otherwise find the size, complexity, and seeming tracklessness of the corpus daunting. I had originally intended to organize the collection chronologically, with Epicharmus followed by Cratinus, followed by Pherecrates, and so forth. But I soon realized that this approach ran the risk of producing a difficult and disjointed book, defeating my own purposes. I have chosen instead to take advantage of one of the most striking characteristics of Attic comedy in particular, the access it grants us to otherwise largely inaccessible aspects of literary, political, intellectual, and social history, and have organized much of the book thematically. Readers who prefer to approach the material in a diachronic manner, by period and poet, can do so with the aid of Sections A–C and Appendix II § A. The themes I have chosen reflect not just the concerns of the comic poets but those of our sources; Athenaeus' interest in anything connected with dinner parties, for example, means that we are disproportionately well informed in this area. But such is the evidence, and I have done my best with it. I have with some regret ignored the large and intriguing question of the relationship between individual Roman comedies and the Greek models from which they appear to have been adapted, on the ground that the fragments shed little specific light on this matter.

In contrast to Arnott's monumental *Alexis*, for example, or my own *Acharnians* or the Austin–Olson *Thesmophoriazusae*, the commentary in this volume is not intended to be exhaustive. Instead, I have attempted to help the reader make his or her way through what is occasionally very difficult material, to bring out some intriguing aspects of the texts, and to offer suggestions for further reading, especially within the corpus of Greek comic poets. I have also generally avoided speculation as to the identity of speakers, larger plot-structures, or the 'theatricality' of what are, in the end, isolated bits and pieces of individual plays about which we know almost nothing else. That further work could profitably be done on all the texts treated here is emphatically true. But my hope is that the reader will take this as a challenge to his or her own ingenuity rather than as a fault of the present edition.

At the urging of the Delegates of the Press, I have included a translation of the fragments as Appendix IV. These translations are occasionally more free than those implied or offered in my notes, and have no great literary merit. I none the less hope that they will be of help and interest for readers with limited Greek, while not too much diminishing the text's value for classroom use.

My text is derived from Kassel–Austin, from whom I none the less diverge at a number of points, generally in minor ways. I would like to thank the Walter de Gruyter Verlag, and Sabine Vogt in particular, for permission to use the K–A text. Wherever possible, I have drawn the information in my critical apparatus from the best available edition of the source author rather than straight from *PCG*. I have also chosen to leave unreported most trivial errors, including places where a single witness offers a reading that cannot be correct or is unlikely to have stood in the exemplar. Readers seeking further information on such matters should consult the Kassel–Austin edition, which stands as one of the great scholarly achievements of our time.

I abbreviate the names of ancient authors as in LSJ, except that I use 'H.' for Homer. For the names of the individual comic poets, I have for the reader's convenience generally adopted K–A's transliterations, including 'Rhinton' for the more common 'Rhinthon'. My numbering of fragments follows Bernabé for epic and the Orphic poems; *PMG*'s continuous numbering for the lyric poets; Voigt for Sappho and Alcaeus; West[2] for elegy and iambus except Hipponax, for whom I cite Degani; Maehler for Pindar; Diels–Kranz[10] for the pre-Socratic philosophers; *TrGF* for tragic poets; *PCG* for the fragments of the comic poets, and Arnott's Loeb for Menander's substantially preserved plays; Olson–Sens for Archestratus and Matro; Gigon for Aristotle; Wehrli for other representatives of Aristotle's school; Fortenbaugh for Theophrastus; Pfeiffer for Callimachus; Austin–Bastianini for Posidippus; Gow for Macho; and *CA* and *SH* for other late classical and Hellenistic poets. For epigrams, I give equivalent numbers in *HE*, *GPh*, or *FGE* wherever possible. I cite Harpocration from Keaney; Hesychius α–ο from Latte; Hesychius π–ς from Hansen; Hesychius τ–ω from Schmidt; Moeris from Hansen; Photius α–μ from Theodoridis; Photius ν–ω from Porson; Pollux from Bethe; the *Suda* from Adler; and the *Synagoge* from Cunningham. Major modern commentaries on poetic texts are cited by the editor's name with no further bibliographic information.

Thanks are due my editor at Oxford University Press, Hilary O'Shea; Ian Storey of Trent University, who read an earlier version of the manuscript for the Press; and a second referee, who chose to remain anonymous. Colin Austin of Trinity Hall, Cambridge, Rudolf Kassel of the University of Cologne, and David Sansone of the University of Illinois at Urbana–Champaign read the entire manuscript in various forms and offered scores of important suggestions and corrections. Portions of the manuscript were also read by Richard Hunter and several of his colleagues at Cambridge University; by Ralph Rosen of the University of Pennsylvania; and by Alexander

Sens of Georgetown University, a warm and generous friend to whom this book is dedicated. Bruce Swann of the Classics Library at the University of Illinois provided invaluable research assistance. Timothy Beck read a penultimate draft of the manuscript with great care, caught many minor errors and infelicities, and offered several important suggestions. Rachel Bruzzone made me laugh, and I hope that she will someday find the joke I have hidden in the commentary especially for her—as well as the one I have (as usual) included for everyone else.

Contents

Abbreviations and Bibliography

AGM	M. L. West, *Ancient Greek Music* (Oxford, 1992)
Amyx	D. A. Amyx, 'The Attic Stelai: Part III', *Hesperia*, 27 (1958), 163–310
APF	J. K. Davies, *Athenian Propertied Families 600–300 BC* (Oxford, 1971)
Beavis	I. C. Beavis, *Insects and Other Invertebrates in Classical Antiquity* (Exeter, 1988)
Bechtel	F. Bechtel, *Die Attischen Frauennamen nach ihrem Systeme dargestellt* (Göttingen, 1902)
Bieber	M. Bieber, *The History of the Greek and Roman Theater* (Princeton, 1961)
Birds	D. W. Thompson, *A Glossary of Greek Birds*² (Oxford, 1936)
Blümner	H. Blümner, *Technologie und Terminologie der Gewerbe und Künste bei Griechen und Römern* (4 vols.: vol. i² Leipzig and Berlin, 1912, vols. ii–iv Leipzig, 1879–87)
Boudreaux	P. Boudreaux, *Le Texte d'Aristophane et ses commentateurs* (Paris, 1949)
Breitholtz	L. Breitholtz, *Die Dorische Farce* (Studia Graeca et Latina Gothoburgensia X: Uppsala, 1960)
Bundrick	S. D. Bundrick, *Music and Image in Classical Athens* (New York, 2005)
CA	See Powell
Cassio	A. C. Cassio, 'The Language of Doric Comedy', in A. Willi (ed.), *The Language of Greek Comedy* (Oxford, 2002) 51–83
Casson	L. Casson, *Ships and Seamanship in the Ancient World* (Baltimore and London, 1971)
CGFPR	C. Austin, *Comicorum Graecorum Fragmenta in Papyris Reperta* (Berlin and New York, 1973)
Cohen	D. Cohen, *Law, Sexuality, and Society* (Cambridge, 1991)
Connor	W. R. Connor, *The New Politicians of Fifth-Century Athens* (Princeton, 1971)
Davidson	J. Davidson, *Courtesans and Fishcakes: The Consuming Passions of Classical Athens* (New York, 1997)
Davies and Kathirithamby	M. Davies and J. Kathirithamby, *Greek Insects* (New York and Oxford, 1986)

Denniston	J. D. Denniston, *The Greek Particles*[2] (revised by K. J. Dover) (Oxford, 1954)
DFA	A. Pickard-Cambridge, *The Dramatic Festivals of Athens*[2] (revised by J. Gould and D. M. Lewis) (Oxford, 1968; reissued with supplement and corrections, 1988)
Dickey	E. Dickey, *Greek Forms of Address from Herodotus to Lucian* (Oxford Classical Monographs: Oxford, 1996)
Dobrov	G. W. Dobrov (ed.), *Beyond Aristophanes* (American Classical Studies 38: Atlanta, 1995)
DTC	A. W. Pickard-Cambridge, *Dithyramb Tragedy and Comedy* (Oxford, 1927)
Ehrenberg	V. Ehrenberg, *The People of Aristophanes: A Sociology of Old Attic Comedy* (London, 1943)
FGE	D. L. Page (ed.), *Further Greek Epigrams* (Cambridge, 1981)
FGrHist	F. Jacoby (ed.), *Die Fragmente der Griechischen Historiker* (Leiden, 1923–69)
Fishes	D. W. Thompson, *A Glossary of Greek Fishes* (St. Andrews University Publications, No. XLV: London, 1947)
Forbes	R. J. Forbes, *Studies in Ancient Technology*[2] (9 vols.: Leiden, 1964)
Fragiadakis	C. Fragiadakis, *Die Attischen Sklavennamen* (Diss. Mannheim, 1986)
Gantz	T. Gantz, *Early Greek Myth* (2 vols.: Baltimore and London, 1993)
García Soler	M. J. García Soler, *El arte de comer en la antigua Grecia* (Madrid, 2001)
Gardiner	E. N. Gardiner, *Athletics of the Ancient World* (Oxford, 1930)
Gildersleeve	B. L. Gildersleeve, *Syntax of Classical Greek* (New York, Cincinnati, and Chicago, 1900; repr. Groningen, 1980)
GM	M. L. West, *Greek Metre* (Oxford, 1982)
GPh	A. S. F. Gow and D. L. Page (eds.), *The Greek Anthology: The Garland of Philip* (Cambridge, 1968)
Goodwin	W. W. Goodwin, *Syntax of the Moods and Tenses of the Greek Verb*[3] (Boston, 1890; reprint New York, 1965)
Harrison	A. R. W. Harrison, *The Law of Athens* (2 vols.: Oxford, 1968, 1971)
Hordern	J. H. Hordern, *Sophron's Mimes* (Oxford, 2004)
HCT	A. W. Gomme, A. Andrewes, and K. J. Dover, *A Historical Commentary on Thucydides* (5 vols.: Oxford, 1945–81)
HE	A. S. F. Gow and D. L. Page (eds.), *The Greek Anthology: Hellenistic Epigrams* (Cambridge, 1965)

IG   *Inscriptiones Graecae*

Inventory   M. H. Hansen and T. H. Nielsen (eds.), *An Inventory of Archaic and Classical Poleis* (Oxford and New York, 2004)

K–A   see *PCG*

KG   R. Kühner, *Ausführliche Grammatik der griechischen Sprache*[3], ii. *Satzlehre* (rev. B. Gerth) (2 vols.: Hanover and Leipzig, 1898, 1904)

Kerkhof   R. Kerkhof, *Dorische Posse, Epicharm und Attische Komödie* (Beiträge zur Altertumskunde 147: Munich and Leipzig, 2001)

Körte (1893)   A. Körte, 'Archäologische Studien zur alten Komödie', *Jahrbuch des Kaiserlich Deutschen archäologischen Instituts* 8 (1893), 61–93

Kraay   C. M. Kraay, *Archaic and Classical Greek Coins* (London, 1976)

Labiano Ilundain   J. M. Labiano Ilundain, *Estudio de las Interjecciones en las Comedias de Aristófanes* (Classical and Byzantine Monographs XLVIII: Amsterdam, 2000)

LGPN   P. M. Fraser and E. Matthews (eds., vols. i, iii. A and B, and iv), M. J. Osborne and S. G. Byrne (eds., vol. ii), *A Lexicon of Greek Personal Names* (Oxford, 1994–)

LIMC   *Lexicon Iconographicum Mythologiae Classicae* (Zurich and Munich, 1981–99)

Lissarrague   F. Lissarrague, *The Aesthetics of the Greek Banquet: Images of Wine and Ritual* (Princeton, 1990; originally published in French in 1987)

López Eire   A. López Eire, *La Lengua coloquial de la Comedia aristofánica* (Murcia, 1996)

LSJ   H. G. Liddell and R. Scott, *A Greek-English Lexicon*[9] (rev. H. S. Jones and R. McKenzie, with revised supplement by P. G. W. Glare) (Oxford, 1996)

Maculate Muse   J. Henderson, *The Maculate Muse: Obscene Language in Attic Comedy*[2] (New York and Oxford, 1991)

Miller   M. C. Miller, *Athens and Persia in the Fifth Century BC: A Study in Cultural Receptivity* (Cambridge, 1997)

Nesselrath   H.-G. Nesselrath, *Die attische Mittlere Komödie: Ihre Stellung in der antiken Literaturkritik und Literaturgeschichte* (Untersuchungen zur antiken Literatur und Geschichte 36: Berlin and New York, 1990)

Olivieri   A. Olivieri, *Frammenti della commedia greca e del mimo nella Sicilia e nella Magna Graecia*[2] (2 vols.: Naples, 1946, 1947)

'Owls to Athens'   E. M. Craik (ed.), *'Owls to Athens'* (Festschrift K. J. Dover: Oxford, 1990)

PA   J. Kirchner, *Prosopographia Attica* (Berlin, 1901–3; reprint Chicago, 1981)

PAA	J. Traill (ed.), *Persons of Ancient Athens* (Toronto, 1994–)
Parke	H. W. Parke, *Festivals of the Athenians* (Aspects of Greek and Roman Life: Ithaca, NY, 1977)
Parker	R. Parker, *Miasma: Pollution and Purification in Early Greek Religion* (Oxford, 1983)
PCG	R. Kassel and C. Austin, *Poetae Comici Graeci* (1983–)
Pfeiffer	R. Pfeiffer, *History of Classical Scholarship from the Beginnings to the End of the Hellenistic Age* (Oxford, 1968)
PMG	D. L. Page (ed.), *Poetae Melici Graeci* (Oxford, 1962)
Powell	I. U. Powell (ed.), *Collectanea Alexandrina* (Oxford, 1925; repr. Chicago, 1981)
Pütz	B. Pütz, *The Symposium and Komos in Aristophanes* (Beiträge zum antiken Drama und seiner Rezeption 22: Stuttgart and Weimar, 2003)
RE	*Real-Encyclopädie der classischen Altertumswissenschaft* (Stuttgart, 1893–1970; Munich, 1972–)
Richter–Milne	G. M. A. Richter and M. J. Milne, *Shapes and Names of Athenian Vases* (New York, 1935)
Rivals	D. Harvey and J. Wilkins (eds.), *The Rivals of Aristophanes: Studies in Athenian Old Comedy* (London, 2000)
SH	H. Lloyd-Jones and P. Parsons (eds.), *Supplementum Hellenisticum* (Texte und Kommentare 11: Berlin and New York, 1983)
Sifakis	G. M. Sifakis, *Parabasis and Animal Choruses* (London, 1971)
Stafford	E. Stafford, *Worshipping Virtues: Personification and the Divine in Ancient Greece* (London, 2000)
Stephanis	I. E. Stephanis, *Διονυσιακοὶ Τεχνῖται* (Herakleion, 1988)
Stevens	P. T. Stevens, *Colloquial Expressions in Euripides* (*Hermes* Einzelschriften 38: Wiesbaden, 1976)
Stone	L. M. Stone, *Costume in Aristophanic Comedy* (New York, 1981)
Storey	I. C. Storey, *Eupolis: Poet of Old Comedy* (Oxford and New York, 2003)
Syll.	W. Dittenberger (ed.), *Sylloge Inscriptionum Graecarum*[3] (Leipzig, 1915–24; reprint Hildesheim, 1960)
Taillardat	J. Taillardat, *Les Images d'Aristophane: Études de langue et de style* (Annales de l'Université de Lyon, iii. Lettres 36: Paris, 1962)
Taplin	O. Taplin, *Comic Angels and Other Approaches to Greek Drama through Vase-Paintings* (Oxford, 1993)
Tessere	A. M. Belardinelli *et al.* (eds.), *Tessere. Frammenti della commedia greca: studi e commenti* (Studi e Commenti 12: Bari, 1998)

Thesleff   H. Thesleff, *Studies on Intensification in Early and Classical Greek*
                 (Societas Scientiarum Fennica, Commentationes humanarum
                 litterarum 21.1: Helsingfors, 1954)

Travlos   J. Travlos, *Pictorial Dictionary of Ancient Athens* (New York and
                 Washington, 1971)

Trendall   A. D. Trendall, *Phlyax Vases*² (*BICS* Suppl. 19: London, 1967)

TrGF   B. Snell *et al.* (eds.), *Tragicorum Graecorum Fragmenta* (Göttingen,
                 1971–)

van Straten   F. T. van Straten, *HIERA KALA: Images of Animal Sacrifice in Archaic
                 and Classical Greece* (Leiden, New York, and Cologne, 1995)

Wachter   R. Wachter, *Non-Attic Greek Vase Inscriptions* (Oxford and New York,
                 2001)

Webster (1948)   T. B. L. Webster, 'South Italian Vases and Attic Drama', *CQ* 42 (1948)
                 15–27

Webster (1970)   T. B. L. Webster, *Studies in Later Greek Comedy*² (Manchester and
                 New York, 1970; reprint Westport, CT., 1981)

Whittaker   M. Whittaker, 'The Comic Fragments in their Relation to the
                 Structure of Old Attic Comedy', *CQ* 29 (1935), 181–91

Wilhelm   A. Wilhelm, *Urkunden dramatischer Aufführungen in Athen* (Sonder-
                 schriften des Oesterreichischen archäologischen Institutes in Wien
                 VI: Vienna, 1906; reprint Amsterdam, 1965)

Wilkins   J. Wilkins, *The Boastful Chef: The Discourse of Food in Ancient Greek
                 Comedy* (Oxford and New York, 2000)

Willi (2002)   A. Willi (ed.), *The Language of Greek Comedy* (Oxford, 2002)

Metrical Notes

These are very basic descriptions of the metres used in the texts presented in this edition. For more complete and authoritative discussion, see West, *GM*.

–   position occupied by a long syllable
∪   position occupied by a short syllable
×   position that may be occupied by either a long or a short syllable
○○ two positions of which at least one must be long

1. Iambic (based on the iambic metron *ia*, × – ∪ –); substitution of ∪∪ for – or ∪ is common, except at the end of the verse
    Iambic dimeter × – ∪ – × – ∪ –
    Iambic dimeter catalectic × – ∪ – × – –
    Iambic trimeter × – ∪ – × – ∪ – × – ∪ –
    Iambic tetrameter catalectic × – ∪ – × – ∪ – × – ∪ – ∪ – –
2. Trochaic (based on the trochaic metron *tr*, – ∪ – ×)
    Trochaic tetrameter catalectic – ∪ – × – ∪ – × – ∪ – × – ∪ ×; substitution
    of ∪∪ for – is common, except in the final foot
3. Anapaestic (based on the anapaestic metron *an*, – ∪ ∪ – ∪ ∪); substitution of ∪∪ for – , and of – for ∪∪, is common
    Anapaestic monometer – ∪ ∪ – ∪ ∪
    Anapaestic dimeter – ∪ ∪ – ∪ ∪ – ∪ ∪ – ∪ ∪
    Anapaestic dimeter catalectic – ∪ ∪ – ∪ ∪ – ∪ ∪ –
    Anapaestic tetrameter catalectic – ∪ ∪ – ∪ ∪ – ∪ ∪ – ∪ ∪ – ∪ ∪ – ∪ ∪ – ∪ ∪ –
4. Dactylic (based on the dactylic metron *da*, – ∪ ∪); substitution of – for ∪∪ is common
    Dactylic Hexameter – ∪ ∪ – ∪ ∪ – ∪ ∪ – ∪ ∪ – ∪ ∪ – –
5. Aeolic and related metres
    Glyconic ○ ○ – ∪ ∪ – ∪ –
    Anaclastic glyconic ○ ○ – × – ∪ ∪ –
    Ithyphallic (*ith*) – ∪ – ∪ – ×
    Lekythion (*lek*) – ∪ – × – ∪ –
    Eupolidean ○ ○ – × – ∪ ∪ – ○ ○ – × – ∪ –
6. Dactylo-epitrite (constructed *inter alia* from the following elements)
    D – ∪ ∪ – ∪ ∪ –
    e – ∪ –

7. Other
    Baccheus (*ba*) – ∪ ∪
    Choriamb (*ch*) – ∪ ∪ –
    Cretic (*cr*) – ∪ –
    Paroemiac (*paroem*) – – – – ∪ ∪ – –

Introduction

Comedies were staged in the Greek city of Syracuse in Sicily perhaps as early as 500 BC and certainly by the mid-480s. In Athens, competitions for comic poets were added to the programme at the City Dionysia in 486 or so and at the Lenaia roughly forty years later.[1] Literary, artistic, and inscriptional evidence shows that these competitions continued until the middle of the second century, by which time Attic comedies were being read, studied, and performed (including in Latin translations and adaptations) throughout the Mediterranean world. But of all the many hundreds of plays written and staged by scores of poets during these centuries, only eleven by Aristophanes (c.450–386) and *The Difficult Man* and *The Girl from Samos* of Menander (c.344–292) survive more or less intact. The rest have either been lost entirely or are preserved in fragments quoted by other ancient authors or on papyrus scraps from Egypt. The monumental Kassel–Austin edition (1983–) of the Greek comic fragments has made a definitive scholarly text of this material available. The corpus is none the less vast and difficult, and this book is intended to make some of the most interesting and important portions of it accessible to a non-specialist audience.

Many fragments of Greek comedy consist of only a word or two quoted out of context, and in very few cases can we say anything significant about the plot of a lost play or even reconstruct a scene.[2] But enough survives to shed substantial light on the evolution and the standard forms and themes of the genre, and thus on the limited number of complete texts we have. The primary purpose of any Athenian comedy was to be amusing and win the prize, and the characters who appeared on stage in them were fictional and often quite exaggerated in their outlook and behaviour. The plays, however, are set

---

[1] For a detailed discussion of the evidence, see Appendix I.

[2] But see **B1–B20**. The papyrus fragments of Menander, which preserve large sections of a number of plays, are the obvious exception. As these fragments are readily accessible in Arnott's Loeb, I have made limited use of them in this edition.

in and comment on a world intended to be immediately recognizable to their audiences, and the fragments thus represent one of our most important sources of information about contemporary literary, political, and social life.[3]

THE ORIGINS OF ATTIC COMEDY: PRELIMINARY REMARKS

According to Aristotle (384–322 BC) in the *Poetics*, the origins of comedy are to be traced to iambic (abuse) poetry and 'those who lead forth the phallic processions' (τῶν ἐξαρχόντων τὰ φαλλικά) (1449ᵃ4–5, 11–12). Aristotle also notes that comedy was not taken seriously in Attica as early as tragedy was, and was accordingly awarded a chorus by the eponymous archon (sc. for performances at the City Dionysia) somewhat later, and that as a result of this relative degree of disinterest, the names of the poets who added prologues, fixed the number of actors, and the like were obscure already by his time (1449ᵃ38–ᵇ5). In addition, Aristotle observes elsewhere in the *Poetics* that the Megarians maintained that they rather than the Athenians had invented comedy, with the Megarians from the Greek mainland claiming that this happened at a time when their city was a democracy (i.e. sometime after the beginning of the sixth century), while the Megarians from Sicily pointed to Epicharmus, whom Aristotle (perhaps simply quoting the Megarians) calls 'much earlier than' the early Athenian comic poets Chionides and Magnes (1448ᵃ28–34)—who in fact seem to have been Epicharmus' rough contemporaries (see below). So too in his discussion of what little he knows about the early history of the genre, Aristotle states in a matter-of-fact way that the Athenian playwright Crates (who dates to the middle of the fifth century, although whether Aristotle thought he belonged so late is unclear; see below) introduced 'plots and stories of general interest' under the influence of Sicilian comedy (1449ᵇ5–9).

Aristotle is open about his lack of substantial documentary sources for the early history of comedy (1449ᵇ4–5); and his failure to name any first-generation poets other than Chionides and Magnes and apparent confusion about the dates of Epicharmus (and perhaps Crates) reinforce this. His

---

[3] The most famous systematic attempt to read what survives of Attic comedy as a source of social and political history is Ehrenberg (although his attention was largely confined to the 'Old Comic' poets). The latter portions of this book in particular might profitably be understood as in some ways an inside-out version of Ehrenberg (cf. Ar. *Nu.* 553–4).

remarks about iambic poetry and phallic processions may therefore be speculative. But Aristotle was also much more widely read in Athenian dramatic
literature than we have any chance of being, and his apparent conviction that
comedy derived from choral performances, but that the Megarian claim to
have invented the genre deserved airing (if not explicit support), must be
taken seriously.

The name κωμῳδία, which recalls τραγῳδία while indicating a fundamental affiliation with the κῶμος ('drunken revelling-band'; see **H18**. 8 n.),
strongly suggests that one original component of Attic comedy was choral.[4]
This thesis finds further support in the presence in many (perhaps all) fifth-
century comedies of a parabasis, an extended central choral section addressed
at least in part directly to the audience, which is performed while the actors
are off stage and has a complex, fixed form (see below). Comedy probably
borrowed many basic structural elements, including the prologue and the
parodos, direct from tragedy, whose origins must also be traced at least
in part to archaic choral performances (Arist. *Po.* 1449ᵃ10–11). But there is
no tragic parabasis, and the obvious conclusion is that this is the ossified
remains of an early—most likely distinctly Attic—performance tradition that
evolved directly into comedy. That a further connection exists between such
proto-comic choral performances and a series of mid-sixth-century Attic
vases that portray groups of men dressed in fantastic costumes has been
argued, but is incapable of proof.[5] The source of the non-choral elements in
Attic comedy is even more problematic, although Aristotle's comments again
point the way.

Little can be said about Megarian comedy except that the Athenians knew
of its existence in the fifth century (see **A22** with introductory n.).[6] But
comedies and mimes (brief dramatic representations of scenes from real
life, with the dialogue in prose rather than metre) were staged in Syracuse
probably by the 480s if not earlier (see below); and Körte, followed by many
others, argued that the inspiration for the non-choral sections of Attic

---

[4] Cf. the late 5th-c. comic term τρυγῳδία (e.g. Ar. *Ach.* 499 with Olson ad loc.; cf. Eup.
fr. 99. 29), which puns on τραγῳδία while making it clear, via a reference to τρύξ ('new wine'
or 'wine-lees'), that κωμῳδία was understood to derive from κῶμος rather than κώμη
('village'), as the Megarians claimed (Arist. *Po.* 1448ᵃ35–8). Another ancient etymology
connected the word (improbably) with κῶμα ('deep sleep') (e.g. *de Com.* IV. 17–19).

[5] The thesis was originally advanced by J. Poppelreuter, *De comoediae atticae primordiis
particulae duae* (Diss. Berlin, 1893); cf. *DTC* 244–51. For further bibliography, discussion, and
plates, see Sifakis 15–20, 73–85 (deeply suspicious of the argument).

[6] For Megarian comedy, see in general Körte, *RE* 11 (1921), 1221–2; *DTC* 273–80; Breitholtz
31–82, esp. 34–74; Kerkhof 13–38, esp. 17–24.

comedy must have come from a widespread tradition of Doric farce.[7] The most substantial literary evidence for the existence of such a tradition is the fragment of the antiquarian historian Sosibius of Sparta (*FGrHist* 595 F *7 = com. dor. test. 2) preserved at Athenaeus 14. 621d–f:

παρὰ δὲ Λακεδαιμονίοις κωμικῆς παιδιᾶς ἦν τις τρόπος παλαιός, ὥς φησι Σωσίβιος, οὐκ ἄγαν σπουδαῖος, ἅτε δὴ κἀν τούτοις τὸ λιτὸν τῆς Σπάρτης μεταδιωκούσης. ἐμιμεῖτο γάρ τις ἐν εὐτελεῖ τῇ λέξει κλέπτοντάς τινας ὀπώραν ἢ ξενικὸν ἰατρὸν τοιαυτὶ λέγοντα, ὡς Ἄλεξις ἐν Μανδραγοριζομένῃ διὰ τούτων παρίστησιν· (Alex. fr. 146) . . . ἐκαλοῦντο δ᾿ οἱ μετιόντες τὴν τοιαύτην παιδιὰν παρὰ τοῖς Λάκωσι δεικηλισταί, ὡς ἄν τις σκευοποιοὺς εἴπῃ καὶ μιμητάς. τοῦ δὲ εἴδους τῶν δεικηλιστῶν πολλαὶ κατὰ τόπους εἰσὶ προσηγορίαι. Σικυώνιοι μὲν γὰρ φαλλοφόρους αὐτοὺς καλοῦσιν, ἄλλοι δ᾿ αὐτοκαβδάλους, οἱ δὲ φλύακας, ὡς Ἰταλοί, σοφιστὰς δὲ οἱ πολλοί· Θηβαῖοι δὲ καὶ τὰ πολλὰ ἰδίως ὀνομάζειν εἰωθότες ἐθελοντάς.

Among the Spartans there was an old type of comic entertainment, according to Sosibius, (which was) not particularly respectable, since Sparta pursued simplicity even in matters of this sort. For someone would use unrefined language to imitate people stealing fruit or a foreign doctor saying the types of things Alexis presents in his *The Woman Who Ate Mandrake*: [Alex. fr. 146 follows]. They used to call those who practised this form of entertainment among the Spartans *deikelistai*, which is to say 'tricksters' or 'mimes'. There are many terms for *deikelistai* of this type in different places: the Sicyonians call them 'phallus-bearers'; others call them 'improvisers'; some call them *phlyakes*, as the Italians do; and many call them 'sophists'. But the Thebans, who are generally accustomed to use their own names for things, call them 'volunteers'.

The performances by Spartan δεικηλισταί (presumably cognate with δείκ-νυμι) described by Sosibius are clearly mimes not unlike those composed by Sophron of Syracuse early in the fifth century (see below); the Italian φλύακες have sometimes been associated with the performances of mythological parodies, domestic farces, and the like depicted on an extensive series of fourth-century South Italian vases (see below); the Sicyonian φαλλοφόροι are reminiscent of Aristotle's reference to 'those who lead forth τὰ φαλλικά' (*Po.* 1449ᵃ11–12), while the claim that the Thebans called such performers ἐθελονταί recalls his observation that before comedy was granted a state-funded chorus in Attica, the part was taken by volunteers (ἐθελονταὶ ἦσαν, *Po.* 1449ᵇ2); and Körte (above) noted that a number of Corinthian vases from

---

[7] Körte (1893), esp. 89–93; *RE* 11 (1921), 1251–2. For restatements of and variations on the thesis, e.g. U. von Wilamowitz-Moellendorff (ed.), *Aristophanes: Lysistrate* (Berlin, 1927), 8–15; *DTC* 253–73; Pohlenz, *Nachrichten von der Akademie der Wissenschaften in Göttingen*, Philologisch-Historische Klasse (1949), 31–44. For a sceptical response, see *Maculate Muse*, 223–8.

the early sixth century depict dancers whose oddly shaped bellies and rumps are strikingly reminiscent of the padded costumes worn by fifth- and early fourth-century Athenian comic actors, as well as by the characters on the '*phlyax*-vases'.[8] Pickard-Cambridge, finally, observed that the excavations at the sanctuary of Artemis Orthia in Sparta uncovered a large number of mostly sixth-century terracotta models of what might easily be taken to be theatrical masks, and suggested that some of these recall 'Old Comic' character types and thus represent a further link between Doric mime and Attic comedy.[9] The second halves of Aristophanic comedies typically consist of a series of visits by characters who arrive unexpectedly on stage, interact briefly with the hero, and disappear, while the chorus stay almost entirely out of the action; and Poppelreuter accordingly argued that the disjointed nature of this portion of the action reflects its origins in Doric farce, with which the (fundamentally Attic) chorus not surprisingly has little to do. Most of these arguments fail to stand up to closer scrutiny.

Sosibius dates to the middle of the third century at the earliest, and although he describes the tradition represented by the Spartan δεικηλισταί as 'old', it is impossible to know exactly what this means. The Italian φλύακες, at any rate, belong to the end of the fourth century and appear to have nothing to do with the '*phlyax*-vases', which probably depict revivals of Athenian comedies in the Greek West (see the discussion below); and the other performance traditions to which Sosibius refers are all purely choral, and have little or nothing in common with one another, as the more detailed treatment of some of them by Semus of Delos (*FGrHist* 396 F 24) that follows in Athenaeus makes clear. Indeed, although little of Sosibius' work is preserved, none of the other fragments explains Spartan customs by reference to practices elsewhere, and the randomly agglutinative style of the passage is instead characteristic of Athenaeus (who was working at the very end of the second century AD and certainly added the fragment of Alexis). The long list of other types of performers to whom the Spartan δεικηλισταί are allegedly similar is thus most likely Athenaeus' composition, in which case the passage is worthless as evidence for preclassical Doric mime.[10]

---

[8] For the vases, see H. Payne, *Necrocorinthia* (Oxford, 1931), 118–24, with further bibliography; and cf. Breitholtz 128–9, 136–63. The early 6th-c. Corinthian 'Dümmler crater' (illustrated at Bieber fig. 132; Breitholtz fig. 9–10) is sometimes taken to depict scenes from a Doric farce, but its interpretation is complicated and controversial, and no larger argument ought to be built upon it. Cf. Charlotte Fränkel, *RhM* NF 67 (1912), 94–106; *DTC* 263–4; Breitholtz 163–81; Kerkhof 24–30.

[9] *DTC* 253–61. For the original material, see G. Dickins in R. M. Dawkins, *The Sanctuary of Artemis Orthia* (London, 1929), 163–86, esp. 163–76.

[10] See Breitholtz 114–22.

As for the masks found in the sanctuary of Artemis Orthia, they are not themselves theatrical, for most are too small to be worn and many lack mouth- and nose-holes; they must instead be votive offerings that recall larger originals made of wood or fabric. But even if that is true, nothing suggests a connection with mime rather than masked cultic rituals, dances, or the like, as the original excavators suggest.[11] The argument for a relationship between Attic comedy and the Corinthian 'padded dancers' is more compelling, and the evidence might be taken to suggest that the performance tradition these dancers represent made its way to Attica in the middle of the sixth century, when similar figures appear on Athenian vases in what can reasonably be assumed to be a formative period for the genre. Even so, other forces must also have come into play as well before similar figures appeared on stage in comedy (or proto-comedy), for comic actors wear large theatrical phalluses, as the 'padded dancers'—who are in any case only dancers—do not.[12] The relationship between padded dancers and comic actors might therefore be indirect rather than direct, and is certainly more complex than a simple Athenian borrowing of a Corinthian performance genre. There is thus little evidence for the existence of a widespread late archaic tradition of Doric mime. But comedies and mimes were certainly staged in Syracuse near the beginning of the fifth century, and here a better case can be made for a connection.

COMEDY AND RELATED GENRES IN THE WEST: THE FIFTH CENTURY

The ancient sources disagree on where Epicharmus was from, but consistently associate his dramatic career with the powerful city of Syracuse. As noted above, Aristotle dates Epicharmus to 'well before' Chionides and Magnes, and some late authors claim that he associated with or was a student of Pythagoras (Epich. test. 9; 11–13), who is supposed to have arrived in Croton on the southern coast of Italy in 530. But other sources are more precise and place Epicharmus a generation or so later: the Marmor Parium (*FGrHist* 239 A 55 = test. 7) puts him in 472/1 and associates him with Hieron, tyrant of Syracuse 478–466, who surrounded himself with poets including Aeschylus, Pindar, Simonides, and Bacchylides; the *Suda* (ε 2766 = test. 1. 6–7) claims

---

[11] See Dickins in Dawkins (above n. 9) 174–6; Breitholtz 101–14.

[12] For the stage-phallus as a standard part of the comic actor's costume in the 5th and early 4th centuries, see Körte (1893), 61–9; Stone 72–105.

that he produced plays in 486/5 or 485/4, a date that is most likely in origin a *floruit*; and the anonymous Byzantine *On Comedy* III (= test. 6a. 7) assigns him to the 73rd Olympiad, i.e. 488–484, probably another *floruit*. Internal evidence is limited but supports the same range of dates: fr. 96 refers to events that occurred between 478/7 and 476/5 (see below), while fr. 221 reports that Epicharmus mocked Aeschylus, something most naturally understood as a reaction to the tragedian's visit to Sicily around 470 (A. test. 1. 33–6; 56a; cf. below). There can thus be little doubt that Epicharmus was at the height of his fame in the 480s and 470s, although Aristotle's date can be preserved if one assumes that the poet began composing as a young man before the turn of the century. A number of late sources report that he lived to be at least 90 (D.L. 8. 78 = test. 9. 13–14, with K–A ad loc.).

The *Suda* claims that Epicharmus wrote 52 plays, although a certain Lycon (not securely identified) assigned him only 35 (ϵ 2766 = test. 1. 4). The anonymous *On Comedy* III (test. 6a. 8), presumably drawing on Hellenistic sources, says that 40 of his plays were preserved, i.e. in Alexandria, but that the authenticity of four of them was disputed, leaving 36 undisputed plays, very close to Lycon's count. At least 47 titles and 239 authentic fragments survive; that the plays from which they come were intended as contest-pieces cannot be taken for granted and is nowhere even hinted at before the Roman period. The fragments consist mostly of iambic trimeter (e.g. **A1**; **A9–A11**; **A13**) and trochaic tetrameter catalectic (e.g. **A2–A7**; **A12**; **A14–A17**).[13] But frr. 110 and 114 are anapaestic tetrameter catalectic, **A8** is anapaestic dimeter, and frr. 113. 415 (Homeric parody), *121, and 224 are dactylic hexameter. Many individual plays appear to have contained a mix of metres (hence Hephaestion's interest in noting that *The Victor* and *Dancers* consisted entirely of anapaestic tetrameters catalectic; *Ench.* 8. 2); thus iambic trimeter and trochaic tetrameter catalectic were both used in *Amycus* (frr. 6 and 7, respectively) and *Sphinx* (frr. 126 and 125, respectively); trochaic tetrameter catalectic, anapaestic tetrameter catalectic, and iambic trimeter were all used in *Pyrrha and Promatheus* (frr. 113, 114, and 115, respectively); and dactylic hexameter and trochaic tetrameter catalectic were used in *Sirens* (frr. 121 and 122, respectively). No Epicharmean lyric is preserved, even in fr. 113, which contains tattered scraps of over 500 lines from *Pyrrha and Promatheus* and most likely other plays as well, and the implication is that there was none. The fragmentary state of the evidence and the fact that almost all other fifth-century West Greek literature has been lost makes it difficult to draw firm conclusions about Epicharmus' language. The dialect appears to be a type of

---

[13] The only surviving line of Dinolochus (for whom, see below) is also trochaic tetrameter catalectic (fr. 4).

Doric closely related to Corinthian, with an admixture of Rhodian and Italic (cf. **G8**. 3–4 n.) words and forms.[14]

Over half the preserved titles of Epicharmus' plays are mythological;[15] and the same is true of his contemporary Phormus/Phormis (all six preserved titles mythological), about whom we know almost nothing else, and of Dinolochus (ten of twelve preserved titles mythological), who is variously described as Epicharmus' son, pupil, and rival (Dinol. test. 1–2), and whose work has otherwise perished almost entirely. But other Epicharmean titles[16] are not so easily pigeonholed and seem to hint at a different type of story, which turned on the foibles of everyday characters like the parasite who speaks in **A13** (from *Hope or Wealth*) or the unsophisticated man introduced to the pleasures and dangers of the symposium in **A14–A15**. According to Σ^DEFGQ Pi. *P.* 1. 99a (= Epich. fr. 96), mention was made in *Islands* of the fact that Hieron prevented Anaxilaus, the tyrant of Rhegium, from attacking Epizephyrian Locris sometime between 478/7 and 476/5. This may have been nothing more, however, than a passing allusion designed to flatter Epicharmus' patron (cf. **A7**. 2 n.), and the only other evidence that his comedies had overt political content is the title *Persians*, which is more plausibly explained as a parody of the homonymous Aeschylean tragedy performed in Syracuse when the Athenian poet visited there (A. test. 56a; and see above). A few plays have alternative titles: *Hope or Wealth* (with frr. 33–4 cited simply from *Hope*); *Revellers or Hephaestus* (with frr. 73 and 75 cited simply from *Revellers*); and *Pyrrha and/or Promatheus* or *Deucalion* or *Leucarion* (cited under a variety of titles; see K–A's initial n.). Some of these are perhaps to be explained as evidence of partial rewriting and re-performance, as was certainly the case with *Muses*, which Athenaeus 3. 110b tells us was a revised version (διασκευή) of *The Wedding of Hebe* (= test. ii) and which accordingly shared a substantial number of verses with it (cf. frr. 41. 2; 45; 46).[17]

According to Aristotle (*Po.* 1449^b5–7 = Epich. test. 5), the Sicilian poets' great contribution was to introduce μῦθοι ('stories') into comedy; whatever one makes of this, the implication—amply supported by the fragments—is

[14] See Cassio, esp. 53–5, 66–9, with further bibliography.

[15] e.g., in addition to the Heracles-plays listed in **A1** introductory n. and the Odysseus-plays listed in **A6–A11** n., *Antanor, Bacchants, Revellers or Hephaestus, Medea, Pyrrha and Promatheus or Deucalion or Leucarion, Sciron,* and *The Sphinx*.

[16] e.g. *The Rustic, The Old Woman, The Victor,* and *The Megarian Woman.* Cf. Dinolochus' *The Doctor.*

[17] Note also that the catalogue of Epicharmus' plays partially preserved in POxy. xxxiii 2659 fr. 2 col. ii. 9 (= test. 36; 2nd c. AD) appears to know two plays entitled Ἁρπαγαί, Διόνυσο[, and Ἐπινικ[. That Βάκχαι is missing from the catalogue may mean either that the second Ἁρπαγαί (which is out of place) is an error or that the individual who compiled the catalogue considered Βάκχαι an alternative title for another play (one of the two Dionysus plays?).

that the plays of Epicharmus, Phormus, and their contemporaries and successors (if any) were based on a connected plotline and were not simply strings of jokes and attacks on individuals (presumably = the ἰαμβικὴ ἰδέα Crates is supposed to have abandoned under Sicilian influence). A number of the fragments feature two speakers (e.g. **A6**; **A14–A15**), but none requires three (see K–A on fr. 6), and there are numerous traces of messenger speeches or the like (e.g. **A1–A5**). The only evidence for a chorus is plural titles such as *Atlantas, Bacchants*, and *Revellers*, which might be explained in other ways,[18] and one fragment of anapaestic dimeter which might but need not be choral (**A8** with introductory n.). Although props must have been used (e.g. **A11**; **A14**. 1), nothing else is known about Epicharmus' staging and no standard plot-structure can be reconstructed. But much of the interest in Sicilian comedy may well have been verbal rather than visual, for the fragments are full of puns and witty asides (e.g. **A2**. 3; **A3**. 4; **A14**) and allusions to earlier poets (see **A4–A5** n.), especially Homer, with whose works the audience is assumed to be intimately familiar (see **A6–A11** n.; **A6** introductory n.). That the plays were generally only a few hundred lines long is possible, for the late Hellenistic scholar Apollodorus is supposed to have divided them into ten τόμοι ('papyrus rolls'; test. 34. 3–4), which would mean four or five plays per roll and (if the length of ancient poetic 'books' is any indication of the maximum size of a papyrus roll) suggests an average of no more than 300–400 lines apiece.

Epicharmus' comedies seem to have contained a substantial amount of sententious material (cf. **A16–A17**), and by the fourth century he had come to be identified as the author of a group of didactic trochaic tetrameter catalectic treatises (known collectively today as the *Pseudepicharmeia*), including the Πολιτεία (frr. 240–3; see Kerkhof 112–15), the Γνῶμαι (frr. 244–73; see **A18–A19** with nn.), the almost entirely obscure Κανών (fr. *274; perhaps concerned with the interpretation of dreams, see Kerkhof 105–8), and the Χείρων, probably referred to also as the Ὀψοποιία (frr. 289–95; most likely on medicine, see Kerkhof 108–11). These treatises are written in a very different dialect from the comedies, although they contain a few Doric forms; most of those known in the third century AD contained acrostics (D.L. 8. 78 = test. 9. 11–13), which identifies them as products of the Hellenistic age; and that they were forgeries was recognized already in antiquity (thus Ath. 14. 648d, citing Aristoxen. fr. 45; Philoch. *FGrHist* 328 F 79; Apollod. *FGrHist* 244 F 226). In addition, Diogenes Laertius 3. 9–16 preserves five fragments (two in trochaic tetrameter catalectic, the others in iambic trimeter) supposedly from Epicharmus quoted by the late fourth-century(?) Sicilian

---

[18] See Kerkhof 151–5.

historian Alcimus (*FGrHist* 560 F 6), who offered them in his πρὸς Ἀμύνταν as evidence that Plato stole important elements of his philosophy from the Syracusan comic poet (= Epich. frr. 275–9, to which D.L. 3. 17 has added fr. 280 (trochaic tetrameter catalectic) from a different source). Metrical and linguistic evidence leaves no doubt that the Alcimus fragments too are forgeries, which are dependent on Plato rather than the other way around, although the language is more reminiscent of the real Epicharmus than is that of the other pseudonymous material discussed above; and the mix of metres suggests that Alcimus' source or sources represent a unique strand of the Pseudepicharmic tradition.[19] The early Roman poet Ennius (third/ second century), finally, appears to have drawn on a cosmological work attributed to Epicharmus (cf. D.L. 8. 78 = test. 9. 11 (of Epicharmus) ὑπο- μνήματα καταλέλοιπεν ἐν οἷς φυσιολογεῖ), whose name served as the title of Ennius' poem (Epich. frr. 281–8, with four of the eight fragments dubiously attributed). This work—another forgery—is of interest mainly because Wilamowitz insisted that it may have been known in Athens already in the fifth century (see below).

Aristotle (*Po.* 1449b5–9 = Epich. test. 5) asserts that the type of comedy he associates earlier in the *Poetics* with Epicharmus and Phormus 'came from Sicily' to Attica in time to influence Crates in the middle of the fifth century.[20] If true, this is a precious bit of information about the relationship between the two traditions, and Epicharmus and the plays and poems attributed to him are certainly referred to a number of times in fourth-century Attic sources: aside from Aristotle (who, in addition to the references noted above, quotes several verses most likely from the Γνῶμαι at *Rh.* 1394b11–25 (frr. 250–1)), Plato apparently alludes to the action in one of the comedies at *Tht.* 152d–e (= fr. 136); Xenophon's Socrates quotes Epicharmus twice at *Mem.* ii. 1. 20 (= frr. 236 (probably from an unidentified comedy); 271 (probably from the Γνῶμαι)); and one of Alexis' characters claims to have a copy of some of his works (**G3.** 6, where see n.; probably one of the *Pseud-epicharmeia*). But although echoes of Epicharmus have occasionally been detected in Old Comedy,[21] at none of these points is direct or indirect knowledge of Sicilian comedy required to explain what are more easily taken as obvious simple jokes or social commonplaces.[22] In the case of tragedy,

---

[19] See Kerkhof 65–78.   [20] For Crates' dates, see below.

[21] Thus most famously a student of Körte's, A. von Salis, *De Doriensium ludorum in comoedia Attica vestigiis* (Diss. Basel, 1905), followed by Cassio, *HSCP* 89 (1985), 39–43. The passages generally cited are Ar. *V.* 1252–5 (cf. **A15** with n.); *Pax* 73 (cf. Epich. fr. 65 (thus already Σᵛ)); 185–7 (cf. Epich. fr. 123 (thus already Σᵛ)); frr. 545 (cf. Epich. fr. 147); 636 (cf. Epich. fr. 113. 243); Stratt. fr. 63 (cf. Epich. fr. 76). For a brief history of the question, see Breitholtz 27–9.

[22] See Kerkhof 144–50, 162–73, with further bibliography.

Wilamowitz (followed by Kaibel) argued that Euripides alludes several times to the pseudonymous Epicharmean cosmological poem also known to Ennius (see above).[23] His arguments too, however, fail to hold up to close examination; see **A16–A17** n. Aeschylus probably met Epicharmus when he visited Sicily, and might easily have brought copies of the plays back to Athens; and the Athenians were in constant commercial, political, and intellectual contact with the West throughout the fifth century. But—despite Aristotle—no positive evidence exists to suggest that Sicilian comedy (or other texts assigned to Sicilian comic playwrights) directly influenced any Attic author before the time of Plato and Xenophon.[24]

The only other early fifth-century Syracusan literary figure of whom we have substantial knowledge is Sophron, an author of mimes said by the *Suda* (σ 893 = test. 1) to have been a contemporary of Euripides (480s–407/6) and the Persian king Xerxes (reigned 486–465). 171 fragments of Sophron's mimes survive, along with ten titles. Although most of the fragments consist of a verse or less and often of a single word, there can be no doubt that they were sophisticated compositions that depicted ordinary people doing things just enough out of the ordinary to catch and hold an audience's attention.[25] The mimes were written in prose (perhaps with a rhythmic character; see K–A on test. 19) and were divided by Apollodorus into 'male' and 'female' categories depending on the sex of the individuals depicted (test. 1. 2–3; 22. 2; cf. **A20** introductory n.). They are repeatedly associated with Plato, who Diogenes Laertius reports first brought them to Athens (D.L. 3. 18 = test. 6) and who is repeatedly said to have kept a copy of them under his pillow (test. 1; 6–8; 10–11).[26] Sophron's mimes were also known to Aristotle (*Po.* 1447[b]10–11;

---

[23] *Euripides Herakles*[i] i (Berlin, 1889), 29 n. 54.

[24] Cf. Kerkhof 51–5, 89–93, 133–73. Indeed, the extent to which knowledge of and interest in Epicharmus, Sophron, and the *phlyax*-poet Rhinton of Taras (for whom, see below) is restricted before Apollodorus to other Western authors and to individuals who had themselves visited Magna Graecia (Plato and Polemon) is striking: Epicharmus is known to Archestratus of Gela, Alexis (originally from Thurii), Dionysius II of Syracuse (who produced a work entitled *On the Poems of Epicharmus* (Epich. test. 33)), Alcimus of Sicily, Aristoxenus of Tarentum, and the Roman writer Ennius; Sophron is known to Theocritus of Syracuse; and Rhinton is known to Nossis of Epizephyrian Locris. The main exceptions are Xenophon and the encyclopaedically learned Aristotle. Cf. **A4–A5** n.

[25] Nothing is known of the genre before Sophron (although see above on Sosibius of Sparta). For its subsequent development, see H. Reich, *Der Mimus*, i (Berlin, 1903); Wüst, *RE* 15. 2 (1932), 1727–64, esp. 1730–8; D. L. Page (ed.), *Select Papyri*, iii (Loeb Classical Library 360: Cambridge, MA, and London, 1941), #74–9 (fragments of a number of late mimes).

[26] Duris of Samos even insisted that Plato was inspired by Sophron's mimes when he produced his dialogues (*FGrHist* 76 F 72 = test. 5), an assertion that belongs to the same pattern of hostile invective as Alcimus' claim that the philosopher was dependent on Epicharmus for his ideas (see above).

fr. 15 Gigon = test. 2–3), as well as to Theocritus of Syracuse (early third century BC), who modelled *Idyll* 2 at least in part on *Women Who Say That They Will Drive Out the Goddess* (see **A20–A21** n.), and *Idyll* 15 (the adventures of two Syracusan women resident in Alexandria) on *Women Viewing the Isthmian Games* (arg. Theoc. 15 = Sophr. test. 15).[27] Whether Herodas (mid-third century BC?) knew Sophron's mimes is unclear, but nothing suggests that he drew on them for his own work as aggressively as Theocritus did. A certain Xenarchus (whose mimes Aristotle mentions in the same breath as Sophron's at *Po.* 1447ᵇ10 = Xenarch. test. 1) is identified as Sophron's son in a note shared by Photius and the *Suda* (= Xenarch. test. 2), but none of his work has been preserved.

Comedies were most likely performed in unofficial settings in Attica for many years before the eponymous archon made a place for the genre in the programme at the City Dionysia in the mid-480s (cf. Arist. *Po.* 1449ᵃ38–ᵇ2; Suda χ 318).[28] Despite Aristotle at *Po.* 1448ᵃ33–4, therefore, Epicharmus and Phormus are far too late to have 'invented' comedy; and although we know nothing about Sicilian comedy before them or about literary mime before Sophron, a clear corollary to this conclusion is that these authors were adapting—or perhaps simply giving literary expression to—pre-existing dramatic forms.[29] That comedy and mime were first written down in Syracuse at almost exactly the same time that state-sponsored performances of comedy began in Athens is intriguing and perhaps significant. But the coincidence is best explained not as the result of direct influence of Syracusan authors on the Athenian comic poets, but on the thesis that Syracusan comedy and literary mime, Attic comedy, and most likely Megarian comedy as well are independent expressions of a single, non-choral, late archaic performance tradition, which in Attica was uniquely combined with a separate, probably indigenous choral form perhaps already influenced by Corinthian 'padded dancers'.

[27] See R. Hunter, *Theocritus and the Archaeology of Greek Poetry* (Cambridge, 1996), 110–23.

[28] See Appendix I § B.

[29] The metrician Hephaestion (2nd c. AD?) refers to a certain Aristoxenus of Selinous (included by Kassel–Austin among the comic poets), who he says was older than Epicharmus and (as proof of this) was mentioned in one of his plays (Aristoxenus test. 1, citing Epich. fr. 77). Only one verse of Aristoxenus survives, τίς ἀλαζονίαν πλείσταν παρέχει τῶν ἀνθρώπων; τοὶ μάντεις ('Who supplies the most bullshit? The seers'; an anapaestic tetrameter catalectic), and its authenticity is disputed; but in any case no ancient source claims that Aristoxenus wrote comedies.

COMEDY AND RELATED GENRES IN THE WEST:
THE FOURTH CENTURY AND AFTER

After the shadowy Dinolochus and Xenarchus, the literary record for comedy and related genres in the West goes blank until Rhinton of Taras in the late fourth/early third century and his obscure successors Sciras of Taras (one title and one fragment preserved) and Blaesus of Capri (two titles and five fragments preserved).[30] The sepulchral epigram on Rhinton by Nossis of Epizephyrian Locris (*HE* 2827–30 = *AP* vii. 414 = test. 3) asks the passer-by to laugh as he remembers him, and notes that he gained success in the theatre with his 'tragic *phlyakes*'. So too the *Suda* (ρ 171 = test. 1) calls Rhinton 'the originator of the so-called *hilarotragoidia*, that is *phlyakographia*'; and Stephanus of Byzantium (p. 603. 6–7 Meineke = test. 2) describes him as 'a *phlyax*, who converted tragic materials into humour'. The etymology of φλύαξ is obscure,[31] and only nine titles and twenty-five fragments (including nine lines or partial lines, most in iambic trimeter) from Rhinton's plays have been preserved. But the titles (especially *Iphigenia in Aulis* and *Iphigenia in Tauris*) suggest a close—and doubtless mocking—relationship to Euripidean tragedy, although Rhinton could scarcely have been described as the 'originator' of a new dramatic genre if he was merely staging tragic parodies, which by his time had been produced for at least a century and probably longer.

The literary record thus allows us to say very little about Rhinton's *phlyax*-plays or—even more importantly—about what took place on the West Greek comic stage in the century and a half or so between his time and that of the fifth-century Syracusan authors discussed above. The archaeological record is more revealing. In the final years of the fifth century, production of high-quality red-figure pottery shifted decisively from Athens to southern Italy and Sicily, and almost two hundred South Italian and Sicilian vases (mostly Apulian and from 380–340 BC) depict or otherwise refer to what look like comic performances, including a substantial amount of mythological burlesque and amusing scenes from everyday life.[32] The actors wear padded

---

[30] For Rhinton and his successors, see Olivieri 121–53; M. Gigante, *Rintone e il teatro in Magna Graecia* (Naples, 1971); Taplin 48–52. Sopater of Paphos (late 4th c. BC), of whose work twelve titles and twenty-five occasionally substantial fragments are preserved, is also said by Athenaeus (3. 86a, etc. = Sopat. test. 4) to have written *phlyakes*, but does not seem to belong to the Sicilian tradition.

[31] Probably cognate with φλυαρία ('nonsense, babble'), although Radermacher suggested that it might be derived from φλέω ('teem, swell'), like ῥύαξ < ῥέω, and refer to the stage-phallus.

[32] The standard collection of the material is Trendall (but with a limited number of plates); important additions in Taplin (discussed below). Bieber 129–46 offers a number of illustrations with useful if frequently quite speculative discussion.

body-suits and, in the case of male characters, large theatrical phalluses, exactly as in Athenian Old Comedy. The stages are insubstantial and seemingly temporary, and there is no evidence of a chorus.

Heydemann (the first scholar to study this material systematically) identified these scenes as coming not from Attic comedy, as had previously been thought, but from *phlyax*-plays, and this has been the standard interpretation ever since.[33] But the fact that the '*phlyax*-vases' date from several generations earlier than Rhinton (something of which Heydemann was unaware) complicates the thesis considerably; and Webster argued that they must depict scenes from Athenian 'Middle Comedy', with which they are contemporary and overlap neatly in terms of subject matter, and which, he hypothesized, was routinely reperformed in the West in the fourth century.[34] Webster's thesis received important support from Taplin's demonstration that among the plays depicted on the '*phlyax*-vases' are not just Aristophanes' *Frogs* (on an Apulian crater from the second quarter of the fourth century; Trendall #22, Taplin plate 13. 7), as Panofka had suggested already in the middle of the nineteenth century, but his *Women Celebrating the Thesmophoria* (on an Apulian crater from around 370; Taplin plate 11. 4)[35]; Eupolis' *Demes* (Taplin plate 16. 16); and two otherwise unknown plays accompanied by inscriptions in Attic (in one case apparently a short excerpt from the text), leaving little doubt that they too were composed by Athenians.[36] The first of these unknown comedies is the 'Goose-Play', depicted on two Apulian craters (one from *c*.400 (Taplin plate 10. 2), the other from *c*.370 (Taplin plate 11. 3)). On the older and more intriguing of these appears an old man who holds his hands in the air and says κατέδησ' ἄνω τὼ χεῖρε ('he/she bound my hands above [me]'); an old woman who appears to be in control of a goose and a kid in a basket that on the other vase[37] belong to the old man, and who says ἐγὼ παρhέξω ('I shall furnish, hand over . . . '); and a young man who holds a staff and says *NOPAPETTEBAO*, which has never been explained as Greek and is generally taken to be barbarian-talk (all = adesp. com. fr. 57). To the left and seemingly at a distance from the action is an adolescent boy with

---

[33] Heydemann, *JDAI* 1 (1886), 260–313; cf. Körte (1893), 61–2; *DTC* 266–9; Wüst, *RE* 20 (1950), 292–306; Trendall 9 (who seems, however, to want to have things both ways, by arguing that 'This sort of comedy reached its highest level in the work of . . . Rhinthon', but acknowledging a few sentences later that 'Webster has also shown . . . that some at least of the scenes . . . are direct reflections of Attic comedies of the fourth century, which presumably were performed also in Magna Graecia'); Bieber 129; Taplin 52–4.

[34] Webster (1948), 19–27.

[35] Cf. Austin–Olson, *Thesmophoriazusae*, pp. lxxv–lxxvii (with frontispiece plate).

[36] Taplin 30–47, 55–66; Storey 116–21.

[37] From earlier in the play, since the goose is alive on it, whereas on the vase being described here it is dead.

no stage-phallus, who is labelled Τραγοιδός. The second play (illustrated on an Apulian crater from *c*.380 (Taplin plate 9. 1)) features two *choregoi* (Taplin's eponymous 'Comic Angels'; see below), a 'tragic' character labelled 'Aegisthus' (who, unlike the other characters, does not wear a stage-phallus), and a fourth character labelled 'Pyrrhias'.[38] The *choregoi* appear to be examining the other men, although to what end is unclear.[39]

If Taplin is right, therefore—and there seems no reason to doubt his interpretation—the comedies of Aristophanes and his contemporaries were at least occasionally re-performed in Magna Graecia in the first three decades of the fourth century. In that case, Occam's Razor suggests that Webster's interpretation of the '*phlyax*-vases', as the simplest explanation of the data, must be correct, a fact that might in turn explain both why some fourth-century comic poets wrote too many plays to have staged them all at the City Dionysia and the Lenaia,[40] and why we have no trace of any Sicilian or South Italian comic poets between Dinolochus and Rhinton: there were none, because the plays performed in Syracuse and elsewhere in this period were imports from Athens (even if never staged there). Taplin implies that Athenian 'Old Comedies' were staged in the West even before this, and argues that a willingness to engage with the political and social complexities of the genre is a mark of the cosmopolitanism of audiences in Magna Graecia.[41] But three of the four comedies he identifies on the '*phlyax*-vases' deal with tragedy and (at least in the case of *Women Celebrating the Thesmophoria* and *Frogs*) how it ought to be evaluated and understood, while the fourth is plausibly explained that way;[42] and it is tempting to think that Attic comedy served initially in the West as the literary handmaid of the other, older and grander dramatic genre. Be that as it may, the gates certainly swung open wide in the first half of the fourth century, when Attic comedy took up themes very similar to those of Epicharmus' plays (see below);[43] and Webster even proposes that Rhinton's

[38] The inscriptions giving the characters' names = adesp. com. fr. 59.

[39] On this vase, see also Shapiro, *JHS* 115 (1995), 173–5 (arguing that the comedy in question may be a parody of Aeschylus' *Choephoroi*).

[40] Alexis, for example, is said to have written 245 plays (test. 1).

[41] Taplin 89–99, esp. 95.

[42] Webster (1948) 25 observes that the obvious comparandum for the 'Goose-Play' scene discussed above is *Women Celebrating the Thesmophoria* after Inlaw has been captured and turned over to the Scythian archer for punishment, in which case the mysterious and seemingly off-stage Τραγοιδός is most naturally taken as a counterpart of the Aristophanic Euripides.

[43] It is thus worth considering whether the apparent great success of Athenian 'Middle Comedy' in Sicily and Southern Italy was less the result of the gradual evolution of the genre than a cause of it, as poets began to write with an eye toward the interests of an audience broader than the one that filled the Theatre of Dionysus on local festival days. So too on the level of staging, one of the most obvious differences between the theatrical traditions of Athens and the Greek West is the absence of dramatic choruses in the latter; and a striking phenomenon

new dramatic form may reflect an unfavourable response in Magna Graecia
to the 'New Comedy' of Menander and his contemporaries.[44] The vital point
in any case is that by the fourth century and perhaps earlier Attic comedy
had become the comedy of the Greek world generally, and early Syracusan
comedy and the *phlyakes* of Rhinton did little more than fill theatrical space
occupied in other periods by Athenian plays.

ATHENIAN COMEDY IN THE FIFTH CENTURY

Our knowledge of the earliest Athenian comic playwrights is limited. The
Suda (χ 318 = Chionid. test. 1) reports that Chionides staged a comedy in
487/6 and calls him the πρωταγωνιστὴς . . . τῆς ἀρχαίας κωμῳδίας,
which is presumably intended to mean that he was the 'first (successful)
competitor' in the genre at the City Dionysia.[45] This claim is compatible with
although not directly supported by the inscriptional evidence; see Appendix I
§ B. How many poets competed in this period, how they were selected
and judged, and the like, is unknown, although there is no reason to think
that arrangements were substantially different from how they were a few
generations later (see below). Only three titles (*Heroes, Persians or Assyrians,*
and *Beggars,* all presumably referring to the identities assumed by the chorus)
and seven or eight fragments of Chionides' plays survive. This makes him
more fortunate, however, than the next four men to take the prize, whose
names have not only not been preserved in the Victors' List (*IG* II² 2325; see
Appendix I) but may have been unknown to Aristotle, and the texts of whose
plays apparently failed to find their way to the Library in Alexandria (see
below) and are today entirely lost.

    The first Athenian comic playwright about whom we have any substantial
knowledge is Magnes, who took the prize at the City Dionysia eleven times
(*IG* II² 2325. 44), including in 473/2 (*IG* II² 2318. 8; see Appendix I § B), and
is described at Ar. *Eq.* 520–1 as the dominant poet of his generation. Most
of the titles attributed to Magnes have been reconstructed on the basis of

---

in the development of Attic tragedy (first in the work of Agathon and late Euripides; cf. Arist.
Po. 1456ᵃ25–32) and later of comedy (see below) is the gradual disengagement of the chorus
from the action. One explanation for this is that poets who anticipated re-performance in
Magna Graecia deliberately constructed their plays with an eye to easy conversion to non-choral
performance styles; cf. Slater, in Dobrov 40–1.

[44] Webster (1948), 19.

[45] Cf. Arist. *Po.* 1448ᵃ33–4 (on Chionides as a very early Athenian comic poet). For brief
individual biographies of the poets included in this collection, see Appendix III.

the remarks at *Eq.* 522–3 about his eagerness to entertain his audience by 'plucking his lyre, flapping his wings, playing the Lydian, acting like a gall-insect, and dyeing himself in frog-colours' (all once again presumably references to the costumes and behaviour of his choruses); but we know from other sources that he wrote two plays entitled *Dionysus* and another entitled *The Female Grass-cutter* (Ποάστρια). Seven lines or partial lines of his poetry survive, none of much interest. The names of the three poets who followed Magnes on the City Dionysia Victors' List, all of whom took the prize only once, are lost, although Oehmichen suggested restoring [ΑΛΚΙΜΕ]ΝΗ[Σ]—of whom we know only that he was an Athenian comic poet (S α 1284 = Alcimenes test. 1)—at *IG* II² 2325. 46. Euphronius took the prize in 459/8 (*IG* II² 2318. 48; cf. *IG* II² 2325. 48), but is otherwise obscure; although Ecphantides was victorious four times in the years that followed (*IG* II² 2325. 49), all we have of him are two titles (Πεῖραι ('*Attempts at Seduction*'?) and *Satyrs*) and six mostly unrevealing fragments. Only with Cratinus (first victorious in the mid-450s; cf. *IG* II² 2325. 50) does the historical record become more substantial, and even in this period there are huge gaps in our knowledge. Diopeithes, for example, whose name appears immediately after Cratinus' on the City Dionysia Victors' List and who is recorded there as having taken first place twice (*IG* II² 2325. 51), is otherwise entirely unknown.

Cratinus won the competition for comic poets six times at the City Diony-sia (*IG* II² 2325. 50) and three times at the Lenaia (for which see below) (*IG* II² 2325. 121). He too is recalled as one of the greatest playwrights of Athens' past by Aristophanes in the parabasis of *Knights* (526–36)—although this is in part a calculated insult, since his career extended until at least 424/3, when his *Wineflask* took the prize at the City Dionysia, defeating Amipsias' *Connus* (for which, see **F4** introductory n.) and the original version of Aristophanes' *Clouds*; see **B1–B12** with nn. Cratinus was known for his use of harsh personal abuse in a style reminiscent of Archilochus (e.g. test. 17. 2–3; and note the title *Archilochuses*), and his comedies continued to be read and studied in the Hellenistic and Roman periods (see below). Twenty-nine titles and 514 fragments of his work survive.

Of the other comic poets first active in the late 450s and early 440s, Crates (who took the prize three times at the City Dionysia, with his first victory coming at least two years after Cratinus' (*IG* II² 2325. 52), but apparently never won at the Lenaia) was originally an actor, according to one source for Cratinus (test. 2a. 5–6; 3). Aristotle claims that Crates was the first Athenian poet to abandon the iambic style of comedy in order to produce 'general plots and stories', supposedly under the influence of the Sicilian playwrights (*Po.* 1449ᵇ7–9 = test. 5); it is difficult to say how seriously ought to be taken the assertion that his work represented a distinct change in the character of the genre, given that Aristotle probably knew little about the earliest Attic comedy (see above). Ten of Crates' titles and sixty fragments are preserved; the most interesting are four excerpts from a debate in *Wild Beasts* about an ideal new world (frr. 16–19; see **B32** with introductory n. and **B32–B34**n.), a disparaging reference to tragic poetry from *Games* (fr. 28), and what appears to be a line spoken by a doctor in Doric dialect from an unidentified play (fr. 46). Less is known of Callias, who was victorious at the City Dionysia in 447/6 (*IG* II² 2318. 78) and most likely one other time (*IG* II² 2325. 53), and who seems to have competed at the Lenaia[46] but is absent from the preserved section of the Victors' List for that festival. The inscriptional evidence suggests that Callias' career did not extend much past 430, and only eight titles and forty mostly insubstantial fragments (but including an interesting reference to Socrates from *Men In Shackles*, = **F3**) of his plays survive.

Comic and tragic competitions were added at the Lenaia in the mid-440s or so (see Appendix I § B), and our knowledge of individual poets, the structure of their plays, and the institutional context within which they competed expands enormously in the years that follow. At the beginning of the Athenian year (normally in what we would call early July), two of the city's chief annual officials, the *archon basileus* and the eponymous archon, decided—on what basis we do not know—which of the poets who had applied to stage comedies and tragedies at the Lenaia and the City Dionysia festivals, respectively, would be awarded a chorus and a personal stipend.[47] The City Dionysia drew an international audience and may have been a more prestigious venue than the Lenaia, a largely intra-Athenian affair;[48] the Hellenistic scholar Eratosthenes, at any rate, seems to have said that an unexpected fourth at the City Dionysia caused Plato Comicus (test. 7) to retreat temporarily to the other festival.[49] The archons also selected a number of extremely wealthy citizens to serve as *choregoi* (literally 'chorus leaders') for the poets and charged them with hiring the choruses and chorus-trainers and providing practice facilities, masks, costumes, stage properties, and the like. Most *choregoi* probably spent freely in the hope of bolstering their personal reputation (cf. **E3**. 5–6 'after being selected as *choregos*, he supplies the chorus with golden robes but wears rags himself'); but some must have cut corners, like the men referred to at Ar. *Ach.* 1150–73 and Eup. fr. 329.[50] The relevant

---

[46] At *IG* XIV 1097. 1, 6, he is credited with two comedies in 435/4, which would seem to mean one at each festival.

[47] See *DFA* 84.   [48] Cf. Ar. *Ach.* 504–7 with Olson ad loc.

[49] See Biles, *ZPE* 127 (1999), 182–8 (on Ar. fr. 590. 44–50); and n. 52 below.

[50] 'Did you ever see a *choregos* more miserly than this one?' See [Arist.] *Ath.* 56. 3; *DFA* 86–91; P. Wilson, *The Athenian Institution of the Khoregia* (Cambridge, 2000).

archon also assigned a protagonist (chief actor) to each poet, and perhaps a deuteragonist (second actor) and tritagonist (third actor) as well.[51]

The didascalic notices preserved in the hypotheses to a number of Aristophanes' plays dating from 426/5 (*Acharnians*) to 406/5 (*Frogs*) list results for only three competitors per festival. But inscriptional evidence refers to fourth- and fifth-place finishes for a number of comic poets in the 440s and 430s (see Appendix I § B) and again in the middle of the fourth century (see Appendix I § C); an ancient commentary on an unidentified play by Aristophanes cites Eratosthenes to the effect that Plato Comicus took fourth at the City Dionysia sometime probably in the 410s (Ar. fr. 590. 44– 50); the hypothesis to Aristophanes' *Wealth* lists five competitors at the festival where that play was performed in 389/8 BC; and [Aristotle] treats this as the traditional number, although by his time the *choregia* had been abolished (*Ath.* 56. 3). Luppe argues that we know of too many comedies written during the Peloponnesian War years for it to be possible that the number of poets was reduced to three per festival for a few decades to save money; if he is right, it must instead be the case that the hypotheses to Aristophanes' comedies refer to first, second, and third because these were considered the honourable places, whereas fourth and fifth were not.[52] As for how the ranking was accomplished, we know that sometime before the festivals began, lists of men qualified to serve as judges were drawn up by the ten Athenian tribes, and their names (probably written on pieces of broken pottery) were sealed in jars; and at the beginning of the contest, these jars were opened up and one name drawn from each. But only five votes counted (cf. Zenob. iii. 64, citing Epich. fr. 237; Cratin. fr. 177 with K–A ad loc.), and the mechanics of the rest of the process, and in particular how only five ballots could produce an unambiguous list of five place-rankings, remain obscure.[53]

Although no complete comedies are preserved from the late 440s and 430s, enough survives to make it clear that the plays were already structured like those of Aristophanes and his contemporaries a generation later.[54] The prologue (in which the plot is set up), the parodos (sung or recited by the chorus

---

[51] See *DFA* 93–5. For actors, see J. B. O'Connor, *Chapters in the History of Actors and Acting in Ancient Greece* (Chicago, 1908); P. Ghiron-Bistagne, *Recherches sur les acteurs dans la Grèce antique* (Paris, 1976); P. Easterling and E. Hall (eds.), *Greek and Roman Actors: Aspects of an Ancient Profession* (Cambridge, 2002); N. W. Slater, *Spectator Politics* (Philadelphia, 2002), 22–39; A. Duncan, *Performance and Identity in the Classical World* (New York, 2006), 90–123.

[52] Luppe, *Philologus*, 116 (1972), 53–75, with further bibliography. See also Luppe, *ZPE* 46 (1982), 147–59; *ZPE* 54 (1984), 15–16; *Nikephoros*, 1 (1988), 185–9; Rosen, *ZPE* 76 (1989), 223– 8; Storey, *Drama*, 12 (2002), 146–67.

[53] See in general *DFA* 95–9; Marshall and van Willigenburg, *JHS* 124 (2004), 90–107.

[54] See the detailed discussions in *DTC* 292–328; Whittaker.

as they enter), and the exodos (sung or recited by the chorus as they exit) are all standard elements in tragedy, from which they may have been borrowed, like the iambic trimeter in which most of the dialogue is written. The parabasis, on the other hand, is unique to comedy and consists of seven standard elements:[55]

1. The *kommation* (a line or two of transitional remarks, in Aristophanes' plays often addressed to the characters as they exit the stage).

2. A section Aristophanes routinely refers to as the 'anapaests' (*Ach.* 627; *Eq.* 504; *Pax* 735; *Av.* 684), although aeolic metres (especially Eupolideans; cf. **B38** introductory n.) are used as well;[56] the poet speaks directly to the audience through the chorus or the chorus-leader, or the chorus sing for themselves, or their leader speaks in character.

3. The *pnigos* ('strangling', supposedly because it needed to be pronounced with a single breath), in a shorter unit of the same metre as (2).

4. The ode (lyric and therefore sung), frequently an invocation of the Muse or another god or group of gods.

5. A spoken passage (usually trochaic) called the epirrhema, which generally consists of complaints, advice, or the like addressed to the audience.

6. The antode (sung lyric corresponding to the ode).

7. The antepirrhema (in the same metre and delivered in the same style as the epirrhema).

Elements 2–3 are sometimes called the 'parabasis proper', while elements 4–7 are generally referred to collectively as the 'epirrhematic syzygy'. See **B36–B45** with nn.

A few of Aristophanes' comedies feature a 'second parabasis', i.e. a second epirrhematic syzygy later in the play; how common these were in other poets is unclear.[57] The same is true of the *agon* (a debate or contest involving a crucial point at issue in the plot), which occurs in a number of Aristophanes' comedies and was apparently found in some of those of his predecessors and contemporaries, but does not seem to be as standard a structural element as the parabasis.[58] The structure of the *agon* resembles that of the epirrhematic

---

[55] See in general Körte, *RE* 11. 1 (1921), 1247–51; Sifakis 33–70; O. Imperio, *Parabasi di Aristofane* (Studi e commenti 13: Bari, 2004), 3–11.

[56] See West 95–6.

[57] For a detailed study, see P. Totaro, *Le seconde parabasi di Aristofane* (Drama Beiheft 9: Stuttgart and Weimar, 1999).

[58] See in general T. Gelzer, *Der epirrhematische Agon bei Aristophanes* (Zetemata 23: Munich, 1960), with further bibliography.

syzygy in the parabasis, although in Aristophanes, at least, the characters share the *epirrhema* and the *antepirrhema*, and the chorus merely sing the odes. But Aristophanes always uses anapaestic or iambic tetrameters in the non-lyric sections, and while this may be a matter of individual preference, it can tentatively be used in combination with an analysis of the subject-matter to distinguish between parabasis- and *agon*-fragments in other poets. See **B32–B35** with nn. That all these structures were used by comic playwrights already in the first half of the century seems likely but cannot be proven.

The addition of a competition for comic poets at the Lenaia meant a significant expansion of the genre and thus of the number of poets it could support, since five more plays were now staged at state expense each year. Cratinus (whose name appears fourth in the list of Lenaia victors (*IG* II² 2325. 121)) took advantage of this opportunity, and Callias attempted to (see above). But none of the other poets from the 450s and 440s whose names are given in col. I of the City Dionysia Victors' List also took the prize at the Lenaia. Instead, a new group of men appear in the same order in the City Dionysia and Lenaia lists with initial victories in the mid-440s to mid-430s: Teleclides (*IG* II² 2325. 54, 119), Aristomenes (?) (*IG* II² 2325. 55, 120), Pherecrates (*IG* II² 2325. 56, 122), and Hermippus (*IG* II² 2325. 57, 123).[59] Teleclides in particular, with five victories at the Lenaia and three at the City Dionysia, seems to have been an extremely important figure on the Athenian comic stage in these years, although little of his work has been preserved and the absence of papyri suggests that in the Hellenistic and Roman periods his plays were not much read outside of a few major libraries. Pherecrates (with two victories at the Lenaia and at least one at the City Dionysia) and Hermippus (with four victories at the Lenaia and an unknown number at the City Dionysia), on the other hand, are both represented by a substantial number of titles and fragments but once again by no papyri.[60] The extent to which these men, along with Cratinus and perhaps Crates (cf. Ar. *Eq.* 537–40), dominated the Athenian dramatic festivals during these years can be judged by the fact that no new poet seems to have taken the prize at the City Dionysia for almost a decade after Hermippus in 436/5.

This pattern began to change in 429/8, when Phrynichus took first place at the Lenaia, followed in 428/7 by Myrtilus (Hermippus' brother and otherwise apparently a very minor figure), in 427/6 by Eupolis (as a very young man), and in 426/5 (*Acharnians*) and 425/4 (*Knights*) by Aristophanes (who was

[59] The names of two other poets, one of whom is perhaps Lysippus (see Appendix I), have been lost between Teleclides and Pherecrates in the City Dionysia Victors' List.

[60] Although Aristomenes took the prize twice at the Lenaia (*IG* II² 2325. 120) and perhaps once or more at the City Dionysia (*IG* II² 2325. 58; but see Appendix I § B), he is otherwise almost entirely obscure.

also very young and had taken second at the festival already in 428/7 with his first play, *Banqueters*); while at the City Dionysia Aristophanes took first in 427/6 (with *Babylonians*) and Eupolis took the prize most likely within the next year or two (see Appendix I § B). These men can reasonably be referred to as a 'new generation' of comic poets, who dominated the Athenian stage for much of the final quarter of the fifth century,[61] and who repeatedly competed against one another[62] and traded on-stage barbs often enough to leave no doubt that they regarded one another as serious rivals (see **B40–B42** with nn.). Eupolis (who died probably in 411; see Storey 56–60, esp. 59) and Aristophanes (who lived into the mid-380s) were treated in the Hellenistic period as two of the most important 'Old Comic' poets, the third being Cratinus, and a very large number of fragments of their work (nineteen titles and almost 500 fragments of Eupolis, including a number of papyri, and thrity-three titles and over 900 fragments of Aristophanes, in addition to the eleven complete plays) have been preserved. Other poets active in this period include Amipsias (victorious at least once at both festivals, including at the City Dionysia in 415/4, and second at the City Dionysia in 424/3, behind Cratinus but ahead of Aristophanes) and Plato Comicus (victorious at least once at the City Dionysia, and probably active from *c*.420 into the early years of the fourth century).

'OLD', 'MIDDLE', AND 'NEW COMEDY'

The history of Athenian comedy is generally said to fall into three periods: 'Old Comedy' (to which all the poets discussed above belong, although Aristophanes' two final preserved plays, *Assemblywomen* and *Wealth*, are often said to foreshadow 'Middle Comedy'), 'Middle Comedy' (poets active from roughly the time of Aristophanes' death into the third quarter of the fourth century), and 'New Comedy' (Menander, whose first play was probably staged in 324 or 323, and his successors). The earliest references to 'Middle Comedy' and thus to a tripartite division of this sort are in Athenaeus and Pollux

---

[61] Cf. C. F. Russo, *Aristophanes: An Author for the Stage* (London, 1994; originally published in Italian in 1962), 19–20; Gelzer, *RE* Suppl. XII (1970), 1407; Biles, *ZPE* 136 (2001), 195–200.

[62] Although our sources are very limited, we know that Aristophanes, Cratinus, and Eupolis all competed at the Lenaia in 426/5; Cratinus and Aristophanes both competed at the City Dionysia in 424/3; Eupolis and Aristophanes both competed at the City Dionysia in 422/1 (by which time Cratinus was probably retired); and Aristophanes and Phrynichus both competed at the City Dionysia in 415/4; all of which suggests that head-to-head confrontations of this sort were not the exception but the rule.

(both second century AD; see below). But both authors seem to have taken this language over from their sources, and the idea is probably to be traced to the Hellenistic period and perhaps specifically to Aristophanes of Byzantium.[63] 'Old Comedy' is generally taken to be characterized by overt and pointed discussion of contemporary social and political issues; bitter abuse of prominent individuals, including politicians (cf. **E12–E29**), poets (cf. **D14**), and intellectuals (cf. **F1–F5**); unrestrained obscenity; and a chorus that is directly involved in the action, especially in the first half of the play, but that also delivers a parabasis. 'Middle Comedy' is generally taken to be characterized by a fondness for mythological parody (cf. **C3–C6**); a substantial decrease in the amount of political commentary and personal invective (although see **C2**; **E30**); the emergence of standard character types, such as the parasite (see **A13** initial n.; **C11–C12**), the outspoken slave (see **C7–C8** n.), the garrulous cook (see **C9–C10** n.), and the courtesan (see **I7** introductory n.); and the disappearance of the parabasis and a gradual withdrawal of the chorus from the action.[64] In addition, Nesselrath argues that 'Middle Comedy' was characterized by a routine use of anapaestic dimeter and by a fondness for high-style 'dithyrambic' language.[65] 'New Comedy' is generally taken to be characterized by a superficially apolitical attitude;[66] a cast of characters made up of average men and women taking very typical parts and concerned with quotidian domestic affairs such as love, marriage, and money; an absence of scurrility and obscenity; and an atavistic chorus that merely provides musical interludes between scenes involving the characters. But these are artificial categories invented well after the event, and although they make the history of Athenian comedy more comprehensible, they do so in large part by distorting it.

Hellenistic scholars working in the Library at Alexandria and elsewhere had access to far more Athenian comedies than we do, and the tripartite scheme outlined above must have some significant foundation in reality. All the same, the general problem with it—as with all such schemes—is that it necessarily misrepresents the evidence by implying that comedy evolved in a coherent, linear fashion and that, except in a few marginal (and thus unclassifiable) cases, the work of individual poets falls neatly into one period or another.[67] In fact, new poets appeared on the stage and old ones died or

---

[63] Thus Nesselrath 149–87, esp. 180–7.
[64] On the final point, see Hunter, *ZPE* 36 (1979), 23–38; Rothwell, in Dobrov 99–118.
[65] Nesselrath 241–80.
[66] Although see S. Lape, *Reproducing Athens: Menander's Comedy, Democratic Culture, and the Hellenistic City* (Princeton, 2004).
[67] See the comments of Rosen, in Dobrov 119–37 (on Plato Comicus).

retired constantly and irregularly. Careers thus overlapped in complex ways; in addition, every poet had his own interests and eccentricities, and the fact that many poets in a particular decade or 'generation' were producing one sort of play is unlikely to mean that all of them were.[68] It is thus difficult to divide up the history of a genre into clear, comprehensive, and discrete periods without ignoring a great deal of recalcitrant evidence. Perhaps more important, there are serious difficulties with the tripartite division that reflect the concerns and biases of Hellenistic scholars and the limits of the material available to them.

That Attic comedy remained largely static throughout the fifth century (i.e. for much of the 'Old Comic' period) is unlikely on the face of it, and Aristotle in fact insists that Crates significantly transformed the genre when he abandoned the ἰαμβικὴ ἰδέα (*Po.* 1449b7–9). But the scholars working in the Library in Alexandria are unlikely to have been aware of most of this, for the almost complete absence of any trace of Athenian comedy before the 450s outside of the inscriptional record (see above) strongly suggests that all this material was lost by the Hellenistic period and probably much earlier. Although the *Suda* (tenth century, but drawing on earlier sources) calls Magnes an 'Old Comic' poet (μ 20 = Magnes test. 1), therefore, 'Old Comic' probably functioned as a blanket term for 'Cratinus, Aristophanes, Eupolis, and all other Athenian comic poets contemporary with or earlier than them'. If that is true, the political comedy of the 430s to 410s (the period we know best and tend to refer to as archetypically 'Old Comic') is only one stage in the development of a genre whose earlier styles and tendencies are obscure but likely to have been different. Indeed, another, newer type of 'Old Comedy' becomes prominent around 400, when mythological parody suddenly grows immensely popular—and remains so for about half a century.[69]

This question of what Hellenistic literary historians meant by 'Old Comedy' leads directly to the problem of the definition of 'Middle Comedy'. The latest more or less securely datable poets referred to in ancient sources as belonging to 'Old Comedy' are Xenophon (D.L. 2. 59 = test. 1) and Philyllius (*Suda* φ 457 = test. 1), who appear near the bottom of the preserved portion of col. II of the Lenaia Victors' List (*IG* II² 2325. 135–6, referring to initial victories perhaps c.400), and Theopompus (*Suda* θ 171 = test. 1) and Cephisodorus (*Suda* κ 1565 = test. 1), who appear at the top of col. III of the City Dionysia Victors' List (*IG* II² 2325. 68–9, referring to initial victories probably in the final years of the fifth century). The Hellenistic definition of

[68] Cf. **E31** introductory n. (on Timocles); Nesselrath 197–8 (on Epicrates); Csapo, in M. Depew and D. Obbink (eds.), *Matrices of Genre* (Cambridge, MA and London, 2000), 115–33, esp. 115–21.
[69] See Nesselrath 188–241.

'Old Comedy' must thus have included plays written and performed (or poets active) in the first few decades of the fourth century, as is also apparent from the *Suda*'s observation that Eubulus, whom it dates to the Olympiad 376/2 BC, stood between 'Old' and 'Middle Comedy' (ε 3386 = test. 1). None of the poets above Eubulus in col. III of the Lenaia Victors' List, including Anaxandrides, a major figure whom the *Suda* (α 1982 = test. 1) also dates to 376/2, noting that he 'was the first to introduce love-stories and rapes of girls', is referred to anywhere as belonging to 'Middle Comedy'; but Ephippus, Antiphanes, Mnesimachus, and Alexis, all of whom follow Eubulus, are.[70]

Although this is fragmentary and in some ways dubious evidence, the most straightforward interpretation of it is that Hellenistic scholarship placed the break between 'Old' and 'Middle Comedy' in the mid-370s or so, about a decade after Aristophanes' death. By that time, however, plays of the sort conventionally referred to today as 'Middle Comedies' had been staged in Athens for about twenty-five years, as Nesselrath's long and careful study of the characteristics of the genre in the first half of the fourth century has shown.[71] Exactly what the ancient sources mean by 'Middle Comedy' is unclear, except that it is apparently *not* the same thing as what modern scholars mean; and it is tempting to think that one important part of the actual working definition of the term was 'somewhat later than Aristophanes and somewhat earlier than Menander'.

None of the poets who appear above Menander in col. IV of the Lenaia Victors' List (*IG* II² 2325. 153–9, referring to initial victories dating back to 340 or so) is described in ancient sources as belonging to either 'Middle' or 'New Comedy'. The four poets who follow him in the list (in order, Philemo, Apollodorus, Diphilus, and Philippides; *IG* II² 2325. 161–4), on the other hand, are all referred to as belonging to 'New Comedy', as are Anaxippus (whom the *Suda* (α 1991 = test. 1) calls a contemporary of Antigonus and Demetrius Poliorcetes, and thus places at the very end of the fourth century) and Posidippus (whose name appears at the top of the preserved portion of col. V of the City Dionysia Victors' List (*IG* II² 2325. 71), referring to initial victories probably early in the third century). Menander was clearly regarded as a watershed figure, who invented a type of play that was rapidly—and successfully—adopted by other poets and came to be called 'New Comedy'. Many of the men whose names appear above his in the Lenaia Victors' List must have competed against him, and it is difficult to believe that he did not

---

[70] Other, less securely dated poets described in ancient sources as belonging to 'Middle Comedy' are Amphis, Epicrates, Epigenes, Heniochus, Sophilus, Sotades, Strato Comicus, and Timotheus.

[71] Nesselrath 188–330.

borrow from them or they from him. They none the less seem to have been treated as lying in a literary-historical no-man's-land, stranded between 'Middle' and 'New Comedy' (to which they could by definition not belong, having arrived on the dramatic scene earlier than Menander, even if they were in other ways his contemporaries). Nor are any of the dozens of poets who staged comedies at the festivals in Athens throughout the rest of the third century and well into the second referred anywhere to as belonging to New Comedy. Indeed, their work—much of which was being produced at the same time that research on earlier generations of comic poets was going on in the Library in Alexandria (see below)—was largely ignored by Hellenistic scholarship. Although we therefore know almost nothing about them, it is a safe assumption that the genre in which they worked continued to change in form and content gradually and unpredictably from one festival and decade to the next.

HELLENISTIC SCHOLARSHIP AND THE SOURCES OF OUR FRAGMENTS

Nothing suggests that texts of plays staged at the City Dionysia or the Lenaia were required to be deposited in Athens' official state archives; the city had no public libraries until the Roman period; and although private copies of some comedies doubtless existed, the very earliest plays in particular were most likely only rarely read or copied after the original performances. Many Attic comedies, including all those from the first half of the fifth century, were thus apparently lost early on. But beginning around 450, the situation must have changed, as the city grew wealthy and powerful; high-level literacy, the book-trade,[72] and the market for cultural exports expanded hand in hand, for copies of late fifth-century plays seem to have been available to fourth-century historians such as Theopompus, and large numbers of them survived into the Hellenistic period. Copies of complete plays by Cratinus, Aristophanes, and Eupolis, as well as of Menander and a few other 'New Comic' playwrights (whose work directly influenced the Roman comic poets; cf. **C16–C17**) continued to be produced and widely read well into Roman times, and are the source of almost all the fragments drawn from papyri. But most of the rest of what had been preserved of the Athenian and Sicilian comic poets seems to become the almost exclusive preserve of scholars (especially

---

[72] See **J1. 1** with n.

those working in the Library in Alexandria) and excerptors; and almost all the other fragments (the so-called 'book fragments') come to us from sources of this type, generally at second- or third-hand or worse.

Sometime in the 330s or early 320s, the Athenian statesman Lycurgus arranged for official copies of Aeschylus, Sophocles, and Euripides to be produced and deposited in an official city archive ([Plu.] *Mor.* 841f). These manuscripts were acquired half a century or so later for the Library in Alexandria by King Ptolemy II ('Philadelphus'; reigned 282–246 BC), who according to Galen borrowed them from the Athenians and forfeited a deposit of 15 talents of gold when he returned copies of the official texts rather than the official texts themselves (*CMG* V 10. 2¹ p. 79. 23 Wenkebach). There is no evidence that similar official copies of the works of a select group of comic poets were ever produced, and the plays eventually assembled in Alexandria must instead have made their way there piecemeal from other sources, perhaps including Theophrastus' library.[73] The enormous amount of material available in the Library and the financial support the Ptolemies provided for scholars working there allowed literary texts to be examined in ways and with an intensity that had never been possible before, and a vast amount of detailed work was done on comedy in particular.[74]

Among the Alexandrian scholars who made important contributions to the study of comedy were Lycophron (who organized the collection and may have done some basic textual work, but whose *On Comedy* probably consisted primarily of glosses on difficult words); Callimachus (who included the comic poets in his *Pinakes* (frr. 439–40), from which the lists of plays preserved at e.g. POxy. xxxiii 2659 = Ar. test. 2c; xxxv 2739 = Cratin. test. 7f, must be drawn); Euphronius (who appears to have produced a commentary on Aristophanes' *Wealth*); Eratosthenes (whose *On Old Comedy* was at least twelve books long and covered a far broader range of issues than did

---

[73] Ath. 1. 3a–b (cf. D.L. 5. 52) reports that a certain Neleus inherited Theophrastus' library (which included Aristotle's books) and later sold it to Ptolemy II. Strabo 13. 608–9 (supported by Posidon. *FGrHist* 87 F 36 = fr. 253 Edelstein–Kidd ap. Ath. 5. 214d–e; Plu. *Sull.* 26), on the other hand, offers a long and circumstantial account of the history of Neleus' books and in particular his copies of the works of Aristotle which, Strabo claims, were hidden for many years by Neleus' heirs and finally sold to Apellicon of Teos in the 1st c. BC. That Theophrastus left his library to Neleus suggests that he expected him to become the next head of the Academy; and the stories in Athenaeus and Strabo can be reconciled on the assumption that, when Neleus was passed over for the position, he suppressed the master's works as an act of revenge on his former colleagues, but sold the rest of the books to Ptolemy II, who doubtless paid well for them.

[74] For the individual scholars referred to below, see Boudreaux 25–47 (Aristophanes of Byzantium), 48–51 (Callistratus), 52–74 (Aristarchus), 75–6 (Ammonius); Pfeiffer 105–7, 119–20 (Lycophron), 159–62 (Eratosthenes), 189–96 (Aristophanes of Byzantium), 224 (Callistratus and Aristarchus), 264–5 (Apollodorus); cf. Ar. test. 113–24 (with an extensive collection of further bibliography); Henderson, *Lysistrata*, pp. lxi–lxviii (a general overview of the question).

Lycophron's similarly titled work); Aristophanes of Byzantium (who edited the plays of his Athenian namesake, produced a study of Athenian courtesans that doubtless drew heavily on comedy, and may have been responsible for the division of comedy into three periods); Callistratus (who wrote wide-ranging commentaries on at least six of Aristophanes' plays); Aristarchus (who also wrote commentaries—in his case seemingly of an almost entirely philological character—on at least eight of Aristophanes' plays); and Aristarchus' students Ammonius (who produced a study of individuals mentioned in comedy (κωμῳδούμενοι)) and Apollodorus (who worked *inter alia* on Epicharmus and Sophron; cf. **A12** introductory n., **A18–A19** n.). Alexandria must also be the place where the scholarly hypotheses preserved along with most of Aristophanes' plays and in a papyrus fragment that describes the action in Cratinus' *Dionysalexandros* (**B13**) were produced.[75] At least some work on comedy was done in the Attalid library in Pergamon as well by Crates of Mallos (mid-second century BC), Demetrius Ixion (a student and enemy of Aristarchus, who produced commentaries on at least two Aristophanic comedies), and Crates' student Herodicus (who like Ammonius assembled a catalogue of κωμῳδούμενοι).[76] Perhaps more important, Athenian (and to a lesser extent Sicilian) comedy served as basic source material for, and was therefore frequently quoted at length by, numerous Hellenistic scholars and rhetoricians working on lexicographical, grammatical, metrical, and historical topics.

In the first century BC, the Alexandrian scholar Didymus condensed all this work into comprehensive running commentaries on the texts of some of what were judged the most important comic poets, in the case of Aristophanes at least probably relying on the text established by Aristophanes of Byzantium.[77] A number of papyrus fragments of these commentaries or their descendants survive (Epich. fr. 98; Ar. frr. 590–1; Eup. frr. 192; 259; 268; adesp. com. fr. 1059) and, although badly damaged, suffice to show that they consisted of disconnected lemmata followed by often extensive notes, which routinely cite other texts and the opinions of earlier scholars.[78] Didymus, doubtless drawing once again on earlier scholarship, also compiled a Λέξεις

---

[75] For hypotheses, see Boudreaux 31–5.

[76] For scholarly work on comedy in Pergamon, see Boudreaux 79–90.

[77] For Didymus (nicknamed Χαλκέντερος ('Bronze-guts') for his endless capacity for work, and Βιβλιολάθας ('Book-forgetter') because his output was so prodigious that he was unable to avoid occasionally contradicting himself), see Boudreaux 91–137, esp. 125–37; Pfeiffer 275–9, esp. 276–7; C. A. Gibson, *Interpreting a Classic: Demosthenes and His Ancient Commentators* (Berkeley, Los Angeles, and London, 2002), 26–35, 54–64.

[78] The *scholia* to Aristophanes' plays also preserve a large number of notes drawn from Didymus (see Boudreaux 98–9); cf. Ath. 2. 67d (citing Didymus on Ar. *Pl.* 720).

κωμικαί (*Comic Expressions*),[79] which was used by the first-century AD lexicographer Pamphilus, whose massive lexicon (now lost) was an important source for Hesychius. Didymus' work was used in turn by Symmachus sometime around AD 100 to produce a learned commentary on a select collection of Aristophanes' plays, including (but apparently not limited to) the eleven preserved for us today.[80]

Extracts from these commentaries and others were drawn together in the second and third centuries AD into sets of elementary notes (ὑπομνήματα) designed to help teachers of grammar and rhetoric and their students make sense of the ever-shrinking number of comedies still read in schools.[81] Didymus' commentary probably did not survive this period. But beginning sometime in the fourth or fifth century, selections from the ὑπομνήματα and from Symmachus' commentary on Aristophanes, along with information and annotations drawn from Heliodorus' (mid-first century AD) study of the metrical structure of the comedies,[82] were transferred for convenience's sake into the margins of the manuscripts of the plays themselves or the margins of the manuscripts of other texts to which the note in question seemed germane.[83] These marginal notes (*scholia*) are accordingly a rich source of comic fragments (e.g. **A22**; **B6–B8**; **B12**; **C14**. 1–4; **D11**; **H16**), as well as of invaluable—if frequently garbled—information of other sorts. Most of the other comic book-fragments come from Roman- or Byzantine-era authors writing on specialized topics of one sort or another, and the source of their quotations seems once again generally to be Hellenistic scholarship rather than the texts of the plays themselves.

Far and away the most important such source of book-fragments of comedy is Athenaeus of Naucratis (fl. *c*.200), whose *Deipnosophists* Gulick (the original Loeb translator) rightly calls 'in some respects . . . the most important work of later antiquity' (vol. i p. xv), since it preserves so much that would otherwise be lost (e.g. **A1–A5**; **B32–B35**; **C3–C13**; **E3**; **G1–G18**). The dinner-conversation reported in the *Deipnosophists* is presented as a product of extremely wide reading: Larensius, the host of the party, is said at the beginning of the work to have had the largest personal library ever assembled (1. 3a), and one of his guests claims to have read more than 800 'Middle Comedies' (8. 336d). Athenaeus himself clearly knew numerous Hellenistic

---

[79] For fragments of works of this sort, see *CGFPR* 342–3.

[80] For Symmachus, see Boudreaux 144–60.

[81] See Boudreaux 161–70, and cf. POxy. vi 856 (an elementary commentary on Aristophanes' *Acharnians* 108–671; 3rd c. AD).

[82] For Heliodorus, see Boudreaux 138–43.

[83] See Boudreaux 171–88; Luppe, in W. Geerlings and C. Schulze (eds.), *Der Kommentar in Antike und Mittelalter* (Clavis Commentariorum Antiquitatis et Medii Aevi 2: Leiden, 2002), 55–76 (a general overview of the question).

treatises on topics as diverse as courtesans (13. 583d), cakes (14. 646a), and farming (14. 650e), and the fact that he was originally from Egypt raises the possibility that he spent time in the Library in Alexandria. But that he regularly relies on the text of the comedies he cites rather than drawing on earlier compilations of material cannot be demonstrated, and Nesselrath 66–79, esp. 66–8, argues convincingly that he often simply passes on sets of quotations assembled by earlier scholars,[84] most likely relying on works in the personal library of his literary patron, on whom his character Larensius is modelled.[85]

The same appears to be true of all the other authors who preserve a sub-stantial number of comic fragments presented in this edition. Plutarch's (late first/early second century AD) *Lives* contain numerous comic fragments (e.g. **E11–E14; E20–E23; E25; E28**), and Stadter argues that in *Pericles*, at least, the historian is drawing on his own reading of the plays he quotes.[86] If that is the case in the *Lives* in general, it is striking how vague some of Plutarch's references are,[87] how little knowledge he displays of the comedies from which he quotes,[88] how limited—and occasionally silly—the range of topics is to which the fragments he cites refer,[89] and what restricted use he makes of a genre one would expect to be treated as a rich and significant source for late-fifth-century Athenian political history. The only comedies about which Plutarch offers any information that could not be got from the fragment itself are Eupolis' *Demes* (*Per.* 3. 7, citing Eup. fr. 115, although his interpretation of the verse is dubious) and *Marikas* (*Nic.* 4. 5, citing Eup. fr. 193 = **E23**), both of which, papyrus evidence shows, were still circulating in his time (Eup. frr. 99; 192). Nothing proves, however, that he had read even these two plays, and the fact that both quotations are found in the company of a number of others, including in each case some lines from Teleclides, whose comedies were almost certainly *not* available outside of major libraries (if at all) in the

[84] See also Arnott, in *Rivals*, 4–8. The *Deipnosophists* is preserved in three manuscripts: A represents the unabridged text but is incomplete, whereas C and E are independent copies of an epitomized version, which they preserve in its entirety. A copy of the epitome was also known to Eustathius (12th c. AD), who cites it occasionally in his commentary on Homer. The reports of readings in Athenaeus in my apparatus are dependent on Kaibel's text of the full text of Athenaeus and Peppink's edition of the Epitome.

[85] See D. Braund in D. Braund and J. Wilkins (eds.), *Athenaeus and His World* (Exeter, 2000), 3–22.

[86] P. A. Stadter, *A Commentary on Plutarch's Pericles* (Chapel Hill and London, 1989), pp. lxv–lxvi.

[87] Esp. *Nic.* 11. 6 (citing **E25**) 'as Plato said somewhere'.

[88] Esp. *Nic.* 4. 7, where Ar. *Eq.* 358 is assigned to 'Cleon' rather than the Sausage-seller.

[89] A substantial number of the fragments cited in *Pericles*, for example, refer (or are alleged to refer) to the odd shape of the statesman's head, which is not a topic one would have expected Plutarch to make the centre of his research and thus suggests that this comes from a pre-existing collection of material.

Roman period, suggests that Plutarch took over most—and probably all—
this material wholesale from a Hellenistic catalogue of κωμῳδούμενοι or
the like.[90]

The *Onomasticon* (*'Vocabulary'*) of the rhetorician Julius Pollux (second
half of the second century AD) is a thesaurus of Attic words arranged by topic
and divided into ten books. Among the comic fragments it preserves are
B9; **B14**; **B16**; **B40**; **D2**. 1; and **J1**. Pollux' *Onomasticon* survives only in an
epitome, but was beyond any doubt a collection and distillation of earlier
scholarly sources rather than a product of original research.[91]

Clement of Alexandria (late second/early third century AD) preserves
numerous comic fragments, including **B5**; **I3**. 1–4; **I7**. 1–2, 7–26. He shows no
sign of having read the plays he cites, and the modern scholarly consensus
is that for authors other than Menander he drew on collections of quotations
assembled by earlier compilers.[92]

The *Lives of Eminent Philosophers* of Diogenes Laertius (first half of the
third century AD?) preserves numerous comic fragments, including **F3–F5**;
F7–F9; **F12**; **F14–F15**. Diogenes does not appear to have read the plays from
which this material is drawn; and the fact that the fragments he quotes tend to
appear in clusters supports the conclusion that they have been drawn from
earlier sources.[93]

The anthology of Johannes Stobaeus ('of Stobi', the capital of the late
Roman province of Macedonia Secunda; fifth century AD) preserves an
enormous number of excerpts from Greek texts of a wide range of periods
and genres, including **A8**; **A19**; **B44**; **C2**; **C14**; **D5**; **E1–E2**; **E4**; **I4–I5**; **I11**.

---

[90] The manuscripts of Plutarch's *Pericles* are divided into two families, represented by S, on
the one hand, and UMA (referred to collectively as *Y*), on the other. For *Nicias*, we have only
UMA. For *Alcibiades*, there are again two families, represented by N, on the one hand, and UA
(referred to collectively as *Y*), on the other. For the relevant portions of *Demetrius*, there are
four manuscripts, P, K, L, and r (which has drawn on a manuscript closely related to L to replace
a number of folios lost from R). The reports of readings in Plutarch in my apparatus are drawn
from Ziegler's Teubner edition (I. 2 (1964) for *Pericles*, *Nicias*, and *Alcibiades*; III. 1 (1971) for
Demetrius).

[91] See Nesselrath 79–102; Arnott, in *Rivals*, 8. The manuscripts of the sections of Pollux that
preserve comic fragments included in this edition are divided into three families: FS, A, and
CLM (with L available only for Books 8–10). The reports of readings in Pollux in my apparatus
are drawn from Bethe's edition (1900–37).

[92] Thus Marrou in his edition of the *Paedagogus* (1960), citing Gussen. Clement's *Stromateis*
(*'Miscellanies'*) are preserved in only one manuscript, L. His *Paedagogus* (*'Tutor'*) is also preserved in only one manuscript, P. The reports of readings in Clement in my apparatus are
drawn from Früchtel's revision of Stählin's edition (1960–72).

[93] The three most important manuscripts of Diogenes Laertius are B, P, and F, occasionally
joined by *Φ* (an extensive Byzantine excerpt) and V (representing the 'vulgate'). The reports of
readings in the manuscripts of Diogenes in my apparatus are drawn from Marcovich's Teubner
(1999).

Stobaeus offers these excerpts under chapter or section headings that describe their ostensible subject, and with the author's name and often (but not invariably) the title of the work, but without further comment. The collection was intended for the education and edification of his son, and there is accordingly relatively little 'Old Comedy' (the salaciousness of which must have made it appear unsuitable for this purpose) but a great deal of Menander and Philemon. That Stobaeus knew the 'New Comic' poets at first hand is possible. But the fact that he was working in a provincial city at a relatively late date militates against the possibility that he had access to a large and diverse library and thus that he read plays by obscure poets such as Heniochus (**C2**) and Sosicrates (fr. 3, quoted at iii. 23. 2); and much of the material he quotes is probably drawn from earlier anthologies.[94]

The *Lexicon* of the Byzantine scholar Photius (ninth century AD) contains numerous quotations from comedy, including **B16–B17**; **B19**; **B21**; **B26**; **B33. 2**; **B43**. Photius' report of his voluminous personal reading in the *Bibliotheca* makes it clear that he had no taste for poetry, and the fact that the fragments he preserves are routinely found in other similar sources as well leaves no doubt that the vast majority of this material has been taken over from earlier lexicographic sources.[95]

A few complete comedies by a handful of select authors continued to circulate until the late Roman period. But the evidence makes it very probable that in Hellenistic and Roman times the vast majority of the plays were known even to highly educated readers—to the extent they were known at all—only at second hand through anthologies, commentaries, lexica, specialist essays, and the like. That fewer than a dozen complete plays by a single author survived the Dark Ages is thus understandable; and while the sands of Egypt may continue to yield tattered bits and pieces of Menander and other 'New Comic' authors, and from time to time some Epicharmus, Cratinus, Eupolis, or Aristophanes, the harvest of fresh fragments of other, more emphatically 'lost' poets is likely to be meagre indeed. Our task is accordingly to make as much as we can of what has in one way or another been preserved for us.

---

[94] The manuscripts of Stobaeus Books iii and iv are divided into three families: S, MA, and (in portions of Book 3 only) L. The reports of readings in this portion of Stobaeus in my apparatus are drawn from Hense's edition (1894–1923).

[95] The portions of Photius' *Lexicon* that contains fragments presented in this collection are preserved in two manuscripts, b and z (the epitomized portions of which are filled out in a supplement, S^z), occasionally joined by a. z was discovered only in 1959 and its readings have not yet been reported fully. See in general K. Tsantsanoglou, *New Fragments of Greek Literature from the Lexicon of Photius* (Πραγματειαι της Ακαδημιας Αθηνων 49: Athens, 1984), 11–14; Arnott, in *Rivals*, 8–9. The reports of readings in Photius α–μ in my apparatus are drawn from the first two volumes of Theodoridis' edition (1982, 1998), which takes account of z; while for Photius ν–ω I rely on Porson's posthumous edition (1823).

Section A

Doric Comedy

A1. Epicharmus fr. 18, from *Bousiris* (VI/V)

πρᾶτον μὲν αἴ κ᾽ ἔσθοντ᾽ ἴδοις νιν, ἀποθάνοις·
βρέμει μὲν ὁ φάρυγξ ἔνδοθ᾽, ἀραβεῖ δ᾽ ἁ γνάθος,
ψοφεῖ δ᾽ ὁ γομφίος, τέτριγε δ᾽ ὁ κυνόδων,
σίζει δὲ ταῖς ῥίνεσσι, κινεῖ δ᾽ οὔατα

A2. Epicharmus fr. 48, from *The Wedding of Hebe* (VI/V)

αὐτὸς ὁ Ποτειδὰν ἄγων γαύλοισιν ἐν Φοινικικοῖς
ἷκε καλλίστους † αδητατήγανος ἀγεμὼν † σπάρους
καὶ σκάρους, τῶν οὐδὲ τὸ σκὰρ θεμιτὸν ἐκβαλεῖν θεοῖς

> 1 ἄγων γαύλοισιν Koen: αίων γαυλοῖς Ath. (1)ᴬ   2 ἷκε Meineke: εἰ καὶ Ath. (1)ᴬ
> ἀγεμὼν Ath. (1)ᴬ: ἁλιεύομεν Ath. (2)ᴬᶜᴱ

A3. Epicharmus fr. 40, from *The Wedding of Hebe* (VI/V)

ἄγει δὲ παντοδαπὰ κογχύλια,
λεπάδας ἀσπέδους κραβύζους κικιβάλους τηθύνια
κτένια βαλάνους πορφύρας ὄστρεια συμμεμυκότα,
τὰ διελεῖν μέν ἐντι χαλεπά, καταφαγῆμεν δ᾽ εὐμαρέα,
μύας ἀναρίτας τε κάρυκάς τε καὶ σκιφύδρια,   5
τὰ γλυκέα μέν ἐντ᾽ ἐπέσθειν, ἐμπαγῆμεν δ᾽ ὀξέα,
τούς τε μακρογογγύλους σωλῆνας. ἁ μέλαινά τε
κόγχος, ἅπερ κογχοθηρᾶν παισὶν † ἐστρισώνια †·
θάτεραι δὲ γάιαι κόγχοι τε κἀμαθίτιδες,
ταὶ κακοδόκιμοί τε κηῢωνοι, τὰς ἀνδροφυκτίδας   10
πάντες ἄνθρωποι καλέονθ᾽, ἁμὲς δὲ λεύκας τοὶ θεοί

> 2–3 τηθύνια, | κτένια Meineke, Ahrens: τηθυνάκια Ath.ᴬ   9 δὲ γάιαι Ahrens:
> δέται Ath.ᴬ   10 ταὶ Schweighäuser: τε Ath.ᴬ   κηῢωνοι Ahrens: κηυγονοι Ath.ᴬ

A4. Epicharmus fr. 51, from *The Wedding of Hebe* (VI/V)

καὶ σκιφίας χρόμις θ', ὃς ἐν τῶι ἦρι κὰτ τὸν Ἀνάνιον
ἰχθύων πάντων ἄριστος, ἀνθίας δὲ χείματι

A5. Epicharmus fr. 50, from *The Wedding of Hebe* (VI/V)

ἐντὶ δ' ἀστακοὶ κολύβδαιναί τε χὣς τὰ πόδι' ἔχει
μικρά, τὰς χεῖρας δὲ μακράς, κάραβος δὲ τὤνυμα

A6. Epicharmus fr. 97, from *Odysseus the Deserter* (VI/V)

(Α.)]κ[   ]   πλ[άνον]   τουτόνη
                    *   *   *

α̣[   ]ευονθορως οἷόνπερ ἐπι   συντυχών
                    *   *   *

(Οδ.) – ∪ – × ῥαιστά κα τοῦτ' ἐργασαίμαν ἢ ὅτι
                    *   *   *

(Α.) ἀλλ' ὁρέω (τί, ὦιζύρ', ἀνιῆις;), τοίδε τὠιχαιοὶ πέλας
                    *   *   *

(Οδ.) ὡς ἔω πονηρ<ότ>ατος. (Α.) <ἀλλ'> ἁλιδίως πονηρὸς <εἶ>.   5
                    *   *   *

(Οδ.) οὐ γὰρ ἔμπα[λίν] χ' ἀνύσαιμ' οὕτως· ἀλοιῆσθαι κακόν
                    *   *   *

– ∪ ε]νθὼν τεῖδε θωκησῶ τε καὶ λεξοῦ[μ' ὅπ]ως
ῥάιδιν' εἴμειν ταῦτα καὶ τοῖς δεξιωτέροις ἐμεῦ[ς.
(Α.) – ∪ –]ἐμὶν δοκεῖτε πάγχυ καὶ κατὰ τρόπον
καὶ ἐοικότως ἐπεύξασθ', αἴ τις ἐνθυμεῖν γ[α λῆι.   10
(Οδ.) – ∪ –]γ' ὤφειλον ἐνθὲν ὕσπερ ἐκελήσ[αντό με
– ∪ –]των ἀγαθικῶν κακὰ προτιμάσαι θ[∪ –
τόν τε κίν]δυνον τελέσσαι καὶ κλέος θεῖον λ[αβεῖν
– ∪ –]ν μολὼν ἐς ἄστυ, πάντα δ' εὖ σαφα[νέως
πυθόμεν]ος δίοις τ' Ἀχαιοῖς παιδί τ' Ἀτρέος φί[λωι   15
ἂψ ἀπαγ]γεῖλαι τὰ τηνεῖ καὐτὸς ἀσκηθὴς φ̣[υγεῖν
               ]   ιν̣[

---

5 πονηρ<ότ>ατος Lobel   <ἀλλ'> Kassel   <εἶ> Webster   7 λεξοῦ[μ'] Gomperz [ὅπ]ως Kaibel   9 [μετρίως] Webster   11 [αἴθ' ἐγών]γ' et ἐκελήσ[αντό με] Blass 13 [τόν τε κίν]δυνον Gomperz   14 σαφα[νέως] Blass   15 [πυθόμεν]ος Blass 16 φ̣[υγεῖν] Austin

A7. Epicharmus fr. 99, from *Odysseus the Deserter* (VI/V)

δέλφακά τε τῶν γειτόνων
τοῖς Ἐλευσινίοις φυλάσσων δαιμονίως ἀπώλεσα,
οὐχ ἑκών· καὶ ταῦτα δή με συμβολατεύειν ἔφα
τοῖς Ἀχαιοῖσιν προδιδόμειν τ᾽ὤμνυέ με τὸν δέλφακα

2 ἀπώλεσα Petit: ἀπώλεσας Ath.^A   3 ἔφη Ath.^A: μ᾽ ἔφα pap.   4 προδιδόμειν
Ahrens: προδιδόμην Ath.^A

A8. Epicharmus fr. 100, from *Odysseus the Deserter* (VI/V)

ἁ δ᾽ Ἡσυχία χαρίεσσα γυνά,
καὶ Σωφροσύνας πλατίον οἰκεῖ

A9. Epicharmus fr. 70, from *Cyclops* (VI/V)

ναὶ τὸν Ποτειδᾶν, κοιλότερος ὅλμου πολύ

ναὶ τὸν Meineke: αἰνετὸν Hdn.

A10. Epicharmus fr. 71, from *Cyclops* (VI/V)

χορδαί τε ἁδύ, ναὶ μὰ Δία, χὠ κωλεός

A11. Epicharmus fr. 72, from *Cyclops* (VI/V)

φέρ᾽ ἐγχέας ἐς τὸ σκύφος

A12. Epicharmus fr. 135, from an unidentified play (VI/V)

ἐκ τᾶς τῶ Διός
φαντι κεφαλᾶς ἀπολέσαι πράτιστα πάντων ἐν μάχαι
τᾶι γενομέναι κατὰ Κρόνον Πάλλαντα, τὸ δὲ τούτω δέρος
πὸτ τὸ φοβερὰν εἶμεν εὐθὺς περιβαλεῖν αὐτᾶι κύκλωι·
διόπερ αὐτὰν Παλλάδ᾽ ὀνομασθῆμεν ὑπὸ πάντων τόκα   5

4 εἶμεν εὐθὺς scripsi: εὐθὺς εἶμεν pap.   αὐτᾶι Kassel: αυτας pap.

A13. Epicharmus fr. 32, from *Hope or Wealth* (VI/V)

συνδειπνέων τῶι λῶντι, καλέσαι δεῖ μόνον,
καὶ τῶι γα μηδὲ λῶντι, κωὐδὲν δεῖ καλεῖν.

τηνεῖ δὲ χαρίεις τ᾽ εἰμὶ καὶ ποιέω πολὺν
γέλωτα καὶ τὸν ἱστιῶντ᾽ ἐπαινέω.
καί κα τις ἀντίον <τι> λῆι τήνωι λέγειν,   5
τήνωι κυδάζομαί τε κἀπ᾽ ὦν ἠχθόμαν.
κἤπειτα πολλὰ καταφαγών, πόλλ᾽ ἐμπιὼν
ἄπειμι. λύχνον δ᾽ οὐχ ὁ παῖς μοι συμφέρει,
ἕρπω δ᾽ ὀλισθράζων τε καὶ κατὰ σκότος
ἐρῆμος· αἴ κα δ᾽ ἐντύχω τοῖς περιπόλοις,   10
τοῦθ᾽ οἷον ἀγαθὸν ἐπιλέγω τοῖς θεοῖς, ὅτι
οὐ λῶντι πλεῖον ἀλλὰ μαστιγῶντί με.
ἐπεὶ δέ χ᾽ ἵκω οἴκαδις καταφθαρείς,
ἄστρωτος εὕδω· καὶ τὰ μὲν πρᾶτ᾽ οὐ κοέω,
ἇς κά μ᾽ ἄκρατος οἶνος ἀμφέπηι φρένας   15

2 τῶι γα μηδὲ λῶντι Schweighäuser: τῶι γαμηλιωντι τω γα Ath.ᴬ   5 <τι> Scaliger
12 πλεῖον Ahrens: παιων Ath.ᴬ   14 κοέω Kaibel: κοῶ Ath.ᴬ

A14. Epicharmus fr. 147, from an unidentified play (VI/V)

(*A*.) τί δὲ τόδ᾽ ἐστί; (*B*.) δηλαδὴ τρίπους. (*A*.) τί μὰν ἔχει πόδας
τέτορας; οὐκ ἔστιν τρίπους, ἀλλ᾽ <ἔστιν>, οἶμαι, τετράπους.
(*B*.) ἔστι δ᾽ ὄνυμ᾽ αὐτῶι τρίπους, τέτοράς γα μὰν ἔχει πόδας.
(*A*.) εἰ δίπους τοίνυν ποκ᾽ ἦς, αἰνίγματ᾽ Οἰ<δίπου> νοεῖς.

2 <ἔστιν> Grotefend   4 εἰ δίπους Grotefend: οἰδίπους Ath.ᶜᴱ   αἰνίγματ᾽ Οἰ<δίπου>
Grotefend: αἴνιγμά τοι Ath.ᶜᴱ

A15. Epicharmus fr. 146, from an unidentified play (VI/V)

            † ἐκ μὲν θυσίας θοίνα
ἐκ δὲ θοίνας πόσις ἐγένετο. (*B*.) χαρίεν, ὥς γ᾽ ἐμοὶ <δοκεῖ>.
(*A*.) ἐκ δὲ πόσιος κῶμος, ἐκ κώμου δ᾽ ἐγένεθ᾽ ὑανία,
ἐκ δ᾽ ὑανίας δίκα, <᾽κ δίκας δ᾽ ἐγένετο καταδίκα>,
ἐκ δὲ καταδίκας πέδαι τε καὶ σφαλὸς καὶ ζαμία   5

2 <δοκεῖ> Dindorf   3 ἐγένεθ᾽ ὑανία Dobree: ἐγένετο θυανία Ath.ᶜᴱ   4 δ᾽ ὑανίας
Dobree: δὲ θυανίας Ath.ᶜᴱ   <᾽κ δίκας δ᾽ ἐγένετο καταδίκα> Meineke (praeeuntibus Erasmo et
Stephano)   5 σφαλὸς Bochart: σφάκελος Suda: σφάκελλος Ath.ᶜᴱ

A16. Epicharmus fr. 214, from an unidentified play (VI/V)

νοῦς ὁρῆι καὶ νοῦς ἀκούει· τἆλλα κωφὰ καὶ τυφλά

A17. Epicharmus fr. 213, from an unidentified play (VI/V)

συνεκρίθη καὶ διεκρίθη κἀπῆλθεν ὅθεν ἦλθεν πάλιν,
γᾶ μὲν εἰς γᾶν, πνεῦμα δ᾽ ἄνω· τί τῶνδε χαλεπόν; οὐδὲ ἕν

A18. [Epicharmus] fr. 244, from *Practical Maxims*

τεῖδ᾽ ἔνεστι πολλὰ καὶ παν[τ]οῖα, τοῖς χρήσαιό κα
ποτὶ φίλον, πὸτ ἐχθρόν, ἐν δίκαι λέγων, ἐν ἀλίαι,
ποτὶ πονηρόν, ποτὶ καλόν τε κἀγαθόν, ποτὶ ξένον,
ποτὶ δύσεριν, ποτὶ πάροινον, ποτὶ βάναυσον, αἴτε τις
ἀλλ᾽ ἔχει κακόν τι, καὶ τούτοισι κέντρα τεῖδ᾽ ἔνο.   5
ἐν δὲ καὶ γνῶμαι σοφαὶ τεῖδ᾽, αἷσιν α[ἴ] πίθοιτό τις,
δεξιώτερός τε κ᾽ εἴη βελτίων τ᾽ ἐς πά[ν]τ᾽ ἀνήρ.
κο]ὔτι πολλὰ δεῖ λέγ[ε]ιν, ἀλλ᾽ ἓν μόνον [τ]ούτων ἔπος
πὸτ τὸ πρᾶγμα ποτιφέροντα τῶνδ᾽ ἀε[ὶ] τὸ συμφέρον.
αἰτίαν γὰρ ἦχον ὡς ἄλλως μὲν εἴην [δ]έξιος,   10
μακρολόγος δὲ κοὔ δυναίμαν ἐν β[ρ]αχεῖ γνώμα[ς λέγ]ειν.
ταῦτα δὴ ᾽γὼν εἰσακούσας συντίθημι τὰν τέχναν
τάνδ᾽, ὅ[π]ως εἴπηι τις· "Ἐπίχαρμος σοφός τις ἐγένετο,
πολλὰ δ᾽ εἶ]π᾽ ἀστεῖα καὶ παντοῖα καθ᾽ ἓν [ἔπος] λέγων
πεῖραν] αὑταυτοῦ διδοὺς ὡς καὶ β[ραχ   15
            τάδ]ε μαθὼν ἅπας ἀνὴρ φαν[ήσεται σοφός
      ]ήσει ποτ᾽ οὐδὲν ἔπος απ[
      ]οντα λυπήσει τι τῶνδ[
      ]τρ[   ]α δρῶντα τοῖσδ[
            ]ορητε πολυμαθη[20
      ]ων[   ]ρτ[   ]ἐρῶ δὲ καὶ τ[
      ]ιτε τούτοις γα κακα[ ]χειν[
ἄλλος ἄ]λλωι γὰρ [γ]έγαθε κοὔτι ταὐ[τὰ
            ]ε πάντα δεῖ τάδ᾽ ὡς ε[
            ἔ]πειτα δ᾽ ἐν καιρῶι λέ[γειν   25
            ]ειμα βραχυσοι[

11 δὲ κού van Leeuwen: δουκα pap.   13 τις¹ Grenfell and Hunt: τι pap.
14 [πολλὰ δ᾽ εἶ]π᾽ Latte   [ἔπος] Grenfell and Hunt   15 β[ραχ-] Croenert   16 [τάδ]ε
Page   φαν[ήσεται σοφός] Croenert   23 [ἄλλος ἄ]λλωι Grenfell and Hunt   ταὐ[τὰ]
Croenert   25 λέ[γειν] Croenert

A19. [Epicharmus] fr. 269, from *Practical Maxims*

τὸ δὲ γαμεῖν ὅμοιόν ἐστι τῶι τρὶς ἓξ ἢ τρεῖς κύβους
ἀπὸ τύχης βαλεῖν. ἐὰν μὲν γὰρ λάβηις τεταγμένην
τοῖς τρόποις καὶ τἆλλ' ἄλυπον, εὐτυχήσεις τῶι γάμωι·
εἰ δὲ καὶ φιλέξοδόν τε καὶ λάλον καὶ δαψιλῆ,
οὐ γυναῖχ' ἕξεις, διὰ βίου δ' ἀτυχίαν κοσμουμέναν   5

1 τρὶς ˢStob.ᴬ: τρεῖς Stob.ˢᴹᴬ   κύβους Stob.ˢ: κύβους μόνους Stob.ᴹᴬ

A20. Sophron fr. 4. a, from *Women Who Say That They Will Drive Out the Goddess* (V)

(*A*.) τὰν τράπεζαν κάτθετε
ὥσπερ ἔχει·
λάζεσθε δὲ
ἁλὸς χόνδρον ἐς τὰν χῆρα
καὶ δάφναν πὰρ τὸ ὦας.   5
ποτιβάντες νυν πὸτ τὰν ἱστίαν θωκεῖτε.
δός μοι τὺ τὤμφακες·
φέρ' ὦ τὰν σκύλακα.
πεῖ γὰρ ἁ ἄσφαλτος;
(*B*.) οὕτα.   10
(*A*.) ἔχε καὶ τὸ δάιδιον
καὶ τὸν λιβανωτόν.
ἄγετε δὴ
πεπτάσθων μοι ταὶ θύραι πᾶσαι.
ὑμὲς δὲ ἐνταῦθα ὁρῆτε   15
καὶ τὸν δαελὸν σβῆτε
ὥσπερ ἔχει.
εὐκαμίαν νυν παρέχεσθε
ἇς κ' ἐγὼν πὸτ τάνδε πυκταλεύσω.
πότνια,   20
δείπνου μέν τυ κα[ὶ ξ]ενίων ἀμεμφέων
ἀντά[ ]ν ν· καὶ κα ἀμῶν δέπ [

A21. Sophron fr. 3, from *Women Who Say That They Will Drive Out the Goddess* (V)

ὑποκατώρυκται δὲ ἐν κυαθίδι τρικτὺς ἀλεξιφαρμάκων

τρικτὺς Schweighäuser: τρικτοι Ath.ᴬ: τρικτύα Jahn

A22. Eupolis fr. 261, from *Men from the Deme Prospalta* (V)

(Α.) τὸ δεῖν’, ἀκούεις; (Β.) Ἡράκλεις, τοῦτ’ ἔστι σοι
τὸ σκῶμμ’ ἀσελγὲς καὶ Μεγαρικὸν καὶ σφόδρα
ψυχρόν. † γελᾶς ὁρᾶις τὰ παιδία †

  1 δεῖν’ Meineke: δεινῆς Σ Arist.   3 γελᾶς anon. in Arist.: σέλας Σ Arist.

COMMENTARY

A1–A19. For Epicharmus of Syracuse (early fifth century BC), see Introduction pp. 6–11; *DTC* 353–413; Olivieri i. 3–137 (an edition with commentary); Breitholtz 25–30; Kerkhof 51–177. The standard edition of the fragments is *PCG* I (2001; replacing G. Kaibel, *Comicorum Graecorum Fragmenta*, i. 1 (Berlin, 1899)). **A1–A12** are from mythological comedies, while **A13–A15** are from 'ethical' comedies, i.e. plays built about the personalities of their human characters. **A18–A19** are from *Practical Maxims*, the best attested of the didactic works falsely attributed to Epicharmus already in the fourth century.

A1. Bousiris king of Egypt, a son of Poseidon, had been advised by the seer Phrasius to sacrifice one foreigner every year to Zeus in order to keep his land free of famine. Bousiris made Phrasius his first victim and then, when Heracles came to Egypt in the course of his labours, had him arrested and led to the altar. But Heracles broke his bonds and killed a number of Egyptians, including the king and his son. The most complete account of the story (attested already in sixth-century vase painting) is at [Apollod.] *Bib.* ii. 5. 11; cf. Pherecyd. *FGrHist* 3 F 17; Panyas. fr. 12 with Matthews ad loc. (pp. 126–7); Hdt. ii. 45. 1 (but with no mention of a king); Isocrates, *Bousiris*; D.S. iv. 18. 1; Gantz 418. For other references to Egypt in comedy, see **B35**. 15; Anaxandr. fr. 40; Antiph. fr. 145; Timocl. fr. 1. Comedies entitled *Bousiris* were also composed by Cratinus (fr. 23 (preparations for the sacrifice)), Ephippus (fr. 2 (Heracles announces his identity to someone who declines to be impressed)), Antiphanes (frr. 66–8), and Mnesimachus (fr. 2 (Heracles announces his identity, observing that he is a glutton)), and Euripides wrote a satyr play with the same name (frr. 313–15). Anon. dor. fr. 1 may also belong to Epicharmus' *Bousiris*.

Heracles' extraordinary appetite probably figured in the plots of Epicharmus' *Heracles at Pholus' House* and *The Wedding of Hebe* (see **A2–A5** n.), as well as in anon. dor. com. fr. 1 (note vv. 8–9), and the theme is widely attested in Attic Comedy (e.g. **G2–G3**; **H14**; Ar. *V.* 60; *Pax* 741 (treated in both places as a tired old cliché); *Av.* 567 with Dunbar ad loc., 1583–1692; *Ra.* 62–5, 549–76; Mnesim. fr. 2 (from *Bousiris*); Eub. fr. 6; Trendall # 22, 25, 31, 32 (all presumably illustrations of Middle Comedies)) and satyr play (E. *Alc.* 753–60 ('pro-satyric'); fr. 691; Ion *TrGF* 19 F 29–*30; cf. Trendall plate II.b); cf. **B24** (a personified day of feasting speaks the prologue of a play entitled *Heracles*); Breitholz 66–70. Other plays by Epicharmus in which Heracles must have been a central character include *Antanor*, *Heracles in Search of the Belt* (the

earliest reference to the incident; cf. Pi. fr. 172. 5; Bond on E. *HF* 408–18),
and perhaps *Amycus*; cf. Phormus' *Admetus*; Dinolochus' *Pholus*; DTC 383–9;
G. K. Galinsky, *The Herakles Theme* (Oxford, 1972), 81–100; Wilkins 90–7.

   The speaker is reporting to someone—most likely Bousiris himself—about
the behaviour of Heracles, whom he has seen but his interlocutor has not.
Line 1 makes it clear that this is only the first portion of the description,
which may have been part of an account of the hero's initial arrival in Egypt.
Cf. Kerkhof 117.

   Preserved at Athenaeus 10. 411a–b, as the first of a number of examples of
what the speaker presents as the general literary consensus that Heracles was a
glutton.

   Iambic trimeter.

1.   **πρᾶτον** = Attic *πρῶτον* (cf. **A12**. 2); **αἰ** = Attic *εἰ* (e.g. **A6**. 10; **A13**. 5);
κ(α) = Attic *ἄν* (e.g. **A6**. 6; **A13**. 5); **ἔσθοντ(α)** = Attic *ἐσθίοντα*; and **νιν** =
Attic *μιν*.   **ἀποθάνοις**: i.e. from terror. But if this report is being
offered to Bousiris himself (see introductory n.), the fact that the king was
eventually killed by Heracles adds ironic significance to the remark.

2–4.   Each verse consists of two balanced clauses, which describe complementary parts of Heracles' anatomy (throat and jaw, molar and canine
tooth, nostrils and ears); the description moves in the opposite direction
from the actual process of eating, from the throat (which swallows), to the
jaw and the rear teeth (which grind the food before it is swallowed), to
the canines (which bite and tear), to the nose and the ear (which move
involuntarily along with the jaw). Despite *ἴδοις* in 1, the emphasis until
the second half of 4 is on what the addressee would hear (rather than see) if
he were to come face-to-face with the hero. The verb is always in lead
position, and the effect depends on the repeated discovery of new ways to
communicate the idea 'makes a loud noise' combined with the surprise
generated by each new noun.

2.   **βρέμει . . . ὁ φάρυγξ ἔνδοθ(ι)**: 'his throat roars within', i.e. 'emits a roar',
as the food races down it.   **ἀραβεῖ**: 'rings, rattles'; epic vocabulary
(e.g. H. *Il.* 5. 42, 58; *Od.* 24. 525; [Hes.] *Sc.* 249 (of the Keres gnashing their
teeth)), not attested after this until the Hellenistic period.

3.   A **γομφίος** (sc. *ὀδούς*; a collective singular (KG i. 13–14; cf. **D1**. 4; **G12**.
6 with n.)) is literally a 'peg tooth', i.e. a molar (e.g. Phryn. Com. fr. 73);
more often opposed to a *πρόσθιος ὀδούς* ('front tooth, incisor'; cf. **B17**.
2) than a **κυνόδων** or *κυνόδους* (literally 'dog tooth', i.e. 'canine'). See
Olson on Ar. *Pax* 33–4.   **τέτριγε** is < *τρίζω* ('squeak' *vel sim.*);
perfect with present sense (Goodwin § 49(a)).

4.   **σίζει . . . ταῖς ῥίνεσσι**: literally 'he hisses with his nostrils,' i.e. 'he snorts

loudly' (because his mouth is so full and busy that he is forced to breathe through his nose).   **κινεῖ . . . οὔατα:** sc. because he is chewing so vigorously.

A2–A5. Hebe was a daughter of Zeus and Hera who was given in marriage to Heracles after he accomplished his labours and ascended to Olympus (e.g. H. *Od.* 11. 601–4; Hes. *Th.* 950–4; fr. 25. 28–9; Pi. *N.* 1. 71–2; E. *Heracl.* 915–16 with Wilkins ad loc.); cf. Gantz 81–2, 460–3. Athenaeus preserves twenty-three fragments (totalling forty-seven lines or partial lines, all in trochaic tetrameter) of what appears to be a single speech from Epicharmus' play; that the play consisted of this speech and nothing else is possible but incapable of proof. Athenaeus also informs us (3. 110b) that *Muses* was a revised version (διασκευή) of *The Wedding of Hebe* (= test. ii), and frr. 84–91 (and probably 92 as well) from that play, all of which describe seafood and are in trochaic tetrameter, should perhaps be connected with this speech as well. Archippus wrote a *Wedding-Feast of Heracles* (frr. 8–13), as did Nicochares (fr. 7).

The speaker is a deity (**A3**. 11), who describes a great parade most naturally taken as making its way to the wedding banquet. The guests include Poseidon, who came bringing fish (**A2**)—as befits the god of the sea—as doubtless did the seven Muses, whom Epicharmus identified as the children of 'Fat and Fullness' and to whom he assigned the names of seven great rivers (fr. 39). If fr. 92 (from *Muses*) belongs to another version of the same speech, Athena (who played the pipe) and the Dioscuri (who danced) may also have attended, presumably in the company of the other Olympians. Almost all the fragments of the speech refer to seafood (but birds in fr. 42; bread (brought by Demeter?) in fr. 46), in which Sicily was rich, although this may mean only that Athenaeus or his source has given us an unrepresentative sample of the text. The edible creatures that follow the gods to the celebration, at any rate, seemingly do so without hesitation; and whether the fact that they are going to be eaten (cf. fr. 88 (from *Muses*), where Zeus arranges that 'the much-honoured ἔλοψ' be served to himself and Hera) came as a surprise to them or not, Heracles' traditional gluttony must have played some part in the story. Cf. **A1** with introductory n.; Kerkhof 118–19.

A2. If most of the fragments of *The Wedding of Hebe* preserved by Athenaeus come from the same section of this speech (see **A2–A5** n.), these are most likely its opening lines.

Preserved entire at Athenaeus (1) 7. 320c (manuscript A only), in a collection of literary references to the sea bream, with 2 in the form printed here. In addition, Athenaeus (2) 7. 319f preserves a version of 2–3 that begins with the words ἁλιεύομεν σπάρους (see 2 n.).

Trochaic tetrameter catalectic.

1. **Ποτειδάν:** a Doric form of the god's name (e.g. Ar. *Ach.* 798 (a Megarian); Eup. fr. 149 (a Doric-speaker); *IG* IV 211 (Corinth); XII. 1 4124. 22 (Rhodes); cf. the Corinthian material collected at Wachter 268), also used in **A9** (where see introductory n.); Epich. frr. 113. 218; 186; Sophr. fr. 125.   **ἄγων:** cf. **A3**. 1 with **A3** introductory n.   **γαύλοισιν ἐν Φοινικικοῖς:** A γαῦλος is a merchant-ship of a sort regularly associated with Phoenicians (e.g. Hdt. iii. 136. 1; vi. 17; viii. 97. 1; Call. fr. 384. 50; cf. Casson 66). Fish spoiled too quickly to be transported fresh from one end of the Mediterranean to the other and were therefore routinely converted into saltfish (τάριχος; see **D1**. 5 n.), which was a common trade good, a fact to which this passage perhaps alludes; cf. Ar. fr. 430 with K–A ad loc.

2. **ἵκε** is < ἵκω, a widespread non-Attic form (e.g. **A13**. 13; Epich. fr. 113. 504; Ar. *Ach.* 820 (a Megarian); *Lys.* 87 (a Spartan); Pi. *P*. 4. 126; Corinn. *PMG* 694 fr. 1(a). 7) = Attic ἥκω.   **ἁλιεύομεν** ('we fish for') in Ath. (2) was most likely supplied by an anthologist or copyist to govern the accusatives in the abbreviated version of the text given there. We are thus thrown back on Ath. (1)'s corrupt **αδητατήγανος ἀγεμών**, which may conceal *inter alia* an adjective formed from τάγηνος ('frying pan'; see **G4**. 12 n.).

2–3. **σπάρους | καὶ σκάρους:** 'sea breams and parrot wrasses'; succulent fish, for which see, respectively, *Fishes*, 248–9, and *Fishes*, 238–41 and Olson–Sens on Archestr. fr. 14. 1 (cf. **G11**. 20).

3. **τῶν κτλ.:** an irreverent, witty interjection of a sort typical of this speech (cf. **A3** introductory n.): the fish is so delicious that the gods have no choice but to eat it all—including its droppings!   **τῶν** = ὧν; cf. **A3**. 4 n. **σκάρ** = Attic σκῶρ, 'shit' (Ar. *Ra.* 146; *Pl.* 305; Stratt. fr. 8); a primary obscenity that mockingly recalls the name of the fish itself.

A3. Comparison with **A2**. 1 suggests that the subject of **ἄγει** in 1 is a god, possibly still Poseidon. Catalogues of foodstuffs are common in Attic comedy (cf. 2–7 nn.; **G13** with introductory n.), and audiences apparently enjoyed the ingenuity with which long strings of related words were put into metrical form. Here (as throughout the preserved portions of this speech) monotony is avoided via the insertion every few lines of witty, generally culinarily oriented comments on the creatures mentioned (4, 6, 10–11; cf. **A2**. 3 n.).

Preserved entire at Athenaeus 3. 85c–e, at the beginning of an extended discussion of literary references to shellfish. In addition, the final two words of 3 are quoted at Athenaeus 3. 92f, as an example of the use of the form ὄστρεια by 'the ancients'.

Trochaic tetrameter catalectic.

1.   **παντοδαπὰ κοχγύλια**: 'little shellfish (diminutive < *κόγχη/κόγχος*; see 9 n.) of every sort' (listed in 2–3, 5, 7).

2–7.   For similar catalogues of shellfish and the like (commonly eaten as appetizers), e.g. Philyll. fr. 12. 1–2; Archipp. fr. 24; Anaxandr. fr. 42. 60–2; Posidipp. Com. fr. 15. 2–3.

2.   **λεπάδας**: 'limpets' (see *Fishes*, 147–8), included in catalogues of shellfish also at Philyll. fr. 12. 2; Archipp. fr. 24; Anaxandr. fr. 42. 61; Philippid. fr. 4.   **ἀσπέδους κραβύζους κικιβάλους**: obviously edible shellfish of some sort, but the words are not attested elsewhere and these must be local Sicilian names, like *κολύβδαινα* in **A5**. 1.   **τηθύνια**: an otherwise unattested diminutive < *τήθυον*, 'sea-squirt, ascidian', a simple, sedentary marine animal with leathery skin, implicitly referred to as food already at H. *Il*. 16. 747–8. See *Fishes*, 261–2; Olson–Sens on Archestr. fr. 7. 6–7.

3.   **κτένια**: an otherwise unattested diminutive < *κτείς*, 'scallop' (see *Fishes*, 133–4; Olson–Sens on Archestr. fr. 7. 2), included in catalogues of shell-fish also at Philyll. fr. 12. 2; Archipp. fr. 24; Anaxandr. fr. 42. 62; Alex. fr. 175. 2.   **βαλάνους**: normally 'acorns' (cf. **D1**. 20), but convention-ally translated 'barnacles' when used of shellfish (e.g. Archipp. fr. 24; Arist. *HA* 535^{a}24–5; Diph. Siph. ap. Ath. 3. 91a); exactly what creature is being referred to is unclear (see *Fishes*, 24–5; García Soler 141).   **πορφύρας**: 'purple shellfish' (see *Fishes*, 209–18; Olson–Sens, *Archestratos*, p. 245), most commonly referred to as a source of dye, but mentioned as food also at e.g. Hp. *Vict*. vi. 550. 4–6; Hicesius ap. Ath. 3. 87e; Ennius, *SH* 193. 11.   **ὄστρεια συμμεμυκότα**: 'tightly closed (< *συμμύω*) oysters' (see *Fishes*, 190–2; Olson–Sens on Archestr. fr. 7. 1), included in catalogues of shellfish at Philyll. fr. 12. 1; Anaxandr. fr. 42. 61; Philippid. fr. 4. The participle (contrast the eight preceding nouns, all of which stand alone) sets up the witticism in 4.

4.   **τά** = *ἅ*, as again in 6. Cf. 10 *ταί* = *αἵ*, *τάς* = *ἅς*; **A2**. 3 *τῶν* = *ὧν*; **A18**. 1 *τοῖς* = *οἷς*.   **διελεῖν**: 'to get apart', i.e. 'pry open'.   **ἐντι** is a Doric form = common *εἰσι*; cf. 6; **A5**. 1.   **καταφαγῆμεν**: 'to be gobbled down' (the Doric form of the aorist passive infinitive, like *ἐμπαγῆμεν* in 6 and *ὀνομασθῆμεν* in **A12**. 5), i.e. 'for anyone who gets one open (see above) to gobble down'. For the verb, see **A13**. 7 n.

5.   **μύας**: 'mussels' (for which, see **G18**. 5 n.).   **ἀναρίτας**: an unidenti-fied spiral univalve shellfish also called *νηρίτης* (see *Fishes*, 176). **κάρυκας**: 'whelks' (see *Fishes*, 113–14; Olson–Sens on Archestr. fr. 7. 6–7), included in banquet catalogues and the like at Anaxandr. fr. 42. 60; Alex. frr. 175. 2; 281. 2; Anaxil. fr. 18. 4.   **σκιφύδρια**: an unidentified bivalve shellfish; cf. 6 n.; LSJ s. *τελλίνη*.

6.   The structure of the verse recalls 4, which suggests that the second clause

stands in contrast to the first; the point must be that, although σκιφύδρια taste delicious, their shell has a sharp edge or point (hence the name, cognate with ξίφος (cf. **A4.** 1 n.), 'sword'). **τὰ . . . ἐντ(ι)**: see 4 n. **ἐμπαγῆμεν**: 'to be impaled upon' (< ἐμπήγνυμι); for the form, see 4 n.

7. **μακρογογγύλους**: 'long [and] circular', i.e. 'cylindrical'. Attested only here (merely a conjecture at Sophr. fr. 23. 1, despite LSJ s.v.). **σωλῆνας**: 'razorshell clams' (see *Fishes*, 257–8; García Soler 137–8), included in catalogues of shellfish at Philyll. fr. 12. 2; Arar. fr. 8. 2.

7–11. **ἁ μέλαινα κτλ.**: Despite the shift to the nominative (from the accusa-tive in 1–7), the creatures listed are almost certainly simply additional companions of the subject of the verb in 1. Cf. **A5**.

7–8. **ἁ μέλαινα . . . | κόγχος**: unidentified.

8. **κογχοθηρᾶν παισίν** ('the sons of the shellfish-fishers') is a poetic way of referring to the shellfish-fishers themselves. **ἐστρισώνια** is corrupt; but given (ε)ὔωνοι in 10, what is concealed probably includes a word that means 'brings a fine price' *vel sim.*

9. 'and others that live on land, both shellfish and sand-dwellers'. κόγχη/κόγχος functions as a generic term for primitive, shell-dwelling animals (*Fishes*, 118; cf. 1), and the reference is perhaps to snails and sand-crabs, since (see 10) the latter, at least, both run away when approached and are not much good for eating. **θάτεραι** is a Doric form = common ἔτεραι.

10. **ταί, τάς**: see 4 n. **κακοδόκιμοι** is omitted from LSJ, but the sense is clearly 'having a bad reputation'. **(ε)ὔωνοι**: 'easily bought', i.e. 'cheap, worthless'; cf. 8 n.

10–11. **τὰς ἀνδροφυκτίδας | κτλ.**: an allusion to Homeric passages such as *Il.* 1. 403–4 ὃν Βριάρεων καλέουσι θεοί, ἄνδρες δέ τε πάντες | Αἰγαίων' ('whom the gods call Briareus, but all men call Aigaion'); 2. 813–14; 14. 290–1; 20. 74. Cf. **A6–A11** n.; **E12**. 4–5; **H8**. 6; Cratin. fr. 352 (~ *Il.* 14. 291, where see Janko's n.); Orph. 140. 2–3 F; 155. 1–2 F; 188 F; Pl. *Crat.* 391d–2a; *Phdr.* 252b–c; H. Günteret, *Von der Sprache der Götter und Geister* (Halle, 1921), 89–130. **ἀνδροφυκτίδας** is attested nowhere else, but is < ἀνήρ + φεύγω and must mean 'fugitives-from-men'.

11. **καλέοντ(ι)** is an uncontracted Doric form = Attic καλοῦσι. **ἁμές** is a Doric form = Attic ἡμεῖς. **λεύκας** ('white') draws a contrast with the good 'black shellfish' of 7–8 (where see n.). **τοί** is a Doric form = Attic οἱ.

A4–A5. Further items in the catalogue of seafood also represented by **A2–A3**. For the nominative (rather than the accusative) in **A5**, see **A3**. 7–11 n. These fragments attest to Epicharmus' engagement with earlier, non-Homeric poetry (**A4**) and to an awareness of his work on the part of other poets from the Greek West (**A5**). Epicharmus is also supposed to have criticized Xenophanes (fr. 143; cf. fr. 279 (from the *Pseudepicharmeia*) and Xenoph. 21 B 15), who spent at least part of his adult life in Sicily, as well as Aeschylus (fr. 221 = A. test. 115), who visited Hieron's court; and the fragmentary commentary on **A6**. 8 seems to suggest another reference to tragedy, although it is difficult to know what to make of this.

A4. An adaptation of Ananius fr. 5. 1 (probably sixth century, and perhaps from the West) ἔαρι μὲν χρόμιος ἄριστος, ἀνθίης δὲ χειμῶνι ('the *chromios* is best in spring, but the *anthias* (is best) in winter'), with Ananius' Ionic translated into Doric. The entire fragment of Ananius (ten choliambic tetrameter lines, consisting of a catalogue of different kinds of fish and meat and the times of year when they are best) is given by Athenaeus immediately after he quotes these verses of Epicharmus.

Preserved at Athenaeus 7. 282a–b, at the beginning of an extended discussion of literary references to and the proper identification of the ἀνθίας (2 n.), the κάλλιχθυς ('beauty-fish'), and the ἱερὸς ἰχθύς ('holy fish'), which may all be different names for the same creature.

Trochaic tetrameter catalectic.

1.   **σκιφίας** = common ξιφίας (cf. **A3**. 6 n.), 'swordfish' (see *Fishes*, 178–80; Olson–Sens on Archestr. fr. 41. 1); not normally included in banquet catalogues and the like.   **χρόμις**: an unidentified fish (probably one of the *Sciaenidae*), which Aristotle says made a grunting noise (*HA* 535^{b}16–17), hence presumably its name (cognate with χρεμετίζω, 'whinny'). See *Fishes*, 291–2; Olson–Sens on Archestr. fr. 31. 1.   **ἦρι** is < a contracted form of ἔαρ, 'spring'.   **κὰτ τὸν Ἀνάνιον**: 'according to Ananius, to quote Ananius'. Syncopated κάτ – common κατά; cf. **Λ12**. 1 n.; **A20**. 1 κάτθετε = κατάθετε; fr. 31. 2; anon. dor. com. fr. 16. 1; Ar. *Lys.* 1258/9 (a Spartan). For this use of the preposition, e.g. Ar. *Th.* 134 κατ' Αἰσχύλον ('to quote Aeschylus'); Antiph. fr. 110. 2 κατὰ Τιμόθεον ('to quote Timotheus').
2.   **ἀνθίας**: unidentified; see *Fishes*, 14–16.

A5. Echoed by the early fourth-century gastronomic poet Archestratus of Gela (fr. 25. 2–3, of the lobster) τὸν τὰς χεῖρας ἔχοντα μακρὰς ἄλλως τε βαρείας, | τοὺς δὲ πόδας μικρούς ('the one that has large and also heavy hands, although its feet are small'; dactylic hexameter).

Preserved at Athenaeus 3. 105a–b, as part of a collection of literary references to crayfish, lobsters, and the like, in support of the unlikely hypothesis that the ἀστακός (1) and the κάραβος (2) ought to be identified.

Trochaic tetrameter catalectic.

1.   **ἐντί:** see **A3**. 4 n.   **ἀστακοί:** 'lobsters' (see *Fishes*, 18; Olson–Sens on Matro fr. 1. 66–7), included in seafood catalogues and the like at Philyll. fr. 12. 2; Matro fr. 1. 66.   **κολύβδαιναι:** otherwise unknown (probably a local name; cf. **A3**. 2 with n.), but clearly some sort of crustacean. **χὤς** = καὶ ὅς.   **πόδι(α)** is a rare diminutive < πούς.

1–2.   **τὰ πόδι(α) ἔχει | κτλ.:** The description functions as a riddle, which is resolved in the second half of 2 with the announcement that 'his name is crayfish'.

2.   **τὦνυμα** = Attic τὸ ὄνομα; a West Greek (Doric and Aeolic) form (e.g. **A14**. 3; Men. *Asp.* 445 (a doctor, who therefore speaks Doric; **F6**. 26–9 n.); Alc. fr. 129. 8; Pi. *O.* 6. 57; *N.* 6. 49) and a Doric crasis.   **κάραβος:** 'crayfish' (for which, see **G5**. 5 n.).

A6–A11. For Epicharmus' use of Homer, see also **A3**. 10–11 n.; frr. 98. 126–9 (several Homeric allusions or echoes identified by an ancient commentator); 113. 415 ἀφρ]άτωρ ἀθέμ[ιστος ἀ]νίστιος (a Doricized version of H. *Il.* 9. 63 ἀφρήτωρ ἀθέμιστος ἀνέστιός ἐστιν ἐκεῖνος, quoted also at Ar. *Pax* 1097) with Ath. 15. 698c (= Epich. test. 20); and the titles *Sirens* (frr. *121–2) and *Trojans* (frr. 128–9). Cf. **D1–D4** n. (on the reception of Homer in comedy generally); Cassio (2002) 70–3. Odysseus seems to have been another of Epicharmus' favorite characters; he appeared not just in *Odysseus the Deserter* (**A6–A8**) and *Cyclops* (**A9–A11**), but in *Odysseus Shipwrecked* (frr. 104–5) and probably *Sirens* (frr. *121–2) and *Philoctetes* (frr. 131–2); and cf. fr. 278 (sage remarks addressed to a certain Eumaeus (the name of Odysseus' faithful swineherd in the *Odyssey*) in a pseudepicharmic text cited by Alcimus). Cf. Phormus' *Alcinoos* and *The Sack of Troy or The Horse*; Dinolochus' *Circe or O[dysseus]*; Sopater's *Nekuia* (fr. 13); Phillips, *G&R* 6 (1959), 58–67 (on Odysseus in comedy generally; pp. 58–63 on Epicharmus).

A6–A8. For *Odysseus the Deserter* (Epich. frr. 97–103), see Kerkhof 123–8.

A6. Although the first six lines of the fragment in particular are badly damaged, lacunose, and obscure, it is clear that Odysseus and another character are speaking. 13–16 contain numerous echoes (underlined below) of H. *Il.* 10. 211–12, where Nestor, at a night council of the Achaean commanders after a day during which Hector has run wild, proposes that someone volunteer for a reconnaissance mission to discover the Trojans' plans: ταῦτα τε <u>πάντα πύθοιτο</u> καὶ <u>ἂψ εἰς ἡμέας ἔλθοι</u> | <u>ἀσκηθής</u>· μέγα κέν οἱ ὑπουράνιον <u>κλέος εἴη</u>. (For other echoes of *Il.* 10 in *Odysseus the Deserter*, see fr. 98. 3–4 (cf. *Il.* 10. 251), 83 (cf. *Il.* 10. 511)). In Homer's version of the story, Diomedes agrees to infiltrate the Trojan camp in the plain and chooses Odysseus as his companion, but in

Epicharmus Odysseus seems to have been charged with infiltrating the city itself (14; cf. H. *Od.* 4. 244–58; *Il. Parv.* arg. 1. 15–17; 2. 1–5; fr. 7; S. *Λάκαιναι* (frr. 367–*9a); E. *Hec.* 239–50; Ion *Φρουροί* (*TrGF* 19 F **43a–9a)). Rather than doing so, he has snuck off elsewhere (hence the title of the play) and is seen here, upon his return, expressing regret for his cowardice (11–16) and fearfully preparing a cover-story that will suggest he did what he was supposed to (7–8; cf. the paraphrase in the PVindob. *scholia* 7 προσποιήσομ(αι) πάντ(α) διαπεπρᾶχθ(αι), 'I will pretend that everything has been accomplished'). The identity of Speaker A is uncertain; whoever he is, he is thoroughly unsympathetic to Odysseus' plight (see 1–2 n.). See also Stanford, *CP* 45 (1950), 167–9; Cassio 73–80 (with further bibliography).

Lines 1–10 are preserved in POxy. xxv 2429. 27–55 (second century AD), which contains fragments of a running commentary (= fr. 98) on *Odysseus the Deserter* (as the overlap at 68 with **A7**. 3–4 proves) and perhaps another play as well. In addition, 7–17 are preserved in PVindob. 2321 (second century AD), which contains a fragment of a text of the play with *scholia* on the upper margin. How much (if anything) is missing between 1 and 2, 2 and 3 etc., is impossible to say; but if we did not have PVindob. 2321, 7–8 and 9–10 would also have to be presented as separate bits of text, and it may be that fewer lacunae exist in 1–7 than the text as printed here suggests.

Trochaic tetrameter catalectic.

1–2. The tone is hostile (someone—presumably Odysseus—is accused of or warned against offering a misleading account of things (1) and behaving haughtily (2); cf. 4–5, 9–10), and the lines are better assigned to Odysseus' interlocutor than to Odysseus himself.

1. πλ[άνον] ... τουτόνη: 'this wandering (statement)' (cf. LSJ s. πλάνος II. 2–3), i.e. 'this nonsense you are arguing (or proposing to argue)'. The restoration and translation are based on the POxy. commentator's gloss πλάνην, φλυαρίαν. τουτόνη = common τοῦτό γε.

2. οἱόνπερ ... συντυχών ('as if ... encountering') is obscure, but the POxy. commentator observes ἀπὸ τῶν ἐ[ν] ταῖς ὁδοῖς κατὰ ἀπαξίωσιν τῆ[ι κι]νήσει τοῦ ὀφθαλμοῦ ἀσπαζομένων ('(The image is drawn) from those who greet (others) in the streets with a movement of the eye expressing contempt'; cf. **G6**. 6 n.).

3. Odysseus bemoans his situation: he would have been better off doing what he was told to do in the first place. Cf. 11–16.   ῥᾶιστα ('most easily, very easily') is adverbial. The theme is taken up again in 8.   ὅτι is glossed τὸ τυχόν ('what happened', i.e. 'what I must now do perforce') by the POxy. commentator.

4.   Odysseus' interlocutor offers an unsympathetic response to his complaint (3) and notes that he is going to have to confront the army very shortly.   ὁρέω is a non-Attic form (for the lack of contraction, see **A13**. 1 n.) = Attic ὁρῶ < ὁράω, with what is seen described in the nominative at the end of the line, τοίδε τ(οὶ Ἀ)χαιοὶ πέλας ('here are the Achaeans, close at hand').   τί, ὦ (ὀ)ιζυρ(έ), ἀνιῆις: 'why, O wretch, do you grieve?' (< ἀνιάω, elsewhere transitive in the active); an interjection (thus the POxy. commentary). οἰζυρός is Homeric vocabulary (e.g. *Il.* 1. 417; *Od.* 3. 95).

5.   ὡς ἔω πονηρ<ότ>ατος is equivalent to ὥστε με εἶναι πονηρότατον, 'so that I be most miserable', sc. as a result of the abuse he expects if he returns to the Achaean camp (cf. 6). But the POxy. commentary suggests that Speaker A's response plays on another sense of πονηρός, 'bad, worthless' (as at **A18**. 3).   ἁλιδίως (cognate with ἄλις; see Cassio, *ZPE* 72 (1988), 51–2) is glossed αὐτάρκως ('sufficiently') by the POxy. commentator, and ἱκανῶς, μετρίως ('sufficiently, moderately') by Hesychius (α 2970); Speaker A's point is clearly that Odysseus is already quite πονηρός (see above) and need not worry about being made to seem a bit more so.

6.   The POxy. commentator attests to an ancient scholarly dispute about whether a half-stop should be placed before οὕτως (in which case the sense must be 'for I wouldn't hurry back (sc. to the men who sent him out)— that's how unpleasant being thrashed is') or after it ('for I wouldn't hurry back thus (i.e. without knowing exactly what he is going to say); being thrashed is unpleasant').   χ' = elided κα (see **A1**. 1 n.) before a word beginning with a rough breathing.   ἀλοιῆσθαι is < = ἀλοάω, 'thresh (grain)', i.e. 'give a pounding to'; cf. Taillardat § 138; Austin–Olson on Ar. *Th.* 2.

7–8.   Odysseus offers a plan, although it is unclear whether he proposes to pretend that his mission was in fact accomplished, and very easily at that, or hopes to argue that the task he was set was much more difficult than anyone realizes and was therefore not carried out.

7.   ε]νθών: a Doric form = common ἐλθών (perhaps part of a compound, hence the lack of a breathing mark in the text printed here).   τεῖδε: 'here', i.e. in the Achaean camp (cf. 4). A Doric form (also attested at **A18**. 1, 5, 6; Theoc. 1. 12 with Gow ad loc.) = common ἐνθάδε.   θωκησῶ: Doric future < θωκέω = common θακέω, 'sit'; cf. **A20**. 6.   λεξ-οῦ[μ(αι)]: deponent Doric future < λέγω; the [ὅπ]ως-clause that follows defines the case Odysseus intends to make in his own defence.

8.   'that these things (i.e. the orders he was given to infiltrate Troy) are easy even for people more clever than me'. The POxy. commentator argues

that the final words appear *para prosdokian* ('contrary to expectation, as a surprise') for 'those who are worse than me', i.e. 'even for perfect fools' *vel sim.* Cf. **B29**. 3 n.   ῥᾴδιν(α) (also attested at Epich. fr. 31. 2, but omitted by LSJ) is probably a local Syracusan form = Attic ῥᾴδια (see Cassio 80); εἴμειν is most likely also a local Syracusan form = Attic εἶναι (see Cassio 54–5); and ἐμεῦ[ς] is a Doric form (also attested at Epich. fr. 140) = Attic ἐμοῦ.

9–10 Assigned by the POxy. commentator to ὁ ἕτερος τῶν ὑποκριτῶν ('the other actor'), who Cassio 77 suggests is rehearsing part of the speech he and Odysseus will make to the Achaeans, arguing that, although they agree with the Achaeans' general approach to military discipline, this case is exceptional. Alternatively, the remark might be a cynical comment on the improbability of the defence succeeding, in which case it is perhaps addressed to the audience.   ἐμίν is a Doric form (also attested at e.g. [Epich.] fr. 246. 1; Sophr. frr. 82; 96) = Attic ἡμῖν.   πάγχυ modifies both κατὰ τρόπον and ἐοικότως, 'altogether both fitly and reasonably' (see LSJ s. τρόπος II. 4. b). The praise is sufficiently exaggerated to suggest either insincerity or irony (thus Cassio 77).

10.   ἐπεύξασθ(αι): 'to call down curses', sc. on soldiers who fail to do their duty.   αἴ τις ἐνθυμεῖν γ[α λῆι]: 'if one wishes to consider (the situation)', i.e. 'if one thinks about it'. For αἰ, see **A1**. 1 n. γα (also at **A13**. 2) is a Doric form = common γε. λῆι is < λῶ, a Doric form (also at e.g. **A12**. 1–2; Ar. *Ach.* 749 (a Megarian); *Lys.* 95 (a Spartan)) = common ἐθέλω.

11–16.   Odysseus either laments his situation again (cf. 3) or continues to rehearse what he will say to the Achaeans.

11.   'If only I were (coming) from that place whither they ordered me', i.e. Troy (14).   ὗς is a Doric form (elsewhere at *IG* IV 498. 4; cf. Sophr. fr. 75 πῦς;) = Attic οἷ.

12.   ἀγαθικῶν κακὰ προτιμάσαι ('to have preferred bad things to good'; presumably dependent on ὤφειλον in 11 ('If only I had preferred'), like everything that follows in 13–16) is most naturally taken as referring to an expectation that Odysseus would don rags and give himself a beating, as at H. *Od.* 4. 244–5; *Il. Parv.* fr. 7. But Cassio 81–2, following Blass, suggests that a negative might have stood in the lacuna at the head of the line, in which case Odysseus means 'and (not) to have preferred bad (actions) to decent ones'.   ἀγαθικῶν (= common ἀγαθῶν) is attested only here and in the lexicographers (e.g. Phot. α 74 ἀγαθικά· τὰ σπουδαῖα), and must be a local Syracusan form.

13–16.   For the echoes of Homer, see introductory n.

14.   σαφα[νέως]: 'clearly, plainly'.

15. δίοις ... Ἀχαιοῖς is an Iliadic echo (e.g. 5. 451), as is παιδὶ ... Ἀτρέος as a periphrasis for 'Agamemnon' (e.g. 2. 23).

16. τηνεῖ is a Doric form (also at **A13**. 3; *Syll.*² 438. 150 (Delphi); *IG* XII. 3 537(a) (Thera)) = common ἐκεῖ.

A7. Probably from only slightly further on in the play, if the POxy. editors Grenfell and Hunt are right that the papyrus scrap that preserves part of 3–4 (see below) represents the third column on a page that contains fr. 98 (see **A6** introductory n.) in columns 1–2. The speaker has spent some time in Troy, apparently in a menial position (1–2), but was forced to flee the city when his behaviour inadvertently aroused suspicion (3–4). He is therefore more likely Odysseus, insisting that his mission failed when he was forced to leave the city prematurely (cf. **A6**. 7–8), than a Trojan who has deserted to the Achaean camp, where he is available to expose Odysseus' lies. Cf. Kerkhof 128.

Preserved entire at Athenaeus 9. 374d–e, as evidence that the word δέλφαξ could be used of male piglets. In addition, 1–2 φυλάσσων is quoted in the *Etymologicum Genuinum* in a gloss on δέλφαξ; Hesychius σ 2298 has an entry συμβολατεύειν (almost certainly a reference to 3); and POxy. xxv 2429 fr. 1(c). iii contains the letters]ν μ' ἔφα τοῖς Ἀχα[(= fr. 98. 68), which must represent the end of 3 and the beginning of 4.

Trochaic tetrameter catalectic.

1. δέλφακα: 'a pig'; see **C6**. 6 n.

2. τοῖς Ἐλευσινίοις: 'for the Eleusinia', a local Sicilian festival; to be distinguished from the Eleusinian Mysteries celebrated in Attica, at which piglets were also sacrificed (Olson on Ar. *Pax* 374–5). An anachronistic reference, which shows that Epicharmus was at least occasionally willing to allow contemporary reality to intrude into his epic settings.

2–3. δαιμονίως ('by the action of a deity') is glossed by οὐχ ἑκών ('not of my own free will').

3. ταῦτα δή: 'because of these things, on this account'.   συμβολατεύειν is glossed συναλλαττεύειν ('to barter with') by Hesychius (σ 2298; the only other attestation of the word, and probably a reference to this passage).   K–A retain the papyrus' μ' (metrically unnecessary and omitted by Athenaeus) after συμβολατεύειν. But the word serves no purpose after με before the infinitive (the examples of repeated pronouns given by E. Fraenkel, *Beobachtungen zu Aristophanes* (Rome, 1962), 89–91, involve wider separations, and the repetitions all have a pragmatic function); and since we do not know that the papyrus had the pronoun twice (i.e. rather than merely having it out of place), I have expelled μ' from the text.

4. προδιδόμειν = Attic προδιδόναι.   τὸν δέλφακα: probably a surprise
for τὴν πόλιν *vel sim.*

A8. Unlike the other preserved portions of *Odysseus the Deserter* (all trochaic
tetrameter catalectic, including fr. 101; frr. 102–3 merely preserve individual
words from the text), these lines are in anapaestic dimeter, and were there
solid evidence for the existence of a chorus in Epicharmus, it would be tempting to assign the words to them. In the absence of such evidence (see Introduction, p. 9), the verses ought probably to be given to one of the actors; see
Kerkhof 151–5. The sentiment, at any rate, is appropriate for a play that seems
to have turned on questions of social and political responsibility, and would
fit easily in the mouth of a self-interested deserter (cf. **A6**). For the symbolic
use of the idea of goddesses living near to or far from one another, cf. A. *Ag.*
1003–4; Critias fr. B 6. 20–1; E. *HF* 557.
   Preserved at Stobaeus iv. 16. 3, under the heading 'On quiet'.
   Anapaestic dimeter.

2.   πλατίον is a Doric form = Attic πλησίον, 'near, close to' + genitive.

A9–A11. All three fragments of Epicharmus' *Cyclops* appear to be adapted
from the story of the disastrous encounter of Odysseus and Polyphemus at
H. *Od.* 9. 106–542, and in particular from the scene in which the hero gets the
monster drunk on Maron's wine at 9. 343–74; cf. Euripides' *Cyclops*. Cratinus'
Odysseuses (frr. 143–57; cf. Nesselrath 236–9) told the same story (for Maron's
wine and the trick involving the captive's name, see Cratin. frr. 145–6), as did
a lost satyr play by Aristias (*TrGF* 9 F 4; Polyphemus objects to Odysseus
mixing the wine with water); see also **H8**. 9–10 with nn.; Ar. *V.* 179–87;
Pl. 290–301 (parodying Philoxenus' *Cyclops or Galateia* (*PMG* 815–24));
Matro fr. 1. 15–16, 100–1 (epic parody). Cf. Mastromarco, in *Tessere* 9–42
(on the Cyclops in fifth-century satyr play and comedy generally); Kerkhof
141–2, 156–60; Hordern, *CQ* ns 54 (2004), 285–92.

A9. Poseidon was Polyphemus' father (H. *Od.* 9. 528–9), and Kaibel suggested
that the speaker might be the Cyclops himself, although it could equally well
be Odysseus. In any case, the reference is probably to the cup in which the
hero offered Polyphemus wine (see **A10** with n.), and the speaker is admiring
its dimensions.
   Preserved in Herodian, *On Anomalous Words* (*Grammatici Graeci*, III.
ii. 917. 1–2), along with several other fragments of Epicharmus and Sophron,
as evidence for the Doric forms of the divine name Poseidon.
   Iambic trimeter.

ναί + accusative: 'yes, by . . .'; cf. **A10**.   Ποτειδᾶν: for the form, see **A2**. 1 n.

κοιλότερος ὀλμοῦ πολύ: 'much more concave than a mortar'; πολύ is adverbial. Mortars were used for pounding grain into meal, kneading dough to make bread, and the like (see **G9**. 2 n.; Ar. *V.* 238 with MacDowell ad loc.; Amyx 235–8), and the speaker must be referring not to the vessel's shape but to its enormous size and thus the amount of wine it can hold.

A10. The speaker might be either Polyphemus describing his favourite dishes (cf. H. *Od.* 9. 292–3 (of Polyphemus consuming two of Odysseus' men) ἤσθιε δ' ὥς τε λέων ὀρεσίτροφος—οὐδ' ἀπέλειπεν— | ἔγκατά τε σάρκας τε καὶ ὀστέα μυελόεντα ('he ate like a mountain-bred lion—he left nothing—entrails and flesh and marrowy bones')) or Odysseus naively responding to something the monster has said. But the humour or irony depends in any case on the fact that the words the speaker uses to describe the Cyclops' horrible food could easily be found in a description of the menu at an ordinary dinner party.

Preserved at Athenaeus 9. 366b, in a brief discussion of the grammatical gender of the word κωλεός.

Iambic trimeter.

χορδαί (literally 'entrails') were normally stuffed and made into sausage (see **B34**. 9 with n.; **G13**. 3 n.), while a **κωλεός** (= Attic κωλῆ; Epicharmus' second-declension form of the word is attested elsewhere only at fr. 81 and in Hippocrates) is usually the 'haunch' of a pig or kid (e.g. Ar. fr. 236; Pl. Com. fr. 17; Anaxipp. fr. 1. 38).   **χὡ** = καὶ ὁ; cf. **A6**. 6; **A13**. 2. **ἁδύ**: 'a delicious thing'.

A11. Polyphemus demands some of Maron's wine, as at H. *Od.* 9. 355 (the second bowlful, and accompanied by a request for the stranger's name).

Preserved at Athenaeus 11. 498e, in a discussion of the grammatical gender of the word σκύφος.

Two-thirds of an iambic trimeter.

φέρ(ε) might be a colloquial 'come on!' (see Stevens 42), but is more likely used in the straightforward sense 'bring (me)!'; cf. **A20**. 8.   **ἐγχέας** is < ἐγχέω ('pour [wine] into').   **τὸ σκύφος**: a deep, two-handled cup (Richter–Milne 26–7) mentioned also by Sophron (fr. 14) and occasionally in Attic comedy (e.g. Archipp. fr. 7; Alex. fr. 135; Epig. fr. 3). Euripides uses the word repeatedly in *Cyclops* to describe Polyphemus' immense drinking-vessel (390), out of which he consumes the wine Odysseus gives him (411, 556). The Homeric Odysseus, on the other hand, describes the vessel he offered the monster as a κισσύβιον (*Od.* 9. 346).

A12. An explanation of the origin of Athena's obscure traditional epithet 'Pallas' (5) and perhaps of her aegis (3–4; but see below). [Apollodorus] *Bib.* i. 6. 2 identifies Pallas as one of the Giants and says that, when they rebelled against the Olympian gods (for the story, see Gantz 445–54; and cf. **B33**. 15), Athena killed him, stripped off his skin, and used it to protect herself (τὸ ἴδιον ἐπέσκεπε σῶμα); cf. the fragmentary *Meropis* (sixth century?), esp. frr. 5–6 = *SH* 903A. 18–24 (also preserved in a papyrus scrap of Apollodorus' *On the Gods*), where Athena puts Asterus' skin to a very similar use. But one of the children of the Titan Kreios was also named Pallas (e.g. Hes. *Th.* 376; *h.Merc.* 100), and since Epicharmus refers explicitly to 'the battle that took place against Cronus' (2–3), i.e. to the Titanomachy (cf. **C1** with introductory n., and see Gantz 44–6) rather than the Gigantomachy, he must have conflated the stories, as Euripides does at *Hec.* 466–74. Unlike in [Apollodorus], moreover, Epicharmus' Athena apparently intends to use Pallas' skin for offensive rather than defensive purposes (3–4), as if what was being discussed was her aegis (for which, see Gantz 84–5). For alternative versions of the origin of the goddess's name, see Orph. 315 F; Pl. *Crat.* 406d–7a; [Apollod.] *Bib.* iii. 12. 3.

Preserved in PColon. 126 (first century BC), which apparently represents a scrap of the Alexandrian scholar Apollodorus' lost *On the Gods*.

Trochaic tetrameter catalectic.

1–2. **ἐκ τᾶς τῶ Διὸς | . . . κεφαλᾶς:** '(at the hands of the goddess born) from the head of Zeus,' i.e. Athena (cf. Hes. *Th.* 924 αὐτὸς δ' ἐκ κεφαλῆς γλαυκῶπιδα γείνατ' Ἀθήνην; *h.Hom.* 28. 4–5 τὴν αὐτὸς ἐγείνατο . . . | σεμνῆς ἐκ κεφαλῆς; Musae. 2 B 12; Orph. 263 F; Pi. *O.* 7. 35–7). τῶ is a Doric form = common τοῦ; cf. τούτω = common τούτου in 3 and anon. dor. com. fr. 20 (conjectural). As the text stands, this is an exceedingly awkward periphrasis, and **φαντι** (wanted for the main construction) seems out of place; but perhaps the fault lies with the ancient excerptor.

2. **φαντι** is a Doric form = Attic φασι.   **πράτιστα** (i.e. πρώτιστα; see **A1**. 1 n.)   **πάντων** is adverbial, 'first of all'.

3. **κατὰ Κρόνον:** 'concerning Cronus', i.e. 'against Cronus'.   **τούτω:** see 1–2 n.

4. **πὸτ τὸ φοβερὰν εἶμεν:** 'with an eye toward being frightening'; cf. H. *Od.* 22. 297–9, where the sight of Athena's aegis throws the Suitors into a panic. Syncopated πὸτ τό frequently appears for Doric ποτὶ (= common πρός) τό; cf. **A4**. 1 n.; **A18**. 2 (πότ for ποτί before a vowel), 9; **A20**. 6. **εὐθύς** is adverbial ('straightaway, immediately'; cf. **B17**. 1; **D6**. 10; **I11**. 4) and is to be taken with **περιβαλεῖν αὐτᾶι κύκλωι** ('she threw round about herself').

5. **ὀνομασθῆμεν**: for the form, see **A3**. 4 n. **τόκα** is a Doric form (also attested at e.g. Epich. frr. 113. 146; 145; Pi. *O.* 6. 66) = common τότε; cf. **A14**. 4 Doric ποκ(α) = common ποτε.

A13. Athenaeus reports that the speaker is a parasite (see below) answering a question, obviously about the nature of his calling; perhaps he represents the 'Hope' (sc. of getting a dinner) of the title, while the men he sponges off are the 'Wealth' (thus *DTC* 399). The speaker is a cheerfully shameless character, and the speech as a whole is a good example of self-deprecating humour. His appearance, he admits, is disreputable enough that when the city's guards catch him wandering the streets at night alone and without a light, they assume he is up to no good and give him a beating (8–12), and he several times confesses to being utterly impoverished (8–9, 14). But none of that matters, for he has found a way to fill his belly, and the abuse and abasement required to accomplish this (esp. 3–6) appear to bother him not at all. That he makes only oblique reference to the food and wine he gets by flattering and protecting his host (7, 15) may reflect the question he was asked; more likely he is simply being coy. The fragment begins in the middle of a sentence and breaks off before the account is complete, and the speaker probably went on to describe how he shivered through the night, once the wine he had drunk wore off, and how his hunger drove him out of the house again first thing in the morning to seek another meal. For other descriptions of the parasite's life, e.g. Antiph. fr. 142; Eub. fr. 172; Timocl. fr. 8.

This passage and Epicharmus frr. 33–4 (from the same play) are the first preserved references to parasites (although cf. Archil. fr. 124), who are called κόλακες ('flatterers') in Attic Old Comedy (e.g. **B45**. 1; Ar. *Pax* 756; cf. **F4**. 4) and become stock 'Middle Comic' characters (see **C11–C12** n.). See Ath. 6. 234c–5e (arguing that παράσιτος was originally the term for an individual chosen to participate in a feast held in honour of a god, and that Alexis was the first to use the word disparagingly, although the first certain attestation in this sense is at Arar. fr. 16. 1); Nesselrath 309–17, and *Lukians Parasitendialog: Untersuchungen und Kommentar* (Berlin, 1985); Arnott on Alex. *Παράσιτος* (pp. 542–5); C. Damon, *The Mask of the Parasite* (Ann Arbor, 1997), 11–13, 25–36 (with further bibliography); Kerkhof 165–73 (commenting on this fragment and Eup. fr. 172 in particular); Wilkins 71–86; A. Duncan, *Performance and Identity in the Classical World* (New York, 2006), 104–11.

Preserved along with fr. 31 (which belongs to the same speech) at Athenaeus 6. 235e–6b, as part of an extended discussion of the history of the institution of parasitism that also includes **B45**; **C11**; **F11**; **G14**.

Iambic trimeter.

1–2. Cf. Epich. fr. 34 (also from *Hope or Wealth*) 'for someone invited you to dinner against his will; but you went off (sc. to his house) willingly on the run'.

1. **συνδειπνέων:** an uncontracted form, as often in Doric; cf. 3 ποιέω, 4 ἐπαινέω, 14 κοέω; **A6.** 4 ὁρέω. The main verb (omitted by Athenaeus) must have been ζῶ ('I live, make my living') or the like; alternatively, one might print Casaubon's συνδειπνέω.   **λῶντι:** see **A6.** 10 n., and cf. 2, 5, 12.   **καλέσαι δεῖ μόνον:** '—he only needs to issue an invitation!—'; μόνον is adverbial.

2. Echoes and humorously reverses 1 (not only does the parasite dine with the man who does not want him, but in that case no invitation is necessary—since he comes to the party anyway!), and **γα** (see **A6.** 10 n.) stresses the addition made by **καί** (Denniston 157).   **κ(αὶ ο)ὐδὲν δεῖ καλεῖν:** 'and (then) there's no need at all for an invitation'; οὐδέν is adverbial.

3–6. The parasite makes himself as generally agreeable as he can (3–4). But his overriding interest is in pleasing his host (4), and when a dispute arises between the host and one of the guests—a situation in which other members of the party might be inclined to stay discreetly on the sideline— the parasite emphatically takes the part of the man furnishing the food (5–6). For quarrels and shouting at symposia, cf. **B45.** 15 with n.; **C11.** 3–4; **H18.** 6–7 with nn.

3–4. A series of three independent clauses linked by **τ(ε) . . . καί . . . Ι . . . καί**; but the first clause (**χαρίεις . . . εἰμί**, 'I act ingratiating, am on my best behaviour') is very general and is essentially glossed by those that follow.

3. **τηνεῖ:** 'there' (see **A6.** 16 n., and cf. τήνωι in 5, 6), i.e. at the dinner party referred to obliquely in 1–2.   **ποιέω:** to be scanned – – (for the lack of contraction, see 1 n.), with -εω treated as a single long syllable (synizesis), as in κοέω (∪–) in 14; cf. 11 θεοῖς (–).

4. **ἱστιῶντ(α)** is a non-Attic form (attested elsewhere in Doric comedy at Epich. fr. 76. 1; cf. **A20.** 6 ἱστίαν) = common ἑστιῶντ(α) < ἑστιάω, 'give a feast'.

5. **κ(αὶ) αἴ κα** = Attic καὶ ἐάν; cf. 10.   **ἀντίον <τι> . . . λέγειν:** 'to say something contrary to', i.e. 'to pick a quarrel with' + dative.

5–6. **τήνωι** is a Doric form (cf. 3 n.) = common ἐκείνωι (in 5 the host, in 6 the man quarrelling with him).

6. **κυδάζομαι** + dative: 'I abuse, revile'; a rare, exclusively poetic verb (cf. A. fr. 94; S. *Ai.* 722; in the active + accusative at Epich. fr. 6).   **(ἐ)π' . . . ἠχθόμαν** = ἐπηχθόμαν (in 'tmesis'), 'I am vexed, made unhappy', i.e. 'I get similar abuse, grief back'.   **ὦν** is a Doric form (also attested at e.g. Epich. fr. 35; Sophr. fr. 52. 1) = Attic οὖν; here 'as a result, on that account'.

7.   **κἤπειτα** = κ(αὶ ἔ)πειτα; a Doric contraction.   **πολλὰ καταφαγών,**
πολλ(ὰ) ἐμπιών: implicitly presented as the intended result of the calculat-
ing behaviour described in 3–6. κατεσθίω (whence the strong aorist
κατέφαγον) is generally used in a deprecatory sense ('gobble' *vel sim.*;
cf. **A3**. 4; **C1**. 4; **F1**. 4), and ἐμπίνω is 'drink one's fill' (e.g. Ar. *Pax* 1143).
The parasite does not eat dinner; he stuffs his belly with as much food
and wine as he can.

8–10.   Dinner parties regularly ended after the sun had set; the streets in
Greek cities were dark and full of mud, dung, and garbage; and unless
it was a clear night with a full moon, anyone who went out—and who
was not a thief, a mugger, or extraordinarily reckless—took a light with
him if he could (e.g. Ar. *Nu.* 612–14; *V.* 249, 1330–1; *Pax* 838–41; Alex.
fr. 152; for a description of a mugging at night in a filthy street, see Ar. *Ach.*
1162–73; and cf. **J8**. 3–4 with n.). A **λύχνος** is a 'lamp', which would
normally be set inside a λυχνοῦχος ('lamp-holder', i.e. 'lantern'); more
often what is carried in the street is a δαΐς or φανός ('torch'). But the
speaker has in any case neither a light nor anyone to carry it for him
(another sign of his poverty; cf. **I5**. 3 n.), and he makes his way home
through the dark (**κατὰ σκότος**) and alone (**ἐρῆμος**, = Attic ἔρημος),
stumbling over obstacles he cannot see and slipping and sliding in the
muck (**ὀλισθράζων**).

8.   **μοι συμφέρει**: 'carries along with me', i.e. 'accompanies me carrying'.

9.   **ἔρπω**: in Doric simply 'come, go' (LSJ s.v. 2; cf. Cassio 66).
ὀλισθράζων: a rare form (also used by Hippocrates, according to Galen
(19. 126 Kühn), but here most likely a bit of Syracusan Greek) = common
ὀλισθάνων, 'slipping, slipping and falling'; cf. Cassio 67.

10.   **τοῖς περιπόλοις**: 'those who make the rounds' (< περιπέλομαι), i.e.
'the night-watchmen, the night patrol'.

11.   'I credit this to the gods, as if it were a good thing, that . . .', i.e. 'I credit
the gods with having done me a favour, if . . .'.   **θεοῖς** is to be scanned
as a single long syllable; cf. 3 n.

12.   Literally 'they want nothing more but they whip me', i.e. 'they're satisfied with giving me a whipping'. Whips are generally not deadly weapons
and could therefore be used by state authorities to control their own
citizens, as well as to punish slaves (e.g. **C8**. 7–8); the Scythian police force
of Athens seems to have carried them (Ar. *Th.* 932–4).   **λῶντι** and
μαστιγῶντι are the Doric form of the third-person plural present active
indicative (contrast 1–2).

13.   **ἵκω**: see **A2**. 2 n.   **οἴκαδις** is a Doric form (attested also at Ar.
Ach. 742, 779 (a Megarian)) = common οἴκαδε.   **καταφθαρείς**:
'ruined, in terrible shape', as result not just of the beating he has got from

the night-watchmen (10–12) but of all his other misadventures as he makes his way through the city's streets with no slave or light (8–10 n.).

14. **ἄστρωτος**: 'without bedding'; a mark of extreme poverty (Ar. *Ec.* 418; cf. Ar. *Pl.* 540–3) and an implicit contrast with the dinner party and symposium he attended earlier, where he must have reclined on a couch (κλίνη) fitted with blankets, tapestries, and pillows (see Olson on Ar. *Ach.* 1090; and cf. **B33**. 8; **C3**. 1; **D1**. 23 n.; **F18**. 1; **G11**. 15 with n.; **G12**. 12 n.; **G16**. 11 n.).   **τὰ . . . πρᾶτ(α)** is adverbial, 'at first, initially'. **κοέω**: 'perceive, notice' (thus Hsch. κ 3894–5, 3897; for the uncontracted form and the scansion, see 3 n.); a very rare word, attested also at Call. fr. 232. 1 (conjectural at Anacr. *PMG* 360. 2).

15. **ἇς** is a Doric form (e.g. **A20**. 19; Ar. *Lys.* 173 (a Spartan)) = common ἕως.   **ἄκρατος οἶνος**: Wine was normally drunk mixed with water (see **H9** with introductory n.), making this another indication of just how wonderful a party the speaker has attended.   **ἀμφέπηι**: 'attends, envelops, protects'. The wine acts like the slave boy the speaker does not have (8); but soon enough its effects will vanish and he will be left cold, uncomfortable, and hungry, and the cycle of his life will begin again.

A14. Probably part of a scene in which an unsophisticated character attends his first dinner party or symposium and offers crude but witty comments on the proceedings; cf. **A15** introductory n.; **H3** with introductory n. Speaker B plays the literal-minded 'straight man' (esp. 3).

The adjective τρίπους ('three-footed', i.e. 'three-legged') is sometimes used alone to mean 'table' (cf. τράπεζα < τετράπεζα, 'four-footed'), especially the type of table on which food was served at dinner parties and symposia (e.g. Antiph. frr. 143. 1; 280; Eub. fr. 119. 4; cf. **E3**. 11; **G16**. 2 n.; **H1**. 2 n.). Not all such tables had only three legs, as Speaker A's confusion makes clear; cf. Ar. fr. 545 (A.) 'Bring us out a τράπεζα with three legs, not four!' (B.) 'Where am I going to get a three-legged τράπεζα?' (scarcely evidence of direct dependence of Aristophanes on Epicharmus, particularly since the joke seems already to have been used in the pseudo-Hesiodic *Marriage of Keyx* (fr. 266(a). 5, (b), with Merkelbach and West, *RhM* 108 (1965), 307–16, esp. 310–11)). But the real wit is in the allusion to Oedipus' famous riddle (actually the Sphinx's riddle, but solved by Oedipus), to which this is the earliest surviving explicit reference: 'What goes on four legs in the morning, two legs at noon, and three legs in the evening?' (also mentioned at Anaxil. fr. 22. 25–7; cf. **D3**. 1–3; **E30**; E. *Oedipus* fr. 540a. 20–3; Asclep. Trag. *FGrHist* 12 F 7a; [Apollod.] *Bib.* iii. 5. 8; H. Lloyd-Jones, in R. D. Dawe, J. Diggle, and P. E. Easterling (eds.), *Dionysiaca* (Cambridge, 1978), 60–1; Gantz 496–8). Epicharmus wrote a *Sphinx*, of which only two unrevealing lines (frr. 125–6—

the first a trochaic tetrameter catalectic, the second an iambic trimeter—are
preserved.

Preserved at Athenaeus 2. 49c (manuscripts CE only), as part of a discussion of the word τρίπους.

Trochaic tetrameter catalectic.

1. **μάν** (a Doric form = common μήν) adds liveliness to the question
    (Denniston 332); contrast 3.
2–3. **τέτορας** is a Doric form (e.g. 'Simon.' *FGE* 775; Theoc. 14. 16; 30. 2) =
    Attic τέτταρας.
3. **ὄνυμ(a):** see **A5**. 2 n.   **γα μάν:** adversative (Denniston 348 (2)).
4. The jingle **εἰ δίπους . . . Οἰ‹δίπου›** adds to the humour, but must also be
    responsible for the corruption in the manuscripts.   **ποκ(α) ἦς** = Attic
    ποτε ἦν; cf. **A12**. 5 n.   **αἰνίγματ(a) Οἰ‹δίπου› νοεῖς:** 'you're thinking
    of Oedipus' riddles!'

A15. This might be either a description of something that actually happened
or part of a dyspeptic refusal to consider having a good time, like Philocleon's
unwillingness to attend a dinner party and symposium at Ar. *V*. 1126–8,
1252–5 (where the distant echo scarcely suggests direct dependence of
Aristophanes on Epicharmus), in which case the aorists in 2–4 are gnomic
(Goodwin § 154–5). In either case, Speaker B is of a very different mind from
Speaker A, and the fragment might easily be from the same play as **A14**
(where see introductory n.).

Preserved at Athenaeus 2. 36c–d (manuscripts CE only), immediately after
H18 (where see introductory n.).

Trochaic tetrameter catalectic.

1. **ἐκ μὲν θυσίας θοίνα:** 'after a sacrifice (is/was) a feast', i.e. 'a sacrifice leads/
    led to a feast' (for which, see **G5–G18**).
2. **πόσις:** 'drinking', i.e. 'a drinking party, symposium' (for which, see
    H1–H20).   **χαριέν:** 'a fine thing'.
3–4. Cf. **H18**. 8–9 'The sixth (mixing bowl of wine) belongs to *kômoi*, the
    seventh to black eyes, and the eighth to the summoner'.
3. For the **κῶμος** ('revelling band'), see **H18**. 8 n.   **ὑανία:** 'swinishness,
    boorish behaviour' (cognate with ὗς; cf. Epich. fr. 113. 202 (conjectural);
    Cratin. fr. 77; Olson on Ar. *Pax* 928), i.e. picking fights with passers-by and
    the like, as the drunken *komast* Philocleon does at Ar. *V*. 1322–3, leading to
    the threat of a series of lawsuits (*V*. 1332–4, 1417–18).
4. **‹καταδίκα›:** 'a conviction'.
5. **πέδαι τε καὶ σφαλὸς καὶ ζαμία:** 'shackles, stocks, and a fine'; the series of
    three related terms (contrast 1–4) brings the argument to an emphatic

close. Stocks (known in other periods and places as ἡ ποδοκάκκη and τὸ ξύλον) were used not to allow public display of criminals, as in colonial America, but to provide extra security within jails; see Olson on Ar. *Pax* 479–80.

A16–A17. Wilamowitz argued that E. *Hel.* 122 αὐτὸς γὰρ ὅσσοις εἰδόμην καὶ νοῦς ὁρᾶι (deleted by some editors, including Diggle) ought to be understood as an allusion to **A16**, and that E. *Supp.* 531–4 ἐάσατ᾽ ἤδη γῆι καλυφθῆναι νεκρούς, | ὅθεν δ᾽ ἕκαστον ἐς τὸ φῶς ἀφίκετο | ἐνταῦθ᾽ ἀπελθεῖν, πνεῦμα μὲν πρὸς αἰθέρα, | τὸ σῶμα δ᾽ ἐς γῆν is dependent on **A17**, and assigned both fragments to the pseudonymous cosmological poem also known to Ennius (see Introduction, p. 10). (Nestle cited E. *Hyps.* fr. 757. 923–7a καὶ τάδ᾽ ἄχθονται βροτοὶ | εἰς γῆν φέροντες γῆν. ἀναγκαίως δ᾽ ἔχει | βίον θερίζειν ὥστε κάρπιμον στάχυν, | καὶ τὸν μὲν εἶναι, τὸν δὲ μή· τί ταῦτα δεῖ | στένειν, ἅπερ δεῖ κατὰ φύσιν διεκπερᾶν; | δεινὸν γὰρ οὐδὲν τῶν ἀναγκαίων βροτοῖς as a stronger parallel for **A17**. See in general Kerkhof 79–93.) But 'the suddenness of the quotation, its allusiveness and brevity in the middle of plain dialogue, and the obscurity of the point' make it difficult to believe that Euripides in *Helen* intended an allusion to Epicharmus (thus Dale ad loc.), while the idea that human beings are formed from a mixture of earth and divine or heavenly 'breath', and that at death the two elements separate and the divine portion returns to the upper world, was a fifth-century commonplace (e.g. Xenoph. 21 A 1 (said by Diogenes Laertius 9. 19 to be the earliest reference to the idea); Ar. *Pax* 832–3; E. fr. 839). Even if Euripides read Epicharmus, therefore, there is no positive reason to think that he knew these two fragments in particular, regardless of whether Kassel–Austin are right to assign them to an unidentified comedy rather than one of the pseudonymous works.

A16. The first half of the verse (νοῦς[1] . . . ἀκούει) is cited first at [Arist.] *Pr.* 903ᵃ20–1 without attribution and seemingly as a proverbial expression. But the entire verse is preserved and attributed to Epicharmus in a number of later sources, the earliest of which are Plut. *de Alex. fort. aut virt.* 2. 3 (*Mor.* 336b); Clem. Al. *Strom.* ii. 24. 4; and Olymp. *in Phd.* 65b.
    Trochaic tetrameter catalectic.

ὁρῆι . . . ἀκούει· . . . κωφὰ καὶ τυφλά: note the chiastic order (seeing and hearing vs. not hearing and not seeing).

A17. Preserved at [Plutarch] *Cons. Apoll.* 15 (*Mor.* 110a–b), as one of a number of quotations from classical poetry intended to console a father grieving the death of his son.
    Trochaic tetrameter catalectic.

1. **συνεκρίθη καὶ διεκρίθη:** 'he was formed and dissolved'. Cf. Emped. 31 A 37 D–K (where the verbs, however, appear to be used in precisely the opposite sense) ἡ μὲν Φιλία διακρίνει, τὸ δὲ Νεῖκος συγκρίνει.

2. **χαλεπόν:** 'difficult (to understand)'.

A18–A19. Two fragments of *Practical Maxims* ([Epich.] frr. 244–73), the best attested of the *Pseudepicharmea* (didactic works falsely attributed to Epicharmus in antiquity; see Introduction, pp. 9–10). Athenaeus 14. 648d–e (*Pseudepicharmeia* test. 1) reports that the late fourth-/early third-century scholar and historian Philochorus (*FGrHist* 328 F 79), followed by Apollodorus (*FGrHist* 244 F 226), who worked on Epicharmus and Sophron in the Library in Alexandria in the second century BC (see Introduction, pp. 9, 11), claimed that *Practical Maxims* and the *Canon* ([Epich.] fr. *274) were actually composed by a certain Axiopistus ('Trustworthy'; patently an invented 'speaking name') of Locris or Sicyon. Cf. *DTC* 363–79.

A18. From the introduction to the poem. That the text is pseudonymous is apparent from the fact that 'Epicharmus' speaks of himself and the reception of his work (i.e. his comedies) with an imperfect (10) and makes it clear that he is concerned to be thought wise not by his peers but by posterity (13–14), i.e. by readers of the present work. He was attacked in the past for being long-winded and clever to no useful purpose (10–11), and this poem is intended to redeem his reputation (12–15) by offering the reader appropriate things to say at crucial moments of all sorts (1–5) and by furnishing him with food for thought and thus the opportunity to improve himself (6–7). See Kerkhof 94–5.

Preserved in PHib. 1 (third century BC).
Trochaic tetrameter catalectic.

1–5. A statement of what is implicitly represented as the primary purpose of the poem, i.e. giving the reader exactly the right thing to say in any public situation; contrast 6–7 with n.

1. **τεῖδ᾽ ἔνεστι:** cf. 5 with n., 6 with 6–7 n. For τεῖδ(ε) ('here'), see **A6.** 7 n.   **τοῖς** = Attic οἷς; cf. **A3.** 4 n.

2–4. A list of some of the audiences and occasions for which the many diverse (1 πολλὰ καὶ παντοῖα) sayings collected in the poem might be appropriate. Each verse is structured in a different way: 2 offers two opposed pairs of social situations in which a man might need to speak (to a friend or an enemy; in court or the Assembly); 3 divides potential audiences by social and political rank (someone from the lower classes, someone from the upper class, and someone from another city); and 4 gives a list of three types of men with whom a chance encounter might easily produce trouble.

2.   *ἐν δίκαι*: 'in court'.   *ἐν ἀλίαι*: 'in the Assembly'; the Doric term (e.g. Hdt. vii. 134. 2 (Sparta)) for what was in Athens called the *ἐκκλησία*.

3.   *πονηρόν*: see **A6**. 5 n.

4.   *βάναυσον*: 'a craftsman, artisan', i.e. someone of a lower social station than the implied reader of the poem, and with whom he might reasonably expect to have problems at some point, just as could easily happen with a habitually quarrelsome individual (*δύσηριν*; a variant, attested also at Pi. *O*. 6. 19, of Attic *δύσερις*) or a nasty drunk (*πάροινον*).

5.   *καὶ τούτοισι κτλ.*: 'pointed responses are in here for these things' (i.e. the other trouble(s) referred to in the first half of the line) 'as well'. For *κέντρα* in this sense (omitted by LSJ s.v.), cf. **E10**. 7.   *τεῖδ' ἔνο* recalls 1 *τεῖδ' ἔνεστι*, marking the end of the section. *ἔνο* is a dialectal form of *ἔνεστι*; see Epim. Hom. ε 186, 200 Dyck.

6–7.   A second purpose for the poem (note *ἐν ... τεῖδ'*, echoing *τεῖδ' ἔνεστι* in 1), the summary treatment of which suggests that it is less important than the one defined in 1–5; but cf. **A19** introductory n.   *γνῶμαι* (cf. 11) is the Greek title of the work.

8–9.   For the implicit insistence on brevity as a virtue (as well as an effective rhetorical strategy), cf. 11, 14–15, and perhaps 26.   *οὔτι* is adverbial, 'not at all'.   *ἓν μόνον κτλ.*: 'applying only one of these lines to the matter, (that is) the one of them that is in each instance useful'. Cf. S. *Ph*. 131 *τὰ συμφέροντα τῶν ἀεὶ λόγων*.

10–11.   The charges previously levelled against the poet were that his wisdom was of no help to anyone else and that he went on too long; this poem is therefore intended to be both pithy and practical (12–16).

10.   *αἰτίαν ... ἦχον ὡς ... εἴην*: 'I used to be accused of being ... '. *ἦχον* is a West Greek (Doric and Aeolic) form = Attic *εἶχον*.   *ἄλλως*: 'to no purpose, pointlessly', i.e. 'in a way that benefited no one else'.

11.   *κ(αὶ) οὐ δυναίμαν κτλ.* gives more specific content to *μακρολόγος* ('full of words, verbose'). Cf. 8–9 n.

12.   *ταῦτα ... εἰσακούσας*: 'because those things were said about me'. For the idiom, cf. Austin–Olson on Ar. *Th*. 386–8.   *(ἐ)γών* is a Doric form = Attic *ἐγώ*.   *συντίθημι*: 'I am composing'.

12–13.   *τὰν τέχναν | τάνδ(ε)*: the poem itself, conceived as a device for accomplishing the goal defined in 13–16. For *τέχνη* in this sense, cf. Isoc. 13. 19; and perhaps **G3**. 12.

14.   *κατ(ὰ) ἓν [ἔπος] λέγων*: 'saying', i.e. 'expressing them in a single line'; cf. 8.

15.   *[πεῖραν] αὐταυτοῦ διδοὺς ὡς*: 'giving proof of himself, that ... ', i.e. 'proving that he ... '. *αὐταυτοῦ* is a Doric form (attested elsewhere at e.g. [Epich.] fr. 278. 7; Sophr. fr. 18; *Syll.*³ 1236. 5 (Aegina); *IG* XIV 287

(Segesta)) = common ἑαυτοῦ. β[ραχ-] (if correct) echoes ἐν βραχεῖ in 11. The imaginary quotation apparently concludes at the end of this line.

16. Returning to the point (esp. 4–5) after the explanatory digression in 10–15. For Croenert's φαν[ήσεται σοφός], cf. 13.

17–26. The references to the need to say the right thing at the right time in 23 and 25, and to grief and troubles in 18 and 22, respectively, suggest that the author expanded again here on the idea that his poem contained diverse material and that different parts were appropriate for different audiences and situations (cf. 1–5, 8–9).

A19. A bit of practical wisdom intended for the reader's edification; cf. **A18.** 6–7 with n. For other expressions of misogyny in *Practical Maxims,* see frr. 247; 268; 270, and cf. **B28** introductory n.; **I1–I12** (aspects of misogyny in Attic comedy).

Preserved at Stobaeus iv. 22ᶜ. 84, under the heading 'That the character of the partners makes marriage beneficial for some, but unfortunate for others'.

Trochaic tetrameter catalectic.

1–2. τῶι τρὶς ἓξ ἢ τρεῖς κύβους | . . . βαλεῖν: 'throwing a triple six or three ones', the highest and the lowest possible throws when shooting three dice (cf. **D12.** 3 n.). Zenobius iv. 23, citing Pherecr. fr. 129 and adesp. iamb. fr. 55, identifies this as a proverb that refers to those who take a desperate chance, as also at Pl. *Lg.* 968e. Here the point is that marriage results in either utter felicity or ruin.

2. ἀπὸ τύχης: 'by chance'; but unlike in dice, where three sixes or three ones represent an unusual throw, in marriage there are allegedly only two possible, extreme results.

2–3. τεταγμένην | τοῖς τρόποις: 'orderly in her manners', i.e. 'conventionally well behaved'. For the text, see 5 n.

3. ἄλυπον: 'disinclined to cause you pain'; τ(ὰ) ἄλλ(α) is adverbial, 'in other respects'.

4. A catalogue of some of the most common comic complaints about women. For φιλέξοδον, see **I4.** 10 n.; for λάλον, see **I4.** 13 with n.; for δαψιλῆ ('extravagant'), cf. **I3.** 8.

5. ἀτυχίαν κοσμουμέναν: for women's ornaments (routinely presented as a means to lure men to destruction), e.g. Ar. fr. 332; Nicostr. Com. fr. 32. κοσμουμέναν is the only distinctly Doric form in this fragment (although τεταγμένην in 2 could easily be emended to τεταγμέναν).

A20–A21. For Sophron of Syracuse (first half of the fifth century BC), see Introduction, pp. 11–12; Olivieri ii. 59–143 (an edition with commentary);

Hordern (introduction, translation, and commentary, with text and apparatus taken over from K–A). The standard edition of the fragments is in *PCG* I (2001; replacing G. Kaibel, *Comicorum Graecorum Fragmenta*, i. 1 (Berlin, 1899)).

Two fragments of far and away the best-preserved of Sophron's mimes. Although only the second fragment is expressly assigned to *Women Who Say That They Will Drive out the Goddess*, it seems perverse to deny that the first comes from it as well. Theocritus 2, in which a woman assisted by a slave-girl invokes Hecate in the hope of recovering a delinquent lover, is based at least in part on this mime; cf. Sophr. frr. *5–*7 (all *scholia* on Theoc. 2, citing echoes of a mime by Sophron). Here, however, the goal is not to gain access to the goddess's power but to convince her to leave; cf. Bond on E. *HF* 650–4 (on ἀποπομπή-prayers). See Hordern, *CQ* NS 52 (2002), 164–73, esp. 166–71; and pp. 124–6 of his commentary.

A20. Preparations are being made for a ceremony that will include the sacrifice of a puppy (8) to the dread underworld goddess Hecate (thus Σ Lyc. 77, apparently referring to this passage; cf. Σ^EAG Theoc. 2. 12 = Sophr. fr. *7 (Sophron referred to Hecate as νερτέρων πρύτανις); Plu. *superst.* 10 (*Mor.* 170b) = Sophr. fr. **8 (an invocation of Artemis/Hecate); Ar. frr. 209; 608) and, after that, an attempt to expel her from the house, where she must have been causing trouble. The reservation implicit in the title—the women only *say* they will drive out the goddess—is intriguing; but whether they are deceiving themselves or others is unclear. Speaker A is officiating, and on the most straightforward interpretation of the text five other characters are present, although only one speaks (10); the others may well be mute slaves. Given the title of the piece and the fact that Apollodorus divided Sophron's mimes into 'male' and 'female' varieties (*FGrHist* 244 F 214 = Sophr. test. 22. 1–2), one would expect all the characters to be women, although this would require that the masculine participle **ποτιβάντες** in 5–6 serve as a general form (thus Latte). The setting is a private house and the atmosphere is tense: the goddess is dangerous (3–5 with 4 n.) and difficult (19 with n.), and care must be taken that the ceremony is performed correctly. See in general Hordern 127–37. For purification rituals, see Thphr. *Char.* 16. 14 with Diggle ad loc. (squill or a puppy); Parker 222–34 (223–4 on this fragment). For Hecate, see Chariclid. fr. 1; S. I. Johnston, *Restless Dead* (Berkeley and London, 1999), 203–49; J. S. Clay, *Hesiod's Cosmos* (Cambridge, 2003), 130–8.

Some of the implied action can be reconstructed, and it seems likely (but cannot be proven) that the mime was intended to be performed, although whether by a group or by one actor taking all the parts is impossible to say. Speaker A is either already present when the other characters arrive, or (more likely) is leading a procession in which the others are participants. Two of the women hold a small table (1–2), on which the items referred to in 4–5 and 12 rest. After they set the table down, they take some of the salt in their hands (3–4), put garlands on their heads (5), and sit on the hearth (6). Of the other participants, one woman carries or balances on her head a sacrificial basket (κανοῦν; see Olson on Ar. *Ach.* 244), from which she removes the hatchet she hands to Speaker A in 7; another carries the puppy (8); and Speaker B has the bitumen (9). The κανοῦν most likely contains the other sacrificial implements mentioned in 3–5; who is carrying the torch (11) and the basin of water in which it is dipped (17–18) is not clear. Once the arrangements for the sacrifice are complete, several of the women (the two who carried the table and are seemingly the least active participants in the ceremony (esp. 6)?) are sent to open the outer doors of the house (13–14), while at least two others take charge of dipping the torch in the water (15–16).

Preserved in PSI 1214 (first century AD); the other portions of the papyrus (Sophr. fr. 4. b–d) are unlikely to be from the same mime. In addition, *Σ* Lyc. 77 refers to the sacrifice of dogs to Hecate in Sophron's mimes (8); Ioann. Alex. *De accent.* p. 32. 14, along with other late grammarians, quotes 9 for the sake of the Doric form πεῖ; Et. Gen. AB says that Sophron used δαελός for the common δαλός (16); and Et. Orion p. 62. 31 reports that he used the verb πυκταλεύω (18, where see n.).

Prose.

1. **τὰν τράπεζαν**: a light, moveable table, on which the slaughtered puppy will be placed as a meal for the goddess (cf. **A14** introductory n.; D. Gill, *Greek Cult Tables* (New York and London, 1991)). For the moment it perhaps has on it some small cakes or the like, which will be left as the bloodless portion of the sacrifice (cf. Sophr. fr. 26 'as dinner for the goddesses, oven-bread and bowls of wheat porridge; and a half-loaf for Hecate'; Ar. *Pl.* 594–7).   **κάτθετε** = Attic κατάθετε < κατατίθημι; cf. **A4**. 1 n.

2. **ὥσπερ ἔχει**: 'just as it is', i.e. 'without further ado, right there'; cf. 17.

3. **λάζεσθε**: a largely non-Attic verb (used, however, in the form λάζυμαι at Ar. *Lys.* 209 and frequently by Euripides (e.g. *Ph.* 1660)) equivalent in sense to λαμβάνω.

4. **ἁλὸς χόνδρον**: 'a lump of salt'; cf. **D1**. 6 (χόνδρος used of roughly milled barley); Olson–Sens on Archestr. fr. 37. 8 (on salt). Like the laurel wreath referred to in 5, probably intended to render the bearer ritually pure and thus safe during the ceremony that follows; cf. Parker 226–7.   **χῆρα** is a rare Doric form (attested elsewhere at e.g. Alcm. *PMG* 3. 80; 84) = Attic χεῖρα.

5.   i.e. 'place a laurel garland'—routinely associated with sacrifice—'on your head!'; cf. 4 n. For laurel (**δάφναν**) used to guard against evil, see Parker 228–9.   **πάρ**=Attic παρά.   **ὦας** ('ear'; cf. **A1**.4, where ὤατα would also do) is a rare Doric form = common οὖς.

6.   **ἰστίαν** is a Doric form (cf. **A13**. 4 n.) = common ἑστίαν.   **θωκεῖτε**: see **A6**. 7 n.

7.   **τύ** (like ὑμές in 15) marks the move to a different addressee.   **τ(ὸ ἀ)μφακες**: attested in classical literature only here, and glossed ἀξίνη ('axe' or 'pick-axe' at Hesychius α 3893, perhaps referring specifically to this passage); presumably a hatchet with which the puppy (**σκύλακα**) will be dispatched (thus Hordern). For the contraction, cf. **A13**. 2. For the sacrifice specifically of a puppy, see introductory n.; Plu. *Mor.* 280b–c (a purificatory rite).

8.   **ὦ**: 'from there'; a rare Doric form = common ὦδε (LSJ s.v. II); cf. Doric αὐτῶ = common αὐτόθεν et sim. at Sophr. frr. *22; 81; 121, ap. A.D. *Grammatici Graeci* II. i. 1. 190. 17–22.

9.   **πεῖ** is a rare Doric form (also attested at Sophr. frr. 74; 139) = Attic ποῖ.   **γάρ**: a common—if puzzling—use of the particle to request additional information (Denniston 82–5); cf. Nicostr. Com. fr. 4. 1; Euphr. fr. 3. 3.   **ἁ ἄσφαλτος**: 'the bitumen, oil-tar'. To be burned along with the frankincense (11–12 with n.) to purify the area, like the sulphur Odysseus uses to cleanse his house of bloodshed at H. *Od.* 22. 481–2, 493–4 (cf. Theoc. 24. 96); cf. Diph. fr. 125. 1–5; Parker 227–8, 232.

10.   **οὔτα**: 'Here it is!'; a Doric form (see LSJ s. οὗτος A) = Attic αὕτη.

11–12.   **τὸν λιβανωτόν** is 'the frankincense', which is now burned, along with the bitumen (9 with n.), with the aid of **τὸ δάιδιον** (probably the same object as the δαελός in 16, where see n.). Cf. **D1**. 13 with n.; **H1**. 9 with n.; Ar. *Nu.* 426; Antiph. fr. 162. 2–4; LiDonnici, *Kernos* 14 (2001), 65–79.

13.   **ἄγετε δή**: 'Come on now!, Alright now!' *vel sim.* (urging a group to action, as at Ar. *Lys.* 667). For δή adding emphasis to an imperative, e.g. **F7**. 3; **G4**. 5; **I6**. 11; cf. Denniston 216–17.

14.   The point of the order must be that opening the doors wide offers the goddess an obvious way out of the house; cf. **A21** introductory n. **πεπτάσθων** is < = πετάννυμι.   **μοι** is an ethic dative, 'please' (KG i. 423).

15.   **ὑμές . . . ὁρῆτε**: i.e. in order to ensure their status as full participants in the ceremony; in practical terms, the order amounts to little more than 'Pay attention!' For the use of the pronoun (a Doric form = Attic ὑμεῖς), see 7 n. ὁρῆτε is a Doric contraction < ὁράετε (Attic ὁρᾶτε); cf. 16 σβῆτε.

16.   **τὸν δαελὸν σβῆτε**: 'put out the torch!' Before a sacrifice was made, a

firebrand (cf. 11) was dipped in water and used to sprinkle the altar and the animal (e.g. Ar. *Pax* 959; E. *HF* 928–9; cf. **D3**. 26 with n.). δαελός is an uncontracted Doric form = common δαλός. σβῆτε is a contracted Doric form < σβέω (equivalent to the common σβέννυμι); cf. 15 n.

17. **ὥσπερ ἔχει:** here 'right now, at once' *vel sim.*; cf. 2 n.

18. **εὐκαμίαν** (cognate with κημός, 'muzzle') is identified by the lexi-cographers as a Doric word = common εὐφημία, 'the use of words of good omen only', i.e. 'reverent silence', which is commonly requested before sacrifices and the like (e.g. Ar. *Ach.* 237; *Eq.* 1316).

19. **ᾶς:** see **A13**. 15 n.   **τάνδε:** i.e. Hecate.   **πυκταλεύσω** is attested only here, but is said by Orion (referring to this line) to be equiva-lent to common πυκτεύω, 'box, spar with'.

20–2. **πότνια κτλ.:** Addressed to Hecate. The prayer plays on traditional (especially Homeric) conventions of hospitality by asking the goddess to enjoy her supper and the 'guest-gifts' (a term that implicitly identifies her as only a visitor in the house, if an honoured one) she is being offered— after which the speaker presumably insisted that she go away (cf. 14 with n.). For another prayer to Hecate (addressed as Artemis), see Sophr. fr. **8 (perhaps from the same mime).   **ἀμεμφέων** = ἀμέμπτων, 'faultless, blameless'.

22. **ἀντά[** must be a form of ἀντάω, 'encounter'.

A21. A reference to rites that have already been carried out in preparation for this one, presumably as part of the process of safeguarding the entrance to the house to prevent the goddess from re-entering. See Hordern 126–7.

Preserved at Athenaeus 11. 480b, in the middle of a long, alphabetically organized discussion of drinking vessels, as the sole example of the word **κυαθίς** (defined as 'a vessel resembling a κότυλος', i.e. a cup of some sort).

Prose.

ὑποκατώρυκται: 'has been buried beneath [the threshold]' (thus K–A, citing Sophr. fr. *6, where a *scholium* probably originally on Theoc. 2. 59–62 reports that the idea was borrowed 'from Sophron's mimes'). **τρικτὺς ἀλεξιφαρμάκων:** 'a threefold sacrifice of healing drugs'.

A22. This fragment, Ecphantid. fr. 3 (corrupt), and Ar. *V.* 57 (cf. *Ach.* 738–9) are the only evidence that comedy was performed in Megara in the fifth century, as Aristotle implies at *Po.* 1448ª31–2. See Introduction, pp. 2–6; and cf. **I1** introductory n. (on Susarion).

Preserved along with the other fragments listed above (and originally Myrtil. fr. 1, now lost) in a *scholium* on Aristotle, *Nicomachean Ethics* 1123ª23–4 (= com. dor. test. 7; perhaps drawing on the lost commentary of

Adrastus of Aphrodisias (second century AD)) intended to explain Aristotle's mention of the Megarians' allegedly tasteless fondness for bringing comic choruses on stage dressed in purple. Whether the plays to which Aristotle refers were written by Megarians and were part of their old local dramatic tradition, or were Attic plays revived abroad, as also in the Greek West in this period (see Introduction, pp. 14–16), is impossible to say; but the latter seems more likely. See Breitholtz 71–4.

Iambic trimeter.

1. τὸ δεῖν(α): 'whatchamacallit, thingumabob'. A colloquial word used to avoid naming something that ought not to be mentioned in public, to identify an object or individual the proper name for which has momentarily slipped the speaker's mind (e.g. Ar. *Th.* 620–5), or the like; cf. **D3**. 11 with n.; Olson on Ar. *Pax* 268. Körte suggested that the reference might be to a fart, hence ἀκούεις; and Speaker B's immediate, disgusted response. Ἡράκλεις: Oaths by Heracles are a common colloquial response to an unexpected and generally unwelcome sight, revelation, or remark (e.g. **C18**. 26; Ar. *Ra.* 298 with Dover ad loc.; Antiph. fr. 27. 1).

3. ψυχρόν: literally 'cold', but also a negative term of aesthetic judgment ('strained, forced' *vel sim.*); cf. Ar. *Ach.* 138–40 with Olson ad loc.; *Th.* 168–70 with Austin–Olson ad loc.; Alex. fr. 184. 3; Timocl. fr. 19. 6; Arist. *Rh.* 1405ᵇ34–6ᵇ14.   σέλας ('bright light'; thus Σ Arist.) makes no sense, and a form of γελάω (somehow referring to the childishness of Megarian humour) would fit the context. But γελᾶς (i.e. γελᾶις) ... τὰ παιδία (anon. in Arist.) would have to mean 'you mock the children' rather than 'you make the children laugh'; and what Eupolis actually wrote is unclear.   For the reproachful parenthetic ὁρᾶις (colloquial), cf. Ar. *Th.* 490; Stevens 36–7.

Section B

Attic 'Old Comedy'

B1. Cratinus fr. 193, from *The Wineflask* (423 BC)

ἀλλ᾿ ἐπανατρέψαι βούλομαί γ᾿ εἰς τὸν λόγον·
πρότερον ἐκεῖνος πρὸς ἑτέραν γυναῖκ᾿ ἔχων
τὸν νοῦν κακῶς ἐποίει † πρὸς ἑτέραν, † ἀλλ᾿
ἅμα μὲν τὸ γῆρας, ἅμα δέ μοι δοκεῖ ∪ —
† οὐδέποτ᾿ αὐτοῦ πρότερον †   5

    1 ἐπανατρέψαι Bentley: ἐπαναστρέψαι Σ   βούλομαί γ᾿ Bentley: βούλομαι Σ^{VΕΓ}:
βουλόμενος Σ^Θ   3 κακῶς ἐποίει Bentley, Kaibel: κακὰς εἴποι Σ

B2. Cratinus fr. 194, from *The Wineflask* (423 BC)

γυνὴ δ᾿ ἐκείνου πρότερον ἦ, νῦν δ᾿ οὐκέτι

B3. Cratinus fr. *195, probably from *The Wineflask* (423 BC)

νῦν δ᾿ ἢν ἴδηι Μενδαῖον ἡβῶντ᾿ ἀρτίως
οἰνίσκον, ἕπεται κἀκολουθεῖ καὶ λέγει
"οἴμ᾿ ὡς ἁπαλὸς καὶ λευκός· ἆρ᾿ οἴσει τρία;"

B4. Cratinus fr. 199, from *The Wineflask* (423 BC)

      πῶς τις αὐτόν, πῶς τις ἂν
ἀπὸ τοῦ πότου παύσειε, τοῦ λίαν πότου;
ἐγῶιδα· συντρίψω γὰρ αὐτοῦ τοὺς χοᾶς
καὶ τοὺς καδίσκους συγκεραυνώσω σποδῶν
καὶ τἆλλα πάντ᾿ ἀγγεῖα τὰ περὶ τὸν πότον,   5
κοὐδ᾿ ὀξύβαφον οἰνηρὸν ἔτι κεκτήσεται

B5. Cratinus fr. 197, from *The Wineflask* (423 BC)

τὴν μὲν παρασκευὴν ἴσως γιγνώσκετε

B6. Cratinus fr. 208, from *The Wineflask* (423 BC)

ληρεῖς ἔχων. γράφ' αὐτόν·
ἐν ἐπεισοδίωι γελοῖος ἔσται Κλεισθένης κυβεύων
† ἐν τῆι τοῦ κάλλους ἀκμῆι †

   1 γράφε Σ: γράφων Suda   αὐτὸν Suda^A: αὐτῶι Suda^V: αὐτὸς Σ

B7. Cratinus fr. 209, from *The Wineflask* (423 BC)

Ὑπέρβολον δ' ἀποσβέσας ἐν τοῖς λύχνοισι γράψον

λύχνοισι Runkel: λύχνοις Σ^RVΓ   γράψον Σ^RV: γράψω Σ^Γ: γράφω Triclinius

B8. Cratinus fr. 211, from *The Wineflask* (423 BC)

ὦ λιπερνῆτες πολῖται, τἀμὰ δὴ ξυνίετε

B9. Cratinus fr. 210, from *The Wineflask* (423 BC)

οὐ δύνανται πάντα πυιυῦυαι νεωσοίκων λαχεῖν
οὐδὲ κάννης

B10. Cratinus fr. 200, from *The Wineflask* (423 BC)

ἀτὰρ ἐννοοῦμαι δῆτα τὰς μοχθηρίας
ἠλιθιότητος τῆς ἐμῆς

   1 δῆτα τὰς Runkel: ΔΗΤΑΤΗΣ Prisc.^RMO: ΔΗΤΑΣΤΗΣ Prisc.^V: ΔΕΤΑΤΕΣ Prisc.^D: δή τι τῆς Nauck   2 τῆς^1 ante ἠλιθιότητος Prisc.: del. Pieters   ἠλιθιότητος ed. Ascensiana: ΗΛΙΕΙΟΤΗΤΟΣ Prisc.^RD: ΗΛΙΕΗΟΤΗΤΟΣ Prisc.^V: ΗΙΕΙΟΤΗΤΟΣ vel ΗΙΕΙΟΤΝΤΟΣ Prisc.^M

B11. Cratinus fr. *203, perhaps from *The Wineflask* (423 BC)

ὕδωρ δὲ πίνων οὐδὲν ἂν τέκοις σοφόν

οὐδὲν ἂν τέκοις σοφόν Cobet: οὐδὲν ἂν τέκοι σοφόν AP: χρηστὸν οὐδὲν ἂν τέκοις Ath. Zenob. Phot. Sud. Apost.: καλὸν οὐ τέκοις ἔπος APl

B12. Cratinus fr. 198, from *The Wineflask* (423 BC)

ἄναξ Ἄπολλον, τῶν ἐπῶν τοῦ ῥεύματος,
καναχοῦσι πηγαί· δωδεκάκρουνον <τὸ> στόμα,
Ἰλισὸς ἐν τῆι φάρυγι. τί ἂν εἴποιμ᾽ <ἔτι>;
εἰ μὴ γὰρ ἐπιβύσει τις αὐτοῦ τὸ στόμα,
ἅπαντα ταῦτα κατακλύσει ποιήμασιν   5

  2 <τὸ> Walpole   3 εἴποιμ᾽ <ἔτι> Dindorf: εἴποιμι Σ

B13. Cratinus, *Dionysalexandros* test. i

                        ].
. . . .]ζητ( )
. . . .]παν
. . . .]αυτον μη
. . . . . κ]ρίσιν ὁ Ἑρμ(ῆς)   5
ἀπέρχ]εται κ(αὶ) οὗτοι
μ(ὲν) πρ(ὸς) τοὺς θεατάς
τινα π(ερὶ) τῶν ποιη(τῶν)
διαλέγονται κ(αὶ)
παραφανέντα τὸν   10
Διόνυσον ἐπισκώ(πτουσι) (καὶ)
χλευάζου(σιν)· ὁ δ(ὲ) πα-
ραγενομένων αὐτῶι
παρὰ μ(ὲν) Ἥρα[ς] τυραννίδο(ς)
ἀκινήτου, πα[ρ]ὰ δ᾽ Ἀθηνᾶς   15
εὐψυχί(ας) κ(α)τ(ὰ) πόλεμο(ν), τῆς
δ᾽ Ἀφροδί(της) κάλλιστό(ν) τε κ(αὶ)
ἐπέραστον αὐτὸν ὑπάρ-
χειν, κρίνει ταύτην νικᾶν.
μ(ε)τ(ὰ) δ(ὲ) ταῦ(τα) πλεύσας εἰς   20
Λακεδαίμο(να) (καὶ) τὴν Ἑλένην
ἐξαγαγὼν ἐπανέρχετ(αι)
εἰς τὴν Ἴδην. ἀκού(ει) δ(ὲ) με-
τ᾽ ὀλίγον τοὺς Ἀχαιοὺς πυρ-
πολ]εῖν τὴν χώ(ραν) (καὶ) [ζητεῖν   25
τὸν Ἀλέξαν[δ(ρον). τὴν μ(ὲν) οὖν Ἑλένη(ν)
εἰς τάλαρον ὡς τά[χιστα
κρύψας, ἑαυτὸν δ᾽ εἰς κριὸ[ν
μ(ε)τ(α)σκευάσας ὑπομένει
τὸ μέλλον.   παραγενό-   30

μενος δ' Ἀλέξανδ(ρος) κ(αὶ) φωράσας ἑκάτερο(ν) ἄγειν ἐπὶ τὰς
ναῦς πρ(οσ)τάττει ὡς παραδώσων
τοῖς Ἀχαιοῖ(ς). ὀκνούσης δ(ὲ) τῆς
Ἑλένη(ς), ταύτην μ(ὲν) οἰκτείρας   35
ὡς γυναῖχ' ἕξων ἐπικατέχ(ει),
τὸν δ(ὲ) Διόνυ(σον) ὡς παραδοθη-
σόμενο(ν) ἀποστέλλει, συν-
ακολουθ(οῦσι) δ' οἱ σάτυ(ροι) παρακαλοῦν-
τές τε κ(αὶ) οὐκ ἂν προδώσειν   40
αὐτὸν φάσκοντες. κωμωι-
δεῖται δ' ἐν τῶι δράματι Πε-
ρικλῆς μάλα πιθανῶς δι'
ἐμφάσεως ὡς ἐπαγηοχὼς
τοῖς Ἀθηναίοις τὸν πόλεμον   45

5–6 suppl. Körte   8 π(ερὶ) τῶν ποιη(τῶν) Körte: πυωνποιη pap.   15 ἀκινήτου]
ἀνικήτου Wilamowitz   16 εὐψυχί(ας) Austin: εὐφ- pap.: εὐτ- Grenfell and Hunt
25 suppl. Austin   26 suppl. Grenfell and Hunt   27 suppl. Luppe

B14. Cratinus fr. 42, from *Dionysalexandros* (430 BC?)

παραστάδας καὶ πρόθυρα βούλει ποικίλα

B15. Cratinus fr. 43, from *Dionysalexandros* (430 BC?)

οὔκ, ἀλλὰ βόλιτα χλωρὰ κοισπώτην πατεῖν

οὔκ ἀλλὰ Σᴿ: οὐ καλὰ Σᵞ   βόλιτα Porson: βόλβιτα Σᴿᴦ

B16. Cratinus fr. 327, perhaps from *Dionysalexandros* (430 BC?)

γλῶττάν τε σοι
δίδωσιν ἐν δήμωι φορεῖν
καλῶν λόγων ἀείνων,
ἧι πάντα νικήσεις λέγων

4 νικήσεις Meineke: κινήσεις Phot. An.Bachm.

B17. Cratinus fr. 41, from *Dionysalexandros* (430 BC?)

εὐθὺς γὰρ ἡμώδεις ἀκούων τῶν ἐπῶν
τοὺς προσθίους ὀδόντας

B18. Cratinus fr. 40, from *Dionysalexandros* (430 BC?)

(*A*.) στολὴν δὲ δὴ τίν᾽ εἶχε; τοῦτό μοι φράσον.
(*B*.) θύρσον κροκωτὸν ποικίλον καρχήσιον

   1 εἶχε; τοῦτό Porson: *EIXEN TOYΔO* Macrob.[NP]

B19. Cratinus fr. 45, from *Dionysalexandros* (430 BC?)

ὁ δ᾽ ἠλίθιος ὥσπερ πρόβατον "βῆ βῆ" λέγων βαδίζει

   δ᾽ ἠλίθιος Phot. Et.Gen. Eust.: δὴ λοίσθιος Suda   ὡς προβάτιον Porson

B20. Cratinus fr. 47, from *Dionysalexandros* (430 BC?)

οὐ γάρ τοι σύ γε πρῶτος ἄκλητος φοιτᾷς ἐπὶ δεῖπνον ἄνηστις

   οὐ Ath.: ἰοὺ Phot. Suda Συναγ.[B]   τοι Ath.: om. Phot. Suda Συναγ.[B]   ἄκλητος om. Ath.

B21. Phrynichus Comicus fr. 19, from *The Recluse* (414 BC)

ὄνομα δὲ μοὔστι Μονότροπος
                 ζῶ δὲ Τίμωνος βίον,
ἄγαμον ἄδουλον ὀξύθυμον ἀπρόσοδον
ἀγέλαστον ἀδιάλεκτον ἰδιογνώμονα

   3 ἄδουλον Hermann: ἄζυγον Phot. Συναγ.[B]

B22. Aristophanes fr. 372, from *Lemnian Women* (late 410s BC or after)

Λῆμνος κυάμους τρέφουσα τακερούς καὶ καλούς

B23. Aristophanes fr. 373, from *Lemnian Women* (late 410s BC or after)

ἐνταῦθα <δ᾽> ἐτυράννευεν Ὑψιπύλης πατὴρ
Θόας, βραδύτατος τῶν ἐν ἀνθρώποις δραμεῖν

   1 ἐνταῦθα δ᾽ Bergk: ἐνταῦθ᾽ Ammon.   2 βραδύτατος Bergk: βραδύτερος Ammon.:
βράδιστος Brunck   τῶν] ὦν Bergk: γ᾽ ὦν Edmonds

B24. Philyllius fr. 7, from *Heracles* (V/IV)

βούλεσθε δῆτ᾽ ἐγὼ φράσω τίς εἰμ᾽ ἐγώ;
ἡ τῶν προτενθῶν Δορπία καλουμένη

B25. Aristophanes fr. 403, from *Islands* (V/IV)

(Α.) τί σὺ λέγεις; εἰσὶν δὲ ποῦ;
(Β.) αἰδὶ κατ' αὐτὴν ἣν βλέπεις τὴν εἴσοδον

2 κατ' αὐτήν Σ^{ΓLh} Ar.: κατὰ ταύτην Σ^V Ar.

B26. Aristophanes fr. 410, from *Islands* (V/IV)

ὡς εἰς τὴν γῆν κύψασα κάτω καὶ ξυννενοφυῖα βαδίζει

B27. Eupolis fr. 245, from *Cities* (late 420s BC?)

(Α.) Τῆνος αὕτη.
(Β.) πολλοὺς ἔχουσα σκορπίους ἔχεις τε συκοφάντας

2 ἔχεις] πολλούς Wilamowitz

B28. Eupolis fr. 246, from *Cities* (late 420s BC?)

αὕτη Χίος, καλὴ πόλις ∪ – ×·
πέμπει γὰρ ὑμῖν ναῦς μακρὰς ἄνδρας θ' ὅταν δεήσηι,
καὶ τἆλλα πειθαρχεῖ καλῶς, ἄπληκτος ὥσπερ ἵππος

B29. Eupolis fr. 247, from *Cities* (late 420s BC?)

(Α.) ἡ δ' ὑστάτη ποῦ 'σθ'; (Β.) ἥδε Κύζικος πλέα στατήρων.
(Α.) ἐν τῆιδε τοίνυν τῆι πόλει φρουρῶν <ἐγώ> ποτ' αὐτὸς
γυναῖκ' ἐκίνουν κολλύβου καὶ παῖδα καὶ γέροντα,
κἀξῆν ὅλην τὴν ἡμέραν τὸν κύσθον ἐκκορίζειν

2 <ἐγώ> Hermann   3 γυναῖκ' ἐκίνουν κολλύβου Hermann: ἐκίνουν δὲ γυναῖκα
κολλύβου Σ   4 κύσθον Hermann: σκύθον Σ

B30. Eupolis fr. 13, from *Nanny-Goats* (420s BC?)

βοσκόμεθ' ὕλης ἀπὸ παντοδαπῆς, ἐλάτης πρίνου κομάρου τε
πτόρθους ἁπαλοὺς ἀποτρώγουσαι, καὶ πρὸς τούτοισιν ἔτ' ἄνθην,
κύτισόν τ' ἠδὲ σφάκον εὐώδη καὶ σμίλακα τὴν πολύφυλλον,
κότινον σχῖνον μελίαν λεύκην ἀρίαν δρῦν κιττὸν ἐρίκην
πρόμαλον ῥάμνον φλόμον ἀνθέρικον κισθὸν φηγὸν θύμα θύμβραν   5

2 ἔτ' ἄνθην V. Schmidt: ΕΤΑΛΛΟΗΝ Macrob.: ἔτ' .... Plu.   3 σφάκον Bodaeus:
ΦΑΣΚΟΝ Macrob.: φα .... Plu.   4 λεύκην Kock: ΠΕΥΚΗΝ Macrob.: om.
Plu.

B31. Aristophanes fr. *322, probably from *Heroes* (410s BC?)

πρὸς ταῦτ᾽ οὖν, ὦνδρες, φυλακὴν
ἔχετε τούς θ᾽ ἥρως σέβεθ᾽, ὡς
ἡμεῖς ἐσμεν οἱ ταμίαι
τῶν κακῶν καὶ τῶν ἀγαθῶν,
κἀναθροῦντες τοὺς ἀδίκους   5
καὶ κλέπτας καὶ λωποδύτας
τούτοις μὲν νόσους δίδομεν·
σπληνιᾶν βήττειν ὑδερᾶν
κορυζᾶν ψωρᾶν ποδαγρᾶν
μαίνεσθαι λειχῆνας ἔχειν   10
βουβῶνας ῥῖγος πυρετόν.
...]..[..(.)]. κλέπτα[ις] δίδομεν

12 ταῦ]τα [τοῖ]ς Handley: τοῖ]ς δ[ὲ δ]ὴ Barrett

B32. Crates fr. 16, from *Wild Beasts* (V)

(A.) ἔπειτα δοῦλον οὐδὲ εἷς κεκτήσετ᾽ οὐδὲ δούλην,
ἀλλ᾽ αὐτὸς αὑτῶι δῆτ᾽ ἀνὴρ γέρων διακονήσει;
(B.) οὐ δῆθ᾽, ὁδοιποροῦντα γὰρ τὰ πάντ᾽ ἐγὼ ποήσω.
(A.) τί δῆτα τοῦτ᾽ αὐτοῖς πλέον; (B.) πρόσεισιν αὔθ᾽ ἕκαστον
τῶν σκευαρίων, ὅταν καλῆι τις "παρατίθου τράπεζα·   5
αὐτὴ παρασκεύαζε σαυτήν. μάττε θυλακίσκε.
ἔγχει κύαθε. ποῦ 'σθ᾽ ἡ κύλιξ; διάνιζ᾽ ἰοῦσα σαυτήν.
ἀνάβαινε μᾶζα. τὴν χύτραν χρῆν ἐξερᾶν τὰ τεῦτλα.
ἰχθὺ βάδιζ᾽." "ἀλλ᾽ οὐδέπω 'πὶ θάτερ᾽ ὀπτός εἰμι."
"οὔκουν μεταστρέψας σεαυτὸν ἁλὶ πάσεις ἀλείφων;"   10

3 τὰ Elmsley: ταῦτα Ath.^A   5 τις Casaubon: τι Ath.^A   παρατίθου Heringa: παρατιθῶ
Ath.^A   7 διάνιζ᾽ ἰοῦσα σαυτήν Dindorf: λίανιζουσα σεαυτήν Ath.^A: νίζε σεαυτήν Ath.^CE
8 ἐξερᾶν τὰ Schweighäuser: ἐξαίραντα Ath.^A: ἐξ ἆραι τὰ vel sim. Ath.^CE   9 'πὶ Erfurdt: τἀπὶ
vel sim. Ath.^ACE

B33. Teleclides fr. 1, from *Amphictyonies* (V)

λέξω τοίνυν βίον ἐξ ἀρχῆς ὃν ἐγὼ θνητοῖσι παρεῖχον.
εἰρήνη μὲν πρῶτον ἁπάντων ἦν ὥσπερ ὕδωρ κατὰ χειρός.
ἡ γῆ δ᾽ ἔφερ᾽ οὐ δέος οὐδὲ νόσους, ἀλλ᾽ αὐτόματ᾽ ἦν τὰ δέοντα·
οἴνωι γὰρ ἅπασ᾽ ἔρρει χαράδρα, μᾶζαι δ᾽ ἄρτοις ἐμάχοντο
περὶ τοῖς στόμασιν τῶν ἀνθρώπων ἱκετεύουσαι καταπίνειν,   5
εἴ τι φιλοῖεν, τὰς λευκοτάτας. οἱ δ᾽ ἰχθύες οἴκαδ᾽ ἰόντες

ἐξοπτῶντες σφᾶς αὐτοὺς ἂν παρέκειντ᾽ ἐπὶ ταῖσι τραπέζαις.
ζωμοῦ δ᾽ ἔρρει παρὰ τὰς κλίνας ποταμὸς κρέα θερμὰ κυλίνδων,
ὑποτριμματίων δ᾽ ὀχετοὶ τούτων τοῖς βουλομένοισι παρῆσαν,
ὥστ᾽ ἀφθονία τὴν ἔνθεσιν ἦν ἄρδονθ᾽ ἁπαλὴν καταπίνειν.   10
λεκανίσκαισιν δ᾽ † ἀνάπαιστα † παρῆν ἡδυσματίοις κατάπαστα.
ὀπταὶ δὲ κίχλαι μετ᾽ ἀμητίσκων εἰς τὸν φάρυγ᾽ εἰσεπέτοντο·
τῶν δὲ πλακούντων ὠστιζομένων περὶ τὴν γνάθον ἦν ἀλαλητός.
μήτρας δὲ τόμοις καὶ χναυματίοις οἱ παῖδες ἂν ἠστραγάλιζον.
οἱ δ᾽ ἄνθρωποι πίονες ἦσαν τότε καὶ μέγα χρῆμα Γιγάντων   15

12 ὀπταὶ Ath. (1)ᴬᶜᴱ, (2)ᶜᴱ: αὐτόμαται Ath. (3)ᴬᶜᴱ: αὐταὶ Pierson

B34. Pherecrates fr. 137, from *Persians* (V)

τίς δ᾽ ἔσθ᾽ ἡμῖν τῶν σῶν ἀροτῶν ἢ ζυγοποιῶν ἔτι χρεία
ἢ δρεπανουργῶν ἢ χαλκοτύπων ἢ σπέρματος ἢ χαρακισμοῦ;
αὐτόματοι γὰρ διὰ τῶν τριόδων ποταμοὶ λιπαροῖς ἐπιπάστοις
ζωμοῦ μέλανος καὶ Ἀχιλλείοις μάζαις κοχυδοῦντες ἐπιβλὺξ
ἀπὸ τῶν πηγῶν τῶν τοῦ Πλούτου ῥεύσονται, σφῶν ἀρύτεσθαι.   5
ὁ Ζεὺς δ᾽ ὕων οἴνωι καπνίαι κατὰ τοῦ κεράμου βαλανεύσει,
ἀπὸ τῶν δὲ τεγῶν ὀχετοὶ βοτρύων μετὰ ναστίσκων πολυτύρων
ὀχετεύσονται θερμῶι σὺν ἔτνει καὶ λειριοπολφανεμώναις.
τὰ δὲ δὴ δένδρη τὰν τοῖς ὄρεσιν χορδαῖς ὀπταῖς ἐριφείοις
φυλλοροήσει καὶ τευθιδίοις ἁπαλοῖσι κίχλαις τ᾽ ἀναβράστοις   10

8 θερμῶι Villebrune: θερμοὶ Ath.ᴬᶜᴱ

B35. Aristophanes fr. 581, from *Seasons* (410s BC?)

(Α.) ὄψει δὲ χειμῶνος μέσου σικυοὺς βότρυς ὀπώραν
στεφάνους ἴων— (Β.) <οἶμαι δὲ καὶ> κονιορτὸν ἐκτυφλοῦντα.
(Α.) αὐτὸς δ᾽ ἀνὴρ πωλεῖ κίχλας ἀπίους σχαδόνας ἐλάας
πυὸν χόρια χελιδόνας τέττιγας ἐμβρύεια.
ὑρίσους δ᾽ ἴδοις ἂν νειφομένους σύκων ὁμοῦ τε μύρτων.   5
(Β.) ἔπειτα κολοκύντας ὁμοῦ ταῖς γογγυλίσιν ἀροῦσιν,
ὥστ᾽ οὐκέτ᾽ οὐδεὶς οἶδ᾽ ὁπηνίκ᾽ ἐστὶ τοὐνιαυτοῦ;
(Α.) <ἆρ᾽ οὐ> μέγιστον ἀγαθόν, εἴπερ ἔστι δι᾽ ἐνιαυτοῦ
ὅτου τις ἐπιθυμεῖ λαβεῖν; (Β.) κακὸν μὲν οὖν μέγιστον·
εἰ μὴ γὰρ ἦν, οὐκ ἂν ἐπεθύμουν οὐδ᾽ ἂν ἐδαπανῶντο.   10
ἐγὼ δὲ τοῦτ᾽ ὀλίγον χρόνον χρήσας ἀφειλόμην ἄν.
(Α.) κἄγωγε ταῖς ἄλλαις πόλεσι δρῶ ταῦτα πλὴν Ἀθηνῶν·
τούτοις δ᾽ ὑπάρχει ταῦτ᾽, ἐπειδὴ τοὺς θεοὺς σέβουσιν.

(*B.*) ἀπέλαυσαν ἄρα σέβοντες ὑμᾶς, ὡς σὺ φήις. (*A.*) τιὴ τί;
(*B.*) Αἴγυπτον αὐτῶν τὴν πόλιν πεπόηκας ἀντ' Ἀθηνῶν   15

2 οἶμαι δὲ καὶ add. Kassel   3 αὐτὸς Dindorf: ωνετος Ath.ᴬ: ὠυτὸς Ath.ᶜᴱ
4 χελιδόνας Schweighäuser: -α Ath.ᴬᶜᴱ   5 διδοις Ath.ᴬ: ἴδοις δ' Ath.ᶜᴱ   νιφομένους σύκων
. . . μύρτων Ath.ᴬ: νιφόμενα σῦκα . . . μύρτα Ath.ᶜᴱ   8 ἆρ' οὐ add. Papabasileios: τοῦτ' οὐ
Kaibel   11–14 om. Ath.ᶜᴱ   11 τοῦτ' Coddaeus: τοῦτον Ath.ᴬ   χρήσας Porson:
φήσας Ath.ᴬ   12 δρῶ Casaubon: δρῶν Ath.ᴬ

B36. Plato Comicus fr. 96, from *Wool-Carders or Cercopes* (V/IV)

χαῖρε παλαιογόνων ἀνδρῶν θεατῶν ξύλλογε παντοσόφων

B37. Cratinus fr. 360, from an unidentified play (V)

χαῖρ' ὦ μέγ' ἀχρειόγελως ὅμιλε, ταῖς ἐπίβδαις
τῆς ἡμετέρας σοφίας κριτὴς ἄριστε πάντων·
εὐδαίμον' ἔτικτέ σε μήτηρ ἰκρίων ψόφησις

B38. Plato Comicus fr. 99, from *The Little Child* (V/IV)

εἰ μὲν μὴ λίαν ∪∪– ὦνδρες ἠναγκαζόμην
στρέψαι δεῦρ', οὐκ ἂν παρέβην εἰς λέξιν τοιάνδ' ἐπῶν

B39. Metagenes fr. 15, from *The Man Who Loved Sacrifices* (late 400s ʙᴄ?)

    κατ' ἐπεισόδιον μεταβάλλω τὸν λόγον, ὡς ἂν
καιναῖσι παροψίσι καὶ πολλαῖς εὐωχήσω τὸ θέατρον

B40. Lysippus fr. 4, from *Bacchants* (V)

οὐδ' ἀνακνάψας καὶ θειώσας τὰς ἀλλοτρίας ἐπινοίας

οὐδ' Dobree: σὺ δ' Poll.

B41. Cratinus fr. 342, from an unidentified play, perhaps *The Wineflask*
(423 ʙᴄ)

    "τίς δὲ σύ;" κομψός τις ἔροιτο θεατὴς
ὑπολεπτολόγος γνωμιδιώκτης εὐριπιδαριστοφανίζων

B42. Eupolis fr. 89, from *Dyers* (410s BC?)

> † κἀκεῖνος † τοὺς Ἱππέας
> ξυνεποίησα τῶι φαλακρῶι – ✕ κἀδωρησάμην

   2 <τούτωι> Hermann: <προῖκα> Kirchhoff

B43. Pherecrates fr. 102, from *Small Change* (V)

>   τοῖς δὲ κριταῖς
> τοῖς νυνὶ κρίνουσι λέγω,
> μὴ 'πιορκεῖν μηδ' ἀδίκως
> κρίνειν, ἢ νὴ τὸν φίλιον
> μῦθον εἰς ὑμᾶς ἕτερον   5
> Φερεκράτης λέξει πολὺ τούτου κακηγορίστερον

   6 Φερεκράτης Grotius: Φιλοκράτης Phot. (et al.)

B44. Eupolis fr. 392, from an unidentified play (V)

> ἀλλ' ἀκούετ', ὦ θεαταί, τἀμὰ καὶ ξυνίετε
> ῥήματ', εὐθὺ γὰρ πρὸς ὑμᾶς πρῶτον ἀπολογήσομαι
>
>   *   *   *
>
> ὅ τι μαθόντες τοὺς ξένους μὲν λέγετε ποιητὰς σοφούς·
> ἢν δέ τις τῶν ἐνθάδ' αὐτοῦ, μηδὲ ἓν χεῖρον φρονῶν,
> ἐπιτιθῆται τῆι ποήσει, πάνυ δοκεῖ κακῶς φρονεῖν,
> μαίνεταί τε καὶ παραρρεῖ τῶν φρενῶν τῶι σῶι λόγωι.   5
> ἀλλ' ἐμοὶ πείθεσθε, πάντως μεταβαλόντες τοὺς τρόπους,
> μὴ φθονεῖθ' ὅταν τις ἡμῶν μουσικῆι χαίρηι νέων

   1 τἀμὰ Bergler: πολλά Stob.^(Tr.Voss)   2 ῥήματ' Bergler: χρήματ' vel sim. Stob.^(Tr.Voss)
inter 2 et 3 lac. indic. Kock   5 ἐπιτιθῆται Porson: ἐπιθῆται Stob.^(Tr.Voss)   6 τε Gesner:
τι Stob.^(Tr.Voss)   7 πείθεσθε Voss: πείθεσθαι Stob.^(Tr.)   8 ἡμῶν Morelius: ὑμῶν
Stob.^(Tr.Voss)

B45. Eupolis fr. 172, from *Flatterers* (421 BC)

> ἀλλὰ δίαιταν ἣν ἔχουσ' οἱ κόλακες πρὸς ὑμᾶς
> λέξομεν. ἀλλ' ἀκούσαθ' ὡς ἐσμὲν ἅπαντα κομψοὶ
> ἄνδρες, ὅτοισι πρῶτα μὲν παῖς ἀκόλουθός ἐστιν
> ἀλλότριος τὰ πολλά, μικρὸν δέ τι † κἄμον † αὐτοῦ.
> ἱματίω δέ μοι δύ' ἐστὸν χαρίεντε τούτω,   5
> οἷν μεταλαμβάνων ἀεὶ θάτερον ἐξελαύνω

εἰς ἀγοράν. ἐκεῖ δ' ἐπειδὰν κατίδω τιν' ἄνδρα
ἠλίθιον, πλουτοῦντα δ', εὐθὺς περὶ τοῦτόν εἰμι.
κἄν τι τύχηι λέγων ὁ πλούταξ, πάνυ τοῦτ' ἐπαινῶ,
καὶ καταπλήττομαι δοκῶν τοῖσι λόγοισι χαίρειν.   10
εἶτ' ἐπὶ δεῖπνον ἐρχόμεσθ' ἄλλυδις ἄλλος ἡμῶν
μᾶζαν ἐπ' ἀλλόφυλον, οὗ δεῖ χαρίεντα πολλὰ
τὸν κόλακ' εὐθέως λέγειν, ἢ 'κφέρεται θύραζε.
οἶδα δ' Ἀκέστορ' αὐτὸ τὸν στιγματίαν παθόντα·
σκῶμμα γὰρ εἶπ' ἀσελγές, εἶτ' αὐτὸν ὁ παῖς θύραζε   15
ἐξαγαγὼν ἔχοντα κλωιὸν παρέδωκεν Οἰνεῖ

2 ἅπαντα Hermann: ἅπαντες Ath.ᴬᶜᴱ   3 ὅτοισι Porson: τοῖσι Ath.ᴬᶜᴱ   5–6 τούτω, |
οὖν Porson: τούτοιν Ath.ᴬᶜᴱ   7 τιν' Ath.ᶜᴱ: τι οὖν Ath.ᴬ   8 εἰμι Grotius: εἶμι Ath.ᴬᶜᴱ
12–16 om. Ath.ᶜᴱ   13 εὐθέως Grotius: εὐθὺς Ath.ᴬ   'κφέρεται Bergk: φέρεται Ath.ᴬ
15 εἶπ' ἀσελγές Porson: εἶπας ἔλεγες Ath.ᴬ

B46. Cratinus fr. 255, from *Cheirons* (late 440s–before 429 ʙᴄ)

ταῦτα δυοῖν ἐτέοιν ἡμῖν μόλις ἐξεπονήθη

ἐτέοιν Meineke: ἐτοῖν Ael. Aristid.

COMMENTARY

B1–B20. Cratinus' *The Wineflask* (frr. 193–217) and *Dionysalexandros* (frr. 39–51) are important exceptions to the rule that little can be said about the plots of individual fragmentary fifth-century comedies. Much remains obscure about both plays. But the fragments (only the most interesting of which are printed here) offer a sense of what an 'Old Comedy' by someone other than Aristophanes looked like, and preserve traces of many of the genre's standard structural elements (further discussed in **B21–B46**).

Other late fifth-century comedies whose plots can be at least partially reconstructed include Aristophanes' *Babylonians* (frr. 67–100; first place at the City Dionysia in 426; see Olson, *Acharnians*, pp. xxviii–xxix) and Eupolis' *Demes* (frr. 99–146; mid- to late 410s; see **E10** introductory n.), *Marikas* (frr. 192–217; see **B42** introductory n.), and *Taxiarchs* (frr. 268–85; undated; see Storey 246–60).

B1–B12. At the Lenaia in 425, Aristophanes (who had been victorious for the first time at the City Dionysia the previous year) and Cratinus (who won the first of his nine victories probably in the mid-450s, at the City Dionysia) both staged comedies, and Aristophanes took the prize with a play that included several nasty personal attacks on his older rival (*Ach.* 848–53, 1173). Cratinus took second, with *The Storm-Tossed*. At the same festival the next year, Aristophanes made a pretence of praising Cratinus as a great figure in the history of Attic comedy, while simultaneously characterizing him as a drunk who ought to be encouraged to retire rather than embarrass himself with his increasingly feeble dramatic efforts (*Eq.* 526–36; cf. *Eq.* 400). Aristophanes again took the prize, while Cratinus was again second, with *Satyrs*. According to $\Sigma^{\text{VET}^{3}\Theta\text{M}}$ Ar. *Eq.* 400 (= *The Wineflask* test. ii), at the City Dionysia in 423 Cratinus responded to the attacks in *Knights* with a comedy entitled Πυτίνη (*The Wineflask*), which he wrote 'about himself and his drunkenness, making use of a plot of the following sort. He represented Comedy as his wife, who wanted to give up living with him and had got the right to bring a suit against him for abuse. But Cratinus' friends, when they encountered her, asked her not to do anything rash and enquired about the cause of her hostility; she complained that he was no longer writing comedies but spending his time getting drunk' (or perhaps 'spending his time with Drunkenness', who would then be the 'other woman'); the *scholium* then quotes **B1**. Hellenistic scholars regularly mined literary texts for biographical information about the author, and we cannot be sure that the poet who appeared on stage in *The Wineflask* was actually called 'Cratinus'; and even if he was, the character cannot simply be identified with the historical author of the play. But Cratinus' fondness for wine is treated as notorious not just in *Knights* (534–5) but at Ar. *Pax* 700–3, and it is difficult to escape the impression that *The Wineflask* offered what was intended to be understood as fictionalized autobiography answering Aristophanes' remarks at the Lenaia the previous year; cf. **B1**. 4 n.; **B6**. 1 n.; **B9** introductory n.; **B11** introductory n.; **B12** introductory n. Presumably the action ended with the poet's reconciliation with Comedy and his return to writing plays (cf. **B6–B7**; **B12**); that he made her realize that his love of wine and extramarital adventures (cf. **B3**) were of no significance for his relationship with her seems more likely than that she convinced him to moderate his drinking. *The Wineflask* also included attacks on Aristophanes (fr. 213; see **B42** introductory n.), Socrates' associate Chairephon (fr. 215; cf. **F1–F5** n.), and a number of contemporary democratic politicians (**B6–B7**; frr. 212; 214), and the parabasis took up political matters and probably the Peloponnesian War (esp. **B9**; cf. **B13–B20** n.). The play (test. i) took first place, defeating Amipsias' *Connus* (see **F4** with introductory n.), the original version of Aristophanes' *Clouds*, and two unidentified plays; for Aristophanes' disgusted comments on the outcome, see *Nu.* 520–5; *V.* 1043–50. **B41** is perhaps from *The Wineflask* as well. For further discussion, see Taplin 43–4 with plate 8 (a possible illustration of the play on a mid-fourth-century Apulian vase); Rosen, in *Rivals*, 23–39; Ruffell, *CQ* NS 52 (2002), 138–63, esp. 155–62; Biles, *AJP* 123 (2002), 169–204, esp. 180–8.

B1–B3. From the prologue. For other fragments of 'Old Comic' prologues, see **B21–B24** with nn.

B1. The text is seriously corrupt and is printed here with a number of minor improvements not adopted by Kassel–Austin. But there can be no doubt that Comedy is complaining about 'Cratinus', who used to pursue other women occasionally (2–3) but whose behaviour has deteriorated even further now that he is old (4; and see **B3** introductory n.). The complaint (to which **B2–B3** most likely belong as well) is addressed to 'Cratinus'' friends (see **B1–B12** n.), who were probably represented by other actors as well as by the chorus, like the female conspirators in Ar. *Ec.* (cf. **B4** introductory n.).

Preserved in a *scholium* on Ar. *Eq.* 400, at the end of the note that summarizes the plot of *The Wineflask* (**B1–B12** n.).

Iambic trimeter.

1. τὸν λόγον: 'the story' (cf. **B39**. 1; **D6**. 2; Ar. *V.* 54), i.e. the plot of the play, the speaker having gone off momentarily on a tangent, perhaps as part of the process of warming up the audience at the very beginning of the action (cf. **B24** introductory n.).

2. πρότερον is adverbial, 'before this, in the past', as also in **B2**. ἐκεῖνος: i.e. 'Cratinus', who must have been referred to earlier, before Comedy took up the secondary issue that requires her to return to her main subject in 1.

2–3. πρὸς ἑτέραν γυναῖκ(α) ἔχων | τὸν νοῦν: 'when he was paying attention to another woman'. For the idiom, see **H13**. 2 n.

4. ἅμα μὲν τὸ γῆρας: cf. Ar. *Eq.* 533 (of Cratinus) γέρων ὤν.

B2. Another fragment of Comedy's complaint (see **B1** introductory n.). Her point is not that the marriage is legally over, but that it might as well be: 'Cratinus' no longer takes any interest in her.

Preserved by Porphyry, *Homeric Enquiries*, p. 83. 20 Schr. (on H. *Il.* 5. 533 and *Od.* 8. 186), as evidence for the Attic first-person singular form ἦ < εἰμί.

Iambic trimeter.

πρότερον: see **B1**. 2 n.

B3. Probably another fragment of Comedy's complaint about 'Cratinus'. The imagery is explicitly sexual ('Cratinus' reacts to a fine wine in the way a devoted pederast reacts to a pretty boy; see **B29**. 3 n.) and perhaps helps make sense of **B1** (where see introductory n.): things were not so bad when 'Cratinus' chased women, but now he is driven by other, even more consuming desires.

Preserved at Athenaeus 1. 29d (manuscripts CE only), in an extended collection of literary references to different varieties of wine, but with no mention of the title, and assigned to *The Wineflask* by Runkel.

Iambic trimeter.

1–2. Μενδαῖον . . . | οἰνίσκον: 'a little Mendaean wine'; οἰνίσκος is an affectionate diminutive < οἶνος, like νεανίσκος < νέος. Wine from Mende (a city on the western side of the Chalcidice peninsula) is routinely mentioned, along with Lesbian, Chian, and Thasian, as a particularly fine local variety; see **H7** introductory n.

1. ἡβῶντ(α) ἀρτίως: 'that has just recently reached adolescence' (cf. **J12**. 1–2 with 2 n.), i.e. 'become drinkable'.

3. οἴμ(οι): here an expression of frustrated desire; 'Damn!' *vel sim.* Cf. Ar. *Nu.* 773 with Dover ad loc.; *Th.* 1185; Labiano Ilundain 260.   ὡς is exclamatory, 'how ἁπαλὸς καὶ λευκός (it is)!'; cf. **B26**. Both adjectives can be used of wine, but are commonly applied to attractive women and boys as well (e.g. Ar. *Av.* 668; adesp. com. fr. 735. 2; Pl. *Smp.* 195c, 196a; cf. **I7**. 17 with n.).   οἴσει τρία;: 'will it support three (measures of water for every one of wine)?'; cf. **H10** with nn.; Ar. *Eq.* 1187–8 'Take this wine to drink mixed three and two!'—'How sweet it is, by Zeus, and how well it bears the three!'

B4. Spoken by a male character (note 4 **σποδῶν**), presumably one of 'Cratinus'' friends, who is eager to put an end to his drinking and reconcile him to Comedy.

Preserved at Athenaeus 11. 494b–c, in a collection of comic passages that refer to an *oxybaphon* (6 with n.) as a drinking vessel.

Iambic trimeter.

1–2.   The anaphora (repetition) reflects the speaker's bafflement.
2.   **τοῦ λίαν πότου**: 'his excessive drinking'. λίαν communicates subjective disapproval (Thesleff § 197; cf. **B38**. 1; **C8**. 1–2; **G5**. 10; **J18**. 1).
3.   **ἐγῷδα** = ἐγὼ οἶδα.   **γάρ** is explanatory (Denniston 59), marking what follows as a description of the idea referred to obliquely in ἐγῷδα. **τοὺς χοᾶς**: 'his pitchers' (e.g. Ar. *Pax* 537 with Olson ad loc.; Anaxandr. fr. 33. 1; cf. **G18**. 19 n.).
4.   **τοὺς καδίσκους**: 'his little wine-buckets' (diminutive < κάδος; see **H9**. 12 n.; Amyx 186–90), used for drinking wine at Stratt. fr. 23. **συγκεραυνώσω**: 'I will blast as with a thunderbolt (κεραυνός), smash to bits'. Cf. Archil. fr. 120. 2 'thunderbolt-blasted (συγκεραυνωθείς) in my mind with wine' (the only earlier attestation of the verb) with **B8** introductory n.; Antiph. fr. 193. 4 τύπτειν κεραυνός ('as for passing out blows, I'm a thunderbolt!') Mendelsohn, *CJ* 87 (1992), 105–24.
5.   'and all the other vessels involved in his drinking', i.e. his cups (see **B32**. 7 n.) and mixing bowl (see **H1**. 8 n.).
6.   **ὀξύβαφον**: a small vessel properly used to hold vinegar (ὄξος), in which one could dip (βάπτω) individual bits of food (cf. **G12**. 10 n.; Ar. fr. 158), although this one is to be used for wine (**οἰνηρόν**), as at e.g. Antiph. fr. 161. 5 (preserved in the same section of Athenaeus).

B5. From the beginning of a speech most likely made by 'Cratinus' in response to an attack on him by Comedy, and addressed to his friends (note the plural **γιγνώσκετε**).

Preserved at Clement of Alexandria, *Stromateis* vi. 20. 3, along with a number of parallel passages from the orators, as an example of plagiarism. But this must in fact be a forensic trope; see below.

Iambic trimeter.

τὴν ... παρασκευήν: 'the preparation (of my opponent)', i.e. 'the care with which she made her case'. Orators seem to have been taught to refer to their opponents' παρασκευή (e.g. And. 1. 1; Lys. 19. 2) as a way of painting them as desperate and conniving.

B6–B7. The individual addressed is male (note **B6.** 1 ἔχων; **B7** ἀποσβέσας) and is most likely 'Cratinus', who is engaged in a debate with an unidentified interlocutor (Comedy? one of his friends? another comic poet?) about whom to attack and how in a new play. But γράφω is normally used of adding an item to a list or the like, or of drawing a picture, rather than to describe the process of composing poetry (for which ποιέω is expected; cf. **B12.** 5; **B42.** 2 n.); and 'Cratinus' and the other character are presumably constructing a catalogue of contemporary Athenians he will mock in his next comedy—making it clear that by this point in the play, at any rate, he has chosen to stick with his old trade/wife. Perhaps from the *agon*; cf. **B32–B35** with nn.

B6. 'Cratinus' must have shown some reluctance to mention Cleisthenes in his comedy, and his interlocutor none too respectfully urges him on.

Preserved in a *scholium* on Ar. *Nu.* 355, as evidence that Aristophanes was not the only poet who mocked Cleisthenes for effeminacy. The *Suda* (κ 1758), doubtless drawing on a related source, cites 1–2 only to prove the same thing. Iambic tetrameter catalectic.

1. **ληρεῖς ἔχων:** 'you keep babbling!', a charge reminiscent of Aristophanes' hostile remarks about Cratinus at *Eq.* 531, 536. For the participle of ἔχω used to add 'a notion of duration to that of present action', see LSJ s.v. B. IV. 2; Austin–Olson on Ar. *Th.* 852.
2. **ἐν ἐπεισοδίωι:** defined by ancient lexicographers as 'properly what is added to a play for the sake of laughter, independent of the main thesis' (e.g. *AB* p. 253. 19–21); cf. **B39.** 1 (the only other attestation of the word in comedy); Norwood, *CP* 25 (1930), 217–23.
2–3. **Κλεισθένης** (*PAA* 575540 ~ 575545) must have been a prominent social and political figure, and is ridiculed constantly by Aristophanes for his lack of a beard (which is probably the point of the unmetrical ἐν τῆι τοῦ κάλλους ἀκμῆι, 'at the height of his beauty') and supposed sexual depravity (see Olson on *Ach.* 117–18, with further references). The reason he will be 'laughable' (γελοῖος) if depicted shooting dice (κυβεύων; see **D12.** 3 n.) is most likely that this is generally depicted as a juvenile activity and thus appropriate for a beardless individual; K–A note that the effeminate Amynias is also mocked for his love of dicing at Ar. *V.* 74–6.

B7. For Hyperbolus, a wealthy lampmaker (cf. Ar. *Nu.* 1065 Ὑπέρβολος . . . οὐκ τῶν λύχνων; *Pax* 690; And. fr. 5 Blass) and important political figure, see **B9** introductory n.; **E23–E25** n.

Preserved in a *scholium* on Ar. *Pax* 692, as evidence that Hyperbolus sold lamps.

Iambic tetrameter catalectic.

ἀποσβέσας plays on the idea that Hyperbolus is a lampmaker, who can accordingly be 'snuffed out' (i.e. eliminated from public life), like one of the lamps he sells, and returned to the marketplace. Cf. **E4** introductory n. **ἐν τοῖς λύχνοισι**: 'in the lampmarket'; see **J1** introductory n.

B8–B9. From the epirrhemmatic section of the parabasis; cf. **B36–B45** with nn.

B8. A quotation of Archil. fr. 109 <ὦ> λιπερνῆτες πολῖται, τἀμὰ δὴ συνίετε | ῥήματα (adapted again three years later at Ar. *Pax* 603–4, at the beginning of a nominally serious speech about the origins of the Peloponnesian War, ὦ σοφώτατοι γεωργοί, τἀμὰ δὴ ξυνίετε | ῥήματ', as well as at **B44**. 1–2. The reference to Archilochus is interesting, given the tradition that Cratinus' poetry had a markedly Archilochean character (test. 17. 1–3; and note the title *Archilochoi*); cf. **B4**. 4 n. Probably from the initial address of the chorus (speaking for their poet) to the audience.

Preserved along with Archil. fr. 109 in a *scholium* on Ar. *Pax* 603.

Trochaic tetrameter catalectic.

λιπερνῆτες: obscure; perhaps 'impoverished'.

B9. The subject must be Athens' triremes, which are allegedly denied the protection (or rest?) they deserve. Probably a response to Ar. *Eq.* 1300–15, where personified triremes complain about Hyperbolus' (see **B7** introductory n.) plan to send them against Carthage.

Preserved at Pollux x. 184 (a book of Pollux that is particularly rich in comic fragments and may be directly dependent on Eratosthenes' *On Comedy*; see Nesselrath 87–8), along with several other passages from comedy that mention κάνναι.

Trochaic tetrameter catalectic.

1. **πάντα ποιοῦσαι**: 'no matter what they do'.   **νεωσοίκων**: 'ship-sheds', in which triremes were kept when not in service, both to protect them from damage and in order that their hulls could dry out and repairs could be made; see Olson on Ar. *Ach.* 96; Harrison, *JHS* 119 (1999), 168–71.
2. **κάννης**: 'a reed mat', and thus 'fencing made of reed mats' (cf. Ar. *V.* 394 (κάνναι used to fence off a hero-shrine)) as a temporary substitute for a ship-shed.

B10. The speaker might be either 'Cratinus', who at last sees the error of his ways, or Comedy recognizing that she has treated her husband worse than he deserves.

Preserved at Priscian, *Inst. Gramm.* 18. 209, who remarks *similiter nos: cogito quae sunt difficultates stoliditatis meae* (which would seem to guarantee that he read the text in something very close to the form to which it has been restored here).

Iambic trimeter.

1. **ἀτάρ** marks a break in the thought or a sudden change of tone (Denniston 51–3) and is probably colloquial (Stevens 44–5); **δῆτα** adds emphasis, a function more often performed by δή (cf. Denniston 278–9), hence Nauck's δή τι τῆς.

B11. Meier attributed this line to *The Wineflask*, and if this is correct, the speaker is most likely 'Cratinus'; but see below on the fragment's dubious origin. The idea that intellectual and verbal brilliance (including the ability to write good poetry) is closely associated with drinking wine is a commonplace (Archil. fr. 120; Epich. fr. 131; Phryn. Com. fr. 74), but is developed in particular in the prologue of Aristophanes' *Knights* (esp. 88–96).

Preserved at *AP* xiii. 29. 2 (= *HE* 2712), as the second line in an epigram attributed to Nicaenetus, and identified there as a quotation from Cratinus (τοῦτ' ἔλεγεν ... | Κρατῖνος). In addition, the epigram is quoted at Athenaeus 2. 39c in a variant form known to a number of other witnesses, all of whom cite only the second line (Zenob. 2. 53; Phot. p. 615. 17 = S υ 53 = Apostol. 17. 52), and is referred to by Horace (*Epist.* i. 19. 1–3): *prisco si credis, Maecenas docte, Cratino, | nulla placere diu nec vivere carmina possunt | quae scribuntur aquae potoribus.*

Iambic trimeter.

σοφόν: for σοφία as a basic defining characteristic of good poetry, see Dover, *Frogs*, pp. 12–14; and cf. **B36** with n.; **B37.** 2; **B44.** 3; **D11.** 4 with n.; Ar. *Nu.* 520, 522, 1377–8; *Pax* 798; fr. 392 (ironic).

B12. Someone (Comedy? the chorus?) responds to a rush of verses (5 ποι-ήμασιν), presumably produced by 'Cratinus', who has returned to composing poetry. Comparing a powerful stream of words to a flood is a commonplace (e.g. **B16**; Ar. *Ach.* 379–81; *Ra.* 1005 τὸν κρουνὸν ἀφίει ('send forth your spring of words!'; addressed to Euripides); see Taillardat §504), and it is impossible to know whether Cratinus is being praised or condemned. But the description is strikingly reminiscent of Ar. *Eq.* 526–8 'Cratinus, who once upon a time, pouring forth with much praise, used to flow through the smooth plains and, sweeping from their place the oaks and the plane-trees and his enemies, carried them off, roots and all', to which these line are perhaps a pointed response.

Preserved in a *scholium* on Ar. *Eq.* 526 πολλῶι ῥεύσας ποτ' ἐπαίνωι (of Cratinus), with the—historically impossible—suggestion that Aristophanes may be alluding to this passage, which dates to the year after it.

Iambic trimeter.

1. **ἄναξ Ἄπολλον:** Invocations of Apollo are a common colloquial response
    to an astonishing or horrible sight, sound, or remark (e.g. **C3**. 4; **C17**. 4;
    H11. 6; Men. *Asp.* 86; *Dysc.* 293, 415); often accompanied by a genitive of
    exclamation (e.g. Ar. *V.* 161; *Pax* 238), as here (**τῶν ἐπῶν τοῦ ῥεύματος**,
    'what a stream of words!').

2–3. **δωδεκάκρουνον κτλ.** explains why 'the streams are gurgling': 'Cratinus''
    mouth has twelve springs (or perhaps 'twelve spouts', as if he were a
    fountain-house; in either case, 'twelve' means simply 'a very large
    number') and runs as full as the **Ἰλισός**, the river just outside Athens' walls
    which Socrates and his interlocutor walk along at the beginning of Plato's
    Phaedrus (229a–b).

4–5. A future most vivid condition, of something feared.

4. **ἐπιβύσει:** 'stick a plug into'.

B13–B20. *Dionysalexandros* was a parody of the story of the Judgment of
Paris/Alexandros and the abduction of Helen (see Gantz 567–76), with
Dionysus disguising himself for much of the action as the Trojan hero, hence
the title. The chorus consisted of satyrs (**B13**. 38), as also in the *Satyrs* of
e.g. Callias (Lenaia 438/7?) and Cratinus (Lenaia 425/4; see **B1–B12** n.), and
the action was set on Mt. Ida near Troy (**B13**. 22).

  The claim that *Dionysalexandros* was directed against the Athenian statesman Pericles (**B13**. 40–4; for Pericles and his image in comedy, see **E10–E14**
with nn.) must have had some basis in the text, although how extensive the
identification was and whether Pericles is supposed to have been represented
by Paris or by Dionysus is unclear. The latter possibility finds support in the
peculiar reference to Pericles as 'king of the satyrs' in **E14**. 1 (where see n.);
cf. Revermann, *JHS* 117 (1997), 197–200. But it is Paris who brings war on
Troy in Cratinus' play, by deciding to hold on to Helen (**B13**. 33–5 with n.);
and it may have been he who was identified, if only late in the play, with
Pericles, who was thus indirectly blamed for bringing the Peloponnesian
War on Athens for the sake of his mistress Aspasia, as also in Aristophanes'
Acharnians 526–39. For Aspasia, see **E13** introductory n. *Dionysalexandros* is
normally dated to 430; but if the war in question was instead the one against
Samos around 440 (cf. **E10–E28** n.; **E11**. 2 n.), which Plutarch repeatedly
reports was begun by Pericles to gratify Aspasia, who was from there (*Per.* 24.
2; 25. 1), it might belong a decade earlier. See J. T. M. F. Pieters, *Cratinus*
(Leiden, 1946), 63–131 (on Pericles in Cratinus), 169–72 (on this play) (in
Dutch); J. Schwartze, *Die Beurteilung des Perikles durch die attische Komödie*
(Zetemata 51: Munich, 1971), 6–24; R. M. Rosen, *Old Comedy and the Iambo-
graphic Tradition* (Atlanta, 1988), 49–55; Mattingly, in K. H. Kinzl (ed.),

Greece and the Eastern Mediterranean in Ancient History and Prehistory (Festschrift Fritz Schachermeyr: Berlin and New York, 1977), 243–4; Heath, *G&R* 37 (1990), 144–7; J. F. McGlew, *Citizens on Stage* (Ann Arbor, 2002), 25–56, esp. 46–55; Storey, in L. Kozak and J. Rich (eds.), *Playing Around Aristophanes* (Nottingham, 2005), 105–25 (with extensive bibliography). Eupolis too is reported to have called Aspasia 'Helen' (fr. 267).

B13. A fragmentary hypothesis consisting of an extended plot summary (2–41) and a brief note about the political intentions of the play (41–5). The fragment begins with the departure from the stage of Hermes (5–6), who must already have described the quarrel among the goddesses (most likely in the prologue) and made arrangements to resolve it. Dionysus' discovery of the situation and decision to try to pass as Paris (taken for granted in what follows) must also belong to the first half of the play. The parabasis came next (6–9), followed by a mocking exchange between Dionysus and the chorus (10–12); the disguised Dionysus' judgment among the goddesses (12–19) and exit for Sparta (20–1); his return, accompanied by Helen (21–3); a messenger-speech informing Dionysus and Helen of the arrival of the Achaeans in the land (23–6); Dionysus' desperate attempt to keep the two of them from being captured (26–30); the arrival of the real Paris, accompanied by herdsmen or servants, and his capture of Dionysus and Helen (30–4); her plea not to be returned and his decision to keep her as his wife (34–6); and the dispatch of Dionysus to the Achaean ships, followed by the chorus singing their *exodos*-song (37–41).

Preserved in POxy. iv 663 (second/third century AD; = *CGFPR* 70), in which the text appears in two columns (my 1–25 and 26–45), with the words

Διονυσ[αλέξανδρος
   η [
ΚΡΑΤ[ΕΙΝΟΥ

at the top of the second. (It is unclear whether the *eta* in the second line marks this as the eighth play in the collection (i.e. η′), or means 'or' (i.e. ἤ) and was followed by an alternative title such as Luppe's Ἰδαῖοι; cf. Cratin. fr. 91, which perhaps refers to the Judgment of Paris.)

Prose.

6. οὗτοι: the chorus.

8. π(ερὶ) τῶν ποιη(τῶν): 'the (other) poets', i.e. Cratinus' rivals (not yet including Aristophanes or Eupolis), who were doubtless criticized for their failings of originality, poetic grace, imagination, and the like; cf. **B40–B42** n. This is Körte's expansion and emendment of the papyrus' πυωνποιη. K–A print π(ερὶ) ὑῶν ποιή(σεως), which ought to mean 'about the production of pigs', although Rutherford, *CR* 18 (1904), 440 (followed by Handley, *BICS* 29 (1982), 109–17) argues for taking it 'about the generation of sons (υἱῶν)', in reference to a supposed attempt to legitimize Pericles' bastard son by Aspasia (see **E13** introductory n.), Pericles II. See Luppe, *ZPE* 72 (1988), 37–8; Austin, *QUCC* ns 63 (1999), 39–40.

10–12. The Satyrs' mockery is most likely connected with the fact that Dionysus is now dressed not as a god but as Paris, a simple shepherd. Cf. **B14–B15** with nn.

12–19. Blass (followed by K–A) marked a lacuna after παραγενομένων, which must then have introduced a list of characters present during the next scene (cf. 30–1 παραγενόμενος δ' Ἀλέξανδρος). Alternatively, the word might be taken with παρὰ μ(ὲν) Ἥρα[ς] τυραννίδο(ς) ἀκινήτου, πα[ρ]ὰ δ' Ἀθηνᾶς εὐψυχί(ας) κ(α)τ(ὰ) πόλεμο(ν) to form a genitive absolute ('with unshakeable kingship made available to him from Hera, and courage made available from Athena'), with the construction shifting slightly with τῆς δ' Ἀφροδί(της) (sc. παρά, 'and from Aphrodite that he be . . .'). That the participle ought in that case properly to be present tense rather than aorist is only a weak objection to this interpretation, since this is late and clumsy Greek. Hera and Athena were probably played by mutes (hence a third party's description of Athena's offer in **B16**, which may belong to this scene); but perhaps Aphrodite was represented by an actor. **B17** appears to be a retrospective description of the action in this part of the play.

18. ἐπέραστον: 'sexually desirable'.

19. ταύτην: i.e. Aphrodite.

20–22. The events referred to in πλεύσας εἰς Λακεδαίμο(να) (καὶ) τὴν Ἑλένην ἐξαγαγών take place off stage between scenes.

22. ἐπανέρχεται: 'he returns'.

26–9. Dionysus attempts to conceal himself and Helen in a way that fits the bucolic setting (cf. 23), by putting her in a basket (τάλαρον) of a type used elsewhere for making cheese (H. *Od.* 9. 247; Ar. *Ra.* 560; Theoc. 5. 86 with Gow ad loc.) and storing wool (H. *Od.* 4. 125, 131), and 'changing his own costume/appearance to make himself look like a ram' (ἑαυτὸν ... εἰς κριὸ[ν] μ(ε)τ(α)σκευάσας). Cf. **B19**.

30–2. **B18** may belong to this scene.

31–2. φωράσας: 'after catching (them)'.

32–3. ἑκάτερο(ν) ἄγειν ἐπὶ τὰς ναῦς πρ(οσ)τάττει: 'gives orders (sc. to the individuals who accompany him on stage; cf. fr. 49) to take them both to the (Greek) ships', so as to prove his own innocence and put an end to the quarrel (cf. 23–6).

34–6. The implication would seem to be that Paris expected Helen to want to return to Sparta and Menelaus, but that she was reluctant to do so and took advantage of his good nature, leading to an otherwise avoidable war.

36. ἐπικατέχ(ει): 'he keeps hold of, detains'.

38–41. συνακολουθ(οῦσι) (sc. τῶι Διονύσωι) κτλ.: a description of the *exodos*. Cf. the end of Euripides' *Cyclops*, where the chorus of satyrs exit proclaiming their continuing allegiance to Dionysus (708–9 with Olson, *Hermes*, 116 (1988), 502–4).

39–40. παρακαλοῦντες: 'encouraging (him)'.

43–4. δι(ὰ) Ι ἐμφάσεως: 'via innuendo' *vel sim.* (cf. LSJ s.v. III. 2).

44. ἐπαγηοχώς is perfect active participle < ἐπάγω; a post-classical form.

B14. Someone (the disguised Dionysus? Helen?) is accused of wanting to live like a king (or queen), sc. rather than a cowherd. Pieters took **B15** to be Dionysus' response. Cf. **B13**. 10–12 n.

Preserved at Pollux vii. 122, in a collection of architectural terms.

Iambic trimeter.

παραστάδας καὶ πρόθυρα . . . ποικίλα: 'doorposts and painted porticoes', such as would be found in a palace.

B15. See **B13**. 10–12 n.; **B14** introductory n.

Preserved in a *scholium* on Ar. *Lys.* 575, in a gloss on the rare word οἰσπώτην (the accent on which is disputed).

Iambic trimeter.

βόλιτα . . . κ(αὶ) οἰσπώτην: 'cow-manure and sheep-shit'.   πατεῖν: sc. βούλομαι (cf. **B14**).

B16. If this fragment belongs to *Dionysalexandros* (as Gelzer suggested), it must represent a summary of Athena's offer to Dionysus (disguised as Paris) and an oblique reference to Pericles' rhetorical power (see **E10** introductory n.); see **B13**. 12–19 n.

Preserved at Photius α 414 = Συναγ.ᴮ α 404, in a gloss on the words ἀείνως γλῶττα.

Iambic dimeter (the third verse catalectic).

2. ἐν δήμωι: i.e. 'in the Assembly' (cf. 4 n.), where 'the people' gathered for political purposes.

3. καλῶν λόγων ἀείνων: '(full of) ever-flowing, lovely words' (modifying γλῶτταν in 1). For the image, see **B12** introductory n.

4. πάντα νικήσεις λέγων: 'you will always carry your point when you make a speech'; cf. Ar. *Nu.* 432 (the Clouds' initial offer to Strepsiades) ἐν τῶι δήμωι γνώμας οὐδεὶς νικήσει πλείονας ἢ σύ ('No one will get more motions approved in the Assembly than you'); *V.* 594.

B17. Probably a description of Dionysus' reaction when one of the goddesses attempted to bribe him to judge her the most beautiful and he had trouble containing himself (thus Pieters); see **B13.** 12–19 n.

Preserved at Photius α 629, in a gloss on the rare word αἱμωδεῖν.

Iambic trimeter.

1. **εὐθύς**: 'immediately' (cf. **A12.** 4 n.).   **ἡμώδεις** is < αἱμωδέω, 'grind one's teeth', either to produce a grimace of eager anticipation, as at Timocl. fr. 11. 6, or in terror.
2. **τοὺς προσθίους ὀδόντας**: 'your front teeth'; cf. **A1.** 3 n.

B18. The individual referred to is clearly Dionysus, and Speaker A is probably Paris, who is attempting to discover who assumed his identity in order to judge among the goddesses and then stole Helen from Menelaus. Cf. **B13.** 30–2 with n.

Preserved at Macrobius, *Saturnalia* v. 21. 6, in a collection of poetic passages that mention the drinking vessel known as a καρχήσιον (2).

Iambic trimeter.

1. **δὲ δή**: 'often in surprised, or emphatic and crucial questions' (Denniston 259).   **τοῦτό μοι φράσον** suggests impatience; cf. above.
2. **κροκωτόν**: a saffron-dyed *chiton*, normally worn by women, but part of Dionysus' costume also at Ar. *Ra.* 46; Callix. *FGrHist* 627 F 2 (p. 169. 16; describing the costume of a statue of the god carried in a procession in early third-century Alexandria, which also included a golden καρχήσιον). See Austin–Olson on Ar. *Th.* 137.   **ποικίλον**: defined at Pollux vii. 47 as 'Dionysus' bacchic *chiton*' (cf. Eup. fr. 280) and at Hesychius π 2717 as 'a multi-coloured (ζωγραφητόν) *himation*' (a definition that works better here, since the god's inner garment has already been mentioned). **καρχήσιον**: a tall, two-handled, footless drinking cup (thus Callix. *FGrHist* 627 F 3, cited at Ath. 11. 474e at the beginning of his discussion of the vessel, to which Kaibel added this passage from Macrobius); cf. Boardman, *JHS* 99 (1979), 149–51. According to Pherecydes (*FGrHist* 3 F 13), Charon of Lampsacus (*FGrHist* 262 F 2), and Herodorus of Heracleia (*FGrHist* 31 F 16), Zeus gave a καρχήσιον to Alcmena when he seduced her disguised as Amphitryon; so perhaps Dionysus put his cup to use as a love-gift for Helen.

B19. A mocking description of the disguised Dionysus' attempts to avoid capture by Paris (thus Körte; cf. **B13.** 28–32).

Preserved at Photius β 130 = *Et.Gen.* β 105 = *Suda* β 250, in a gloss on the word βῆ, and at Eustathius pp. 768. 14; 1721. 26 (citing the second-century AD grammarian Aelius Dionysius), in a pair of notes derived from a very similar lexicographic source.

Trochaic tetrameter catalectic.

βῆ βῆ: 'baa!, baa!' (important evidence for ancient Greek pronunciation, since although the sound the letter *beta* represents may have changed, sheep still make the same noise they did two and half thousand years ago).   **βαδίζει:** colloquial vocabulary; cf. **B26**; **B32**. 9; Olson on Ar. *Ach.* 393–4.

B20. Probably an assentient answer ('(Yes), because you're not, in fact, the first . . . '; cf. Denniston 89, 549–50) from the *agon* (cf. **B32–B35** with nn.). Fr. 46 ('after going to dinner † of the uninvited leech-throats themselves †'; also anapaestic tetrameter catalectic) must belong to the same section of the play. But who is speaking and to whom (Dionysus denounced for having abused Menelaus' hospitality?) is unclear. For uninvited guests at dinner parties, see **A13** introductory n.; **B45**.

Preserved at Photius α 1940 = *Suda* α 2443 = Συναγ.ᴮ α 1383, as well as at Athenaeus 2. 47a, in a pair of closely related glosses on the rare word ἄνηστις. In addition, φοιτᾶις κτλ. is preserved at *Et.Gen.* s. ἄνηστις and Συναγ.ᴮ α 2259 (s. ἄσταχυς καὶ ἀσταφίς), in related notes that probably derive from the same source.

Anapaestic tetrameter catalectic.

ἄνηστις: 'fasting', i.e. 'intensely hungry'. The initial α is an intensifier rather than a privative, and the adjective is equivalent in sense to the more common νῆστις.

B21–B24. Additional 'Old Comic' prologue fragments; cf. **B1–B3**; and see Whittaker 181–2; Storey 349–50. Pl. Com. fr. 182 may also be from a prologue.

B21. Addressed to the audience; doubtless the speaker's isolation was invaded shortly after he spoke these words. For *The Recluse* (which took third place at the City Dionysia in 415/4, behind Amipsias' *Revellers* and Aristophanes' *Birds*), see Ceccarelli, in *Rivals*, 461–2. For the political ideology at least glancingly referred to here, cf. **E2** with introductory n.

Preserved at Photius α 375 (ἄδουλος βίος ἐρεῖς, τούτεστιν ὁ μὴ δοῦλον ἔχων) = Συναγ.ᴮ α 374, in a note about the use of βίος with various adjectives that appears to be little more than a prose version of this fragment.

Iambic trimeter.

1. **Μονότροπος**: 'Mr Recluse, He-who-lives-alone'.
2. **Τίμωνος βίον**: 'a life of Timon', i.e. 'a life like Timon's' (further defined in 3–4). Timon was a notorious misanthrope mentioned repeatedly by the comic poets (Ar. *Av.* 1548–9; *Lys.* 808–20 (he never shaved, and lived by himself, cursing other men); Pl. Com. fr. 237; Antiphanes' *Timon* (fr. 204); cf. Neanth. *FGrHist* 84 F 35; Luc. *Timon* (based at least in part on Antiphanes' play?); Hawkins, *GRBS* 42 (2001), 143–62). Most likely he was a proverbial character rather than a real person (despite Armstrong, *G&R* 34 (1987), 7–11).
3–4. The manuscripts' ἄζυγον in 3 is unmetrical, and if Hermann's **ἄδου-λον** (supported by the lemma in Photius) is right, the first six adjectives fall neatly into complementary pairs ('with no wife or slave; easily angered and unapproachable; never laughing or speaking with anyone'), with **ἰδιογνώμονα** ('keeping my own counsel') summing up the description.

B22–B23. Two fragments of a mock-Euripidean prologue; the reference to Euripides' *Iphigenia in Tauris* in **B23** dates the play to no earlier than 414/13 or so. For the story of Hypsipyle and the Lemnian women, who murdered all the men on their island except Hypsipyle's father Thoas (whom she concealed) and later used the services of Jason and the Argonauts to repopulate the place, cf. H. *Il.* 7. 467–9; Pi. *P.* 4. 251–7; Hdt. vi. 138. 4; [Apollod.] *Bib.* i. 9. 17; Gantz 345–6. Ar. frr. 374–6 may also be from the prologue, in which case the Argonauts have already arrived on Lemnos (fr. 375) and Hypsipyle has fallen in love with Jason (cf. fr. 377 with K–A ad loc.), and the speaker is most likely Hypsipyle's old nurse (thus Kaibel), who has left her mistress inside the palace in the bath (cf. fr. 376) and come outside to complain about her troubles, like Phaedra's Nurse in the opening scene of Euripides' *Hippolytus*. For the reception of Euripides in Attic comedy, see **D11–D12** n.

B22. The speaker identifies the setting of the play ('(This is) Lemnos . . . '), but refers to the land not in a dignified, heroic way (e.g. E. *HF* 4–7; *Hel.* 1–3) but as a source of excellent . . . beans. Lemnos (a large but mostly barren volcanic island in the north-east Aegean) had been subject to Athens since the beginning of the fifth century (Hdt. vi. 140 with How and Wells ad loc.) and remained so through the 320s, except for a brief period of independence in the aftermath of the Peloponnesian War. See *Inventory*, 756–7.
    Preserved at Athenaeus 9. 366c–d, along with Pherecr. fr. 89, in response to a request at 9. 366a for examples of literary uses of the adjective τακερός.
    Iambic trimeter.

κυάμους: 'fava beans', often eaten as symposium dainties (τραγήματα; see **H2**. 3 n.); cf. Ephipp. fr. 13. 2; Olson–Sens on Archestr. fr. 60. 15.

B23. A parodic reference to Euripides, *IT* 30–3 Ταύρων χθόνα, Ι οὗ γῆς
ἀνάσσει βαρβάροισι βάρβαρος Ι Θόας, ὃς ὠκὺν πόδα τιθεὶς ἴσον πτεροῖς Ι ἐς
τοὔνομ' ἦλθε τόδε ποδωκείας χάριν ('the land of the Taurians, over which
country rules, as a barbarian over barbarians, Thoas, whose foot is as fast as
wings, and who got his name on account of his swiftfootedness').

Preserved at Ammonius Grammaticus, *Adfin. Voc. Diff.* 480, as an example
of the word τύραννος used to refer to a king (βασιλεύς).

Iambic trimeter.

1.　**ἐνταῦθα:** i.e. 'on Lemnos'.
2.　**βραδύτατος … δραμεῖν:** As the passage of Euripides parodied here (see
　　introductory n. and Platnauer ad loc.) makes clear, the personal name
　　Θόας can be punningly connected with θοός ('quick'), hence the humour
　　in claiming that he is not swift-footed but, in fact, the slowest runner there
　　is.　　**τῶν ἐν ἀνθρώποις:** 'of all those among human beings', i.e. 'of
　　human beings'; a deliberately absurd paratragic periphrasis, echoing
　　passages such as E. *Med.* 471; *Ph.* 440; frr. 403. 7; 1030.

B24. The prologue-speaker is a personified festival-day (2), like Calligeneia
in Aristophanes' second *Women Celebrating the Thesmophoria* (fr. 331). For
the way she identifies herself to the audience (not necessarily at the very
beginning of her speech; cf. **B1.** 1 n.), cf. Men. *Asp.* 146–8. At the Apatouria
festival, boys were introduced into their father's *phratry* ('brotherhood',
i.e. 'kin-group'). But Heracles (the title character of the play) was a bastard
and thus ineligible for *phratry*-membership, a point that may have been at
issue in the play (cf. Ar. *Av.* 1641–75, esp. 1667–70)—along with his gluttony
(see **A1** introductory n.).

Preserved at Athenaeus 4. 171d, along with Ar. *Nu.* 1196–1200; Pherecr. fr.
7; and an Attic decree from either 366/5 or (less likely) 323/2, all of which
refer to προτένθαι, as part of an extended catalogue of the names of classes of
individuals involved in preparing or serving food.

Iambic trimeter.

1.　For **βούλεσθε;** addressed to the audience in similar situations, cf. Men.
　　Dysc. 46; Philem. fr. 50.　　**δῆτ(α)** marks some logical connection with
　　what preceded (Denniston 269–70).
2.　According to Hesychius (δ 2222), **Δορπία** (cognate with δόρπον, 'meal')
　　was the name of the first day of the Apatouria festival, which must have
　　involved a common meal and was followed the next day by a sacrifice to
　　Zeus Phratrios and Athena Phratria and a feast; see Parke 88–92; Olson on
　　Ar. *Ach.* 145–6 (with further bibliography). The first day of the
　　festival probably belongs to **τῶν προτενθῶν** (literally 'the anticipators', i.e.

'foretasters') because they had the right to eat the food before anyone else, although who these men were and why this privilege was extended to them is unclear; see Dover on Ar. *Nu.* 1198.

B25–B31. Parodos fragments (**B25–B29** spoken by characters observing the chorus' entrance, **B30–B31** spoken by the chorus itself). Cf. Cratin. frr. 133; 171; 253; Eup. fr. 207; and see Whittaker 183–4.

B25. Speaker B has just announced that he can see some of the Islands (sc. that belong to the Athenian empire; cf. **B26** introductory n.; **B27–B29** n.), and Speaker A—who is expecting to see real islands rather than women— expresses puzzlement. Ar. *Nu.* 323–8, esp. 325–6, is similar.

Preserved in a *scholium* on Ar. *Av.* 296, as an example of the use of the word εἴσοδος (2) to refer to the passageway by which the chorus entered the Theatre.

Iambic trimeter.

1. **τί σὺ λέγεις;**: 'What are you talking about?, What do you mean?' (e.g. Ar. *Ach.* 768; *Nu.* 207).
2. **αἰδί**: accompanied by a gesture. **κατ(ὰ) αὐτὴν ἣν βλέπεις τὴν εἴσοδον**: '(who are) coming down the very entrance-way you're looking toward'.

B26. A character comments on the appearance of an individual member of the chorus, whose posture reflects the mistreatment she has suffered at the hands of the Athenians (thus Bergk). Cf. **B25**; **B27–B29** n.

Preserved at Photius p. 311. 16 = *Suda* ξ 129, along with Ar. fr. 46, in a gloss on the verbal form ξυννένοφεν.

Anapaestic tetrameter catalectic.

ὡς is exclamatory ('how . . . !'); cf. **B3**. 3 n. **κύψασα** is < κύπτω, 'stoop', sc. in shame or dejection, as at Ar. *Eq.* 1354; *Th.* 930; Eup. fr. 192. 120. **ξυννενοφυῖα** is < ξυννέφω, 'cloud over' (e.g. Ar. *Av.* 1502; fr. 46) and thus metaphorically in the perfect 'with a gloomy expression on her face' (also E. *El.* 1078; cf. E. *Ph.* 1308 with Mastronarde ad loc.).

B27–B29. Individual members of the chorus of Eupolis' *Cities* (sc. *That Belong to the Athenian Empire*; probably late 420s) are introduced as they come on stage for the first time, and a witty remark is made about each. Most likely each 'city' wears a costume appropriate to 'her' (cf. **B29**. 1 with introductory n.). **B29** shows that two characters are on stage as the chorus enters, but **B28** makes it clear that the introductions are carried out primarily for the benefit of the audience in the theatre. Ar. *Av.* 268–304, esp. 294–304, where the chorus of birds enters, seemingly accompanied by four lavishly costumed specialized dancers, is similar, as are Ar. fr. 71 (a comment on the tattoos worn by one member of the chorus of Babylonians/allied states) and Eup. fr. 298 (part of a catalogue of at least eighteen men with disabilities who most likely represent the chorus of *The Golden Race*). Cf. **F4** introductory n.; Wilson, *CQ* NS 27 (1977), 278–83 (on individualized choruses generally); Rosen, in G. W. Dobrov (ed.), *The City as Comedy* (Chapel Hill, NC, and London, 1997), 149–76, esp. 153–64 (on the sexual dynamics of the poet's decision to present Athens' subject-allies as women); Storey 216–30, esp. 217–21.

B27. The first two words (1) are presumably to be assigned to the same character as **B28**, who must be Speaker B in **B29**. The rude remark that follows, on the other hand, most likely belongs to his interlocutor, i.e. Speaker A in **B29**. Tenos (one of the Cyclades) appears in the Athenian tribute lists at e.g. *IG* I³ 281. II. 50 (paying 2 talents in 430/29; for the tribute, see **E11**. 1 n.); 287. I. 13, and is listed at Th. vii. 57. 4 among the allied states participating in the Sicilian Expedition in 414. See *Inventory*, 776–8. The island seems to have been notorious for harbouring venomous snakes and the like (cf. Antim. fr. 91 Matthews (preserved by the same source as this fragment); Plin. *Nat.* 4. 65), and the claim that it was also full of political informers (2) must have had some contemporary significance that escapes us.

Preserved in a *scholium* on Ar. *Pl.* 718, as evidence that 'Tenos appears to be infested with savage creatures'.

Iambic tetrameter catalectic.

2. συκοφάντας: literally 'fig-revealers', according to Istrus, *FGrHist* 334 F 12 in reference to an early embargo on the export of figs from Attica that led to denunciations of those who violated it. But the true etymology of the word is obscure, and the term functioned above all else as an imaginative category (routinely appealed to in comedy, e.g. Ar. *Ach.* 818–28, 910–58) that allowed the Athenians to discuss perceived problems of legal excess and abuse; see M. R. Christ, *The Litigious Athenian* (Baltimore and London, 1998), 48–71 (with further bibliography). For the implicit comparison of a sycophant to a scorpion or other poisonous creature, see **E9**. 1–4; Ar. *Pl.* 883–5 (a magic ring that protects the wearer against 'informer stings'); and cf. Ar. *Th.* 528–30 (a proverb about scorpions lurking under every stone, but adapted to refer to politicians).

B28. Unlike **B27**, addressed to the audience in the theatre (2 ὑμῖν; cf. **B44**. 2; **B45**. 1). The city of Chios (located on the island of the same name just off the coast of Asia Minor) was large and wealthy. As 2–3 make clear, Chios was an exceptionally loyal Athenian ally (cf. Ar. *Av.* 877–80, with Theopomp. Hist.

FGrHist 115 F 104), which paid no tribute and furnished ships and men instead (Th. ii. 9. 5; vi. 31. 2; vii. 57. 4), although it finally revolted from the empire at Alcibiades' urging in 412 (Th. viii. 14. 1–2). See *Inventory*, 1064–9. The lacuna in 1 (at least ∪ – × and perhaps × – ∪ – ∪ – ×) must have contained another adjective, a participial clause, or the like that emphasized Chios' cooperative attitude or docility, and which was then glossed (note 2 **γάρ**) in 2–3. Unlike Tenos, who brings only trouble (**B27**), Chios is presented as an ideal woman, in that she offers the man or men in her life access to enormous resources but none the less remains completely submissive; cf. **A19**. 2–5 with nn.; **I4**. 7 n.

Preserved in a *scholium* on Ar. *Av*. 880, in a note on Athenian relations with Chios.

Iambic tetrameter catalectic.

2.   **ναῦς μακράς:** i.e. 'warships, triremes' (e.g. Ar. *Eq*. 1366).
3.   **τ(ὰ) ἄλλα:** accusative of respect.   **ἄπληκτος:** literally 'unstruck', i.e. 'that needs no goad (to make it do as its master wants)'.

B29. Cyzicus (located on the Asian side of the Propontis) was another extremely wealthy allied city (e.g. *IG* I³ 281. III. 9 (paying over 8.5 talents tribute in 430/29; cf. **E11**. 1 n.); Th. viii. 107. 1), and was known for its electrum coinage (referred to in 1, where see n.). See *Inventory*, 983–6. 'Full of *staters*' in 1 perhaps describes some aspect of 'Cyzicus'' costume.

Preserved in a *scholium* on Ar. *Pax* 1176, as support for the thesis that Cyzicus had a reputation for sexual depravity.

Iambic tetrameter catalectic.

1.   **στατήρων:** a generic term for large coins; see **I11**. 12 n. For Cyzicene staters in particular, e.g. *IG* I³ 378. 21; 383. 108–9; D. 34. 23 (equal in value to 28 Athenian drachmas); Kraay 260–5.
2.   **τοίνυν** ('Well, . . .') marks this as a comment that responds to Speaker B's remark (Denniston 572–3), and the point would seem to be that, even if Cyzicus is full of money now, things were not always so (3–4). **φρουρῶν:** 'standing watch', i.e. as part of an Athenian garrison, as at Ar. *V*. 236–7 (where the chorus describe similar mischief they got into on guard-duty in Byzantion in their youth).
3.   **ἐκίνουν:** 'I screwed'; a metaphorical use of the verb (literally 'move') and thus perhaps less offensive than the unambiguously obscene βινέω ('fuck'; cf. **I6**. 21 with n.; **I8**. 22). Cf. *Maculate Muse*, § 205–6.   **κολλύβου:** gen. of price. κόλλυβοι were tiny bronze coins (cf. Ar. *Pax* 1200 with Olson ad loc.), and the point is that the price for sex was ridiculously low; cf. **I6**. 17 n.; **I11**. 18 n.   **καὶ παῖδα καὶ γέροντα:** That an adult male

might want to have sex with a handsome boy is routinely treated as normal (e.g. **B3**; **C11**. 7; **J12** with introductory n.; Ar. *Eq.* 1384–7; *Av.* 137–42). But the claim to have buggered an old man as well is different; the local inhabitants were desperate, and the speaker was able to run absolutely wild as a result, and καὶ γέροντα is accordingly reserved for the end of the verse as a punchline (cf. **A6**. 8; **B41** introductory n.; **D1**. 7; **D14**. 5 n.; **E7**. 17–21 n.; **E9**. 2, 4; **E15**. 2; **E22**. 2 n.; **F2** introductory n.; **F11** introductory n.; **H8**. 12 n.).

4.   τὸν κύσθον is a primary obscenity, 'its cunt' (see *Maculate Muse*, 35 and § 107); and regardless of whether ἐκκορίζειν is cognate with κόρη ('girl'), κορέω (A) ('sweep'), or κόρις ('bedbug'), it must be a colloquial term for sexual activity, as also at Ar. fr. 277.

B30. The chorus of nanny-goats describe their habits. See in general Wilkins and Rackham, in *Rivals*, 341–54, esp. 348–50; Storey 67–74. Rackham (whose identification of the individual plants mentioned I have followed) notes that Eupolis' catalogue includes a number of things real goats either refuse to eat or eat with great reluctance (marked in the translations below with an asterisk). Presumably the poet was more interested in finding plausible words of the right metrical shapes than with strict zoological accuracy.

Preserved at Plutarch, *Quaestiones convivales* iv. 1. 3 (= *Mor.* 662d–e), as evidence that animals do not live on an exceedingly simple diet, and taken over from him by Macrobius, *Saturnalia* vii. 5. 8, whose text of Plutarch was much better than what we have.

Anapaestic tetrameter catalectic.

1.   ἐλάτης πρίνου κομάρου τε: 'of fir, prickly-oak, and strawberry tree'.
2.   καὶ πρὸς τούτοισιν ἔτ(ι): 'and, moreover, in addition to these things', i.e. the πόρθους ('shoots').   ἄνθην: 'greenery, leaves'; but the text is uncertain.
3.   'and also tree-medick and fragrant sage* and leafy yew(?)'.
4–5.   The leisurely, adjective-filled pace of 3 yields to a straightforward catalogue style: 'wild olive, lentisk*, manna-ash, white poplar, holm oak, oak, ivy, heather, | (unknown; LSJ suggest willow), (a thorny shrub of some sort), Jerusalem sage*, asphodel*, rock-rose*, Valonia oak, thyme, savory*'.

B31. The chorus of heroes offer the audience (1 ἄνδρες) a warning in the course of introducing themselves. For heroes causing sickness for those who offend them, see Hp. *Morb.Sacr.* 4 (vi. 362. 3–6 Littré); Ar. *Av.* 1490–3 with Dunbar ad loc.; and cf. Ar. fr. 712; Men. fr. 348; L. R. Farnell, *Hero Cults of the Greeks* (Oxford, 1921), 71–94. A list of benefits reserved for those who behaved well must have followed eventually (but see 7 n.).

Preserved in P.Mich. 3690 (second/third century AD; = *CGFPR* *58).
Anaclastic glyconics ('Wilamowitzians') (○ ○ − × − ∪∪ −).

1. **πρὸς ταῦτ(α):** 'wherefore' (in reference to something said in the preceding lines).
3–4. **οἱ ταμίαι | τῶν κακῶν καὶ τῶν ἀγαθῶν:** 'the stewards of bad things and good', the point being that they can deal these out to whomever they wish.
5. **ἀναθροῦντες** is < ἀναθρέω, 'keep a close watch on'.
5–6. **καὶ κλέπτας καὶ λωποδύτας** gives specific content to **ἀδίκους**. κλέπται are thieves (who, in contrast to robbers, work discreetly and without violence), while λωποδύται were a specialized type of mugger who stripped their victims of their clothes; cf. Ar. *Av.* 496–8 with Dunbar on 497; Austin–Olson on Ar. *Th.* 816–18.
7. **τούτοις** might be either all the evil-doers referred to in 5–6, in which case 12 must have resumed the point (hence Handley's [ταῦ]τα [τοῖ]ς κλέπτα[ις]) and a δέ-clause referring to the treatment of the just was offered within a verse or two, or the λωποδύται only (hence Barrett's [τοῖ]ς δ[ὲ δ]ὴ κλέπτα[ις] in 12).
8–11. A catalogue of ugly chronic conditions, all in apposition to **νόσους** in 7: 'to have an enlarged spleen (i.e. malaria) (or) a cough (i.e. tuberculosis or the like) (or) suffer from dropsy | (or) have a runny nose (or) mange (see **D1**. 7 n.) (or) gout | (or) be mad (or) have eruptions on one's skin | (or) swollen glands (or) a chill (or) a fever'.
12. For the text, see 7 n.

B32–B35. *Agon*-fragments; cf. **B6–B7**; **B20**; **B44** introductory n.; **D2**; **E4**; Phryn. Com. fr. 73; Pl. Com. frr. 132; 167; Theopomp. Com. frr. 56–7; and see Whittaker 184–7. For the formal structure of the *agon*, see Introduction pp. 20–1.

B32–B34. The theme of *Schlaraffenland* (the land of Cockaigne, Big Rock Candy Mountain, Katroo, Woodunzburunzy), a fantastic place where all good things are available free and in enormous quantities, is ill represented in Aristophanes' preserved plays (although cf. **B35** and *Tagênistai* (*Frying-Pan Men*) test. iii) but common in the fragments of the other 'Old Comic' poets. Athenaeus 6. 267e–70a preserves an extensive collection of such passages, which also includes Cratin. fr. 176 (from *Gods of Wealth*); Pherecr. fr. 113 (from *Miners*); Nicophon fr. 21 (from *Sirens*); and Metag. fr. 6 (from *Thuriopersians*), and which Athenaeus cites in the order (retained here) in which they were performed (6. 268e), except for the plays by Nicophon and Metagenes, which were never produced (6. 270a). For further discussion, see Baldry, *G&R* 23 (1953), 49–60; J. C. Carrière, *Le Carnaval et la politique* (Annales litteraires de l'Université de Besançon 212: Paris, 1979), 85–118; Ceccarelli and Ruffell, in *Rivals*, 453–8 and 473–506, esp. 474–86 (with further bibliography), respectively; M. Farioli, *Mundus alter: Utopie e distopie nella commedia greca antica* (Milan, 2001), 27–137 (pp. 57–74 on Crates' *Wild Beasts*, pp. 74–91 on Teleclides' *Amphictyonies*, pp. 104–15 on Pherecrates' *Persians*).

B32. The plot of *Wild Beasts* seems to have involved a dispute over whether a life of extraordinary luxury (described in part in Crates fr. 17, which Athenaeus says followed 'immediately after' fr. 16) or a relatively spare and simple style of existence would be more likely to make men happy. Speaker B has advanced some radical proposal to transform human existence, but Speaker A is dubious; **B35** is at least superficially similar. Although the meal Speaker B describes in 5–10 includes a fish (see **G6** introductory n.), the food he mentions is in general very plain and homely. He must therefore be arguing in favour of simplicity (thus Kock), and 1–2 probably represent an accurate if slanted summary of what he said in the immediately preceding verses: in the ideal new world he imagines, no one will own slaves (cf. Pherecr. fr. 10; contrast Ar. *Pl.* 510–18)—but only because there will be no need for them.

Preserved at Athenaeus 6. 267e–f.

Trochaic tetrameter catalectic.

2. **δῆτ(α)** indicates that the question springs from what the other speaker has just said (Denniston 269, 271–2), as again in 4.

3. **οὐ δῆθ'** ('Certainly not!' see Denniston 274–5) negates the assertion made in 2, but not the one made in 1.   **ὁδοιπορούντα:** i.e. 'capable of moving itself'.

4. **τί δῆτα τοῦτ(ο) αὐτοῖς πλέον;:** 'What advantage will they get from this?' For the use of δῆτα, see 2 n.   **αὔθ'** = αὐτό, 'of its own accord', like αὐτή in 6. Automatism is a common theme in *Schlaraffenland*-descriptions; cf. **B33.** 3 αὐτόματ(α); **B34.** 3 αὐτόματοι; Ar. *Ach.* 36 with Olson ad loc.

5. **τῶν σκευαρίων:** 'of his household equipment', as at e.g. **C1.** 12; Ar. *Pax* 201; *Ec.* 753.

5–9. **ὅταν καλῆι τις κτλ.:** Although abbreviated, the orders trace the normal course of preparations for a drinking party: the table is put in position and set (5–6; cf. **G16.** 2 n.; **H1.** 2 n.); cakes are made (6, 8; cf. **H4.** 3); wine is poured (7); and food is served (8–9; cf. **H2.** 3 n.).

5. **παρατίθου:** 'set yourself beside (me)!'

6. **αὐτή:** see 4 n.   **μάττε θυλακίσκε:** 'Knead (some barley-cakes), my little grainsack!'; cf. 8 with n. For the use of a grainsack (θύλακος) to bring barley groats (ἄλφιτα; cf. **J2.** 3 n.) home from the marketplace, see Ar. *Ec.* 819–20.

7.   A particularly lighthearted moment: the ladle (**κύαθε**; see Richter–Milne
      30–1, with figs. 183–4) is ready to get to work drawing wine out of the
      central mixing-bowl (see **H1**. 8 n.), but the drinking cup (**κύλιξ**; see
      Richter–Milne 24–5 and figs. 152–66) into which it will pour itself is miss-
      ing; when the cup does finally appear, it is dirty and has to be sent to wash
      up.
8.   **ἀνάβαινε**: 'get up (onto the table)!'   **μᾶζα**: 'barley-cake', the product
      of the order (now successfully completed) given to the grainsack in 6.
      μᾶζαι were made of rough-cut barley-meal (**ἄλφιτα**; see 6 n.) mixed with
      milk, wine, oil, or the like, and were eaten unbaked, as a staple food; see
      B33. 4–6 n.; **B45**. 12 (a metonymy for 'food'); **G1**. 1–3; Olson on Ar. *Pax* 1;
      Olson–Sens on Matro fr. 1. 91–2.   **τὴν χύτραν χρῆν ἐξερᾶν τὰ τεῦτλα**:
      'the cookpot should have been pouring out the beets!', which have been
      stewing in it. χύτραι are common lidless cookpots used for making soup
      (e.g. Epich. fr. 30) and boiling and stewing foods of all kinds (e.g. Alc. Com.
      fr. 24 (cabbage); Timocl. fr. 23. 3–4 (beans); Matro fr. 1. 48 (blackened from
      having been placed over a fire)); see Amyx 211–12. For beets, see García
      Soler 54–5. χρῆν/ἐχρῆν (also **C8**. 10; **H1**. 5–6 with n.), like ἔδει (**D3**. 29;
      E18. 3; **H10**. 5; **H17**. 1; **I4**. 1), indicates unfulfilled obligation (KG i. 204–5;
      Gildersleeve § 364): the cookpot (like the drinking cup in 7 and the fish in
      9–10) is running behind schedule, as slaves generally were routinely
      accused of doing (**G9**. 5 n.).
9–10.   The behaviour of the fish at **B33**. 6–7 is similar.
9.   **(ἐ)πὶ θάτερ(α)**: 'on the other side'.
10.   **οὔκουν ... πάσεις**: is equivalent to an imperative (KG i. 176–7; cf.
      Gildersleeve § 198); cf. **C3**. 1; **D3**. 23; **H20**. 9. πάσεις is future indicative <
      πάσσω, 'sprinkle' (the *vox propria* for seasoning food). For the use of salt
      as a seasoning, see **G7**. 7; Olson–Sens on Archestr. fr. 14. 7; García Soler
      327–32; and cf. **A20**. 4 n.   **σεαυτόν** is the common object of both
      participles and the main verb.   **ἀλείφων**: 'basting yourself (with olive
      oil)'.

B33. A god (Dionysus?) or perhaps an ancient king of Attica (Amphictyon,
the son of Deucalion and Pyrrha?) is speaking.
      Preserved entire at Athenaeus (1) 6. 268a–d. In addition, 1 is quoted by
Sextus Empiricus, *Against the Grammarians* 6. 15; 2 is quoted by Photius
κ 393 = Suda κ 863; and 12 is quoted again by Athenaeus at (2) 2. 64f
(manuscripts CE only) and (3) 14. 644f.
      Anapaestic tetrameter catalectic.

1.   **τοίνυν** ('Well') followed by emphatic **ἐγώ** suggests that this is all a pointed
      response to a very different programme described by the previous speaker

(Denniston 572–3).   **ἐξ ἀρχῆς**: 'from of old, in the old days'; to be taken with **παρεῖχον**.

2. **πρῶτον ἁπάντων** is adverbial, 'first of all'.   **ὥσπερ ὕδωρ κατὰ χειρός**: 'just like water (poured) down over one's hand(s)', sc. to wash with; i.e. 'widely and easily available'. The image is borrowed from banqueting (see **G12**. 3 n.) and sets up the idea (developed in 4–13) that life in the speaker's day was an endless feast.

3. **οὐ δέος οὐδὲ νόσους**: perhaps to be taken to mean 'no dangerous creatures or poisonous plants'. But the larger point is that nothing bad or troublesome for men had yet come into existence; cf. Hes. *Op.* 90–2 (on life before Pandora opened the vessel of troubles) 'For before this the tribes of men used to live on the earth separate, apart from troubles, harsh toil, and baneful sicknesses, which bring doom to men'.   **αὐτόματ(α)**: see **B32**. 4 n.; **B34**. 3.

4. **ἅπασ(α) . . . χαράδρα**: 'every torrent-gully', which are normally dry but flow with tremendous force when full. For similar images, see 9; **B34**. 6.

4–6. **μᾶζαι δ(ὲ) ἄρτοις ἐμάχοντο | κτλ.**: The idea is taken up again in 13; cf. Nicophon fr. 21. 4 (another passage cited by Athenaeus in this section of the *Deipnosophists*) 'Let a cake urge (the diner) to eat him!' ἄρτος is 'baked bread' (normally made of wheat flour), as opposed to unbaked μᾶζα (made of barley); cf. **B32**. 8 n.; **F10**. 10 with n.; **J3**. 1; Cratin. fr. 176. 2 (also cited by Athenaeus in this section of the *Deipnosophists*).

5. **καταπίνειν**: 'to gulp down' (also in 10); τὰς λευκοτάτας in 6 is the object of the infinitive. Cf. **B33**. 10; **G11**. 11.

6. **εἴ τι φιλοῖεν**: 'if they would be so kind'.   **τὰς λευκοτάτας**: i.e. 'the very best (of them)', since high-quality flour and meal were sifted to remove the bran, producing bread or cakes that were whiter than those made with less expensive ingredients; cf. **F10**. 10 n.; **G1**. 1–2 n.   **οἴκαδ(ε) ἰόντες**: i.e. from the marketplace, where one would normally have to go to fetch them (**G5–G6**; **J6–J7**).

7. For self-roasting fish, see **B32**. 9–10.   **ἂν παρέκειντ(ο)**: 'would lie beside (the dinner guests)'.

8. Cf. **B34**. 3–4; Metag. fr. 6. 1–8; Nicophon fr. 21. 3 ζωμὸς διὰ τῶν ὁδῶν κυλινδείτω κρέα ('Let broth roll chunks of meat through the streets!') (all cited by Athenaeus in this section of the *Deipnosophists*).   **ζωμοῦ**: 'broth', which naturally contains numerous chunks of warm meat (κρέα θερμά). Cf. **C11**. 3 n.; **G9**. 1–2 with n.; Olson on Ar. *Pax* 715–17.   **τὰς κλίνας**: 'the couches', on which banqueters reclined to eat; cf. **A13**. 14 n.

9. **ὑποτριμματίων**: 'little sauces'; see **G10**. 3 n.   **ὀχετοί**: 'streams'; cf. **B34**. 7.   **τούτων τοῖς βουλομένοισι**: 'for those who wanted (to eat some) of these things'.

10. 'with the result that there was no reason to begrudge a man for soaking his mouthful (in the sauces (cf. 9), to make it) soft, and gulping it down'; cf. 5 n.; **E3**. 12 (for another use of ἔνθεσις in this sense); **G12**. 10 n. Monopolizing the tastiest portions of the meal (in this case the ὑποτριμμάτια) is generally represented as bad—if understandable—behaviour (cf. **C12**; **G11**. 11–18; **G17**); but in the speaker's day there was more than enough to go around.

11. **λεκανίσκαισιν**: 'little dishes' (diminutive < λεκάνη, 'basin'). As the text stands, this must be the vessel in which the food further described as **ἡδυσματίοις κατάπαστα** ('sprinkled with seasonings'; cf. **B32**. 10 n.) was served; but something has gone badly wrong somewhere, and what is preserved may be the beginning of one verse and the end of the next. ἥδυσμα is a generic term for seasonings of all sorts; see Olson–Sens on Archestr. fr. 23. 3–4.

12. **κίχλαι**: see **B34**. 10 n. **ἀμητίσκων**: diminutive < ἄμης, a type of cake made with milk (e.g. Ar. *Pl.* 999; Ephipp. fr. 8. 3; Alex. fr. 168. 5 with Arnott ad loc.).

13. See 4–6 n. **πλακούντων**: a generic term for unbaked cakes of all sorts; cf. **J3**. 3; Olson–Sens on Archestr. fr. 60. 15. **ἀλαλητός**: 'an uproar, shouting' (despite LSJ s.v. I. 3).

14. Cf. Cratin. fr. 176. 2 (of Cronus' time; also quoted by Athenaeus in this section of the *Deipnosophists*) 'when they played knucklebones with loaves of bread'; Ar. *Pl.* 816–17. **μήτρας . . . τόμοις καὶ χναυματίοις**: 'with slices of sow's womb'—a delicacy, here served stuffed like a sausage; cf. Antiph. fr. 219. 3 'sow's womb, the most delicious meat'; Olson–Sens on Archestr. fr. 60. 7–8—'and little trimmings (of meat)'. **ἂν ἠστραγάλιζον**: 'they used to play neckbones, knucklebones' (ἀστράγαλοι), which were used much like dice (κύβοι); see **D12**. 3 n.

15. **πίονες ἦσαν**: For the Greeks (unlike for us), being fat was a good thing; cf. Ar. *Pax* 1170. **μέγα χρῆμα Γιγάντων**: literally 'a big affair of Giants'; a colloquialism (Stevens 21) equivalent to 'big Giants' and thus here 'as big as the Giants, immensely tall'. For the Giants, see **A12** introductory n.

B34. Someone has just praised agriculture and the craftsmen that make it possible (1–2). But getting food that way involves hard work, and the speaker of this fragment describes instead a world of spontaneous natural abundance, where delicious things stream forth like water from springs (3–5), rain off a roof during a storm (6–8), or leaves from the proverbially countless trees in the mountains (9–10).

Preserved at Athenaeus 6. 269c–e.

Anapaestic tetrameter catalectic.

1–2. 'Ploughs' (ἀροτῶν) and 'yokemakers' (ζυγοποιῶν) go naturally together in 1 to refer to the preparation of the soil at the beginning of planting-season, just as the matched pairs 'sicklemakers' (δρεπανουργῶν; also mentioned at Ar. *Pax* 548) and 'smiths' (χαλκοτύπων, sc. to make agricultural tools generally), and 'sowing' (σπέρματος) and 'staking' (χαρακισμοῦ, sc. to support vines and small trees) in 2 describe—in no particular order—the back-breaking work that follows.

3. αὐτόματοι: 'spontaneous, of their own accord'; see **B32.** 4 n.; **B33.** 3.

3–4. ζωμοῦ μέλανος is to be taken with ποταμοί, 'rivers of black broth' (a traditional delicacy made with blood, whence its colour, and often described as eaten with μᾶζαι or another starch; see Eup. fr. 380; Alex. fr. 145. 7–8; Olson–Sens on Matro fr. 1. 93–4). For the image, cf. **B33.** 8 with n.   λιπαροῖς ἐπιπάστοις | ... καὶ Ἀχιλλείοις μάζαις κοχυδοῦντες ἐπιβλύξ: 'gushing abundantly with rich sprinkle-bread'—whatever that may be—'and cakes of the finest barley'. For 'Achillean' (i.e. top-quality) barley-groats and the cakes made from them, see Ar. *Eq.* 819; Thphr. *HP* viii. 4. 2, 10. 2; Ath. 3. 114f.

5. τοῦ Πλούτου: for the personified god Wealth (e.g. Hes. *Th.* 969–74; carm. conv. *PMG* 885; Hippon. fr. 44; Timocr. *PMG* 731; cf. Cratinus' *Gods of Wealth*), see Sommerstein's edition of Aristophanes' *Wealth*, pp. 5–8. σφῶν ἀρύτεσθαι: 'to draw for ourselves from them', i.e. 'so that we can draw from them'; an epexegetic infinitive (KG ii. 4).

6. ὕων οἴνωι καπνίαι: 'raining with καπνίας wine', i.e. rather than with mere water. καπνίας οἶνος (mentioned also at Pl. Com. fr. 274; Anaxandr. fr. 42. 71) is most likely 'wine that has been treated with smoke' (καπνός) (thus Hsch. κ 716); cf. Colum. i. 6. 20; **H8.** 6 n. For the image, cf. Nicophon fr. 21. 1–2 (one of the other passages quoted by Athenaeus in this section of the *Deipnosophists*), 'Let it snow barley! let it drizzle loaves of baked bread! let it rain pea-soup!'   κατὰ τοῦ κεράμου βαλανεύσει: 'will pour (it, i.e. the wine) down over the tiling'—i.e. the roof—'like a bathman' as he ladles water over his customers. For bathmen (a common urban occupation), see Pl. *R.* 344d; Thphr. *Char.* 9. 8 with Diggle ad loc.; Olson on Ar. *Pax* 1103.

7–8. ὀχετοὶ βοτρύων ... | ὀχετεύσονται: 'streams of grape-clusters will pour forth'.

7. μετὰ ναστίσκων πολυτύρων: sc. πλακούντων (cf. **B33.** 13 n.), 'accompanied by little (cakes) stuffed with a lot of cheese' (a common ingredient; see Olson on Ar. *Ach.* 1124–5). ναστίσκος is a diminutive < νάστος, 'stuffed (cake)'; see Dunbar on Ar. *Av.* 567.   ἔτνει: 'pea-soup, bean-soup' (e.g. Crates fr. 11. 1; Call. Com. fr. 26; Ar. *Ach.* 246 with Olson ad loc.).   λειριοπολφανεμώναις is obscure. But a λείριον is a delicate flower of some type, perhaps a lily (Cratin. fr. 105. 2), πολφός is a type of porridge (Metag. fr. 18. 2 with Pellegrino, in *Tessere* 336–7), and Hesychius α 4882 glosses ἀνεμώνη as 'a type of barley-cake'; so these must be fancy cakes of a perhaps imaginary kind.

9. **χορδαῖς . . . ἐριφείοις**: 'sausages' (literally 'intestines'; see **G13**. 3 n., and cf. **A10**) 'stuffed with kid-meat' (for which, see **B35**. 3–4 n.).

10. **φυλλοροήσει**: 'will shed leaves with' + dat., i.e. 'will drop (dat.) rather than leaves'.   **τευθιδίοις**: 'baby squid' (*Fishes*, 260–1); a delicacy (e.g. **G5**. 4; Pherecr. fr. 50. 3; Metag. fr. 6. 6; Eub. fr. 14. 8; Archestr. fr. 55. 1 with Olson–Sens ad loc.).   **κίχλαις . . . ἀναβράστοις**: 'stewed thrushes' (*Birds*, 148–50), another delicacy (e.g. **B33**. 12; **B35**. 3; **I6**. 8–9; Pherecr. fr. 113. 23; Ar. *Nu.* 339; Alex. fr. 168. 3–5 with Arnott ad loc.).

B35. Speaker A is a god (note ὑμᾶς in 14), who proposes to make good food of every sort available to the Athenians throughout the year as a reward for their piety (13); in contrast to **B32–B34**, the fantasy is firmly and emphatically set within a modern cash-economy (3, 9, 10). But Speaker B (more likely a god of a different, more traditional sort rather than a human being) is dubious of the plan, which he characterizes as confusing (6–7), expensive (10), and likely to make the city a very different place from what it ought to be (15); and the gods to whose worship Speaker A refers are most likely foreign deities such as Sabazius (mentioned in Ar. fr. 578, from the same play), whose cult was introduced into Athens probably sometime in the 420s (MacDowell on Ar. *V.* 9). For the phenomenon of 'new gods' in late fifth- and fourth-century Athens, see **J19**; R. Parker, *Athenian Religion: A History* (Oxford and New York, 1996), 152–98. The chorus of Seasons (for whom, see **G16**. 6 n.) was doubtless sympathetic to Speaker B's case (esp. 6–7, 15 with n.) and hostile to Speaker A, whose plan would have eliminated them.

Preserved at Athenaeus 9. 372b–d, where the speaker claims that he and his fellow-diners were reminded of the passage when gourds (κολοκύνται; see 6 with n.) were unexpectedly served in mid-winter. Nicander fr. 72 Schneider follows.

Trochaic tetrameter catalectic.

1. **ὄψει**: sc. 'if I am allowed to carry out my programme'; cf. 5 ἴδοις ἄν. **σικυοὺς βότρυς ὀπώραν**: 'cucumbers, grape-clusters, summer fruit generally'. Theophrastus' Dolt quarrels with his slave when the latter fails at the impossible task of purchasing cucumbers in winter (*Char.* 14. 9). For eating cucumbers and grapes, see Olson–Sens on Matro frr. 4; 1. 113, respectively; García Soler 49, 116–17, respectively.

2. **στεφάνους ἴων**: for garlands of violets (to be worn at symposia; see **H1**. 7 n.), cf. Ar. *Ach.* 637 with Olson ad loc.; Thphr. *HP* vi. 8. 1. **οἶμαι κτλ.**: a cynical aside, which Speaker A ignores; contrast 6–7.

κονιορτὸν ἐκτυφλοῦντα: 'a blinding dust-storm' (cf. **F11**. 8; **J13**. 6); normally a far more common sight in mid-winter than fresh produce in the market-place, but also a pointed response to ὄψει in 1 ('What I really expect my eyes to be full of is . . . dust!').

3–4. αὐτὸς δ' ἀνὴρ πωλεῖ: Many individual vendors in Athens' marketplace handled specific, limited categories of items (see **J1–J3** with nn.), and Speaker A's point is that he will produce such a super-abundance of goods (cf. 1–2, 5, 8–9) that this will no longer be true and everyone will sell delicious food of every sort. The present tense verb (contrast 1) produces a vivid picture of what is likely to happen (Goodwin § 32). κίχλας κτλ.: 'thrushes, pears, honey-comb, olives, I beestings, after-birth pudding, swallow-figs, cicadas, still-born kids'. For thrushes (a delicacy), see **B34**. 10 n. Beestings (another delicacy) are the rich, yellowish milk produced by a she-goat immediately after she gives birth; see Olson on Ar. *Pax* 1150; García Soler 272–3. For after-birth pudding (honey and milk cooked in the foetal envelope of a sheep or goat), see Arnott on Alex. fr. 178. 13. For 'swallow-figs', see Epigen. fr. 1. 2; Macho 427; Poll. vi. 80–1. For eating cicadas, see Ar. fr. 53. 1; Alex. fr. 167. 13 with Arnott ad loc. Still-born lambs and kids were presumably valued as food because their meat was so tender.

5. ὑρίσους . . . νειφομένους σύκων ὁμοῦ τε μύρτων: 'harvest-baskets full of a mixture of figs and myrtle-berries, pouring down thick as snow'. For ὕρισοι, see Arnott on Alex. fr. 133. 3 (where the word appears in the form υὑριχυς). For figs, see **G1**. 4 n. For myrtle-berries (a dainty), e.g. Ar. *Pax* 575; Theopomp. Com. fr. 68; Thphr. *Char*. 11. 4 with Diggle ad loc.; and see García Soler 118. For the image 'thick as snow', see H. *Il*. 3. 222; Taillardat § 661. ἴδοις ἄν: sc. 'should I be allowed to do what I propose'. Contrast the use of the future indicative in 1.

6–7. The point of the question is that turnips (ταῖς γογγυλίσιν) were a winter crop, gourds (κολοκύντας) a summer crop (cf. Thphr. *HP* vii. 1. 2), so that sowing (ἀροῦσιν < ἀρόω) them simultaneously is a sign of not knowing 'what time of the year it is' (ὁπηνίκ(α) ἐστι τοῦ (ἐ)νιαυτοῦ). For turnips (simple, inexpensive food), see Austin–Olson on Ar. *Th*. 1185. For gourds (in a catalogue of homely foods at Metag. fr. 18. 2), see Heller, *ICS* 10 (1985), 102–11; Pellegrino, in *Tessere*, 337–8; García Soler 48–9; and cf. **F6**. 16.

8. <ἆρ' οὐ> μέγιστον ἀγαθόν;: sc. ἐστι, 'Isn't this the greatest good (there could be)?' ἔστι: 'it is (possible)'. δι(ὰ) ἐνιαυτοῦ: 'throughout the year, at any time of year'.

9. λαβεῖν: here 'to buy', as also at **G5**. 5–7. μὲν οὖν: 'to the contrary' (cf. **D2**. 3; **F15**. 3; Denniston 475).

10.   **εἰ μὴ ... ἦν:** 'If this weren't the case', i.e. if one couldn't buy whatever food one wanted whenever one wanted it (cf. 8–9).   **ἐδαπανῶντο** is middle (rather than passive), 'spend money'.

11.   **τοῦτ(ο) ὀλίγον χρόνον χρήσας:** 'after lending (LSJ s. χράω B) this'—i.e. the opportunity described in 8–9—'for a short time'.

13.   **τούτοις:** i.e. the Athenians.   **τοὺς θεοὺς σέβουσιν:** Although Athenian authors often refer to the city's supposed great piety (see Dover on Ar. *Nu.* 310), the gods in question must be not the traditional Olympians but 'new' deities, and the good things promised above are offered only on condition that Athens accepts these new gods.

14.   **ἀπέλαυσαν κτλ.:** an ironic remark, as 15 makes clear.   **ἄρα** conveys scepticism about the assertion attributed to the other party (**ὡς σὺ φής**); see Denniston 38–9.   **τιὴ τί;:** '*Why?*' or 'What do you *mean?*' An emphatic expression of puzzlement; cf. Austin–Olson on Ar. *Th.* 84.

15.   For Egypt as a land without seasons, see Hdt. ii. 77. 3. But the claim that, under the speaker's proposal, Athens will have been transformed into another Egypt, is implicitly hostile, and the more substantial point is that the city has no need of Egypt's plethora of absurd deities; cf. **A1** introductory n. (on Egypt in comedy); Anaxandr. fr. 40 (on the impossibility of an alliance between Athenians and Egyptians because of religious differences).

B36–B45. Parabasis fragments, in many of which 'the poet' speaks directly to the audience through his chorus. Cf. **B8–B9**; **B13**. 6–9; **E19** (but apparently not from a parabasis); Cratin. frr. 105; 182 (probably from a 'second parabasis'); 251; *361; Crates fr. 18 (from the *pnigos*); Telecl. fr. 4; Pherecr. frr. 34; 52; Ar. frr. 30–1; 58–9; 112–13 (probably from a 'second parabasis'); 264–5; 428–31; Eup. frr. 99. 1–34 (the antode and antepirrhema); 173 (probably from a 'second parabasis'); Philonid. frr. 4–5; adesp. com. fr. 209; and see Whittaker 188–90.

B36. A flattering initial address to the audience in the 'parabasis proper', like **B37** (even more obviously tongue-in-cheek).

Preserved at Hephaestion, *Enchiridion* 15. 12, on account of the metre.

Hephaestion identifies this as a 'Platonikon', which he describes as two and a half dactylic feet, an iambic central section, and two and a half dactylic feet, i.e. in Maas' terminology D – e – D.

For the initial greeting **χαῖρε**, cf. **B37**. 1.   **παλαιογόνων:** probably an allusion to the Athenian claim to be an autochthonous people (e.g. Ar. *V.* 1076; fr. 112. 1; Th. i. 2. 5; cf. N. Loraux, *The Children of Athena* (Princeton,

1993; originally published in French in 1984), 37–71). But the idea that the members of the audience are very old also serves to explain their allegedly extraordinary wisdom; cf. Ar. *Av.* 688–90 (the birds use the great antiquity of their race as a basis to demand that the audience pay attention to their words).   παντοσόφων: 'clever in every way'. For the audience (or a portion thereof) addressed as σοφοί at the beginning of a parabasis section, see Ar. *Nu.* 575; and cf. **B11** n.; **B37**. 2 (of the poet); Ar. *Nu.* 535; *V.* 1049; *Ra.* 1118.

B37. Another flattering initial address to the audience (cf. **B36** with n.) who, the chorus claim, are routinely taken in by bad material, but are then full of insights as to who ought to have got the prize—one day too late. Cf. Introduction, p. 19 (on the judging at the festivals); **B43** with nn.

Preserved at Hephaestion, *Enchiridion* 15. 2, on account of the metre.
× D × ith (see *GM* 97).

1.   μέγα is adverbial, 'loudly'.   ἀχρειόγελως: 'that laughs to no purpose, for no good reason', i.e. 'at bad jokes'—which is to say, 'at the jokes of our poet's rivals'. Cf. **B40–B42** with nn.; Ar. *Nu.* 560 (of the unoriginal rubbish staged by the poet's rivals) 'may anyone who laughs at these things take no pleasure in mine'.   ταῖς ἐπίβδαις: 'on the days that follow festivals'; cf. Braswell on Pi. *P.* 4. 140.
2.   τῆς ἡμετέρας σοφίας: see **B11** n.; **B36**.
3.   εὐδαίμον(α) is ironic, and the point is that the spectators have the luxury of being offered wonderful comic material by the poet for whom the chorus speaks; clamouring for the prize to be given to someone else; and then archly criticizing the decision after the festival is over.   ἰκρίων ψόφησις: 'the noise produced by the benches, bleachers', i.e. by the spectators who sit on them in the theatre. The term ἴκρια ('planks, decking') was used of the temporary stands of scaffolding set up to accommodate spectators for processions and (at least before an infamous collapse sometime early in the fifth century) theatrical shows in the Agora (Pratin. *TrGF* 4 T 1. 3–4; Hsch. α 1695; ι 501; π 513; Phot. ι 95). After the dramatic festivals were transferred to the theatre of Dionysus, the word continued to be used of the rows of seats there; cf. Ar. *Th.* 395 with Austin–Olson ad loc. In apposition to μήτηρ.

B38. 'The poet' explains his supposedly reluctant decision to address the audience in his own defence (i.e. against the slanders of his rivals); cf. **B40–B42** n.; Ar. *Ach.* 628–32; *Pax* 734–8. **J17** is from the same play.

Preserved in a *scholium* on Ar. *Pax* 734, as part of an extended note on the staging of parabases.

Eupolideans (○ ○ – × – ∪ ∪ – ○ ○ – × – ∪ –); also used in the 'parabasis proper' at e.g. **B42**; **B43**. 6; Cratin. fr. 105; Pherecr. fr. 34; Ar. *Nu.* 518–62. Cf. Poultney, *AJP* 100 (1979), 133–44.

1. **ὦνδρες**: for the audience addressed thus, e.g. Pherecr. fr. 84. 1; Ar. *Pax* 13; *Lys.* 1044; Pl. Com. fr. 182. 7. That women are ignored does not necessarily mean that they were not present in the theatre.   **εἰ μὲν μὴ λίαν . . . ἠναγκαζόμην**: 'were I not under terrible pressure' *vel sim.*; cf. **B4**. 2 n.

2. **στρέψαι δεῦρ(ο)** ('to turn around in this direction'), like **παρέβην** (< παραβαίνω, cognate with παράβασις), refers both to the chorus's movements, as they turn to face the audience after the actors have left the stage, and to the 'direction' in which circumstances have forced the poet to go in this section of his play.

B39. 'The poet' reminds his audience of the constant novelty that distinguishes his productions, and the pleasure they get from them, the implication being that his rivals are not generally so original. Cf. **B40** with introductory n.; Pherecr. fr. 84 'Pay attention, gentlemen, to this new invention: folded anapaests!'; Ar. *Nu.* 546–8 (also from a parabasis) 'nor do I try to deceive you, by bringing the same things on stage two or three times; instead, I display my skill by always introducing new ideas, utterly unlike one another and all of them clever' (followed in 551–9 by a denunciation of other comic poets for endlessly reworking the same material); *V.* 56–66; *Pax* 739–47 (also from a parabasis; 'the poet' lists some of the tired jokes and typical scenes his rivals use but he does not). See in general Pellegrino, in *Tessere*, 326–32 (detailed commentary on this fragment).

Preserved at Athenaeus 10. 459b–c, as a parallel in support of the main narrator's plan to have his characters move on to a different topic of discussion the next night.

Anapaestic tetrameter catalectic, also used in the 'parabasis proper' at e.g. **B40–B41**; Cratin. fr. 251; Ar. *Ach.* 628–58; Philonid. frr. 4–5.

1. **κατ(ὰ) ἐπεισόδιον μεταβάλλω τὸν λόγον**: 'I vary my plot ἐπεισόδιον by ἐπεισόδιον' (see **B6**. 2 n.), i.e. 'I add variety to my plot by inserting ἐπεισόδια'. For this distributive use of κατά + accusative, e.g. **C2**. 1; **D3**. 11; **E3**. 9. For λόγος in this sense, see **B1**. 1 n.

2. **καιναῖσι παροψίσι καὶ πολλαῖς**: 'with many novel appetizers'; καί is to be left untranslated when it links a form of πολύς and another adjective. For παροψίδες (appetizers or secondary side-dishes, which add interest to a meal but are not its focus, just as ἐπεισόδια, enjoyable as they may be, make only a peripheral contribution to a play), see **G12**. 6–7 n.

εὐωχήσω: for comedy as a feast served to the audience, see also Cratin. fr. 182; Ar. *Eq.* 538 (of Crates) 'who used to give you an inexpensive breakfast and send you off'; fr. 347; cf. **F5** (of tragedy).   τὸ θέατρον: 'the audience', as at e.g. Ar. *Ach.* 629; *Eq.* 233; Amphis fr. 14. 3; cf. **B44**. 1.

B40–B42. Aristophanes repeatedly asserts the superiority of his own poetry to that of his rivals (e.g. *Nu.* 524–5, 537–44, 551–60; *V.* 54–66; *Pax* 736–74), whom he occasionally mentions by name (*Ach.* 848–53, 1173; *Eq.* 400, 531–6 (all Cratinus; see **B1–B12** n.); *Nu.* 553–6 (Eupolis; see **B42** introductory n.), 557 (Hermippus); *Pax* 700–3 (Cratinus)), and these fragments make it clear that on-stage attacks of this sort were scarcely unusual among the 'Old Comic' poets. Cf. **B13**. 8 with n.; Ar. *V.* 1025 ~ *Pax* 762–3 (personal criticism of Eupolis); Eup. fr. 62 (criticism of the staging of Ar. *Pax*); Pl. Com. fr. 86 (criticism of the staging of Ar. *Pax*).

B40. The imagery is borrowed from fulling, a process in which dirty clothes were trampled in a basin containing water and a crude detergent; beaten with rods, rinsed, and dried; brushed (κνάπτω, whence κναφεύς, 'fuller') to raise the nap (cf. ἀνακνάψας); bleached with sulphur (θεῖον, whence θειώσας); and pressed. See Blümner i². 170–90; Forbes iv. 82–90, 93–5. In this way an old garment could be made to look new (or at least newer), and the point of the assertion made in this fragment is that 'the poet' does not merely recycle ideas already put on stage by others (cf. **B42** introductory n.), but comes up with new ones of his own. For the image (poetry as a garment), cf. Ar. *Nu.* 553; fr. 58 (both from the parabasis).

Preserved in Pollux at (1) vii. 41, in a discussion of terms related to fulling; and (2) vii. 77, in a discussion of names for different types of clothing.

Anapaestic tetrameter catalectic.

B41. If a full stop is placed at the end of the first verse (thus K–A), the second verse becomes a response to the spectator's question ('[I'm] someone . . .'). But more likely no punctuation is wanted and the adjectives in 2 represent a series of increasingly elaborate glosses on κομψός (here 'subtle, clever' (as at **C9**. 1; Cratin. fr. 182. 3; Ar. *Ra.* 967), but with overtones of 'haughty'; contrast **B45**. 2 with n.), with εὐριπιδαριστοφανίζων reserved for the end as the punch-line (cf. **B29**. 3 n.; Ar. *Eq.* 18 κομψευριπικῶς). In any case, the final word amounts to a public slap at one of Cratinus' most important rivals during the final years of his career (cf. **B1–B12** n.) by 'the poet', who indirectly represents himself as most emphatically *not* a 'Euripidaristophanizer'. Cf. Luppe, in *Rivals*, 15–20. For the reception of Euripides in comedy, see **D11–D12** n. For comments (imaginary or not) from the audience, cf. **C2**. 4–5 n.

Preserved in a *scholium* on Pl. *Ap.* 19c (Socrates claims that much of the prejudice against him can be traced to the—allegedly utterly false—portrait presented in Aristophanes' *Clouds*), as evidence in support of the observation that 'Aristophanes was made fun of in comedy for mocking Euripides but imitating him'.

Anapaestic tetrameter catalectic.

2. **ὑπολεπτολόγος:** λεπτολογέω is 'quibble about ideas', and the prefix adds the sense 'somewhat, a bit' (LSJ s. ὑπό F. II). **γνωμιδιώκτης:** formed from the contemptuous diminutive γνωμίδιον (cf. Ar. *Eq.* 100; *Nu.* 321) rather than γνώμη, which would produce γνωμοδιώκτης. **εὐριπιδαριστοφανίζων:** Aristophanes constantly criticizes Euripides for being a chatterer (e.g. *Ach.* 414–47 (which Cratinus will have known); *Ra.* 1069–73; fr. 392), and after ὑπολεπτολόγος and γνωμιδιώκτης, part of the point must be that he is just as much of one himself.

B42. At *Clouds* 553–4, Aristophanes insists that Eupolis wrote *Marikas* (a satire on the demagogue Hyperbolus, probably Lenaia 422/1; see **E5**; **E23–E25** n.; **E23** introductory n.; Storey 197–214) 'by turning our *Knights* (Lenaia 424) clumsily inside out' (cf. fr. 58, which may be another allusion to the quarrel), and an ancient commentator on the passage offers this fragment (probably from the early 410s) to show that Eupolis argued the opposite. (The dispute may have been older and more complicated than this, for Cratinus in *The Wineflask* (fr. 213) at the City Dionysia in 423 is said to have 'abused Aristophanes for using Eupolis' words' (see **B1–B12** n.; and cf. **E19** introductory n.; Hermipp. fr. 64 (a similar charge directed against Phrynichus)). There can be no doubt that the comic poets saw one another's plays performed, and occasionally borrowed (or 'stole') ideas from their rivals; for examples, see **C7** introductory n.; **G5**. 3–4 with n.; **I2** introductory n.; **I8** introductory n.; Ar. *Th.* 215 with Austin–Olson ad loc. But the seemingly autobiographical remarks by 'the poet' at Ar. *V.* 1017–22 (cf. *Eq.* 512–17, 542–4) suggest that they also worked together on occasion, reviewing drafts, suggesting jokes, and the like (cf. Halliwell, *GRBS* 30 (1989), 515–28; Storey 278–300); and Eupolis and Aristophanes may thus both be right about the tangled origins of *Knights*, *Marikas*, and the 'demagogue-comedy' (for which, see **E23** introductory n.). **J19** (where see introductory n.) is from the same play.

Preserved entire in a *scholium* on Ar. *Nu.* 554, and in an incomplete form in *scholia* on *Eq.* 1291 and *Nu.* 540.

Eupolideans (see **B38** introductory n.).

2. **ξυνεποίησα:** 'I collaborated with'. ποιέω in the compound has the specific sense 'write poetry'; cf. **D4**. 3; **D9**. 3. **τῶι φαλακρῶι:** 'the bald guy', i.e. Aristophanes (*Eq.* 550; *Nu.* 545; *Pax* 771–4).

B43. The phrasing of the threat in 5–7 makes it clear that these remarks were preceded by hostile comments about the judges at a previous festival (in contrast to τοῖς δὲ κριταῖς | τοῖς νυνὶ κρίνουσι, 'the judges judging now' (1–2)), at which Pherecrates failed to take the prize. For similarly pointed 'advice' to the judges in the theatre, see Pherecr. fr. 126; Ar. *Nu.* 1115–30; *Av.* 1102–17; *Ec.* 1154–62; and cf. **B37**. The speaker throughout the fragment is 'the poet', with the reference to Pherecrates in the third person in 6 merely adding solemnity to the threat.

Preserved at Photius p. 647. 22 = *EM*, p. 793. 43 = Suda φ 342, in a gloss on Φίλιος Ζεύς.

Line 6 is a Eupolidean (see **B38** introductory n.), and 1–5 are a variant thereof, = the first half of a Eupolidean (i.e. an anaclastic glyconic) ○ ○ – × – ∪∪–

3–4. μὴ (ἐ)πιορκεῖν μηδ(ὲ) ἀδίκως | κρίνειν: The second order gives specific content to the first. Cf. Ar. *Ec.* 1160 (also addressed to the judges) μὴ 'πιορκεῖν, ἀλλὰ κρίνειν τοὺς χοροὺς ὀρθῶς ἀεί ('not to violate their oath, but to always judge the choruses properly').

4. ἤ: 'or (else)', i.e. if they fail to follow this advice.   νὴ τὸν φίλιον: 'by the god of friendship', a cult-title of Zeus (e.g. Diod. Com. fr. 2. 5; Men. fr. 53; Pl. *Phdr.* 234e); probably invoked here because Pherecrates and the judges (or the audience generally?) have been said in the immediately preceding verses to have always maintained a close and amicable relationship, which the alleged treachery of awarding the prize to someone else has betrayed and which ought now to be emphatically reaffirmed (sc. by voting for the current play). Cf. Ar. *Nu.* 518–62; *V.* 1043–59.

5. εἰς ὑμᾶς: 'in regard to you, about you'.

B44. 'The poet' reproaches the audience for their failure to show adequate appreciation for young Athenian playwrights (presumably including himself, given ἀπολογήσομαι in 2 and ἡμῶν … νέων in 8). The trochaic metre would seem to identify this as part of an epirrhema or antepirrhema, although Storey 300–3, suggests that it belongs to an *agon* instead. In any case, 1 is clearly the beginning of the section, while the appeal in 8 to the audience (or the other party) to change their ways probably comes at the end; and up to a dozen verses or so containing a more specific description of the complaint might easily have been lost between 2 and 3.

Preserved at Stobaeus iii. 4. 32 (only in Tr and Voss, which are in turn dependent on a lost portion of S), under the heading 'Concerning folly'.

Trochaic tetrameter catalectic.

1. For the audience addressed as θεαταί ('spectators') in the parabasis, e.g. Ar. *Nu.* 575; *V.* 1071; *Av.* 753; cf. **B39**. 2 with n.

1–2. τὰ (ἐ)μὰ καὶ ξυνίετε | ῥήματ(α): an allusion to Archil. fr. 109; cf. **B8** (also from an epirrhema or antepirrhema) with n.

2. εὐθύ and πρῶτον are both adverbial, 'immediately at the beginning' (sc. of this section of my parabasis). The priority the topic is given reflects how seriously 'the poet' takes it, and although the lacuna makes it impossible to know what charge (or implied charge) he defended himself against, the obvious conclusion from 3–8 is that he insisted he ought to have been awarded a prize that went to someone else. Cf. Ar. *Nu.* 524–5 (from the 'parabasis proper'); *V.* 1015–59, esp. 1051–5 (from the 'parabasis proper' and the *pnigos*).

3. ὅ τι μαθόντες: 'what got into your heads, that . . .'. Colloquial; cf. Dover on Ar. *Nu.* 402; Olson on Ar. *Ach.* 826.   τοὺς ξένους: Meineke suggested taking this as a hostile reference to Aristophanes, who may have been from Aegina (*Ach.* 652–4). But Eupolis and Aristophanes were about the same age (cf. Eup. test. 7), and given τις ἡμῶν . . . νέων ('one of us young men', apparently contrasted with the 'foreigners') in 8 (corrupt?), the target must be someone else, although none of the comic poets of the previous generation are known to have come from outside Attica. (Contrast tragic poets such as Neophron of Sicyon (*TrGF* 15) and Ion of Chios (*TrGF* 19); and cf. **B45**. 14 n.)

4. ἐνθάδ(ε) αὐτοῦ: 'right here', i.e. from Athens itself.   μηδὲ ἓν χεῖρον φρονῶν: 'thinking nothing worse', i.e. 'who is no less brilliant'; echoed in 5 δοκεῖ κακῶς φρονεῖν and 6 παραρρεῖ τῶν φρενῶν.

5. ἐπιτιθῆται is middle, 'applies himself to' + dat.

6. παραρρεῖ τῶν φρενῶν: 'drifts away from his senses'.   τῶι σῶι λόγωι: 'according to you', as at X. *Mem.* iii. 10. 12.

7. μεταβαλόντες τοὺς τρόπους: found in the same position in the line in a similar request at Ar. *Ra.* 734 (near the end of the antepirrhema).

8. μὴ φθονεῖτ(ε) κτλ.: cf. μὴ φθονεῖθ' ἡμῖν at the end of the epirrhema at Ar. *Eq.* 580.   μουσικῆι: used here as a general term for 'poetic activity', as at e.g. Ar. *Ach.* 851; Antiph. fr. 207. 6; Anaxil. fr. 27. 1.

B45. The chorus of 'flatterers' (i.e. parasites; see **A13** introductory n.; **C11–C12**; **G14–G17**) explain their way of life to the audience (1 πρὸς ὑμᾶς; cf. **B28**. 2; **B44**. 2); cf. Cratin. fr. 105 (from the 'parabasis proper'); Ar. *V.* 1071–90, 1102–21 (the epirrhema and antepirrhema); *Av.* 753–68 (the epirrhema). *Flatterers* (test. i) was performed at the City Dionysia in 421 and took first place, defeating Aristophanes' *Peace*, Leucon's *Phratries*, and most likely two unidentified plays. Much of the play was apparently devoted to mocking the wealthy and extravagant Callias son of Hipponicus (*PAA* 554500).

Preserved at Athenaeus 6. 236e–7a, as evidence that 'the ancient poets' called parasites 'flatterers', as part of an extended history of the institution of parasitism that also includes **A13**; **C11**; **F11**; **G14**.

– ∪∪–×–∪×–∪∪–∪–, like **F2** (perhaps from the same play), where see introductory n.; Ar. frr. 30–1 (from the parabasis of *Amphiaraus*).

1–2. ἀλλ(ά)² is progressive ('Well . . ., So . . .'; Denniston 21–2) and marks the request that follows as fulfilling the proposal put forward in ἀλλὰ . . . λέξομεν. κομψοί: here 'elegant, smart' (e.g. Ar. *Lys.* 89; Arar. fr. 8. 1); contrast **B41**. 1.

3. For the παῖς ἀκόλουθος (a slave who accompanied his master when he went out, carried whatever goods the master might need or purchase, and the like), e.g. Ar. *Ec.* 593; fr. 145; D. 54. 4; Thphr. *Char.* 9. 3; 21. 4; and cf. **A13**. 8.

4. ἀλλότριος τὰ πολλά ('generally belonging to someone else!') is a humorous gloss on παῖς ἀκόλουθος in 3; cf. μᾶζαν ἐπ' ἀλλόφυλον at the beginning of 12, capping ἐπὶ δεῖπνον in 11.

5–10. The description moves abruptly into the singular; contrast 11, and cf. **J7**. 5–6 n.

5. ἱματίω . . . μοι δύ(ο) ἐστὸν χαρίεντε τούτω: 'I have these two lovely *himatia* (outer garments)', which Fritzsche took as a mocking reference to the inside and the outside of a single robe, which the impoverished speaker turns inside-out on alternate days (6); cf. **A13**. 14.

6. οἷν μεταλαμβάνων . . . θάτερον: 'changing one for the other of which'; cf. 5 n.

7. εἰς ἀγοράν: sc. because that is where one can see who is buying food (cf. **G5–G6**) or hiring a cook (see **G7** introductory n.) for a dinner party to be held later in the day, and thus pick one's target (a man wealthy enough to be purchasing something worth eating, but foolish enough to be easily buttered up). Cf. **G15**; **J1–J4** with nn.

8. εὐθὺς περὶ τοῦτόν εἰμι: 'I'm all over him immediately'.

9. κ(αὶ ἐ)άν τι τύχηι λέγων: i.e. 'whatever he says, no matter what he says'. ὁ πλούταξ: 'the rich guy' (colloquial; attested elsewhere only at Men. fr. 351. 10).

10. 'and I pretend that I'm stunned with pleasure at his words'.

11. ἐπὶ δεῖπνον ἐρχόμεσθ(α): sc. because the strategy described in 9–10 has been successful and invitations to share the meals for which the shopping was being done (7–8) have been obtained. Note the abrupt return to the plural (contrast 5–10). ἄλλυδις ἄλλος: a snatch of Homeric language (e.g. *Il.* 11. 486; *Od.* 5. 71).

12 μᾶζαν ἐπ(ὶ) ἀλλόφυλον: see 4 n.; **B32**. 8 n.

12–13. For the parasite's need to flatter his host and be gracefully amusing, e.g. **A13**. 3–4; Antiph. fr. 80. 9–10; Anaxandr. fr. 10. 2; Alex. frr. 188; 229. 1–2; Diod. Com. fr. 2. 35–40.

14. Acestor (*PAA* 116685; *TrGF* 25) was a tragic poet active in the final third of the fifth century. The comic poets repeatedly refer to him as a foreigner and a barbarian (Ar. *V*. 1221; *Av*. 31 with Dunbar ad loc.; Metag. fr. 14; Theopomp. Com. fr. 61; cf. **B44**. 3 n.), hence the claim that he has been tattooed (τὸν στιγματίαν; cf. **D1**. 19 n.).

15. σκῶμμα . . . ἀσελγές: 'an insolent joke', i.e. one at the host's expense; cf. **A13**. 5 with **A13**. 3–6 n.   ὁ παῖς: i.e. the doorkeeper at the house where the party was being held (cf. **C9**. 16).

16. ἔχοντα κλωιόν: 'wearing a collar' of a sort fitted around the necks and hands of condemned criminals also at e.g. Ar. *V*. 897; adesp. com. fr. *618; X. *HG* iii. 3. 11.   Οἰνεῖ: i.e. 'to death', since τὸ βάραθρον, a gully into which individuals condemned of crimes against the state were cast, sometimes alive (e.g. Ar. *Eq*. 1362; Alex. fr. 159. 1 with Arnott ad loc.; X. *HG* i. 7. 20), was located in the deme Oinoe.

B46. Probably a boast about the immense amount of effort invested in the play by the poet (cf. **B39–B40**), and thus interesting evidence for how far in advance an author might begin to plan for a festival; but perhaps Cratinus simply failed to get a chorus the first time around, and self-serving exaggeration must be suspected in any case. Identified by Aelius Aristides (below) as coming from the *exodos*. For other *exodos*-fragments, cf. **B13**. 37–40; Whittaker 190–1. **E12–E13** are also from *Cheirons*, which must date to sometime between Pericles' rise to power in the late 440s or early 430s and his death in 429.

Preserved at Aelius Aristides, *Oration* 29. 92, as an example of the comic poets' habitual boastfulness.

Dactylic hexameter, like the *exodos*-song in Aristophanes' *Frogs* (1528–33).

ταῦτα: i.e. the play now coming to an end.   ἡμῖν is probably a dative of advantage ('worked out for us', i.e. the chorus).

Section C

'Middle' and 'New Comedy'

C1. Adespota comica fr. 1062, from an unidentified play

"τί οὖν ἐμοὶ τῶν σ[ῶν μέ]λει;" φαίη τις ἂν
ὑμῶν. ἐγὼ δ' ἐρῶ [τ]ὸ Σοφοκλέους ἔπος·
"πέπονθα δεινά." πάντα μοι γέρων Κρ[όνος
τὰ παιδί' ἐκπίνει τε καὶ κατεσθίει,
ἐμοὶ δὲ τούτων προσδίδωσιν οὐδὲ ἕν,   5
ἀλλ' αὐτὸς ἔρδει χειρὶ καὶ Μεγαράδ' ἄγων
ὅ τι ἂν τέκω 'γὼ τοῦτο πωλῶν 'σθίει.
δέδοικε γὰρ τὸν χρησμὸν ὥσπερ κυν[
ἔχρησε γὰρ Κρόνωι ποθ' Ἀπόλλων δραχ[μήν,
κἇιτ' οὐκ ἀπέλαβε. ταῦτα δὴ θυμὸν πνέ[ων   10
ἑτέραν ἔχρησε[ν οὐκέτι] δρα[χ]μῶ[ν ἀ]ξ[ίαν,
οὐ σκευάρια, μὰ τὸν Δί', οὐδὲ χρήματα,
ἐκ τῆς βασιλείας δ' ἐκπεσεῖν ὑπὸ π[αιδίου.
τοῦ]τ' οὖν δεδοικὼς πάντα καταπί[νει τέκνα

8 κύν[α λαγώς] Immisch   11 suppl. Pfeiffer et Körte

C2. Heniochus fr. 5, from an unidentified play (IV)

ἐγὼ δ' ὄνομα τὸ μὲν καθ' ἑκάστην αὐτίκα
λέξω· συνάπασαι δ' εἰσὶ παντοδαπαὶ πόλεις,
αἳ νῦν ἀνοηταίνουσι πολὺν ἤδη χρόνον.
τάχ' ἂν τις ὑποκρούσειεν ὅ τι ποτ' ἐνθάδε
νῦν εἰσι κἀνέροιτο· παρ' ἐμοῦ πεύσεται.   5
τὸ χωρίον μὲν γὰρ τόδ' ἐστὶ πᾶν κύκλωι
Ὀλυμπία, τηνδὶ δὲ τὴν σκηνὴν ἐκεῖ
σκηνὴν ὁρᾶν θεωρικὴν νομίζετε.
εἶέν· τί οὖν ἐνταῦθα δρῶσιν αἱ πόλεις;
ἐλευθέρι' ἀφίκοντο θύσουσαί ποτε,   10

ὅτε τῶν φόρων ἐγένοντ' ἐλεύθεραι σχεδόν.
κἄπειτ' ἀπ' ἐκείνης τῆς θυσίας διέφθορεν
αὐτὰς ξενίζουσ' ἡμέραν ἐξ ἡμέρας
Ἀβουλία, κατέχουσα πολὺν ἤδη χρόνον.
γυναῖκε δ' αὐτὰς δύο ταράττετόν τινε   15
ἀεὶ συνοῦσαι· Δημοκρατία θατέραι
ὄνομ' ἐστί, τῆι δ' Ἀριστοκρατία θατέραι,
δι' ἃς πεπαρωινήκασιν ἤδη πολλάκις

3 ἀνοηταίνουσι Canter: -ουσαι Stob.S   7 τηνδὶ δὲ Valckenaer: τὴν δ' εἰ δὲ Stob.S
8 νομίζετε Grotius: νομίζεται Stob.S   15 αὐτὰς Grotius: αὐτὴν Stob.S   δύο ταράττετόν
Meineke: δῦ' ἐταράττετόν Stob.S

C3. Eubulus fr. 89, from *Procris* (IV)

(Α.) οὔκουν ὑποστορεῖτε μαλακῶς τῶι κυνί;
κάτω μὲν ὑποβαλεῖτε τῶν Μιλησίων
ἐρίων, ἄνωθεν δ' ἐπιβαλεῖτε ξυστίδα.
(Β.) Ἄπολλον. (Α.) εἶτα χόνδρον αὐτῶι δεύσετε
γάλακτι χηνός. (Β.) Ἡράκλεις. (Α.) καὶ τοὺς πόδας   5
ἀλείψετ' αὐτοῦ τῶι Μεγαλλείωι μύρωι

6 ἀλείψετ' Meineke: ἀλείψατ' Ath.A

C4. Anaxilas fr. 12, from *Circe* (IV)

τοὺς μὲν ὀρειονόμους ὑμῶν ποήσει δέλφακας ὑλιβάτας,
τοὺς δὲ πάνθηρας, ἄλλους ἀγρώστας λύκους,
λέοντας

C5. Anaxilas fr. 13, from *Circe* (IV)

δεινὸν μὲν γὰρ ἔχονθ' ὑὸς
ῥύγχος, ὦ φίλε, κνησιᾶν

2 κνησιᾶν Meineke: κινησία Ath.A

C6. Antiphanes fr. 131, from *Cyclops* (IV)

τῶν χερσαίων δ' ἡμῖν ἥξει
παρ' ἐμοῦ ταυτί·
βοῦς ἀγελαῖος τράγος ὑλιβάτης
αἲξ οὐρανία κριὸς τομίας

κάπρος ἐκτομίας ὗς οὐ τομίας   5
δέλφαξ δασύπους ἔριφοι, ...
τυρὸς χλωρὸς τυρὸς ξηρὸς
τυρὸς κοπτὸς τυρὸς ξυστὸς
τυρὸς τμητὸς τυρὸς πηκτός

1 ἡμῖν Nesselrath: ὑμῖν Ath.ᴬᶜᴱ   3 τράγος Ath.ᴬ: ταῦρος Ath.ᶜᴱ   ὑλιβάτης Casaubon:
ὑλιβάτας Ath.ᴬ: ὑληβάτας Ath.ᶜᴱ: ἠλιβάτης Eust.

C7. Epicrates fr. 5, from *Difficult to Sell* (IV)

τί γὰρ
ἔχθιον ἢ "παῖ παῖ" καλεῖσθαι παρὰ πότον,
καὶ ταῦτ' ἀγενείωι μειρακυλλίωι τινί,
<καὶ> τὴν ἀμίδα φέρειν, ὁρᾶν τε κείμενα,
ἄμητας ἡμιβρῶτας ὀρνίθειά τε,   5
ὧν οὐδὲ λειφθέντων θέμις δούλωι φαγεῖν,
ὥς φασιν αἱ γυναῖκες; ὃ δὲ χολᾶν ποεῖ,
γάστριν καλοῦσι καὶ λαμυρὸν ἡμῶν ὃς ἂν
φάγηι τι τούτων

4 <καὶ> τὴν Morel: τὴν Ath.ᴬ: τὴν τ' Ath.ᶜᴱᴾ: τήνδ' Ath.ᴱˣ: <ἢ> τὴν Porson
7 χολᾶν Porson: χοααιν Ath.ᴬ: om. Ath.ᶜᴱ   8–9 ἡμῶν ὃς ἂν | φάγηι Porson: ὃς ἂν
φάγηι | ἡμῶν Ath.ᴬ: om. Ath.ᶜᴱ

C8. Antiphanes fr. 75, from *Ganymede* (IV)

(Α.) οἴμοι περιπλοκὰς
λίαν ἐρωτᾶις. (Λα.) ἀλλ' ἐγὼ σαφῶς φράσω·
τῆς ἁρπαγῆς τοῦ παιδὸς εἰ ξύνοισθά τι,
ταχέως λέγειν χρὴ πρὶν κρέμασθαι. (Α.) πότερά μοι
γρῖφον προβάλλεις τοῦτον εἰπεῖν, δέσποτα,   5
τῆς ἁρπαγῆς τοῦ παιδὸς εἰ ξύνοιδά τι,
ἢ τί δύναται τὸ ῥηθέν; (Λα.) ἔξω τις δότω
ἱμάντα ταχέως. (Α.) εἶέν· οὐκ ἔγνων ἴσως.
ἔπειτα τοῦτο ζημιοῖς με; μηδαμῶς·
ἅλμης δ' ἐχρῆν τι περιφέρειν ποτήριον.   10
(Λα.) οἶσθ' οὖν ὅπως δεῖ τοῦτό σ' ἐκπιεῖν; (Α.) ἐγώ;
κομιδῆι γε. (Λα.) πῶς; (Α.) ἐνέχυρον ἀποφέροντά <σου>.
(Λα.) οὐκ ἀλλ' ὀπίσω τὼ χεῖρε ποιήσαντα δεῖ
ἕλκειν ἀπνευστί

5 προβάλλεις Musurus: προβαλεῖς Ath.ᴬ   6–7 τι, | ἢ Dindorf et Dobree: τιν Ath.ᴬ
8 εἰέν Schenkl: οἶον Ath.ᴬ   11 τοῦτό σ' Casaubon: σε τοῦτ' Ath.ᴬ   12 <σου>
Hermann

C9. Dionysius Comicus fr. 3, from *Men Who Shared a Name* (IV)

ἄγε δὴ Δρόμων νῦν, εἴ τι κομψὸν ἢ σοφὸν
ἢ γλαφυρὸν οἶσθα τῶν σεαυτοῦ πραγμάτων,
φανερὸν ποήσον τοῦτο τῶι διδασκάλωι.
νῦν τὴν ἀπόδειξιν τῆς τέχνης αἰτῶ σ' ἐγώ.
εἰς πολεμίαν ἄγω σε· θαρρῶν κατάτρεχε.   5
ἀριθμῶι διδόασι τὰ κρέα καὶ τηροῦσί σε·
τακερὰ ποήσας ταῦτα καὶ ζέσας σφόδρα
τὸν ἀριθμὸν αὐτῶν, ὡς λέγω σοι, σύγχεον.
ἰχθὺς ἁδρὸς πάρεστι· τἀντός ἐστι σά.
κἂν τέμαχος ἐκκλίνηις τι, καὶ τοῦτ' ἐστὶ σόν,   10
ἕως ἂν ἔνδον ὦμεν· ὅταν ἔξω δ', ἐμόν.
ἐξαιρέσεις καὶ τἆλλα τἀκόλουθ' ὅσα
οὔτ' ἀριθμὸν οὔτ' ἔλεγχον ἐφ' ἑαυτῶν ἔχει,
περικόμματος δὲ τάξιν ἢ θέσιν φέρει,
εἰς αὔριόν σε κἀμὲ ταῦτ' εὐφρανάτω.   15
λαφυροπώληι παντάπασι μεταδίδου,
τὴν πάροδον ἵν' ἔχηις τῶν θυρῶν εὐνουστέραν.
τί δεῖ λέγειν με πολλὰ πρὸς συνειδότα;
ἐμὸς εἶ μαθητής, σὸς δ' ἐγώ διδάσκαλος.
μέμνησο τῶνδε καὶ βάδιζε δεῦρ' ἅμα   20

1 Δρόμων Musurus: δρίμων Ath.ᴬ   7 τακερὰ Casaubon: τὰ κρέα Ath.ᴬ   11 ἔξω δ'
Schweighäuser: δ' ἔξω Ath.ᴬ   13 οὔτ' ¹ Dindorf: οὐδὲ Ath.ᴬ

C10. Antiphanes fr. 180, from *The Parasite* (IV)

                    (Α.) ἄλλος ἐπὶ τούτωι μέγας
ἥξει τις ἰσοτράπεζος εὐγενής— (Β.) τίνα
λέγεις; (Α.) Καρύστου θρέμμα, γηγενής, ζέων—
(Β.) εἶτ' οὐκ ἂν εἴποις; ὕπαγε. (Α.) κάκκαβον λέγω·
σὺ δ' ἴσως ἂν εἴποις λοπάδ'. (Β.) ἐμοὶ δὲ τοὔνομα   5
οἴει διαφέρειν, εἴτε κάκκαβόν τινες
χαίρουσιν ὀνομάζοντες εἴτε σίττυβον;
πλὴν ὅτι λέγεις ἀγγεῖον οἶδα

6–7 τινες | χαίρουσιν ὀνομάζοντες Sylburg: τινες χαίρουσιν ὀνομάζειν Poll.ꟳ: χαίρουσίν
τινες ὀνομάζοντες Poll.ᴬᴮᶜᴸ: τινες χαίροντες ὀνομάζουσιν Ath.ᴬ: τινες ὀνομάζουσιν
Ath.ᶜᴱ

C11. Aristophon fr. 5, from *The Doctor* (IV)

βούλομαι δ' αὐτῶι προειπεῖν οἷός εἰμι τοὺς τρόπους.
ἄν τις ἑστιᾶι, πάρειμι πρῶτος, ὥστ' ἤδη πάλαι
– ∪ – Ζωμὸς καλοῦμαι. δεῖ τιν' ἄρασθαι μέσον
τῶν παροινούντων, παλαιστὴν νόμισον Ἀργεῖόν μ' ὁρᾶν.
προσβαλεῖν πρὸς οἰκίαν δεῖ, κριός· ἀναβῆναί τι πρὸς   5
κλιμάκιον × – ∪ Καπανεύς· ὑπομένειν πληγὰς ἄκμων·
κονδύλους πλάττειν δὲ Τελαμών· τοὺς καλοὺς πειρᾶν καπνός

3 <παρὰ νέων> Grotius: <τοῖς νέοις> Bailey: <εἰκότως> Stephanopoulos   4 Ἀργεῖόν
Grotius: αὐταργεῖον vel sim. Ath.^ACE   5 προσβαλεῖν Grotius: προσβάδην Ath.^A: προσβαίνειν
Ath.^CE   7 κονδύλοις Ath.^CE

C12. Crobylus fr. 8, from an unidentified play (IV)

(Α.) ἐγὼ δὲ πρὸς τὰ θερμὰ ταῦθ' ὑπερβολῆι
τοὺς δακτύλους δήπουθεν Ἰδαίους ἔχω
καὶ τὸν λάρυγγ' ἥδιστα πυριῶ τεμαχίοις.
(Β.) κάμινος, οὐκ ἄνθρωπος

3 λάρυγγ' Ath.^CE: φάρυγγ' Suda

C13. Antiphanes fr. 200, from *The Soldier or Tycho* (IV)

(Α.) ἐν Κύπρωι φήις, εἰπέ μοι, διήγετε
πολὺν χρόνον; (Β.) τὸν πάνθ' ἕως ἦν ὁ πόλεμος.
(Α.) ἐν τίνι τόπωι μάλιστα; λέγε γάρ. (Β.) ἐν Πάφωι,
οὗ πρᾶγμα τρυφερὸν διαφερόντως ἦν ἰδεῖν
ἄλλως τ' ἄπιστον. (Α.) ποῖον; (Β.) ἐρριπίζετο   5
ὑπὸ τῶν περιστερῶν, ὑπ' ἄλλου δ' οὐδενός,
δειπνῶν ὁ βασιλεύς. (Α.) πῶς; ἐάσας τἆλλα γὰρ
ἐρήσομαί σε τοῦθ'. (Β.) ὅπως; ἠλείφετο
ἐκ τῆς Συρίας ἥκοντι τοιούτου μύρωι
καρποῦ σύχν' οἷόν φασι τὰς περιστερὰς   10
τρώγειν. διὰ τὴν ὀσμὴν δὲ τούτου πετόμεναι
παρῆσαν, οἷαί τ' ἦσαν ἐπικαθιζάνειν
ἐπὶ τὴν κεφαλήν· παῖδες δὲ παρακαθήμενοι
ἐσόβουν. ἀπαίρουσαι δὲ μικρόν, οὐ πολύ,
τοῦ μήτ' ἐκεῖσε μήτε δεῦρο παντελῶς,   15
οὕτως ἀνερρίπιζον, ὥστε σύμμετρον
αὐτῶι τὸ πνεῦμα, μὴ περίσκληρον, ποεῖν

C14. Philemon fr. 95, from an unidentified play (IV/III)

ὃν οὐδὲ εἷς λέληθεν οὐδὲ ἓν ποῶν
οὔτε κακὸν οὔτε γ' ἐσθλόν, οὗτός εἰμ' ἐγώ,
Ἀήρ, ὃν ἄν τις ὀνομάσειε καὶ Δία.
ἐγὼ δ', ὃ θεοῦ 'στιν ἔργον, εἰμὶ πανταχοῦ,
ἐνταῦθ' ἐν Ἀθήναις, ἐν Πάτραις, ἐν Σικελίαι,   5
ἐν ταῖς πόλεσι πάσαισιν, ἐν ταῖς οἰκίαις
πάσαις, ἐν ὑμῖν πᾶσιν· οὐκ ἔστιν τόπος,
οὗ μή 'στιν Ἀήρ. ὁ δὲ παρὼν ἁπανταχοῦ
πάντ' ἐξ ἀνάγκης οἶδε

C15. Adespota comica fr. 1084, from an unidentified play

(recto)
(A.) δεινότ[ερ]ά τις πέπονθε τῶν ἐν τῆι πόλει
ἐμοῦ; μ[ὰ] τὴν Δήμητρα καὶ τὸν Οὐρανόν.
πέμπτ[ο]ν γεγάμηκα μῆνα, πεισθεὶς τῶι πατρί·
ἀφ' ἧς γ[εγά]μηκα νυκτός (ὦ δέσποινα Νύξ,
σὲ μά[ρτυρ' ὀ]ρθὴν ἐπάγομ' οὗ λέγω λόγου)   5
μί[αν οὐ γε]γένημαι νύκτ' ἀπόκοιτ[ο]ς πώποτ[ε
ἀπὸ τῆ[ς γυναι]κὸς † οσονηνεχεινεδ.[
οὔποτ[......]ος γεγον..ουκ...[
μετὰ τοὺς γάμους[
δίκαιον ἥρων· καὶ οτ..[   ]εται.ε[10
αὐτῆς ἐλευθέρωι γὰρ ἤθει καὶ βίωι
δεθεὶς ἀπλάστωι τὴν φ[ι]λοῦσαν ἠγάπ[ων.
τί προσφέρεις μοι δει[κ]νύουσα καθ' ἓν[
ἅπαντ', [ἐπεὶ τὴν κ]αρδίαν ἀλγῶ γ' ὁρ[ῶν;
τιθε.[   ]....οῦ καὶ νῦν[15
(B.) ἵν' ἦι[   ]πριν[
αλ.[

(verso)

(A.) ἐμ]ῆς γυναι[κὸς

(B.) τῆς μη]τρὸς . [. . . . . . .] . ιδε τῆι γυ[ναικὶ   20

ἔδωκε· καὶ δι[. . . . .]βεβλητ[

ὁ δακτύλιος [. . . .] ἐκείνης· ου . [

(A.) ἄνοιξον, εἴ τι καὶ φυλάττει χρήσιμο[ν

ἵν' ἴδωμεν. (B.) αἴ. (A.) τί ἐστι; (B.) χλαμύδο[ς] ἥμισυ

διεσπαραγμένης παλαιᾶς, ὑπὸ [σέ]ων   25

σχέδον τι καταβεβρωμ[έν]ης. (A.) ἄ[λ]λ' οὐδὲ ἕν;

(B.) καὶ περιδέραια καὶ περισκελὶς [μ]ία.

(A.) ἐμοὶ προσένεγκε τὸν λύχνον τε φ[αῖν'] ἅμα.

οὐκ εἶδες ἐπιγεγραμμένα[. . . . .]δια;

ὠή,

ἄνοιγ' ἄνωθεν. (B.) γρα[μματ . . . . .]τάλαν   30

.] . . . γράμματ' εἶδον. (A.) τί [. . . . . .]βούλεται;

. . . .]ἔνεστ' ἐν αὐτῶι παιδίου

γ]νωρί[σμαθ', ἡ] μήτηρ δ' ἐτήρει ταῦτα. θὲς

πάλιν ὡς ἔκειτο, σημανοῦμαι δ' αὖτ' ἐγώ.

ο]ὐ νῦν ἐπιτηδείως ἔχει, μὰ τὸν Δία,   35

ζ]ητεῖν ἄφαντ'· οὐχ ἡμέτερον· τὴν ἐμποδὼν

τα]ραχὴν ἱκανῶς θεῖμέν ποτ'· ἂν ἐντός ποτε

γέ]νωμ' ἐμαυτοῦ κ[. . . . . . ἀνο]ίξω πάλιν

. . .]ητες . [ο]ὐδὲ ἕν

(two extremely fragmentary lines follow)

5 μά[ρτυρ' ὀ]ρθὴν Pfeiffer   14 [ἐπεὶ] Lloyd-Jones   19 [ἐμ]ῆς Mette
20 τῆς μ]ητρὸς Roberts   28 φ[αῖν'] Lloyd-Jones   33 [γ]νωρί[σμαθ', ἡ] Maas
38 [ἀνο]ίξω Barns

C16. Menander fr. 296, from *The Necklace* (IV/III)

(Λα.) ἐπ' ἀμφότερα νῦν ἡ 'πίκληρος ἡ κ<αλὴ>

μέλλει καθευδήσειν. κατείργασται μέγα

καὶ περιβόητον ἔργον· ἐκ τῆς οἰκίας

ἐξέβαλε τὴν λυποῦσαν, ἣν ἐβούλετο,

ἵν' ἀποβλέπωσιν πάντες εἰς τὸ Κρωβύλης   5

πρόσωπον ἧι τ' εὔγνωστος οὖσ' ἐμὴ γυνὴ

δέσποινα. καὶ τὴν ὄψιν ἣν ἐκτήσατο·

ὄνος ἐν πιθήκοις, τοῦτο δὴ τὸ λεγόμενον,

ἔστιν. σιωπᾶν βούλομαι τὴν νύκτα τὴν

πολλῶν κακῶν ἀρχηγόν. οἴμοι Κρωβύλην   10

λαβεῖν ἔμ', εἰ καὶ δέκα τάλαντ' <ἠνέγκατο,

τὴν> ῥῖν᾽ ἔχουσαν πήχεως. εἶτ᾽ ἐστὶ τὸ
φρύαγμα πῶς ὑποστατόν; <μὰ τὸν> Δία
τὸν Ὀλύμπιον καὶ τὴν Ἀθηνᾶν, οὐδαμῶς.
παιδισκάριον θεραπευτικὸν δὲ καὶ λόγου   15
τάχιον· ἀπαγέσθω δέ. † τισαρανπισαγοι †

1 κ<αλὴ> Ribbeck   11 <ἠνέγκατο> Kaibel   12 <τὴν> ῥῖν᾽ ἔχουσαν Kock:
ΓΕΙΝΕΣΟΥΣΑΝ Gell.ᵛ   13 πῶς Spengel: ΕΙΚΤΩΣΑΝ Gell.ᵛ   <μὰ τὸν> Gronovius
16 τίς ἄρ᾽ ἂν εἰσάγοι; Spengel: τί ἄρ᾽ ἄν τις λέγοι; Thierfelder

C17. Menander fr. 297, from *The Necklace* (IV/III)

(Λα.) ἔχω δ᾽ ἐπίκληρον Λάμιαν· οὐκ εἴρηκά σοι
τουτὶ γάρ; (Α.) οὐχί. (Λα.) κυρίαν τῆς οἰκίας
καὶ τῶν ἀγρῶν καὶ † πάντων ἀντ᾽ ἐκείνης †
ἔχομεν. (Α.) Ἄπολλον, ὡς χαλεπόν. (Λα.) χαλεπώτατον.
ἅπασι δ᾽ ἀργαλέα ᾽στίν, οὐκ ἐμοὶ μόνωι,   5
υἱῶι πολὺ μᾶλλον, θυγατρί. (Α.) πρᾶγμ᾽ ἄμαχον λέγεις.
(Λα.) εὖ οἶδα

1 ΕΛΩΔΕΠΙΚΑΛΗΡΟΝ Gell.ᵛ   2 τουτὶ γάρ; — οὐχί Lloyd-Jones:
ΤΟΥΓΕΙΤΑΡΟΥΧΙ Gell.ᵛ   4 ΛΑΛΕΠΟΝ Gell.ᵛ

C18. Adespota comica fr. 1063. 1–34, from an unidentified play

col. i
(Α.) . . . πε]πιστευκώς. (Με.) βάδιζε μὴ δεδοικὼς μηδὲ ἕν.
. . . . .]ει μὲν ἔνδον ἐστίν· ὥστ᾽ ἔγειρ᾽, ἔγειρε δὴ
νῦν σε]αυτὸν μὴ παρέργως. νῦν ἀνὴρ γενοῦ, Μέγα.
μὴ ᾽γκ]αταλίπηις Μοσχίωνα. βούλομαι, νὴ τοὺς θεούς,
βούλομ᾽,] ἀλλ᾽ ἀπροσδοκήτως εἰς κλύδωνα πραγμάτων   5
ἐμπε]σὼν ἠγωνίακα καὶ πάλαι ταράττομαι
μή πο]θ᾽ ἡ Τύχη λάβηι μου τὴν ἐναντίαν κρίσιν.
δειλὸ]ς εἶ, νὴ τὴν Ἀθηνᾶν, δειλὸς εἶ· βλέπω· σύ γε
τὸν π]όνον φεύγων προσάπτεις τῆι Τύχηι τὴν αἰτίαν.
τοῖς π]λέουσιν (οὐ θεωρεῖς;) πολλάκις τὰ δυσχερῆ   10
ἀντίκει]ται πάντα· χειμὼν πνεῦμ᾽ ὕδωρ τρικυμία
ἀστραπ]αὶ χάλαζα βρονταὶ ναυτίαι σύναγ[μα] νύξ.
ἀλλ᾽ ὅμω]ς ἕκαστος αὐτῶν προσμένει τὴν ἐλπίδα
καὶ τὸ μέ]λλον οὐκ ἀπέγνω· τῶν κάλων τις ἥψατο
. . . .] . ἐσκέψαθ᾽· ἕτερος τοῖς Σαμόθραιξιν εὔχετα[ι   15
τῶι κυβερνή]τηι βοη[θεῖν], τοὺς πόδας προσέλκεται
(three badly damaged lines containing only scattered letters follow)

col. ii

..........]εις ἅπασιν εὐγενῶς προθυμ[ία]ν   20
..........]ορῶ γὰρ τουτονὶ τὸν δεσπότη[ν
....]γ[.....]νον μετ᾽ αὐτοῦ. θᾶττον εἴσειμ᾽ ἐνθάδε
παρα]φ[ανήσ]ομαί τε τούτοις καιρὸν εὐφυῆ λαβών.
(Β.) ἐγὼ μὲν ὕβρισμαι, Λάχης, ὡς οὐδὲ εἷς
ἄνθρωπος ἕτερος πώποθ᾽, ὕβρικας δέ με   25
σὺ δεῦρο πέμψας. (Λα.) μὴ λέγ᾽ οὕτως. (Β.) Ἡρά[κ]λεις.
ἐγὼ δὲ πῶς σχοίην ἂν ἑτέρως; πολλάκ[ι]ς
ἔλεγον ἐκεῖ σοι· "ποῖ με πέμπεις—" (Λα.) καὶ μάλα.
(Β.) "υἱῶι φέροντα περὶ γάμου καὶ θυγατέρα
δώσοντ᾽; ἐὰν δὲ μὴ προσέχηι μοι, πῶς ἐγὼ   30
ἀναγκάσω σου μὴ παρόντος λαμβάνειν;"
.]...δε[.]σει πραγμάτων κατήκοος
         ]μψεθ᾽ ἡ μήτηρ [
         ]ἐπείσθη μοι λέ[γειν
(two badly damaged lines containing only scattered letters follow)

5 βούλομ᾽,] Maas   13 [ἀλλ᾽ ὅμω]ς Maas   16 [τῶι κυβερνή]τηι Wilamowitz
23 [παρα]φ[ανήσο]μαί Körte

COMMENTARY

C1–C13. For 'Middle Comedy', see Introduction, pp. 22–6; Webster (1970), 10–97: Nesselrath (1990); Rothwell, in Dobrov 99–118.

C1–C2. Fragments of 'Middle Comic' prologues; see also Antiph. fr. 166; and cf. **G6** introductory n.

C1. Perhaps from Philiscus' *Birth Of Zeus* (of which nothing else except the title survives); see Nesselrath 229–33, and in Dobrov 1–27, esp. 22–6. The goddess Rhea is speaking. The story she tells is adapted from Hes. *Th.* 453–67 (the beginning of the struggle between the Titans and the Olympians), which ends with the observation that 'Rhea was gripped by unforgettable pain'; cf. in general Gantz 41–4. For mythological parody as a common type of 'Middle Comic' plot, see **C3–C6** n. For other echoes of Hesiod in comedy, e.g. **H20** with introductory n.; Cratin. fr. 349 (~ Hes. *Op.* 299–300); Ar. fr. 239 (cf. Hes. fr. 284); adesp. com. fr. 1086. 9–10 (cf. Hes. *Op.* 765–828); and cf. **E12–E13**; **F13**. 3 with n.; **G3**. 5; Ar. *Av.* 693–702 (the Birds' theogony).
    Preserved in PSI 1175 (first century AD).
    Iambic trimeter.

1–2. *τί οὖν ἐμοὶ τῶν σ[ῶν μέ]λει;:* 'Why then should *I* be concerned about *your* affairs?'; what preceded must have been a general complaint giving rise to this hypothetical response from a member of the audience (*τις . . . | ὑμῶν*; cf. **C2**. 4–5 n.). Cf. **D12**. 10 *τί δέ σοι μέλει;*

3. *πέπονθα δεινά:* a quotation of S. *OC* 892 (401 BC, a posthumous performance; Oedipus denounces Creon to Theseus) 'I have suffered terrible things at this man's hands just now'. For the reception of Sophocles in comedy, see **D8–D10** n.

4. *ἐκπίνει* and *κατεσθίει* ('gulps down' and 'gobbles up') are undignified verbs (cf. **A13**. 7 n.), and cast Cronus as a glutton from the very first; cf. 7 with n., 14 with n.

6. *ἔρδει χειρί:* 'produces (a gesture) with his hand', i.e. 'gives me the finger'; cf. **J14**. 2 n.   *Μεγαράδ(ε):* Megara is located at the north-east end of the Isthmus of Corinth, about 20 miles from Athens as the crow flies; Cronus (implicitly presented as residing in Athens) perhaps chooses it as the place to sell his children simply because it is close, convenient, and 'other'.

7. *τοῦτο πωλῶν ἐσθίει:* a rationalization of the myth presented in a more traditional form in 3–4: Cronus does not swallow the children themselves, as Hesiod would have it, but sells them and uses the money to buy food, which he eats. Cf. 9–14 n.

8.   Immisch suggested ὥσπερ κύν[α λάγως], 'in the same way a hare fears a dog'.

9–14.   The humour depends on χράω being used in two different senses, 'give an oracle' and 'lend', and the effect is to reduce a grand cosmic conflict to a petty domestic quarrel over a trivial sum of money. Hesiod (*Th.* 463–4) reports that Earth and Sky told Cronus 'that it was fated he be subdued by his son', which need not mean that they gave him an oracle but could easily be taken that way. After δέδοικε γὰρ τὸν χρησμόν in 8, ἔχρησε γὰρ Κρόνωι ποτ(ε) Ἀπόλλων in 9 is most naturally taken 'for Apollo'— appropriately, as god of prophecy, although, strictly speaking, he ought not to have been born yet; cf. the similarly anachronistic oath by Zeus in 12—'once gave an oracle to Cronus'. But accusative δραχ[μήν] at the end of the line requires that the verb be understood in retrospect 'loaned', as κα(ὶ ε)ἶτ(α) οὐκ ἀπέλαβε ('and then he didn't get it back') in 10 makes clear. The same sense is required for the verb in 11–12 (where the internal object χρείαν must be supplied with ἑτέραν: 'he no longer made him another (loan) with any monetary value, (and he loaned him) no household items, by Zeus, and no money'). But in 13 the reference is unmistakably to the content of an oracle.

10.   οὐκ ἀπέλαβε: an unsurprising result, given Cronus' profligate tendencies (7).   ταῦτα . . . θυμὸν πνέ[ων]: 'breathing wrath as regards these things', i.e. 'very angry about these events'. A momentary irruption of high poetic style (see Taillardat § 123), abruptly deflated by the prosaic content of 11–12.

12.   σκευάρια: see B32. 5 n. For lending household items to friends and neighbours (common practice), see Olson on Ar. *Pax* 261.   μά + accusative: 'no, by . . .' (e.g. C15. 2; C16. 13).

14.   Resumes the story in 3–13 (with specific echoes of 4 and 8) and sets the stage for the next element in Rhea's story (presumably the birth of Zeus and her plan to conceal him and offer Cronus something—or someone— else in his place; cf. Hes. *Th.* 468–91).   πάντα καταπί[νει τέκνα]: 'he swallows down all his children'; cf. Hes. *Th.* 459 τοὺς μὲν κατέπινε, 467 παῖδας ἑοὺς κατέπινε, 473 παίδων <θ' > οὓς κατέπινε (all of Cronus); Orph. 200 F; Pl. *Euthphr.* 6a.

C2. From an allegorical play about contemporary political events. The speaker is most likely a divinity (cf. **C1**; **C14** introductory n.), and has already completed the first part of his or her exposition. The tribute collected from the cities has abruptly been lifted (10–11), which is to say that the dominant military power in the Greek world has been broken, and the result has been a series of extended quarrels among the individual states about how they ought to be governed (15–18). Breitenbach dated the fragment to after the Battle of Chaeronea in 338, when Athens and Thebes were crushed by Philip of Macedon, while Wilamowitz put it sometime around the beginning of the Second Athenian League in 379/8; Heniochus himself is known only to have been a 'Middle Comic' poet (*Suda* η 392 = Henioch. test. i). The members of the chorus had individual identities (1–2), as apparently in Eupolis' *Cities* (cf. **B27–B29** n.) and possibly Aristophanes' *Islands* (**B26** with n.), and were perhaps divided into opposed hemichoruses of democratic and aristocratic states (cf. **E23** introductory n.). For political content in 'Middle Comedy', see **E29** introductory n. (also from an allegorical play); Webster (1970) 24–34, 37–50.

Preserved at Stobaeus iv. 1. 27 (manuscript S only), under the heading 'Concerning government'.

Iambic trimeter.

1. **τὸ . . . κατ(ὰ) ἑκάστην**: 'on an individual basis, one by one'. For this use of κατά + accusative, see **B39**. 1 n.   **αὐτίκα**: 'in a moment'.

3. **νῦν . . . πολὺν ἤδη χρόνον** ('now . . . for a long time') + present **ἀνοηταίνουσι** ('are confused, are acting foolishly') is equivalent to a present and a perfect combined (Goodwin § 26); cf. **C11**. 2–3 ἤδη πάλαι | . . . καλοῦμαι; **C18**. 6 πάλαι ταράττομαι; **D12**. 2; **I6**. 1–2.

4–8. A digression; the speaker returns to a description of the cities (cf. 1–3) in 9.

4–5. **ὑποκρούσειεν . . . | . . . κ(αὶ) ἀνέροιτο**: 'might interrupt and ask', i.e. 'to ask'. For the idea, cf. **B41**; **C1**. 1–2; Ar. *Pax* 43–5 (a member of the audience is imagined interrupting the prologue to ask what is 'really' happening on stage); Timocl. Com. fr. 19. 6–7 (spectators likely to whistle or hiss in derision at a weak joke; cf. **D6**. 22 with n.).   **ὅ τι . . . | νῦν εἰσι**: literally 'what (the things you see before you) here now are', i.e. 'what you are supposed to be seeing'. For **ποτ(ε)** used to add emphasis, e.g. **C18**. 7; **E14**. 1; **F6**. 18.

6. **τὸ χωρίον . . . τόδ(ε)**: i.e. the theatrical space generally.   **κύκλωι** is adverbial, 'round about'.

7–8. i.e. 'and as for the **σκηνή** over there, you should imagine you're seeing a **σκηνὴ . . . θεωρική**'; cf. Men. *Dysc.* 1 τῆς Ἀττικῆς νομίζετ' εἶναι τὸν τόπον ('Imagine that the setting is in Attica'). The **σκηνή** the audience can see is the permanent stage-building, in front of which the action of the play takes place. But they are to take it for an actual 'tent' of the sort erected and inhabited—and doubtless used for entertaining—by the

official representatives (θεωροί) of Athens and presumably other cities as
well at the Olympic Games (see And. 4. 30).

9.   εἰέν: 'Alright!', indicating that the speaker is ready to move on to another
point (cf. 4–8 n.). A colloquial interjection, attested elsewhere in comedy at
e.g. **C8.** 8 (where the sense is slightly different); Ar. *Eq.* 1077; Eup. fr. 385. 5;
Eub. fr. 2. 1; see Stevens 34; Labiano Ilundain 152–4.

10.   ἐλευθέρι(α) . . . θύσουσαι: 'in order to make thanksgiving offerings for
their liberation'.   ποτε is correlative with ὅτε at the beginning of 11
('at the time when').

11.   σχεδόν modifies ἐλεύθεραι, 'almost free, about to be freed'. The point is
that only after the sacrifices are complete will the cities be finally and
formally free.

12.   ἀπ' ἐκείνης τῆς θυσίας: 'after that sacrifice', i.e. once they were defini-
tively free and the fact had been publicly recognized.

12–13.   αὐτάς is the object of both διέφθορεν and ξενίζουσ(α).
ξενίζουσ(α): i.e. in her tent, which must be the σκηνὴ θεωρική represented by the stage-building (7–8 n.).   ἡμέραν ἐξ ἡμέρας: 'from one
day to the next,' i.e. 'day after day'.

14.   Ἀβουλία: probably 'Ms Irresolution' rather than 'Ms Folly', since the
point of 15–18 is that the cities are unable to decide which form of
government to adopt. Ἀβουλία must have been a character in the play,
along with Ms Democracy and Ms Aristocracy (16–17).   κατέχουσα
πολὺν ἤδη χρόνον ('keeping (them) spellbound for a long time now', echoing 3) amounts to an emphatic reiteration of ξενίζουσ(α) ἡμέραν ἐξ ἡμέρας
in 13.

16–17.   θατέραι = τῆι ἑτέραι.

17.   τῆι δ(ὲ) Ἀριστοκρατία θατέραι: 'and for her, that is the other of the two,
Ms Aristocracy'.

18.   διὰ ἅς: both 'on whose account' and 'by whose agency'.
πεπαρωινήκασιν: '(the cities) have got drunk and acted badly' (< παροινέω;
cf. **C11.** 4; Ar. *Ec.* 143; Amphis fr. 29; Alex. fr. 160. 6), i.e. 'have quarrelled
and fought'. For the comic trope that women are habitual drunks, see **H10**
introductory n.

C3–C6. Mythological parody in which gods and heroes were represented
acting like average Athenians was common in Attic comedy in the first half
of the fourth century; cf. **C1**; **C8**; **G2–G3**; **H18–H19**; **J13**; and see Nesselrath
188–241.

C3. Cephalus had an extraordinary hunting dog that no animal could escape,
which is presumably the creature being pampered here. Cephalus' wife Procris
(a daughter of King Erechtheus of Athens) became suspicious of his frequent

absences to hunt, with disastrous results; and she may well be Speaker B, who overhears Cephalus giving orders to the household's slaves. For Cephalus and Procris (probably also the subject of Philetaerus' *Cephalus*), see Pherecyd. *FGrHist* 3 F 34; [Apollod.] *Bib.* iii. 15. 1; Ov. *Met.* 7. 672–862; Gantz 245–6 (but without reference to the comic evidence). For Eubulus' play, see Nesselrath 221–3.

Preserved at Athenaeus 12. 553b (manuscript A only), as an example of the Athenians' fondness for having their feet rubbed with perfumed oil (see 5–6 n.).

Iambic trimeter.

1.   **οὔκουν ὑποστορεῖτε μαλακῶς;:** 'Spread a soft bed!', with more specific directions given in 2–3; cf. **A13.** 14 n. For **οὔκουν;** + future as equivalent to an imperative, see **B32.** 10 n.
2–3.   **τῶν Μιλησίων | ἐρίων:** '(one) of our Milesian wool blankets', Milesian wool being famously soft; cf. Ar. *Lys.* 729; *Ra.* 543a; Amphis fr. 27. 1; Gow on Theoc. 15. 126–7.
3.   **ξυστίδα:** a fancy, saffron-dyed *himation* of a type worn by well-dressed women and tragic kings, but also used to cover a bed at Eub. fr. 132. Cf. Cratin. fr. 294; Ar. *Nu.* 70 with Σ^RVEN; *Lys.* 1189–90; fr. 332. 7.
4.   **Ἄπολλον** expresses shock; see **B12.** 1 n.
4–5.   **χόνδρον:** 'wheat-pudding'; elsewhere treated as a delicacy (see **H4.** 1 n.) and here made even more special by being mixed with the impossible luxury **γάλακτι χηνός** ('goose milk'; cf. 'bird milk' at e.g. Ar. *Av.* 734; Eup. fr. 411 with K–A ad loc.).
5.   **Ἡράκλεις:** see **A22.** 1 n.
5–6.   For having one's feet massaged with perfume (cf. **H1.** 6 n.) as a sign of luxury, e.g. Cephisod. fr. 3; Anaxandr. fr. 41; Eub. fr. 107; Antiph. fr. 105. 2–3.
6.   **τῶι Μεγαλλείωι μύρωι:** for 'Megalleian' perfume (supposedly named after the man who first produced it), see Ar. fr. 549; Stratt. fr. 34. 1–3; Anaxandr. fr. 47; Amphis fr. 27. 2; Thphr. *Od.* 29.

C4–C5. For the reception of Homer in comedy, see **A6–A11** (Epicharmus); **D1–D4** with nn. Comedies entitled *Circe* were also composed by the 'Middle Comic' poet Ephippus (fr. 11) and the Sicilian playwright Dinolochus (test. 3. 3).

C4. An adaptation of Eurylochus' warning at H. *Od.* 10. 432–3 to the other members of Odysseus' crew about the danger posed by Circe: 'She will make you all into pigs, wolves, or lions!'

Preserved at Athenaeus 9. 374e–f, as an example of the word δέλφαξ treated as masculine.

1 D – e – D; 2 4cr; 3 ∪ – ∪.

1.   **ὀρειονόμους** ('mountain-ranging') and **ὑλιβάτας** ('mud-treading', < ὗλις? (thus LSJ); attested elsewhere only at **C6**. 3, where emendation should perhaps be considered) are examples of high-style, 'dithyrambic' vocabulary of a sort typical of 'Middle Comedy'; cf. 2 n.; **C10** with nn.; **G2**. 3–6; Nesselrath 241–66.

2.   **ἀγρώστας**: another high-style word (e.g. S. fr. 94; E. *HF* 377 (lyric)).

C5. Either a complaint by someone who has been transformed into a pig or a warning about the consequences of letting this happen.

    Preserved at Athenaeus 3. 95b, in a catalogue of comic references to pigs' feet, ears, and snouts.

    Glyconics.

1.   **δεινόν**: 'it's a terrible thing . . .'

2.   **ῥύγχος**: 'snout'.   **κνησιᾶν**: 'to have an itch, need to scratch'; but the verb can also mean 'feel sexual desire' (Ar. *Ec.* 919), which might be appropriate in a story involving Circe and Odysseus (cf. H. *Od.* 10. 333–47).

C6. The love-smitten Cyclops lists the products of the mainland he will furnish for the wedding banquet, if the sea-nymph Galateia will have him as her lover; fr. 130 (different types of fish, presumably to be supplied by Galateia from her own realm) probably comes from earlier in the speech. What the Cyclops offers are mostly herd-animals (3–6) and cheese (7–9), and his concern with exactly which animals will be castrated and which will not (4–5) and the painfully extended catalogue of all the different styles of cheese he has available (7–9) combine to characterize him as a hopelessly unreflective bumpkin who has no chance of getting the girl he wants. For Polyphemus and Galateia, cf. Philox. Cyth. *PMG* 815–24 (parodied at Ar. *Pl.* 290–5); Nicoch. *Galateia* (frr. 3–6); Alex. *Galateia* (frr. 37–40) with Arnott ad loc.; Gow on Theoc. 6.

    Preserved at Athenaeus 9. 402e, as an example of a dinner that is more pleasant to hear described than it would be to eat, and quoted from there by Eustathius (see 3 n.).

    Anapaestic dimeter (common in 'Middle Comic' lists of this sort; cf. **G13**; **J2**; Anaxandr. fr. 42; Eub. fr. 63; Ephipp. frr. 12–13; Mnesim. fr. 4; Nesselrath 267–80, esp. 272–4).

1–2.   **τῶν χερσαίων δ(ὲ) . . . | παρ(ὰ) ἐμοῦ**: in contrast to the seafood Galateia will provide (fr. 130).   **ἥξει**: cf. **C10**. 2; **H4**. 1 n.

3.   **τράγος ὑλιβάτης**: 'a mud-treading he-goat' (see **C4**. 1 n.). But perhaps Eustathius' ἠλιβάτης ('high-walking', i.e. 'cliff-walking'; not attested

elsewhere, although ἠλίβατος ('high, steep') is common poetic vocabulary) should be printed.

4. **αἶξ οὐρανία**: 'a heavenly she-goat', with a glancing allusion to the story of how Amaltheia nourished the infant Zeus on the milk of a she-goat, whose broken horn (our 'Cornucopia') furnished food and drink of every sort (e.g. Cratin. fr. 261 with K–A ad loc.; adesp. com. fr. 708; Anacr. *PMG* 361. 1–2; Pherecyd. *FGrHist* 3 F 42; cf. Gantz 41–2; Bernabé on Orph. 209 F).

4–5. **τομίας** and **ἐκτομίας** (< τέμνω) both mean 'castrated'.

6. **δέλφαξ**: a full-grown pig, as opposed to a χοῖρος ('piglet'); cf. **A7**. 1; Schaps, *JHS* 116 (1996), 169–71.   **δασύπους**: 'hare'; see **G5**. 9 n. **ἔριφοι**: 'kids'; see **G10**. 6–7 n.

7–9.   Cheese was simple, inexpensive food; cf. **G16**. 3 with n. For cheese-making technology, see Olson on Ar. *Pax* 368. For the Homeric Cyclops making cheese, see *Od.* 9. 219, 232; and cf. **D1**. 9 n. **τυρὸς χλωρός** is cheese that has been set out in baskets to dry but from which whey is still draining, as opposed to **τυρὸς ξηρός** ('dry cheese'), on the one hand, and **τυρὸς πηκτός** (cottage cheese or the like; see Gow on Theoc. 11. 20), on the other. **τυρὸς κοπτός** is cheese that has been chopped up into small pieces; **τυρὸς ξυστός** is grated cheese; and **τυρὸς τμητός** is cheese cut into slabs or slices.

C7–C13. Some standard 'Middle Comic' types (most also found in 'New Comedy'). For another stock character (the courtesan), see **I11** introductory n.

C7–C8. Outspoken and occasionally disrespectful slaves appear in Aristophanes' *Frogs* (Xanthias; 405 BC; and cf. *Ra.* 12–15 with Dover on 15) and *Wealth* (Cario; 388 BC), and gradually become stock 'Middle Comic' characters. Cf. **F7**; **F19**; **G5**; **J4**; Antiph. fr. 69; Eub. fr. 123; Alex. fr. 125; Nesselrath 283–96. For slaves and slaveholding generally, Ehrenberg 165–91 (with particular attention to 'Old Comedy'); M. I. Finley, *Ancient Slavery and Modern Ideology* (London, 1980); V. Hunter, *Policing Athens: Social Control in the Attic Lawsuits, 420–320 B.C.* (Princeton, 1994).

C7. The speech partially preserved here is intended to amuse rather than to evoke pity, and the audience likely wasted little sympathy on the resentment expressed by the speaker (esp. 1–2, 7), who might easily be the 'difficult to sell' title-character of the play. But it is hard to escape the sense that his words capture some of what many real slaves thought on a daily basis; that slaves routinely ate more poorly than their masters, and that some of them responded by stealing food when opportunity arose (as the speaker of this fragment seems oddly disinclined to do) is beyond doubt. Cf. **G12**. 10; Ar. *Pax* 13–14 with Olson ad loc.; Anaxandr. fr. 58 (Zeus' servant Ganymede speaks as if he were an ordinary domestic slave stealing some of the food he prepares for his masters).

Antiphanes fr. 89 is identical to 4 ὁρᾶν–9. But which poet borrowed from the other is impossible to say; cf. **B42** introductory n.

Preserved at Athenaeus 6. 262d, near the beginning of a long discussion of slaves, with specific reference to their self-control when they serve food they are not allowed to eat.

Iambic trimeter.

2. **"παῖ παῖ" καλεῖσθαι:** 'to be summoned (with the cry) "Boy! Boy!"' The vocative παῖ (often repeated, as here, to add emphasis) is used routinely in comedy when a free character summons a slave or gives him orders (e.g. Ar. *Ach.* 395 with Olson ad loc.; Eup. fr. 385. 5 (see 4 n.); Alex. fr. 116. 1; Diph. fr. 57. 2). **παρὰ πότον:** 'to where the drinking is going on', i.e. into the room where the symposium is being held, the slaves being expected to stay outside except when serving, cleaning up, or the like, as in **H1**.

3. **καὶ ταῦτ(α):** 'and . . . at that!' **ἀγενείωι μειρακυλλίωι τινί:** dative of advantage, 'for the benefit of some beardless little boy'.

4. What follows continues the imaginary scene described in 1–3 rather than beginning a new one, and Morel's <καί> is therefore better than Porson's <ἤ>. **τὴν ἀμίδα:** 'the piss-pot', an earthenware vessel into which men urinated at drinking parties, saving them the trouble of leaving the room (e.g. Ar. *Th.* 633 with Austin–Olson ad loc.; *Ra.* 544a; Eup. fr. 385. 5 'Who was the first man to say "(Bring me) a piss-pot, boy!" when he was drinking?' (treated as a brilliant discovery); Diph. fr. 42. 34–5). **κείμενα** ('(food) lying there') is to be taken in loose apposition to the nouns in 5.

5. **ἄμητας . . . ὀρνίθειά τε:** 'milk-cakes (see H4. 3 n.) and bird-meat', typical symposium dainties (see H2. 3 n.). **ἡμιβρῶτας** ('half-eaten') agrees with the first noun, but is to be taken with both.

6. **οὐδὲ λειφθέντων:** 'not even if they're abandoned, left over'; the speaker is now thinking not so much of the situation within the dining room (contrast 3–4) as of what goes on outside it after the 'second tables' have been carried out (see H1. 2 n.) and the coast would seem to be clear for the slaves to finish off any food that remains on them (but see 7–8 n.).

7–8. The point of **ὥς φασιν αἱ γυναῖκες** must be that the free female members of the household—who were excluded from the symposium— insist that the first right to any leftover dainties is *theirs* (cf. Men. *Dysc.* 568–70). But the speaker's phrasing leaves it ambiguous whether they get their way, and 8–9 make it clear that the slaves at least occasionally succeed

in stealing some of the food.   **ὃ δὲ κτλ.**: 'and what ... (is that) ...'
χολᾶν ποεῖ: 'makes me crazy (with anger)'; see **D3**. 7 n. Athenaeus' χοααιν
is a nice example of what must originally have been a majuscule error
(*ΧΟΛΑΙΝ* (with an ι wrongly included in the infinitive ending)
mistaken for *ΧΟΑΑΙΝ*).   **γάστριν ... καὶ λαμυρόν**: 'a glutton and
impudent'. γάστρις is a colloquial term of abuse, attested also at Ar. *Av.*
1604; *Th.* 816; Pl. Com. fr. 219; Hes. *Th.* 26 with West ad loc. For λαμυρός,
cf. X. *Smp.* 8. 24.   **ἡμῶν** (sc. τούτου) **ὅς**: 'anyone of us who ...'

C8. Laomedon, the king of Troy, is cross-examining a slave about the abduction (ἁρπαγή) of his son Ganymede; the slave (presumably Ganymede's
παιδαγωγός, 'attendant') first claims to have no idea what his master is
talking about and then refuses to take the threat of punishment seriously. For
the kidnapping of Ganymede, see H. *Il.* 5. 265–6; 20. 231–5; *h.Ven.* 202–17;
E. *Tr.* 820–4; *Cyc.* 582–8; Gantz 557–60 (but without reference to the comic
evidence). Plays entitled *Ganymede* were also written by Alcaeus Comicus
(frr. 2–9) and Eubulus (frr. 16–17), although nothing significant is known
about either, and Ganymede himself seems to have served as the prologue
speaker in an unidentified comedy by Anaxandrides (fr. 58; cf. **C7** introductory n.).

Preserved at Athenaeus 10. 458f–9b (manuscript A only), at the end of a
long discussion of literary riddles and the like that also includes **E7**; **E30**, as
evidence that 'those (at symposia) who failed to solve the riddle put to them
drank saltwater mixed into their wine and were compelled to finish the cup
without taking a breath'.

Iambic trimeter.

1–2. **περιπλοκὰς | λίαν ἐρωτᾷς**: 'You're asking much too complicated
questions'; cf. **D3**. 22 with n. For the disapproving tone of λίαν, see **B4**. 2 n.
2. **ἀλλ(ά)**: 'Well ..., Alright ... '; marking assent to the request for simplicity and straightforwardness implicit in Speaker A's protest (Denniston
17–18).
3. Repeated in slightly modified form in 6, in the slave's quotation of what
he has been asked.
4. **πρὶν κρέμασθαι**: 'before being hung up', sc. to be whipped; cf. 8–9.
4–5. **πότερά μοι | γρῖφον προβάλλεις τοῦτον εἰπεῖν**: 'are you propounding
this to me as a riddle to answer?'; cf. 10–14 with n. For riddles as symposium entertainment, cf. **E7** with introductory n.; Ar. *V.* 20–3; Antiph.
fr. 122. 1–7; Diph. fr. 49; Pl. *R.* 479b; and see Pütz 242–63. For examples of
such riddles preserved in comedy, e.g. **E30**; Antiph. fr. 192; Alex. fr. 242.
6. Cf. 3 with n.
7. **ἢ τί δύναται τὸ ῥηθέν;**: 'or (if not,) what's the point of what you said?'

7–8. ἔξω τις δότω | ἱμάντα ταχέως: Laomedon ignores Speaker A's uncooperative question and addresses himself to the stage-house, from which a mute slave emerges, carrying a whip (cf. 4 with n.). For orders to anonymous slaves expressed as third-person imperatives + τις ('let someone . . . !'), see e.g. Cratin. fr. 271. 2; Ar. *Ach.* 805; and cf. **H1.** 8.

8–10. The slave continues to treat Laomedon's request for information about the abduction of Ganymede as a riddle (cf. 4–6) and therefore insists that he ought to be treated like someone who has failed to answer one correctly.

8. εἰέν: 'alright!' (see **C2.** 9 n.), indicating the slave's recognition that the implication of Laomedon's remark in 7–8 is that he could not solve the riddle and therefore deserves to be punished. οὐκ ἔγνων ἴσως: 'maybe I didn't recognize (the riddle)', i.e. 'solve it'.

9. τοῦτο is an internal accusative with ζημιοῖς, 'exacting this punishment'.

10. ἐχρῆν τι περιφέρειν ποτήριον: 'you should have been passing a cup around' (sc. the circle of couches; cf. **A13.** 14 n.). For the use of ἐχρῆν, see **B32.** 8 n.

12. κομιδῇ is a colloquial Attic intensifier (cf. **D6.** 14; Thesleff § 272; Austin–Olson on Ar. *Th.* 3), to which γε adds further emphasis; 'absolutely!', i.e. 'I certainly do!' ἐνέχυρον ἀποφέροντά <σου>: 'Taking a surety from you!', sc. against the possibility that Laomedon will mistreat him.

13. ὀπίσω τὼ χεῖρε ποιήσαντα: 'putting your hands behind you', meaning that someone else will hold the cup, to prevent the drinker from taking it away from his lips. But the description has a menacing tone, since a captive's hands were bound this way as well (e.g. Ar. *Lys.* 434).

14. ἕλκειν ἀπνευστί: 'to drain it without taking a breath'.

C9–C10. Garrulous, self-congratulatory, and untrustworthy cooks who express themselves in elaborate, riddling words are stock 'Middle Comic' and 'New Comic' characters. Cf. **D3** with introductory n.; **G3** introductory n.; **G8**; **G11–G13**; Anaxandr. fr. 34; Sotad. fr. 1; Euphro fr. 1; Athenio fr. 1; Nesselrath 297–309. According to Aristophanes of Byzantium (fr. 363 Slater ap. Ath. 14. 659a = Dor. com. test. 11. 4–7), a Megarian actor named Maison invented what became the standard comic cook's mask, and characters of this type were called μαίσονες on that account. But Maison is undated, and which Megara he came from is uncertain (Polemon Periegetes (fr. 46 Preller ap. Ath. 14. 659c = Dor. com. test. 11. 8–10; early second century BC) argued that it was Megara Hyblaea in Sicily); and even if Aristophanes is right that Maison invented the cook's mask, the story provides no support for the thesis that comedy was staged in Megara before it was staged in Athens (cf. Introduction, pp. 3–5). See Körte, *RE* xiv. 1 (1928), 609; Breitholtz 87–95; Kerkhof 30–7.

C9. A thievish cook offers last-minute instructions to his pupil and assistant Dromon (1) before the two of them enter their employer's house and get down to business; cf. **G7** introductory n., 7. Euphro fr. 9 is very similar; see also Euphro fr. 1. 13–35; Men. *Asp.* 226–32; adesp. com. frr. 1073; 1093. 221–30.

Preserved at Athenaeus 9. 381c–e (manuscript A only), in a speech full of comic quotations by a cook who cites this passage for the sake of the word ἐξαίρεσις ('offal'; see 12 with n.).

Iambic trimeter.

1. **ἄγε δή**: 'Come on!'; a colloquial form of encouragement.
1–2. **εἴ τι κομψὸν κτλ.**: 'if you know any of your own affairs (to be) subtle (see **B41** introductory n.), wise, or elegant', i.e. 'if you have any subtlety, wisdom, or elegance in you'; ironic preparation for what follows, since what interests the speaker is subtlety in . . . stealing.
3. **τῶι διδασκάλωι**: i.e. the speaker himself, who taught Dromon all the bad tricks he is capable of (19–20). Comic cooks routinely refer to the master with whom they trained or the culinary 'school' to which they belong (e.g. Sosip. fr. 1. 10–19; Euphro fr. 1. 1–15).
5. **εἰς πολεμίαν**: sc. χώραν, 'into enemy territory' (in reference to the house in which they will soon be cooking). Cf. 16 with n.   **κατάτρεχε**: 'lay (it) to waste!'
6. (like the first three words in 9) is equivalent to an 'if'-clause; cf. **D5**. 13–16 n.   **ἀριθμῶι διδόασι**: 'they give the chunks of meat to you by number', i.e. 'they count them as they give them to you' (since no one trusts a cook); cf. 12–13; adesp. com. fr. 1073. 5–6 (a thievish cook is speaking) 'They counted out the chunks of meat to me; I made them smaller, but kept the number the same'.
7–8. **καὶ ζέσας σφόδρα** ('and by stewing them intensely', i.e. for a long time over a hot fire; cf. Thesleff § 120) is actually an explanation of how the chunks of meat are to be rendered **τακερά** ('soft, tender').   **ὡς λέγω σοι** points back to the participial phrases in 7, and the point is that, if meat is stewed long enough and on a hot enough fire, the individual structure of the pieces will break down and it will be impossible to tell if a few have been stolen.   **σύγχεον**: 'confuse, confound'.
9. **ἰχθὺς ἁδρὸς πάρεστι**: see 6 n. ἁδρός is 'big, fat', i.e. large enough to be cut into steaks (10 with n.).   **τὰ (ἐ)ντός**: 'its guts, entrails'; cf. adesp. com. fr. 1073. 10–11 (a thievish cook is speaking) 'I gave (the guests) a fish, but apportioned the entrails to myself.'

10.   **ἂν τέμαχος ἐκκλίνῃς τι**: 'and if you filch a steak' (cognate with τέμνω), i.e. a slab of the fish's body, in addition to its guts (9). For fish steaks, cf. C12. 3; G4. 15 with n.; G10. 6; G13. 2; Olson–Sens on Archestr. fr. 38. 5.

11.   **ὅταν ἔξω δ(έ), ἐμόν**: a nice, rogueish twist: Dromon should not forget who is working for whom, which is to say who is the master thief (cf. 3).

12.   **ἐξαιρέσεις**: 'the offal', i.e. the heart, kidneys, liver, etc., of whatever animals are killed for dinner.   **τ(ὰ) ἄλλα τ(ὰ) ἀκόλουθ(α)**: 'the other items that go along with them', i.e. scraps of all sorts.

12–13.   **ὅσα | κτλ.**: 'however many as by their nature can't be counted or checked' (cf. 7–8 n.) and can thus be stolen easily.

14.   'but have the rank and station of mincemeat, trimmings' (cognate with κόπτω; see Arnott on Alex. fr. 137). Cf. 16–17 n.

15.   **εἰς αὔριον**: 'on the morrow, tomorrow'.

16–17.   **λαφυροπώληι . . . μεταδίδου**: 'give a share to the dealer in plunder' (resuming the image of warfare from 5; cf. 14 τάξιν). That this will assure a 'more friendly passage through the doors' suggests that the reference is to the doorkeeper (cf. B45. 15), who will need to be bribed in order for the operation to go as smoothly as possible, or perhaps the dog. **παντάπασι**: 'by all means'.

18–19.   These lines recall the speaker's initial request at 1–4, as he brings his speech to a conclusion.

20   **δεῦρ(ο)**: i.e. into the house.

C10. A cook (Speaker A) offers a longwinded catalogue of the dinner he proposes to serve to the increasingly aggravated man who has hired him (Speaker B); cf. C7; G10 with introductory n. This is at least the second item in his great 'parade of dishes'.

Preserved at Athenaeus 4. 169e–f, in a catalogue of comic passages that mention cookpots and casserole-dishes of various sorts.

Iambic trimeter.

2.   **ἥξει**: for the image, see C6. 1; H4. 1 n.   **ἰσοτράπεζος**: 'as large as the table', sc. on which it is served; cf. G16. 2 n.

3.   **Καρύστου θρέμμα**: 'spawn of Carystus', the point being that the Euboean city of Carystus exported cooking-ware to Athens; cf. Matro fr. 1. 48–9. Dithyrambic style; cf. C4. 1 n.; Pl. Com. fr. 132; Philyll. fr. 4; Anaxandr. fr. 6; Antiph. fr. 55 (a cook is speaking); Nausicr. fr. 1; Epicr. fr. 7. 3–4. That the vessel is made of baked clay allows it to be described as **γηγενής** ('earthborn'), another 'poetic' word.

4.   **ὕπαγε**: 'Get a move on!', i.e. 'Spit it out!'

4–5.   **κάκκαβον κτλ.**: According to Phot. κ 84, a κάκκαβος (or κακκάβη) was 'a vessel like a λοπάς' (a lidded casserole-dish used for boiling, stewing, and braising; see **G4**. 12 n.) 'having three feet attached to it'. The cook uses the word because it is technically more precise than **λοπάδ(α)**, although the distinction is of no significance for his employer (5–8).

7. **σίττυβον**: an otherwise unattested word, perhaps invented by the speaker (< *σιτέω*) on the model of *κάκκαβος*.

8. Literally 'Except that I know you're talking about a (cooking-)vessel!', i.e. 'All I know is that . . . !'

C11–C12. For the parasite as a stock 'Middle Comic' character, see **A13** introductory n.: and cf. **C12**; **G14**; **G16**; Nesselrath 309–17.

C11. A parasite lists the services (most connected with the symposium or the *κῶμος* that followed; see **H18**. 6–10 with nn.) he can render in return for what he eats and drinks. Cf. Antiph. frr. 80; 193; Axionic. fr. 6; Men. *Dysc.* 58–68. The potential host is referred to in the third person in 1 and may not be on stage.

Preserved at Athenaeus 6. 238b–c, as part of an extended discussion of the history of the institution of parasitism that also includes **A13**; **G14**.

Trochaic tetrameter catalectic.

1. **αὐτῶι προειπεῖν**: 'to tell him'—the man giving the party—'in advance', i.e. before the meal begins.

2. **πάρειμι πρῶτος**: cf. **G15**. 8.   **ἤδη πάλαι**: 'for a long time now'; see 3 n.

3. **Ζωμὸς καλοῦμαι**: 'my nickname has been "Meat-broth"'. The implication is that broth (for which, see **B33**. 8 with n.; **B34**. 4 with n.; **G9**. 1–2 with nn.) was routinely the first thing served at a meal; contrast **J13**. 5. For the perfective use of the present, see **C2**. 3 n. For nicknames, see **J13** with nn.

3–4. **δεῖ κτλ.**, like *προσβαλεῖν κτλ.* in 5 and *ἀναβῆναί τι κτλ.* in 5–6, functions as equivalent to an 'if'-clause; cf. **C5**. 13–16 n.

3. **ἄρασθαι μέσον**: 'to be raised up about the middle', i.e. 'to be grabbed about the waist, lifted off the ground (sc. and carried out of the room)', after he has drunk too much and got out of control; cf. **A13**. 3–4 n.; Antiph. fr. 193. 5 (a parasite is speaking) 'as for picking someone up and carrying him off, I'm a windstorm'. The language is drawn from the wrestling-ring (cf. 4 with n.), where seizing one's opponent this way and throwing him down was a standard winning move; see Olson on Ar. *Ach.* 274–5.

4. **παροινούντων**: for the verb, see **C2**. 18 n.   **παλαιστὴν νόμισον Ἀργεῖόν μ(ε) ὁρᾶν**: 'reckon that you see an Argive wrestler in me!', i.e. 'you'll think I resemble an Argive wrestler' (for whom, see Damag. *HE* 1427; Diotim. *HE* 1764; Theoc. 24. 111–12).

5. **προσβαλεῖν πρὸς οἰκίαν δεῖ**: 'suppose' (see 3–4 n.) 'it's necessary to attack

a house', sc. to get access to an attractive boy or girl who is locked up safe inside. Cf. Antiph. fr. 193. 6 (a parasite is speaking) 'as for prying doors open, I'm an earthquake'.   **κριός**: '(I'm) a battering-ram'. But perhaps the word (like the identities the speaker claims for himself in 6–7) ought to be capitalized ('call me "Ram"'; cf. 3; Simon. *PMG* 507); cf. **J13**. 2–11 (on nicknames).

5–6. **ἀναβῆναί τι πρὸς | κλιμάκιον**: sc. δεῖ, and see 3–4 n.; '(suppose it's necessary) to go upwards on a ladder' (for this use of πρός, see Ar. *Pax* 69–70), sc. to get to a window; cf. **I8**. 10; Trendall #36 (illustrated at Bieber fig. 501).   **Καπανεύς**: one of the Seven Against Thebes, who attempted to scale the city's walls on a ladder but was blasted by Zeus; cf. A. *Th.* 422–56 with Hutchinson ad loc.; S. *Ant.* 131–7; E. *Ph.* 1172–86; Gantz 515–19.

6–7. **ὑπομένειν πληγὰς κτλ.**: probably a reference to the fistfights that routinely accompanied adventures of the sort described in 5–6. Cf. Antiph. fr. 193. 3–4 (a parasite is speaking) 'as for being struck, I'm red-hot iron; as for striking (others), a lightning-bolt'.   **κονδύλους πλάττειν . . . Τελαμών**: 'as for forming knuckles'—i.e. fists—'(I'm) Telamon'. Telamon, king of Salamis and father of the Homeric Ajax, was one of the Argonauts and accompanied Heracles when he sacked Troy and fought against the Amazons (see Gantz 221–5), and the lexicographer Hesychius defines 'Telamonian knuckles' as 'large (and) hard' (τ 394). See also **H15**. 4 n.   **πειρᾶν**: 'making passes at' + accusative. For pederasty, see **B29**. 3 n.   **καπνός**: i.e. because he can get in anywhere, no matter what is done to keep him out; cf. **I8**. 10–12. Or perhaps the point is that the speaker knows how to make convincing promises on which he has no intention of delivering; cf. Ar. *Ra.* 148; Eup. fr. 135.

C12. Speaker A is a devoted glutton and most likely a parasite. Cf. **G17**.
Preserved complete at Athenaeus 1. 5f (manuscripts CE only), in a comment on a story about the notorious glutton Philoxenus preserved by the Stoic philosopher Chrysippus, who reports that Philoxenus practised plunging his hand into hot water and gargling with it in order to be able to get to food before anyone else could touch or swallow it; cf. **G16**. 11 n. (on eating with one's fingers). In addition, the *Suda* (perhaps drawing direct on Athenaeus) preserves 1–3 at ο 1091; τ 599, and 1–2 at ι 93.
Iambic trimeter.

1–3. **δήπουθεν** ('of course'; colloquial Attic) marks this as a response to a question (presumably by Speaker B) about how Speaker A can handle such hot food; see Denniston 267–9.

1. **πρός**: 'against', i.e. 'to deal with'.   **ὑπερβολῆι** is to be taken with **θερμά**, 'extraordinarily hot'.

2. **Ἰδαίους**: 'like Mt Ida' (here most likely a reference to the mountain range in Crete; contrast **B13**. 22), i.e. 'covered in snow' (Thphr. *HP* iv. 1. 3) and thus 'able to endure immense heat'. But there is also a punning allusion to the Idaean Dactyls, small magical creatures who invented ironworking and protected the infant Zeus (e.g. Paus. v. 7. 6).

3. **τὸν λάρυγγ(α) ἥδιστα** (adverbial) **πυριῶ**: 'I take the greatest pleasure in giving my oesophagus (cf. **F13**. 2 n.) a steambath'.   **τεμαχίοις**: an affectionate diminutive < τέμαχος ('steak'; see **C9**. 10 n.).

4. **κάμινος**: '(you're) a kiln!'

C13. For the soldier as a stock 'Middle Comic' character, see **I11**. 4–10 with nn.; Alex. fr. 63 with Arnott ad loc.; Nesselrath 325–9; Kerkhof 162–5.

Speaker B, a braggart, is in the midst of describing his troops' adventures (note plural **διήγετε** in 1) during a war (1–2). *Τύχων* (the alternate title of the play) might be the soldier's name or nickname ('Lucky'). But since Paphos, where Speaker B and his men spent their time (1–3), was one of Aphrodite's most important cult centres, the reference is more likely to the *daimon* by this name that was associated with her (Phot. α 3404, citing Ar. fr. 325). Why Speaker A is so intrigued by the fact that Speaker B spent time in Cyprus (1–3 with 1 n.) is unclear; probably this was part of an elaborate chain of coincidences that bound the plot together. In the fourth century, Cyprus was under Persian authority but was divided into a number of small kingdoms (including Paphos), the most powerful of which was Salamis; see Maier, *CAH* vi² 312–17, 326–36. **E3** is from the same play.

Preserved at Athenaeus 6. 257d–f, in a wandering discussion (much of this portion of which is drawn from the late fourth-century Peripatetic philosopher Clearchus) about flattery and luxury.

Iambic trimeter.

1. **εἰπέ μοι**, like λέγε γάρ in 3, indicates the speaker's impatient interest in the answer to the question he is asking. Cf. **D10**. 1; **H12**. 2.

2. **τὸν πάντ(α)** (sc. χρόνον) **ἕως ἦν ὁ πόλεμος**: '(Yes,) all the (time) the war was going on', i.e. 'Yes, the whole war'.

3. **ἐν τίνι τόπωι μάλιστα;**: 'Where precisely?'   **λέγε γάρ**: see 1 n.; **A20**. 9 n. (for the idiomatic use of γάρ in requests for further information, as again in 7); **D3**. 6 n.

4. **διαφερόντως** modifies **τρυφερόν**, 'pre-eminently luxurious'. Colloquial; see Gow–Page on Philodem. *GPh* 3244.

5–17. Cf. the less extravagant story at Alex. fr. 63 (where the speaker is probably another braggart soldier; see Arnott ad loc.), where scented oil is put on the wings of four pigeons, which fly about the room and sprinkle the guests and the couches with it.

5. **ἄλλως τ' ἄπιστον**: 'and incredible, beyond belief besides'. **ἐρριπίζετο** is < *ῥιπίζω*, 'fan'; cf. 16. For fans (often made of feathers) and fan-bearers as a symbol of Oriental luxury, see E. *Or.* 1426–30; Miller 198–206.

6. **ὑπ(ὸ) ἄλλου δ(ὲ) οὐδενός** ('and by no one else') merely adds emphasis to **ὑπὸ τῶν περιστερῶν** and is thus equivalent in sense to 'I'm not kidding!' *vel sim.* For pigeons (a common domestic animal, but also sacred to Aphrodite), see *Birds* 238–47, esp. 245–6.

7–8.　　For the indirect interrogative **ὅπως;** picking up the direct interrogative **πῶς;**, cf. Ar. *Th.* 203 with Austin–Olson ad loc.

7.　　**ἐάσας τ(ὰ) ἄλλα**: 'letting everything else go, ignoring everything else' (sc. having to do with the stay in Paphos).　　　For the use of **γάρ**, see 3 with n.

9.　　**ἐκ τῆς Συρίας ἥκοντι**: for perfumed oil from Syria, see Anaxandr. fr. 42. 36; Theoc. 15. 114 with Gow ad loc.; and cf. **D1**. 13 n. (on Syria as a source of frankincense).

9–11.　　**τοιούτου μύρωι | καρποῦ σύχν(α) οἷον . . . τὰς περιστερὰς | τρώγειν**: 'with perfume scented with the sort of fruit that pigeons often eat'. For the use of perfume at banquets, see **H1**. 6 n.

12.　　The point of **οἷαι . . . ἦσαν ἐπικαθιζάνειν** is not that the pigeons were *capable* of landing on the king's head (on which the oil was poured; cf. Ar. *Ec.* 1117), but that they were close enough to do so, had they not been constantly warded off by the king's slaves (13–14).

14.　　**ἐσόβουν** is < *σοβέω*, 'shoo away'.

14–15.　　**ἀπαίρουσαι δὲ κτλ.**: 'and departing a bit, not a lot, from neither altogether in that direction nor in this one', i.e. 'and staying just a bit away from him, not too far in either direction'. But this is difficult sense, and the verses may be corrupt.

16.　　**ἀνερρίπιζον**: 'they fanned up (the air)'; cf. 5 n.

16–17.　　**ὥστε σύμμετρον | κτλ.**: 'so as to make the breeze the same size as him (and) not too strong', i.e. so that the cloud of scent entirely surrounded him but went no further and was not overpowering.

C14–C18. For 'New Comedy', see Introduction, pp. 22–6; Webster (1970), 98–252; W. G. Arnott, *Menander*, i (Loeb Classical Library 132: Cambridge, Mass., 1979), pp. xxx–xlv (on Menander).

C14–C15. Fragments of 'New Comic' prologues; see also **D7**; Men. fr. 129; adesp. com. fr. 1008.

C14. The speaker (a deity who most likely plays no further part in the action, like *Τύχη* in Menander's *The Shield*, Pan in Menander's *The Difficult Man*, and Dionysus (?) in adesp. com. fr. 1008; cf. **C2** introductory n.) explains how he knows the information he will offer the audience about the other characters in the play and the—doubtless complicated and confused—situation into which they have got themselves. The mention of Athens in 5 proves only that the play is being performed there. But the most natural interpretation of the verse is that the action is set either in Athens or in Patras or Sicily, and that the other two places are part of the background story.

Preserved entire at Stobaeus (1) i. 1. 32, under the heading 'That god (is) creator of everything that exists and manages the universe with reason born of foreknowledge, and of what substance he is'; (2) i. 10. 10, under the heading 'Concerning the beginnings and constituent elements of the whole'. In addition, 1–4 are cited in *scholia* on Aratus 1 and on Germanicus Caesar's translation of Aratus; and 4 is cited at *EM*, p. 389. 38–9 (but attributed there to Plato Comicus).

Iambic trimeter.

1–3. The relative clause in 1–2 is typical of hymnic style, as is the specification in 3 of an alternative name for the deity; cf. 5–7 n.; Austin–Olson on Ar. *Th.* 316. But putting the description of the god first adds a playful touch, by transforming the first two verses into a riddle, with the answer given at the beginning of the third. The specification that Aêr is well aware of both the good and the evil men does strongly suggest that someone in the play is responsible for some sort of crime, for which satisfaction will be given in the end.

3. *Ἀήρ* is the moist 'Lower Air', as opposed to the fiery 'Upper Air' (*Αἰθήρ*), which is referred to as a cosmogonic deity very early on (e.g. Orph. 1 B 12 (p. 11. 10); Musae. 2 B 14) and is identified with Zeus at e.g. E. frr. 877; 941. *Ἀήρ* is a Zeus-like god also in Philemon's contemporary Diphilus (fr. 125. 6–7), which may suggest that the distinction between the Upper and the Lower Air was breaking down in the popular mind in this period. But the more significant point is that only the Lower Air can be 'in' all the places listed in 5–7.

4. *ὃ θεοῦ (ἐ)στιν ἔργον*: 'which is a god's deed', i.e. '—something (only) a god is capable of—'; in apposition to the rest of the verse.

5–7. A list of places where the god might be found is another typical hymnic feature (cf. 1–3 n.), trivialized to good comic effect in 6–7 in 'in every house, in all of you' (*bathos*).

5. *ἐν Πάτραις, ἐν Σικελίαι*: Patras was a port in western Achaea just outside the Gulf of Corinth, and is thus a logical mid-point for a story involving events in both Sicily and Athens (see introductory n.).

8.　ὁ δὲ παρὼν ἁπανταχοῦ echoes ἐγὼ δ᾽ . . . εἰμὶ πανταχοῦ in 4 after the digression in 5–8 Ἀήρ.

9.　πάντ(α) picks up on ἁπανταχοῦ in 8 and converts the preceding discussion into evidence in favour of the assertion made in 1–2: someone who is everywhere naturally knows everything—and can thus introduce a complicated story of this sort.

C15. The names of five characters (Lysippus, Cantharus, Gorgias, Philinus, and a slave-woman) are listed on the top right-hand side of the page, and the names of others (all lost except Cratinus) seem to have been given on the left. In the centre are traces of what might easily be Μενάνδρου, which will then have been followed by the title (now almost entirely lost, except for a single *sigma*; Austin, *CR* NS 17 (1967), 134, suggests restoring Ἄπιστος, *The Suspicious Man*). Most likely this is the beginning of the play. The appeal to Νύξ to serve as witness in 4–5 and the need for a lamp at 28 suggest that the action takes place at night. The beginning of Menander's *The Man Who Was Hated* is similar; cf. Men. fr. 129; Austin–Olson on Ar. *Th.* 1065–9a (on plays beginning as dawn is about to break).

A young man (Speaker A) is on stage, complaining about his troubles (1–2) and in particular his relationship with his wife. The marriage was apparently arranged rather than a love-match (3; see **C18** introductory n.). But he has been faithful to her (4–7) and had come to love her, thinking that she loved him back (9–12). Something went terribly wrong, however, and his insistence on his own sexual fidelity (6–7) and his pointed initial observation that he has been married only four months (3) combine to suggest that she has given (or is about to give) birth to a child which, he is sure, cannot be his; the situation at the beginning of Menander's *Men at Arbitration* seems to have been similar. The young man's soliloquy is interrupted by the arrival on stage of a slave-woman (Speaker B), who is bringing him a series of objects (apparently household property) that cause him grief when he looks at them (13–14). The obvious conclusion is that these are items his wife left behind when she fled the house (or he expelled her) and which he is now rummaging through before discarding, on the chance that they might contain something 'useful' (23–4). What the slave-woman (Speaker B) has brought him now, at any rate, is a jar or the like, which appears to have belonged first to his mother and then his wife (19–21), and is sealed closed with an impression from a woman's ring (21–2).

After she opens the jar, the slave-woman reports that it contains items that, the young man quickly realizes, must be tokens of a long-ago birth (24–7). One object is inscribed (29–31); and although the text is badly damaged at this point, it seems clear that the slave-woman is alarmed at the sight of it and does her best to keep the young man from examining it. He does not insist, and instead decides to seal the jar up again: he has enough trouble, and the secrets the jar contains are—so he thinks—none of his business (33–7). But Menander (or whoever the poet was) would scarcely have had a set of birth-tokens brought onstage at the beginning of a play, ostentatiously ignored, and then carefully sealed up again, except in order that the jar that contained them could be brought back at the end of the play in order to establish the identity of an abandoned baby—perhaps the young man himself. Cf. **C16–C17** n. Doubtless the young man is also the father of his wife's child, having got her pregnant in a brief, anonymous premarital encounter. This in turn may explain the hesitation about getting married that he hints at in 3: his concern for the anonymous girl made him reluctant to commit himself to someone else, but rather than tell his father the story, he gave in and took a wife.

Adesp. com. frr. 1085 and 1122 may belong to the same play. See Webster, *CR* NS 2 (1952), 57–8; NS 3 (1953), 237–40; Barns and Lloyd-Jones, *JHS* 84 (1964), 21–34 (reprinted in *The Academic Papers of Sir Hugh Lloyd-Jones*, ii (Oxford, 1990), 94–114); *CGFPR* # 240; W. G. Arnott, *Menander*, iii (Loeb Classical Library 460: Cambridge, Mass. and London, 2000), 505–27; Handley, *ZPE* 155 (2006), 23–5.

Preserved in PAnt. 15 (two sides of a badly damaged page from a codex dating to the third or fourth century AD); only the most substantial and significant conjectures and corrections are recorded in my apparatus. At least a dozen lines have been lost between the bottom of the recto and the top of the verso, so that the continuous numbering is somewhat misleading.

Iambic trimeter.

1–2. τῶν ἐν τῆι πόλει is to be taken with τις, ἐμοῦ with δεινότ[ερ]α ('more terrible than I have').

2. For μ[ά] + accusative, see **C1**. 12 n.

3. The asyndeton (lack of a connective particle) adds urgency and excitement.   πεισθεὶς τῶι πατρί: see introductory n. Most likely the old man appeared on stage later in the play.

4. ὦ δέσποινα Νύξ: see introductory n., and cf. the similar appeal at Asclep. *HE* 866. For Night as all-knowing, cf. Orph. 113. 2 F.

5. μά[ρτυρ(α) ὀ]ρθήν: 'as an upright, honest witness'.   οὗ λέγω λόγου: i.e. λόγου ὃν λέγω, 'of the story I am telling'; the relative pronoun has been attracted into the case of the antecedent.

10. ἤρων is < ἐράω, and δίκαιον is an internal accusative, 'I felt a just (love)', with this remark (along with whatever is lost in the second half of the line) explained in 11–12.

11–12. αὐτῆς ἐλευθέρωι ... ἤθει καὶ βίωι δεθεὶς | ἀπλάστωι: 'I was enchanted by her straightforward manner and honest way of living', a characterization—implicitly rejected here—that must have been vindicated at the end of the play.

12. τὴν φ[ι]λοῦσαν ἠγάπ[ων]: 'I grew fond of her, who showed affection for me', i.e. 'and she seemed to love me back'.

13–15. Addressed to the slave-woman, who has just entered carrying a jar or the like and a lamp (28).

13. κατ(ὰ) ἕν: 'individually, one by one'; see **B17.** 1 n.

16. ἵν(α) ἦι: the beginning of an answer to the question posed in 13.

19–22. The assignment of these verses is difficult; but if the supplements are correct, the young man speaks 19 and the slave-woman probably speaks 20–2.

21–2. ὁ δακτύλιος [...] ἐκείνης: 'her signet ring', which was used to seal the jar closed.   ]βεβλητ[above is probably a form of ἐπιβάλλω, the *vox propria* for 'applying' seals. Cf. Austin–Olson on Ar. *Th.* 415, 424–6.

24. αἶ: 'Oh!, Aah!'; an inarticulate cry of astonishment and surprise, as the slave-woman sees what is in the jar she has just opened up. Cf. Labiano Ilundain 69–77.   χλαμύδο[s] ἥμισυ: 'half of a *chlamys*' (a fancy woollen outer garment, normally worn by wealthy men; see Stone 169), the other half having been retained by a second party—presumably the father of the child, to whom it had belonged and who left a piece of it with the mother after they had sex (cf. 27 n.).

25–6. διεσπαραγμένης κτλ.: 'torn to shreds (and) old, and nearly eaten up by moths'.

27. περιδέραια καὶ περισκελὶς [μ]ία: 'necklaces and a single ankle-bracelet' (cf. Nicostr. Com. fr. 32. 2), which must be tokens intended to identify the mother (contrast 24 with n.).

28. 'Bring (them) to me, and shine the lamp'—which the slave-woman is apparently holding—'at the same time!'

29. ὠή: 'Hey!' (extrametrical). An inarticulate cry (common in tragedy; see Seaford on E. *Cyc.* 51), registering a protest against what the slave-woman is doing (see 30–1 n.).

30–1. The jar containing the tokens was opened at 23, and the fact that the young man must say ἄνοιγ(ε) ἄνωθεν ('open it on top!', or perhaps 'open (it) again!') suggests that the slave-woman hurriedly put the lid back on when she noticed the inscription referred to in 29 and recognized its significance. What follows looks like a dispute about whether there was actually writing on one of the tokens, with the slave-woman insisting that there was not and the young man quickly yielding to her and letting the matter go (32–8).

33. [ἡ] μήτηρ must be 'my mother' rather than '(the baby's) mother'. Why the young man's mother was keeping these tokens, and why she passed them on to his wife (if something to that effect is concealed in 19–21) is unclear. He seems to assume that she was keeping the items safe for someone else. But the slave-woman's reaction to the inscription one of them offers (30–1) suggests that they conceal a secret that belongs to their household and about which she knows something the young man does not. Doubtless she revealed her dead mistress's secret at the end of the play, as part of the process leading to a happy ending.

34. σημανοῦμαι δ(ὲ) αὐτ(ά): 'and I will seal them up'.

36. οὐχ ἡμέτερον: 'it's not our problem, our business'.

36–7. τὴν ἐμποδὼν | [τα]ραχὴν ἱκανῶς θεῖμέν ποτ(ε): 'Might we reckon sufficient the trouble in our way!', i.e. 'we have enough trouble; let's not ask for more!'

37–8. ἂν ἐντός ποτε | [γέ]νωμ(αι) ἐμαυτοῦ: 'If I should ever regain control of myself', i.e. 'get myself together, recover from my current grief and despair' (cf. 1–2).

C16–C17. Aulus Gellius ii. 23 preserves these fragments (along with Men. fr. 298, for which see below; the Greek is badly mangled) as part of an extended comparison of Menander's Πλόκιον (*Necklace*) with Caecilius Statius' free Latin adaptation of the play, for which Gellius expresses great contempt. The speaker's name is known from a third-century AD Mytilenean mosaic (= Πλόκιον test. ii), which identifies the characters in the second act as Laches, Moschion (Laches' son?), and Crobyle (the speaker's wife; cf. 5, 10). Laches' conflict with Crobyle over the slave-girl expelled from his house was only one aspect of Menander's plot, which also involved the daughter of a poor man (cf. frr. 298–9, laments for the life of the urban pauper) who was raped during a festival (Gell. ii. 23. 15; cf. Caecil. v. 167 Ribbeck³ *properatim in tenebris istuc confectum est opus*, 'the business was done quickly in the dark'). The girl kept what happened secret even after she realized that she was pregnant (Gell. ii. 23. 16; cf. Caecil. v. 166 Ribbeck³ *pudebat, credo, commemoramentum stupri*, 'I suppose she was ashamed of any mention of the assault'), and gave birth during the course of the play (Gell. ii. 23. 17–19). Most likely the rapist was Laches' son (see **C17**. 6), who was supposed to marry the girl before she gave birth (for problems involving a marriage that has had to be cancelled at the last minute in Caecilius' play, see vv. 178/9–80 Ribbeck³), and the eponymous necklace served as a token that allowed the two to recognize one another. What happened to the slave-girl referred to in **C16** is unclear; but doubtless the two parts of the plot were intricately interwoven and in the end her situation and Laches' were both improved.

C16. Laches describes the situation in his house and his resentment of his wife.

Preserved at Aulus Gellius ii. 23. 9, where the verses are followed by Caecilius' adaptation (vv. 142–57 Ribbeck³). Gellius' text contains numerous errors; only the most substantial and significant conjectures and corrections are recorded in my apparatus.

Iambic trimeter.

1–2. **ἐπ(ὶ) ἀμφότερα** (sc. τὰ ὦτα) ... | ... **καθευδήσειν:** 'to sleep on both (ears)', i.e. 'with no cares' (App. Prov. ii. 78; cf. Ter. *Heaut.* 342; Plaut. *Pseud.* 122).

1. **(ἐ)πίκληρος:** 'heiress', specifically a woman whose father had no son, and who therefore inherited his property when he died (Harrison i. 10–11, 132–8), giving her considerable leverage in her relationship with her husband; cf. **I4.** 7 n.   **κ<αλή>** is sarcastic; cf. 5–6 n.

3. **περιβόητον:** 'notorious', as at adesp. com. fr. 78. 1 = Men. *Epitr.* 667 Martina (cited by the grammarian Ammonius to prove that the word is properly used of someone or something widely condemned). Crobyle has got the attention she wants (cf. 5–7), although according to Laches it is entirely unfavourable.

4–6. In Caecilius' version of the story, the wife's actions are motivated by a belief that her husband is sleeping with the girl (vv. 149, 156 Ribbeck³), whereas in Menander she appears simply to be driven by jealousy of the younger woman's good looks and her own need to dominate.

4. **ἣν ἐβούλετο:** 'whom she was wanting (to expel)', i.e. 'just as she had been wanting to do'.

5–6. **ἵν(α) κτλ.:** another sarcastic reference to Crobyle's ugliness; cf. 1, 7–9, 12. The subjunctives express Crobyle's purpose as she originally conceived it (Goodwin § 318).   **ἀποβλέπωσιν:** 'stare, gaze admiringly'.

6–7. **ἐμὴ γυνὴ | δέσποινα:** 'my lady mistress', i.e. 'my wife and queen', the point being that Crobyle is in charge and everyone knows it.

7. **καὶ τὴν ὄψιν ἣν ἐκτήσατο:** i.e. 'and as for what she looks like', sc. to her 'admirers' (cf. 5–6).

8. **ὄνος ἐν πιθήκοις:** 'a donkey among monkeys', a proverbial expression meaning 'ugly even among the ugly' (App. Prov. iv. 24).   **τοῦτο δὴ τὸ λεγόμενον:** 'as the saying goes'.

9. **σιωπᾶν βούλομαι:** 'I wish to make no mention of' + accusative; having nothing good to say about the subject, the speaker prefers not to discuss it at all.

9–10. **τὴν νύκτα τὴν | πολλῶν κακῶν ἀρχηγόν:** i.e. his wedding night;

cf. Strepsiades' curse on the matchmaker who brought him and his wife together, at Ar. *Nu.* 41b–2.

10–11.   **Κρωβύλην Ι λαβεῖν ἔμ(ε)** is an accusative of exclamation after **οἴμοι,** 'Alas, that I married Crobyle!'

11.   **δέκα τάλαντ(α):** sc. as her inheritance (see 1 n.). Ten talents (= 60,000 drachmas) is an enormous sum of money, which will have made Laches very wealthy (if none the less very unhappy).

12.   **<τὴν> ῥῖν(α) ἔχουσαν πήχεως:** 'with her cubit-long nose' (genitive of measure).

12–13.   **εἶτ(α) ἐστὶ τὸ Ι φρύαγμα πῶς ὑποστατόν;:** 'So how is her insolence endurable?' **φρύαγμα** is literally 'whinnying, snorting', as if Crobyle were a proud, high-spirited horse.

15.   **παιδισκάριον** is a pathetic diminutive < **παιδίσκη** (itself a diminutive < **παῖς**), 'a poor little slave-girl'.

15–16.   **λόγου Ι τάχιον:** 'swifter than a word', i.e. 'who got her work done before the order was even out of one's mouth'.

C17.   Gellius reports that in the scene from which these lines are taken Laches 'is speaking with another old man who is his neighbour, and cursing the pride of his wealthy wife'.

Preserved at Aulus Gellius ii. 23. 12, followed by Caecilius' adaptation (vv. 158–62 Ribbeck³).

Iambic trimeter.

1.   **ἔχω δ(ὲ) ἐπίκληρον Λάμιαν:** 'I'm married to an heiress ogre!' Lamia was a disfigured bogey-monster invoked *inter alia* to terrify children; cf. Ar. *V.* 1177; *Pax* 758 with Olson ad loc.

4.   **Ἄπολλον:** see **B12.** 1 n.

6.   **πρᾶγμ(α) ἄμαχον:** 'an impossible situation'.

C18.   Megas (who speaks 1 βάδιζε–23) is a slave (note 21) who has taken on the responsibility of protecting the interests of Moschion, his master's son. But matters have gone disastrously wrong, and a new initiative is necessary. Speaker A (who exits in 1) is a co-conspirator, perhaps Moschion himself. At 21–2, Laches (Moschion's father) and another man enter from the wing, and their conversation reveals that (as the audience in the theatre was probably already aware) Laches is eager to marry Moschion to his daughter, who must be the young man's half-sister (29–30). But Moschion has refused to go along with the proposal (30–1), doubtless because he prefers to take a different girl as his wife, hence the need for Megas to save the day. Lines 32–4 suggest that Moschion's mother is involved in the intrigue as well. For 'love' (ἔρως) and the conflict between love-matches and arranged marriages as a theme in

'New Comedy', see Brown, *CQ* NS 43 (1993), 189–205; and cf. **C15**. 3–12 with introductory n.

The names of several of the main characters are the same as in Menander's *Necklace* (**C16–C17**), but this is more likely an accident (cf. **D3**. 10 n.) than evidence that this fragment as well ought to be assigned to that play (as Corbato believed). Changes of speaker are indicated in the papyrus with capital letters (*A* = 'protagonist' (Megas), *B* = 'deuteragonist' (Speaker B), *Γ* = 'tritagonist' (Laches)), leaving little doubt that 1 βάδιζε–23 is a soliloquy. See W. G. Arnott, *Menander*, iii (Loeb Classical Library 460: Cambridge, Mass. and London, 2000), 453–63.

Preserved in PSI 1176 (first century AD; = *CGFPR* 255); only the most substantial and significant conjectures and corrections are recorded in my apparatus. Col. iii of the papyrus contains the first word or so of seventeen additional lines, which continue the dialogue between Laches and Speaker B, although Megas must eventually have broken into the conversation (cf. 23).

1–23 are trochaic tetrameter catalectic, 24–34 are iambic trimeter.

2, 4–5, 8. The repetitions (ἔγειρ(ε), ἔγειρε, βούλομαι, . . . [βούλομ(αι)], [δειλὸ]ς εἶ, . . . δειλὸς εἶ) reflect the speaker's agitation.

3. μὴ παρέργως: 'not as if this were a secondary matter', i.e. 'with full seriousness', as at Men. *Sam.* 638.

4. [(ἐ)γκ]αταλίπηις: 'leave in the lurch'.

4–7. βούλομαι κτλ.: Megas wavers momentarily and talks back to himself.

5–6. εἰς κλύδωνα πραγμάτων | [ἐμπε]σών: for the paratragic image of a 'wave of troubles' (setting up 10–16), cf. A. *Pers.* 599–600; S. *OT* 1527; E. *Tr.* 696; *Ph.* 859–60 with Mastronarde ad loc.

6. ἠγωνίακα: 'I've grown distressed'; further defined in what follows. πάλαι ταράττομαι: see C2. 3 n.

7. 'lest Fortune take the decision that is unfavourable to me', i.e. 'lest my luck run out'.

8–16. Megas once again (cf. 2–4) tries to talk himself into taking action.

8. βλέπω: 'I see (what's going on)!'

8–9. σύ γε | κτλ.: 'although *you're* trying to avoid trouble, you're assigning the blame to Fortune'.

10–16. For a storm at sea as an analogy for a sudden onset of personal troubles (picking up on εἰς κλύδωνα ... | [ἐμπε]σών in 5–6), cf. Philem. fr. 28; Men. *Sam.* 206–10; fr. 420 (where a sailor responds to the sight of a whirlwind by crying (7) 'Zeus the Saviour! Grab hold of the ropes!'; cf. 14–15); adesp. com. fr. 1126; E. *Tr.* 686–96.

10. οὐ θεωρεῖς;: 'don't you see (what I'm getting at)?'

11–12. The general term χειμών is glossed first with three words that list the fundamental elements of the storm (the wind, the water, and the waves produced by their violent interaction); then with three more words that describe its meteorological aspects (lightning, hail, and thunder); and finally with a grab-bag of three items that reflect its effect on the sailors, ship, and sky.

11. *τρικυμία:* literally 'a third wave', i.e. 'a huge wave', reflecting the popular belief that waves came in series of three, the third being the largest; cf. Men. fr. 420. 8; E. *Hipp.* 1213 with Barrett ad loc.

12. *ναυτίαι:* 'bouts of seasickness'.   *σύναγ[μα]:* 'a gathering together' (sc. of clouds), i.e. 'a thunderhead' *vel sim.* (cognate with συνάγω; attested only here).   *νύξ:* here 'darkness', as in a description of a storm at sea at H. *Od.* 5. 294.

13. *ἕκαστος αὐτῶν:* referring to the sailors mentioned in 10.

13–14. *προσμένει τὴν ἐλπίδα | [καὶ τὸ μέ]λλον οὐκ ἀπέγνω:* 'clings to his hope and doesn't despair of the future'. ἀπέγνω is a gnomic aorist (Goodwin §154–5); cf. 14 ἥψατο, 15 ἐσκέψατ(ο).

14. *τῶν κάλων . . . ἥψατο:* 'lays hold of the brails', in an attempt to shorten the sails; cf. Ar. *Eq.* 756; Epicr. fr. 9. 5; E. *Med.* 278 with Page ad loc.; Casson 259 n. 3.

15. *τοῖς Σαμόθραιξιν:* The 'Samothracian deities' (often identified with the Cabeiri) were thought to have the power to protect sailors during storms; cf. Alex. fr. 183. 4–6 with Arnott on 5; Thphr. *Char.* 25. 2 with Diggle ad loc.; Olson on Ar. *Pax* 276–9.

16. *τοὺς πόδας προσέλκεται:* 'pulls in the sheets', thus tightening the sail. But what the sailor ought to do is loosen the sail (Ar. *Eq.* 436–7; S. *Ant.* 715–17; E. *Or.* 706–7); and either the poet or his character is confused. For πούς in this sense, see LSJ s.v. II. 2.

20. Obscure; but Megas has apparently recovered his courage.

21. Laches and Speaker B enter from a wing, engaged in conversation.

23. *καιρὸν εὐφυῆ λαβών:* 'seizing a favourable moment', i.e. 'when the time is right'. Megas exits into the stage-house without being seen by Laches and his companion.

24–25. *ὡς οὐδὲ εἷς | ἄνθρωπος ἕτερος πώποτ(ε):* for the hyperbole, cf. C15. 1–2.

26. *δεῦρο πέμψας:* i.e. on an unsuccessful initial solo mission to Moschion, this being a second attempt, with Laches himself now in attendance. *μὴ λέγ(ε) οὕτως* is intended as a soft response to the complaint in 24–6 ('Don't talk this way!', i.e. 'Please don't characterize my treatment of you so unkindly!, Don't think this is my intent!'). But Speaker B remains unmollified.   *Ἡρά[κ]λεις:* see A22. 1 n.

27. **ἐγὼ δὲ πῶς σχοίην ἂν ἑτέρως;:** 'How else am I supposed to feel?'

28. **ποῖ με πέμπεις;:** i.e. 'What do you think you're doing, sending me . . . ?' Speaker B was confused not about his destination but about the reasoning behind Laches' plan.   **καὶ μάλα:** 'Yes indeed', affirming the truth of the preceding statement (e.g. Ar. *Nu.* 1326; Philem. fr. 67. 2; Men. *Dysc.* 754; cf. Thesleff § 41). Another attempt to mollify Speaker B (cf. 26 with n.)— who, however, ignores the interruption.

29–30. **υἱῶι φέροντα κτλ.** ('bringing news to your son about his marriage and intending to offer your daughter', sc. to him as his wife; cf. 31) continues the construction of ποῖ με πέμπεις in 28 after Laches' interruption.

30–1. K–A end Speaker B's quotation of his earlier remarks after **δώσοντ(α).** But **ἐὰν δὲ κτλ.** must belong to them as well.

30. **προσέχηι** (sc. τὸν νοῦν) **μοι:** 'pay attention to me, heed my orders/ advice'; cf. **H13.** 2 n.

31. **σου μὴ παρόντος** is a genitive absolute, 'if you're not present'. **λαμβάνειν:** sc. αὐτήν, 'to take (her), marry (her)'.

Section D

The Reception of Other Poetry

D1. Hermippus fr. 63, from *Porters* (late 430s/early 420s BC)

ἔσπετε νῦν μοι, Μοῦσαι Ὀλύμπια δώματ' ἔχουσαι,
ἐξ οὗ ναυκληρεῖ Διόνυσος ἐπ' οἴνοπα πόντον,
ὅσσ' ἀγάθ' ἀνθρώποις δεῦρ' ἤγαγε νηῒ μελαίνηι.
ἐκ μὲν Κυρήνης καυλὸν καὶ δέρμα βόειον,
ἐκ δ' Ἑλλησπόντου σκόμβρους καὶ πάντα ταρίχη,   5
ἐκ δ' αὖ Θετταλίας χόνδρον καὶ πλευρὰ βόεια·
καὶ παρὰ Σιτάλκου ψώραν Λακεδαιμονίοις,
καὶ παρὰ Περδίκκου ψεύδη ναυσὶν πάνυ πολλαῖς.
αἱ δὲ Συράκουσαι σῦς καὶ τυρὸν παρέχουσαι
     *   *   *

καὶ Κερκυραίους ὁ Ποσειδῶν ἐξολέσειε   10
ναυσὶν ἐπὶ γλαφυραῖς, ὁτιὴ δίχα θυμὸν ἔχουσι.
ταῦτα μὲν ἐντεῦθεν· ἐκ δ' Αἰγύπτου τὰ κρεμαστά,
ἱστία καὶ βίβλους, ἀπὸ δ' αὖ Συρίας λιβανωτόν.
ἡ δὲ καλὴ Κρήτη κυπάριττον τοῖσι θεοῖσιν,
ἡ Λιβύη δ' ἐλέφαντα πολὺν παρέχει κατὰ πρᾶσιν,   15
ἡ Ῥόδος ἀσταφίδας <τε> καὶ ἰσχάδας ἡδονείρους.
αὐτὰρ ἀπ' Εὐβοίας ἀπίους καὶ ἴφια μῆλα,
ἀνδράποδ' ἐκ Φρυγίας, ἀπὸ δ' Ἀρκαδίας ἐπικούρους.
αἱ Παγασαὶ δούλους καὶ στιγματίας παρέχουσι.
τὰς δὲ Διὸς βαλάνους καὶ ἀμύγδαλα σιγαλόεντα   20
Παφλαγόνες παρέχουσι· τὰ γάρ <τ'> ἀναθήματα δαιτός.
Σιδὼν δ' αὖ καρπὸν φοίνικος καὶ σεμίδαλιν,
Καρχηδὼν δάπιδας καὶ ποικίλα προσκεφάλαια

6 Θετταλίας Kock: ἰταλίας Ath.CE   9 σῦς . . . παρέχουσαι Ath.CE: σῖτον . . .
παρέχουσι Eust.   16 <τε> Musurus   21 <τ'> Musurus   22 Σιδὼν
Desrousseaux: Φοινίκη Ath.CE

D2. Aristophanes fr. 233, from *Banqueters* (427 BC)

(*A.*) πρὸς ταύτας δ' αὖ λέξον Ὁμήρου γλώττας· τί καλοῦσι κόρυμβα;
‿‿–‿‿–‿‿–‿‿– τί καλοῦσ' ἀμενηνὰ κάρηνα;
(*B.*) ὁ μὲν οὖν σός, ἐμὸς δ' οὗτος ἀδελφὸς φρασάτω· τί καλοῦσιν ἰδύους;
‿‿–‿‿–‿‿–‿‿–‿‿– τί ποτ' ἐστὶν ὀπύειν;

3 ἰδύους Seidler: ἰδοῦσί τε vel sim. Gal.   4 ποτ' ἐστὶν ὀπύειν Kaibel: ποτέ ἐστι τὸ εὖ ποιεῖν Gal.

D3. Strato Comicus fr. 1, from *Phoenicides* (IV)

⌊σφίγγ' ἄρρεν', οὐ μάγειρον, εἰς τὴν οἰκίαν⌋
⌊εἴληφ'. ἁπλῶς γὰρ οὐδὲ ἕν, μὰ τοὺς θεούς,⌋
⌊ὧν ἂν λέγηι συνίημι. καινὰ ῥήματα⌋
⌊πεπορισμένος⌋ πά⌊ρ⌋ε⌊στιν. ὡς εἰσῆλθε γά⌋ρ,
⌊εὐθύς μ' ἐ⌋πηρώτησε ⌊προσβλέψας⌋ μέγα·   5
⌊"πόσους κ⌋έκληκας μέροπα⌊ς ἐπὶ δεῖ⌋πνον; λέγε."
"ἐγ⌊ὼ κέκ⌋ληκα Μέροπας ἐπ⌊ὶ δεῖπνο⌋ν; χολᾶις.
τοὺς δὲ Μέροπας τούτους με γ⌊ιν⌋ώσκειν δοκεῖς;"
"οὐδ' ἄρα παρέσται δαιτυμὼν οὐθεὶς ὅλως;"
"ἥξει Φιλῖνος, Μοσχίων, Νικήρατος,   10
ὁ δεῖν', ὁ δεῖνα." κατ' ὄνομ' ἐπεπορευόμην·
οὐκ ἦν ἐν αὐτοῖς οὐδὲ εἷς μοι Δαιτυμών.
ὁ δ' ἠγανάκτησ' ὥσπερ ἠδικημένος
ὅτι οὐ κέκληκα Δαιτυμόνα. καινὸν σφόδρα.
"οὐδ' ἄρα θύεις ῥηξίχθον';" "οὐκ", ἔφην, "ἐγώ."   15
"βοῦν εὐρυμέτωπον;" "οὐ θύω βοῦν, ἄθλιε."
"μῆλα θυσιάζεις ἆρα;" "μὰ Δί', ἐγὼ μὲν οὔ."
"τὰ μῆλα πρόβατα." "μῆλα πρόβατ'; οὐκ οἶδ'", ἔφην,
"μάγειρε, τούτων οὐθέν, οὐδὲ βούλομαι.
ἀγροικότερός εἰμ', ὥσθ' ἁπλῶς μοι διαλέγου."   20
⌊"τὰς οὐλοχύτας φέρε δεῦρο." "τοῦτο δ' ἐστὶ τί;"⌋
⌊"κριθαί." "τί οὖν, ἀπόπληκτε, περιπλοκὰς λέγεις;"⌋
⌊"πηγὸς πάρεστι;" "πηγός; οὐχὶ λαικάσει,⌋
⌊ἐρεῖς σαφέσ⌋τερ⌊όν θ' ὃ βούλει μοι λέγε⌋ιν;"
⌊"ἀτάσθα⌋λός γ' εἶ, πρέσβυ" φ⌊ησίν. "ἄλ⌋α φέρε·   25
⌊τοῦτ' ἔ⌋σθ' ὁ πηγός, τοῦτο δεῖξον." χέρνιβον
⌊παρῆ⌋ν· ἔθυεν, ἔλεγεν ἕτερα μυρία
τ⌊ο⌋ι⌊αῦ⌋θ' ἅ, μὰ τὴν Γῆν, οὐδὲ εἷς συνῆκεν ἄν,
μίστυλλα μοίρας δίπτυχ' ὀβελούς· ὥστ' ἔδει
τὰ τοῦ Φιλίτα λαμβάνοντα βυβλία   30

σκοπεῖν ἕκαστον τί δύναται τῶν ῥημάτων.
ἀλλ' ἱκέτευον αὐτὸν ἤδη μεταβαλὼν
ἀνθρωπίνως λαλεῖν τι. τὸν δ' οὐκ ἄν ποτε
ἔπεισεν ἡ Πειθὼ παραστᾶσ' αὐτόθι.
καί μοι δοκεῖ ῥαψῳδοτοιούτου τινὸς   35
δοῦλος γεγονὼς ἐκ παιδὸς ἀλιτήριος
εἶτ' ἀναπεπλῆσθαι τῶν Ὁμήρου ῥημάτων

3 ὧν ἄν λέγηι Dindorf: ὧν λέγει Ath. (2)ᴬᶜᴱ: ὅσ' ἄν λέγηι Ath. (1)ᴬᶜᴱ   9 ουθεις pap.: οὐδὲ
εἷς Ath. (1)ᴬᶜᴱ   11 επεπορευομην pap.: ἀνελογιζόμην Ath. (1)ᴬᶜᴱ   13 ο δ pap.:
σφόδρα Ath. (1)ᴬᶜᴱ   14 οτι ου pap.: εἰ μὴ Ath. (1)ᴬᶜᴱ   δαιτυμονα pap.: δαιτυμόνας Ath.
(1)ᴬᶜᴱ   καινον σφοδρα pap.: καινὸν πάνυ Ath. (1)ᴬ: om. Ath. (1)ᶜᴱ   16 βουν pap.: βοῦν δ'
Ath. (1)ᴬᶜᴱ   17 ου pap.: om. Ath. (1)ᴬᶜᴱ   18 μηλα προβατ ουκ οιδ εφη pap.: οὐ
μανθάνω Ath. (1)ᴬ: om. Ath. (1)ᶜᴱ   19–20 vers. om. Ath.ᶜᴱ   19 μαγειρε pap.: om.
Ath. (1)ᴬ   ουθεν pap.: οὐδὲν Ath. (1)ᴬ   21 τὰς Ath. (1)ᴬ: τοὺς Ath. (1)ᶜᴱ
23 λαικάσει Coraes: λεκας εἰ Ath. (1)ᴬ: om. Ath. (1)ᶜᴱ   24 ἐρεῖς σαφεστερον θ' Ath. (1)ᴬ:
σαφέστερον λέγε Ath. (1)ᶜᴱ   25 [αλ]α pap.: ἅλας Ath. (1)ᴬᶜᴱ   26 [ε]σθ ο pap.: ἐστι Ath.
(1)ᴬᶜᴱ   post πηγός defic. Ath. (1)ᶜᴱ   τουτο pap.: ἀλλὰ Ath. (1)ᴬ   χερνιβον pap. (ο ex α corr.)
χέρνιβα Ath. (1)ᴬ   27 ετερα μυρια pap.: ἀλλὰ ῥήματα Ath. (1)ᴬ   28 συνηκεν αν pap.:
ἤκουσεν ἄν Ath. (1)ᴬ   29 ωστ εδει pap.: ὥστε με Ath. (1)ᴬ   30 τα του Φιλιτα . . .
βυβλια pap.: τῶν τοῦ φιλτα . . . βιβλίων Ath. (1)ᴬ   31 εκαστον pap.: ἔκαστα Ath. (1)ᴬ   τῶν
ῥημάτων Ath. (1)ᴬ: τωμβυβλιων pap   32 αλλ ικετευον pap.: πλὴν ἱκετεύω γ' Ath. (1)ᴬ
μεταβαλων pap.: μεταβαλεῖν Ath. (1)ᴬ   33 τι pap.: τε Ath. (1)ᴬ   αμποτε pap.: ἂν ταχὺ
Ath. (1)ᴬ   34 παραστας αυτοθι pap.: μὰ τὴν γῆν οἶδ' ὅτι Ath. (1)ᴬ   37 εἶτ'
ἀναπεπλῆσθαι Kassel: επε[ιτ]α πεπλησθαι pap.

D4. Eubulus fr. 118, from an unidentified play (IV)

ἰχθὺν δ' Ὅμηρος ἐσθίοντ' εἴρηκε ποῦ
τίνα τῶν Ἀχαιῶν; κρέα δὲ μόνον ὤπτων, ἐπεὶ
ἕψοντά γ' οὐ πεπόηκεν αὐτῶν οὐδένα,
ἀλλ' οὐδὲ μικρόν. οὐδ' ἑταίραν εἶδέ τις
αὐτῶν, ἑαυτοὺς δ' ἔδεφον ἐνιαυτοὺς δέκα·   5
πικρὰν στρατείαν δ' εἶδον, οἵτινες πόλιν
μίαν λαβόντες εὐρυπρωκτότεροι πολὺ
τῆς πόλεος ἀπεχώρησαν ἧς εἷλον τότε

1 δ' . . . εἴρηκε ποῦ Morelius: δὲ που . . . εἴρηκε Ath.ᶜᴱ   4 οὐδ' Hunter, praeeunte Kaibel:
ἀλλ' Ath.ᶜᴱ

D5. Timocles fr. 6, from *Women Celebrating the Dionysia* (IV)

ὦ τᾶν, ἄκουσον ἤν τι σοι δοκῶ λέγειν.
ἄνθρωπός ἐστι ζῷον ἐπίπονον φύσει,

καὶ πολλὰ λυπήρ' ὁ βίος ἐν ἑαυτῶι φέρει.
παραψυχὰς οὖν φροντίδων ἀνεύρετο
ταύτας· ὁ γὰρ νοῦς τῶν ἰδίων λήθην λαβὼν   5
πρὸς ἀλλοτρίωι τε ψυχαγωγηθεὶς πάθει,
μεθ' ἡδονῆς ἀπῆλθε παιδευθεὶς ἅμα.
τοὺς γὰρ τραγωιδοὺς πρῶτον, εἰ βούλει, σκόπει
ὡς ὠφελοῦσι πάντας. ὁ μὲν ὢν γὰρ πένης
πτωχότερον αὑτοῦ καταμαθὼν τὸν Τήλεφον   10
γενόμενον ἤδη τὴν πενίαν ῥᾶιον φέρει.
ὁ νοσῶν τι μανικὸν Ἀλκμέων' ἐσκέψατο.
ὀφθαλμιᾶι τις· εἰσὶ Φινεῖδαι τυφλοί.
τέθνηκέ τωι παῖς· ἡ Νιόβη κεκούφικε.
χωλός τις ἐστι· τὸν Φιλοκτήτην ὁρᾶι.   15
γέρων τις ἀτυχεῖ· κατέμαθεν τὸν Οἰνέα.
ἅπαντα γὰρ τὰ μείζον' ἢ πέπονθέ τις
ἀτυχήματ' ἄλλοις γεγονότ' ἐννοούμενος
τὰς αὑτὸς αὑτοῦ συμφορὰς ἧττον στένει

1 δοκῶ Stob.ˢᴹᴬ: μέλλω Ath.ᴬ: vers. om. Ath.ᶜᴱ   4 οὖν Stob.ˢᴹᴬ: γοῦν Ath.ᴬᶜᴱ
9 ὁ μὲν ὢν Ath.ᶜᴱ: ὁ μένων Ath.ᴬ: ὢν μὲν Stob.ˢᴹᴬ   11 ἤδη Ath.ᴬᶜᴱ: οὕτω Stob.ˢᴹᴬ
12 τι μανικὸν Stob.ˢᴹᴬ: δὲ μανικῶς Ath.ᴬᶜᴱ   19 ἧττον στένει Stob.ˢᴹᴬ: ῥᾶιον φέρει
Ath.ᴬᶜᴱ

D6. Antiphanes fr. 189, from *Poetry* (IV)

      μακάριόν ἐστιν ἡ τραγωιδία
ποίημα κατὰ πάντ', εἴ γε πρῶτον οἱ λόγοι
ὑπὸ τῶν θεατῶν εἰσιν ἐγνωρισμένοι,
πρὶν καί τιν' εἰπεῖν· ὥσθ' ὑπομνῆσαι μόνον
δεῖ τὸν ποιητήν. Οἰδίπουν γ' ἂν φῆι <μόνον>,   5
τὰ δ' ἄλλα πάντ' ἴσασιν· ὁ πατὴρ Λάιος,
μήτηρ Ἰοκάστη, θυγατέρες, παῖδες τίνες,
τί πείσεθ' οὗτος, τί πεπόηκεν. ἂν πάλιν
εἴπηι τις Ἀλκμέωνα, καὶ τὰ παιδία
πάντ' εὐθὺς εἴρηχ', ὅτι μανεὶς ἀπέκτονε   10
τὴν μητέρ', ἀγανακτῶν δ' Ἄδραστος εὐθέως
ἥξει πάλιν τ' ἄπεισι – × – ∪ ×
ἔπειθ' ὅταν μηθὲν δύνωντ' εἰπεῖν ἔτι,
κομιδῆι δ' ἀπειρήκωσιν ἐν τοῖς δράμασιν,
αἴρουσιν ὥσπερ δάκτυλον τὴν μηχανήν,   15
καὶ τοῖς θεωμένοισιν ἀποχρώντως ἔχει.

ἡμῖν δὲ ταῦτ' οὐκ ἔστιν, ἀλλὰ πάντα δεῖ
εὑρεῖν, ὀνόματα καινά, – × – ∪ ×
× – ∪ – κἄπειτα τὰ διωιχημένα
πρότερον, τὰ νῦν παρόντα, τὴν καταστροφήν,   20
τὴν εἰσβολήν. ἂν ἕν τι τούτων παραλίπηι
Χρέμης τις ἢ Φείδων τις, ἐκσυρίττεται·
Πηλεῖ δὲ πάντ' ἔξεστι καὶ Τεύκρωι ποεῖν

5 γ' ἂν φῆι <μόνον> Coulon: γὰρ φῶ Ath.^ACE   13 ἔπειθ' Casaubon: ταπεισεθ' Ath.^A: vers.
om. Ath.^CE   18–19 e.g. <καινὰ πράγματα, | καινοὺς λόγους> Kaibel   19 διωιχημένα
van Herwerden: διωικημένα Ath.^ACE   23 πάντ' Ellebodius: ταῦτ' Ath.^A: vers. om. Ath.^CE

D7. Timocles fr. 27, from *Orestautocleides* (IV)

περὶ δὲ τὸν πανάθλιον
εὕδουσι γρᾶες, Νάννιον Πλαγγὼν Λύκα
Γνάθαινα Φρύνη Πυθιονίκη Μυρρίνη
Χρυσὶς † Κοναλὶς † Ἱερόκλεια Λοπάδιον

D8. Cratinus fr. 17, from *Cowherds* (V)

ὃς οὐκ ἔδωκ' αἰτοῦντι Σοφοκλέει χορόν,
τῶι Κλεομάχου δ', ὃν οὐκ ἂν ἠξίουν ἐγὼ
ἐμοὶ διδάσκειν οὐδ' ἂν εἰς Ἀδώνια

D9. Phrynichus Comicus fr. 32, from *Muses* (405 BC)

μάκαρ Σοφοκλέης, ὃς πολὺν χρόνον βιοὺς
ἀπέθανεν εὐδαίμων ἀνὴρ καὶ δεξιός·
πολλὰς ποήσας καὶ καλὰς τραγωιδίας
καλῶς ἐτελεύτησ', οὐδὲν ὑπομείνας κακόν

D10. Antiphanes fr. 228, from an unidentified play (IV)

τὸ δὲ ζῆν, εἰπέ μοι,
τί ἐστι; – ∪ – τὸ πίνειν φήμ' ἐγώ.
ὁρᾶις παρὰ ῥείθροισι χειμάρροις ὅσα
δένδρων ἀεὶ τὴν νύκτα καὶ τὴν ἡμέραν

βρέχεται, μέγεθος καὶ κάλλος οἷα γίγνεται,　　　　　　　5
τὰ δ᾿ ἀντιτείνοντ᾿ αὐτόπρεμν᾿ ἀπόλλυται

6 sic Naber: ἀντιτείνοντ᾿ οἱονεὶ δίψαν τινὰ | ἢ ξηρασίαν ἔχοντ᾿ αὐτόπρεμν᾿ Ath.ᶜᴱ

D11. Eubulus fr. 26, from *Dionysius* (IV)

Εὐριπίδου δ᾿ "ἔσωσά σ᾿ ὡς ἴσασ᾿ ὅσοι"
καὶ "παρθέν᾿, εἰ <σώσαιμί> σ᾿, ἕξεις μοι χάριν;"·
καὶ τοῖς ἐμοῖσιν ἐγγελῶσι πήμασι
τὰ σίγμα συλλέξαντες, ὡς αὐτοὶ σοφοί

3 ἐγγελῶσι Porson: ἀγγελοῦσι Σ Eur.

D12. Diphilus fr. 74, from *Synoris* (IV/III)

(Α.) ἄριστ᾿ ἀπαλλάττεις ἐπὶ τούτου τοῦ κύβου.
(Β.) ἀστεῖος εἶ. δραχμὴν ὑπόθες. (Α.) κεῖται πάλαι.
(Β.) πῶς ἂν βάλοιμ᾿ Εὐριπίδην; (Α.) οὐκ ἂν ποτε
Εὐριπίδης γυναῖκα σώσει᾿. οὐχ ὁρᾷς
ἐν ταῖς τραγῳδίαισιν αὐτὰς ὡς στυγεῖ;　　　　　　　5
τοὺς δὲ παρασίτους ἠγάπα. λέγει γέ τοι·
"ἀνὴρ γὰρ ὅστις εὖ βίον κεκτημένος
μὴ τοὐλάχιστον τρεῖς ἀσυμβόλους τρέφει,
ὄλοιτο, νόστου μή ποτ᾿ εἰς πάτραν τυχών."
(Β.) πόθεν ἐστὶ ταῦτα, πρὸς θεῶν; (Α.) τί δέ σοι μέλει;　　10
οὐ γὰρ τὸ δρᾶμα, τὸν δὲ νοῦν σκοπούμεθα

9 τυχών E. *IT* 535: μολεῖ Ath.ᴬ: om. Ath.ᶜᴱ　　　　　10 σοι] μοι Meineke

D13. Eupolis fr. 148, from *Helots* (early 420s ʙᴄ?)

τὰ Στησιχόρου τε καὶ Ἀλκμᾶνος Σιμωνίδου τε
ἀρχαῖον ἀείδειν, ὁ δὲ Γνήσιππος ἔστ᾿ ἀκούειν.
κεῖνος νυκτερίν᾿ ηὗρε μοιχοῖς ἀείσματ᾿ ἐκκαλεῖσθαι
γυναῖκας ἔχοντας ἰαμβύκην τε καὶ τρίγωνον

D14. Pherecrates fr. 155, from *Cheiron* (V)

(Μουσ.) λέξω μὲν οὐκ ἄκουσα· σοί τε γὰρ κλυεῖν
ἐμοί τε λέξαι θυμὸς ἡδονὴν ἔχει.
ἐμοὶ γὰρ ἦρξε τῶν κακῶν Μελανιππίδης,

ἐν τοῖσι πρῶτος ὃς λαβὼν ἀνῆκέ με
χαλαρωτέραν τ᾽ ἐπόησε χορδαῖς δώδεκα.   5
ἀλλ᾽ οὖν ὅμως οὗτος μὲν ἦν ἀποχρῶν ἀνὴρ
ἔμοιγε – × – ∪ πρὸς τὰ νῦν κακά.
Κινησίας δέ <μ᾽> ὁ κατάρατος Ἀττικὸς
ἐξαρμονίους καμπὰς ποῶν ἐν ταῖς στροφαῖς
ἀπολώλεχ᾽ οὕτως, ὥστε τῆς ποιήσεως   10
τῶν διθυράμβων, καθάπερ ἐν ταῖς ἀσπίσιν,
ἀριστέρ᾽ αὐτοῦ φαίνεται τὰ δεξιά.
ἀλλ᾽ οὖν ἀνεκτὸς οὗτος ἦν ὅμως ἐμοί.
Φρῦνις δ᾽ ἴδιον στρόβιλον ἐμβαλών τινα
κάμπτων με καὶ στρέφων ὅλην διέφθορεν,   15
ἐν πέντε χορδαῖς δώδεχ᾽ ἁρμονίας ἔχων.
ἀλλ᾽ οὖν ἔμοιγε χοῦτος ἦν ἀποχρῶν ἀνήρ·
εἰ γάρ τι κἀξήμαρτεν, αὖτις ἀνέλαβεν.
ὁ δὲ Τιμόθεός μ᾽, ὦ φιλτάτη, κατορώρυχε
καὶ διακέκναικ᾽ αἴσχιστα. (Δικ.) ποῖος οὑτοσὶ   20
<ὁ> Τιμόθεος; (Μουσ.) Μιλήσιός τις πυρρίας.
κακά μοι παρέσχεν οὗτος, ἅπαντας οὓς λέγω
παρελήλυθεν, ἄγων ἐκτραπέλους μυρμηκιάς.
κἂν ἐντύχηι πού μοι βαδιζούσηι μόνηι,
ἀπέδυσε κἀνέλυσε χορδαῖς δώδεκα   25
        *   *   *

ἐξαρμονίους ὑπερβολαίους τ᾽ ἀνοσίους
καὶ νιγλάρους, ὥσπερ τε τὰς ῥαφάνους ὅλην
καμπῶν με κατεμέστωσε

4 πρῶτος Meineke: πρώτοις Plu.   8 <μ᾽> Meineke   10 ἀπολώλεχ᾽ οὕτως
Meineke: ἀπολώλεκέ με οὕτως Plu.   13 οὖν Wyttenbach: οὐκ Plu.   ἀνεκτὸς
Emperius: ἂν εἴποις Plu.   ὅμως ἐμοί Wyttenbach: ὅμως ὅμως Plu.   16 ἐν] εἰς West
21 <ὁ> Meineke   25 δώδεκα] ἔνδεκα Méziriac   26 τ᾽ del. Bothe

COMMENTARY

D1–D4. For other allusions to or echoes of Homer in comedy, e.g. **A6–A11** with nn.; **C4–C6**; **E12**. 4; **E14**. 7; **E30**. 2; **F13**. 1; **G3**. 6; **G17**. 6; **H8**; **I2**. 9–10 with 9–12 n.; **I10**. 3–4; **J14**. 3; Cratin. fr. 352 (~ *Il*. 14. 291); Pherecr. frr. 159. 1 (~ *Il*. 9. 270–1; cf. **H20** introductory n.); 261. 1 (cf. *Il*. 9. 264); Ar. *Ach*. 1171–3 with Olson ad loc.; *Nu*. 1056–7; *Av*. 575, 908–14; *Ra*. 1034–6; *Pl*. 290–308; Theopomp. Com. frr. *34 (~ *Od*. 19. 232–3); 48–9; Antiph. fr. 248 (see **D4** introductory n.); Philem. fr. 99; and cf. **B13–B20**; **C1** (on Hesiod in comedy); Silk, in *Rivals*, 305–8.

D1. A Homeric-style catalogue, in epic metre, of the extraordinary variety of goods imported into Athens by sea, with several topical political jokes thrown in (7–8, 10–11). For the idea, see Ar. frr. 428–31 (from the parabasis of *Merchantships*); Th. ii. 38. 2; [X.] *Ath*. 2. 7. The first verse is borrowed direct from the *Iliad*, and 10–11, 14, 17, and 21 seem to refer to or quote specific epic passages. But the Homeric words and formulae in 2, 3, 11, 17, and 20 (cf. 4, 6) are all generic, and full appreciation of substantial portions of the parody requires only a broad familiarity with epic diction. The items mentioned range from luxury goods (e.g. 13–15, 23) to basic commodities (e.g. 5–6), and most fall into obvious clusters of two to four items (4–6 food; 7–8 lies and mange (a joke); 13–15 Eastern luxury goods dedicated in various ways to the gods; 16–17 food; 18–19 slaves and mercenaries; 20–2 food); some geographic grouping is also apparent (6–9 places to the north and north-east of Athens; 9–11 places to the west; 12–16 places to the south and south-east), as in the Homeric Catalogue of Ships. Further interest is added by the constant variation of syntactic structure (4–6; 7–8; 9 (followed by a lacuna); 12–13; 14–16; 17–18; 19–23). Dionysus was conventionally said to have introduced wine to mankind; here he is given credit for even more substantial gifts.

According to the second-century BC geographer and antiquarian Polemon of Ilium (fr. 45 Preller ap. Ath. 15. 699a), Hermippus composed parodies; but whether Polemon is referring to passages such as this and Cratin. fr. 349 (~ Hes. *Op*. 299–300), or to non-dramatic epic parodies like those of Hegemon of Thasos (late fifth century; see Ath. 15. 698c–9a), is unknown. *Porters* (literally '*Basketbearers*'; referring to the men who carried goods like those in this catalogue from the docks to where they were sold or consumed) is undated but clearly belongs to the early Peloponnesian War years (cf. 7 n., 10–11 n., 18 n.), and the death of King Sitalces (7) in winter 424/3 provides a *terminus ante quem*. See Gilula, in *Rivals*, 75–90, esp. 77–82; M. Pellegrino, *Utopie e immagini gastronomiche nei frammenti dell'Archaia* (Bologna, 2000),

195–225. H8 (in which Dionysus is the speaker; also mock-Homeric dactylic hexameters) may belong to the same play.

Preserved entire at Athenaeus 1. 27e–8a (manuscripts CE only; many of the verses are also cited at scattered points by Eustathius), with the poet identified but not the play (as typically in the Epitome), along with a number of other texts that list commodities that are best in particular places. Hesychius δ 1922 quotes 20 alone, in a gloss on Διὸς βάλανοι, and is the source for the attribution of the fragment to *Porters*.

Dactylic hexameter.

1. = *Il.* 2. 484 (the introduction to the Catalogue of Ships), a famous verse (echoed also at Timo *SH* 775) from a famous section of the poem (e.g. **H8**. 4–5 ~ *Il.* 2. 673–4; Th. i. 10. 3–5; Matro frr. 1. 119–20 ~ *Il.* 2. 489–90; 3. 1 ~ *Il.* 2. 488).

2–3. Dionysus is routinely represented as a wanderer, and is a sailor already (perforce) in the seventh Homeric Hymn. The idea surfaces elsewhere in Comedy in the Aristophanic title Διόνυσος ναυαγός ('*Dionysus Shipwrecked*') and is perhaps connected with a ceremony (part of the Anthesteria festival?) in which the god was escorted through the city in a cart that resembled a ship (*DFA* 12–13). Zielinski took these verses to be an oblique reference to Athens' establishment of naval supremacy in the Eastern Mediterranean in the middle of the fifth century; the allusion might just as well be simply to the beginning of sailing season, which fell around City Dionysia time in late March or early April.

2. ἐξ οὗ: 'ever since, starting at the time when'. The words appear at the beginning of Homeric lines at e.g. *Il.* 1. 6; 13. 778; *Od.* 2. 27, but are used with the present (as here) only at *Od.* 8. 539 ἐξ οὗ δορπέομεν. ναυκληρεῖ is properly 'serves as ship-owner'. But ship-owners often doubled as captains, and the activity of a captain is at issue. οἴνοπα πόντον: a common Homeric line-end formula (e.g. *Il.* 2. 613; 5. 771; *Od.* 2. 421), but in Homer with ἐπί (respecting the original digamma at the beginning of οἴνοπα) rather than ἐπ᾽ (metrically necessary here). The epithet is particularly appropriate in a description of the activity of the wine god Dionysus.

3. δεῦρ(ο) ἤγαγε: found in the same position in the line at *Od.* 4. 312. But here δεῦρ(ο) is 'to Athens', and ἤγαγε is a timeless ('gnomic') aorist (Goodwin § 154–5). νηὶ μελαίνηι: a common Homeric line-ending formula (e.g. *Il.* 1. 300, 329; 8. 222; *Od.* 3. 365). The colour of the ship results from the use of pitch to seal its hull; cf. Olson on Ar. *Ach.* 188–90.

4–8. Supply ἤγαγε throughout.

4. Κυρήνης: an old Greek city located on what is today the Libyan coast.

καυλόν: 'silphium-stalk' (a collective singular (**A1**. 3 n.), like many other items in the catalogue), which was eaten either stewed or roasted. Silphium (Greek σίλφιον; said to be imported from North Africa also at Antiph. frr. 88; 216. 13; Eub. fr. 18. 3–4) was gathered so aggressively that it was driven into extinction and thus remains unidentified. But its stalk, root, leaf, and gummy juice or sap are repeatedly referred to in culinary contexts (e.g. Anaxandr. fr. 42. 58; Antiph. fr. 71. 1; Alex. fr. 132. 5; cf. **G12**. 6–7 n.). See Andrews, *Isis* 33 (1941), 232–6; Olson–Sens on Archestr. frr. 9. 1; 46. 14; García Soler 365–7.   **δέρμα βόειον**: 'ox hides' (another collective singular; see above). Cf. 6 πλευρὰ βόεια |; *Il.* 4. 122 νεῦρα βόεια |; *Od.* 14. 24 δέρμα βόειον (but in a different *sedes*). For δέρμα in this *sedes*, see *Il.* 6. 117; 10. 23, 177; *Od.* 4. 440.

5.   The Hellespont (i.e. the Dardanelles, the long strait that links the Sea of Marmara and the Aegean Sea) was lined on both sides with Greek cities and was famous as a source of saltfish (τάριχος; cf. **A2**. 1 n.; **G18**. 4, 9, 14 n.; R. I. Curtis, *Garum and Salsamenta* (Leiden, 1991), 6–26; Olson–Sens on Archestr. fr. 39. 1–2; García Soler 204–15), which was produced from mackerel (**σκόμβρους**; cf. *Fishes* 243–5), tuna (see **G4**. 6 n.), and doubtless almost anything else that made its way into the nets.   **πάντα ταρίχη**: 'saltfish of every sort', i.e. 'made from every sort of fish'; see above.

6.   For Thessaly (a large, fertile region in northern Greece) as a source of grain, see Antiph. fr. 36. 3; X. *HG* vi. 1. 11.   **χόνδρον**: 'small chunks' (cf. **A20**. 4), here of roughly milled barley, which was made into a porridge called by the same name (cf. **C3**. 4–5; **H4**. 1 n.).   **πλευρὰ βόεια**: 'sides of beef', presumably packed in salt to keep them from spoiling during transport. Cf. 4 n.

7.   A reference to the Thracian king Sitalces (d. winter 424/3) would be particularly appropriate in or after winter 429/8, when he mounted a huge expedition against Perdiccas of Macedon (8 n.) but eventually withdrew, when the Athenian support he had been promised failed to materialize (Th. ii. 95–6, 98–101).   **ψώραν Λακεδαιμονίοισι**: 'mange'—a contagious condition caused by mites that burrow into the skin, lay their eggs there, and cause intense itching; cf. **B31**. 9—'for the Spartans' (a surprise at the end of the line; cf. **B29**. 3 n.).

8.   **παρὰ Περδίκκου ψεύδη**: Perdiccas of Macedon made and renounced numerous alliances with Athens during the Peloponnesian War years, depending on where his own advantage lay; he is accordingly denounced here as a notorious liar (rather than as a shrewd political survivor, as a more objective observer might have put it).   **ναυσὶν πάνυ πολλαῖς**: 'with very many ships', i.e. 'by the boatload'; marking a return to the idea of nautical commerce after the jokes about Sitalces and Perdiccas.

9.   Sicily (the most important city on which was Syracuse) was well known for its cheese (e.g. Ar. *V.* 838, 896–7; Antiph. fr. 233. 4; cf. **C6.** 7–9 with Olson–Sens on Matro fr. 1. 24 (Sicily as the Cyclops' island)), and the late-classical historian Clytus refers to Sicilian pigs as a delicacy (*FGrH* 490 F 2). There is a gap of uncertain size in the text between 9 and 10.

10–11.   The island of Corcyra (just off the west coast of mainland Greece) was a major naval power (11) and was identified by the fifth century with Homeric Phaeacia (Th. i. 25. 4). Corcyra became an Athenian ally in 433, just before the Peloponnesian War broke out (Th. i. 44), and δίχα θυμὸν ἔχουσι ('they have a divided heart'; an adaptation of H. *Il.* 20. 32 δίχα θυμὸν ἔχοντες |) must allude to the ugly civil war between pro- and anti-Athenian (or democratic and aristocratic) factions that followed and came to a climax in 427 (Th. iii. 70–85).

10.   ὁ Ποσειδῶν ἐξολέσειε: cf. Men. *Dysc.* 504 (but with no verb); H. *Od.* 17. 597 τοὺς Ζεὺς ἐξολέσειε (a curse on the Suitors). Perhaps an allusion to the story of the vengeance taken by Poseidon on the Phaeacians (i.e. the Corcyreans; see 10–11 n.) for ferrying Odysseus home to Ithaca (*Od.* 13. 125–64). But the mid-420s were a period of intense seismic activity in Greece (Th. iii. 87. 4, 89; cf. Ar. *Ach.* 510–11), and this is more likely a reference to Poseidon's power as lord of earthquakes (e.g. Ar. *Nu.* 566–8).

11.   ναυσὶν ἐπὶ γλαφυραῖς is an adaptation of the common Iliadic line-initial formula νηυσὶν ἐπὶ γλαφυρῇσιν (e.g. 5. 327; 8. 531; cf. 9. 425).

12.   ταῦτα μὲν ἐντεῦθεν: 'these things are from there'. Either this is an awkward way of saying 'That's where all the items mentioned so far are from', or whatever was lost between 9 and 10 made the point clear. In any case, the catalogue of goods begins again in the second half of the verse, with ἤγαγε (cf. 3) to be supplied, as again in 17–18.

12–13.   τὰ κρεμαστά, | ἱστία καὶ βίβλους: 'the hanging gear'—to be distinguished from 'the wooden gear' (τὰ ξύλινα), such as oars, ladders, and masts (X. *Oec.* 8. 12)—'(that is) sails and papyrus (ropes)'; cf. *IG* II² 1610. 5–30 (a catalogue of κρεμαστά); J. S. Morrison and R. T. Williams, *Greek Oared Ships 900–322 B.C.* (Cambridge, 1968), 289–307. Sails were made of linen (e.g. [A.] *PV* 468), an Egyptian commodity; see Casson 233–5. For papyrus (also produced in Egypt; cf. Hdt. ii. 92. 5), see V. Täckholm and M. Drar, *Flora of Egypt*, ii (Cairo, 1950), 102–33, esp. 117–18; N. Lewis, *Papyrus in Classical Antiquity* (Oxford, 1974).

13.   λιβανωτόν: 'frankincense', the aromatic gum of an Arabian tree, which was burned in honour of the gods (e.g. Ar. *Nu.* 426; cf. **A20.** 12; **H1.** 9 with n.); also said to be imported through Syria at A. *Ag.* 1312; E. *Ba.* 144; Anaxandr. fr. 42. 36–7; Mnesim. fr. 4. 57–61. Cf. **C13.** 9 n. (on scented oil from Syria).

14.   ἡ δὲ καλὴ Κρήτη: perhaps an allusion to H. *Od.* 19. 172–3 'there is a land named Crete in the midst of the wine-dark sea, καλὴ καὶ πίειρα'. κυπάριττον: 'cypress-wood', which was strong, sweet-smelling, and largely immune to insects, and was accordingly used for roof-beams, doors, and the like in temples (hence τοῖσι θεοῖσιν, 'for the gods'). Cf. *IG* I³ 461. 35 (cypress-wood purchased for the construction of the Parthenon doors).

15.   ἐλέφαντα: Ivory was used for inlay work on luxury items such as instruments and furniture (e.g. Ar. *Av.* 218–19; Pl. Com. fr. 230. 1; carm. conv. *PMG* 900. 1) and for statues such as the chryselephantine ('gold and ivory') statue of Athena Parthenos on the Acropolis (cf. Ar. *Eq.* 1169). For Libya as a land of extraordinary creatures (including elephants), cf. Anaxil. fr. 27; Hdt. ii. 32. 4; iv. 191. 2–192; Arist. *HA* 606ᵇ9–14.   κατὰ πρᾶσιν is literally 'in accord with sale', i.e. 'for sale'.

16.   ἀσταφίδας: 'raisins'; see García Soler 116–17.   ἡδυονείρους: 'that cause sweet dreams'; the word is attested nowhere else. Rhodian figs are also praised by the early Hellenistic author Lynceus of Samos (fr. 12 Dalby ap. Ath. 3. 75e, cf. 14. 652d).

17.   αὐτὰρ ἀπ(ὸ) Εὐβοίας (sc. ἤγαγε; cf. 3, 12 n.) is adapted from Hes. fr. 204. 52 | αὐτὰρ ἀπ' Εὐβοίης (of Elephenor, one of Helen's suitors), which is also the source of the parody at Matro fr. 1. 49. αὐτάρ is epic vocabulary (commonly line-initial) and is attested nowhere else in comedy. ἀπίους καὶ ἴφια μῆλα: 'pears and goodly apples'; see García Soler 101–5. Modelled on H. *Il.* 5. 556 βόας καὶ ἴφια μῆλα |), although there μῆλα means 'sheep'. Cf. **D3**. 17–18, and the very similar joke at Matro fr. 1. 112 ἐν δ' αὐταῖσιν ἐπῆν ἄπιοι καὶ πίονα μῆλα ('on (the tables) were pears and fat apples').

18.   ἀνδράποδ(α) ἐκ Φρυγίας: Phrygia (a region in west central Asia Minor) was an important source of Athenian slaves, as is clear from the common use in comedy of the Phrygian personal name Μανῆς (fem. Μανία; cf. **F19**. 6; **H13**. 13; Austin–Olson on Ar. *Th.* 728; Fragiadakis 358–9) and the ethnic Φρύξ (e.g. Ar. *Av.* 762 with Dunbar ad loc.; cf. Fragiadakis 378) as slave-names.   ἀπὸ δ(ὲ) Ἀρκαδίας ἐπικούρους: 'and mercenaries from Arcadia', a poor, backward region in the central Peloponnese. Arcadian mercenaries were hired by the Athenians *inter alia* in 427 BC (Th. iii. 34. 2).

19.   αἱ Παγασαί: a Thessalian city. For Thessalians as slave-dealers (at least in part a consequence of their easy access to Thrace, another major source of Greek slaves), see Ar. *Pl.* 521 ('from Thessaly, where there are the most slave-dealers').   στιγματίας: 'individuals with tattoos' (similarly contrasted with δοῦλοι at Ar. *Lys.* 330–2), i.e. 'barbarians' of the sort who, while they might not be slaves, would certainly be seen in Athens

performing the lowest forms of manual labour; cf. Jones, *JRS* 77 (1987), 140–50, esp. 144–7 (showing that the word does not refer to branding). Cf. **B45**. 14; **E25**. 2 with n.; Ar. fr. 71 (one of the eponymous 'Babylonians').

20–1. Paphlagonia was a region in northern Asia Minor.

20. τὰς ... Διὸς βαλάνους: 'Zeus' acorns', i.e. nuts that look like but taste better than acorns (which are extremely bitter); perhaps hazelnuts. Cf. Ath. 2. 53b–d (preserving ancient scholarly references to various nuts supposedly referred to alternatively as Διὸς βάλανοι).   σιγαλόεντα: commonly found at the end of Homeric lines (e.g. *Il.* 5. 226, 328; *Od.* 6. 26; 11. 189), but used there of more appropriate objects, such as reins and robes.

21. τὰ γάρ <τ'> ἀναθήματα δαιτός: 'for these are the accessories of a feast'; a quotation of *Od.* 1. 152 (of song and dance); 21. 430 (of song and the lyre) (both line-final). For nuts and other dainties eaten during symposia, see **H2**. 3 n.

22–3. Supply παρέχει (cf. 21) in both verses.

22. Σιδών: a major commercial city on the Phoenician coast. The paradosis Φοινίκη is unmetrical and most likely represents a superlinear gloss that drove out the word beneath it.   καρπὸν φοίνικος: 'the fruit of the palm tree', i.e. 'dates'; see Thphr. *HP* ii. 6. 2–8; iii. 3. 5; García Soler 119. σεμίδαλιν: 'hard wheat, durum wheat' (as opposed to σιτανίας πυρός, 'soft wheat'); see Olson–Sens on Archestr. fr. 5. 14. For Phoenicia as a producer of wheat, see A. *Supp.* 554–5; Antiph. fr. 36. 4–5; Herod. 2. 16–17.

23. δάπιδας καὶ ποικίλα προσκεφάλαια: 'rugs and embroidered pillows' (luxury goods used at dinner parties and symposia (e.g. Ar. *V.* 676; *Ec.* 840; Eub. fr. 119. 3); cf. **A13**. 14 n.).

D2. The plot of *Banqueters* (Aristophanes' first comedy; second place in 428/7) involved an old countryman and his two sons, referred to by the chorus (speaking for 'the poet') at Ar. *Nu.* 529 as ὁ σώφρων τε χὠ καταπύγων ('the decent one and the depraved one'). The depraved son studied law and rhetoric with the sophists, while the decent son got a traditional education, which in the late fifth century meant memorizing old-fashioned poetry (cf. **D13** introductory n.; Ar. *Nu.* 966–7)—one of Xenophon's characters claims to have learned all of Homer by heart (*Smp.* 3. 5)—but also, this passage makes clear, the meaning of obscure items of epic vocabulary. These verses come from a scene in which the father (Speaker A) questions his depraved son (Speaker B) in a style reminiscent of a teacher examining a student, and asks him to gloss a series of Homeric words and phrases (1–2). Rather than doing so, the depraved son demands that his brother give the meaning of a number of archaic legal and forensic terms (3–4). For the play, see A. C. Cassio, *Aristofane Banchettanti* (Pisa, 1977).

Preserved at Galen, *Hippocratic Glosses* xix. 65 Kühn, as part of an attempt to show that γλῶττα in the sense 'obscure word requiring explanation' was a traditional if rare usage. Galen has preserved only those portions of the passage that serve his immediate purposes, and more may have been lost than our text implies. In addition, Pollux ii. 109 preserves 1 as evidence that 'they called poetic words γλῶτται'.

Anapaestic tetrameters catalectic; probably from the *agon*.

1. **γλώττας:** 'obscure terms'. **τί καλοῦσι κόρυμβα,:** 'What do (the poets) refer to as κόρυμβα?', i.e. 'What does κόρυμβα mean?'; cf. 2, 3 ('What do (the ancient authorities) refer to as . . . ?'). κόρυμβα appears in Homer only at *Il.* 9. 241, where it seems to have the sense 'stern-posts'; subsequently at A. *Pers.* 411; E. *IA* 258.
2. **ἀμενηνὰ κάρηνα:** 'strengthless heads'; used of the dead in the Underworld at H. *Od.* 10. 521, 536; 11. 29, 49.
3. **ὁ . . . σός:** 'your (son)'. **μὲν οὖν:** 'to the contrary'; see B35. 9 n. **τί καλοῦσιν;:** see 1 n. **ἰδύους:** 'witnesses'; an obscure word said by late sources to have been used in the law-codes attributed to Draco (late seventh century) and Solon (early sixth century).
4. **ὀπύειν:** 'to wed'; an archaic verb supposedly used in one of Solon's laws— although also attested in Homer (e.g. *Il.* 13. 379; cf. Orph. 22. 2 F).

D3. An old man (cf. 25) emerges from his house and complains to the world at large about the haughty, pretentious cook he has hired to prepare a dinner party (cf. **C9–C10** n.; **G7** with introductory n.): the fellow insists on using Homeric vocabulary and is virtually incomprehensible. But most of the words and phrases the cook uses are less unusual than the genuine rarities referred to in **D2**, so that the humour depends on the audience understanding them even if his unsophisticated employer (20 with n.) does not; and many of the cook's 'Homeric' terms are used in odd, un-Homeric ways (6, 9, 23, 25, 29; cf. 15, 17), lending his 'learning' an air of absurdity. For other cooks' speeches, see **C10**; **G8**; **G11–G12**; and perhaps **G13**.

Preserved in the form printed here in PCair. 65445 (third century BC); the numerous gaps in the text (marked ⌊ . . . ⌋) have been filled in by reference to Athenaeus (1) 9. 382b–3b, where the passage is quoted by a slave cook in the course of a discussion about bombastic cooks. Lines 1–4 πάρεστιν are also quoted at Athenaeus (2) 14. 659b–c, in a collection of literary references to cooks that includes **G7**, but are attributed there to Philemon. The version of the text at Athenaeus (1) includes thirteen additional verses, which contribute little to the sense and probably represent an expansion of the speech by someone who liked it and wanted to make it even longer.

Iambic trimeter.

1. **σφίγγ(α) ἄρρεν(α)**: 'a male Sphinx', since the Sphinx was famous for her riddle (cf. **A14**. 3–4 with **A14** introductory n.) and the cook insists on using words the speaker cannot understand.

2. **ἁπλῶς ... οὐδὲ ἕν**: 'not a single thing'.

3. **ὧν** = τούτων ἅ.

3–4. **καινὰ ῥήματα | πεπορισμένος πάρεστιν**: What the cook *should* have come equipped with, of course, is pans, knives, spices, and the like (cf. **G9**). καινά is 'strange, bizarre', as again in 14.

4. **ὡς**: 'as soon as, the moment that'.   **εἰσῆλθε**: i.e. into the speaker's house, after they came back from the Agora, where the cook was hired (cf. **G7** introductory n.).

5. **προσβλέψας μέγα**: 'looking me boldly in the eye'; like his impatient tone (6 with n.), a mark of the cook's aggressive and decidedly unservile character. μέγα might be taken as adverbial with **ἐπηρώτησε** ('in a loud voice'), but is probably better treated as an internal accusative with the participle.

6. **κέκληκας**: 'you have invited', as at e.g. 14; **G12**. 2 οἱ κεκλημένοι ('the guests'); **G14**. 4; **H18**. 5.   **μέροπας** is an obscure Homeric word used routinely as an epithet of ἄνθρωποι and βροτοί (e.g. *Il*. 1. 250; 2. 285; 3. 402; cf. Pi. *N*. 4. 26, where it refers to the inhabitants of the island of Cos). The cook clearly means 'human beings', but the speaker thinks he is being offered a personal name (7–8); cf. 11–12 (a very similar joke). **λέγε** ('Tell me!') indicates the speaker's impatience, as at e.g. **C13**. 3; **E7**. 16; Ar. *Ach*. 812; Pl. Com. fr. 204. 1; Antiph. fr. 192. 14. Cf. 5 with n., 12–13.

7–8. **ἐγὼ κτλ.** is a baffled echo of 6 (where see n.) and equivalent to an emphatic negative response to the question ('I certainly have *not* invited any Μέροπας!').   **χολᾷς**: 'you're suffering from excessive bile!', i.e. 'you're crazy!'; cf. **C7**. 7; Taillardat § 478.

9. **δαιτυμὼν οὐθεὶς ὅλως**: 'not one single guest at all'. δαιτυμών is Homeric vocabulary, but is always used in epic poetry in the plural (e.g. *Od*. 4. 621; 7. 102, 148). The papyrus' οὐθείς (also **F16**. 4) is a fourth-century form of Athenaeus' οὐδείς; cf. οὐθέν (pap.) = οὐδέν (Ath.) in 19; **E3**. 9; **F16**. 10; **I3**. 5; μηθέν = μηδέν at **D6**. 13; **I4**. 3; Arnott, in Willi (2002) 200–1.

10. **Φιλῖνος, Μοσχίων, Νικήρατος**: common personal names (at least 58, 24, and 28 fifth- and fourth-century examples, respectively, in *LGPN* ii s.vv.; cf. **C15** introductory n. (Philinus); **C18** introductory n. (Moschion)).

11. **ὁ δεῖν(α), ὁ δεῖνα**: 'thus-and-such (and) thus-and-such' (cf. **A22**. 1 n.); the point is not that the speaker cannot recall the names, but that they are not germane to his point and need not be recited for his auditors.   **κατ(ὰ) ὄνομ(α) ἐπεπορευόμην**: 'I went through them name by name' (cf. **B39**. 1 n.).

13–14.   These lines do little more than repeat the joke in 9–12, this time with the emphasis on the cook's overbearing attitude rather than the perplexity of his employer.

14.   **καινὸν σφόδρα:** '—an extremely strange, very strange (thing)!' (cf. 3 n.).

15.   **ῥηξίχθον(α):** 'an earth-breaker', i.e. 'an ox'; the word is not attested elsewhere, but is intended to sound impressively 'epic'. The cook wrongly imagines that this is going to be a grand affair (cf. 16 n.), and is therefore shocked to learn that apparently no guests are invited (13–14). **ἄρα** expresses his amazement and disillusionment (Denniston 35–6).

16.   **βοῦν εὐρυμέτωπον:** 'a cow with a wide forehead'; a Homeric phrase (e.g. *Il.* 20. 495 βόας . . . εὐρυμετώπους; *Od.* 3. 382 βοῦν . . . εὐρυμέτωπον). Cows and oxen (15) were very expensive and furnished far more meat than a private individual could consume, making this an absurd question, as the response shows.   **ἄθλιε:** 'you miserable creature!'; a colloquial form of abuse also at e.g. Men. *Epitr.* 394; *Pk.* 390.

17–18.   **μῆλα** is poetic vocabulary (not restricted to Homer); the everyday equivalent is **πρόβατα**. But μῆλον can also mean 'tree-fruit', especially 'apple', hence the narrator's confused exasperation; cf. **D1.** 17 with n.

17.   **θυσιάζεις:** a very rare verb (first attested here) and used by the cook on that account; equivalent in sense to the common θύω.   **ἆρα** (here equivalent in sense to ἄρα) marks this as a conclusion the speaker has drawn (Denniston 45).

18.   **μῆλα πρόβατ(α);:** 'Apples are sheep?'

19.   **οὐθέν:** see 9 n.

20.   **ἀγροικότερος:** 'quite rural', i.e. 'quite unsophisticated'.   **ὥστ(ε):** 'therefore'.

21–2.   **τὰς οὐλοχύτας:** a Homeric term for the barley-grains (**κριθαί**) that were mixed with salt (23–6) and thrown at the victim or the altar before a sacrifice was made (e.g. *Il.* 1. 449; 2. 410; *Od.* 3. 447). See Olson on Ar. *Pax* 948–9.

22.   **ἀπόπληκτε:** 'one who has been knocked out of his wits, stunned' (< ἀποπλήσσω; cf. Pl. Com. fr. 138. 2; Amphis fr. 23. 5), i.e. 'idiot, lunatic' *vel sim.*   **περιπλοκάς:** 'entanglements, intricacies', and thus 'riddling phrases' (cf. **C8.** 1); in contrast to the simplicity and clarity requested in 20, 24.

23.   **πηγός** ('solid'; cognate with πήγνυμι) is a rare adjective applied to the sea's wave at *Od.* 5. 388; 23. 235, hence the cook's—very odd—use of it as a metonym for ἅλς (25).   **οὐχὶ λαικάσει;:** 'Take my cock in your mouth!' (for this use of οὐ + future indicative, see **B32.** 10 n.), i.e. 'Suck me!' A crude, colloquial insult; cf. Jocelyn, *PCPhS* 206 (1980), 12–66; Bain, *CQ* NS 41 (1991), 74–7.

24. σαφέστερον is adverbial, 'more clearly'. θ' (= τε) links λαικάσει in 23 with ἐρεῖς and thus belongs one position earlier, but has been post-poned for the sake of the metre.

25. ἀτάσθαλος: properly 'reckless', although what follows suggests that the cook intends it to mean something more like 'ignorant'. Homeric vocabulary (e.g. *Il.* 13. 634; *Od.* 7. 60). ἅλα φέρε: see 21–2 n.

26. δεῖξον: 'show (me)!', i.e. 'make available to me, give (me)!' χέρνιβον: 'a basin containing water to wash one's hands (χέρνιψ)' before sacrifice, and in which the sacrificial torch was dipped (see **A20**. 16 n.). The word is attested elsewhere before the fourth century only at H. *Il.* 24. 304 and is thus a bit peculiar in the mouth of the narrator, given his annoyance at the cook's use of recherché epic vocabulary.

27. παρῆν: i.e. 'was brought to him'. μυρία: 'countless, a million'; cf. **J7**. 1.

28. μὰ τὴν Γῆν: Solemn oaths by Earth are common in comedy (e.g. **E27**. 1; **F6**. 7; Ar. *Pax* 188 with Olson ad loc.; Ephipp. fr. 11. 2; Alex. fr. 128. 3; Men. *Dysc.* 908).

29. As the animal is butchered and the meat prepared, the cook continues to use vocabulary reminiscent of (but not necessarily restricted to) Homeric scenes of sacrifice: μίστυλλα is attested nowhere else but is cognate with Homeric μιστύλλω, 'cut meat into chunks (for spitting)' (e.g. *Il.* 24. 623; *Od.* 3. 462); μοίρας are the 'portions' into which roasted meat was divided before a meal began (e.g. *Od.* 3. 66; 8. 470); δίπτυχ(α) refers to the 'double-folded (fat)' in which the thighbones were wrapped before being burned as an offering to the gods (e.g. *Il.* 1. 461; *Od.* 3. 458); and ὀβελούς are the 'spits' on which the chunks of meat (above) and entrails were roasted (e.g. *Il.* 1. 465; *Od.* 3. 462–3; see **G9**. 1 n.). ἔδει: 'it would have been necessary, one would have had to'; see **B32**. 8 n.

30. τὰ τοῦ Φιλίτα . . . βυβλία: a reference to the Ἄτακτοι γλῶσσαι (*Miscellaneous Glosses*) of the late fourth-century poet and scholar Philetas of Cos (= Philet. test. 15 Sbardella); about thirty fragments of the work survive. Cf. Bing, *CP* 98 (2003), 330–48, esp. 343–6 (on this fragment).

31. 'to consider each of the words, what it means', i.e. 'to understand what each of the words meant' (prolepsis; see KG ii. 577–8, and cf. **D6**. 7; **F6**. 16–17; **F7**. 1; etc.).

32. ἤδη μεταβαλών: 'now taking a different tack', i.e. by pleading for cooperation (ἱκέτευον) rather than relying on abuse (cf. 22–4) to change the cook's behaviour.

33. ἀνθρωπίνως: 'like a human being'. In the fifth century λαλεῖν carries a strong sense of subjective disapproval ('chatter'; cf. Dover, *Frogs*, p. 22), but in the fourth it is often merely a colloquial equivalent of λέγω,

as here; cf. **E7**. 19; **F11**. 6 (where the point is not so much that the cicada—like a Pythagorean philosopher—talks nonsense, as that it 'talks' at all at midday).

34. **ἡ Πειθώ**: 'the goddess Persuasion'; personified already at Hes. *Op.* 73 and Orph. 15 F, and worshipped in Athens in the company of Aphrodite Pandemos (Isoc. 15. 249; Paus. i. 22. 3; cf. **E10**. 5; D. *Prooem.* 54; Stafford 111–45).

35. **ῥαψῳδοποιούτου τινός**: 'of some sort of rhapsode'. Rhapsodes performed epic poetry at public festivals and the like and served as significant repositories of 'Homeric learning' (cf. Pl. *Ion* 530c–d).   **ἐκ παιδός**: 'since boyhood, ever since he was a boy'.

36. **(ὁ) ἀλιτήριος**: 'the dirty bastard' *vel sim.* A strong term of abuse, drawn from the language of religious pollution; cf. Eup. fr. 103. 3; Eub. fr. 87. 2; Men. *Epitr.* 894; Olson on Ar. *Ach.* 907.

D4. Fish and whores were luxuries, and stewing is routinely presented cross-culturally as a more sophisticated style of cooking than roasting; and the speaker's point is that the Homeric heroes had a less pleasant life than epicures of his own day. Similar observations are made about the Homeric diet by Plato (*R.* 404b–c) and Antiphanes (fr. 248 '(Homer) didn't stew chunks of meat or brain, and he even roasted the guts; that's how old-fashioned he was'); so the first half of the speaker's characterization, at least, was probably a fourth-century *topos*. See Davidson 11–20.

Preserved at Athenaeus 1. 25b–c (manuscripts CE only), in a discussion of the Homeric lifestyle.

Iambic trimeter.

1–2. Just before he quotes this passage (which he dismisses as a joke), Athenaeus' speaker cites H. *Il.* 5. 487–8, where Sarpedon compares defeated warriors to 'those captured in the mesh of a fine net', in an attempt to show that Homer's characters knew about fishing and must therefore have eaten fish. There are numerous other Homeric references to catching fish (e.g. *Il.* 16. 406–8; 24. 80–2; *Od.* 10. 124; 12. 251–5; 19. 113; 22. 384–8), and Odysseus' men are said to eat fish at *Od.* 12. 330–2. But they do so only because the alternative is starvation, and Eubulus' character has the basic point right: although Homeric heroes are familiar with fishermen and fishing, if they have any choice in the matter, they prefer meat.

2. **κρέα δὲ μόνον ὤπτων**: 'And as for chunks of meat, all they did was roast them' (adverbial μόνον; ὤπτων is < ὀπτάω). Cf. **D3**. 29 n.

3. **ἕψοντα**: 'stewing (it)', thus making it softer (cf. **C9**. 6–8)—and to the speaker's way of thinking, more palatable—as roasting (2) generally does not.   **πεπόηκεν**: 'represented in his poetry'; see **B42**. 2 n.

4.　ἀλλ(ά) is progressive rather than adversative (Denniston 22).

4–5.　οὐδ(ὲ) ἑταίραν εἶδέ τις | αὐτῶν: In fact, Homer's Achaeans routinely sleep with women taken from captured cities, and the plot of the *Iliad* turns on a quarrel involving one. But Eubulus' character is technically correct that the poem never mentions prostitutes (for whom, see **I7–I12** with nn.), who must have followed in the train of any real army.

5.　ἑαυτοὺς . . . ἔδεφον: 'they jerked off' (a primary obscenity; cf. *Maculate Muse*, p. 35); the verb is used elsewhere only in the middle (Ar. *Eq.* 24, 29; *Pax* 290; *Ec.* 709).　　ἐνιαυτοὺς δέκα: 'for ten years', the traditional length of the siege of Troy.

6.　πικρὰν στρατείαν . . . εἶδον: 'to their cost they saw the expedition!', i.e. 'the expedition turned out badly for them!' For the idiom, e.g. Ar. *Av.* 1045; *Th.* 853; H. *Od.* 17. 448; S. *El.* 470–1; E. *Ba.* 357.　　δ(έ) is not really needed, but marks this as a passionate exclamation (Denniston 172).

6–7.　πόλιν | μίαν λαβόντες: 'after capturing a single city'; a rare use of λαμβάνω. A dismissive qualification: in ten years of war (5), Homer's heroes took only one city—and paid a substantial personal price for their accomplishment. In fact, many other cities were sacked in the course of the expedition (e.g. H. *Il.* 1. 163–4) and Troy was only the last and biggest.

7–8.　εὐρυπρωκτότεροι πολὺ | κτλ.: 'they left having been fucked harder than the city they captured'. εὐρύπρωκτος (literally 'with a wide arsehole', sc. as a result of having been repeatedly and vigorously buggered) is a colloquial insult (e.g. Ar. *Ach.* 716; *Nu.* 1083–99; *Th.* 200), and sexual violence functions easily as an image of military conquest, since rape was common when cities were captured. But the speaker's more significant— and more amusing—point is that, because the Achaeans had no 'normal' outlet for their sexual energies (4–5), they must have resorted to making aggressive use of one another.

8.　ἧς ought properly to be ἥν, but has been attracted into the case of its antecedent.

D5. A defence of the practice of telling and listening to sad tales, with particular attention to tragedy (see 5 n.), as having a simultaneously educational and consolatory function. Cf. **D14**. 1–2. Whether women attended theatrical performances in Athens in the classical period is unclear (see Henderson, *TAPA* 121 (1991), 133–47; Gerö and Johnsson, *Eranos* 99 (2001), 87–99); but all the members of the audience referred to here are in any case male.

Preserved at (1) Athenaeus 6. 223b–d, along with **D6** and Diph. fr. 29, both of which also discuss the nature of tragic art; and (2) Stobaeus iv. 56. 19, in a section entitled 'Consolatory (Passages)'.

Iambic trimeter.

1. **ὦ τᾶν**: 'my good sir'. A colloquial form of address, ostensibly polite but normally bossy, impatient, or condescending (as here); cf. Stevens 42–3. **ἄκουσον κτλ.**: 'listen (and judge) if I seem to you to be saying anything (worthwhile)', i.e. 'if what I say makes sense to you'. Colloquial; cf. Ar. *V.* 1409; E. *HF* 279; Stevens 25.

2. 'Man is a creature doomed to trouble by his very nature'. A typical 'New Comic' gnome (e.g. Philem. fr. 121. 3; Philippid. fr. 18. 3; Nicostr. Com. fr. 29. 1; cf. **E3.** 1–3).

3. A sententious restatement of the thesis put forward in 2: troubles are a normal part of human existence.

4. **παραψυχὰς ... φροντίδων**: 'consolations of anxious thoughts, distractions from anxious thoughts'.   **ἀνεύρετο**: 'invented for itself' (cf. **E25.** 3; E. *Med.* 194, 196); supply ὁ βίος (3) or more likely ὁ ἄνθρωπος (2) as subject.

5. **ταύτας** shows that the activity the speaker calls a 'consolation' (4) has already been referred to (unfavourably) by his or her interlocutor, while **8–16** treat seeing tragic performances as only one example of this sort of thing (presumably an elevated example, lending the behaviour in question more dignity); and the topic under discussion must therefore be simply listening to tales of the woes of others.

5–6. **ὁ γὰρ κτλ.**: complementary phenomena, since one forgets one's own troubles (5) as a result of becoming fascinated by accounts of the sufferings endured by others (6). But the effect is more signficant and enduring than that; see 7 n.

5. **τῶν ἰδίων**: 'its own affairs', i.e. 'its own troubles'.

6. **πρὸς ἀλλοτρίωι ... ψυχαγωγηθεὶς πάθει**: 'entranced in the presence of', i.e. 'at the sight of another person's suffering'. For the verb (which hints at wizardry), cf. Ar. *Av.* 1555 with Dunbar ad loc.

7–16. The first verse describes the results of the phenomena referred to in 5–6: the listener (strictly speaking his νοῦς; cf. **H13.** 2 n.) 'goes away'—sc. from the discussion or show implicitly referred to in the preceding verses— 'happy' (**μετ(ὰ) ἡδονῆς**), because he has forgotten his own troubles, and 'simultaneously educated' (**παιδευθεὶς ἅμα**), because he has learned something new about the world. But 8–16 develop the argument in a different way: what a man learns from experiences of this sort can have a permanent effect on his sense of his own position, by proving that his griefs are less significant than he was inclined to think (cf. 17–19).   **ἀπῆλθε**: a gnomic aorist (Goodwin § 154–5) expressing a general truth.

8. **πρῶτον** is adverbial, 'first of all'.   **εἰ βούλει**: 'if you will, if you please'. Impatient rather than accommodating; cf. Philem. fr. 113. 1 (also introducing an individual item intended to help prove a larger point).

9. ὁ μέν refers to a member of the audience (not one of the tragic poets). For the delayed position of γάρ, cf. **E26**. 1; Denniston 97.

10. καταμαθών: 'after he sees, recognizes . . .'; cf. 16 κατέμαθεν with n. τὸν Τήλεφον: Telephus was king of the Mysians, a barbarian people in north-west Asia Minor, and was wounded in the leg by Achilleus when the Achaeans mistakenly attacked his country rather than Troy in a pre-liminary raid on the region. When Telephus' leg failed to heal, he was advised by an oracle to seek the assistance of 'the one that had done the wounding' or the like, and he therefore disguised himself as a beggar and infiltrated the Achaean camp. Cf. Hes. fr. 165; [Apollod.] *Epit.* 3. 17–19; Gantz 428–31, 576–80; Olson, *Acharnians*, pp. liv–lxi (with bibliography). Aeschylus (frr. 238–40; see **J7**. 6 n.), Euripides (frr. 696–727c; cf. Ar. *Ach.* 414–70), Iophon (*TrGF* 22 F 2c), Agathon (*TrGF* 39 F 4), Cleophon (*TrGF* 77 F 11), and Moschion (*TrGF* 97 F 2) all wrote tragedies about Telephus.

11. ἤδη: 'at once'. τὴν πενίαν echoes ὢν . . . πένης in 9. ῥᾷον is adverbial, 'more easily'.

12. ὁ νοσῶν τι μανικόν: 'the fellow who suffers from some sort of madness'. Ἀλκμέων(α) ἐσκέψατο: 'considers Alcmeon', sc. 'and realizes he's not as badly off as he might be' (cf. 9–11); for the aorist, cf. 16. Alcmeon was the son of the seer Amphiaraus, who ordered him to kill his mother Eriphyle because she forced Amphiaraus to accompany Adrastus on the expedition of the Seven against Thebes, despite her knowing that he would die there. Alcmeon later accompanied Adrastus and the sons of the other original 'Seven' (the Epigoni) in a second expedition against Thebes; after he had taken revenge for his father by sacking the place (cf. 16 n.), he killed Eriphyle. Her Furies then drove him mad, and he wandered from city to city until he was purified by the river-god Acheloos, who gave him his daughter Callirhoe in marriage. Cf. **D6**. 8–12 (a typical tragic theme) with nn.; Th. ii. 102. 5–6; Asclep. Trag. *FGrHist* 12 F 29; [Apollod.] *Bib.* iii. 6. 2, 7. 5; Paus. viii. 24. 7–10; Gantz 522–7. Tragedies entitled *Alcmeon* were written by Sophocles (frr. 108–10), Euripides (two plays; frr. 65–87a), Agathon (*TrGF* 39 F 2), Timotheus (*TrGF* 56 F 1), Astydamas II (*TrGF* 60 F 1b–c), and Theodectes (*TrGF* 72 F 1a).

13–16. The initial proposition in each line functions like an 'if'-clause, as at **C9**. 6, 8; **C11**. 3–6; **I7**. 7–20; **J13**. 4–8; cf. **D12**. 7–8. See KG ii. 233–4.

13. ὀφθαλμιᾶι: 'has an eye-infection', a different matter from being per-manently blind, as what follows makes clear. Cf. Olson on Ar. *Ach.* 1027. εἰσὶ Φινεῖδαι τυφλοί: 'the sons of Phineus'—who was king of Salmydessus and was visited by the Argonauts, who drove away the Harpies that were plaguing him—'are blind', as a result of the machinations of their step-mother Idaia. Cf. S. *Ant.* 970–6; [Apollod.] *Bib.* iii. 15. 3; Gantz 349–56. The story does not appear to have been popular among the tragic poets, and this is most likely a specific reference to a play by Sophocles (esp. frr. 704; 710; 715) praised at Arist. *Po.* 1455ª10–12.

14. *ἡ Νιόβη κεκούφικε*: 'Niobe has given him relief, lifted his spirits'. Niobe, the wife of King Amphion of Thebes, had a large number of children; but when she boasted that she was more fortunate than the goddess Leto (who had only two), Leto's children Apollo and Artemis killed them all. Cf. H. *Il.* 24. 602–17; [Apollod.] *Bib.* iii. 5. 6; Gantz 536–9. Plays entitled *Niobe* were written by Aeschylus (frr. 154a–67b; cf. Ar. *Ra.* 911–26) and Sophocles (frr. **441a–51).

15. *τὸν Φιλοκτήτην*: Philoctetes was one of the original Achaean commanders in the expedition against Troy, but was abandoned on the desert island of Lemnos after he was struck on the foot by a viper and the wound began to fester and stink. Odysseus and a companion (Neoptolemus in some sources, Diomedes in others) fetched him again in the ninth year of the war; after one of Asclepius' sons healed him, he killed Paris with his bow. Cf. H. *Il.* 2. 718–24; Gantz 589–90, 635–8; Olson on Ar. *Ach.* 424–5. Tragedies concerned with Philoctetes' escape from Lemnos were written by Aeschylus (frr. 249–57), Sophocles (the preserved *Philoctetes*), Euripides (frr. 787–803), and Philocles (*TrGF* 24 T 1); cf. Olson, *Hesperia*, 60 (1991), 269–83; C. W. Müller, *Philoktet* (Beiträge zur Altertumskunde 100: Stuttgart and Leipzig, 1997).

16. *κατέμαθεν*: 'he learns about, observes'; cf. 7 n., 12.   *τὸν Οἰνέα*: In his old age, Oineus king of Calydon was driven into exile by the sons of his brother Agrius and suffered endless humiliations until his grandson Tydeus returned from sacking Thebes (cf. 12 n.) and either restored him to power or took him off into exile. Cf. Pherecyd. *FGrHist* 3 F 122; [Apollod.] *Bib.* i. 7. 10–8. 6; Gantz 328–33; Olson on Ar. *Ach.* 418–19 (where Oineus is referred to as ὁ δύσποτμος γεραιός ('the ill-fated old man')). Euripides (frr. 558–70), Ion (*TrGF* 19 F 36–41b), Philocles (*TrGF* 24 T 1), and perhaps Sophocles (fr. 470 Pearson = adesp. tr. fr. 327c) all wrote plays entitled *Oineus*.

17–19. These lines sum up the argument in 8–16; see 7 n.

17. *ἢ πέπονθέ τις*: 'than someone has suffered', i.e. 'than he himself has suffered'.

19. *ἧττον* is adverbial, 'less'.

D6. A comic poet's complaint about the advantages enjoyed by tragedians; perhaps part of a debate in which representatives of the two genres argued for the superiority of their own art. Nothing else is preserved of the play; but the obvious response to the arguments put forward here is that the very familiarity of the material with which tragic poets worked demanded greater ingenuity to make the story interesting. Aristotle in the *Poetics* says in regard to tragedy that 'even the well-known myths are known to only a few, although they give pleasure to everyone' (1451^{b}25–6), an argument whose initial thesis contrasts strikingly with what is asserted here. Cf. Crates fr. 28, with Whittaker 188; Nesselrath 240–1 (who notes that Antiphanes' play probably dates to a period when mythological parody was no longer the dominant style of Attic comedy); Rosen, in L. Kozak and J. Rich (eds.), *Playing around Aristophanes* (Oxford, 2006), 27–47.

Preserved at Athenaeus 6. 222a–3a, in a speech that also includes **D5** (where see introductory n.).

Iambic trimeter.

1–2.   μακάριον . . . | ποίημα: 'an enviable type of poetry'. But the 'praise' that follows is both bitter and ironic, as 13–16 in particular make clear.
2.   κατὰ πάντ(α): 'in every respect'.   εἴ γε: 'since, given that'. πρῶτον is adverbial, 'first of all'.   οἱ λόγοι: 'the plots'; cf. **B1**. 1.
4.   πρὶν καί τιν(α) εἰπεῖν: 'before anyone even speaks a word (on stage)'. ὑπομνῆσαι: 'to offer (the audience) a reminder', sc. by announcing the hero's name (5, 9).
5.   Οἰδίπουν γ(ε) ἂν φῆι <μόνον>: 'if (the poet) merely says "Oedipus"'. The mss' Οἰδίπουν γὰρ φῶ is metrically deficient, and 9 suggests that a third-person rather than a first-person verb is wanted.
6–8.   The story most obviously alluded to here is the one told in Sophocles' *Oedipus the King*; cf. **D8–D10** n. But there are also glancing allusions (esp. in the second half of 7) to related myths, such as the expedition of the Seven against Thebes and Antigone's confrontation with Creon, that help fill out Oedipus' biography in the audience's mind. Aeschylus (test. 78. 12b) and Euripides (frr. 539a–57) also wrote plays entitled *Oedipus*, as did e.g. Achaeus (*TrGF* 20 F 30–1), Philocles I (*TrGF* 24 T 1), and Xenocles I (*TrGF* 33 F 1).
7.   θυγατέρες, παῖδες τίνες: 'his daughter (and) his sons, who they are', i.e. 'who his sons and daughters are'. For the prolepsis, cf. **D3**. 31 n.
8.   τί πείσετ(αι) οὗτος: sc. when he blinds himself.   τί πεπόηκεν: sc. by killing his father and sleeping with his mother (hence the reference to them in 6–7) before the action begins.
8–12.   For Alcmeon's story, see **D5**. 12 n.
8.   πάλιν: 'on the other hand'.
9–10.   τὰ παιδία | πάντ(α): a reference to Acarnan and Amphoterus, Alcmeon's sons by Callirhoe, who took vengeance for him after he was murdered by agents of King Phegeus of Psophis ([Apollod.] *Bib*. iii. 7. 6).

10. εὐθύς is adverbial, 'at once, immediately' (**A12**. 4 n.), i.e. 'without saying another word'.

10–11. μανεὶς ἀπέκτονε | τὴν μητέρ(α): 'he went mad and killed his mother', with the madness treated as having come first, although it was actually the consequence of the killing.

11. ἀγανακτῶν δ(ὲ) Ἄδραστος: for a quarrel between Alcmeon and Adrastus, presumably before they agreed to march together against Thebes, cf. S. fr. **187. In Sophocles, Alcmeon has already murdered his mother before the quarrel, as also here, if the speaker is giving the standard elements of the story in order, as εὐθέως ('at once'; cf. εὐθύς in 10) perhaps implies. Or is the point that Adrastus appears at the very beginning of the play?

12. πάλιν τ(ε) ἄπεισι: The second half of the line is lost, and Adrastus' destination (his native city of Argos, after he has temporarily lost the argument with Alcmeon? or Thebes?) is unclear.

13. ἔπειτ(α): 'next'; introducing the second main item in the complaint (13–16).   μηθέν: see **D3**. 9 n.   δύνωντ(αι): sc. οἱ τραγωιδοί ('the tragic poets').

14. κομιδῆι ... ἀπειρήκωσιν: 'they have utterly collapsed from exhaustion'; see 15 n. For κομιδῆι ('absolutely, entirely'), see **C8**. 12 n.

15. αἴρουσιν ... τὴν μηχανήν: 'they raise the theatrical crane' (for which, see Mastronarde, *CA* 9 (1990), 268–72), bringing a god on stage and thus putting an abrupt—and, the speaker implies, artificial—end to the action, as e.g. in Euripides' *Ion* or Sophocles' *Philoctetes*. Cf. the criticism implicit in Socrates' comparison at Pl. *Crat.* 425d of a desperate argumentative ploy to the behaviour of 'the tragic poets, who when they are at a loss about something, flee to the theatrical cranes and raise up gods (upon them)'. ὥσπερ δάκτυλον: a reference to the gesture used by a competitor in a boxing or *pankration* match to signal that he had been defeated and did not wish to continue; cf. Gardiner figs. 173, 180, 186; M. B. Poliakoff, *Combat Sports in the Ancient World* (New Haven and London, 1987), plates 62, 71.

16. τοῖς θεωμένοισιν ἀποχρώντως ἔχει: 'it's enough for the spectators', i.e. 'the spectators are satisfied'—as they ought not to be. Cf. the similarly disgusted comments in 21–3.

17. ἡμῖν ... ταῦτ(α) οὐκ ἔστιν: 'we (comic poets) lack these advantages'.

18–19. The lacuna must have contained several other items that comic poets (unlike tragic poets; cf. 5–12) are forced to invent.

19–20. τὰ διωιχημένα | πρότερον: 'what has gone by, occurred (< διοίχο-μαι) earlier', i.e. 'the background', in contrast to τὰ νῦν παρόντα, 'the current situation'.

20–1. τὴν καταστροφήν is 'the conclusion', as opposed to τὴν εἰσβολήν, 'the introduction'.

22.   **Χρέμης τις ἢ Φείδων τις**: 'some(one called) Chremes or Pheidon', treated here as typical comic names (cf. Ar. *Nu.* 134; *Ec.* 477). **ἐκσυρίττεται**: 'he's hissed off the stage'. For hissing or whistling as a sign of derisive disapproval, e.g. Timocl. Com. fr. 19. 6–7; X. *Smp.* 6. 5; D. 18. 265; and cf. Pl. *Lg.* 700c–1a.

23.   **Πηλεῖ ... καὶ Τεύκρωι**: two more heroes of the sort typically seen on stage in tragedy, the former the father of Achilleus, the latter the brother of Telamonian Ajax.   **πάντ(α)**: 'everything', i.e. 'whatever they want'; cf. **D1**. 5.

D7.   Aristophanes refers a number of times to Aeschylus, often as an example of a very 'old-fashioned' sort of poetry (*Ach.* 10; *Nu.* 1364–7; *Lys.* 188–9a (cf. A. *Th.* 42ff.); *Ra. passim*; also e.g. *Th.* 134–40 (cf. A. fr. 61) with Austin–Olson ad loc.; *Ec.* 391–3 (~ A. fr. 138); fr. 696 (a character in an unidentified play, perhaps *Gerytades*)), and to the pseudo-Aeschylean *Prometheus Bound* (e.g. *Eq.* 836 ~ *PV* 613; see Olson on *Pax* 319–20); Eupolis seems to quote him at fr. 207 (~ A. *Pers.* 65; perhaps the first verse of the parabasis); and he appeared on stage not only in Aristophanes' *Frogs* but also as a character in Pherecrates' *Small Change* (fr. 100, probably from the *agon*; cf. Whittaker 186). But Aeschylus otherwise receives relatively little attention from the comic poets, who—presumably reflecting the tastes and experience of their audiences—show more interest in Sophocles and especially Euripides. See in general Silk, in *Rivals*, 302–5. (But cf. **A4–A5** n.; **I10**. 3–4 n.; **J7**. 6 n.; Cratinus' *Eumenides* (frr. 69–70); Anaxil. fr. 19. 1–2.)

   This fragment (presumably from the prologue) is a parody of the opening scene of *Eumenides*, in which the Delphic priestess emerges in terror from Apollo's temple to announce that she has found a suppliant with bloody hands (Orestes) within 'and in front of this man sleeps an extraordinary band of women', who turn out to be the Furies (40–7). In Timocles' play, however, the women are prostitutes (see 2–4 n.), and Orestes' place is taken by someone named Autocleides (hence the title; cf. Cratinus' *Dionysalexandros* (see **B13–B20** n.), Aristophanes' *Aeolosicon* (see **F19**. 4 n.), and Eubulus' *Sphinx-Carion* (**E30**)), about whom nothing certain is known, although Aeschines (a contemporary of Timocles) refers to an Autocleides (*PAA* 238785) who, Harpocration informs us, was a notorious pederast (Aeschin. 1. 52; Harp. *A* 267). The only other fragment of *Orestautocleides* is the word παράβυστον (Timocl. Com. fr. 28), which Harpocration *Π* 21 says was used for the lawcourt in which the Eleven (who had the power to arrest, try, and execute certain classes of criminals; see Harrison ii. 17–18) met; and the fact that precisely eleven women are named in fr. 27. 2–4 suggests that Autocleides was tried for his life, like Orestes in Aeschylus' tragedy (thus Maidment). For the strikingly personal style of Timocles' comedies (330s–310s BC), see **E31** introductory n.

Preserved at Athenaeus 13. 567e–f, in a discussion of prostitutes and prostitution (for which, see **I7–I12**).

Iambic trimeter.

2–4. Many of these names are used for prostitutes elsewhere in contemporary sources. For *Νάννιον*, see Eub. fr. 67 (the title-character); Amphis fr. 23. 3; Anaxil. fr. 22. 15; Alex. fr. 225. 1; Hyp. fr. 141 Jensen; Antiphanes' *On Courtesans* (*FGrHist* 349 F 2a) ap. Ath. 13. 587b. For *Πλαγγών*, see Eub. fr. 86 (the title-character); Anaxil. fr. 22. 8. For *Λύκα*, see Amphis fr. 23. 3. For *Γνάθαινα*, see Philippid. fr. 5. 3; Lync. ap. Ath. 13. 584b–e; Macho 258–332, etc. For *Φρύνη*, see Timocl. Com. fr. 25. 2; Lync. ap. Ath. 13. 584c. For *Πυθιονίκη*, see Antiph. fr. 27. 20; Timocl. Com. frr. 15–16; and cf. Asclep. *AP* v. 164. 2 = *HE* 867. For *Μυρρίνη*, see Ath. 13. 590c ('the most expensive prostitute in Athens'). For *Χρυσίς*, see Antiph. frr. 223–4 (the title-character). But it is impossible to know whether there was (e.g.) one Nannion or many, which is to say if these are simply generic names used by any number of women.

4. *Λοπάδιον* ('Little Casserole-Dish') seems an odd name, although cf. *Πλαθάνη* ('Bread-pan'; a female cook's name at Ar. *Ra.* 549) and *Πατανίων* ('Little Casserole' (see **G8.** 3–4 n.); a cook's name at Philetaer. fr. 14. 1). Perhaps the implication is that, when the woman was younger, she worked in a kitchen—or simply that she was delectable.

D8–D10. For other comic references or allusions to Sophocles (generally favourable), see **C1.** 3; **D6.** 6–8; Phryn. Com. fr. 68 ap. D.L. 4. 20; Ar. *Pax* 531, 695–9; *Ra.* 76–82, 664–7 (~ S. fr. 371), 786–94, 1515–19; frr. 427 (cf. S. fr. 890) with K–A ad loc.; 598; 958; Eup. frr. 41. 2 (cf. S. fr. 890); 268. 7; cf. **E5.** 2 (cf. S. *OT* 629); **J7.** 6 n. Strattis' *Philoctetes* (frr. 44–5) may have been a parody of Sophocles' play; and cf. Taplin 83–8 with his pl. 22 (an Apulian *phlyax*-vase (= Trendall #59 with pl. IV. a) apparently illustrating a parody of *Antigone*). Antiph. fr. 1. 6 probably refers to the younger Sophocles (*TrGF* 62, Sophocles' grandson?).

D8. An attack on an *archon* (doubtless named in the preceding lines) who failed to favour Sophocles in the selection of poets for one of the city's dramatic festivals; cf. Introduction, p. 18.

Preserved at Athenaeus 14. 638e–f, in a collection of comic references to musicians and poets named Gnesippus that also includes (in order) Chionid. fr. 4; Eup. fr. 148 (= **D13**); Cratin. frr. 104; 276; and Telecl. fr. 36, as part of a larger discussion of authors of disreputable poetry.

Iambic trimeter.

2.　Cratinus also refers to 'the son of Cleomachus' as a depraved tragic poet in fr. 276. 1–2 (3 n.), and Athenaeus or his source apparently had reason to believe that the individual in question was named Gnesippus (*PAA* 279690; *TrGF* 27). This is a very rare name (only two other examples in *LGPN* ii, including the man referred to below), and if the identification with 'the son of Cleomachus' is correct, Cratinus' tragedian is probably the same person as the citharode Gnesippus referred to in the other comic fragments Athenaeus cites (*PAA* 279680; Stephanis #556), who must then belong to the first half of the fifth century, if Chionides mentioned him. Cf. **D13**. 3–4 n.; and see Davidson, in *Rivals*, 41–64 (a highly speculative discussion of a very complex question; cf. Hordern, *CQ* ns 53 (2003), 608–13). In any case, no fragments attributed to anyone known to have been the son of Cleomachus (or to have been named Gnesippus) have been preserved, and it is impossible to say how fair the attack mounted here is; perhaps Sophocles offered weak material and was quite appropriately refused a chorus.

2–3.　For the colloquial repetition of ἄν (which does not substantially affect the sense), see Slings, *CP* 87 (1992), 102–4.

3.　ἐμοὶ διδάσκειν: 'to serve as my διδάσκαλος, my trainer'; but the term is routinely used of the poet (e.g. Cratin. fr. 276. 1–2 τραγωιδίας | ὁ Κλεομάχου διδάσκαλος; Ar. *Ach.* 628; *Pax* 738), whether he trained the chorus himself or not.　　　εἰς Ἀδώνια: 'for the Adonia', a festival (not officially sponsored by the Athenian state) in which the city's women mourned the premature death of Aphrodite's mortal lover Adonis; cf. Ar. *Lys.* 389–96; Pherecr. fr. 181; Men. *Sam.* 38–46; Olson on Ar. *Pax* 420 (with bibliography); Dillon, *Hermes*, 131 (2003), 1–16. The Adonia featured drinking and dancing, and the speaker's point is not that it also included dramatic choruses but that the poetry of 'the son of Cleomachus' is better suited for crude, lascivious occasions of that sort—and perhaps not even for them. Cf. **E5**. 1–2; Ar. *Ra.* 732–3.

D9. Phrynichus' *Muses* took second place at the Lenaia in 405, behind Aristophanes' *Frogs* (in which Sophocles (d. 406) is spoken of in similarly laudatory terms at 82, cf. 1515–19), and Meineke suggested that the plots of the two plays may have been similar. This is a μακαρισμός, and much of it might have been pronounced in remembrance of any man who had lived a long and happy life and died well and easily; indeed, 1 and 4 could easily stand alone together, without 2–3. But the end of 2 introduces, at the last possible moment, the idea of Sophocles as poet, and this is developed in 3 before the return to more conventional sentiments in 4.

Preserved in the second hypothesis to Sophocles' *Oedipus at Colonus*, in the context of a discussion of the date of the tragedy and (if Sophocles was dead by the time it was staged, as he certainly was) who produced it.

Iambic trimeter.

1. **βιούς**: masculine nominative singular aorist active participle < βιόω.
2. **δεξιός** is commonly used of poets (Dover, *Frogs*, pp. 13–14; cf. **D14**. 12) and thus serves to introduce 3.
3–4. **καλάς** is picked up in **καλῶς**, just as **πολλάς** echoes **πολὺν χρόνον** in 1.
4. **ὑπομείνας**: 'after enduring'.

D10. Lines 3–6 are a witty adaptation of S. *Ant.* 712–14 ὁρᾶις παρὰ ῥείθρ-οισι χειμάρροις ὅσα | δένδρων ὑπείκει, κλῶνας ὡς ἐκσώιζεται, | τὰ δ' ἀντιτείνοντ' αὐτόπρεμν' ἀπόλλυται ('you see beside streams swollen with rain that the trees that bend save their branches, but those that resist are ripped out by the roots'; Haemon's advice to Creon), which was famous enough to be adapted (somewhat less aggressively) also at Eup. fr. *260. 23–5.

Preserved at Athenaeus 1. 22f–3a (manuscripts CE only), in a collection of literary passages that praise drinking as a cure for heat and dryness.

Iambic trimeter.

1–2. **τὸ ... ζῆν, ... | τί ἐστι;**: 'What's the point of being alive?' A rhetorical rather than a real question, as the impatient **εἰπέ μοι** (cf. **C13**. 1 n.) makes clear.
4–5. **ἀεὶ τὴν νύκτα κτλ.**: An abrupt divergence from the Sophoclean exemplar: the trees in question are drenched with flood-water all day and all night, just as the speaker wishes to be constantly drenched with wine; and such trees do not merely survive, but flourish.
5. **βρέχεται**: As parallels for the use of this verb to refer to drinking wine ('wetting one's whistle' *vel sim.*), Athenaeus (1. 23a–b) cites Antiph. fr. 279; Eub. fr. 123.

D11–D12. For other comic quotations, references, or allusions to Euripides, see **D11** introductory n.; **D12**. 7–9 with n. (with further citations); **D13**. 1–2 n.; **F3** with introductory n.; **F5** (associated with Socrates); **G11**. 1–2 (~ E. *Med.* 57–8); **I2**. 9–12 with n.; **J16**. 1 (~ E. *Ph.* 546); Cratin. fr. 299. 4 (~ E. fr. 664. 2); Ar. *Ach.* 394–479; *Lys.* 368–9; *Th. passim*; *Ra. passim*; frr. 53. 1 (~ E. *Hipp.* 219); 570 with K–A ad loc.; 574 (~ E. *Ph.* 182) (the last two from a play entitled *Phoenician Women*, probably a parody of Euripides' tragedy); 694; Stratt. frr. 46 (cf. E. fr. 752); 47 (cf. E. *Ph.* 460–1) (like **J16**, both from a play entitled *Phoenician Women*, probably a parody of Euripides' tragedy); Anaxandr. fr. 66 (~ E. fr. 265a); Eub. frr. 6. 2 (~ E. *Andr.* 369) with K–A ad loc.; 9–12 (a parody of E. *Antiope*) with Nesselrath 223–7; 64. 2 (~ E. *Or.* 37); Antiph. frr. 19–20 (a parody of E. *Aeolus*) with Nesselrath 205–9; 205. 6–8;

Alex. fr. 3. 1 (~ E. *Or.* 255); Axionic. frr. 3–4 (from *The Man Who Loved Euripides*); Philem. frr. 118; 153; Men. *Asp.* 424–5 (~ E. *Or.* 1–2), 427; Diph. fr. 60. 1–3 (~ E. fr. 915); Nicostr. Com. fr. 29 (= E. fr. 661. 1); adesp. com. fr. 1111. 7; Rhint. *Iphigenia in Aulis, Iphigenia in Tauris, Medea,* and *Orestes.* For Euripides' influence on typical 'New Comic' plots, see Nesselrath, *HSCP* 95 (1993), 181–95 (arguing that parody was the fundamental means by which Euripidean plot-devices entered the comic poets' dramatic repertoire).

D11. Dionysius I, tyrant of Syracuse from 405 to 367 BC, competed in the dramatic festivals in Athens with his own tragedies and was finally victorious with *The Ransom of Hector* at the Lenaia just before he died (*TrGF* 76 T 1). Eubulus' comedy was clearly devoted to mocking Dionysius' literary pretensions (cf. the similarly hostile attitude expressed at Ephipp. fr. 16. 1), and most likely Dionysius himself is the speaker and 1–2 (which lack a verb) represent the conclusion of his quotation of remarks by his critics, who mockingly compare his alleged tendency to sigmatism with Euripides'. But it is also possible that 1–2 and 3–4 are separate fragments which have been run together by a copyist, and that 3–4 are spoken by Euripides himself (having presumably come back from the dead to confront modern pretenders to his art); or the corruption may run even deeper than this.

Preserved in a *scholium* on E. *Med.* 476 ἔσωσά σ' ὡς ἴσασιν Ἑλλήνων ὅσοι (Medea to Jason), along with Pl. Com. fr. 29, as evidence of Euripides' reputation for an overfondness for the letter *sigma.* The charge is ill founded (see Clayman, *TAPA* 117 (1987), 69–84) and is probably based on a few famous—or notorious—verses like those quoted (in carefully altered form) in 1–2.

Iambic trimeter.

1. **Εὐριπίδου δ(έ):** sc. ἐστι, 'Euripides has', i.e. 'is responsible for'. **ἔσωσά σ(ε) ὡς ἴσασ(ι) ὅσοι:** an abbreviated quotation of E. *Med.* 476 (above), the asigmatic Ἑλλήνων having been omitted.
2. **παρθέν(ε) εἰ <σώσαιμί> σ(ε), ἕξεις μοι χάριν;:** a slightly altered quotation of E. *Andromeda* fr. 129 ὦ παρθέν', εἰ σώσαιμί σ', εἴσηι μοι χάριν; (Περσευσ το Ανδρομεδα), ωιτη τηε συβστιτυτιον οφ ἕξεις for Euripides' εἴσηι adding one more sibilant (thus Hunter).
3. **ἐγγελῶσι:** 'they mock at, make fun of' + dative.
4. **ὡς αὐτοὶ σοφοί:** 'as if they were wise themselves', i.e. 'particularly good poets'; cf. **B11** n.

D12. Synoris (the title-character of the play) was an Athenian courtesan (thus Athenaeus in his introduction to this fragment and at 13. 583e) and may well be Speaker B. Cf. **I11** introductory n. (on courtesans as stock

'Middle' and 'New Comic' characters). Speaker A is a parasite with whom she is shooting dice (1).

Preserved at Athenaeus 6. 247b–c, as part of an extended discussion of parasites that also includes **A13** (where see introductory n.).

Iambic trimeter.

1.   'You come off very well as regards (cf. LSJ s. ἐπί A. III. 3) this die', i.e. 'this throw'; probably a sarcastic remark, given Speaker B's response in 2.

2.   **ἀστεῖος εἶ**: flat and perfunctory praise ('Ha-ha. You're very funny'), as is clear from the rapidity with which the speaker (who has apparently lost her money and wants to win it back) changes the subject.   **ὑπόθες** is 'Bet!, Up the stakes!' (LSJ s.v. VII. 2), and the prefix ὑπο- is to be supplied with **κεῖται** ('It's been put up!'; cf. LSJ s. ὑπόκειμαι II. 7) as well.

3.   **Εὐριπίδην**: Pollux ix. 101 reports that in games of *astragaloi* ('knuckle-bones', which had only four sides, valued 1, 3, 4, and 6; cf. **B33**. 14; Olson–Sens on Archestr. fr. 16. 6–9) a throw that totalled 40 was called 'Euripides', and the same was most likely true of dice, in which case at least seven dice (= five 6s and one 4) must have been thrown at one time. Probably a pun on εὖ ῥίπτω, hence Speaker B's eagerness to make the throw. For a catalogue of twenty-five names of dice-throws (but with no values specified), see Eub. fr. 57 (from *Dice-Players*). For other comic references to shooting dice, see **A19**. 1–2; **B6**. 2–3 with n.; Pherecr. fr. 129; Hermipp. fr. 27; Diph. fr. 77.

3–5.   **οὐκ ἂν κτλ.**: For Euripides' alleged hostility toward women, see Ar. *Lys.* 368–9 with Henderson on 12; *Th.* 85, 385–94, 545–8.

6.   **γέ τοι**: 'at any rate'; 'Giving a reason, valid so far as it goes, for accepting a proposition: a colloquial idiom' (Denniston 550).

7–9.   The first verse is borrowed from Euripides' *Antiope* (= fr. 187. 1), the third from *Iphigenia in Tauris* 535. But the second verse (which is crucial to Speaker A's argument) seems to be made up out of whole cloth. For other aggressive comic quotations (or misquotations) of Euripides, e.g. Ar. *Lys.* 368–9 (~ E. fr. **882b); Theopomp. Com. fr. 35 (= E. fr. 894); Antiph. fr. 205 (E. fr. 1098); Philem. fr. 153; Diph. fr. 60. 1–3 (~ E. fr. 915); adesp. com. fr. 1048. 1–3 (cf. E. fr. 1056). For the construction, with 7–8 equivalent to an if-clause, see **D5**. 13–16 n.

7.   **εὖ βίον κεκτημένος**: i.e. 'is well-to-do'.

8.   **τὸ (ἐ)λάχιστον τρεῖς**: 'three at the very least'.   **ἀσυμβόλους**: 'who have made no contribution (to the dinner-expenses)'; see **G14** introductory n.

10.   **τί δέ σοι μέλει;**: 'What does it matter to you?, What do you care?'; cf. **C1**. 1.

11. τὸ δρᾶμα puns on two senses of the word: 'the play' (responding
to the question in 10) and 'the deed' (in contrast to τὸν . . . νοῦν, 'the
intent').

D13. The idea that the great music of the past is being forgotten and replaced
by something morally and aesthetically worse is a commonplace in 'Old' and
'Middle Comedy' (cf. 1–2 n.; **D14**; Eup. fr. 398 (Pindar's poetry said to be
'condemned to silence' on account of the crudity of popular taste); Pl. Com.
fr. 138 (on tragic dancing); Antiph. fr. 207)—and perhaps in all societies in all
times, as fans of the allegedly decadent and depraved Elvis Presley condemn
the Rolling Stones without ever really listening to them, and their children in
turn condemn Eminem without ever really listening to him, and so on and on
for ever. For informal performances of lyric and elegiac poetry (including
lyric sections from tragedy and comedy) at dinner parties and symposia,
e.g. **F2** (Stesichorus); **H20**. 10–12 (Theognis); Ar. *Eq.* 529–30, quoting Cratin.
fr. 70; *V.* 1222–48 (Alcaeus and several *scholia* (see **H1**. 11 n.)); Amips. fr. 21
(a *scholium*); Lissarrague 123–39; Csapo and Miller, *Hesperia*, 60 (1991), 381–
2 (singers of lyric on Attic red-figure vases); and see in general Bowie,
Rhetorica, 11 (1993), 355–73 (on 'table talk' of all sorts). Stesichorus (quoted
or alluded to elsewhere in comedy at Ar. *Nu.* 967 (?; ~ Lamprocles *PMG* 735);
Pax 775–7 (~ *PMG* 210), 796–801 (~ *PMG* 212)) dates to the first half of the
sixth century; Alcman (quoted at Ar. *Av.* 250–1 (cf. *PMG* 26. 2–3)) to the
mid- to late seventh; and Simonides (quoted or alluded to at Ar. *Eq.* 406
(*PMG* 512); *Pax* 736–7 (~ fr. 86 West²)) to the late sixth and first half of the
fifth. For other comic references to early poets, see **E7** (Sappho); **H5** introductory n. (Sappho, Archilochus, and Hipponax); C. Kugelmeier, *Reflexe früher
und zeitgenössischer Lyrik in der alten Attischen Komödie* (Beiträge zur Altertumskunde 80: Stuttgart and Leipzig, 1996). For *Helots*, see Storey 176–9; at
least one character in the play spoke Doric Greek (frr. 147; 149).
    Preserved at Athenaeus 14. 638e, in a collection of comic references to
musicians and poets named Gnesippus that also includes **D8** (where see
introductory n.).
    Metrically problematic. Lines 1 and 4 are archilocheans (× D – ith); 2 and
3 conclude with ith, but do not correspond to 1 and 4 or even precisely to one
another, and have never been convincingly analysed or emended.

1–2.   Cf. **D2** introductory n.; Ar. *Nu.* 1355–72, where Strepsiades urges his
son Pheidippides to sing him some Simonides or Aeschylus, but the sophis-
tically educated young man refuses on the grounds that both men are
terrible poets and singing to a lyre is ἀρχαῖον (cf. 2 with n.), and insists on
singing instead what strikes his father as a depraved song by Euripides.
2. ἀρχαῖον: '(is) old-fashioned'; a disgusted report of common sentiment

rather than an endorsement of it, as 3–4 make clear.   **ἐστ(ὶ) ἀκούειν**: 'can be heard'.

3–4. According to Athenaeus, Teleclides claimed that Gnesippus 'often involved himself in μοιχεία' (fr. 36), which is presumably a confused reference to the content of his poetry; see below. For adultery and the laws relating to it, see **I8.** 22 n.   **ἐκκαλεῖσθαι | γυναῖκας**: 'to summon out women to themselves' (middle, not passive), i.e. 'so that they could summon . . . '. For the idea of a lover calling a woman out into the street at night (hence **νυκτερίν(α)**) to have sex, see Ar. *Th.* 479–82; and cf. **I4.** 10 n. (on the conventional limits on married women's movements). But more likely Gnesippus composed *paraclausithyra* (songs sung by excluded lovers) or dramatic adaptations thereof; cf. Ar. *Ec.* 952–75 with Olson, *CQ* ns 38 (1988), 328–30; Cummings, *Scholia*, ns 10 (2001), 38–53; Pranscello, *CP* 101 (2006), 52–66, esp. 53–6.   **ἔχοντας** is to be taken with **μοιχοῖς**, having been drawn into the normal case of a noun that serves as subject of an infinitive.

4. The **ἰαμβύκη** (also σαμβύκη; cf. **H17.** 5) and the **τρίγωνος** or τρίγωνον (cf. **J19.** 2) were exotic harps of some sort (*AGM* 72, 75–7).

D14. The final decades of the fifth century saw the emergence of a new musical style characterized by novel tunings, elaborate rhythms, and greatly increased melodic variety; see Ar. *Th.* 101–29 (parody of the tragic poet Agathon) with Austin–Olson ad loc.; Anaxil. fr. 27; *AGM* 356–7; Restani, *Rivista Italiana di Musicologia*, 18 (1983), 139–92 (a detailed music-historical treatment of this fragment); A. Barker, *Greek Musical Writings*, i (Cambridge, 1984), 93–5, 236–8; Imperio, in *Tessere*, 75–95; Csapo, *ICS* 24–25 (1999–2000), 399–426; cf. Eup. frr. 326; 398. According to [Plutarch], the first speaker in this fragment is Μουσική ('Music'), whom he also calls Ποίησις ('Poetry') and who he says came on stage dressed in women's clothes and badly beaten up (cf. 19–20); while the second speaker (20–1) is Δικαιοσύνη ('Justice'). Music is presented as a courtesan (i.e. a high-class prostitute who attaches herself to only one or two men at a time and is supported by them; cf. **I7** introductory n.), and 1–4 make it clear that her complaint is a response to a question asked by Justice about the lovers she has taken and thus about how she was reduced to such a miserable condition. **I11** is similar. For the social background (men beating their wives or lovers when they think they have misbehaved), cf. Ar. *Lys.* 160–2, 515–16, 519–21; Pl. Com. fr. 105; Semon. fr. 7. 16–18, 43–6 (satire, but clearly with a background in social reality); D. 25. 57; and see in general Hall, in *Rivals*, 407–18, esp. 414–15. **H20** (where see introductory n.) is also from *Cheiron*.

Preserved at [Plutarch], *On Music* 30 (*Mor.* 1141d–2a), as part of a potted history of the development and decline of the art.

Iambic trimeter.

1.   **οὐκ ἄκουσα:** 'not unwilling', i.e. 'quite willingly' (litotes).

1–2.   **σοί τε κτλ.:** 'for your heart gets pleasure from listening, and mine from speaking'. For the idea, cf. **D5**. 4–7.

3.   For explanatory **γάρ** used 'after an expression denoting the giving or receiving of information' ('Well, … ' *vel sim.*), see Denniston 59. **Μελανιππίδης:** a dithyrambic poet (*fl. c.*440–415) from a distinguished Melian musical family, who according to Aristotle abandoned antistrophic composition (*Rh.* 1409^b26–9) and whom [Plutarch] (citing this fragment) charges with having made the pipe-player independent of the singers (*Mor.* 1141d). Cf. *AGM* 357–8. Ten fragments of Melanippides' poetry (the longest seven corrupt lines from *Danaids*) survive (*PMG* 757–66).

4.   **ἐν τοῖσι πρῶτος ὃς λαβών … με:** literally 'who, being the first of these men'—probably referred to collectively in the preceding verses—to get control of me'; *με* serves as the object of both the participle and the main verb.   **ἀνῆκε:** 'relaxed me', in reference to both Melanippides' freeing Music from traditional constraints and tunings (see 3 n.) and the physical 'loosening up' she got from taking him as her first lover (cf. 5).

5.   **χαλαρωτέραν:** 'slacker, looser'.   **χορδαῖς δώδεκα:** dative of degree of difference, 'by a dozen strings', i.e 'a dozen notes'; contrast 25. A surprise in place of a measure of physical size of some sort (abandoning sexual imagery in favour of musical), and therefore reserved for the end of the line; cf. **B29**. 3 n.

6–7.   Echoed in 13 and, much more emphatically, in 17.

6.   **ἀλλ᾽ οὖν** (also 13, 17) emphatically counters the speaker's own words; 'but the fact is, but actually' (Denniston 442).   **ἀποχρῶν:** 'sufficient', i.e. 'not too bad'.

7.   **πρός:** 'in comparison with' (LSJ s.v. C. III. 4).

8.   **Κινησίας:** a dithyrambic poet (*PAA* 569985; Stephanis #1406; *fl. c.*425–390) mocked at length on stage at Ar. *Av.* 1372–1409 (where see Dunbar's n.) and referred to elsewhere in comedy (never favourably) at Ar. *Ra.* 153, 366 (see Dover ad loc.), 1437; *Ec.* 329–30; Pl. Com. fr. 200, and the title-character in a play by Strattis (frr. 14–22). Cf. 14 n.; *AGM* 359. Only three insignificant scraps of Cinesias' poetry survive (*PMG* 774–6). Of all the poets referred to in Music's speech, he is the only Athenian, hence the specification **ὁ … Ἀττικός.**   **κατάρατος** is literally 'subject to a curse' (i.e. the speaker's own), but is here only a general colloquial form of abuse ('goddamned' *vel sim.*), as often (e.g. **H10**. 3; **I10**. 1; **J7**. 4; **J11**. 3; Ar. *Lys.* 530; Pherecr. fr. 76. 3).

9.   **ἐξαρμονίους καμπάς:** 'discordant changes of (musical) direction'; cf. 26 ἐξαρμονίους. κάμπτω ('bend') and its cognates are frequently used in unfavourable comic descriptions of poetic composition (15, 28 n.; Ar. *Nu.*

333, 969–71 (see 14 n.); *Th.* 53; cf. Eup. fr. 366 (corrupt)). But cf. 15, 25, where the reference to physical abuse becomes more explicit. στροφαῖς: cognate with στρέφω; see 12 n.

10–11. τῆς ποιήσεως | τῶν διθυράμβων: i.e. 'of his dithyrambic poems'; to be taken with τὰ δεξιά in 12.

11. καθάπερ ἐν ταῖς ἀσπίσιν: sc. if they are well polished, allowing them to function like mirrors, as at Ar. *Ach.* 1128–9 and in the story of Perseus and the Gorgons.

12. τὰ δεξιά is both 'his right-hand sections', i.e. those strophes (cf. 9) in which the chorus 'turned' to the right, and 'the clever portions of his poetry' (cf. **D9**. 2 n.). ἀριστερ(ά) thus means both 'left-hand' (as if the strophes in question were being seen in reflection) and 'clumsy'.

13. See 6–7 n. ἀλλ' οὖν: see 6 n.

14. Φρῦνις: a Mytilinean citharode (Stephanis #2583) also referred to at Ar. *Nu.* 971, where the Just Argument condemns his poetry for its difficult, new-fangled 'twists' (see 9 n.), and depicted on a mid-fourth-century *phlyax*-vase that probably illustrates Eupolis' *Demes* (Trendall #*58; illustrated at Taplin pl. 16. 16; cf. Storey 169–70). An ancient commentator on *Clouds* dates Phrynis' first victory at the Panathenaic festival to sometime around the middle of the fifth century, and Timotheus (19 n.) boasts of defeating him and calls him an ἰωνοκάμπτας ('Ionian-style bender (of verses)'; = *PMG* 802. 3; cf. 8 n.). See *AGM* 360–1. No fragments of Phrynis' poetry survive. ἴδιον στρόβιλον . . . τινα ('a kind of personal whirl-wind') suggests both a wild and incoherent flurry of notes (thus *AGM* 360) and the power that produces elaborate musical 'twists' (cf. 16). But see 15 n.

15. κάμπτων με καὶ στρέφων describes both Phrynis' fondness for modulations between scales or the like (cf. *AGM* 360) and, on a different level, his physically abusive treatment of his lover; cf. 9, 24–5. με also functions as the object of διέφθορεν.

16. ἐν πέντε χορδαῖς: The standard number of strings on a *kithara* (a type of lyre; see *AGM* 50–6) was seven, and Phrynis is said by Plutarch (*Agis* 10. 4; *Mor.* 84a; 220c) to have increased it to nine. It is thus unclear why Music assigns him only five, although the basic point is obviously that he is over-inventive. ἁρμονίας: 'tunings, modes'; see *AGM* 177–9.

17. See 6–7 with n.

18. κα(ί) is to be taken with εἰ, 'even though' (Denniston 300). αὖτις ἀνέλαβεν: 'he made it good again, repaired the damage'.

19. ὁ . . . Τιμόθεος: a Milesian (cf. 21) citharode and dithyrambic poet (Stephanis #2417; also referred to at Anaxandr. fr. 6; Antiph. fr. 110), who was born *c.*450 and lived into his nineties; the perfects in 19–20 suggest that he is supposed to be Music's most recent lover. Timotheus boasts of increasing the number of strings on the *kithara* (see 16 n.) to eleven (*PMG* 791. 229–31; cf. 25 (which speaks of an even dozen)), and the complexity of his language was probably matched by that of the music he wrote to accompany it; cf. 24 with n. Eleven titles and nineteen fragments of Timotheus' poems (*PMG* 777–804, plus part of a line preserved by Philodemus), including several hundred verses of his *Persai*, survive. Cf. *AGM* 361–4; J. H. Hordern, *The Fragments of Timotheus of Miletus* (Oxford Classical Monographs: Oxford and New York, 2002). Justice's response in 20–1 makes it clear that she is familiar with Melanippides, Cinesias, and Phrynis, but not with Timotheus; but the audience must know who he is, and the point is presumably to ostentatiously treat him as a social and poetic nobody.   **μ(ε) . . . κατορώρυχε**: 'he has buried me in the earth', i.e. 'made me vanish'; but perhaps there is a sexual *double-entendre*, 'he has dug down into me, penetrated me deeply' (*Maculate Muse*, § 292).

20.   **διακέκναικ(ε)**: 'he has ground me down to nothing', i.e. 'reduced me to insignificance'; perhaps also 'he has rubbed me, fucked me very hard' (*Maculate Muse*, § 322).   **αἴσχιστα** is adverbial, 'in a thoroughly shameful fashion'.

22–3.   **ἄπαντας οὓς λέγω | παρελήλυθεν** is parenthetic; '—he's outstripped all the (other) men I'm discussing—'.

24.   **ἐκτραπέλους μυρμηκιάς** ('perverse anthills') is an internal accusative with **ἄγων**, with **με** to be supplied as direct object from **μοι** in 23; 'dragging (me) along, through . . .'. The reference must be to the complex, meandering character of Timotheus' melodies; cf. Ar. *Th.* 100 (where trills sung by the tragic poet Agathon, another advocate of the 'new music', are compared to 'ant-paths') with Austin–Olson ad loc.

25.   **χορδαῖς δώδεκα**: 'with a dozen strings', i.e. those on his *kithara* (cf. 19 n.); but on another level a reference to bondage, to which Timotheus subjects his helpless victim. Cf. 9, 15–16.

26–8.   After quoting 25, [Plutarch] observes 'And Aristophanes the comic poet mentions Philoxenus'—another contemporary dithyrambic poet; see **G4** introductory n.; Antiph. fr. 207; *AGM* 364–6—'and says that he introduced . . . songs into cyclic choruses (= Ar. fr. 953). But Music speaks thus'. Lines 26–8 follow and clearly belong to the same speech as 1–25. Most likely Music is still describing Timotheus, but she might have moved on—as [Plutarch's] remarks are most naturally taken to imply—to denouncing Philoxenus, presumably as another nasty man from her past. How many verses are missing is in any case impossible to say.

26.   The position of **τ(ε)** is problematic, and it seems best to take **ἐξαρμονίους** (see 9 n.) as modifying a lost noun in the previous line; **ἀνοσίους** as

modifying *ὑπερβολαίους*; and *ὑπερβολαίους* as substantival ('added (notes)', i.e. 'treble (notes)').

27. *νιγλάρους*: an obscure word used to describe a musical sound of some sort; cf. Ar. *Ach.* 554 with Olson ad loc. *ὥσπερ . . . τὰς ῥαφάνους*: 'just as happens with cabbages'. Cf. Arist. *HA* 551ᵃ13–16 (καμπαί generated on the leaves of cabbages and related vegetables); Beavis 125–6; Davies and Kathirithamby 102–3.

28. *καμπῶν*: 'with caterpillars' (καμπή; cf. 27 n.; **F11**. 4); a pun on κάμπη ('bend, turn'; see 9 n.). *κατεμέστωσε*: 'he filled me full of' + gen.

Section E

Politics and Politicians

E1. Nicostratus Comicus fr. 30, from an unidentified play (IV)

† ἆρ᾽ οἶσθα ὅτι τῆς πενίας ὅπλον ἐστὶν ἡ
παρρησία; ταύτην ἐάν τις ἀπολέσηι,
τὴν ἀσπίδ᾽ ἀποβέβληκεν οὗτος τοῦ βίου

E2. Amphis fr. 17, from *Day-Labourers* (IV)

εἶτ᾽ οὐχὶ χρυσοῦν ἐστι πρᾶγμ᾽ ἐρημία;
ὁ πατήρ γε τοῦ ζῆν ἐστιν ἀνθρώποις ἀγρός,
πενίαν τε συγκρύπτειν ἐπίσταται μόνος·
ἄστυ δὲ θέατρον ἀτυχίας σαφοῦς γέμον

E3. Antiphanes fr. 202, from *The Soldier or Tycho* (IV)

ὅστις ἄνθρωπος δὲ φὺς
ἀσφαλές τι κτῆμ᾽ ὑπάρχειν τῶι βίωι λογίζεται,
πλεῖστον ἡμάρτηκεν· ἢ γὰρ εἰσφορά τις ἥρπακεν
τἄνδοθεν πάντ᾽, ἢ δίκηι τις περιπεσὼν ἀπώλετο,
ἢ στρατηγήσας προσῶφλεν, <ἢ> χορηγὸς αἱρεθεὶς   5
ἱμάτια χρυσᾶ παρασχὼν τῶι χορῶι ῥάκος φορεῖ,
ἢ τριηραρχῶν ἀπήγξατ᾽, ἢ πλέων ἥλωκέ ποι,
ἢ βαδίζων ἢ καθεύδων κατακέκοφθ᾽ ὑπ᾽ οἰκετῶν.
οὐ βέβαιον οὐθέν ἐστι, πλὴν ὅσ᾽ ἂν καθ᾽ ἡμέραν
εἰς ἑαυτὸν ἡδέως τις εἰσαναλίσκων τύχηι.   10
οὐδὲ ταῦτα σφόδρα τι· καὶ γὰρ τὴν τράπεζαν ἁρπάσαι
κειμένην ἄν τις προσελθών· ἀλλ᾽ ὅταν τὴν ἔνθεσιν
ἐντὸς ἤδη τῶν ὀδόντων τυγχάνηις κατεσπακώς,
τοῦτ᾽ ἐν ἀσφαλεῖ νόμιζε τῶν ὑπαρχόντων μόνον

5 <ἢ> add. Casaubon   6 χρυσᾶ Grotius: καὶ χρυσί᾽ Ath.ACE   10 εἰσαναλίσκων
Stephanus: εἰσαναλίσκειν Ath.A: ἀναλίσκειν Ath.CE

E4. Eupolis fr. 384, from an unidentified play (V)

καὶ μὴν ἐγὼ πολλῶν παρόντων οὐκ ἔχω τί λέξω.
οὕτω σφόδρ᾽ ἀλγῶ τὴν πολιτείαν ὁρῶν παρ᾽ ὑμῖν.
ἡμεῖς γὰρ οὐχ οὕτω τέως ᾠκοῦμεν οἱ γέροντες,
ἀλλ᾽ ἦσαν ἡμῖν τῆι πόλει πρῶτον μὲν οἱ στρατηγοὶ
ἐκ τῶν μεγίστων οἰκιῶν, πλούτωι γένει τε πρῶτοι,   5
οἷς ὡσπερεὶ θεοῖσιν ηὐχόμεσθα· καὶ γὰρ ἦσαν.
ὥστ᾽ ἀσφαλῶς ἐπράττομεν· νυνὶ δ᾽ ὅπηι τύχωμεν
στρατευόμεσθ᾽ αἱρούμενοι καθάρματα στρατηγούς

2 ὑμῖν van Herwerden: ἡμῖν Stob.^SMA   3 οἱ Brunck: ᾧ Stob.^SMA   7 τύχωμεν
Kaibel: τύχοιμεν Stob.^SMA

E5. Eupolis fr. 219, from *Marikas* (Lenaia 421 BC)

οὓς δ᾽ οὐκ ἂν εἴλεσθ᾽ οὐδ᾽ ἂν οἰνόπτας πρὸ τοῦ,
νυνὶ στρατηγοὺς <ἔχομεν>. ὦ πόλις, πόλις,
ὡς εὐτυχὴς εἶ μᾶλλον ἢ καλῶς φρονεῖς

2 στρατηγοὺς <ἔχομεν> Hermann: στρατηγήσουσιν Austin

E6. Eupolis fr. 262, from *Men from the Deme Prospalta* (probably 429 BC)

μήτηρ τις αὐτῶι Θρᾶιττα ταινιόπωλις ἦν

ἦν Schweighäuser: τὴν Ath.^ACE

E7. Antiphanes fr. 194, from *Sappho* (mid-360s?)

(Σα.) ἔστι φύσις θήλεα βρέφη σώιζουσ᾽ ὑπὸ κόλποις
αὐτῆς, ὄντα δ᾽ ἄφωνα βοὴν ἵστησι γεγωνὸν
καὶ διὰ πόντιον οἶδμα καὶ ἠπείρου διὰ πάσης
οἷς ἐθέλει θνητῶν, τοῖς δ᾽ οὐδὲ παροῦσιν ἀκούειν
ἔξεστιν· κωφὴν δ᾽ ἀκοῆς αἴσθησιν ἔχουσιν   5
        *   *   *

(Β.) ἡ μὲν φύσις γὰρ ἦν λέγεις ἐστὶν πόλις,
βρέφη δ᾽ ἐν αὐτῆι διατρέφει τοὺς ῥήτορας.
οὗτοι κεκραγότες δὲ τὰ διαπόντια
τἀκ τῆς Ἀσίας καὶ τἀπὸ Θράικης λήμματα
ἕλκουσι δεῦρο. νεμομένων δὲ πλησίον   10
αὐτῶν κάθηται λοιδορουμένων τ᾽ ἀεὶ
ὁ δῆμος οὐδὲν οὔτ᾽ ἀκούων οὔθ᾽ ὁρῶν.

(Σα.) × – ∪ – πῶς γὰρ γένοιτ' ἄν, ὦ πάτερ,
ῥήτωρ ἄφωνος; (Β.) ἦν ἁλῶι τρὶς παρανόμων.
× – ∪ – καὶ μὴν ἀκριβῶς ᾠόμην   15
ἐγνωκέναι τὸ ῥηθέν. ἀλλὰ δὴ λέγε.
(Σα.) θήλεια μέν νυν ἐστὶ φύσις ἐπιστολή,
βρέφη δ' ἐν αὐτῆι περιφέρει τὰ γράμματα·
ἄφωνα δ' ὄντα <ταῦτα> τοῖς πόρρω λαλεῖ
οἷς βούλεθ'· ἕτερος δ' ἂν τύχηι τις πλησίον   20
ἑστὼς ἀναγιγνώσκοντος οὐκ ἀκούσεται

2 ὄντα Porson: ητα Ath.^A: ταῦτα Ath.^CE   10 δεῦρο–16 om. Ath.^CE   13 <οὐδὲν
λέγεις> Jacobs   14 ἦν ἁλῶι Cobet (ἁλῶι iam Casaubon): ην αλλω Ath.^A
15 ᾠόμην Scaliger: ὤιμην Ath.^A   17 νυν Erfurdt: οὖν Ath.^ACE   19 <ταῦτα>
Grotius

E8. Diphilus fr. 101, from an unidentified play (IV/III)

ὅρκος δ' ἑταίρας ταὐτὸ καὶ δημηγόρου·
ἑκάτερος αὐτῶν ὀμνύει πρὸς ὃν λαλεῖ

1 δ' Stob.^L: om. Stob.^SMA

E9. Plato Comicus fr. 202, from an unidentified play (V/IV)

                    ἦν γὰρ ἀποθάνηι
εἷς τις πονηρός, δύ' ἀνέφυσαν ῥήτορες·
οὐδεὶς γὰρ ἡμῖν Ἰόλεως ἐν τῆι πόλει,
ὅστις ἐπικαύσει τὰς κεφαλὰς τῶν ῥητόρων.
κεκολλόπευκας· τοιγαροῦν ῥήτωρ ἔσηι   5

E10. Eupolis fr. 102, from *Demes* (412 bc?)

(Α.) κράτιστος οὗτος ἐγένετ' ἀνθρώπων λέγειν·
ὁπότε παρέλθοι <δ'>, ὥσπερ ἀγαθοὶ δρομῆς,
ἐκ δέκα ποδῶν ἧιρει λέγων τοὺς ῥήτορας.
(Β.) ταχὺν λέγεις γε. (Α.) πρὸς δέ <γ'> αὐτοῦ τῶι τάχει
πειθώ τις ἐπεκάθιζεν ἐπὶ τοῖς χείλεσιν·   5
οὕτως ἐκήλει καὶ μόνος τῶν ῥητόρων
τὸ κέντρον ἐγκατέλειπε τοῖς ἀκρωμένοις

2 <δ'> Toup   δρομῆς Canter: δρομεῖς Σ^RQT Ael. Arist.   3 ἐκ δέκα Σ Il.:
ἐκκαίδεκα Σ^RQT Ael. Arist. Olympiod.   4 <γ'> Musurus

E11. Teleclides fr. 45, from an unidentified play (late 440s/early 430s?)

πόλεών τε φόρους αὐτάς τε πόλεις τὰς μὲν δεῖν, τὰς δ᾽ ἀναλύειν,
λάινα τείχη τὰ μὲν οἰκοδομεῖν, τὰ δὲ τἄμπαλιν αὖ καταβάλλειν,
σπονδὰς δύναμιν κράτος εἰρήνην, πλοῦτόν τ᾽ εὐδαιμονίαν τε

2 τὰ δὲ τἄμπαλιν αὖ Kock: τὰ δὲ αὐτὰ πάλιν Plu.[SY]

E12. Cratinus fr. 258, from *Cheirons* (late 440s–429 BC)

Στάσις δὲ καὶ πρεσβυγενὴς
Χρόνος ἀλλήλοισι μιγέντε
μέγιστον τίκτετον τύραννον
ὃν δὴ κεφαληγερέταν
θεοὶ καλέουσι   5

2 Χρόνος] Κρόνος anon.

E13. Cratinus fr. *259, probably from *Cheirons* (late 440s–429 BC)

Ἔραν τέ οἱ Ἀσπασίαν τίκτει Καταπυγοσύνη
παλλακὴν κυνώπιδα

1 Καταπυγοσύνη Emperius: καὶ Καταπυγοσύνην Plu.[SY]

E14. Hermippus fr. *47, probably from *Fates* (430 BC?)

βασιλεῦ σατύρων, τί ποτ᾽ οὐκ ἐθέλεις
δόρυ βαστάζειν, ἀλλὰ λόγους μὲν
περὶ τοῦ πολέμου δεινοὺς παρέχηι,
ψυχὴ δὲ Τέλητος ὕπεστιν;
κἀγχειριδίου δ᾽ ἀκόνηι σκληρᾶι   5
παραθηγομένης βρύχεις κοπίδος,
δηχθεὶς αἴθωνι Κλέωνι

4 ψυχὴ ... ὕπεστιν Emperius: ψυχὴν ... ὑπέστη Plu.[Y]: ψυχὴν ... ὑπέστης Plu.[S]
6 παραθηγομένης Dacier: -μένη Plu.[Y]: -μένην Plu.[S]   βρύχεις anon.: βρύχει Plu.[Y]:
βραχεῖ Plu.[S]   κοπίδος Coraes: κοπίδας Plu.[SY]: παραθηγομένη ... κόπις ὣς Kraus

E15. Adespota comica fr. 957, from an unidentified play

<ὁ> Φορμίων τρεῖς <ἀργυροῦς> στήσειν ἔφη
τρίποδας, ἔπειτ᾽ ἔθηκεν ἕνα μολύβδινον

1 <ὁ> et <ἀργυροῦς> Meineke

E16. Adespota comica fr. 461, from an unidentified play (424–422 BC)

Κλέων Προμηθεύς ἐστι μετὰ τὰ πράγματα

E17. Eupolis fr. 331, from an unidentified play (424–422 BC)

πρῶτος γὰρ ἡμᾶς, ὦ Κλέων,
χαίρειν προσεῖπας, πολλὰ λυπῶν τὴν πόλιν

E18. Eupolis fr. 316, from *The Golden Race* (429–422 BC)

ὦ καλλίστη πόλι πασῶν ὅσας Κλέων ἐφορᾶι,
ὡς εὐδαίμων πρότερόν τ᾽ ἦσθα, νῦν δὲ μᾶλλον ἔσηι
    *   *   *

ἔδει πρῶτον μὲν ὑπάρχειν πάντων ἰσηγορίαν
    *   *   *

πῶς οὖν οὐκ ἄν τις ὁμιλῶν χαίροι τοιᾶιδε πόλει
ἵν᾽ ἔξεστιν πάνυ λεπτῶι κακῶι τε τὴν ἰδέαν   5

E19. Plato Comicus fr. 115, from *In Terrible Pain* (429–422 BC)

ὃς πρῶτα μὲν Κλέωνι πόλεμον ἠράμην

E20. Aristophanes fr. 102, from *Farmers* (late 420s BC)

(Α.) ἐθέλω γεωργεῖν. (Β.) εἶτα τίς σε κωλύει;
(Α.) ὑμεῖς. ἐπεὶ δίδωμι χιλίας δραχμάς,
ἐάν με τῶν ἀρχῶν ἀφῆτε. (Β.) δεχόμεθα·
δισχίλιαι γάρ εἰυι υὺν ταῖς Νικίου

E21. Phrynichus Comicus fr. 62, from an unidentified play
(late 420s–413 BC)

ἦν γὰρ πολίτης ἀγαθός, ὡς εὖ οἶδ᾽ ἐγώ,
κοὐχ ὑποταγεὶς ἐβάδιζεν, ὥσπερ Νικίας

E22. Teleclides fr. 44, from an unidentified play (probably mid-410s BC;
before 413)

Χαρικλέης μὲν οὐκ ἔδωκε μνᾶν, ἵν᾽ αὐτὸν μὴ λέγηι
ὡς ἔφυ τῆι μητρὶ παίδων πρῶτος ἐκ βαλλαντίου;

τέσσαρας δὲ μνᾶς ἔδωκε Νικίας Νικηράτου·
ὧν δ' ἕκατι τοῦτ' ἔδωκε, καίπερ εὖ εἰδὼς ἐγώ,
οὐκ ἐρῶ, φίλος γὰρ ἀνήρ. σωφρονεῖν δέ μοι δοκεῖ   5

1 *Χαρικλέης* Reisig: χαρικλῆς Plu.ᵁᴹᴬ   4 ἔδωκε] ἔδρασε Cobet

E23. Eupolis fr. 193, from *Marikas* (Lenaia 421 BC)

(*Μα.*) πόσου χρόνου γὰρ συγγεγένησαι Νικίαι;
(*Β.*) οὐδ' εἶδον, εἰ μὴ 'ναγχος ἑστῶτ' ἐν ἀγορᾶι.
(*Μα.*) ἀνὴρ ὁμολογεῖ Νικίαν ἑορακέναι.
καίτοι τί μαθὼν ἂν εἶδεν, εἰ μὴ προυδίδου;
(*Χο. Πενήτων*) ἠκούσατ', ὦ ξυνήλικες,   5
ἐπ' αὐτοφώρωι Νικίαν εἰλημμένον;
(*Χο. Πλουσίων*) ὑμεῖς γάρ, ὦ φρενοβλαβεῖς,
λάβοιτ' ἂν ἄνδρ' ἄριστον ἐν κακῶι τινι;

8 ἐν] ἐπὶ Kock

E24. Plato Comicus fr. 183, from *Hyperbolus* (late 420s/early 410s BC; before 417)

ὁ δ' οὐ γὰρ ἠττίκιζεν, ὦ Μοῖραι φίλαι,
ἀλλ' ὁπότε μὲν χρείη "διηιτώμην" λέγειν,
ἔφασκε "δηιτώμην", ὁπότε δ' εἰπεῖν δέοι
"ὀλίγον", <"ὀλίον"> ἔλεγεν

1 ὁ δ' οὐ γὰρ ἠττίκιζεν Bloch: ὁδοῦ γὰρ ἥττη κιζεῦν Hdn.   *Μοῖραι*] Μοῦσαι Meineke
3 δηιτώμην Dindorf: δὴ τῶι μὴν Hdn.   4 <ὀλίον> Bloch

E25. Plato Comicus fr. 203, from an unidentified play (after 417 BC)

καίτοι πέπραγε τῶν τρόπων μὲν ἄξια,
αὑτοῦ δὲ καὶ τῶν στιγμάτων ἀνάξια·
οὐ γὰρ τοιούτων οὕνεκ' ὄστραχ' ηὑρέθη

E26. Pherecrates fr. 164, from an unidentified play (V)

οὐκ ὢν ἀνὴρ γὰρ Ἀλκιβιάδης, ὡς δοκεῖ,
ἀνὴρ ἁπασῶν τῶν γυναικῶν ἐστι νῦν

E27. Adespota comica fr. 123, from an unidentified play (415–412 BC)

Ἀλκιβιάδην τὸν ἁβρόν, ὦ Γῆ καὶ θεοί,
ὃν ἡ Λακεδαίμων μοιχὸν ἐπιθυμεῖ λαβεῖν

E28. Phrynichus Comicus fr. 61, from an unidentified play (after 415 BC)

(Α.) ὦ φίλταθ᾽ Ἑρμῆ, καὶ φυλάσσου, μὴ πεσὼν
αὑτὸν περικρούσηι καὶ παράσχηις διαβολὴν
ἑτέρωι Διοκλείδηι βουλομένωι κακόν τι δρᾶν.
(Ερμ.) φυλάξομαι· Τεύκρωι γὰρ οὐχὶ βούλομαι
μήνυτρα δοῦναι τῶι παλαμναίωι ξένωι   5

   2 σαυτὸν Meineke   περικρούσηι Meineke: παρακρούσηι Plu.: περικρούσηις Kock

E29. Plato Comicus fr. 201, from an unidentified play (early 380s?)

(Δημ.) λαβοῦ λαβοῦ τῆς χειρὸς ὡς τάχιστά μου·
μέλλω στρατηγὸν χειροτονεῖν Ἀγύρριον
      *   *   *

προσίσταταί μου πρὸς τὸ βῆμα Μαντίας
     *   *   *

βόσκει δυσώδη Κέφαλον, ἐχθίστην νόσον

   4 βόσκει] βόσκω Meineke: βόσκεις Cobet

E30. Eubulus fr. 106. 1–9, from *Sphinx-Carion* (IV)

(Α.) ἔστι λαλῶν ἄγλωσσος, ὁμώνυμος ἄρρενι θῆλυς,
οἰκείων ἀνέμων ταμίας, δασύς, ἄλλοτε λεῖος,
ἀξύνετα ξυνετοῖσι λέγων, νόμον ἐκ νόμου ἕλκων·
ἓν δ᾽ ἐστὶν καὶ πολλά, καὶ ἂν τρώσηι τις, ἄτρωτος.
τί ἔστι τοῦτο; τί ἀπορεῖς; (Β.) Καλλίστρατος.   5
(Α.) πρωκτὸς μὲν οὖν οὗτός <γε>· σὺ δὲ ληρεῖς ἔχων.
οὗτος γὰρ αὑτός ἐστιν ἄγλωττος λάλος,
ἓν ὄνομα πολλοῖς, τρωτὸς ἄτρωτος, δασὺς
λεῖος. τί βούλει; πνευμάτων πολλῶν φύλαξ

   2 λεῖος Musurus: δειος Ath.^ACE   5–9 om. Ath.^CE   5 τί¹ Musurus: τίς Ath.^A
6 <γε> add. Kaibel   9 βούλει; πνευμάτων Morelius: βουλεπινευμάτων Ath.^A

E31. Timocles fr. 4, from *Delos* (*c.*324 BC)

(Α.) Δημοσθένης τάλαντα πεντήκοντ᾽ ἔχει.

(Β.) μακάριος, εἴπερ μεταδίδωσι μηδενί.
(Α.) καὶ Μοιροκλῆς εἴληφε χρυσίον πολύ.
(Β.) ἀνόητος ὁ διδούς, εὐτυχὴς δ᾽ ὁ λαμβάνων.
(Α.) εἴληφε καὶ Δήμων τι καὶ Καλλισθένης.   5
(Β.) πένητες ἦσαν, ὥστε συγγνώμην ἔχω.
(Α.) ὅ τ᾽ ἐν λόγοισι δεινὸς Ὑπερείδης ἔχει.
(Β.) τοὺς ἰχθυοπώλας οὗτος ἡμῶν πλουτιεῖ·
<ἔστ᾽> ὀψοφάγος γάρ, ὥστε τοὺς λάρους <δοκεῖν>
εἶναι Σύρους   10

  5 εἶτ᾽ εἴληφε Ath.^ACE: corr. Musurus   τι Dobree: τε Ath.^ACE   9 <ἔστ᾽> et <δοκεῖν>
Tucker

E32. Philippides fr. 25, from an unidentified play (*c.*300 BC)

ὁ τὸν ἐνιαυτὸν συντεμὼν εἰς μῆν᾽ ἕνα,
ὁ τὴν ἀκρόπολιν πανδοκεῖον ὑπολαβὼν
καὶ τὰς ἑταίρας εἰσαγαγὼν τῆι παρθένωι,
δι᾽ ὃν ἀπέκαυσεν ἡ πάχνη τὰς ἀμπέλους,
δι᾽ ὃν ἀσεβοῦνθ᾽ ὁ πέπλος ἐρράγη μέσος,   5
τὰς τῶν θεῶν τιμὰς ποοῦντ᾽ ἀνθρωπίνας·
ταῦτα καταλύει δῆμον, οὐ κωμωιδία

  6 τιμὰς ποοῦντ᾽ anon.: ποιοῦντα τιμὰς Plu.^PKLr

COMMENTARY

E1–E32. That some comedies in the second half of the fifth century in particular had substantial political content is clear; cf. **B27–B29**; **E10–E28** n. (with additional bibliography on 'Old Comic' politics); Gomme, *CR* 52 (1938), 97–109 (repeatedly reprinted, most recently in E. Segal (ed.), *Oxford Readings in Aristophanes* (Oxford and New York, 1996), 29–41); Henderson, in G. W. Dobrov (ed.), *The City as Comedy* (Chapel Hill and London, 1997), 135–48 (with specific attention to Aristophanes' *Birds*); and in K. A. Morgan (ed.), *Popular Tyranny* (Austin, 2003), 155–79. But the fragments provide relatively little access to the larger arguments advanced in the plays, and instead either preserve scattered bits and pieces of conventional political and social ideology (**E1–E9**) or focus on individual personalities (**E10–E32**). Specific political content seems to have been much rarer in fourth- and third-century comedy; but cf. **C2**; **E29–E32** with **E31** introductory n.

E1–E3. Two fundamental divides in Athenian political rhetoric were between 'the rich' and 'the poor', on the one hand, and 'the city' and 'the country', on the other. Comedy refers frequently to both issues, idealizing life in the countryside (e.g. Ar. frr. 111; 402) while simultaneously acknowledging how difficult and in many ways undesirable it is (e.g. **G1** with introductory n.; adesp. com. frr. 895–6), and aggressively confusing the question of what it means to be 'poor' (and thus, almost by definition, a 'good democrat').

E1. παρρησία (i.e. παν-ρησία, the freedom to say whatever one likes about matters of public concern) was fundamental to the Athenian understanding of democracy; cf. **E18**. 3 with n.; E. *Supp.* 438–41 with Collard ad loc.; Moschion *TrGF* 97 F 4. 2–4; Austin–Olson on Ar. *Th.* 540–1 (with further references). Although this is presented, however, in this fragment as πενίας ὅπλον ('poverty's armour'), i.e. as the average citizen's defence against the intrusions of the wealthy, the metaphor in 1 and 3 is borrowed from hoplite fighting, in which only the relatively wealthy (who also provided the bulk of the city's political leadership) engaged.

The first verse is unmetrical and can be mended only through very aggressive rewriting.

Preserved at Stobaeus iii. 13. 26, under the heading 'Concerning free speech'.

Iambic trimeter.

1. ἆρ(α) οἶσθα;: 'Don't you realize?' (Denniston 46–7).

2. ἀπολέσηι: here 'loses', although 3 leaves no doubt that what is referred to is instead an active abandonment of one's political rights.
3. τὴν ἀσπίδ(α) ἀποβέβληκεν: picking up on ὅπλον in 1. The shield was the hoplite's most basic piece of defensive equipment and, because of its weight, was often abandoned during retreats (V. D. Hanson, *The Western Way of War* (New York, 1989), 55–71; cf. Archil. fr. 5. 1–2 (quoted at Ar. *Pax* 1298–9); Alc. fr. 428). To be a ῥίψασπις (literally 'shield-thrower') was thus to be a coward and—much more to the point here—someone deserving of being stripped *inter alia* of his right to speak in the Assembly via a sentence of ἀτιμία (cf. Olson on Ar. *Pax* 446).

E2. A less extreme version of the attitude towards life also taken by the title-character of Phrynichus' *The Recluse* (**B21**); cf. **E20**. Menander fr. 299 is similar. For quietism as a widespread political ideology in the late fifth and fourth centuries, see L. B. Carter, *The Quiet Athenian* (Oxford, 1986), and cf. **E3** with introductory n.; **F19** with introductory n. For similar praise of life in the countryside in one's own fields (ἀγρός), see Philem. frr. 100 (but with a cynical twist at the end); 105; contrast **G1**.

Preserved at Stobaeus iv. 15ᵃ. 4, under the heading 'Concerning farming, that it is a good thing'.

Iambic trimeter.

1. χρυσοῦν . . . πρᾶγμ(α): 'something as good as gold'; the point is that this makes up for the speaker's otherwise all-too-obvious impoverishment (3–4).
2–3. These lines expand on the sentiment expressed in 1 (which might just as easily have been followed directly by 4).
2. ὁ πατήρ: 'the origin, fundamental source'.   τοῦ ζῆν: 'of living (well, happily)'.
3 gives more specific content to the idea put forward in 2.
4. θέατρον ἀτυχίας σαφοῦς γέμον: 'a theatre full of patent poverty', i.e. a place full of paupers, whose unhappy situation is on constant, painful display to the world at large.

E3. The view of life articulated here is initially presented as applying equally to all human beings (1–2). But the obligations, honours, and dangers mentioned in 3–8 have to do specifically with the situation of wealthy, politically active individuals; and the fundamental message of the speech is that public life brings only loss and trouble, and that one ought to focus on private pleasures to the extent one can (9–14). Cf. **F18**. **C13** is from the same play.

Preserved at Athenaeus 3. 103e–4a, as an example of Epicurean hedonism.

Trochaic tetrameter catalectic.

1–3. *ἄνθρωπος* … *φύς* marks *ὅστις* … *ἡμάρτηκεν* as a typical gnomic statement; cf. **D5**. 2 with n.; Choeril. Ias. *SH* 335. After the illustration in 3–8, the idea is resumed and expanded, and a practical conclusion drawn in 9–14.

2. *ἀσφαλές τι κτῆμ' ὑπάρχειν* … *λογίζεται*: echoed in 14 *τοῦτ' ἐν ἀσφαλεῖ νόμιζε τῶν ὑπαρχόντων*.

3. *εἰσφορά τις*: 'an extraordinary tax', levied on capital (and thus exclusively on the rich) in times of financial crisis; see Ar. *Eq.* 773–6, 923–6; Eup. fr. 300; Gomme on Th. iii. 19. 1; de Ste Croix, *C&M* 14 (1953), 30–70, esp. 31–6.   *ἥρπακεν*: a wildly hyperbolic verb, chosen because it presents the man being taxed as an innocent victim of what amounts to strong-arm robbery (cf. 11 *ἁρπάσαι*).

4. *δίκηι* … *περιπεσών*: 'falling in with, encountering a lawsuit' (LSJ s. *περιπίπτω* II. 3 ('mostly of evil')). The underlying point is once again (cf. 3 n.) that the victim would never have initiated this sort of thing himself or even have done anything to deserve it.

4–8. *ἀπώλετο, προσῶφλεν, ἀπήγξατ(ο)*: Given the presence elsewhere in this section of a number of presents (6 *φορεῖ*) and perfects (3 *ἥρπακεν*, 7 *ἥλωκε*, 8 *κατακέκο(πται)*), these aorists are probably best treated as unmarked for tense and translated respectively 'he has been ruined', 'he owes', and 'he strangles himself'.

5. *στρατηγήσας προσῶφλεν*: The generalship was an elective annual office ([Arist.] *Ath.* 44. 4; 61. 1), and candidates were drawn not from the populace at large but from a select pool of mostly wealthy men ([X.] *Ath.* 1. 2–3); see in general D. Hamel, *Athenian Generals* (*Mnemosyne* Supplement 182: Leiden, Boston, and Cologne, 1998), and cf. **E4**. 4 with n. At the beginning of each prytany (i.e. ten times every year), the Assembly voted as to whether the generals were performing their office satisfactorily; anyone whose service was condemned could be fined (hence *προσῶφλεν*, 'he owes additional money', sc. in addition to what he spent out of his own pocket performing the office) or punished in some other way ([Arist.] *Ath.* 61. 2).

5–6. *χορηγὸς αἱρεθεὶς* | *κτλ.*: For *choregoi* (like trierarchs (7 n.), chosen from the city's wealthiest ('liturgical') class), see Introduction p. 18.

7. *τριηραρχῶν ἀπήγξατ(ο)*: 'while serving as trierarch, he strangles himself', i.e. 'hangs himself'. Each year 400 trierarchs were appointed from Athens' liturgical class (cf. 5–6 n.), and those unable to obtain an exemption were assigned responsibility for manning, outfitting, and maintaining a fighting ship from the city's fleet. Depending on the condition of the ship, the amount of time it spent at sea, and the difficulty of recruiting and retaining an adequate crew, the office was potentially quite expensive, hence the despair of the man referred to here. See V. Gabrielsen, *Financing the Athenian Fleet* (Baltimore and London, 1994), 43–169.   **πλέων ἥλωκέ ποι** ('he's been captured as he sails to somewhere') is most naturally taken as a reference to service on board the trireme mentioned in the first half of the verse. But what follows in the next verse raises the possibility that the point is instead that the man referred to is travelling on personal business or for pleasure when he is set on by pirates or by warships belonging to a hostile state; cf. Diggle on Thphr. *Char.* 25. 2.

8.   **βαδίζων ἢ καθεύδων**: i.e. as he is going innocently about his business (cf. 3 n., 4 n., 7 with n.), with no suspicion that trouble is in store for him. **κατακέκο(πται)**: another hyperbolic verb (cf. 3 n.); the victim is not simply murdered but 'butchered, cut to pieces'.

9.   **οὐ βέβαιον οὐθέν ἐστι** repeats the thesis advanced in 1–3, before putting forward a tentative—and rapidly modified—solution to the problem. For οὐθέν (= οὐδέν), see **D3**. 9 n.   **καθ' ἡμέραν**: 'on a daily basis'; cf. **B39**. 1 n.

10.   'a person happens to enjoy spending on himself', i.e. 'a person spends on enjoying himself'; the implicit contrast is with the money wasted on public goods and duties in the scenarios imagined in 3–7.

11.   **οὐδὲ ταῦτα σφόδρα**: sc. βέβαιά ἐστι, 'and not even this' (i.e. whatever he spends on his own pleasure) 'is particularly secure'. **τι** is adverbial ('really, at all').   **τὴν τράπεζαν**: see **G16**. 2 n.

11–12.   **ἁρπάσαι** is third-person singular aorist active optative, and is to be taken with **ἄν**.

12.   **τὴν ἔνθεσιν**: 'the mouthful'; cf. **B33**. 10.

13.   **κατεσπακώς** is < κατασπάω, 'devour' (Ar. *Eq.* 718; *Ra.* 576; Antiph. fr. 86. 3).

14.   Cf. 2 with n.

E4–E9. Some common comic slanders having to do with politics and politicians.

E4. An old man, speaking as a representative of his peers (3), complains about how much better governed Athens was in his youth; for similar sentiments, see **E5**. 1–2; Ar. *Eq.* 191–3; *Ra.* 727–33, and cf. **E6**; **E18**. 4–5; **E24** with introductory n. The social decline of which the speaker complains is better understood as evidence for the extent to which the radical democracy of the late fifth century opened up political opportunities for talented men from a variety of backgrounds—which is not to say either that any chance comer could be elected general by the Assembly (despite 7–8; **E29**. 1–2; Eup. fr. *104; cf. **E3**. 5 n.) or that everyone awarded the office in any period turned out to be competent. The more significant point is that 'Old Comedy' regularly attacks contemporary politicians as worthless self-seekers and reserves whatever praise it offers for men of the 'good old days'. Probably the beginning of a speech in an *agon*. See Storey, *MCr* 30–1 (1995–6), 150–4.

Preserved at Stobaeus iv. 1. 9, under the heading 'Concerning government'. Iambic tetrameter catalectic.

1. **καὶ μήν**: 'indeed', introducing a new point (Denniston 351–2). **πολλῶν παρόντων**: genitive absolute; 'although there are many (arguments) available', i.e. 'although I have many options, although there are many possibilities'. But 'since there are many (people) present' is also possible. **οὐκ ἔχω τί λέξω**: 'I don't know what to say' (cf. LSJ s. ἔχω A. III. 2), sc. because he is so disgusted and furious.

2. Despite the first-person plurals in 7–8, the paradosis ἡμῖν is impossibly awkward before ἡμεῖς . . . οἱ γέροντες in 3, and I print van Herwerden's **παρ(ὰ) ὑμῖν**, 'among you', i.e. 'in your time'. The error is so common that the emendation is better referred to simply as a correction.

3. **τέως**: 'up to this time', i.e. 'in the past, previously' (LSJ s.v. III). **ᾠκοῦμεν**: 'we ran our affairs'.

4. **ἡμῖν** and **τῆι πόλει** are both datives of advantage dependent on **ἦσαν**; 'for us for the city', i.e. 'for the city in our time'. **πρῶτον μέν** suggests that the attack on the city's generals that follows in 4–7 is only the first in a projected list of complaints; cf. **E18**. 3; **E19** with n. **οἱ στρατηγοί**: For Athens' generals, see **E3**. 5 n. For other hostile comments about them, see **E5**. 2; **G6**. 1–4; **J7**. 1–3.

5. **πλούτωι γένει τε πρῶτοι** is little more than a gloss on **ἐκ τῶν μεγίστων οἰκιῶν**.

6. **καὶ γὰρ ἦσαν**: 'for in fact' (Denniston 108–9) 'they *were* (gods)'.

7. **ἐπράττομεν**: 'we conducted our (political) business, governed ourselves'. **ὅπηι τύχωμεν**: 'in whichever way we happen to', i.e. 'any which way, seemingly at random'.

8. **καθάρματα**: literally 'what is thrown away in rites of purification', but used colloquially as a form of abuse ('scum' *vel sim.*; cf. Ar. *Pl.* 454; D. 21. 185 with MacDowell ad loc.; Men. *Sam.* 481). To be taken in apposition to **στρατηγούς**.

E5. For the sentiments, see **E4** introductory n. For *Marikas*, see **E23** introductory n.

Preserved at Athenaeus 10. 425a–b, along with a fragment of the fourth-century orator Philinus, as evidence that certain Athenian officials were referred to as οἰνόπται (1 with n.).

Iambic trimeter.

1. οὓς δ᾽ οὐκ ἂν εἵλεσθ(ε) κτλ.: For the idea, cf. **D8**. 2–3.   οἰνόπτας:
    According to Athenaeus (cf. Poll. vi. 21–2; Hsch. ο 332), οἰνόπται (literally
    'wine-watchers') supervised what went on at dinner parties, making sure
    that the guests drank equal amounts; he adds, on the authority of Philinus,
    that this was a minor magistracy (ἀρχὴ εὐτελής) occupied by three men,
    who supplied diners with lamps and wicks. Cf. the 'Supervisors of Women'
    (referred to at e.g. Timocl. Com. fr. 34), whose job was to ensure that the
    number of guests at dinner parties and symposia did not exceed the legal
    limit.   πρὸ τοῦ: 'before this'.
2. ὦ πόλις, πόλις: probably paratragic; cf. S. *OT* 629; Ar. *Ach.* 27 (in the same
    position in the line in both places).
3. An allusion to the tradition that, although the Athenians blundered
    routinely, even their worst mistakes somehow worked out well for them
    (Ar. *Nu.* 587–9; *Ec.* 473–5; cf. fr. 308 with K–A ad loc.).   ὡς is
    exclamatory, 'How . . .!'

E6. Prominent individuals were frequently attacked both in comedy and the
lawcourts via claims that their mothers were foreigners (e.g. *Ach.* 704–5 with
Olson ad loc.; Pl. Com. fr. 61; Aeschin. 3. 172) or common market-vendors
(e.g. Ar. *Ach.* 478 with Olson ad loc.; *Th.* 387; D. 57. 31, 34 (where the fact that
the defendant's mother currently sells ribbons in the Agora and has in the
past served as a wet-nurse has been presented by the prosecution as evidence
that the family is not Athenian)), who could expect to be subject to sexual
advances by men other than their husbands and might therefore be alleged
to be likely to bear illegitimate children. Cf. **E22**. 1–2; **E23–E25** n. This is
accordingly most likely a slanderous assault on some public figure, probably a
politician. The play probably dates to the early 420s and may well be Eupolis'
first comedy; see Storey 230–46.
    Preserved at Athenaeus 7. 326a, in a discussion of the fish known as the
ταινία ('ribbon').
    Iambic trimeter.

Θρᾶιττα ταινιόπωλις: 'a Thracian ribbon-vendor'. A large percentage of
Athenian slaves were Thracians, as inscriptional evidence (e.g. *IG* I³ 421.
34–6, 40–1) and the common use of the ethnic Θρᾶιττα as a slave-name
in comedy (e.g. Ar. *Ach.* 272–3; *V.* 828; cf. Archipp. fr. 27) make clear. The
ribbons in question are to be used as grave-goods (Ar. *Ec.* 1032; fr. 205. 1;
Alex. fr. 147. 2–3 with K–A ad loc.) or worn around the guests' heads at
symposia (e.g. Ar. *Ra.* 392; Eub. fr. 2. 3 with K–A ad loc.).

E7. Athenaeus identifies the first speaker as the poetess Sappho, the title-
character of the play, and 13 shows that Speaker B is an older man. What

Sappho offers is an αἴνιγμα ('conundrum'), i.e. a description of a common object set in obscure and seemingly self-contradictory language (cf. 2, 4–5); for other examples of comic riddles, see **E30**; Antiph. fr. 192 (from a play entitled Πρόβλημα); Alex. fr. 242; and note Cratinus' *Cleoboulinas* (test. i reports that Cleoboulina wrote hexameter riddles). But Speaker B converts the riddle into political commentary, explaining it as a denunciation of demagogues for their self-serving behaviour and of the city's people for their inability to see through this. Compare Aristophanes' *Knights*, where Demos (the personified Athenian people) is presented as an old fool who fails to detect the blatant misdeeds of his conniving Paphlagonian slave ~ Cleon (esp. 40–70, 1337–55; cf. **E16–E19** n.), and *Wasps*, in which the old juryman Philocleon belatedly discovers that the extraordinary power he thinks he exercises over the city's affairs is a mirage and that the city's politicians have been fooling and stealing from him for years (esp. 655–718). The reference to events in Asia Minor and Thrace suggests a date in the mid-360s, when Athens was involved in fighting (and thus presumably in raising revenue) in both places; see Roy, *CAH*² vi. 200–3. Probably from a symposium scene, with Sappho presented as a courtesan; see **C8**. 4–5 (for riddles at symposia); **H5** introductory n. (for Sappho in comedy); **I7** introductory n. (for courtesans).

Preserved at Athenaeus 10. 450e–1b, as part of a long discussion of riddles (γρῖφοι) that also includes **C8**; **E30**, and most of the other fragments mentioned above.

Lines 1–5 are dactylic hexameter, the traditional metrical form for riddles (e.g. **E30**. 1–4; Antiph. fr. 192. 1–4, 7–8, 15–19; Eub. fr. 106. 10–11, 16–17, 21–5; Hermipp. Hist. fr. 77). 6–12 are iambic trimeter.

1. For **ἔστι** ('(What I'm thinking of) is . . . ') at the beginning of a riddle, see **E30**. 1; Antiph. fr. 192. 7; and cf. Ar. *Eq.* 1059.   **φύσις θήλεια:** 'a female creature' (cf. 6 'The creature you're talking about . . . '), i.e. 'something feminine', so that both πόλις (6) and ἐπιστολή (17) will do as solutions to this part of the riddle.

1–2. **βρέφη σώιζουσ(α) ὑπὸ κόλποις | αὐτῆς:** 'who keeps her children safe beneath the fold of her garment', which Speaker B takes to mean 'at her breast' *vel sim.* (see 7). Cf. H. *Il.* 6. 400 παῖδ᾽ ἐπὶ κόλπωι ἔχουσ(α) (of Andromache carrying the infant Astyanax); *h.Cer.* 187 παῖδ᾽ ὑπὸ κόλπωι ἔχουσ(α) (of Metaneira with baby Demophon on her lap).

2. **βοὴν ἵστησι:** 'raises a cry'. A poetic expression (cf. Ar. *Th.* 696–7 with Austin–Olson ad loc.; E. *Hipp.* 903 with Barrett ad loc.); the subject is τὰ βρέφη (supplied from 1, and paradoxically modified by ὄντα . . . ἄφωνα). **γεγωνόν:** 'loud, resounding'; a rare, poetic, two-termination adjective, modifying **βοήν**.

3. **διά** + acc. in the sense 'through (a space)' is poetic; contrast the more common use of the preposition with the gen. in the second half of the verse.   **πόντιον οἶδμα**: 'the sea-swell'. Elevated poetic vocabulary; cf. Ar. *Av.* 250 ἐπὶ πόντιον οἶδμα θαλάσσης (lyric) with Dunbar ad loc., 1339 (lyric); Austin–Olson on Ar. *Th.* 322 (lyric).

4. **θνητῶν** is not needed for the sense and is accordingly omitted in the 'less poetic' paraphrase in 20.

5. **κωφὴν δ(ὲ) ἀκοῆς αἴσθησιν ἔχουσιν**: 'but they' (the mortals referred to in 4) 'have a perception of hearing that is deaf', i.e. they perceive the 'loud cry' (2), but without hearing it.

6–12. **γάρ** ('(Yes), for . . .') in 6 marks this as an explanation or justification of something omitted by Athenaeus or his source, most likely a claim by Speaker B to be able to interpret the riddle, to which Sappho offered a sceptical response. Speaker B explains most of the elements in Sappho's riddle in the order in which she gave them (cf. 17–21 n.): the **φύσις** ('creature') in question is a city (which is possible; see 1 n.); the **βρέφη** are its politicians, whose shouting (**κεκραγότες**; cf. 2 βοὴν ἴστησι γεγωνόν) fills the sea and the earth (3) because it concerns revenues brought in from the lands scattered about the Aegean coast; and the mention of deafness in 5 refers to the habitual obtuseness of the Athenian people. But the explanation fails to account for ὄντα . . . ἄφωνα in 2, as the audience must have realized immediately and Sappho points out in 13–14, and thoroughly garbles 4–5; and it may be that the explanation is not offered seriously and that the protest in 15–16 is therefore made tongue-in-cheek.

7. **βρέφη δ(ὲ) ἐν αὐτῆι διατρέφει**: see 1–2 n.   **τοὺς ῥήτορας**: 'the speakers (in the Assembly)'; but already by the late fifth century the noun frequently has the more specific sense 'habitual speakers, politicians' (e.g Ar. *Eq.* 358; *Th.* 382; cf. **E9**. 2, 4).

8. **κεκραγότες** is perfect with present sense < κράζω, 'shout'; used of politicians or characters representing them at e.g. Ar. *Ach.* 711; *Eq.* 256, 274.

8–9. **τὰ διαπόντια** | . . . **λήμματα**: 'the overseas revenues' (cognate with λαμβάνω); see introductory n.

10–11. **νεμομένων** . . . | . . . **λοιδορουμένων τ(ε) ἀεί**: 'splitting (the money) up among themselves and constantly abusing one another'. The implication is that what look like disputes over policy and principles are in fact driven only by concern about who will pocket the largest share of the cash. **πλησίον** + genitive modifies **κάθηται** ('sits near them'). Average members of the Assembly sat to listen to the speakers, who stood before them (e.g. Ar. *Ach.* 29; *Eq.* 749–50, 783–5; *Ec.* 86, 152; cf. **E10**. 2 with n.).

12. **οὔτ(ε) ἀκούων οὔτ(ε) ὁρῶν**: cf. the description of Demos as 'half-deaf' (ὑπόκωφος) at Ar. *Eq.* 43.

13.   The lacuna must have contained something like Jacobs' οὐδὲν λέγεις, since what follows gives the ground (**γάρ**) for Sappho's dismissal of her interlocutor's explanation of the riddle.   **ὦ πάτερ** is simply a polite form of address for an older man (see **H11**. 4 n.) and does not suggest that Speaker B is Sappho's father.

14.   **ἢν ἁλῶι τρὶς παρανόμων:** 'If he's convicted (< αἱρέω) three times for (proposing and carrying a motion containing) things contrary to the laws' (genitive of charge), sc. *'then* he will be!' A reference to the rule (attested at D.S. xviii. 18. 2) that anyone convicted three times on a γραφὴ παρανόμων (for which, see [Arist.] *Ath.* 45. 4 with Rhodes ad loc.) was deprived of his civic rights and thus of his 'voice', i.e. the opportunity to participate in the debate in the Athenian Assembly.

15.   **καὶ μήν:** 'and yet' (Denniston 357–8); but see 6–12 n.

15–16.   **ἀκριβῶς** is to be taken with **ἐγνωκέναι.** For γιγνώσκω used of 'recognizing' (the answer to) a riddle, cf. Nausicr. fr. 1. 5 (*B.*) Γλαῦκον λέγεις. (*A.*) ἔγνωκας ('You're talking about Glaucus.' 'You've solved it!').

16.   **ἀλλὰ δή:** 'brushing aside a digression or irrelevancy'—here Speaker B's insistence, sincere or not (cf. 6–12 n.), that he had thought his idea was a good one (15–16)—'and coming to the point' (Denniston 241). **λέγε:** see **D3**. 6 n.

17–21.   Sappho's own solution to her riddle also cites and explains its key elements in the order they were given (cf. 6–12 n.): **θήλεια ... φύσις** (~ 1 φύσις θήλεια) is glossed by **ἐπιστολή**, and **βρέφη** (cf. 1) is glossed by **τὰ γράμματα** (with the 'answer' in each case reserved for the end of the line as a surprise; cf. **B29**. 3 n.), with **ἐν αὐτῆι περιφέρει** offered as a less obscure paraphrase of σώιζουσ(α) ὑπὸ κόλποις | αὐτῆς (1–2); the sense of **ἄφωνα δ(ὲ) ὄντα** (~ 2 ὄντα δ' ἄφωνα) is thus made clear (cf. E. *IT* 763 (of a letter) φράσει σιγῶσα, and **τοῖς πόρρω λαλεῖ | οἷς βούλετ(αι)** condenses and clarifies 2 βοήν–4 οἷς ἐθέλει θνητῶν; and finally **ἕτερος δ(ὲ) ἂν κτλ.** decodes the mantic κωφὴν κτλ. in 5.

17–18.   Although Sappho refers to the object in question as an **ἐπιστολή** ('letter'), what she describes is the pair of wax-covered writing tablets on which the letter was inscribed and which were then folded together and tied closed to protect the text in transit. See E. G. Turner, *Greek Manuscripts of the Ancient World*[2] (ed. P. J. Parsons; *BICS* Supplement 46: London, 1987) #4; Austin–Olson on Ar. *Th.* 778–80.

20–1.   These lines suggest that by the middle of the fourth century most people read silently rather than aloud; cf. **G4**. 1–3; Knox, *GRBS* 9 (1968), 432–4; Gavrilov, *CQ* ns 47 (1997), 56–73, esp. 68.

E8. For the faithlessness of politicians (a comic trope), cf. **E7**. 10–12; **E15**; **E31**. For courtesans (who had little choice but to say whatever their customers wanted to hear), see **I7** introductory n.

Preserved at Stobaeus iii. 28. 10, under the heading 'Concerning perjury'. Iambic trimeter.

1. τ(ὸ) αὐτὸ καὶ δημηγόρου: 'is the same thing', i.e. 'identical to a politician's'.

2. ὀμνύει is < ὀμνύω, a regularized, alternative form of ὄμνυμι. πρὸς ὃν λαλεῖ: '(to suit the person) to whom he is speaking'.

E9. For the comparison of politicians to vipers (implicit in 1–4), cf. **B27**. 2 n. For the idea that a willingness to be fucked by other men is a fundamental qualification for a life in politics, cf. Ar. *Eq.* 417–28, 878–80; *Nu.* 1089–90, 1093–4; *Ec.* 112–13; Eup. fr. *104; Pl. *Smp.* 191e–2a.

Preserved at Stobaeus ii. 3. 3, under the heading 'Concerning rhetoric'. Iambic trimeter.

2. ἀνέφυσαν is a gnomic aorist (Goodwin § 154–5).   ῥήτορες (cf. **E7**. 7 n.) is reserved for the end of the line as a *para prosdokian* joke (cf. **B29**. 3 n.), as again in 4 ῥητόρων.

3–4. Iolaus was Heracles' cousin and charioteer (cf. [Hes.] *Asp.* 77–121), and assisted him in his battle against the monstrous Lernaean Hydra, which grew two heads for every one that was cut off, by cauterizing the stumps (E. *HF* 419–21; Palaeph. 38; [Apollod.] *Bib.* ii. 5. 2; Gantz 384–6 (but without reference to this passage); cf. Pl. *Euthd.* 297c–d)—as unfortunately cannot be done with politicians, even today.

5. κεκολλόπευκας: 'you've been a κόλλοψ', i.e. 'you've allowed someone to bugger you'. For the noun and its cognates, cf. Eub. fr. 10. 3; Diph. fr. 42. 22; Diosc. *AP* xii. 42. 6 = *HE* 1528; Taillardat § 209; *Maculate Muse*, § 469; Pohlmann and Tichy, in *Serta Indogermanica* (Festschrift G. Neumann; Innsbruck, 1982), 287–315, esp. 296–7.   τοιγαροῦν is strongly emphatic, 'that's why . . .!, and as a result . . .!' (Denniston 566–8).

E10–E28. 'Old Comedy' routinely comments on political events and personalities, generally in a manner that is supportive of the theory of democracy but scathingly critical of the contemporary practice of it. See Henderson, in J. J. Winkler and F. I. Zeitlin (eds.), *Nothing to Do with Dionysos?: Athenian Drama in its Social Context* (Princeton, 1990), 271–313, and in A. H. Sommerstein *et al.* (eds.), *Tragedy, Comedy and the Polis* (Bari, 1993), 307–19; Carey, in R. Osborne and S. Hornblower (eds.), *Ritual, Finance, Politics* (Festschrift D. Lewis: Oxford, 1994), 69–83; Olson, *TAPA* 126 (1996), 129–50 (with particular attention to Ar. *V.*); Sommerstein, *CQ* ns 46 (1996),

327–56 (with a complete catalogue of late fifth-century κωμωιδούμενοι), and in J. A. López Férez (ed.), *La comedia Griega y su influencia en la literatura Española* (Estudios de filología Griega 3: Madrid, 1998), 43–62 (all with further bibliography). That the freedom to engage in such criticism was ever systematically restricted, as Hellenistic scholars believed, seems unlikely, although some limits may have been imposed in 440–437 (thus Σ^REΓ Ar. *Ach.* 67) in connection with the Samian War (cf. **B13–B20** n.); see Halliwell, *JHS* 111 (1991), 48–70, esp. 54–66.

E10–E14. Pericles son of Xanthippus of the deme Cholargus (*PAA* 772645) belonged to Athens' most distinguished poltical family, the Alcmaeonidae (cf. **E26–E27** n.), and served as *choregos* for Aeschylus in 473/2, when the tetralogy that included *Persians* took the prize at the City Dionysia (*IG* II² 2318. 9–11). He dominated Athenian political life from the late 440s until his death in 429. Cf. *APF* 457–60; Thucydides regarded him as the greatest man of his generation (ii. 65. 5–10). But the 'Old Comic' poets, although aware of his gifts (**E10** (posthumous)), are also extremely critical of him, expressing concern about his immense personal authority (**E11**) and allegedly divisive approach to politics (**E12**), blaming him for the outbreak of the Peloponnesian War (**B13–B20** n. with **B13**. 33–5; **B13**. 40–4; cf. Ar. *Ach.* 530–9; *Pax* 606–11), and questioning his conduct of it (**E14**). Other comic references to Pericles (most preserved by Plutarch in his *Life*) include **F19**. 12; Cratin. frr. 73; 118; 326; Telecl. frr. 18; 47; Eup. fr. 115; Pl. Com. fr. 207; adesp. com. fr. 703; and perhaps Hermipp. fr. 42. For Pericles' political style and the significance of his career, see in general Connor 119–28; A. J. Podlecki, *Perikles and his Circle* (London, 1998). For his image in comedy, see J. Schwartze, *Die Beurteilung des Perikles durch die attische Komödie* (Zetemata 51: Munich, 1971) (an eccentric treatment).

E10. *Demes* (Eup. frr. 99–146) was performed sometime between 417 BC (since fr. 99. 30–2 refers to events in summer 418) and 411 (when Eupolis most likely died), and thus at least a decade after the death of Pericles, who is accordingly referred to with past tenses. The plot involved the return from the dead of four prominent statesmen from Athens' past, the others being Solon, Aristides 'the Just', and Miltiades; despite the existence of a substantial papyrus fragment, which raises more questions than it answers (fr. 99, containing portions of 120 lines), most of what went on in the play remains obscure. See Storey 111–74, esp. 133–4 (on this fragment). For Pericles' brilliance as an orator, cf. **B16** introductory n.; **E14** introductory n.; Ar. *Ach.* 530–1 with Olson ad loc.; adesp. com. fr. 701; Th. i. 139. 4 'a man . . . with the greatest ability both to speak and to get things done'; Pl. *Phdr.* 269e.
  This passage must have been famous in antiquity (doubtless in part

because its topic is the power of rhetoric), and our sources quote only those portions of it that suit their purposes: 1–5 are preserved in a *scholium* on Ael. Arist. *Or.* 3. 51, which also contains Eup. fr. 103; 4 πρὸs–7 are preserved at Pliny, *Epistles* i. 20. 17; 5–7 are preserved at Diodorus Siculus xii. 40. 6; and other authors preserve smaller bits and pieces.

Iambic trimeter.

2. **παρέλθοι:** 'came forward', sc. to the speaker's stand (βῆμα) in the front of the Assembly; cf. Th. i. 139. 4 (for this use of παρέρχομαι); E7. 10–11 n.; E29. 3.

3. **ἐκ δέκα ποδῶν:** 'from ten feet (back)', i.e. despite their having what looked like an impossible initial advantage in the debate; see 7 n.

4. **γε** adds emphasis to **ταχύν** ('You're describing someone *fast*!'), but has been put in third position *metri gratia*.   **πρὸs ... αὐτοῦ τῶι τάχει:** 'and in addition to his speed'.   **δέ <γ'>** picks up the thread of the argument after the interjection by Speaker B (Denniston 154).

5. More often it is honey or the like that sits on the lips of a brilliant speaker or poet (Hes. *Th.* 83–4 with West on 83; Ar. frr. 598; 679; cf. Taillardat § 741), and that image is taken up (with a twist) in the allusion to bees in 7 (where see n.). For the goddess Peitho, to whom there is at least a glancing allusion (hence Welcker's Πειθώ), see D3. 34 n.

6. **οὕτως ἐκήλει:** 'that's how bewitching (< κηλέω) he was'.

7. **τὸ κέντρον:** 'his stinger' (see 5 n.), but also 'his response' (cf. A18. 5 with n.). The basic point is that the audience quickly forgot what other Assembly speakers said, whereas Pericles' words lingered in their ears. But what stays with them is painful rather than pleasant, and the implication of this verse, especially when taken together with 3, is that Pericles alone was able to tell the Athenian people things they did not wish to hear, and to convince them to make difficult choices, as Thucydides also maintains (ii. 65. 8–9).

E11. According to Plutarch, this is a catalogue of things the Athenians 'had turned over' (παραδεδωκέναι) to Pericles, sc. by docilely adopting whatever policies he proposed. The description sounds like it belongs to the 440s or early 430s rather than to the Peloponnesian War years.

Preserved at Plutarch, *Life of Pericles* 16. 1, as part of a discussion of the extent of Pericles' authority and influence that also cites adesp. com. fr. 703 (see E12. 3 n.).

Anapaestic tetrameter catalectic; probably from a parabasis.

1. **πόλεων ... φόρους:** 'the tribute payments of the (allied) cities', which funded Athens' fleet and the imperial enterprise generally; see R. Meiggs,

The Athenian Empire (Oxford, 1972), 234–54; and cf. **B29**. 1. The reference
might be either to the use of the tribute after it had been collected or (more
likely, given what follows) to Pericles' authority over the city-by-city
reassessment of tribute levels that took place every four years. See also
E18. 1 with n.

1–2.   δεῖν, ἀναλύειν, οἰκοδομεῖν, καταβάλλειν: infinitives of purpose (Goodwin § 770), 'so that he could bind them', etc.

2.   λάινα τείχη: i.e. the fortification walls that surrounded most major cities
in the second half of the fifth century. Thasos was required to demolish her
walls after an unsuccessful revolt from the Empire in the late 460s (Th.
i. 101. 3), as was Samos by Pericles in 439 (Th. i. 117. 3; cf. **B13–B20** n.),
and the implication is that similar orders to subject-allies were common
in the pre-Peloponnesian War years.   τὰ (ἔ)μπαλιν is adverbial,
'contrariwise, instead'.

3.   Three pairs of synonyms (σπονδάς and εἰρήνην, δύναμιν and κράτος,
πλοῦτον and εὐδαιμονίαν), all positive, apparently intended to emphasize
that the Athenians' happiness and prosperity depend—for good or bad—
entirely on Pericles' authority.

E12. A fragment of a mock theogony (cf. Ar. *Av.* 685–702 with Dunbar's nn.)
culminating in the birth of the 'greatest tyrant'—who is not Zeus but Pericles.
E13 probably comes from the same song. For *Cheirons* (undated), see **B46**
introductory n.
    Preserved at Plutarch, *Life of Pericles* 3. 5, in a collection of comic fragments
that refer to the odd shape of the statesman's head (see 4).
    1 ia ch; 2 paroem; 3 ba cr ba; 4 – D, 5?

1.   Στάσις: 'Political Division' of the sort, the implication is, that Pericles'
policies have engendered.   πρεσβυγενής: 'eldest-born, first-born';
elevated poetic vocabulary (H. *Il.* 11. 249; E. *Tr.* 593 (lyric)).

2.   Why Χρόνος ('Time'; a cosmogonic figure or the like at Pherecyd. frr. 14;
60 Schibli; Pi. *O.* 2. 17; E. *Heracl.* 900; *Supp.* 787; fr. 303. 4; Pl. *Ti.* 37d–8c, as
well as in Orphic poetry (e.g. 76 F with Bernabé ad loc.; 109 F), is one of
Pericles' divine parents is unclear, hence the conjecture Κρόνος. Perhaps
the point is that Pericles had exercised enormous political power for years
and seemed likely to go on doing so 'for ever'. See Noussia, *PCPhS* 49
(2003), 74–88.   ἀλλήλοισι μιγέντε: 'after having sex'; an epicism
(e.g. H. *Il.* 14. 295; Hes. *Th.* 927; *h.Ven.* 150).

3.   τύραννον: In late fifth-century Athens, τύραννος and its cognates are
highly charged terms, which can be used in a neutral sense of Zeus and his
dominion (e.g. Ar. *Nu.* 564; *Pl.* 124) but not of one's fellow citizens or their
aspirations (esp. Ar. *V.* 487–502; *Lys.* 618/19 with Henderson on 616–35;

Th. 338 with Austin–Olson ad loc.); cf. Raaflaub and Henderson, in K. A. Morgan (ed.), *Popular Tyranny: Sovereignty and its Discontents in Ancient Greece* (Austin, 2003), 59–93 and 155–79, respectively. According to Plu. *Per.* 16. 1, some of the comic poets went so far as to call Pericles' associates 'the new Peisistratids' (in reference to the family of tyrants who controlled the city before the establishment of a democracy in 510) and to urge him to swear an oath that he was not aiming at a tyranny (= adesp. com. fr. 703).

4–5. ὃν δὴ . . . | θεοὶ καλέουσι: see **H8**. 6 n.

4. κεφαληγερέταν: 'head-gatherer'; an allusion to Pericles' deformity (see introductory n.) and a pun on Zeus' Homeric epithet νεφεληγερέτα, 'cloud-gatherer' (e.g. *Il.* 5. 631; *Od.* 1. 63). For other comic references to Pericles as 'Zeus', see Cratin. frr. 73. 1–2; 118; Telecl. fr. 18; Ar. *Ach.* 530–1; and cf. **B13**. 40–4 with nn.

E13. Sometime in the 440s Pericles divorced his wife and began to live with a free Milesian woman named Aspasia (*PAA* 222330), who the comic poets claim exercised considerable power over his political decisions, and whom they describe as a whore and a madame (Ar. *Ach.* 526–34 with Olson on 526–7; Eup. fr. 110. 2). According to Plutarch in his introduction to this fragment, certain comic poets also referred to Aspasia as 'a new Omphale' and 'Deianeira' (= adesp. com. fr. 704; cf. Eup. fr. 294 (corrupt)), with Pericles presumably cast as Heracles and thus her victim (cf. Gantz 439–40, 458–9). Plutarch also reports that the comic playwright Hermippus prosecuted Aspasia for impiety on the ground that she arranged sexual liaisons for Pericles with free women (= Hermipp. test. 2), although this seems more likely to be a garbled report of something said or done on stage in a comedy; cf. Dover, *Talanta*, 7 (1976), 27–9. See in general *APF* 458; M. M. Henry, *Prisoner of History: Aspasia of Miletus and her Biographical Tradition* (New York and Oxford, 1995), esp. 9–56; A. J. Podlecki, *Perikles and his Circle* (London, 1998), 109–17; and cf. **B8**. 8 n.

Preserved at Plutarch, *Life of Pericles* 24. 9, in a discussion of Aspasia's character and influence. Plutarch does not explicitly assign this fragment to *Cheirons*, but it likely belongs to the same mock theogony as **E12**.

1 – D – D; 2 lek or e ∪ e.

1. Ἥραν τέ οἱ Ἀσπασίαν τίκτει: 'and as his Hera she bears for him (i.e. Pericles) Aspasia'.   Καταπυγοσύνη: 'Buggery', i.e. 'Depravity' *vel sim.*

2. παλλακήν: 'a concubine', a woman with whom a man lives but to whom he is not married; see Harrison i. 13–15.   κυνώπιδα: 'dog-eyed', i.e. 'shameless'. Poetic and especially Homeric vocabulary (e.g. *Il.* 3. 180; *Od.* 4. 145 with S. West ad loc.).

E14. When the Spartans and their allies invaded Attica in summer 431, Pericles—who was not only one of the generals, but far and away the most influential man in the city—convinced the Athenians not to go out of the city to confront them. Thucydides reports that this policy created tremendous resentment among the citizens who were forced to watch their personal property being destroyed, as well as among the younger men (Th. ii. 21. 2–3), and their hostility is apparent in this passage, which most likely dates to 430.

Preserved at Plutarch, *Life of Pericles* 33. 8, as part of a gossipy account of the statesman's behaviour during the early Peloponnesian War years that interweaves elements of Thucydides' account with material from 'Old Comedy' (especially Cratinus) and other sources. Cf. P. A. Stadter, *A Commentary on Plutarch's Pericles* (Chapel Hill and London, 1989), pp. lviii–lxxxv.

Anapaestic dimeter (4 and 7 catalectic).

1. *βασιλεῦ σατύρων*: The 'king of the satyrs' ought to be Dionysus, and if this is not a direct reference to Cratinus' *Dionysalexandros* (see **B13** with introductory n.)—to which van Leeuwen suggested the fragment ought perhaps to be reassigned—the point eludes us.   *ποτ(ε)* adds emphasis to *τί*, 'why ever, why in the world?'; cf. **C2**. 4–5 n.
2. *βαστάζειν*: 'to balance, weigh in your hand'; elevated poetic vocabulary (e.g. H. *Od.* 21. 405 (a bow); Pi. *P.* 4. 296; A. *Ag.* 35 with Frankel ad loc.).
2–3. *λογοὺς κτλ.*: i.e. 'you *talk* big'.
4. *ψυχὴ . . . Τέλητος ὕπεστιν*: 'Teles' spirit is in you'. Teles is mentioned nowhere else but must have been a notorious coward; a rare name, otherwise attested in Athens only in the mid- to late sixth century (five examples in *LGPN* ii s.v.).
5–6. *(ἐ)γχειριδίου . . . ἀκόνηι σκληρᾶι | παραθηγομένης . . . κοπίδος*: genitive absolute; 'if a little hand-knife, (that is) a chopping knife, is whetted with a hard whetstone'. If Pericles is represented as a coward who refuses to take up his spear to confront the Spartans (1–4), it perhaps makes sense that he objects even when a knife is sharpened in his presence. But 7 suggests that these verses are intended primarily as a riddling reference to the behaviour of Cleon (**E16–E19** n.), who was said by the third-century historian Idomeneus (*FGrHist* 338 F 9 ap. Plu. *Per.* 35. 5) to have prosecuted Pericles when Pericles was fined and removed as general in summer 430 (Th. ii. 65. 3), and who must already by this time have been manoeuvring to take his place as 'leader of the people'. *κοπίδος* (cf. **G9**. 3 with n.) may therefore be intended to suggest *κόπιδος*, 'glib talker' (E. *Hec.* 132).
6. *βρύχεις*: 'you gnash your teeth'.

7.   δηχθείς: literally 'bit', and thus by extension 'grieved'; cf. Ar. *Ach.* 325
with Olson ad loc.; Taillardat § 296.   αἴθωνι Κλέωνι: 'by shining
Cleon' (see 5–6 n.); a reworking of the Homeric αἴθωνι σιδήρωι
(e.g. *Il.* 4. 485; 7. 473) which casts Pericles' political rival as a dagger being
sharpened to kill him—or perhaps to flay him (since Cleon' wealth came
from leather-tanning), in which case there may be a reference to the story
of the satyr Marysas.

E15. Phormio son of Asopius (*PA* 14958) was a distinguished military
commander and a contemporary of Pericles (Th. i. 64. 2, 117. 2; ii. 68. 7, 69. 1,
83–92). Aristophanes refers to him repeatedly in his early plays (*Eq.* 562; *Pax*
347b with Olson ad loc.; frr. 88 (*Babylonians*); 397 (the original *Clouds*); also
Lys. 804), and a character representing him played a leading part in Eupolis'
Taxiarchs ('*Tribal Military Commanders*'), in which he taught Dionysus about
a soldier's life (esp. fr. 269). He most likely died in spring or early summer of
428 BC, making all these references posthumous.
    Preserved at Zonaras p. 1366, as evidence that Attic used the form
μολύβδινος.
    Iambic trimeter.

1–2. στήσειν ἔφη | τρίποδας: sc. in commemoration of a military victory,
like the gold tripod dedicated at Delphi by the Greek forces after the Battle
of Plataea (Hdt. ix. 81. 1), or the two bronze tripods dedicated at Amyclae
by the Spartans after the Battle of Aegospotamoi (Paus. iii. 18. 7–8);
cf. W. H. D. Rouse, *Greek Votive Offerings* (Cambridge, 1902), 145–8.
Probably a report of a vow made in advance of a battle rather than a boast
after it (for military vows, see W. K. Pritchett, *The Greek State at War*,
iii (Berkeley, Los Angeles, and London, 1979), 230 9), in which case the
charge is not just of lying to the public (cf. **E8**) and general cheapness, but
of impiety as well.
2. ἔθηκεν: 'set up, dedicated' (LSJ s.v. A. III. 2).   ἕνα μολύβδινον:
'one—of lead'. That Phormio dedicated only one tripod after promising
two is bad enough. But his offering was not of silver but of lead, which was
virtually worthless (e.g. Ar. *Nu.* 913; Hdt. iii. 56. 2), and the crucial word
gains impact from having been reserved for final position in the line
(cf. **B29**. 3 n.).

E16–E19. After the death of Pericles in 429, Cleon son of Cleaenetus of
the deme Cydathenaion (*PAA* 579130) became Athens' leading politician.
Cleon's greatest political coup came in summer 425, when his rival Nicias
(cf. **E20–E22** n.) resigned command of the Athenian forces at Pylos in his
favour; cf. **E20** with introductory n. To universal surprise, Cleon (who had no

previous command experience) won a great victory, capturing 292 Peloponnesian hoplites, including 120 full-blooded Spartiates, on the island of Sphacteria (see **E16–E17** with nn.); he was rewarded with the honour of a front-row seat at the city's dramatic festivals (Ar. *Eq.* 702) and the right to eat at public expense in the Prytaneion (Ar. *Eq.* 280–1, 709, 766, 1404). Cleon died in battle in summer 422, according to Thucydides (who hated him and can reasonably be suspected of malice), while running away (v. 10. 9). Other 'Old Comic' references to Cleon include **E14.** 7; Cratin. fr. 228; Ar. *Ach.* 6, 299–302, 377–82, 659–64; *Eq. passim*; *Nu.* 584–94; *V.* 62, 596–7; *Pax* 47–8, 647–56; Eup. frr. 192. 135; 211; and perhaps **E21.** For his political style and the significance of his career, see in general Connor 91–8, 128–34, 151–83.

E16. A sneering reference to the adulation Cleon received after the victory at Sphacteria.

Preserved at Lucian *Prom. Es* 2, where the character who quotes the verse worries that a man who has called him a 'Prometheus' means this no more sincerely than the anonymous comic poet did when describing Cleon.

Iambic trimeter.

Προμηθεύς: i.e. 'a genius'. But the joke depends on 'Prometheus' being understood to mean 'He who plans in advance', as already in Hesiod (see West on *Th.* 510, 511).   **μετὰ τὰ πράγματα:** 'after the events, after the fact', the implication being that Cleon blundered into victory and got undeserved credit for brilliant planning. Thucydides offers much the same analysis at iv. 39. 3 ('Cleon's promise, insane though it was, was fulfilled'; cf. the bitterly satirical account of the meeting of the Assembly that got Cleon joint command of the Athenian forces at iv. 27–8), while Aristophanes claims at *Eq.* 54–7, 1200–1, that Cleon stole credit for the victory from the other generals, who were actually responsible for it.

E17. Preserved at Moeris χ 37, where the fragment is offered in support of the thesis (put forward by a number of late sources) that Cleon was the first person to use the term χαίρειν ('Rejoice!', i.e. 'Greetings!') in a letter, having done so after (other authorities say in the course of announcing) his victory on Sphacteria. As Fritzsche noted, Cleon's innovation may actually have been to include a common colloquial expression in a formal state communication; or we may be dealing with 'one of those scholiastic fictions derived from a misunderstanding or misexplanation of the comic text', and the connection with Sphacteria may be illusory (thus Storey, *MCr* 30–31 (1995–96), 141–3).

Iambic trimeter.

1–2. **ἡμᾶς . . . | χαίρειν προσεῖπας:** 'you addressed us with the word χαίρειν'. Similar puns occur elsewhere in both comedy (e.g. Ar. *Ach.* 176 with Olson ad loc.) and tragedy (e.g. E. *Hec.* 426–7).

E18. Three fragments of a single parabasis-section (see **B36–B45** n.), which is addressed to Athens and offers mocking praise of her as 'lucky enough' to be dominated by Cleon (i.e. in the period after the death of Pericles). For the play, see Storey 266–77, esp. 269–71 (on this fragment).

Preserved at Priscian, *de metr. Ter.* 26, who cites the verses for the sake of the metre (attested nowhere else) and names the metrician Hephaestion as his source. But our text of Hephaestion (*ench.* 16. 4) contains only 1–2, and it seems clear that Priscian had a fuller version of the work. A metrical *scholium* to Pi. *O.* 13 also preserves 1 for the sake of the metre.

×–––∪∪––×–∪–∪∪–; see *GM* 97.

1. The cities Cleon 'watches over' must be those of the Athenian empire (for the idea, cf. **E11**. 1), and the demagogue himself is presented as resembling a god or the sun (e.g. H. *Il.* 3. 277; *Od.* 13. 213–14); cf. Ar. *Eq.* 75 (also of the Paphlagonian/Cleon) ἐφορᾶι ... οὗτος πάντ(α).
2. ὡς εὐδαίμων πρότερόν τ(ε) ἦσθα must refer to the time before Cleon's ascendancy, so that νῦν δὲ μᾶλλον ἔσηι is either deeply sarcastic or anticipates his imminent fall from power.
3. πρῶτον μέν: see **E4**. 4 n.; **E19** n.   πάντων ἰσηγορίαν: 'an equal right to speak belonging to all', i.e. 'for all'. In Aristophanes' *Knights*, the Paphlagonian slave (who stands in for Cleon) is repeatedly accused of—and indeed confesses to—shouting down his opponents (e.g. 137, 275, 286, 303–4, 311–12; cf. *V.* 596; *Pax* 314), which must be the point of the complaint here. For the right of free speech (more often referred to as παρρησία) as fundamental to the Athenian concept of democratic freedom, see **E1** introductory n.
5. πάνυ λεπτῶι κακῶι τε τὴν ἰδέαν: 'someone very thin and ugly'. Probably a description of Cleon, in which case the marvellous thing he is able to do (ἵν(α) ἔξεστιν ...) must be to control the city and all its affairs.

E19. Reminiscent of—and perhaps a response to—the parabasis in Aristophanes' *Clouds*, where the chorus, speaking for their poet, claim that he was the first to 'hit Cleon in his belly, when he was at his greatest' (i.e. with the production of *Knights*, staged the year after the battle on Sphacteria), and that the other comic playwrights merely piled on unimaginatively afterwards (*Nu.* 549–59). Cf. **B42** introductory n. But the fact that the verse is in iambic trimeter suggests that a character is speaking, perhaps standing in for the poet in the same way Dicaeopolis stands in occasionally for Aristophanes in *Acharnians* (thus Kock).

Preserved by the late Latin grammarian Priscian (*inst. gramm.* xviii. 221), as an example of the Attic idiom πόλεμον ἠράμην + dative (also Ar. *Ach.* 913).
Iambic trimeter.

πρῶτα μέν: like πρῶτον μέν in **E4**. 4; **E18**. 3, introducing the first item in a list (here presumably of the speaker's—or the poet's—accomplishments or virtues).   **πόλεμον ἠράμην**: 'I attacked'.

E20–E22. After Pericles' death in 429 (see **E10–E14** n.), Nicias son of Niceratus of the deme Cydantidae (*PAA* 712520; referred to elsewhere in comedy at **E23**; Ar. *Av.* 363, 639; Phryn. Com. fr. 23), a moderate democrat, emerged as the chief political rival of the radical Cleon (see **E16–E19** n.) and then, after Cleon's death in 422, of Hyperbolus (**E23–E25** n.) and Alcibiades (**E26–E27** n.). Although Nicias opposed Alcibiades' plan for an expedition against Sicily in 415, he was chosen as one of its leaders (Th. vi. 8. 2–4); in 413 he was captured in the battle at the river Assinaros and executed by the Syracusans (Th. vii. 85. 1, 86. 2–5).

E20. Generals were selected and appointed to commands by the Athenian people in Assembly (cf. **E4**. 4 n.), and the group Speaker B represents (2–3) must be some especially influential group among them, perhaps 'the demagogues', as at fr. 75 (from *Babylonians*). *Farmers* probably dates to the late 420s.
Preserved at Plutarch, *Life of Nicias* 8. 4, and said there to allude to Nicias' surrender of his command at Pylos to Cleon (see **E16–E19** n.).
Iambic trimeter.

1.   **γεωργεῖν**: i.e. 'to live on my country estate in peace', rather than being involved in public duties in the city; cf. 2–3; **E2** introductory n.   **εἶτα** ('So . . ., Well . . .') marks this as a hostile question (LSJ s.v. II).
2–3.   **ἐπεὶ κτλ.**: sc. 'and you've failed to take the money and do as I ask!' **δίδωμι** is 'I'm offering'.   For an attempt to catalogue Athens' various ἀρχαί ('magistracies'), see D. S. Allen, *The World of Prometheus* (Princeton, 2000), 305–16.
4.   **σὺν ταῖς Νικίου**: 'when added to the (drachmas) we got from Nicias'.

E21. Perhaps posthumous praise of Cleon by one of his admirers.
Preserved at Plutarch, *Life of Nicias* 4. 8, in a collection of 'Old Comic' quotations that also includes **E22–E23** and Ar. *Eq.* 358, all intended to illustrate Nicias' cowardice and openness to blackmail.
Iambic trimeter.

2.   **ὑποταγείς**: literally 'subjected' (< ὑποτάσσω), i.e. 'timidly, looking frightened'.

E22. Regardless of who is described in 1–3 as taking bribes from leading politicians to hush up ugly secrets, the speaker of this fragment is doing his malicious best to keep the rumours circulating.

Preserved at Plutarch, *Life of Nicias* 4. 5, along with **E21** (where see introductory n.) and **E23**.

Trochaic tetrameter catalectic.

1.   Charicles son of Apollodorus of the deme Oinoe (*PA* 15407) became one of the Thirty Tyrants of 404/3 (X. *HG* ii. 3. 2; Lys. 12. 55). He appears first elsewhere in the historical record in 415, when he and Peisander (another radical democratic politician, active in the 420s and 410s; see Olson on Ar. *Pax* 395) are said to have been chosen as commissioners to investigate the Affair of the Herms (see **E28** introductory n.), 'since they seemed at that time to be very well disposed towards the people' (And. 1. 36). Charicles must thus already have been prominent in Athenian politics, as is also suggested by the fact that he served as general in 413 (Th. vii. 20, 26). μνᾶν = 100 drachmas or one sixtieth of a talent; a substantial amount of money (although only one tenth of the bribes offered in **E20**. 2–4!).

2.   τῆι μητρὶ παίδων πρῶτος ἐκ βαλλαντίου: 'first-born of his mother's money-purse', with the crucial word (in place of the expected 'womb') reserved for the end of the line; cf. **B29**. 3 n. The point is that Charicles is not his father's child but an unwanted infant purchased by the woman who claims to be his mother, and has been pawned off by her on her husband. Cf. D. 21. 149 (where the same thing is alleged of Meidias; Austin–Olson on Ar. *Th.* 339–41 (on supposititious children generally). For money-purses (βαλλάντια), see Olson on Ar. *Ach.* 130–1.

3–5.   What Nicias is trying to keep secret is left tantalizingly unspecified. But the fact that Charicles paid only one *mna* to suppress news of his illegitimacy, whereas Nicias has paid four, makes it clear that he is hiding something very bad indeed.

5.   Given the gossipy, knowing tone of these remarks, φίλος γὰρ ἀνήρ must be utterly insincere.   σωφρονεῖν δέ μοι δοκεῖ: i.e. because whatever is alleged is true, and paying for it to be kept quiet is thus a wise thing to do.

E23–E25. Hyperbolus son of Antiphanes of the deme Perithoidae (*PA* 13910) was active in the lawcourts and the Assembly already by the mid-420s (e.g. **B7** with introductory n.; **B9** introductory n.; Cratin. fr. 283; Ar. *Ach.* 846–7; *Eq.* 1303–4; *IG* I³ 82. 5), if not earlier, and became prominent after Cleon's death in 422; cf. Ar. *Pax* 680–4 (City Dionysia 422/1), where he is described as the προστάτης τοῦ δήμου. The comic poets attack him and his mother (Hermipp. frr. 8–9 (from *Female Bread-Sellers*) with K–A ad loc.; Ar. *Th.* 839–45) incessantly (esp. Ar. *Nu.* 551–8, where this is treated as a commonplace); cf. **E23** introductory n.; Olson on *Pax* 681; Casanova, *Prometheus*, 21 (1995), 102–10. Hyperbolus, Nicias (**E20–E22** n.), and Alcibiades (**E26–E27** n.) were all political rivals (see **E23**), and sometime between 418 and 415 Nicias and Alcibiades joined forces to bring about Hyperbolus' ostracism (see **E25** with n.). He went into exile on Samos, where he was murdered in 411 (Th. viii. 73. 3; cf. Ar. *Ra.* 570 (406/5), where he is said to be resident in Hades).

E23. Eupolis' *Marikas* (probably Lenaia 422/1), along with Aristophanes' *Knights* (Lenaia 425/4), Hermippus' *Female Bread-Sellers* (frr. 7–12; 420 or 419 BC?), and Plato's *Peisander* (frr. 102–13; undated, but perhaps 423/2 or 422/1) and *Hyperbolus* (frr. 182–7, including **E24**; before 417 BC), form a small cluster of comedies in which the central character is a leading Athenian demagogue or a thinly disguised representative of one, who is systematically criticized and humiliated. See **B42** introductory n.; **E5** (from the same play); **E24** introductory n.; Sommerstein, in *Rivals*, 437–51; Storey 197–214 (207–8 on this fragment). *Marikas* attacked Hyperbolus, presenting him as the eponymous barbarian (for the name, which appears to come from Old Persian *marika*, 'boy, slave, rogue', see Cassio, *CQ* NS 35 (1985), 38–42; Morgan, *CQ* NS 36 (1986), 529–31), much like the Paphlagonian slave ~ Cleon in *Knights*. The chorus was divided in half, with one hemichorus representing poor men, who were most likely elderly (cf. 5 with n.) and supported Marikas, and the other representing wealthy men, who were most likely younger and more sympathetic to Marikas' opponents. For divided choruses, see also **C2** introductory n.; Ar. *Lys.*; Taplin 57–9 (an early fourth-century BC Apulian vase illustrating what appears to be a comedy with two opposed hemichoruses differentiated by age). Marikas' words in this fragment parody the wild charges of political conspiracy that became a staple of democratic discourse around this time (e.g. Ar. *Eq.* 235–8; *V.* 488–9; *Pax* 403–15); the character being browbeaten cannot be identified, but must be a decent citizen.

Preserved at Plutarch, *Life of Nicias* 4. 6, along with **E21** (where see introductory n.); **E22**. Portions of 5 and 7 are also preserved in POxy. 2741 (= Eup. fr. 192; substantial portions of an ancient commentary on *Marikas*, which includes lemmata drawn from about thirty-eight scattered verses), and Pollux vi. 159 cites the word συνήλικες (*sic*; cf. 5).

Lines 1–4, 6, and 8 are iambic trimeter, 5 and 7 are iambic dimeter.

1. πόσου χρόνου;: 'within how much time?', i.e. 'how recently?'
2. εἰ μή: 'unless' (cf. 4), here 'except'.   (ἔ)ναγχος: 'just now'. Colloquial Athenian vocabulary, attested elsewhere in comedy at Ar. *Nu.* 639; Men. *Epitr.* fr. 1. 3.

3.   Addressed to the chorus (or the world at large).
4.   τί μαθών; ('what has put it into his head to . . .?') is the colloquial equivalent of a reproachful 'why?' (e.g. Pherecr. fr. 70. 1; Ar. *Ach.* 826; *Nu.* 402; Nicol. Com. fr. 1. 17).   εἰ μή: see 2 n.   προυδίδου: 'he was engaged in treachery'.
5.   That a representative of the first hemichorus appeals to the others as 'agemates' (ξυνήλικες) suggests that they are not distinguished from the second hemichorus by socioeconomic status alone, and probably the poor (and more radically democratic) men are old, the wealthy (and more moderate) men young, as in Aristophanes' *Wasps*.
6.   'that Nicias has been caught redhanded', sc. engaged in a treacherous plot with Speaker B. A misguided, knee-jerk conclusion, as a member of the second hemichorus immediately points out (7–8).
7.   φρενοβλαβεῖς: 'lunatics, fools' (cognate with βλάπτω).
8.   λάβοιτ(ε) ἄν: 'would you convict?'; echoing εἰλημμένον in 6.   ἐν κακῶι τινι: probably 'on the judgment of some awful fellow' (i.e. Marikas), sc. 'and him alone' (thus Kaibel, taking κακῶι as masculine). But this is difficult sense, and Kock suggested emending to ἐπὶ κακῶι τινι ('on some base (charge)', taking κακῶι as neuter; cf. [A.] *PV* 194; D. 25. 94).

E24. The individual described must be Hyperbolus himself (thus Cobet), who was denounced repeatedly in Plato's play as a foreigner (frr. 182. 4–5; 185; cf. Polyzel. fr. 5); cf. **E6** introductory n.; **E25.** 2 with n. But the faults of pronunciation criticized in 2–4 probably represent the way many real Athenians talked, and the main point is that Hyperbolus does not speak like an educated person (see **J7.** 11–14 for an expression of a similar class-based prejudice against speakers of 'non-standard' Attic; Halliwell, in *'Owls to Athens'*, 69–79, esp. 74–7; and cf. **E4** introductory n.) and ought therefore not to exercise any substantial political influence. Cf. Ar. *Eq.* 191–3 'Political leadership is no longer reserved for the refined man with good manners; it's for the uneducated and base'. Eupolis in *Marikas* (see **E23** introductory n.) also called Hyperbolus uneducated (fr. 208), while in his *Demes* (fr. 99. 25; probably 413/2) someone says of one of the city's demagogues κοὐδ᾽ ἂν ἡττίκιζεν, εἰ μὴ τοὺς φίλους ἠισχύν[ετο] ('and he wouldn't even have spoken Attic, except that he felt ashamed before his friends').
       Preserved at Herodian, *On Anomalous Vocabulary* 20 (*Grammatici Graeci* III. ii p. 926. 3–8), in a discussion of ὀλίγος, with the comment that Plato mocked the use of the word without a γ as βάρβαρον ('barbarous').
       Iambic trimeter.

1.   οὐ . . . ἡττίκιζεν: 'he didn't speak Attic'; but see introductory n.   ὦ Μοῖραι φίλαι: The Fates (see Gantz 7–8; referred to elsewhere in comedy at

Ar. *Av.* 1734; *Th.* 700; *Ra.* 453, and the title-characters in a play by Hermippus (frr. 42–50)) are presumably invoked as guarantors of the eventual punishment of Hyperbolus for his crimes (cf. Fraenkel on A. *Ag.* 1535–6). Emendation to Meineke's Μοῦσαι (on the ground that verbal elegance is in question) is thus not just unnecessary but inappropriate.

2–3. **διῃτώμην** is < διαιτάομαι, 'lead one's life, live', but Hyperbolus converts the first ι into a consonant and pronounces the word **δῃτώμην**; cf. *GM* 14 'a feature of vulgar speech'. It may well be that the speaker is reporting on a specific speech delivered offstage by Hyperbolus, from which this word (like ὀλίον in 4) is quoted; if the demagogue was required to render an account of himself, the word preserved here perhaps suggests that he was forced to argue that he was a real Athenian (see introductory n.).

4. For Hyperbolus' **ὀλίον** in place of the 'expected' **ὀλίγον**, see L. Threatte, *The Grammar of Attic Inscriptions*, i (Berlin and New York, 1980), 440, documenting the use of ὀλι- for ὀλιγ- in Attic inscriptions beginning in the second half of the fourth century; and cf. Rhinton fr. 2.

E25. Hyperbolus was the last victim of the political process of ostracism, which was called after the pot-sherds (**ὄστρακα** (3)) on which the candidates' names were scratched (see in general Rhodes on [Arist.] *Ath.* 22. 3–4; and cf. Cratin. fr. 73. 3); his name is preserved on three such sherds from the Athenian Agora (#307–9 Lang). See Rhodes, in R. Osborne and S. Hornblower (eds.), *Ritual, Finance, Politics* (Festschrift D. Lewis: Oxford, 1994), 85–98; Heftner, *RhM* NF 113 (2000), 32–59; S. Forsdyke, *Exile, Ostracism, and Democracy* (Princeton, 2005). Plutarch (1), building on Thucydides' brief but hostile remarks (viii. 73. 3), claims that the Athenians' failure to ostracize anyone after Hyperbolus reflected popular revulsion at the use of a system intended to deal with great men like Thucydides son of Melesias and Aristides 'the Just' to expel someone so base. But more likely ostracism was finally judged an inefficient means of dealing with the city's internal political conflicts, and was replaced with measures such as the *graphê paranomôn* (for which, see **E7**. 14 n.; first known to have been used in 415 BC).

Preserved at Plutarch (1) *Life of Nicias* 11. 6–7, where this is said to represent the popular reaction to Hyperbolus' ostracism; (2) *Life of Alcibiades* 13. 9, where a less detailed analysis is offered and the reader is referred to *Nicias*.

Iambic trimeter.

1–2. **καίτοι** ('yet, but') 'covers the **μέν** clause only: so that **δέ**, while formally balancing μέν, really goes behind μέν to answer καίτοι' (Denniston 558, quoting R. W. Chapman).

2. **τῶν στιγμάτων**: 'his tattoos'. The implication is that Hyperbolus is a barbarian foreigner or a slave (see **C1**. 19 n.; **E24** introductory n.), who ought in either case never to have been involved in Athenian politics. **ἀνάξια**: i.e. 'too good for'.
3. **τοιούτων**: 'men of this sort'.   **ηὑρέθη**: 'invented'; cf. **D5**. 4.

E26–E27. Alcibiades son of Cleinias of the deme Scambonidae (*PAA* 121630), another Alcmaeonid (cf. **E10–E14** n.) and a political rival of Nicias (see **E20–E22** n.) and Hyperbolus (see **E23–E25** n.), was handsome, wealthy, extravagant, and well known for his love-affairs. The Sicilian expedition was largely his idea, and he was chosen as one of the three original generals, along with Nicias and Lamachus (Th. vi. 8. 2; And. 1. 11; cf. *IG* I³ 370. 52, etc.); but shortly after the expedition began, he was called back to Athens to stand trial in the Affair of the Herms (see **E28** introductory n.). He fled instead to Sparta and spent the rest of the Peloponnesian War playing the various sides off against each other, never with any lasting success. He was murdered in Phrygia in 404/3 (Plu. *Alc.* 38–9). Other references to Alcibiades in comedy include Ar. *Ach.* 716; *V.* 44–6; *Ra.* 1422–32; fr. 205. 6; Eup. *Baptai* ('*Dyers*') test. iii–iv, vi; fr. 385 (a character in the play); Archipp. fr. 48; and see **E26** introductory n.; D. Gribble, *Alcibiades and Athens* (Oxford, 1999); Wohl, *CA* 18 (1999), 349–85; Storey 101–5, 194–6.

E26. On Alcibiades' sexual attractiveness (and presumed success at seduction), cf. **E27** with n.; Ar. fr. 244; Eup. fr. 171. Here the wit depends on a pun on two senses of **ἀνήρ**, 'adult male' (1) and 'husband/lover' (2).
    Preserved at Athenaeus 12. 535b, as part of a long account of Alcibiades' personal behaviour that draws at least in part on the Hellenistic (?) biographer Satyrus' lost *Life* (see 12. 534b; how far the quotation (= F 20 Schorn) extends is unclear).
    Iambic trimeter.

1. **οὐκ ὢν ἀνήρ** is concessive, 'although not (yet) a man'.   For the postponement of **γάρ**, cf. **D5**. 9 with n.

E27. The idea of Alcibiades' attractiveness to women (cf. **E26**) is extended to the political sphere: Sparta (grammatically feminine) longs for an irregular relationship with him, and the irony (marked by the oath at the end of 1) is that his notorious fondness for luxury makes him the most inappropriate lover possible for her. The image was perhaps inspired by what Plutarch, *Alc.* 23. 7–8, reports was a common rumour that Alcibiades seduced Timaea, the wife of the Spartan king Agis, and got her pregnant (cf. Athenaeus' less detailed account after he quotes this fragment, as well as at 12. 535b, quoting **E26** and Eup. fr. 171 (from *Flatterers*, City Dionysia 421)). The fragment dates most likely to between 415 BC (when Alcibiades fled to Sparta to avoid being tried for involvement in the scandals centering around the mutilation of the Athenian herms; see **E28** introductory n.) and 412 (when he broke with the Spartans and moved to the court of the Persian satrap Tissaphernes).

Preserved at Athenaeus 13. 574d, in the course of a long and wandering discussion of prostitutes that also includes **I7–I9; I12**.

Iambic trimeter.

1. **τὸν ἁβρόν**: 'the dainty one'. The adjective is used of that which is sexually attractive at Pl. *Smp.* 204c (cf. 197d), but would not normally be applied in praise by one adult male to another, especially in Sparta (cf. Antiph. fr. 46); used of the notoriously effeminate Ionians (see Olson on Ar. *Pax* 932–3) at Antiph. fr. 91. 2. For the oath by Earth, see **D3**. 28 n.
2. **μοιχόν**: 'adulterous lover' *vel sim.*; see **I8**. 22 n.

E28. One night in spring 415, shortly before the Athenian fleet was to sail against Sicily, most of the ithyphallic statues of Hermes that stood throughout the city were mutilated. (Th. vi. 27. 1 says only that the statues' faces were damaged; but Ar. *Lys.* 1093–4 suggests that their phalluses were knocked off as well.) This was interpreted as an expression of hostility toward the democracy itself, and large rewards and immunity from prosecution were offered to anyone who could provide information about the crime or 'any other act of impiety' (Th. vi. 27. 2). Alcibiades (see **E26–E27** n.) was rapidly implicated in the scandal by his slave Andromachus (*PAA* 128425), who testified that his master had taken part in a parody of the Eleusinian Mysteries conducted in a private house (And. 1. 11–12). A metic named Teucrus also confessed to participation in the mock mysteries, and after being granted immunity named a number of other men and apparently gave information about what had been done to the herms (And. 1. 15). Eventually an Athenian citizen named Diocleides (*PAA* 331975) claimed to have witnessed a secret meeting of about three hundred men in the Theatre of Dionysus on the night the herms were damaged; he was subsequently caught in a lie, admitted making the story up, and was executed (And. 1. 37–42, 65–6). Cf. Th. vi. 27–9, 53, 60–61. 1, with *HCT* iv. 264–88; W. D. Furley, *Andokides and the Herms* (*BICS* Suppl. 65: London, 1996), 131–45 (a discussion of other possible echoes of the events of 415 in comedy). Hermes also appears on stage in Aristophanes' *Peace* and *Wealth* as a god who, although craven and greedy, is generally well disposed to human beings; see also Ar. *Nu.* 1478–85; Timocl. fr. 14.

Preserved at Plutarch, *Life of Alcibiades* 20. 6, as an example of 'the other (authors)' who identified Diocleides and Teucrus as among the informers (left unnamed at Th. vi. 53. 2) in the scandals of 415.

Iambic trimeter.

1.　καί adds emphasis to φυλάσσου, 'be *careful!*' (Denniston 320–1).

2.　αὐτὸν (here = σεαυτόν; see Fraenkel on A. *Ag.* 1672f.) περικρούσηι: 'knock a piece off yourself, break yourself'—as had happened to the god's statues.　　　διαβολήν: 'an (opportunity for) slander'.

3.　κακόν τι δρᾶν: 'to cause some trouble'.

5.　μήνυτρα: 'a reward for information' (cognate with μηνύω, 'be an informer'); always plural in Attic.　　　παλαμναίωι: 'murderous'; a reference to the fact that a number of men thought guilty of involvement in the affair of the herms were executed as a result of the evidence Teucrus provided (Th. vi. 60. 4).　　　ξένωι: cf. E6 introductory n.

E29. Three fragments of a single speech from a comedy dating probably to the early 380s; see 2 n. For a general overview of Athenian politics in this period, see B. S. Strauss, *Athens after the Peloponnesian War* (Ithaca, NY, 1986). According to Plutarch, the speaker was Δῆμος ('the People') himself, and the play must have been an allegory like Aristophanes' *Knights* (in which Δῆμος also appears on stage) or the unidentified 'Middle Comedy' from which C2 comes. For another reference to political invective on the comic stage in the early fourth century, see Lys. fr. 53 Thalheim.

Preserved at Plutarch, *Precepts of Statecraft* 4 (= *Mor.* 801b), as evidence that democratic states often make use of leaders the people despise.

Iambic trimeter.

1.　λαβοῦ . . . τῆς χειρός . . . μου: i.e. to keep him from putting it up to vote in the Assembly; cf. M. H. Hansen, *The Athenian Ecclesia* (Copenhagen, 1983), 103–21 (on voting by show of hands). The repetition is an indication of the speaker's agitation.　　　ὡς τάχιστα: 'as quickly as possible'.

2.　στρατηγὸν χειροτονεῖν: cf. E4 with nn.　　　Agyrrhius of the deme Collytus (*PAA* 107660; mentioned elsewhere in comedy at Ar. *Ec.* 102, 184), a member of a wealthy family, was prominent in Athenian politics in the post-Peloponnesian War years. He appears first in the historical record in 403/2, when he served as secretary of the Council and the Assembly (*IG* II² 1. 41), although a *scholium* on Ar. *Ra.* 367 (406/5) notes that he may be the man responsible for the attempt to cut the comic poets' pay alluded to there. Agyrrhius seems to have been elected as general only once, in 389/8 (X. *HG* iv. 8. 31), which must be the event referred to here. Cf. E30 introductory n.; *APF* 277–82, esp. 278–9.

3.　According to Plutarch, Demos asked for a basin and a feather to make himself vomit (cf. Cratin. fr. 271; Ar. *Ach.* 583–6; *Nu.* 907) when he spoke this line.　　　μου πρὸς τὸ βῆμα: 'beside my speaker's stand' (i.e. in the Pnyx); cf. E10. 2 with n.　　　Mantias son of Mantitheus of the deme Thoricus (*PAA* 632545) appears first elsewhere in the historical record in

377/6 at *IG* II² 1622. 435–7 (cf. *IG* II² 1604. 10, 46), as the treasurer of the naval yards. His complicated personal affairs are the subject of D. 39–40.

4. **βόσκει** 'is properly used of beasts, and is transferred to men only with a sense of irksomeness or contempt' (Neil on Ar. *Eq.* 255–7); cf. **H4**. 6. The subject is unclear (hence the various suggestions for emendation), but Plutarch's presentation of the verse immediately after 3 suggests that it may be Mantias. For the idea of 'nourishing' a plague, cf. S. *OT* 97–8 with Dawe ad loc.   **δυσώδη** is probably intended literally (cf. Ar. *Ach.* 850–3; *Pax* 811–13, where several contemporary poets are attacked for their nasty 'goatish' smell) rather than figuratively ('disgusting' *vel sim.*); this is in any case an extremely hostile characterization.   Cephalus of the deme Collytus (*PAA* 566650), another major player in post-Peloponnesian War Athenian politics, appears first in the historical record in 399, when he spoke on behalf of Andocides after the latter's return from exile (And. 1. 150 with MacDowell on 1. 115). Aristophanes mentions him at *Ec.* 248–53 (393/2), by which time he appears to exercise decisive influence over the city's affairs.   For the metaphorical use of **νόσον**, cf. φθόρος (literally 'destruction') at Ar. *Eq.* 1151; *Th.* 535; D. 13. 24; ὄλεθρος (literally 'death, ruin') at Ar. *Lys.* 325; Eup. fr. 406; λοιμός (literally 'plague') at D. 25. 80.

E30. Callistratus son of Callicrates of the deme Aphidna (*PAA* 561575; also mentioned in comedy at Anaxandr. fr. 41. 3; Eub. fr. 10; Antiph. fr. 293. 4) was a prominent Athenian politician in the first half of the fourth century BC; cf. Wankel on D. 18. 219; Sealey, *Historia,* 5 (1956), 178–203; *APF* 280. Agyrrhius (**E29**. 2 n.) was his uncle.

The riddle (1–4) consists of a series of paradoxes ('What is both X and not X?'), and the correct answer is 'an arsehole' (6–9). But most of the humour consists in Speaker B's conclusion that a number of the clues fit Callistratus (5). Speaker A is most likely the title-character Sphinx-Carion (i.e. 'Carion the Riddler'; cf. **A14** introductory n.; **D7** introductory n.; for Carion as a common slave-name, see Fragiadiakis 354–5) himself.

Preserved at Athenaeus 10. 449e–f, as part of a long discussion of riddles (γρῖφοι) that also includes **C8** and **E7**.

1–4 are dactylic hexameter (see **E7** introductory n.), 5–9 are iambic trimeter.

1. **ἔστι:** see **E7**. 1 n.   For the paradox **λαλῶν ἄγλωσσος** ('that lacks a tongue but speaks'), cf. **E7**. 2; Antiph. fr. 192. 15–19. The riddle uses the epic form ἄγλωσσος, whereas the dialogue in 7 has the normal Attic ἄγλωττος.   Unlike most of the other terms of the riddle (but see 3 n.), **ὁμώνυμος ἄρρενι θῆλυς** is not taken up in the explanation in 7–9,

although the point (that all arseholes are the same) is resumed in ἐν δ᾽ ἐστὶν καὶ πολλά in 4, and cf. 8 ἐν ὄνομα πολλοῖς.

2. **οἰκείων ἀνέμων ταμίας:** a reminiscence of H. *Od*. 10. 21 ταμίην ἀνέμων.

3. **ἀξύνετα ξυνετοῖσι λέγων** does little more than resume λαλῶν in 1, and therefore does not receive an independent gloss in the explanation of the intended sense of the riddle in 7–9.   It is not clear how **νόμον ἐκ νόμου ἕλκων** (not commented on in 7–9) fits into Speaker A's explanation of the riddle—although it makes sense when applied to Callistratus.

5. **Καλλίστρατος:** 'It's Callistratus!', since, as Speaker B sees it, Callistratus is a babbler (1–3), an effeminate (1), devoted to generating endless legislation (3), and impervious to criticism (4).

6. **πρωκτός** (a primary obscenity; see *Maculate Muse*, p. 35, and § 449; and cf. **G4**. 22) does not appear to have been used as an insult in the way 'arsehole' is today; but Callistratus none the less suffers by the comparison. For a modern parallel (esp. 3 ἀξύνετα ξυνετοῖσι λέγων), see Janko, *JHS* 118 (1998), 206–7.   **μὲν οὖν:** 'to the contrary!' (Denniston 475); cf. **F15**. 3.   **ληρεῖς ἔχων:** 'you're always talking nonsense' (Goodwin § 837).

7. **ἄγλωττος λάλος:** because it produces farts, which is also the point of οἰκείων ἀνέμων ταμίας in 2 and ἀξύνετα ξυνετοῖσι λέγων in 3.

8. **ἐν ὄνομα πολλοῖς:** since all arseholes are referred to without distinction as 'an arsehole'.   **τρωτὸς ἄτρωτος:** a reference to anal intercourse, in which the πρωκτός is pierced but not wounded.

8–9. **δασὺς | λεῖος:** i.e. depending on whether the individual in question is an adult or a child.

9. **τί βούλει;:** 'What (more) do you want?', i.e. 'That's everything!'—although one last gloss (**πνευμάτων πολλῶν φύλαξ**, on οἰκείων ἀνέμων ταμίας in 2) is then provided. Athenaeus' βουλεπινευμάτων is in origin a simple majuscule error (ΠΙ mistaken for ΙΠ).

E31. In 324 BC Alexander the Great's treasurer Harpalus (*PAA* 204010), who had lived in grand style while the king was in the East, fled with 5000 talents of Alexander's money (D.S. xvii. 108. 6). Harpalus had been made an Athenian citizen in the early 320s and was eventually admitted into the city with 700 talents; when Macedonian ambassadors arrived, demanding his surrender, Hypereides son of Glaucippus of the deme Collytus (*PA* 13912), an important politician and a bitter enemy of Macedonia, argued against giving him up. But Demosthenes son of Demosthenes of the deme Paeania (*PAA* 318625), who was the leading man in the city and whose policy at this point seems to have been to avoid direct confrontation with Alexander if possible, won the day with the suggestion that Harpalus be arrested and his money deposited on the Acropolis for safekeeping. When Harpalus fled Athens a few weeks later, half the money was discovered to be missing; and Demosthenes and a number of other politically active men were convicted of having been bribed with some of it (see 1 n.). Moerocles (3), Demon (5), and Callisthenes (5) were important enough in Athenian public life to be among the ten men whose surrender Alexander demanded in 335 after the shortlived revolt against Macedonia that followed Philip's death. But they are nowhere else said to have taken money from Harpalus, and given that Hypereides— who helped prosecute Demosthenes—is attacked on the same charge in 7–9, these are most likely only typical comic smears (cf. **E7**. 9–11), which ought not to be treated as reliable historical evidence. Harpalus was murdered by his lieutenant Thibron later in 324. See Badian, *JHS* 81 (1961), 16–43.

The fragments of the comedies of Timocles contain far more personal and political commentary than otherwise seems typical of the final decades of the fourth century (references to other contemporary politicians at e.g. frr. 7; 12; 19). But note **D7** with introductory n.; **E32**; Alex. fr. 116. 4–5 (a mention of Antigonus and Demetrius); Arched. fr. 4; and cf. Introduction, pp. 22–6. Had Menander's new style not carried the day, Timocles' easily might have instead.

Preserved at Athenaeus 8. 341e–2a, as evidence that Hypereides was an ὀψοφάγος (see 9 n.).

Iambic trimeter.

1. Demosthenes (also mentioned at Timocl. fr. 12. 3, from a different play) was convicted of taking twenty talents from Harpalus (Din. 1. 6, 53, etc); how much he actually got is anyone's guess. He was fined fifty talents and went into exile, but was recalled shortly thereafter (see 5 n.).

2. The implication is that only by bribing others in turn will Demosthenes be able to hold onto the money Harpalus gave him.

3. Moerocles son of Euthydemus of the deme Eleusis (*PAA* 658480) was wealthy and politically active; see MacDowell on D. 19. 293 for what little is known of his career.   χρυσίον: 'gold coinage, gold money'.

4. ἀνόητος ὁ διδούς: because Moerocles is either untrustworthy or unlikely to be able to accomplish anything.

5. εἴληφέ . . . τι is to be taken with both proper names.   Demon of the deme Paeania (*PAA* 322735) is otherwise known only for proposing the motion to recall his cousin Demosthenes from exile (Plu. *Dem.* 27. 6; [Plu.] *Mor.* 846d; cf. 1 n.). Callisthenes (*PAA* 559815) had been active in Athenian politics since the early 350s (D. 20. 33), and is probably referred to also at Antiph. fr. 27. 10.

7. ὅ τ(ε) ἐν λόγοισι δεινὸς Ὑπερείδης: perhaps a sneering reference to the fact

that Hypereides (whose alleged over-fondness for fish is also mentioned in Timocl. fr. 17, from a different play) began his career writing speeches for other men.   ἔχει: 'has (a share)'.

8.   For fishmongers and their allegedly outrageous prices, see **G6** with nn.

9–10.   'For he's an **ὀψοφάγος**—enough of one to make the seagulls appear to be Syrians', since devotees of the Syrian goddess Atargatis were forbidden to eat fish; see Men. fr. 631; J. L. Lightfoot (ed.), *Lucian: On the Syrian Goddess* (Oxford and New York, 2003), 65–72 (with further references). ὄψον was the portion of a meal that served to add interest to the main course (normally bread, porridge, or the like), although the term is most often applied to fish (e.g. **F10**. 2 with n.; **G11**. 2; **G12**. 3; **J8**. 1). An ὀψοφάγος is someone who consumes more ὄψον than he should, displaying a lack of self-control and an unwillingness to behave like an ordinary citizen; cf. Davidson 3–35, esp. 20–6; Olson–Sens, *Archestratos*, pp. l–li.

E32. In 307 BC Demetrius (later styled Poliorcetes, 'Besieger of Cities'), the son of Antigonus I 'the One-Eyed', liberated Athens from the dictator Demetrius of Phaleron, and in 303/2 he broke a siege of the city by the Macedonian king Cassander. The Athenians, led by Stratocles son of Euthydemus of the deme Diomeia (*PA* 12938; see Olson–Sens on Matro fr. 1. 30 for what is known of his political career), showered honours of every sort on Demetrius and Antigonus, *inter alia* establishing annual games in their honour (D.S. xx. 46. 2), referring to them as gods and dedicating an altar to Demetrius (Plu. *Demetr*. 10. 4–6; D.S. xx. 46. 2; cf. 6), ordering that images of them be woven into Athena's sacred *peplos* (Plu. *Demetr*. 10. 5; 12. 3; D.S. xx. 46. 2; see 4–5 n.), rearranging the calendar so that Demetrius could be initiated into the Eleusinian Mysteries out of season (Plu. *Demetr*. 26; see 1 n.), entertaining him on his visits to the city as if he were Demeter or Dionysus (Plu. *Demetr*. 12. 1; cf. 6), and turning a portion of the Parthenon over to him as his personal residence, where—at least according to Plutarch— he threw parties and had sex not just with prostitutes but with free boys and citizen women (Plu. *Demetr*. 24. 5–25. 1; cf. 2–3). See Scott, *AJP* 49 (1928), 137–66, 217–39; R. A. Billows, *Antigonos the One-Eyed and the Creation of the Hellenistic State* (Hellenistic Culture and Society, V: Berkeley, Los Angeles, and London, 1990), 148–50, 169–70, 226–7, 234–6 (on the divine cult). Plutarch twice reports (*Demetr*. 12. 6; 26. 5) that these verses were directed against Stratocles, who may well have alleged that the comedies of Philippides (an influential partisan of Demetrius' enemy Lysimachus; see Philippid. test. 2–3) were doing harm to Athens by damaging her relationship with Demetrius (see 7). But there can be little doubt that the poet's primary target is Demetrius himself. Most late fourth-century comedy appears to have been studiously 'apolitical'; but cf. **E31** introductory n.

Preserved by Plutarch, who cites 4–7 at *Demetrius* 12. 7 (after a description of the phenomena to which the poet is supposed to refer in 4–5), and 1 and 2–3, separated by a brief explanatory note, at *Demetrius* 26. 5 (after accounts of Demetrius' debauchery on the Acropolis at 24. 1, and of the manipulation of the calendar in his favour at 26. 1–4). Meineke brought the bits and pieces together into a single fragment. Kock noted that there might be material missing between e.g. 3 and 4; but if Plutarch had more of the text, it is difficult to understand why he did not cite it, and it seems likely that he has given us everything he knew, although he has broken the quotation up to fit his own narrative purposes.

Iambic trimeter.

1. The Lesser Eleusinia were held in the month of Anthesterion (Parke 122–4), the Greater Eleusinia in Boedromion seven months later (Parke 55–72), and individuals who wished to enter the highest stage of initiation, the ἐποπτεία, were required to wait at least a year after their initiation into the Greater Mysteries; see in general G. E. Mylonas, *Eleusis and the Eleusinian Mysteries* (Princeton, 1961), 237–85. But when Demetrius expressed a desire to complete all the ceremonies as rapidly as possible, Plutarch reports (*Demetr.* 26), the Athenians, at Stratocles' urging, changed the name of the current month to Anthesterion and performed the Lesser Mysteries for him, and then changed it again to Boedromion and performed the Greater Mysteries, initiating him into the ἐποπτεία at the same time.

2. πανδοκεῖον: 'as an inn'; in apposition to τὴν ἀκρόπολιν. Inns and inn-keepers are routinely presented as disreputable (e.g. Ar. *Ra.* 549–604 with Dover ad loc.; *Pl.* 426–8; Pl. *Lg.* 918d–19b; Thphr. *Char.* 6. 5 with Diggle ad loc.; D. 19. 158).

3. εἰσαγαγὼν τῆι παρθένωι: 'introducing to the virgin', i.e. Athena, whose residence on the Acropolis Demetrius shared. Implicitly contrasted with τὰς ἑταίρας ('his courtesans, whores').

4–5. Plutarch (*Demetr.* 12. 4–5) reports that, after various divine honours were awarded to Antigonus and Demetrius, signs from the gods made their displeasure clear: the sacred robe (πέπλος) that was woven for Athena every year (or perhaps every fourth year, at the Greater Panathenaia, in which case the reference must be to events in either 306 or 302 BC; cf. **F6**. 9 n.; Parke 38–41; Barber, in J. Neils, *Goddess and Polis* (Hanover, NH and Princeton, 1992), pp. 103–17, esp. 113–17) and carried in a procession at the Panathenaia was torn by a gust of wind, and the procession at the

Dionysia (now called the Demetria!) had to be cancelled because of an unseasonable ice-storm and the cold associated with a heavy frost (πάχνη; cf. **F16**. 3), which damaged the city's crops.   For the (seemingly paradoxical but readily comprehensible) use of *ἀπέκαυσεν* to refer to damage done by cold, cf. Thphr. *CP* ii. 3. 1 ἀποκάει τὰ ψυχρά.

Section F

Philosophy and Philosophers

F1. Eupolis fr. 386, from an unidentified play (V)

μισῶ δὲ καὶ <τὸν> Σωκράτην
τὸν πτωχὸν ἀδολέσχην,
ὃς τἆλλα μὲν πεφρόντικεν,
ὁπόθεν δὲ καταφαγεῖν ἔχοι,
τούτου κατημέληκεν   5

1 μισῶ δὲ καὶ <τὸν> Σωκράτην Dindorf: μισῶ δὲ καὶ Σωκράτην Asclep. Procl.: τί δῆτα ἐκεῖνον
Olymp.   3 τἆλλα Olymp.: τῶν ἄλλων Asclep.   4 καταφαγεῖν ἔχοι Olymp.: φάγηι
Asclep.

F2. Eupolis fr. 395, from an unidentified play (V)

δεξάμενος δὲ Σωκράτης τὴν ἐπιδέξι᾽ <ἄιδων>
Στησιχόρου πρὸς τὴν λύραν οἰνοχόην ἔκλεψεν

1 ἐπιδέξι᾽ Fritzsche: ἐπίδειξιν Σ   <ἄιδων> Meineke

F3. Callias Comicus fr. 15, from *Men In Shackles* (V)

(Α.) τί δὴ σὺ σεμνὴ καὶ φρονεῖς οὕτω μέγα;
(Β.) ἔξεστι γάρ μοι· Σωκράτης γὰρ αἴτιος

1 τί δὴ Runkel: ἤδη D.L.BPFΦ

F4. Amipsias fr. *9, perhaps from *Connus* (City Dionysia 423 BC)

Σώκρατες ἀνδρῶν βέλτιστ᾽ ὀλίγων, πολλῶν δὲ ματαιόταθ᾽, ἥκεις
καὶ σὺ πρὸς ἡμᾶς; καρτερικός γ᾽ εἶ. πόθεν ἄν σοι χλαῖνα γένοιτο;
          *   *   *

τουτὶ τὸ κακὸν τῶν σκυτοτόμων κατ᾽ ἐπήρειαν γεγένηται
          *   *   *

οὗτος μέντοι πεινῶν οὕτως οὐπώποτ' ἔτλη κολακεῦσαι

1 ὀλίγωι, πολλῶι Dobree　　　2 γ' Cobet: τ' D.L.^BPF: om. D.L.^Φ　　　4 οὕτως ... οὗτος D.L.^Φ

F5. Teleclides fr. 41, from an unidentified play (V)

Μνησίλοχός ἐστ' ἐκεῖνος <ὃς> φρύγει τι δρᾶμα καινὸν
Εὐριπίδηι, καὶ Σωκράτης τὰ φρύγαν' ὑποτίθησιν

1 Μνησίλοχός ἐστ' ἐκεῖνος <ὃς> Dindorf: Μνησίλοχος δὲ ἐκεῖνος Vit. Eur.: Μνησίλοχος οὕτω φησί (ut nomen poetae) D.L.^BPFΦ　　　φρύγει τι Dindorf: φρύγειον τι Vit. Eur.: Φρύγες ἐστὶ D.L.^BPFΦ　　　δρᾶμα καινὸν Vit. Eur.: καινὸν δρᾶμα τοῦτ' D.L.^BPFΦ　　　2 καὶ Vit. Eur.: ὧι καὶ D.L.^BPFΦ: χὢ Hermann

F6. Epicrates fr. 10, from an unidentified play (IV)

　　　　　　(Α.) τί Πλάτων
καὶ Σπεύσιππος καὶ Μενέδημος;
πρὸς τίσι νυνὶ διατρίβουσιν;
ποία φροντίς, ποῖος δὲ λόγος
διερευνᾶται παρὰ τούτοισιν;　　　　　　　　　　5
τάδε μοι πινυτῶς, εἴ τι κατειδὼς
ἥκεις, λέξον, πρὸς Γᾶς < >.
(Β.) ἀλλ' οἶδα λέγειν περὶ τῶνδε σαφῶς.
Παναθηναίοις γὰρ ἰδὼν ἀγέλην
< > μειρακίων　　　　　　　　　　　　　10
ἐν γυμνασίοις Ἀκαδημείας
ἤκουσα λόγων ἀφάτων, ἀτόπων,
περὶ γὰρ φύσεως ἀφοριζόμενοι
διεχώριζον ζώιων τε βίον
δένδρων τε φύσιν λαχάνων τε γένη.　　　　　15
κἆιτ' ἐν τούτοις τὴν κολοκύντην
ἐξήταζον τίνος ἐστὶ γένους.
(Α.) καὶ τί ποτ' ἄρ' ὡρίσαντο καὶ τίνος γένους
εἶναι τὸ φυτόν; δήλωσον, εἰ κάτοισθά τι.
(Β.) πρώτιστον μὲν πάντες ἀναυδεῖς　　　　20
τότ' ἐπέστησαν καὶ κύψαντες
χρόνον οὐκ ὀλίγον διεφρόντιζον.
κἆιτ' ἐξαίφνης, ἔτι κυπτόντων
καὶ ζητούντων τῶν μειρακίων,
λάχανόν τις ἔφη στρογγύλον εἶναι,　　　　　25

ποίαν δ' ἄλλος, δένδρον δ' ἕτερος.
ταῦτα δ' ἀκούων ἰατρός τις
Σικελᾶς ἀπὸ γᾶς
κατέπαρδ' αὐτῶν ὡς ληρούντων.
(Α.) ἦ που δεινῶς ὠργίσθησαν χλευάζεσθαί τ' ἐβόησαν;   30
τὸ γὰρ ἐν λέσχαις τοιαῖσδε ποεῖν τοιαῦτ' <οὐκ> εὐπρεπές <ἐστιν>.
(Β.) οὐδ' ἐμέλησεν τοῖς μειρακίοις.
ὁ Πλάτων δὲ παρὼν καὶ μάλα πράιως,
οὐδὲν ὀρινθείς, ἐπέταξ' αὐτοῖς
πάλιν <   >   35
ἀφορίζεσθαι τίνος ἐστὶ γένους.
οἱ δὲ διῄρουν

2 Μενέδημος Musurus: Μενέθυμος Ath.^CE   5 τούτοισιν Dindorf: τοῖσι Ath.^CE: τοῖσιν Porson   20 πρώτιστον μὲν Meineke: πρώτιστα μὲν Ath.^CE: πρώτιστα μὲν <οὖν> Scaliger   23 κᾆτ' ἐξαίφνης Porson: κᾀξαίφνης Ath.^CE   31 τοιαῖσδε Musurus: τῷδε ^sAth.^E: τόῗδε Ath.^C   ποεῖν τοιαῦτ' <οὐκ> εὐπρεπές <ἐστιν> Kassel–Austin, ducente Dindorfio: τοιαῦτα ποιεῖν εὐπρεπές Ath.^CE

F7. Amphis fr. 6, from *Amphicrates* (IV)

(Α.) τὸ δ' ἀγαθὸν ὅ τι ποτ' ἐστίν, οὗ σὺ τυγχάνειν
μέλλεις διὰ ταύτην, ἧττον οἶδα τοῦτ' ἐγώ,
ὦ δέσποτ', ἢ τὸ Πλάτωνος ἀγαθόν. (Β.) πρόσεχε δή

3 ὦ δέσποτ', ἢ D.L.^FP²Q: ὡς δεσπότη D.L.^BP¹

F8. Theopompus Comicus fr. 16, from *The Hedonist* (V/IV)

ἓν γάρ ἐστιν οὐδὲ ἕν,
τὼ δὲ δύο μόλις ἕν ἐστιν, ὥς φησιν Πλάτων

2 τὼ D.L.^BΦ: τὸ D.L.^PFV

F9. Amphis fr. 13, from *Dexidemides* (IV)

ὦ Πλάτων,
ὡς οὐδὲν οἶσθα πλὴν σκυθρωπάζειν μόνον,
ὥσπερ κοχλίας σεμνῶς ἐπηρκὼς τὰς ὀφρῦς

2 οἶσθα D.L.^F: ᾖσθα D.L.^BPVΦ Suda: ᾔσθα ed. Basil. 1907

F10. Alexis fr. 223, from *Men from Tarentum* (IV)

(Α.) οἱ πυθαγορίζοντες γάρ, ὡς ἀκούομεν,

οὔτ᾽ ὄψον ἐσθίουσιν οὔτ᾽ ἄλλ᾽ οὐδὲ ἓν
ἔμψυχον, οἶνόν τ᾽ οὐχὶ πίνουσιν μόνοι.
(B.) Ἐπιχαρίδης μέντοι κύνας κατεσθίει,
τῶν Πυθαγορείων εἷς. (A.) ἀποκτείνας γέ που·   5
οὐκέτι γάρ ἐστ᾽ ἔμψυχον
          *   *   *
               πυθαγορισμοὶ καὶ λόγοι
λεπτοὶ διεσμιλευμέναι τε φροντίδες
τρέφουσ᾽ ἐκείνους, τὰ δὲ καθ᾽ ἡμέραν τάδε·
ἄρτος καθαρὸς εἷς ἑκατέρωι, ποτήριον   10
ὕδατος· τοσαῦτα ταῦτα. (B.) δεσμωτηρίου
λέγεις δίαιταν. πάντες οὕτως οἱ σοφοὶ
διάγουσι καὶ τοιαῦτα κακοπαθοῦσιν; (A.) οὔ·
τρυφῶσιν οὗτοι πρὸς ἑτέρους. ἆρ᾽ οἶσθ᾽ ὅτι
Μελανιππίδης ἑταῖρός ἐστι καὶ Φάων   15
καὶ Φυρόμαχος καὶ Φᾶνος, οἳ δι᾽ ἡμέρας
δειπνοῦσι πέμπτης ἀλφίτων κοτύλην μίαν;

4–9 om. Ath.CE   4 μέντοι Jacobs: μὲν τὰς Ath.A   5 γέ που Kock: γενοῦ Ath.A: μὲν οὖν Casaubon   12 οὕτως Villebrune: οὗτοι Ath.ACE   13 καὶ–17 om. Ath.CE   13 κακοπαθοῦσιν; —οὔ Kock: κακοπαθοῦσί που Ath.A   14 οὗτοι Cobet: ἕτεροι Ath.A   ἆρ᾽ οἶσθ᾽ Musurus: ἄρισθ᾽ Ath.A   16 ἡμέρας Musurus: ἡμέρας μιᾶς Ath.A

F11. Aristophon fr. 10, from *The Pythagorean* (IV)

πρὸς μὲν τὸ πεινῆν ἐσθίειν τε μηδὲ ἓν
νόμιζ᾽ ὁρᾶν Τιθύμαλλον ἢ Φιλιππίδην.
ὕδωρ δὲ πίνειν βάτραχος, ἀπολαῦσαι θύμων
λαχάνων τε κάμπη, πρὸς τὸ μὴ λοῦσθαι ῥύπος,
ὑπαίθριος χειμῶνα διάγειν κόψιχος,   5
πνῖγος ὑπομεῖναι καὶ μεσημβρίας λαλεῖν
τέττιξ, ἐλαίωι μήτε χρῆσθαι μήτε ὁρᾶν
κονιορτός, ἀνυπόδητος ὄρθρου περιπατεῖν
γέρανος, καθεύδειν μηδὲ μικρὸν νυκτερίς

F12. Aristophon fr. 12, from *The Pythagorean* (IV)

(A.) ἔφη καταβὰς εἰς τὴν δίαιταν τῶν κάτω
ἰδεῖν ἑκάστους, διαφέρειν δὲ πάμπολυ
τοὺς Πυθαγοριστὰς τῶν νεκρῶν· μόνοισι γὰρ
τούτοισι τὸν Πλούτωνα συσσιτεῖν ἔφη

δι' εὐσέβειαν. (B.) εὐχερῆ θεὸν λέγεις   5
εἰ τοῖς ῥύπου μεστοῖσιν ἥδεται συνών

      *   *   *

                   (A.) ἐσθίουσί τε
λάχανά τε καὶ πίνουσιν ἐπὶ τούτοις ὕδωρ.
(B.) φθεῖρας δὲ καὶ τρίβωνα τήν τ' ἀλουσίαν
οὐδεὶς ἂν ὑπομείνειε τῶν νεωτέρων   10

1 ἔφη D.L.ᴰ Cobet: ἔφη τε D.L.ᴮᴾᶠ: om. Suda   5–6 λέγεις εἰ τοῖς D.L.ᴾ²Q Sudaᴹ: λέγει
σίτοις D.L.ᴮ: λέγεις ἐν τοῖς D.L.ᶠ: λέγειν τοῖς D.L.ᴾ¹: λέγεις ὃς σίτοις D.L.ᴰ: λέγειν σίτοις Sudaᴬⱽ
7 ἐσθίουσί τε ᵐᵍD.L.ᶠᴰᴾ¹: om. D.L.ᴮᴾ¹ Suda   8 τε om. D.L.ᶠᴰᴾ⁴   9 καὶ τρίβωνα] κατὰ
τρίβωνα Kaibel

F13. Eubulus fr. 137, from an unidentified play (IV)

οὗτοι ἀνιπτόποδες χαμαιευνάδες ἀερίοικοι
ἀνόσιοι λάρυγγες,
ἀλλοτρίων κτεάνων παραδειπνίδες, ὦ λοπαδάγχαι
λευκῶν ὑπογαστριδίων

4 <τῶν> λευκῶν Meineke

F14. Menander fr. 114, from *Twin Girls* (IV/III)

συμπεριπατήσεις γὰρ τρίβων' ἔχουσ' ἐμοί,
ὥσπερ Κράτητι τῶι κυνικῶι ποθ' ἡ γυνή

      *   *   *

καὶ θυγατέρ' ἐξέδωκ' ἐκεῖνος, ὡς ἔφη
αὐτός, ἐπὶ πείραι δοὺς τριάκονθ' ἡμέρας

post 2 lac. ind. Kock   3 ἐκεῖνος Cobet: ἐκείνοις vel sim. D.L.ᴮᴾᶠ: -ε κεῖνος Grotius

F15. Menander fr. 193, from *The Horse-Groom* (IV/III)

(A.) Μόνιμός τις ἦν ἄνθρωπος, ὦ Φίλων, σοφός,
ἀδοξότερος μικρῶι δ'. (Φί.) ὁ τὴν πήραν ἔχων;
(A.) πήρας μὲν οὖν τρεῖς. ἀλλ' ἐκεῖνος ῥῆμά τι
ἐφθέγξατ' οὐδὲν ἐμφερές, μὰ τὸν Δία,
τῶι γνῶθι σαυτὸν οὐδὲ τοῖς βοωμένοις   5
τούτοις, ὑπὲρ δὲ ταῦθ', ὁ προσαιτῶν καὶ ῥυπῶν·
τὸ γὰρ ὑποληφθὲν τῦφον εἶναι πᾶν ἔφη

3 ἀλλ' ἐκεῖνος Menagius: ἀλλὰ καὶ εἰκόνος D.L.ᴮᴾᶠ

F16. Theognetus fr. 1, from *The Phantom or The Man Who Loved Money* (III)

ἄνθρωπ᾽, ἀπολεῖς με· τῶν γὰρ ἐκ τῆς ποικίλης
στοᾶς λογαρίων ἀναπεπλησμένος νοσεῖς.
"ἀλλότριόν ἐσθ᾽ ὁ πλοῦτος ἀνθρώπωι, πάχνη·
σοφία δ᾽ ἴδιον, κρύσταλλος. οὐθεὶς πώποτε
ταύτην λαβὼν ἀπώλεσ᾽." ὦ τάλας ἐγώ·   5
οἵωι μ᾽ ὁ δαίμων φιλοσόφωι συνώικισεν.
ἐπαρίστερ᾽ ἔμαθες, ὦ πόνηρε, γράμματα·
ἀνέστροφέν σου τὸν βίον τὰ βιβλία.
πεφιλοσόφηκας γῆι τε κοὐρανῶι λαλῶν,
οἷς οὐθέν ἐστιν ἐπιμελὲς τῶν σῶν λόγων   10

1–6 om. Ath. (1)[CE]   2 νοσεῖς Morelius: νοσεῖς· ἐρεῖς Ath. (1)[A]   3 πάχνη Casaubon: πάχνης Ath. (1)[A]   8 ἀνέστροφέν Porson: ἀντέστροφέ(ν) Ath. (1–2)[ACE]   σου Ath. (1–2)[A]: σοι Ath. (1)[CE]

F17. Hegesippus Comicus fr. 2, from *Men Who Were Fond of Their Comrades* (III)

Ἐπίκουρος ὁ σοφὸς ἀξιώσαντός τινος
εἰπεῖν πρὸς αὐτὸν ὅ τι ποτ᾽ ἐστὶ τἀγαθόν,
ὃ διὰ τέλους ζητοῦσιν, εἶπεν ἡδονήν.
εὖ γ᾽, ὦ κράτιστ᾽ ἄνθρωπε καὶ σοφώτατε·
τοῦ γὰρ μασᾶσθαι κρεῖττον οὐκ ἔσθ᾽ οὐδὲ ἓν   5
ἀγαθόν· πρόσεστιν ἡδονῆι γὰρ τἀγαθόν

3 εἶπεν Casaubon: εἰπεῖν Ath.[ACE]

F18. Bato fr. 3, from *The Murderer* (III)

ἐξὸν γυναῖκ᾽ ἔχοντα κατακεῖσθαι καλὴν
καὶ Λεσβίου χυτρῖδε λαμβάνειν δύο·
ὁ φρόνιμός ἐστι <τοῦτο,> τοῦτο τἀγαθόν.
Ἐπίκουρος ἔλεγε ταῦθ᾽ ἃ νῦν ἐγὼ λέγω.
εἰ τοῦτον ἔζων πάντες ὃν ἐγὼ ζῶ βίον,   5
οὔτ᾽ ἄτοπος ἦν ἂν οὔτε μοιχὸς οὐδὲ εἷς

3 ἐστι <τοῦτο> Casaubon: <οὗτός> ἐστι Kaibel

F19. Alexis fr. 25, from *The Instructor in Profligacy* (IV/III)

τί ταῦτα ληρεῖς, φληναφῶν ἄνω κάτω
Λύκειον Ἀκαδήμειαν Ὠιδείου πύλας,

λήρους σοφιστῶν; οὐδὲ ἓν τούτων καλόν.
πίνωμεν, ἐμπίνωμεν, ὦ Σίκων, <Σίκων>,
χαίρωμεν, ἕως ἔνεστι τὴν ψυχὴν τρέφειν.   5
τύρβαζε, Μάνη· γαστρὸς οὐδὲν ἥδιον.
αὕτη πατήρ σοι καὶ πάλιν μήτηρ μόνη.
ἀρεταὶ δέ, πρεσβεῖαί τε καὶ στρατηγίαι,
κόμποι κενοὶ ψοφοῦσιν ἀντ᾽ ὀνειράτων.
ψύξει σε δαίμων τῶι πεπρωμένωι χρόνωι·   10
ἕξεις δ᾽ ὅσ᾽ ἂν φάγηις τε καὶ πίηις μόνα,
σποδὸς δὲ τἆλλα, Περικλέης, Κόδρος, Κίμων

4 <Σίκων> Casaubon   6 Μάνη Muretus: μανην Ath.^A: om. Ath.^CE   8 ἀρεταί] ἀρχαὶ Jacobs   δὲ Ath.^CE: τε Ath.^A   12 σποδὸς Dobree: σποδοὶ Ath.^ACE

COMMENTARY

F1–F19. For the image of philosophers in comedy, see in general Webster 50–6, 110–13; Galy, *Annales de la Faculté des lettres et sciences humaines de Nice*, 35 (1979), 109–30; Imperio, in *Tessere*, 43–130; Carey, in *Rivals*, 419–36. For other attacks on individual philosophers in 'Old Comedy', see **F4** introductory n.; Cratin. fr. 167 (Hippon (D–K 38); from a play apparently directed against the sophists); Ar. fr. 506 (Prodicus (D–K 84); see **F1**. 2 n.); Eup. frr. 91 (Democritus (D–K 68)); 157–8 (Protagoras (D–K 80); from *Flatterers*; see **F2** introductory n.).

F1–F5. Socrates (*PA* 13101; 469–399 BC) was both eccentric and highly visible in Athens, and the Comic poets handle him roughly. But although they allude repeatedly to his reputation for clever talk and subtle ideas (**F1**. 2–3; **F3**; **F5**), most of what is preserved of their criticism has to do with his personal eccentricities, and it is not clear that they expected their audience to be familiar with the specifics of his thought; cf. Dover, *Clouds*, pp. xxxii–lvii; Patzer, in A. Bierl and P. von Möllendorff (eds.), *Orchestra: Drama-Mythos-Bühne* (Festschrift H. Flashar: Stuttgart and Leipzig, 1994), 50–81; Imperio, in *Tessere*, 99–114. Socrates is also mentioned at Ar. *Nu. passim*; *Av.* 1282, 1554–5; *Ra.* 1491–9; adesp. com. fr. 940 (referring to one of his accusers, perhaps Meletus). His associate Chairephon of the deme Sphettos (*PA* 15203) is attacked at Cratin. fr. 215 (from *The Wine-Flask*; see **B1–B12** n.); Ar. *Av.* 1296, 1562–4; fr. 295 (see **F2** introductory n.); Eup. frr. 180; 253.

F1. A fragment of an iambic abuse-song (for other examples, e.g. Ar. *Ach.* 836–59; *Ra.* 416–30; Eup. fr. 99. 1–22), which καί in 1 makes apparent had other targets as well. For other comic references to Socrates' poverty, see **F2** with nn.; **F4**. 4; Ar. *Nu.* 835–7.

Preserved entire at Asclepius, *On Aristotle's Metaphysics* p. 135. 21 Hayduck, along with *Nu.* 831, as evidence that Aristophanes (sic) abused the philosophers for concerning themselves with trivial matters but neglecting the more important things in life; and at Olympiodorus, *On Plato's Phaedo*, on *Phd.* 70b–c, where Socrates asserts that 'not even a comic poet would say now that I am chattering and talking about things that are none of my concern'. In addition, 1–2 are quoted at Proclus, *On Plato's Parmenides* iii. 656. 16 Cous., and (in corrupt and fragmentary form) at *Et. Gen.* α 81 = *EM*, p. 18. 8 = *Et. Sym.*, p. 64. 5.

Iambic dimeters, 2 and 5 catalectic. Alternatively, the lines could be analysed as two iambic tetrameters catalectic separated by one iambic dimeter.

2. **τὸν πτωχὸν ἀδολέσχην**: 'the impoverished chatterer'. For Socrates' ἀδολεσχία ('idle talk, chatter'), see also Ar. *Nu.* 359 (hailed by the Clouds as 'priest of the most subtle babblings'), 1480, 1485; and cf. Ar. fr. 506 ('either a book has corrupted this fellow, or Prodicus' (a sophist contemporary with Socrates) 'or at any rate someone τῶν ἀδολεσχῶν'); Eup. fr. 388 ('But teach him ἀδολεσχεῖν, sophist!'); Alex. fr. 185 ('or ἀδολεσχεῖν privately with Plato').

5. **κατημέληκεν** is < καταμελέω, 'pay no attention to, neglect' + genitive.

F2. Socrates, presumably impelled by his poverty (cf. **F1**), attends a drinking party only to steal the serving vessels. The joke at Ar. *Nu.* 175–9 (where the punchline θοἰμάτιον ὑφείλετο is reserved for the end, like **οἰνοχόην ἔκλεψεν** in 2 here; cf. **B29**. 3 n.) is similar. Aristophanes presented Chairephon as a thief in *Dramas or Niobe* (fr. 295).

Preserved entire in an Aldine *scholium* (apparently drawn from a lost manuscript of the play) on Ar. *Nu.* 96. In addition, 2 alone is quoted in a *scholium* on Ar. *Nu.* 179.

– ∪ ∪ – × – ∪ × – ∪ ∪ – ∪ – – (iambo-choriambic), like **B45** (from the parabasis of *Flatterers* (City Dionysia 422/1), to which Bergk suggested attributing these verses as well); cf. *GM* 96; L. P. E. Parker, *The Songs of Aristophanes* (Oxford, 1997), 79.

1. **δεξάμενος . . . τὴν ἐπιδέξι(α)**: sc. κύλικα. A reference to a common style of symposium drinking, in which a 'friendship cup' (φιλοτησία κύλιξ) was passed around the group from left to right (ἐπιδέξια; see Braunlich, *AJP* 57 (1936), 245–60); cf. Eup. fr. 354 ὅταν δὲ δὴ πίνωσι τὴν ἐπιδέξια ('whenever they drink the left-to-right (cup)'); Ar. *Ach.* 983 λαβὲ τήνδε φιλοτησίαν ('Take this friendship (cup)!') with Olson ad loc. But Socrates betrays the company (2). For drinking toasts at symposia, see **H11** introductory n.

1–2. **<ᾄδων> | Στησιχόρου**: 'while singing (a bit) of Stesichorus'. For Stesichorus and singing lyric poetry at symposia, see **D13**. 1–2 with **D13** introductory n.

2. **πρὸς τὴν λύραν**: 'to the accompaniment of the lyre' (LSJ s. πρός C. III. 6; cf. **H16**. 1). For lyres (which have strings of equal length, distinguishing them from harps), see *AGM* 49–70; *Stringed Instruments*, 79–128; Bundrick 14–29.   **οἰνοχόην**: 'the wine-jug', used for dipping wine out of the mixing-bowl (cf. **H9** introductory n.) and pouring it into individual cups; see Richter and Milne 18–20, with figs. 114–34.

F3. For Socrates' haughtiness, see also Ar. *Nu.* 362–3 (the Clouds heed his summons 'because you swagger in the streets and meet no-one's gaze . . . and present a proud face on our account'; echoed at Pl. *Smp.* 221b); and cf. Ar. *Ra.* 1496 σεμνοῖσιν λόγοισιν (of Socrates' conversation); **F9** (of Plato). The playwright Callias appears to have been active from the mid-440s until the early 420s or so, making this perhaps our earliest reference to Socrates. See in general Imperio, in *Tessere*, 222–8 (detailed commentary on this fragment).

Preserved at Diogenes Laertius 2. 18, along with **F5** (where see introductory n.); Ar. fr. 392; and Telecl. fr. 42 (the name 'Euripides' in the nominative, followed by the masculine accusative plural adjective σωκρατογόμφους, 'pegged together by Socrates'), as evidence that Socrates 'seemed to have assisted Euripides in his writing'. Perhaps the speaker (a woman) represents Euripidean tragedy, like the Euripidean Muse called on stage at Ar. *Ra.* 1305–7 (a mute).

Iambic trimeter.

1. **φρονεῖς οὕτω μέγα:** ('(why) are you so big-headed, proud?'; for the idiom, e.g. **G6**. 4; E. *Hipp.* 6; *IT* 503) is little more than a restatement in different words of τί . . . σὺ σεμνή;
2. For **γάρ** 'giving . . . the motive for action' ('Because I can!') and thus responding to the question in 1, see Denniston 58 (with other examples of the particle occurring twice in a single line).

F4. Diogenes reports that when these words were spoken, Socrates was on stage dressed in a poor man's robe (τρίβων; cf. Pl. *Prt.* 335d; *Smp.* 219b; Stone 162–3; also worn by Pythagoreans at **F12**. 9, by a Cynic at **F14**. 1, and by a generic 'philosopher' at **I11**. 17). Casaubon attributed the fragment to *Connus* (City Dionysia 424/3; see **B1–B12** n.), the title-character of which was a musician who taught Socrates to play the lyre (*PAA* 581470; Stephanis #1478; cf. Ar. *V.* 675 with *scholia*; Pl. *Euthd.* 272c). According to Athenaeus 5. 218c, the chorus of *Connus* (test. ii) was made up of 'thinkers' (φροντισταί) but did not include Protagoras (apparently dead by then), suggesting that its members were recognizable individuals (cf. **B27–B29** n.). Kaibel, building on Casaubon's theory, suggested that the chorus is speaking here, mocking Socrates for teaching free of charge; and that he responded to 1–2 by saying 'My τρίβων is good enough for me', and to 3 by saying 'I am satisfied to go barefoot'. Cf. X. *Mem.* i. 6. 1–14. For Socrates' tendency to go without shoes or sandals, see Ar. *Nu.* 103–4, 363; Pl. *Phdr.* 229a; *Smp.* 174a, 220b; X. *Mem.* i. 6. 2; and cf. **F11**. 8 (of Pythagoreans). For his lack of what others might regard as enough to eat, see Ar. *Nu.* 175–9, cf. 416–17; and cf. **F1** introductory n.; X. *Mem.* i. 3. 5–7, 6. 2. See in general Totaro, in *Tessere*, 157–64 (detailed commentary on this fragment).

Preserved at Diogenes Laertius 2. 28, along with several passages from

Aristophanes' *Clouds*, all intended to show that the comic poets actually praised Socrates when they mocked him.

Anapaestic tetrameter catalectic.

1. **ἀνδρῶν βέλτιστ(ε) ὀλίγων, πολλῶν δὲ ματαιότατ(ε)**: 'best of a few men, and most foolish of many'. A riddling phrase, perhaps to be taken to mean 'best of the few who share your interests, and most foolish of men generally' (thus Fritzsche, who understood the 'few' to be the chorus) or 'best of the few who are good, and most foolish of the many fools' (thus Kaibel).

2. **καρτερικός**: 'quite tough', in reference to Socrates' going about in all sorts of weather dressed only in a *τρίβων* (see introductory n.) rather than a *χλαῖνα* ('heavy wool *himation*'; see Stone 160–2). Adjectives in -ικος were fashionable among intellectuals in the late 420s (cf. Ar. *Eq.* 1375–81), and if the speaker is in fact a member of the chorus of *Connus*, use of a word of this sort is part of their characterization; cf. A. Willi, *The Languages of Aristophanes* (Oxford and New York, 2003), 139–45, esp. 142.   **πόθεν ἂν κτλ.;**: literally 'Whence could you get yourself a *χλαῖνα*?', but really a hostile comment that means something like 'Why don't you earn some money and buy yourself decent clothing?'

3. A mocking suggestion about the reason Socrates goes barefoot. **τῶν σκυτοτόμων κατ(ὰ) ἐπήρειαν**: 'as an insult to the leather-cutters', i.e. 'the shoemakers'. For shoemakers and shoemaking, see Ar. *Lys.* 414–19; *Pl.* 162; Herod. 7; and cf. Blümner i. 273–92; Olson on Ar. *Ach.* 299–302.

4. Addressed to the world at large.   **μέντοι** adds emphasis to **πεινῶν οὕτως**, 'even *hungry* as this' (Denniston 400).   **οὐπώποτ(ε) ἔτλη κολακεῦσαι** is most likely a reference not just to something specific Socrates said in the lost preceding line or lines about his unwillingness to market his services to make money to buy better clothes (cf. 3 n.), but to the blunt and uncompromising way he responded to the chorus' general hostility. For the *κόλαξ* ('flatterer', i.e. 'parasite'), see **A13** introductory n.

F5. For Socrates' supposed connections to Euripides, see also **F3**; Ar. *Ra.* 1491–2; fr. 392 (from the original *Clouds*); *Suda* ε 3695 ((of Euripides) 'He was at first a painter, and then a student of Prodicus in rhetoric, and of Socrates in ethics and philosophy; he was also a disciple of Anaxagoras of Clazomenae'); and cf. Ar. *Nu.* 1354–72, 1377–8, where the Socratically educated Pheidippides refuses to sing anything by Simonides or Aeschylus, and instead praises Euripides; **D11–D12** n. (on the reception of Euripides in comedy).

Preserved (1) in the anonymous ancient *Life of Euripides* 2 (pp. 1. 12–2. 2 Schwartz), in support of the assertion that 'Socrates the philosopher seems to have assisted him in his writing, as did Mnesilochus', and followed by the observation 'but some say that Cephisophon wrote his lyrics for him, or that Timocrates of Argos did' (for Cephisophon's (*PAA* 569015; see Olson on Ar. *Ach*. 395–6) supposed involvement in the composition of Euripides' poetry, see also Ar. *Ra*. 944, 1452–3; fr. 596); and (2) in garbled form and without attribution to an author at Diogenes Laertius 2. 18, along with **F3** (where see introductory n.).

Iambic tetrameter catalectic.

1.   Mnesilochus (*PAA* 657020) was Euripides' father-in-law (*Vit. Eur.* 5 (p. 5. 5 Schwartz); cf. Austin–Olson on Ar. *Th*. 74).   φρύγει: 'is roasting', as if the play were food being prepared by the poet for his audience (cf. **B39**. 2 n.; Ar. *Ra*. 510–11; *Ec*. 844); but exactly what part of the process of writing and production Mnesilochus is imagined assisting in is unclear.
2.   τὰ φρύγαν(α) ὑποτίθησιν: 'is putting the sticks' (cognate with φρύγω) 'under it', i.e. 'is feeding the fire' and thus 'is providing ideas, inspiration'.

F6–F9. Plato (*PAA* 775000; *c*.429–347 BC) was from an old and distinguished family (see *APF* 322–35, esp. 333, 335; he was related to both Solon and Critias (see **H11** introductory n.)) and did not adopt an ascetic lifestyle; the Comic poets' remarks about him and his school accordingly lack much of the vitriol of their assaults on Socrates and his associates (**F1–F5** with nn.). **F7** (where see introductory n.) assumes a limited acquaintance with one important aspect of Plato's thought; **F8** refers to an argument odd and interesting enough to have captured public attention (and ridicule); and the communist scheme described in Aristophanes' *Assemblywomen* (392 BC) has often been understood as a reaction to Book 5 of Plato's *Republic*. But none of this means that the average member of the audience in the Theatre of Dionysus had more than a vague, nodding acquaintance with what was being discussed and written about in the Academy; cf. **F6** introductory n. Other comic references to Plato, most preserved at D.L. 3. 26–8, include Cratin. Jun. fr. 10; Anaxandr. fr. 20; Alex. frr. 1; 151; 185 (see **F1**. 2 n.); 247 (a speech about love, from a play entitled *Phaedrus*; but see Arnott, *Alexis*, pp. 691–4); Aristophon's *Plato* (fr. 8); Ophelio fr. 3; and cf. **F6** introductory n.; **F7** introductory n. For Plato's own reaction to comedy, see Brock, in '*Owls to Athens*', 39–49.

F6. A conversation between two men, set somewhere other than Athens. Speaker A knows the city and its inhabitants, and is eager to have news of it from Speaker B, who has just returned from the Panathenaic festival (9 with n.) and offers an account of an incident involving Plato and his disciples. Both characters employ Doric forms at one point (7, 28), and Speaker B's use of ἀγέλη in 9 to refer to a group of boys is a Lakonism (or at least a

Doricism); but they otherwise speak ordinary comic Attic, and Speaker B employs colloquial Atticisms at e.g. 10, 16. The Doricisms could easily be emended away; but most likely both men use something close to the standard 'Middle Comic' dialect, and their words have been given just enough exotic colouring to remind the audience that these are not Athenians; cf. **I10**. 2–3 (also from a play by Epicrates).

Both speakers display some familiarity with Platonic vocabulary and usage (e.g. 5; cf. 13 n., 14 n.). But the Academy—unlike the Aristotelian Peripatos— is not normally associated with research in natural history, and whether our understanding of what went on there is defective or an allegedly foolish interest in such matters was a convenient charge to bring against any philosopher or school (as against Socrates and his disciples at Ar. *Nu.* 144– 234, although cf. Pl. *Phd.* 96a–d) is impossible to say. For other comic references to the Academy and its members, **F19**. 2; Ephipp. fr. 14; Antiph. fr. 35; Alex. fr. 99. 1.

Preserved at Athenaeus 2. 59c–f (manuscripts CE only), immediately after **G16** in a collection of literary references to gourds (16–17 with n.).

Mostly anapaestic dimeter (27 catalectic). Lines 18–19 are iambic trimeter, 28 anapaestic monometer, and 30–1 (as restored here) anapaestic tetrameter catalectic. See Nesselrath 276–8, esp. 277.

1–2. τί κτλ.;: 'What (about) . . .?'; a very general question, expanded in 3–5.
2. Speusippus son of Eurymedon of the deme Myrrhinous (*PA* 12847) was Plato's nephew and student, as well as his successor in 347 as head of the Academy. See D.L. 4. 1–5; L. Tarán, *Speusippus of Athens* (Philosophia antiqua 39: Leiden, 1981) (a collection of the fragments and testimonia). Menedemus of Pyrrha was also one of Plato's students, and when Speusippus died in 339, some of the younger members of the Academy supported him for head. But Xenocrates was elected instead, and Mene- demus withdrew to found his own school. No fragments of Menedemus' work survive, although he appears to have written Socratic dialogues. See von Fritz, *RE* xv (1931), 788 (Menedemos 8); Austin–Bastianini on Posidipp. 104.
3. πρὸς τίσι . . . διατρίβουσιν;: 'With what matters do they occupy them- selves, pass their time?'
4. For φροντίς and λόγος used together to describe philosophical activity, cf. **F10**. 7–8.
5. διερευνᾶται: 'is examined, investigated'; Platonic vocabulary (e.g. *Phd.* 78a; *Tht.* 168e λόγωι διερευνωμένωι, 174b).
6. πινυτῶς ('with understanding'; cf. σαφῶς in 8 with n.) is poetic vocabulary and thus lends the request an elevated tone, particularly in

combination with the interwoven word-order and the solemn oath by Earth (7 n.).

6–7. εἴ τι κατειδὼς | ἥκεις, λέξον: cf. 19 δήλωσον, εἰ κάτοισθά τι.

7. Γᾶς is a Doric form; cf. 28, and see introductory n. For the oath, see **D3**. 28 n.

8. ἀλλ(ά) ('Well . . .') marks the speaker's consent to act in the way requested (Denniston 17–18).   Speaker B echoes the crucial elements of his interlocutor's request in 6–7 (cf. Denniston 17): οἶδα ~ κατειδώς, λέγειν ~ λέξον, τῶνδε ~ τάδε, σαφῶς ~ πινυτῶς.

9–11. For adult males gathering in gymnasia and the like to ogle the boys, see **J12** with introductory n.

9. Παναθηναίοις: 'at' (i.e. during) 'the Panathenaic festival', held every year in Hecatombaeon (July/August), probably at the end of the month. But the reference is almost certainly to the Greater Panathenaia, which took place only every four years and featured musical and athletic competitions that drew spectators from all over the Greek world; see introductory n.; **E32.** 4–5 n.; Parke 33–50; J. Neils (ed.), *Goddess and Polis* (Hanover, NH and Princeton, 1992); and *Worshipping Athena: Panathenaia and Parthenon* (Madison and London, 1996).   ἀγέλην ('herd') is used a number of times by Plato of groups of human beings (e.g. *Plt.* 275a, 276c; *Lg.* 794a), but is probably to be understood as a Lakonism (LSJ s.v. II).

10. μειρακίων: a colloquial Attic word (also in 24), perhaps intended as a bit of local linguistic colour; but see introductory n.

11. ἐν γυμνασίοις Ἀκαδημείας: 'in the exercise grounds of the Academy'. The Academy was located about a mile north-west of the city walls, near Plato's house, and was one of Athens' three gymnasia (the others being Cynosarges and the Lyceum, where Aristotle's school eventually came to be located; cf. **F19.** 2 n.) and the place where his students gathered. See introductory n., and cf. Anaxandr. fr. 20 ('when he ate the sacred olives, like Plato', in reference to the groves in the Academy); Travlos 42–51. For pre-Platonic mentions of the place in comedy, see Ar. *Nu.* 1005; Eup. fr. 36.

12. λόγων ἀφάτων, ἀτόπων: 'horrible (and) bizarre discussions'; the adjectives serve to colour the audience's reaction to the otherwise superficially neutral narrative in 13–26; see also 27–9 with n. For the use of the genitive with ἀκούω, see Olson on Ar. *Ach.* 238 and *Pax* 61.

13. περὶ . . . φύσεως: see introductory n.; Pl. *Phd.* 96a (Socrates refers to περὶ φύσεως ἱστορία as the conventional term for 'natural philosophy', i.e. what we today would call 'natural history').   ἀφοριζόμενοι: 'as they were drawing distinctions, offering definitions' (also 36; cf. 18, 37); used in this sense by Plato at e.g. *Chrm.* 173e.

14.   **διεχώριζον**: 'they were putting in separate categories, discriminating between'; used in this sense by Plato at e.g. *Phlb.* 17a.

14–15.   **ζώιων τε βίον | κτλ.** is a high-style way of saying 'animals, trees, and vegetables'. The pomposity of the language (presumably intended to echo that of Plato's students) is undercut by the humble nature of the object taken up for study in 16–17.   **λάχανα** are cultivated vegetables and pot-herbs of all kinds; cf. 25; **F11.** 4.

16.   The temporal use **κα(ὶ ϵ)ἶτ(α)** ('and then'; also e.g. 23; **H20.** 7) is an Attic colloquialism; see K. J. Dover, *Greek and the Greeks* (Oxford and New York, 1987), 233–4.   **ἐν τούτοις**: 'in the course of these (discussions)', i.e. those described with an imperfect in 14.

16–17.   **τὴν κολοκύντην | ... τίνος ἐστὶ γένους**: literally 'the gourd' (see **B35.** 6–7 n.), 'of what category it is', i.e. 'what category the gourd belongs to' (prolepsis; cf. **D3.** 31 n.; **F7.** 1; **G3.** 1–2, 7–8; **G4.** 5; **I7.** 21; etc.).

17.   **ἐξήταζον**: 'they were scrutinizing, giving careful consideration to'.

18–19.   'And what definition did they settle on, and to what category (did they define) the gourd as belonging?' The question echoes Speaker B's account of what he witnessed (**ὡρίσαντο** ~ 13 ἀφοριζόμενοι, **τίνος γένους εἶναι** ~ 17 τίνος ἐστὶ γένους) but does not add to it, and serves instead to indicate Speaker A's continuing interest in the story and (perhaps more important) to avoid the monotony of a long, uninterrupted speech. **ἄρ(α)** adds liveliness to the question (Denniston 39–40).   **δήλωσον, εἰ κάτοισθά τι**: cf. 6–7 εἴ τι κατειδὼς | ἥκεις, λέξον.

21.   **τότ(ε)**: in distinction from the situation a few minutes earlier when, the speaker implies, the discussion was fast and lively (14–15).   **κύψαντες**: 'stooped over' (cf. **B26** n.), and thus here 'gazing at the ground', like Socrates' disciples 'pondering the gloom beneath Tartarus' at Ar. *Nu.* 191–2. Echoed in 23 κυπτόντων.

22.   **διεφρόντιζον**: 'they were thinking the matter through'.

25–9.   All of the students' attempts at categorizing the gourd are appropriate in one way or another (the first because the plant bears round fruit, although it is not round itself; the second because it is soft and leafy, rather than woody; the third because it climbs upright and dangles its fruit). But the humour depends on the fact that none of the answers is really adequate and the enterprise as a whole is patently absurd.

25.   **λάχανον ... στρογγύλον εἶναι**: 'that it was a round vegetable'.

26.   **ποίαν**: '(a type of) grass'.

27–9.   The Sicilian doctor is introduced very abruptly (cf. 33–6 n.), and his reaction to the students' discussion represents the narrator's own feelings (cf. 12 with n.), as the latter's willingness to interpret the doctor's gesture in

29 (ὡς ληρούντων, 'on the ground that they were talking nonsense') makes clear. Doctors in comedy (for whom, see **A21–A22** n.; **I**11. 11–15; Arnott on Alex. fr. 146; Imperio, in *Tessere* 63–75; Olson on Ar. *Ach.* 1030) frequently speak Doric Greek (Crates fr. 46; Alex. fr. 146; Men. *Asp.* 439–41, 444–6, etc.; cf. Euphro fr. 3), doubtless because there were famous medical schools in Sicily (home to many Doric-speakers) and on the island of Cos (Doric-speaking). But whether that association is enough to evoke the Doric forms Σικελᾶς and γᾶς, or whether Speaker B is simply being marked (very inconsistently) as a non-Athenian, is impossible to say; see introductory n.

29. **κατέπαρδ(ε) αὐτῶν**: 'farted on them' (< καταπέρδομαι), as a sign of contempt, as at Ar. *V.* 618; *Pax* 547; *Pl.* 617–18.

30. **ἦ που;**: 'I imagine . . .?' (Denniston 286). Speaker A's common-sense observation that the students must have grown angry and protested when treated so grossly, sets up Speaker B's observation in 32 that they did nothing of the sort.   **χλευάζεσθαί τ(ε) ἐβόησαν**: 'and shouted (sc. in protest) that they were being scoffed at, mocked'.

31. What the speaker is saying is apparently that buffoonish behaviour of the sort described in 29 has no place in a solemn, serious intellectual environment. But the real point of the passage as a whole is that a loud and well-aimed fart is exactly the right response to the ridiculous deliberations that go on in Plato's school.   **λέσχαις**: 'conversations'.

32. See 30 n.

33–6. If Plato's students fail to react when their research is openly denigrated, one would at least expect Plato himself to do so. But he intervenes only to order—very mildly (**καὶ μάλα πρᾴως**) and calmly (**οὐδὲν ὀρινθείς** (< ὀρίνω))—his disciples back to work.   Plato appears in the narrative almost as abruptly as the Sicilian doctor (see 27–9 n.). The reference to Speusippus and Menedemus in 2 may suggest that they too took part in the action that followed, although Athenaeus or his source has chosen to omit that portion of the text.

36. **ἀφορίζεσθαι** (sc. τὴν κολοκύντην) **τίνος ἐστὶ γένους**: see 13 n., 16–17.

37. **διῄρουν**: 'began to draw distinctions'; cf. 13 with n. The verb and its cognates are common in rhetorical and philosophical contexts (e.g. Ar. *Nu.* 742; Pl. *Phdr.* 266b).

F7. A slave (3) argues with his master against a plan involving a woman (2 **ταύτην**), which he believes will prove disastrous, and the master prepares to respond; cf. **C7–C8** n. (on outspoken 'Middle Comic' slaves). What is at issue is presumably a marriage or at least an erotic liaison. For other vague comic references to the Platonic 'good', see Alex. fr. 98. 2–3 ('Plato says that the good is good everywhere'); Philippid. fr. 6. 2 (also in the context of advice against marriage); cf. **F17**. 1–2; **F18**. 3.

Preserved at Diogenes Laertius 3. 27, in a collection of comic references to Plato that also includes **F8**; **F9**.

Iambic trimeter.

1. *τὸ δ(ὲ) ἀγαθὸν ὅ τι ποτ(ε) ἐστίν*: for the prolepsis, see **D3**. 31 n.
2. *ἧττον* is adverbial.
3. *πρόσεχε*: sc. *τὸν νοῦν*, 'Pay attention!'; cf. **H13**. 2 n.   For *δή* with an imperative, see **A20**. 13 n.

F8. Probably a reference to *Phaedo* 96e–7b (one of the 'middle' dialogues), where Plato's Socrates expresses confusion both about what happens when one thing is added to another to produce two, and about how one of those things can be divided but none the less also produce two things (thus Meineke).

Preserved at Diogenes Laertius 3. 26, as the first in a collection of comic references to Plato that also includes **F7**; **F9**.

Iambic trimeter.

1. *ἕν*: 'one thing'.
2. *μόλις*: 'scarcely, hardly'.

F9. For the charge of arrogance, cf. **F3** (of Socrates).

Preserved at (1) Diogenes Laertius 3. 28, immediately after **F7** (where see introductory n.), and (2) *Suda* σ 706 (in a gloss on *σκυθρωπάζω*).

Iambic trimeter.

2. *ὡς* is exclamatory, *μόνον* adverbial; 'how (true it is that) you know nothing except only how ... !'   *σκυθρωπάζειν*: 'to look angry, scowl'; cf. Ar. *Lys.* 7–8 'Don't *σκυθρώπαζε*, child; arching your brows doesn't become you'.
3. *ὥσπερ κοχλίας*: 'just like a snail', when it raises its optical tentacles. *σεμνῶς*: cf. **F3**. 1 (of Socrates) with introductory n.   *ἐπηρκώς* is < *ἐπαίρω*, 'lift up, raise'. For elevated eyebrows as part of a haughty demeanour, e.g. Cratin. fr. 348 *ἀνελκταῖς ὀφρύσι σεμνόν* ('haughty with raised eyebrows'); Ar. *Ach.* 1069 with Olson ad loc.; Alex. fr. 16 (= **G6**) with Arnott on 16. 1–2; Bato fr. 5. 13 (of philosophers); Hegesander of Delphi fr. 2 (*FHG* iv. 413) ap. Ath. 4. 162a *ὀφρυανασπασίδαι* ('eyebrow-up-drawers'; of philosophers generally).

F10–F12. Pythagoras (born sometime around the middle of the sixth century) was himself most likely not a vegetarian. But by the early fourth century, one branch of his movement had adopted a rigorously ascetic lifestyle, and these ostentatiously non-conforming Pythagoreans, with their refusal to bathe, wear shoes, eat meat, or drink wine, are mocked relentlessly (normally as a group rather than as individuals) in 'Middle Comedy'. Cf. W. Burkert, *Lore and Science in Ancient Pythagoreanism* (Cambridge, Mass., 1972), 97–208. For other comic references to Pythagoras and Pythagoreans (most preserved at either D.L. 8. 37–8 or Ath. 4. 160f–1f), see **F10**. 2–3 n., 5–6 n.; **F11**. 3 n.; Eup. frr. 156–7; Imperio, in *Tessere*, 122–4.

F10. Two fragments, most likely of a single dialogue (but see 9–10 n.), connected in Athenaeus by the words προελθών τέ φησι ('and going forward', i.e. 'and after this he says').

Preserved at Athenaeus 4. 161b–c, in a collection of literary references (most from comedy) to Pythagoreans.

Iambic trimeter.

2–3. For the simple Pythagorean diet, see also **F11**. 1–4; **F12**. 7–8; Mnesim. fr. 1; Antiph. frr. 133; 158; Alex. fr. 201; Archestr. fr. 24. 19–20; cf. Aristophon fr. 9.   ὄψον: 'fish', as the contrast with οὔτ(ε) ἄλλ(ο) οὐδὲ ἓν | ἔμψυχον ('nor anything else animate') makes clear; see **E31**. 9–10 n.

4–5. An Epicharides is mentioned also in Alex. fr. 248, where he is said to have run through his estate in five days; if this is the same man (*PAA* 399660), his profligacy explains why he has been reduced to eating dog-meat. That Epicharides was actually a Pythagorean is unlikely; the point is that he eats as poorly as one. Cf. 15–16 with n.

4. μέντοι: 'and yet' (Denniston 405).   κύνας: Dogs were not normally eaten in Athens, although cf. Ar. *Eq.* 1398–9 (dog-meat mixed with donkey-meat in cheap sausages).

5–6. τῶν Πυθαγορείων εἷς: '(although he's) one of the Pythagoreans'. ἀποκτείνας κτλ.: The joke in Alex. fr. 27 is very similar: the speaker announces that he has followed the teaching of a wise man (i.e. Pythagoras) by buying οὐδὲ ἓν | ἔμψυχον ('nothing alive') at the market, although he concedes that he purchased several large fish, some mutton, and a roast liver—all of which items, however, were already dead (and thus no longer in possession of a ψυχή) when he bought them.   που: 'I suppose'; but no real doubt is intended (Denniston 490–1).   γάρ: 'for (in that case)' (Denniston 60–1).

7–8. πυθαγορισμοί: 'Pythagorisms' (a hapax legomenon), i.e. 'odd Pythagorean terms for things'.   λόγοι | λεπτοὶ διεσμιλευμέναι τε φροντίδες: 'over-subtle arguments and finely chiselled thoughts'; see **F6**. 4; Cratin. Jun. fr. 7. For the σμίλη ('straight-edged cutting tool, chisel'), see Austin–Olson on Ar. *Th.* 779.

9–10.   ἑκατέρωι ('for each of the two, both of them') in 10 makes it clear that
ἐκείνους in 9 refers not to Pythagoreans generally (contrast 1–6) but to a
specific pair of individuals.   τὰ δὲ κατ(ὰ) ἡμέραν τάδε: 'but their daily
provisions are as follows'.   ἄρτος καθαρὸς εἷς: 'a single loaf of white
bread', i.e. bread made of flour sifted 'clean' of grain-husks; cf. **B33**. 4–6 n.,
6 n. But perhaps this is a joke, Pythagoreans naturally being concerned
with 'cleanliness' in their way of life generally (if not in their persons).

11.   τοσαῦτα ταῦτα: 'that's it, that's all'.   δεσμωτηρίου: 'a prisoner',
living on the proverbial bread and water.

14.   τρυφῶσιν οὗτοι πρὸς ἑτέρους: 'these men' (the Pythagoreans) 'live in
luxury compared to others'.   ἆρ(α) οἶσθ(α): 'Don't you know . . .?';
expecting a positive answer, but dubious as to whether it will be given
(Denniston 46–7).

15–16.   Melanippides (*PAA* 638480), Phaon, and Phanus are otherwise
unknown. But a man named Phyromachus is mentioned by Alexis' contemporary Euphanes (**G17**. 6) in a list of ὀψοφάγοι ('gluttons'), as well as
by the third-century epigrammatist Posidippus (121. 1 Austin–Bastianini =
HE 3134); and given that the name is rare, it seems likely that these are all
references to the same individual, and that he and the other men mentioned here regularly attended dinner parties and could accordingly, on the
slanderous logic of comedy, be presented as impoverished 'parasites'
dependent on the patronage of others to survive. Cf. **F11**. 2 with n. That
Melanippides, Phaon, and Phanus were really Pythagoreans is no more
likely than that Epicharides (4–5 n.) was.

15.   ἑταῖρος: 'a disciple' (LSJ s.v. I. 3), sc. of Pythagoras.

16–17.   δι(ὰ) ἡμέρας | . . . πέμπτης: 'over the course of four days, every four
days' (on Greek inclusive counting).   ἀλφίτων κοτύλην μίαν: 'a single
cup of barley groats' (see **J2**. 3 n.), which were both cheaper and coarser
than white flour (cf. 10); see Olson–Sens on Archestr. fr. 5. 7. A κοτύλη
is one-fourth of a χοῖνιξ, the standard daily ration of grain for a man,
making this an exceedingly small amount of food.

F11. A list of someone's qualifications (most likely the speaker's own) to live
like a Pythagorean; cf. Ar. *Nu.* 414–19, 439–56 (the Clouds demand and
Strepsiades offers very similar qualifications for entering Socrates' school).
The area of expertise is given first, with the thing or creature the individual is
to resemble reserved for the end of the clause as the punchline (cf. **B29**. 3 n.),
as at **C11**. 3–7; Antiph. fr. 193. 3–7; Aristophon fr. 5. 5–7.

Preserved at Athenaeus 6. 238c–d, as part of an extended discussion of the
history of the institution of parasitism that also includes **A13** (where see
introductory n.); **B45**; **C11**; **G14**.

Iambic trimeter.

1. 'as regards going hungry and eating nothing' represents the same idea expressed in two different ways. For this use of πρός + articular infinitive, see also 4.

2. **νόμιζ(ε) ὁρᾶν κτλ.**: 'reckon that you're looking at Tithymallus and Philippides'. Tithymallus is referred to repeatedly in comedies from the second half of the fourth century as a starving parasite (Antiph. fr. 208; Alex. frr. 155; 161; 164; Dromo fr. 1; Timocl. Com. frr. 10. 2–3; 20–1). Philippides (*PA* 14351) was a politician and extremely thin (Alex. frr. 2. 8; 93; 148; Aristophon fr. 8; Men. fr. 266), hence the mocking mention of him here.

3. **ὕδωρ ... πίνειν βάτραχος**: sc. εἰμι (or ἐστι), as throughout 3–9; 'When it comes to drinking water, I'm'—or 'he's'—'a frog'. For the idea, cf. **H10**. 5 'You ought to be pouring wine for frogs!' (addressed to someone who mixed too much water into the wine).　　　　**θύμων**: probably not 'thyme' but a garlic-like plant eaten by impoverished peasants at Ar. *Pl.* 253, by Pythagoras himself at Antiph. fr. 166. 7–8, and 'not even by those who act like Pythagoreans, if meat's available' at Antiph. fr. 225. 6–7.

4. **λαχάνων**: see **F6**. 14–15 n.; **F12**. 8.　　　　**κάμπη**: 'a caterpillar'; cf. **D15**. 27–8 with nn.　　　　**ῥύπος**: 'filth, dirt'. For the Pythagoreans' disinclination to bathe, see also **F12**. 6, 9; Alex. fr. 201. 5–6 ῥύπον, | ... ἀλουσίαν; Aristophon fr. 9. 2 ῥυπᾶν.

5. **κόψιχος**: 'a blackbird' (called κόσσυφος (a dissimilated form of *κόψυφος, which features the -φος suffix typical of animal-names, e.g. ἔλαφος, ἔριφος) outside of Attica), which is not migratory and therefore spends the winter exposed to the elements (**ὑπαίθριος**, 'under the open sky'); see *Birds* 174–6. For the idea, cf. **F13**. 1 (of Cynics); Pl. *Smp.* 203c–d (of Love) 'he is always poor ..., unanointed, shoeless, and homeless, always lying on the ground with no bed, sleeping in doorways and the streets under the open sky'.

6. **πνῖγος**: 'stifling heat' (neuter accusative); balancing the reference to winter in 5.　　　　**μεσημβρίας**: 'at midday', when normal human social life came to a halt but the cicada sings (e.g. Ar. *Av.* 1095–6; Pl. *Phdr.* 258e–9a). **λαλεῖν**: see **D3**. 33 n.

7. **τέττιξ**: 'a cicada' (see Davies and Kathirithamby 113–33; Beavis 91–103). **ἐλαίωι κτλ.**: 'for neither using olive oil' (to anoint oneself after a bath; see **J13**. 6 n.) 'nor even giving it a second glance'.

8. **κονιορτός**: 'a dust-cloud'; cf. **B35**. 2; **J13**. 6 (a man who refuses to bathe or anoint himself receives this as a nickname).　　　　**ἀνυπόδητος**: for shoelessness as typical of ascetic philosophers, see **F4** introductory n.

ὄρθρου: 'before dawn' (Wallace, *TAPA* 119 (1989), 201–7), earlier than any reasonable person would be up and about.

9.   γέρανος: 'a crane', which is typically seen out walking around (naturally with no shoes) at first light; see *Birds* 68–75.   μηδὲ μικρόν is adverbial, 'not even a little'.   νυκτερίς: 'a bat', which is awake at night and can thus be imagined as never sleeping.

F12. Two fragments, not necessarily from the same speech, connected in Diogenes by the words ἔτι ἐν τῶι αὐτῶι ('again in the same (play)'). In the first fragment, Speaker A offers a second-hand account of a descent to the Underworld that includes an admiring description of the Pythagoreans' eating habits (1–5), and Speaker B responds with a witty comment that indicates his dislike for their filthiness (5–6). The second fragment is structured in a similar way, with 7–8 describing the Pythagoreans' diet in a seemingly neutral fashion, and 9–10 referring with implicit disgust to their lack of personal hygiene; these lines too are probably best divided between two speakers.

    Preserved at (1) Diogenes Laertius 8. 38, in a collection of literary references to Pythagoras and his disciples that also includes Cratin. Jun. frr. 6–7; Mnesim. fr. 1, and at (2) *Suda* π 3124, in a long entry on Pythagorean norms and prohibitions.

    Iambic trimeter.

1.   τὴν δίαιταν τῶν κάτω: 'the abode of those below'.
2.   ἑκάστους: probably 'each group of philosophers', the idea being that the schools keep to themselves even in the Underworld.   πάμπολυ is adverbial, 'greatly, immensely'.
3.   τῶν νεκρῶν: 'the (other) dead'.
4.   For the belief that the dead (or at least the good among the dead) spend their time in the Underworld feasting, see Pherecr. fr. 113; Ar. fr. 504. 8–9; Pl. *R.* 363c–d (where the idea is attributed to 'Musaeus and his son'); cf. Ar. *Ra.* 85, 761–5. For Pluto/Hades (the lord of the Underworld; confounded with Ploutos (**B34**. 5 n.) at e.g. Ar. fr. 504. 1–5), see Austin–Olson on Ar. *Th.* 299.
5.   δι(ὰ) εὐσέβειαν: 'on account of their piety', sc. in practising a vegetarian diet and abstaining from wine (see 7–8; **F10**. 2–3 n.).   εὐχερῆ θεὸν λέγεις: 'you're talking about a tolerant god . . .!'
6.   τοῖς ῥύπου μεστοῖσιν: 'full of', i.e. 'covered with dirt, filth'; cf. 9–10; **F11**. 4, 7–8.
7–8.   Something (another accusative object of ἐσθίουσι parallel to λάχανα?) appears to be missing from the text, which as it stands has one τε too many.
8.   ἐπὶ τούτοις: 'to go with these things' (LSJ s. ἐπί B. I. 1. e).

9–10. Cf. 5–6.

9. φθεῖρας: 'lice' (see Davies and Kathirithamby 168–76; Beavis 112–20), which serve here as symbols of personal filthiness.   τρίβωνα: see **F4** introductory n.; Aristophon fr. 9. 3 (typical clothing for Pythagoreans).

10. οὐδεὶς . . . τῶν νεωτέρων: presumably because young men are more concerned with having a fashionable appearance than their elders, and are also less able to endure discomfort.

F13–F15. Diogenes of Sinope (*c.*412/03–*c.*324/321 BC), the original Cynic ('Dog-like', i.e. 'Shameless One'; cf. **E13**. 2 n.), lived in Athens and Corinth beginning sometime after 362, and was a student of Antisthenes. His philosophy was based on a complete rejection of civilized life in favour of a 'natural' existence, and thus on a hostility to material possessions and normal social conventions; see D.L. 6. 70–3. Although numerous (often very funny) anecdotes about Diogenes are preserved by Diogenes Laertius (6. 20–81), the comic poets ignore the man himself and refer only a few times to his students, whom they seem to know mostly by reputation.

F13. Preserved at Athenaeus 3. 113f, as part of an attack on Cynulcus, a member of the dinner party who is a Cynic. Athenaeus' use of the fragment does not prove that in its original context it denounced Cynic philosophers (cf. **F16**, a fragment of an attack on the Stoics similarly used against Cynulcus); and since Eubulus' career is slightly too early for it to be likely that Cynics are in question, these remarks are perhaps directed at a different ascetic group. The characterization of the individuals in question as greedy eaters of fish (3–4), at any rate, rules out a reference to Pythagoreans.

Line 1 is divided from 2–3 παραδειπνίδες by the words κατὰ τὸν κωμικὸν Εὔβουλον ('as the comic poet Eubulus puts it'), and 3 ὢ λοπαδάγχαι–4 follow after a brief discussion of Diogenes' gluttony. It is thus possible that the words originally stood as printed here. But 4 (– – ∪ ∪ – ∪ ∪ –) is metrically problematic, and Meineke suggested adding <τῶν> before λευκῶν, converting the line into the beginning of a dactylic hexameter, in which case another line (an ithyphallic?) probably stood between 3 and 4.

Lines 1 and 3 are dactylic hexameter; 2 is an ithyphallic. For 4, see above.

1. ἀνιπτόποδες χαμαιευνάδες is adapted from H. *Il.* 16. 235 ἀνιπτόποδες χαμαιεῦναι | (of the Selloi or Helloi, Zeus' prophets at Dodone; see Janko ad loc.); cf. **D1–D4** n. But χαμαιευνάδες is used of pigs in the same metrical position at H. *Od.* 10. 243; 14. 15 (elsewhere only at Nic. *Th.* 532 (as a Homeric rarity); cf. Emped. 31 B 127 χαμαιεῦναι), to which an allusion must also be intended, since the comparison is both apt and unflattering.   **ἀερίοικοι:** 'living in the open air'; a hapax legomenon (cf. 3 n., 3–4 n.). For the idea, cf. **F11**. 5 (of an aspiring Pythagorean ascetic) with n.

2.   **λάρυγγες:** properly 'windpipes'; but used at e.g. **C12**. 3; Pherecr. fr. 113. 7 to mean 'gullets, oesophaguses', and thus here by extension 'gluttons'.

3.   **ἀλλοτρίων κτεάνων παραδειπνίδες:** 'guests who dine on others' possessions'; an echo of the comic set phrase τἀλλότρια δειπνεῖν used to describe the parasite's way of life (see **G14**. 1 n.). But here the judgement is unambiguously negative, and in an epicizing context (1 n.) it is tempting to hear a reference to the bad behaviour of Penelope's suitors (e.g. H. *Od.* 18. 280). ἀλλοτρίων κτεάνων is preserved in early epic at Hes. *Op.* 315 (cf. Hes. *Op.* 34; Thgn. 1149). παραδειπνίς is another hapax legomenon (see 1 n., 3–4 n.), but is modelled on and clearly equivalent in sense to παράσιτος (for which, see **A13** introductory n.).

3–4.   **λοπαδάγχαι Ι λευκῶν ὑπογαστριδίων:** 'who seize tight hold of casserole-dishes that contain the white belly-sections (of fish)', i.e. 'who grab the best food the minute it is brought to the table, and try to hold on to it'. λοπαδάγχης (< λοπάς + ἄγχω) is a hapax legomenon; cf. 1 n., 3 n., and the hapax λοπαδαρπαγίδαι ('casserole-dish-snatchers'; also of philosophers) in anon. *FGE* 1753 (quoted by Hegesander of Delphi (fr. 2, *FHG* iv. 413) ap. Ath. 4. 162a). For casserole-dishes, cf. **G4**. 12 n. For belly-sections (a delicacy), see Olson–Sens on Archestr. fr. 24. 1–2.

F14. Crates of Thebes (*c.*368/5–288/5 BC) is said by Diogenes Laertius to have been a student of Diogenes (6. 85, cf. 87) and to have written epistles in a style that resembled Plato's, as well as tragedies (6. 98), one dubious fragment of which survives (*TrGF* 90 with Snell ad loc.). Hipparchia, the sister of Crates' disciple Metrocles (D.L. 6. 94), became entranced by his teachings, married him despite her wealthy family's misgivings, and adopted his way of life (D.L. 6. 96–8, cf. 88); Diogenes claims that there were 'countless stories' about her (6. 98). Their son was named Pasicles (D.L. 6. 88), but nothing else is known of their daughter (3–4), if they actually had one. According to Diogenes Laertius 6. 87, Philem. fr. 134 ('and in the summer he used to wear a thick *himation*, to practise self-control, and in the winter something full of holes') also referred to Crates. Diogenes (7. 2–4) reports that Zeno (the founder of Stoicism; see **F16** n.) was originally Crates' student, and Monimus of Syracuse is said to have studied with him as well (see **F15** introductory n.). Cf. Criscuolo, *Maia*, 232 (1970), 360–7.

In 1–2, a man who believes he has been ruined describes to his wife their future of poverty and homelessness; 3–4, on the other hand, cannot easily be made to fit in this context, but are an odd and amusing anecdote of the sort told about fools and philosophers. If everything printed here is drawn from comedy, these must be two separate fragments originally connected in Diogenes Laertius or his source either by (1) καί (lost via haplography before the καί at the beginning of 3), in which case both are from Menander's *Twin Girls*; or else by (2) the name of another author and/or play, which has fallen out of the text. But it might also be that 3–4 (accepting Diogenes' implication that the anonymous subject of the verb is still Crates), although easily put in metrical form, are simply Diogenes' final comment on Crates' behaviour (thus Körte).

Preserved at Diogenes Laertius 6. 93, at the end of the section devoted specifically to Crates himself.

Iambic trimeter.

1. τρίβων(α) ἔχουσ(α): 'wearing a τρίβων'; see **F4** introductory n. ἐμοί is to be taken with συμπεριπατήσεις, 'you will walk about with me'.
3. After θυγατέρ(α), the expected sense of ἐξέδωκ(ε) is 'gave in marriage'. But the verb can also mean 'hire out', and the wit of Crates' remark depends on his willingness to treat this as merely a straightforward commercial transaction (4). For the idea, cf. **I4**. 13–17.
4. ἐπὶ πείραι: 'on approval', as only someone utterly unconcerned with social convention would do, since once the girl was no longer a virgin, it would be much harder to find another man to marry her.

F15. The Cynic philosopher Monimus of Syracuse was a disciple of both Diogenes and Crates (D.L. 6. 82; see **F14** introductory n.). Diogenes Laertius (almost our only source for Monimus) seems to know little about him except that he wrote some didactic παίγνια ('light poetic pieces'), a work *On Impulses* in two books, and an *Exhortation to Philosophy* (D.L. 6. 83). The saying mentioned in 7 is alluded to also at Sext. Emp. *adv. Math.* 8. 5, in the form τῦφον τὰ πάντα.

Philo (the second speaker) has apparently just quoted a famous philosopher to Speaker A to encourage him. Speaker A responds by referring to Monimus, who he knows is a less distinguished thinker, but who addresses his own situation better by articulating his sense that nothing in his life is as he thought it was.

Preserved at Diogenes Laertius 6. 83, as evidence that Monimus was ἐλλόγιμος ('distinguished').

Iambic trimeter.

1. ἄνθρωπος ... σοφός is to be taken in apposition to Μόνιμός τις, 'There was a certain Monimus, a wise person'.   Φίλων: a very common name (over a hundred fifth- and fourth-century examples in *LGPN* ii s.v.).

2. **ἀδοξότερος μικρῶι δ':** 'but a bit less well known', sc. than the person referred to by Philo in the immediately preceding verses.   **τὴν πήραν:** 'the pouch', traditionally carried by beggars (e.g. Ar. *Nu.* 921–4; cf. 6 'the beggar') and Cynic philosophers (e.g. by Diogenes at D.L. 6. 22; by Crates in the anecdote from the second-century BC (?) historian and biographer Sosicrates (fr. 22, *FHG* iv. 503) preserved at Ath. 10. 422c–d; cf. Luc. *Fug.* 20 τῆι πήραι τῆι Κράτητος).

3. **πήρας μὲν οὖν τρεῖς:** 'To the contrary' (see **E30**. 6 n.) '—*three* pouches!', the point being that Monimus was that many times more devoted to the Cynic lifestyle than were his contemporaries (thus Meineke).

4. **οὐδέν** is adverbial, 'in no way'.

5. **γνῶθι σαυτόν:** 'Know thyself', a traditional adage inscribed (along with μηδὲν ἄγαν, 'Nothing to excess') on Apollo's temple at Delphi (Pl. *Prt.* 343b) and cited repeatedly in late fourth-century comic poets (Men. *Asp.* 191; *Con.* fr. 1. 1; fr. 181. 2; Philem. fr. 139). The definite article **τῶι** functions like quotation marks; cf. Austin–Olson on Ar. *Th.* 392–4.

5–6. **τοῖς βοωμένοις | τούτοις:** 'these (other) bruited, famous things', i.e. 'other similarly famous sayings'.

6. **ὑπὲρ δὲ ταῦτ(α):** 'but beyond these things, superior to them'. When placed immediately after the lavish praise of Monimus' saying, **ὁ προσαιτῶν καὶ ῥυπῶν** has what amounts to concessive force, 'filthy beggar though he was'.

7. **τὸ … ὑποληφθέν:** 'what is believed, generally taken to be true' (< ὑπολαμβάνω).   **τῦφον:** 'delusion, nonsense'.

F16. Zeno of Citium (*PAA* 461700; 335–263 BC) came to Athens in 313 and studied with Crates (**F14** introductory n.), among others. He taught in the Stoa Poikile (see 1–2 n.), as a result of which he and his students came to be called Stoics (D.L. 7. 5). Zeno appears to have been much respected by the Athenians (D.L. 7. 6, 10–12 (an honorary decree in his favour)) and is referred to in what survives of Attic Comedy only here and at Posidipp. Com. fr. 16 ('so that within ten days he will appear to me more self-controlled than Zeno'; from *Men Who Tried to Change*); Philem. fr. 88 ('For this fellow practises a strange kind of philosophy: he teaches people to be hungry and gets students. A single loaf of bread, a dried fig as relish, and water to drink with it'; from *Philosophers*); cf. the *phlyax*-writer Sopater fr. 6. 9–12. For a summary of Stoic teachings, see D.L. 7. 39–159.

The speaker offers a disgusted response to an attempt to argue in favour of something resembling the Stoic doctrine that material wealth is of no significance (1–5). Most likely he is 'The Man Who Loved Money' himself, and his interlocutor is his son (note 6 συνώικισεν, and see 9–10 n.), who wants to marry without a dowry (see **I4**. 7 n.) or the like.

Preserved at Athenaeus (1) 3. 104b–c, as the last in a series of comic fragments that refer to Epicurus or try to justify a hedonistic approach to life. Athenaeus also quotes 6–10 alone at (2) 15. 671b–c (manuscript A only), at the beginning of an attack on the Cynic Cynulcus; cf. **F13** introductory n.

Iambic trimeter.

1–2. As the characters appear to know one another (esp. 6), the use of ἄνθρωπ(ε) as a form of address communicates hostility (Dickey 152). ἀπολεῖς με: 'you'll be the death of me!', i.e. 'you're driving me crazy!' (colloquial), as at e.g. Ar. *V.* 1202; *Th.* 1073. Cf. **G10**. 8.　　τῆς ποικίλης | στοᾶς: The Stoa Poikile (or 'Painted Stoa', called after the collection of large paintings it contained) was most likely located along the north side of the Agora; see J. M. Camp, *The Athenian Agora* (London, 1986), 68–72. λογαρίων: 'little speeches'; a contemptuous diminutive < λόγος.

3–4. ἀλλότριον . . . ἀνθρώπωι: 'something foreign to a person', i.e. 'something capable of being lost', as opposed to ἴδιον, 'something that is actually one's own' and is thus a permanent possession (cf. 4–5).　　πάχνη: 'frost' (cf. **E32**. 4–5 n.), which resembles κρύσταλλος ('ice') but vanishes much more rapidly.　　οὐθείς: see **D3**. 9 n.; and cf. 10 οὐθέν.

5. ὦ τάλας ἐγώ: a paratragic expression of despair; cf. Ar. *Th.* 1038 with Austin–Olson ad loc.

6. οἴωι is exclamatory; 'What a . . . !'　　ὁ δαίμων is here virtually 'Fortune' in its malevolent aspect; cf. **F19**. 10.

7. ἐπαρίστερ(α) ἔμαθες . . . γράμματα: 'You learned backwards'—literally 'right-to-left'—'letters!', i.e. 'Everything you learned is perverse!'; cf. **I3**. 2.

8. ἀνέστροφεν: perfect active indicative < ἀναστρέφω, 'turn upside-down'. For the idea of sophistic or philosophical books 'ruining' a person, see Ar. fr. 506 (quoted in **F1**. 2 n.); and cf. E. *Hipp.* 952–7.

9–10. Perhaps a reference to what went on onstage just before this: the son delivered a soliloquy describing his situation (cf. **G11**. 1–2 for γῆι τε κοὐρανῶι plus a verb of speaking in a similar context), and his father, having overheard at least part of the speech, is now rebuking him.

10. οἷς οὐθέν ἐστιν ἐπιμελές: 'who feel no concern for' (+ genitive); sc. 'unlike me, to whom you decline to speak'?

F17–F18. Epicurus son of Neocles of the deme Gargettus (*PAA* 393335; 341–270 BC) was born on Samos to Athenian parents, moved to Athens around 307/6, and spent most of the rest of his life there. His moral philosophy—drastically simplified in comedy—was founded on the notion that 'pleasure is the beginning and the end of living happily' (Epic. *Men.* 128).

Epicurus is referred to elsewhere in comedy at Damox. fr. 2. 1–4 (a braggart cook claims to be a student of Epicurus—and thus someone perfectly qualified to produce pleasure for anyone who eats his food), cf. 15; and cf. **E3**.

F17. Most likely spoken by a parasite (see **A13** introductory n.).
Preserved at Athenaeus 7. 279d, in a collection of literary references to the Epicurean doctrine of pleasure that also includes **F18**; Bato fr. 5.
Iambic trimeter.

1. **ὁ σοφός**: echoed in 4 σοφώτατε. Cf. Damox. fr. 2. 1–2 Ἐπικούρου ... | ... τοῦ σοφοῦ.
1–2. **ἀξιώσαντός τινος | εἰπεῖν πρὸς αὐτόν**: 'when someone thought it right', i.e. 'demanded that (Epicurus) tell him (the interlocutor)'.
2–3. **τ(ὸ) ἀγαθόν, | ὃ διὰ τέλους ζητοῦσιν**: see **F18**. 3 n. διὰ τέλους is 'always, constantly' (LSJ s. τέλος II. 2. c). The implied subject of the verb might be either 'people generally' or 'philosophers generally'.
4. **εὖ γ(ε)**: 'Well (said)!' (e.g. Ar. *Ach.* 447; *Ec.* 213).
5. **τοῦ ... μασᾶσθαι**: 'chewing (food)'.
6. **πρόσεστιν**: 'belongs to', i.e. 'is an attribute of'; probably intended to echo philosophical language.

F18. Athenaeus reports that the speaker first made fun of a 'decent' (ἐπιεικής) philosopher (a Stoic?), apparently for declining to take advantage of the pleasures described in 1–2, and then spoke these words. For the sentiment, cf. Philem. fr. 74.
Preserved at Athenaeus 7. 279c–d, along with **F17** (where see introductory n.).
Iambic trimeter.

1. begins in mid-sentence.   **γυναῖκ(α) ... καλήν**: i.e. a prostitute; see **H1**. 5 n.   **κατακεῖσθαι**: i.e. on a couch at a symposium (see **A13**. 14 n.), as 2 makes clear.
2. **Λεσβίου**: sc. οἴνου. Lesbian wine was much admired; cf. **H7** introductory n.   **χυτρίδε ... δύο**: 'two little pots' (diminutive < χύτρα, normally 'cookpot'; see Amyx 211–12; Olson on Ar. *Ach.* 284), presumably one for the speaker and one for his female companion.
3. **ὁ φρόνιμος, τ(ὸ) ἀγαθόν**: see **F17**. 1–3; **F19**. 1–4. Presumably echoes of language used by the 'decent' philosopher mocked in the preceding lines. Cf. Bato frr. 2. 3–4 ~ 5. 14–15, where philosophers are described as τοὺς τὸν φρόνιμον ζητοῦντας ... | ... ὥσπερ ἀποδεδρακότα ('those who seek for the wise man as if he were a runaway slave').

6.   ἄτοπος: 'strange, odd', and thus here 'unsociable'.   οὔτε μοιχός: because he would be getting all the sex he needed from prostitutes; but cf. **I9** with introductory n.

F19. Athenaeus reports that the speaker is a slave named Xanthias ('Blondy', presumably used mostly for northerners such as Thracians; cf. **D3**. 19 n.; Fragiadakis 363), who is encouraging his fellow-slaves to enjoy a life of luxury; cf. **C7–C8** n. Philosophy is referred to in 1–3; but what the speaker is most concerned to reject is political ambition (8–12); see 8 n.; **E2** introductory n.; **E3**. No other fragments of *The Instructor in Profligacy* are preserved, and Athenaeus (who says that he got these verses from *On Timo's Silloi* by the early second-century BC Peripatetic Sotion of Alexandria) notes that it was apparently not included in the catalogues of the Libraries at Alexandria and Pergamon. The fragment may thus be a forgery (cf. 1 n., 4 n.), and Arnott (*Alexis*, p. 821) suggests that it was produced by a Cynic in the third or second century BC 'to illustrate the enemy viewpoint in an anti-Epicurean pamphlet'.

Preserved at Athenaeus 8. 336e–f, in a collection of literary sources espousing hedonism.

Iambic trimeter.

1.   φληναφῶν ἄνω κάτω: 'babbling up (and) down, every which way', i.e. 'mixing up, confusing'; the verb is elsewhere always intransitive in the active. For ἄνω κάτω (colloquial), cf. Ar. *Ach.* 21 with Olson ad loc.

2.   Λύκειον: The Lyceum (one of Athens' gymnasia; see **F6**. 11 n.; Travlos 345–7) was used by sophistic teachers already by the middle of the fourth century (cf. Antiph. fr. 120. 3 'in the Lyceum with the sophists'; Isoc. 12. 18), but the reference here is probably to Aristotle's school. Ἀκαδήμειαν: i.e. Plato's school; see **F6**. 11 n.   Ὠδείου πύλας: The Odeion (a multi-columned, roofed building constructed in Pericles' time and used for concerts and musical contests; see Cratin. fr. 73; Travlos 387–91; J. M. Camp, *The Archaeology of Athens* (New Haven and London, 2001), 100–1) is not known to have been used for philosophical instruction before Chrysippus (D.L. 7. 184), who arrived in Athens around 260 and became head of the Stoa in 232, a fact that counts against assigning this fragment to Alexis (d. *c.*275). Nor is it clear why the speaker refers to the gates of the Odeion rather than the Odeion itself.

4–12.   For the sentiment, cf. Alex. frr. 222. 14–17; 273; Philetaer. fr. 7.

4.   πίνωμεν, ἐμπίνωμεν: 'Let's drink! Let's really drink!' The compound verb reinforces or intensifies the sense of the simplex that precedes it; cf. R. Renehan, *Studies in Greek Texts* (Hypomnemata 43: Göttingen, 1976), 22–7.   Σίκων: a very rare name (only seven examples in *LGPN* ii,

including those given here), used for slaves also at Ar. *Ec.* 867; Men. *Dysc.* 889; and probably Eub. fr. 123. 1, as well as in the compound name Aeolosicon ('Sicon playing Aeolus', the title of two plays by Aristophanes; see *PCG* iii. 2, p. 34).

5. τὴν ψυχὴν τρέφειν: 'to nourish our soul(s)', sc. with every sort of luxury (thus Daléchamp); or perhaps this is simply a stilted way of saying 'remain alive'.

6. τύρβαζε: 'stir up', i.e. 'revel, have a wild time'; an otherwise unattested sense of the word.   *Μάνη*: a stock name for comic slaves; cf. **D1**. 18 n.; **H13**. 13 n.   ἥδιον: '(is) more pleasant', i.e. 'gives more pleasure'.

7. πάλιν: 'moreover, as well'.   μόνη is to be taken with αὕτη, 'this alone'.

8–9.   'Personal excellences, (that is) both ambassadorships and generalships, have the sound of empty boasts equivalent to dreams'.   ἀρεταί seems at first to refer to the teachings of the philosophical schools (see 1–3), but the gloss that follows (πρεσβεῖαί τε καὶ στρατηγίαι) converts it into a description of political service (cf. 12). For generals, see **E4**. 4 n. For ambassadors (elected on an ad hoc basis, and seemingly drawn almost exclusively from the rich and well connected, as generally today), see D. J. Mosley, *Envoys and Diplomacy in Ancient Greece* (Historia Einzelschriften 22: Wiesbaden, 1973), esp. 43–9; Olson on Ar. *Ach.* 610–11.

10. ψύξει σε: 'will make you cold' (< ψύχω), i.e. 'bring about your death'; an otherwise unattested sense of the verb (perhaps colloquial). δαίμων: see **F16**. 6 n.

12. Cf. the opening verses of the epitaph ascribed to the Assyrian king Sardanapallus (i.e. Ashurbanipal) by the Stoic philosopher Chrysippus at Ath. 8. 335f–6a (= Choeril. Ias. *SH* 335. 1–5): 'Recognize that you are mortal and enjoy yourself by having a pleasant time at feasts; nothing is any good once you are dead. For I am dust (σποδός), although I was king of mighty Babylon; all I have is what I ate, and the wild behaviour I indulged in, and the pleasure I had in bed'.   *Περικλέης, Κόδρος, Κίμων*: examples of the sort of men who got allegedly empty honours like those referred to in 8; to be taken in apposition to τ(ὰ) ἄλλα. For Pericles, see **E10–E14** n. Codrus was a mythical king of Athens, who sacrificed himself to save the city during the Dorian invasion (Lycurg. *Leocr.* 86–7; Pherecyd. *FGrHist* 3 F 154; Paus. i. 19. 5) and was worshipped at a substantial sanctuary most likely somewhere within the walls (*IG* I³ 84). Cimon son of Miltiades (*PAA* 569795; d. 450/49) was one of Athens' most distinguished military and political leaders in the first half of the fifth century; Aristophanes mentions him at *Lys.* 1144, and Eupolis referred to him in *Cities* (fr. 221).

Section G

Food and Dining

G1. Poliochus fr. 2, from an unidentified play (V)

μεμαγμένην
μικρὰν μελαγχρῆ μᾶζαν ἠχυρωμένην
ἑκάτερος ἡμῶν εἶχε δὶς τῆς ἡμέρας
καὶ σῦκα βαιά, καὶ μύκης τις ἐνίοτ᾽ ἂν
ὠπτᾶτο, καὶ κοχλίας γενομένου ψακαδίου   5
ἠγρεύετ᾽ ἄν. καὶ λάχανα τῶν αὐτοχθόνων
θλαστή τ᾽ ἐλαία, καὶ πιεῖν οἰνάριον ἦν
ἀμφίβολον

6 ἠγρεύετ᾽ Brunck: ἀνηγρεύετ᾽ Ath.^CE

G2. Antiphanes fr. 174, from *Omphale* (IV)

πῶς γὰρ ἄν τις εὐγενὴς γεγὼς
δύναιτ᾽ ἂν ἐξελθεῖν ποτ᾽ ἐκ τῆσδε στέγης,
ὁρῶν μὲν ἄρτους λευκοσωμάτους ἱπνὸν
καταμπέχοντας ἐν πυκναῖς διεξόδοις,
ὁρῶν δὲ μορφὴν κριβάνοις ἠλλαγμένους,   5
μίμημα χειρὸς Ἀττικῆς, οὓς δημόταις
Θεαρίων ἔδειξεν;

2 ποτ᾽ ἐκ τῆσδε Porson: ποτε δ᾽ ἐκ τῆς Ath.^A   3 ὁρῶν μὲν Musurus: ὁρῶμεν Ath.^A
ἄρτους Porson: ἄρτους· τοὺς δὲ Ath.^A   6 δημόταις Porson: δηγοναις Ath.^A

G3. Alexis fr. 140, from *Linus* (IV/III)

(Λι.) βιβλίον
ἐντεῦθεν ὅ τι βούλει προσελθὼν γὰρ λαβέ,
ἔπειτ᾽ ἀναγνώσει— (Ηρ.) πάνυ γε. (Λι.) διασκοπῶν
ἀπὸ τῶν ἐπιγραμμάτων ἀτρέμα τε καὶ σχολῆι.

Ὀρφεὺς ἔνεστιν, Ἡσίοδος τραγωιδίαι 5
Ἐπίχαρμος Ὅμηρος Χοιρίλος συγγράμματα
παντοδαπά· δηλώσεις γὰρ οὕτω τὴν φύσιν
ἐπὶ τί μάλισθ᾽ ὥρμηκε. (Ηρ.) τουτὶ λαμβάνω.
(Λι.) δεῖξον τί ἐστι πρῶτον. (Ηρ.) ὀψαρτυσία,
ὥς φησι τοὐπίγραμμα. (Λι.) φιλόσοφός τις εἶ, 10
εὔδηλον, ὃς παρεὶς τοσαῦτα γράμματα
Σίμου τέχνην ἔλαβες. (Ηρ.) ὁ Σῖμος δ᾽ ἐστὶ τίς;
(Λι.) μάλ᾽ εὐφυὴς ἄνθρωπος. ἐπὶ τραγωιδίαν
ὥρμηκε νῦν καὶ τῶν μὲν ὑποκριτῶν πολὺ
κράτιστός ἐστιν ὀψοποιός, ὡς δοκεῖ 15
τοῖς χρωμένοις, τῶν δ᾽ ὀψοποιῶν ὑποκριτής
          *   *   *

(Λι.) βούλιμός ἐσθ᾽ ἄνθρωπος. (Ηρ.) ὅ τι βούλει λέγε·
πεινῶ γάρ, εὖ τοῦτ᾽ ἴσθι

6 Ἐπίχαρμος Ὅμηρος Χοιρίλος Scaliger: Χοιρίλος Ὅμηρος Ἐπίχαρμος Ath.ᴬ: Χοιρίλου Ἐπιχάρμου Ὁμήρου Ath.ᶜᴱ   post 16 lac. ind. Jacobs

G4. Plato Comicus fr. 189, from *Phaon* (391 BC)

      (A.) ἐγὼ δ᾽ ἐνθάδ᾽ ἐν τῆι ἐρημίαι
τουτὶ διελθεῖν βούλομαι τὸ βιβλίον
πρὸς ἐμαυτόν. (Β.) ἔστι δ᾽, ἀντιβολῶ σε, τοῦτο τί;
(Α.) Φιλοξένου καινή τις ὀψαρτυσία.
(Β.) ἐπίδειξον αὐτὴν ἥτις ἔστ᾽. (Α.) ἄκουε δή. 5
ἄρξομαι ἐκ βολβοῖο, τελευτήσω δ᾽ ἐπὶ θύννον.
(Β.) ἐπὶ θύννον; οὐκοῦν † τῆς τελευτ † πολὺ
κράτιστον ἐνταυθὶ τετάχθαι τάξεως.
(Α.) βολβοὺς μὲν σποδιᾶι δαμάσας καταχύσματι δεύσας
ὡς πλείστους διάτρωγε· τὸ γὰρ δέμας ἀνέρος ὀρθοῖ. 10
καὶ τάδε μὲν δὴ ταῦτα· θαλάσσης δ᾽ ἐς τέκν᾽ ἄνειμι
          *   *   *

οὐδὲ λοπὰς κακόν ἐστιν· ἀτὰρ τὸ τάγηνον ἄμεινον,
οἶμαι
          *   *   *

ὀρφὼν αἰολίαν συνόδοντά τε καρχαρίαν τε
μὴ τέμνειν, μή σοι νέμεσις θεόθεν καταπνεύσηι, 15
ἀλλ᾽ ὅλον ὀπτήσας παράθες· πολλὸν γὰρ ἄμεινον.
πουλύποδος † πλεκτὴ δ᾽ ἂν ἐπιλήψηι † κατὰ καιρόν,
ἐφθὴ τῆς ὀπτῆς, ἢν ἦι μείζων, πολὺ κρείττων·

ἦν ὀπταὶ δὲ δύ᾽ ὦσ᾽, ἐφθῆι κλαίειν ἀγορεύω.
τρίγλη δ᾽ οὐκ ἐθέλει νεύρων ἐπιήρανος εἶναι· 20
παρθένου Ἀρτέμιδος γὰρ ἔφυ καὶ στύματα μισεῖ.
σκορπίος αὖ— (Β.) παίσειέ γε σου τὸν πρωκτὸν ὑπελθών

6 ἐκ Casaubon: δ᾽ ἐκ Ath.ᶜᴱ   10 ἀνέρος ὀρθοῖ Dindorf: ἀνορθοῖ Ath.ᶜᴱ
19 ἀγορεύω] ἀγόρευε Kock

G5. Ephippus fr. 15, from *Men Who Looked Like One Another or Spitbearers* (IV)

      (Α.) ἀλλ᾽ ἀγόρασον εὐτελῶς·
ἅπαν γὰρ ἱκανόν ἐστι. (Β.) φράζ᾽, ὦ δέσποτα.
(Α.) μὴ πολυτελῶς, ἀλλὰ καθαρείως, ὅ τι ἂν ἦι,
ὁσίας ἕνεκ᾽· ἀρκεῖ τευθίδια σηπίδια,
κἂν κάραβός τις ἦι λαβεῖν, εἷς ἀρκέσει 5
ἢ δύ᾽ ἐπὶ τὴν τράπεζαν. ἐγχελύδια
Θήβηθεν ἐνίοτ᾽ ἔρχεται· τούτων λαβέ.
ἀλεκτρυόνιον φάττιον περδίκιον,
τοιαῦτα. δασύπους ἄν τις εἰσέλθηι, φέρε.
(Β.) ὡς μικρολόγος εἶ. (Α.) σὺ δέ γε λίαν πολυτελής. 10
πάντως κρέ᾽ ἡμῖν ἔστι. (Β.) πότερ᾽ ἔπεμψέ τις;
(Α.) οὐκ ἀλλ᾽ ἔθυσεν ἡ γυνή· τὸ μοσχίον
τὸ τῆς Κορώνης αὔριον δειπνήσομεν

3–4 ὅ τι ἂν ἦι, | ὁσίας Schweighäuser: ὅτι ἀνοησίας Ath.ᴬ: om. Ath.ᶜᴱ   9–13 om.
Ath.ᶜᴱ   9 εἰσέλθηι Porson: ἐπέλθηι Ath.ᴬ   10 δέ γε Casaubon: λέγε Ath.ᴬ

G6. Alexis fr. 16, from *The Man Who Had a Cataract* (IV/III)

τοὺς μὲν στρατηγοὺς τὰς ὀφρῦς ἐπὰν ἴδω
ἀνεσπακότας, δεινὸν μὲν ἡγοῦμαι ποεῖν,
οὐ πάνυ τι θαυμάζω δὲ προτετιμημένους
ὑπὸ τῆς πόλεως μεῖζόν τι τῶν ἄλλων φρονεῖν.
τοὺς δ᾽ ἰχθυοπώλας τοὺς κάκιστ᾽ ἀπολουμένους 5
ἐπὰν ἴδω κάτω βλέποντας, τὰς δ᾽ ὀφρῦς
ἔχοντας ἐπάνω τῆς κορυφῆς, ἀποπνίγομαι.
ἐὰν δ᾽ ἐρωτήσηις "πόσου τοὺς κεστρέας
πωλεῖς δύ᾽ ὄντας;" "δέκ᾽ ὀβολῶν" φησίν. "βαρύ·
ὀκτὼ λάβοις ἄν;" "εἴπερ ὠνεῖ τὸν ἕτερον." 10
"ὦ τᾶν, λαβὲ καὶ μὴ παῖζε." "τοσουδί· παράτρεχε."
ταῦτ᾽ οὐχὶ πικρότερ᾽ ἐστὶν αὐτῆς τῆς χολῆς;

4 μεῖζόν τι Wakefield: μείζω Ath.^A: vers. om. Ath.^{CE}   11 τοσουδί Dobree: τοὺς
ὀνδεῖ Ath.^A: τοῦ, σοι δεῖ Ath.^{CE}

G7. Posidippus fr. 1, from *The Man Who Tried to Recover His Sight* (III)

ἐγὼ μάγειρον ἀναλαβὼν ἀκήκοα
τὰ τῶν μαγείρων πάνθ᾽ ἃ καθ᾽ ἑκάστου κακὰ
ἀντεργολαβοῦντος ἔλεγον· ὁ μὲν ὡς οὐκ ἔχει
ῥῖνα κριτικὴν πρὸς τοῦψον, ὁ δ᾽ ὅτι <τὸ> στόμα
πονηρόν, ὁ δὲ τὴν γλῶτταν εἰς ἀσχήμονας   5
ἐπιθυμίας ἐμίαινε τῶν ἡδυσμάτων,
κάθαλος κάτοξος χναυστικὸς προσκαυστικός,
καπνὸν οὐ φέρων, πῦρ οὐ φέρων. ἐκ τοῦ πυρὸς
εἰς τὰς μαχαίρας ἦλθον. ὧν εἷς οὑτοσὶ
διὰ τῶν μαχαιρῶν τοῦ πυρός τ᾽ ἐλήλυθεν   10

1 ἀναλαβὼν] ἕνα λαβὼν Coraes: λαμβάνων Meineke   2 πάνθ᾽ ἃ Hirschig: πάντα
Ath.^A   3 ἔλεγον· ὁ μὲν Scaliger: ἐλέγομεν Ath.^A   4 <τὸ> Grotius
6 ἐμίαινε Cobet: ἔνιά τε Ath.^A   8 πῦρ οὐ φέρων Grotius: οὐ πῦρ οὐ φέρων δ᾽ Ath.^A

G8. Alexis fr. 24, from *Asclepiocleides* (IV/III)

οὕτως δ᾽ ὀψοποιεῖν εὐφυῶς
περὶ <τὴν> Σικελίαν αὐτὸς ἔμαθον ὥστε τοὺς
δειπνοῦντας εἰς τὰ βατάνι᾽ ἐμβάλλειν ποῶ
ἐνίοτε τοὺς ὀδόντας ὑπὸ τῆς ἡδονῆς

2 <τὴν> Casaubon   3 βατάνι᾽ Schweighäuser: βατάνια Phot.: βατάνεια Ath.^A: βατάνειον
Ath.^{CE}: πατάνια Poll.

G9. Anaxippus fr. 6, from *The Citharode* (IV/III)

ζωμήρυσιν φέρ᾽, οἷσ᾽ ὀβελίσκους δώδεκα
κρεάγραν θυείαν τυρόκνηστιν παιδικὴν
στελεὸν σκαφίδας τρεῖς δορίδα κοπίδας τέτταρας.
οὐ μὴ πρότερον οἴσεις, θεοῖσιν ἐχθρὲ σύ,
τὸ λεβήτιον τἀκ τοῦ λίτρου; πάλιν ὑστερεῖς;   5
καὶ τὴν κύβηλιν τὴν ἀγωνιστηρίαν

4 οἴσεις Villebrune: νεύσεις Ath.^A: om. Ath.^{CE}   6 ἀγωνιστηρίαν] ταγηνιστηρίαν
Meineke

G10. Antiphanes fr. 221, from *Philotis* (IV)

(*A.*) οὐκοῦν τὸ μὲν γλαυκίδιον, ὥσπερ ἄλλοτε,
ἕψειν ἐν ἅλμηι φημί. (*B.*) τὸ δὲ λαβράκιον;
(*A.*) ὀπτᾶν ὅλον. (*B.*) τὸν γαλεόν; (*A.*) ἐν ὑποτρίμματι
ζέσαι. (*B.*) τὸ δ᾽ ἐγχέλειον; (*A.*) ἅλες ὀρίγανον
ὕδωρ. (*B.*) ὁ γόγγρος; (*A.*) ταὐτόν. (*B.*) ἡ βατίς; (*A.*) χλόη.   5
(*B.*) πρόσεστι θύννου τέμαχος. (*A.*) ὀπτήσεις. (*B.*) κρέας
ἐρίφειον; (*A.*) ὀπτόν. (*B.*) θάτερον; (*A.*) τἀναντία.
(*B.*) ὁ σπλήν; (*A.*) σεσάχθω. (*B.*) νῆστις; (*A.*) ἀπολεῖ μ᾽ οὑτοσί

2 ἕψειν Ath. (1)ᴬᶜᴱ: ἑλεῖν Ath. (2)ᴬ

G11. Philemo fr. 82, from *The Soldier* (IV/III)

ὡς ἵμερός μ᾽ ὑπῆλθε γῆι τε κοὐρανῶι
λέξαι μολόντι τοὖψον ὡς ἐσκεύασα.
νὴ τὴν Ἀθηνᾶν ἡδύ γ᾽ ἔστ᾽ εὐημερεῖν
ἐν ἅπασιν. ἰχθὺς ἁπαλὸς οἷος γέγονέ μοι,
οἷον παρατέθεικ᾽, οὐ πεφαρμακευμένον   5
τυροῖσιν οὐδ᾽ ἄνωθεν ἐξηνθισμένον,
ἀλλ᾽ οἷος ἦν ζῶν, κὠπτὸς ὢν τοιοῦτος ἦν·
οὕτως ἁπαλὸν ἔδωκα καὶ πρᾶιον τὸ πῦρ
ὀπτῶν τὸν ἰχθύν. οὐδὲ πιστευθήσομαι
      *   *   *
ὅμοιον ἐγένετ᾽, ὄρνις ὁπόταν ἁρπάσηι   10
τοῦ καταπιεῖν μεῖζόν τι· περιτρέχει κύκλωι
τηροῦσα τοῦτο, καταπιεῖν δ᾽ ἐσπούδακεν,
ἕτεραι διώκουσιν δὲ ταύτην· ταὐτὸν ἦν.
τὴν ἡδονὴν ὁ πρῶτος αὐτῶν καταμαθὼν
τῆς λοπάδος ἀνεπήδησε κἄφευγεν κύκλωι   15
τὴν λοπάδ᾽ ἔχων, ἄλλοι δ᾽ ἐδίωκον κατὰ πόδας.
ἐξῆν ὀλολύζειν· οἱ μὲν ἥρπασάν τι γάρ,
οἱ δ᾽ οὐδέν, οἱ δὲ πάντα. καίτοι παρέλαβον
ἰχθῦς ποταμίους ἐσθίοντας βόρβορον·
εἰ δ᾽ ἔλαβον ἀρτίως σκάρον, ἢ ᾽κ τῆς Ἀττικῆς   20
γλαυκίσκον, ὦ Ζεῦ σῶτερ, ἢ ᾽ξ Ἄργους κάπρον,
ἢ ᾽κ τῆς Σικυῶνος τῆς φίλης ὃν τοῖς θεοῖς
φέρει Ποσειδῶν γόγγρον εἰς τὸν οὐρανόν,
ἅπαντες οἱ φαγόντες ἐγένοντ᾽ ἂν θεοί.
ἀθανασίαν εὕρηκα· τοὺς ἤδη νεκρούς,   25
ὅταν <μόνον> ὀσφρανθῶσι, ποιῶ ζῆν πάλιν

lac. inter 9 et 10 stat. Meineke   20 ἀρτίως Bentley: ἄρτι Ath.ᴬ: om. Ath.ᶜᴱ
26 ⟨μόνον⟩ Casaubon: ὅτανπερ Porson

G12. Archedicus fr. 2, from *The Treasure* (IV/III)

πρῶτον ὠμῶν κειμένων
τῶν ἰχθύων πάρεισιν οἱ κεκλημένοι.
"δίδου κατὰ χειρός." "τοὖψον οἰχήσει λαβών."
τὰς λοπάδας ἐπιθεὶς ἐπὶ τὸ πῦρ τοὺς ἄνθρακας
ἔρραν᾽ ἐλαίωι πάντα καὶ ποιῶ φλόγα.   5
ἐν ὧι τὸ λάχανον αἵ τε τῶν παροψίδων
τὸν ἄνδρα δριμύτητες εὐφραίνουσί μου,
ἑφθὸν τὸν ἰχθὺν ἀποδίδωμ᾽ ἔχοντα τοὺς
χυμοὺς ἐν αὑτῶι τήν τε τῆς ἅλμης ἀκμήν,
εἰς ἣν ἂν ἐμβάψαιτο πᾶς ἐλεύθερος·   10
ἐλαιδίου κοτύλης τε παραναλωμένης
σέσωκ᾽ ἐμοὶ τρίκλινα πεντήκοντ᾽ ἴσως

6–10 et 12 om. Ath.ᶜᴱ   10 πᾶς Musurus: πᾶς ἀνὴρ Ath.ᴬ   12 σέσωκ᾽ ἐμοὶ
Schweighäuser: σέσωκέμου Ath.ᴬ

G13. Eubulus fr. 63, from *Spartans or Leda* (IV)

πρὸς τούτοισιν δὲ παρέσται σοι
θύννου τέμαχος κρέα δελφακίων
χορδαί τ᾽ ἐρίφων ἧπάρ τε κάπρου
κριοῦ τ᾽ ὄρχεις χόλικές τε βοός
κρανία τ᾽ ἀρνῶν νῆστίς τ᾽ ἐρίφου   5
γαστήρ τε λαγώ φύσκη χορδὴ
πνεύμων ἀλλᾶς τε

G14. Eubulus fr. 72, from *Oedipus* (IV)

ὁ πρῶτος εὑρὼν τἀλλότρια δειπνεῖν ἀνὴρ
δημοτικὸς ἦν τις, ὡς ἔοικε, τοὺς τρόπους.
ὅστις δ᾽ ἐπὶ δεῖπνον ἢ φίλον τιν᾽ ἢ ξένον
καλέσας ἔπειτα συμβολὰς ἐπράξατο,
φυγὰς γένοιτο μηδὲν οἴκοθεν λαβών   5

G15. Alexis fr. 259, from *The Exile* (IV/III)

ἀεί γ᾽ ὁ Χαιρεφῶν τιν᾽ εὑρίσκει τέχνην
καινὴν πορίζεταί τε τὰ δεῖπν᾽ ἀσύμβολα.

ὅπου γάρ ἐστιν ὁ κέραμος μισθώσιμος
ὁ τοῖς μαγείροις, εὐθὺς ἐξ ἑωθινοῦ
ἕστηκεν ἐλθών. κἂν ἴδηι μισθούμενον   5
εἰς ἑστίασιν, τοῦ μαγείρου πυθόμενος
τὸν ἑστιῶντα, τῆς θύρας χασμωμένης
ἂν ἐπιλάβηται, πρῶτος εἰσελήλυθεν

2 καινὴν Naber: καὶ νῦν Ath.^{ACE}   τε Naber: γε Ath.^{ACE}

G16. Alexis fr. 263, from an unidentified play (IV/III)

ἔλαθον γενόμενος οὗ τὸ πρᾶγμ' ἠβούλετο.
κατὰ χειρὸς ἐδόθη· τὴν τράπεζαν ἧκ' ἔχων,
ἐφ' ἧς ἐπέκειτ' οὐ τυρὸς οὐδ' ἐλαῶν γένη
οὐδὲ παρέχουσαι κνῖσαν ἡμῖν πίονα
παροψίδες καὶ λῆρος, ἀλλὰ παρετέθη   5
ὑπερηφάνως ὄζουσα τῶν Ὡρῶν λοπάς,
τὸ τοῦ πόλου τοῦ παντὸς ἡμισφαίριον.
ἅπαντ' ἐνῆν τἀκεῖ γὰρ ἐν ταύτηι καλά,
ἰχθῦς, ἔριφοι, διέτρεχε τούτων σκορπίος,
ὑπέφαινεν ὠιῶν ἡμίτομα τοὺς ἀστέρας.   10
ἐπεβάλομεν τὰς χεῖρας. ὁ μὲν ἐμοὶ λαλῶν
ἅμα καὶ διανεύων ἠσχολεῖθ'· ὁ πᾶς δ' ἀγὼν
ἐπ' ἐμὲ κατήντα. τὸ πέρας οὐκ ἀνῆχ' ἕως
τὴν λοπάδ' ὀρύττων ἀποδέδειχα κόσκινον

4 πίονα Meineke: πλείονα Ath.^{CE}   6 ὑπερηφάνως Casaubon: ὑπερήφανος Ath.^{CE}

G17. Euphanes fr. 1, from *Muses* (IV)

Φοινικίδης δ' ὡς εἶδεν ἐν πλήθει νέων
μεστὴν ζέουσαν λοπάδα Νηρείων τέκνων,
ἐπίσχετ' ὀργῆι χεῖρας ἠρεθισμένας·
"τίς φησιν εἶναι δεινὸς ἐκ κοινοῦ φαγεῖν;
τίς ἐκ μέσου τὰ θερμὰ δεινὸς ἁρπάσαι;   5
ποῦ Κόρυδος ἢ Φυρόμαχος ἢ Νείλου βία;
ἴτω πρὸς ἡμᾶς, καὶ τάχ' οὐδὲν μεταλάβοι"

5 δεινὸς Musurus: δεινός γ' Ath.^A

G18. Alexis fr. 15, from *The Man Who Had a Cataract* (IV/III)

(Α.) παρ' ἐμοῦ δ', ἐὰν μὴ καθ' ἓν ἕκαστον πάντα δῶις,
χαλκοῦ μέρος δωδέκατον οὐκ ἂν ἀπολάβοις.

(B.) δίκαιος ὁ λόγος. (A.) ἀβάκιον ψῆφον. λέγε.

(B.) ἔστ᾽ ὠμοτάριχος πέντε χαλκῶν. (A.) λέγ᾽ ἕτερον.

(B.) μῦς ἑπτὰ χαλκῶν. (A.) οὐδὲν ἀσεβεῖς οὐδέπω.   5

λέγε. (B.) τῶν ἐχίνων ὀβολός. (A.) ἁγνεύεις ἔτι.

(B.) ἆρ᾽ ἦν μετὰ ταῦθ᾽ ἡ ῥάφανος, ἣν ἐβοᾶτε; (A.) ναί·

χρηστὴ γὰρ ἦν. (B.) ἔδωκα ταύτης δύ᾽ ὀβολούς.

(A.) τί γὰρ ἐβοῶμεν; (B.) τὸ κύβιον τριωβόλου.

(A.) † ονεῖλκε χειρῶν γε † οὐκ ἐπράξατ᾽ οὐδὲ ἕν;   10

(B.) οὐκ οἶσθας, ὦ μακάριε, τὴν ἀγοράν, ὅτι

κατεδηδόκασιν τὰ λάχαν᾽ <αἱ> τρωξαλλίδες.

(A.) διὰ τοῦτο <τὸ> τάριχος τέθεικας διπλασίου;

(B.) ὁ ταριχοπώλης ἐστίν· ἐλθὼν πυνθάνου.

γόγγρος δέκ᾽ ὀβολῶν. (A.) οὐχὶ πολλοῦ. λέγ᾽ ἕτερον.   15

(B.) τὸν ὀπτὸν ἰχθὺν ἐπριάμην δραχμῆς. (A.) παπαῖ,

ὥσπερ πυρετὸς ἀνῆκεν, εἶτ᾽ † ἐν ἐπιτέλει †

(B.) πρόσθες τὸν οἶνον <ὃν> μεθυόντων προσέλαβον

ὑμῶν, χοᾶς τρεῖς, δέκ᾽ ὀβολῶν ὁ χοῦς

10 ονεῖλκε] ὅ γ᾽ εἷλκε Desrousseaux   12 λάχαν᾽ <αἱ> Erfurdt: λάχανα Ath.ᴬ
13 <τὸ> Schweighäuser   18 <ὃν> Musurus: <οὗ> Blaydes

COMMENTARY

G1–G18. For Greek culinary and dining practices and their significance, see in general A. Dalby, *Siren Feasts* (London and New York, 1996); and *Food in the Ancient World from A to Z* (London and New York, 2003); Davidson (1997), 3–35; Olson–Sens, *Archestratos*, pp. xlvi–lv; Wilkins, esp. 257–311; García Soler (2001); R. I. Curtis, *Ancient Food Technology* (Technology and Change in History, 5: Leiden, Boston, and Cologne, 2001), 275–322. Banquet scenes, long catalogues of food, and the like seem to be more typical of 'Middle' and 'New Comedy' than of 'Old Comedy'; but see e.g. **B33**; Call. Com. fr. 6; Pherecr. fr. 113; Ar. *Ach.* 1085–93; frr. 333; 520.

G1. A description of the simple traditional diet of the countryside, about which the speaker is clearly unenthusiastic, given that every item in the catalogue has a negative qualifier of some sort: the barley-cakes he and his friends or family (3) used to eat were of low quality and few in number, as were the figs; mushrooms and snails—neither referred to elsewhere as a delicacy—were available only occasionally; the vegetables and greens they got were wild rather than cultivated; the olives and wine were of the type no one would consume if given a choice; and there was no meat or fish (a point never made explicitly but basic to the complaint as a whole). Cf. **G16**. 3 with n.; Antiph. fr. 225; Alex. fr. 167; Philem. fr. 100 (all even more pointed denunciations of an impoverished rural diet); T. W. Gallant, *Risk and Survival in Ancient Greece* (Stanford, 1991), esp. 34–59; P. Garnsey, *Food and Society in Classical Antiquity* (Key Themes in Ancient History: Cambridge, 1999), 12–61 (on food-supply and hunger); contrast **E2**. Most likely the description served to develop a contrast with the luxurious (urban?) life the speaker was now enjoying.

Preserved at Athenaeus 2. 60b–c (manuscripts CE only), in a collection of literary references (many from comedy, including Antiph. fr. 225, and most of them disparaging) to mushrooms.

Iambic trimeter.

1–2. 'a small, swarthy, kneaded barley-cake full of bran'; cf. **B32**. 8 n. (on μᾶζα); Antiph. fr. 225. 1–2 (a starving farmer is speaking) 'our dinner is a barley-cake fortified with bran, cheaply prepared'. The dark colour reflects the high percentage of bran (ἄχυρα; cf. **I8**. 12 with n.; Olson on Ar. *Ach.* 507–8) in the meal and thus its low quality; contrast **B33**. 4–6; **G2**. 3 with n.; Alex. fr. 145. 7 'we're eager for our barley-cake to be white'.

3. δὶς τῆς ἡμέρας: 'twice each day', i.e. 'for both our meals'.

4. **σῦκα βαιά**: 'a few figs'. For figs (simple, inexpensive food), see Olson on Ar. *Pax* 558–9; García Soler 111–15; and cf. **J2**. 2 n. For βαιός (poetic vocabulary; rare in comedy), see Olson on Ar. *Ach.* 2.   **μύκης**: 'a mushroom'; also in a catalogue of 'wretched' rural food at Antiph. fr. 225. 4. See García Soler 63–4.

5. **ὠπτᾶτο**: For roasting (ὀπτάω) as a means of preparing mushrooms, see Antiph. fr. 225. 10–11.   **κοχλίας**: For snails as food, see Arnott on Alex. fr. 281. 1–2; García Soler 132.   **γενομένου ψακαδίου**: genitive absolute, 'if there was a bit of rain' (since snails like moist weather).

6. **λάχανα τῶν αὐτοχθόνων**: 'wild pot-herbs and vegetables', such as water-cress, mustard greens, and chicory. See Gallant (introductory n.) 115–19 (with extensive bibliography).

7. **θλαστή**: 'bruised'. For eating olives, see **G12**. 6–7 n.; García Soler 64–6.

8. **ἀμφίβολον**: 'dubious', i.e. 'vinegary'.

G2. The speaker is most likely Heracles, who is enjoying himself in the house of the title-character Queen Omphale, to whom he was sold as a slave (S. *Tr.* 248–53, 274–8; Pherecyd. *FGrHist* 3 F 82b; cf. Gantz 439–40) and whom he has no intention of deserting (thus Meineke). For Heracles as glutton, see **A1** introductory n.; **G3**. Satyr plays entitled *Omphale* were written by Ion (*TrGF* 19 F 17a–33a) and Achaeus (*TrGF* 20 F 32–5).

Large-scale commercial baking of wheat bread (ἄρτος; see **B33**. 4–6 n.) is first attested in Athens at the very end of the fifth century, when the creation of the industry is repeatedly associated with a certain Thearion (*PAA* 501987; mentioned in 7, as well as at Ar. frr. 1; 177; Pl. *Grg.* 518b (all cited by Athenaeus immediately after this fragment)).

Preserved at Athenaeus 3. 112c–d (manuscript A only), as evidence of the excellence of Attic bread.

Iambic trimeter.

1. **εὐγενής** is properly 'well-born', but here (as often) the adjective means little more than 'decent, good'; see K. J. Dover, *Greek Popular Morality in the Time of Plato and Aristotle* (Oxford, 1974), 94–5.

3–6. High-style, 'dithyrambic' language; cf. **C4**. 1 n.

3. **λευκοσωμάτους**: The colour of the loaves is an indication of the high quality of the flour used to make them; see **G1**. 1–2 n.; Ar. fr. 129. 3; Philyll. fr. 4.

3–4. **ἱπνὸν | καταμπέχοντας ἐν πυκναῖς διεξόδοις**: 'occupying the oven in frequent passages back and forth', sc. as one set of loaves is pulled out and another shoved in.

5. **μορφὴν κριβάνοις ἠλλαγμένους**: 'changed in form by baking-shells'. For baking-shells (warmed by means of coals or a fire set around the outside),

see Cubberley, in J. Wilkins, D. Harvey, and M. Dobson (eds.), *Food in Antiquity* (Exeter, 1995), 55–68. For baking-shells used specifically to produce bread, see Ar. *Ach.* 1123 with Olson ad loc. and on 84–7; fr. 1; Ephipp. fr. 1. 2; Archestr. fr. 5. 17.

6. μίμημα χειρὸς Ἀττικῆς: 'the artwork, moulding of an Attic hand'; in apposition to ἄρτους (3–5; picked up again by the relative οὕς).

G3. Athenaeus reports that the first speaker is Linus, the second Heracles, who is taking music lessons in Linus' house; this appears to be the first encounter of teacher and student (7–8 with n.). Heracles eventually murdered Linus, after Linus struck him when he had difficulties with his studies; see Nesselrath 227–9. The story is illustrated on a number of red-figure vases (see Bundrick 71–4) and was presumably the subject of Achaeus' satyr play *Linus* (*TrGF* 20 F 26) and perhaps Anaxandrides' *Heracles* (fr. 16 with K–A ad loc.). Cf. Hes. fr. 305; D.S. iii. 67. 2; [Apollod.] *Bib.* ii. 4. 9; Paus. ix. 29. 9; M. L. West, *The Orphic Poems* (Oxford, 1983), 56–67; Gantz 378–9. For Heracles as glutton (8–9, 17–18), see **A1** introductory n.; **G2**.

The first cookbook (see 9–10) of which we know was composed in prose around 400 BC by a certain Mithaecus, whom Plato's Socrates refers to as 'the author of the Sicilian recipe-book' (*Grg.* 518b; cf. **G8**. 2 n.). Only one fragment survives (ap. Ath. 7. 325f): 'As for the ribbon-fish, after you gut it, cut its head off, rinse it, and cut it into slices, pour cheese and olive oil over it'. Other early cookbook authors include Heracleides of Syracuse and Glaucus of Locris. Athenaeus 7. 308f; 12. 516c, and Pollux vi. 70–1 preserve additional names. Cf. **G4** with **I6** introductory n.; Anaxipp. fr. 1. 1–5, 21–5 (a braggart cook claims that his teacher helped 'rub the old-fashioned spices out of the books', and declares that he studies the works of others and intends to compose συγγράμματα of his own someday); Bato fr. 4 (a braggart cook claims to stay up late studying the treatises of his predecessors); Olson–Sens, *Archestratos*, pp. xxxvi–xxxvii.

Preserved at Athenaeus 4. 164b–d, in support of the assertion that 'you philosophers always have your minds on dinner parties', the speaker having missed the irony in Linus' claim in 10–11 that Heracles is patently a philosopher.

Iambic trimeter.

1–2. βιβλίον Ι ... ὅ τι βούλει: 'whichever papyrus-roll you want'. For the prolepsis, cf. 7–8; **F6**. 16–17 n.

2. γάρ is assentient and most likely marks Linos' λαβέ as an echo of something Heracles said in the immediately preceding verses; 'yes indeed, take ... ' (Denniston 86–8; cf. Denniston 97 for the position of the particle).

3. The second-person future indicative **ἀναγνώσει** is equivalent in sense to an imperative (Goodwin § 69; Gildersleeve § 269); cf. **G10**. 6; **G12**. 3; **H13**. 17.   **πάνυ γε**: 'By all means!' A colloquial expression of enthusiastic assent (e.g. Ar. *Th.* 749, 1191; Men. *Sam.* 115; Pl. *Ap.* 20b) with which Heracles interrupts his teacher's orders.

3–4. **διασκοπῶν | κτλ.**: 'examining (them) on the basis of their labels, quietly and at your leisure'. The closing words represent an implicit response to Heracles' aggressive eagerness to get his hands on the books in 3; see 8 n.

5–7. Linus was an epic singer, and his collection of texts therefore consists largely of epic and epicizing poetry. But it also contains tragedies and **συγγράμματα | παντοδαπά** ('prose treatises of every sort') typical of fourth-century Athens but not the heroic age, and which will not do for instruction in music but are needed for the joke in 8–9.

5. For Orpheus and the poetry attributed to him in the classical period, see M. L. West, *The Orphic Poems* (Oxford, 1983); Dover on Ar. *Ra.* 1032; Gantz 721–5. For the reception of Hesiod in comedy, see **C1** introductory n.

6. **Ἐπίχαρμος** is probably included not as a comic poet but as the author of works of pseudo-philosophical 'wisdom' such as *Practical Maxims* (**A18–A19**) (thus Wilamowitz).   For the reception of Homer in comedy, see **D1–D4** n.   **Χοιρίλος**: Since the works of the tragedians are referred to collectively at the end of 5, this must be the late fifth-century Samian epic poet, twelve fragments of whose *Persica* survive (Bernabé, *Poetae Epici Graeci*, i. 191–6), rather than the early (and almost entirely obscure) Athenian tragic poet (*TrGF* 2).

7–8. **δηλώσεις . . . οὕτω**: sc. 'by the choice you make'. Linus intends to tailor Heracles' lessons to his personality, and he accordingly allows his student to select material he finds appealing; for a parallel but more extended scene, see Ar. *Nu.* 636–93 (Socrates assesses Strepsiades' interests and abilities when the old man attempts to enrol in the Phrontisterion). **τὴν φύσιν | ἐπὶ τί μάλιστ(α) ὥρμηκε**: 'your nature, toward what it has turned' (for this use of ὁρμάω ἐπί + accusative, cf. 13–14), i.e. 'what subject-matter you are naturally inclined to'. For the prolepsis, cf. 1–2 with n.

8. **τουτὶ λαμβάνω**: In 4, Linus told his student to take his time selecting a text to work on; but Heracles knows immediately which book suits him best.

9. **πρῶτον** is adverbial.   **ὀψαρτυσία**: 'a cookbook' (< ὄψον (see **E31**. 9–10 n.) + ἀρτύω ('prepare')); cf. **G4**. 4.

10. **τὸ (ἐ)πίγραμμα**: 'the label' (cf. 4).

11. **εὔδηλον**: '(it's) quite clear!'

12–15. Simus (Stephanis #275) is known only from this passage. That he gets a mention on stage in comedy suggests that (despite the question in 12) he was well known, and there is no need to take Alexis' (or Linus') assessment of his abilities as an actor—or a cook—at face value.

12. For τέχνη in the sense '(rhetorical) handbook', cf. **A18.** 12 n.

13. μάλ(α) εὐφυὴς ἄνθρωπος: 'a very clever individual' (setting up the nasty undercutting of the assertion in 14–16). For εὐφυής in this sense, cf. Alex. fr. 37. 4 with Arnott ad loc.; Isoc. 7. 49.

13–14. ἐπὶ τραγῳδίαν Ι ὥρμηκε: see 7–8 n.

15–16. ὡς δοκεῖ Ι τοῖς χρωμένοις: 'as it seems to those who employ him', i.e. to the *choregoi* and playwrights who have the bad luck to be awarded his services.

16. ὑποκριτής: sc. πολὺ κράτιστος from 14–15, '(by far the best) actor'. Something is missing after 16, but Linus' comment in 17 makes it clear that Heracles showed no interest in anything but the food his book described.

17. βούλιμος: 'ravenously hungry'; but the sense is of an insatiable hunger that is virtually a disease, as at Ar. *Pl.* 873.

18. εὖ τοῦτ(ο) ἴσθι: 'know this well!', i.e. 'you can be sure of that!, that's for sure!'

G4. For the story of Phaon, and the plot and date of Plato's play, see **I6** introductory n.; Speaker A is most likely Phaon himself (thus Kaibel). Whether the lines quoted at 6, 9–22 are drawn from an actual poem by a contemporary author named Philoxenus (4; see below) or not, they are the earliest example of a genre of epicizing gastronomic literature otherwise preserved only in the fragments of Archestratus of Gela, to which they bear some close if obscure relationship; see 15 n., 16 n., 19 n.; Olson–Sens, *Archestratos*, pp. xl–xliii. Most of the foods recommended in the preserved portions of the poem are supposed to be aphrodisiacs (10 n., 17 n.; cf. 20 n.). But the addressee is also implicitly treated as a glutton: he is to 'gobble up' as many purse-tassel hyacinth bulbs as he can (10), consume large fish whole (14–16), and prefer a stewed octopus to a roasted one if it is bigger—unless he can get two roasted ones (18–19). Cf. Degani, *Eikasmos*, 9 (1998), 81–99; Pellegrino, *Utopie*, 237–61.

Preserved entire at Athenaeus 1. 5b–d (manuscripts CE only), in a discussion of the 'descriptions of dinner parties' (δείπνων ἀναγραφαί) produced by various authors and in particular the one composed by Philoxenus of Leucas (*PMG* 836; dactylo-epitrite), to whom Athenaeus argues Plato is referring here. (Cf. **H6.** 3–4 n.; Ath. 4. 146f, where the speaker raises the possibility that the poet in question is Philoxenus of Cythera instead.) Lines 11 and 12, and 13 and 14 are separated in Athenaeus by the words εἶτα μετὰ μικρόν ('then after a little') and καὶ μετ᾽ ὀλίγα ('and after a few (lines)'), respectively; cf. 7–8 n. In addition, 20–1 alone are preserved separately at Athenaeus 7. 325a, in a collection of literary references to the red mullet.

Lines 6 and 9–22 are dactylic hexameter, the other verses are iambic trimeter.

1–3. Speaker A thinks he is alone on stage (ἐν τῆι ἐρημίαι, πρὸς ἐμαυτόν) and is surprised—although seemingly not discomfited—by the appearance of Speaker B, who has overheard him and wants to know what he is up to. Although Speaker A eventually reads a portion of the text aloud, he clearly intends initially to read silently to himself; cf. **E7**. 20–1 n.

3. **ἀντιβολῶ σε** in the sense 'I implore you' is an Attic colloquialism; see López Eire 58–9; Olson on Ar. *Ach.* 414.

4. **ὀψαρτυσία:** see **G3**. 9 n.

5. **ἄκουε δή:** 'Listen carefully' *vel sim.*; cf. Denniston 216–17.   **αὐτὴν ἥτις ἔστ(ι):** for the prolepsis, see **F6**. 16–17 n.

6. A programmatic statement from the opening section of the poem, which plays on the dactylic hexameter saying ἄρξομαι ἐξ ἀγαθοῖο, τελευτήσω δ᾽ ἐς ἄμεινον ('I will begin with the good, and end with something bettter'; identified by the fourth-century AD rhetorician Libanius as a παροιμία ('proverb')).   **βολβοῖο:** 'a bulb'. But the word is generally used in gastronomic contexts to refer to the onion-like bulb of the purse-tassel hyacinth (*Muscari comosum*); see 9–10 with nn.; Olson–Sens on Archestr. fr. 9. 1. 'Philoxenus' mentions the βολβός first not only because it was commonly served as an appetizer at the beginning of meals (e.g. Mnesim. fr. 4. 29; Nicostr. fr. 1. 3; cf. **G12**. 6–7 n.), but also because it is simple food, in contrast to the much more luxurious tuna with which he will conclude. But see also 10 n.   **θύννον:** 'tuna'; a delicacy (in banquet catalogues and the like at e.g. Eub. fr. 36. 1–2; Aristophon fr. 7. 3), and so large that it was routinely bought and served in slices, as at **G10**. 6; **G13**. 2. See *Fishes*, 79–90; Olson–Sens on Archestr. fr. 35. 2.

7–8. A gluttonish, bomolochic ('buffoonish') interjection of a sort probably made repeatedly in this scene by Speaker B (i.e. somewhere in the gaps between 11 and 12, and 13 and 14), although Athenaeus or his source has eliminated those portions of the text.   The manuscripts' **τῆς τελευτ(αίας)** appears to be a superlinear gloss on **ἐνταυθὶ ... τάξεως** that has driven a word or words with the metrical shape – ∪ – × – out of the text (thus Meineke). The sense of **οὐκοῦν κτλ.** is none the less clearly 'So then' (sc. if the tuna comes last), 'it's by far the best thing to have been stationed in this spot in the ranks', although why Speaker B says that he has been posted in the rear (putting him near the tuna) is obscure. Perhaps the point is that he is looking over Speaker A's shoulder as Speaker A reads the poem.

9. **σποδιᾶι δαμάσας**: 'after mastering them with ash', i.e. 'baking them in the coals'.   **καταχύσματι**: 'a sauce' (cognate with καταχέω), with which βολβοί are served also at Nicostr. Com. fr. 1. 3; Philem. fr. 113. 1–3.

10. **ὡς πλείστους διάτρωγε**: 'gobble up as many possible'. The prefix serves to intensify the sense of the verb; see LSJ s. διά D. IV.   **τὸ γὰρ δέμας ἀνέρος ὀρθοῖ**: 'for (eating many purse-tassel bulbs) makes a man's body stand upright', i.e. 'gives him an erection'. For βολβοί as an aphrodisiac, see **I6**. 12 (also from *Phaon*); Ar. *Ec.* 1089–92; Xenarch. fr. 1; Alex. frr. 175; 281; and cf. 20 n. The initial syllable in ἀνέρος is to be scanned long, as regularly in trisyllabic forms of the word.

11. **καὶ τάδε μὲν δὴ ταῦτα**: i.e. 'so much for items of this sort' (vegetables and the like). δή is connective and strengthens the μὲν . . . δ(ἐ) antithesis; see Denniston 257–9.   **θαλάσσης . . . τέκν(α)**: cf. πόντου τέκνα (also of seafood) at Archestr. fr. 50. 3 with Olson–Sens ad loc. The combination of mute and liquid in τέκν' does not make position in the epicizing poetry of 'Philoxenus', as it normally would in comedy.   **ἄνειμι**: 'I move on', as at Ar. *Nu.* 1058.

12. For the opposition between wet and dry cooking, see 18–19 n. **λοπάς**: 'a casserole-dish', used for boiling, braising, and stewing, especially of seafood; see also **G11**. 15–16; **G12**. 4; **G16**. 6; and cf. **C10**. 4–5 n.; Arnott on Alex. fr. 115. 21–3; Olson–Sens on Matro fr. 1. 36–7.   **κακόν**: predicative of λοπάς, 'a bad thing'.   **τὸ τάγηνον**: 'the frying-pan' (often τήγανον); used for cooking seafood at e.g. Ar. *Eq.* 929–30; Eub. fr. 108. 3; Archestr. fr. 11. 8–9 with Olson–Sens ad loc.

14. 'as for speckled sea-perch' (see *Fishes*, 187–8) 'and dentex' (see *Fishes*, 255–6; Olson–Sens on Archestr. fr. 18. 1–2) 'and shark' (see *Fishes*, 106–7; Olson–Sens on Archestr. fr. 24. 1–2). These are all large fish that were normally purchased and eaten in pieces, hence the prohibition in 15.

15. **μὴ τέμνειν** functions as an imperative, 'don't cut them up (into steaks; cf. **C9**. 10 n.)!' (Goodwin § 784. 1); the prohibition ensures that the implicitly gluttonous addressee will be served the entire fish rather than only a portion of it. Cf. Alex. fr. 175. 3, where ἰχθῦς ἁδροὺς ('fat fish') are referred to as an aphrodisiac.   In context, **μή σοι νέμεσις θεόθεν καταπνεύσηι** can only mean 'lest you be rendered impotent'. The words are echoed at Archestr. fr. 16. 3–4 μή σοι νέμεσις καταπνεύσηι | δεινὴ ἀπ' ἀθανάτων (a warning against failure to buy the boar-fish, no matter how much it costs), where see Olson–Sens.

16. **ὅλον ὀπτήσας παράθες** ('roast it and serve it whole!') occurs in the same position in the line at Archestr. fr. 13. 4 (of the gilthead); cf. 15 n. For

παρατίθημι in the sense 'serve', e.g. **G11**. 5; **G16**. 5; Pherecr. fr. 198; Anaxipp. fr. *1. 33; Theophil. fr. 4. 2.

17. The line is incurably corrupt. But **κατὰ καιρόν** is more likely 'in season' than 'when it is perfectly cooked'.   **πουλύποδος**: For octopus (see *Fishes*, 204–8; Olson–Sens on Archestr. fr. 54. 1) as an aphrodisiac, cf. Xenarch. fr. 1. 7–10; Alex. fr. 175. 3.

18–19. The opposition between frying, roasting, and baking (ὀπτάω), on the one hand, and poaching, braising, and stewing (ἕψω), on the other, is fundamental to Greek culinary thought; cf. 12; **G10**. 2–3, 7; **G12**. 4–5 with n.; Olson–Sens on Archestr. fr. 11. 8–9. In this case, however, what matters most is the quantity of food rather than how it is prepared; see introductory n.

19. **κλαίειν**: 'to wail', i.e. 'to go to hell'; cf. Archestr. fr. 39. 3 σαπέρδηι δ' ἐνέπω κλαίειν ('I say to hell with the *saperdē*'). A colloquial sense of the verb; cf. Stevens 15–16.

20. **τρίγλη**: 'red mullet' (common in banquet catalogues and the like); see *Fishes*, 264–8; Olson–Sens on Archestr. fr. 42. 1. Athenaeus 7. 325d cites the περὶ Ἀφροδίσια ('*On Sexual Matters*') of a certain Terpsicles to the effect that, if a man drank wine in which a red mullet had been smothered, he would be unable to attain an erection, while a woman who drank the same wine would be unable to conceive.   **νεύρων ἐπιήρανος**: 'an assistant of cord-muscles' (i.e. those that are conceived as producing and maintaining a man's erection); cf. Ar. *Lys.* 1078 with Henderson ad loc.; Ath. 2. 64b, citing the proverb (pp. 94–5 Stromberg) οὐδέν σ' ὀνήσει βολβός, ἂν μὴ νεῦρ' ἔχηις ('A purse-tassel bulb will do you no good (cf. 10 n.), if you don't have νεῦρα'; an iambic trimeter).

21. **παρθένου Ἀρτέμιδος**: '(devoted to) Artemis the Virgin'. Athenaeus 7. 325a–f cites a number of texts, including Nausicr. fr. 1. 6–11 and Charicl. fr. 1, for the association of the red mullet with the Underworld goddess Hecate (see **A20** introductory n.), who was often identified with Artemis. **στύματα**: 'hard-ons'. A primary obscenity (*Maculate Muse*, p. 35, and § 7).

22. **σκορπίος**: 'bullhead, sculpin', called 'scorpion' on account of the poisonous spines around its head; cf. *Fishes*, 245–6; Olson–Sens on Archestr. fr. 30. 1.   **παίσειέ γε κτλ.**: a disgusted interjection (contrast 7–8), which makes it clear that Speaker B has had enough of Speaker A and his poem.   **τὸν πρωκτόν**: 'your arsehole' (cf. **E30**. 6 n.), and thus by extension 'your arse'. Another primary obscenity (*Maculate Muse*, p. 35, and § 449).

G5. Athenaeus reports that Speaker A is a young man κατασμικρύνων ἅπαντα τὰ περὶ τὴν ὀψωνίαν ('making light of'—or perhaps 'trying to reduce the cost of'—'everything that has to do with buying ὄψον'); Speaker B is his slave (2), who is being sent off to the Agora to purchase supplies for a great dinner party in a courtesan's house (12–13 with n.; for courtesans, see I7 introductory n.). The young man repeatedly insists that the slave—whom he seems not to trust (esp. 10)—should be careful not to spend too much money (1–3, 10). But the shopping list keeps growing longer (esp. 6 with n.), and most of the items on it are luxuries in any case; Speaker A thus rapidly emerges as someone who wants to have things both ways—and who knows he is going to have a good meal no matter what he does (12–13). See Nesselrath 285–93, esp. 285–6. Nicostr. Com. fr. *4 is very similar, and Eub. frr. 109; 120; Antiph. fr. 69 (cf. Ephipp. fr. 21) all appear to come from the same type of scene, in which one character sends another off to the marketplace with a list of items to purchase. Cf. **G18**, in which two men settle up accounts after the party for which one did the communal buying.

     Preserved at Athenaeus 8. 359a–b, in a brief collection of comic fragments having to do with purchasing fish.

     Iambic trimeter.

1.   For **ἀλλά** in a command marking 'a transition from arguments for action to a statement of the action required', see Denniston 13–15. **εὐτελῶς**: 'cheaply', i.e. 'parsimoniously, without spending much money'.

2.   **ἅπαν … ἱκανόν ἐστι**: 'anything is acceptable'.   **φράζ(ε)**: 'tell (me what to buy)!'

3–4 are virtually identical to Eub. fr. 109. 1–2; cf. **B42** introductory n. **μὴ πολυτελῶς** (sc. ἀγόρασον) **κτλ.** does little more than repeat the sense of 1–2, underlining Speaker A's anxiety to get his point across. **καθαρείως**: 'simply', as at Nicostr. Com. fr. *4.   **ὅ τι ἂν ἦι**: 'whatever there is, whatever's available'.   **ὁσίας ἕνεκ(α)**: 'for form's sake, appearance's sake', the point being that the slave is to buy enough to make it clear to bystanders that his master is neither cheap nor poor—but absolutely nothing more than this.   **τευθίδια σηπίδια**: 'squid (and) cuttlefish' (both common in banquet catalogues and the like). For squid, see **B34**. 10 n. For cuttlefish, e.g. Ar. *Ach.* 1041; fr. 333. 1; Anaxandr. fr. 42. 47; Anaxipp. fr. *1. 33; and see *Fishes*, 231–3; Olson–Sens on Archestr. fr. 56.

5.   **κάραβος**: 'a crayfish' (in banquet catalogues and the like at e.g. Ar. fr. 164; Eup. fr. 174. 2; Philyll. fr. 12. 1; cf. **A5**. 2); see *Fishes*, 102–3; Olson–Sens on Matro fr. 1. 66–7.   **ἦι λαβεῖν**: 'can be got', i.e. 'purchased', as also in 7; cf. **B35**. 9.

6.   **ἢ δύ(ο)** at the head of the line catches Speaker A in the act of gradually expanding his shopping list despite his initial insistence on frugality (1–4). **ἐπὶ τὴν τράπεζαν**: for the use of tables at dinner parties, see **G16**. 2 n.

6–7. ἐγχελύδια | Θήβηθεν: Eels (a delicacy; see **G10**. 4 n.) are repeatedly said to have been imported into Athens from Lake Copais in Boeotia (Ar. _Ach._ 880 with Olson ad loc.; Eub. fr. 36. 3; Antiph. fr. 191. 1), where the chief city was Thebes. For the diminutive ἐγχελύδιον, see 8 n. For the use of ἔρχεται (as if the eels enter the marketplace of their own accord), see also 9 εἰσέλθηι; and cf. **H4**. 1 n.

7. τούτων: '(some) of these'.   λαβέ: see 5 n.

8. 'a little rooster, a little ringdove, a little partridge!' (all dependent on an implied λαβέ); the diminutives (like ἐγχελύδια in 6) serve to make the requests sound less substantial. For eating roosters, see Mnesim. fr. 4. 48; and cf. _Birds_, 33–44; Dunbar on Ar. _Av._ 483–4. For ringdoves, e.g. Ar. _Ach._ 1104, 1106; Eub. fr. 148. 5; and cf. _Birds_, 300–2; Dunbar on Ar. _Av._ 303. For partridges, e.g. Antiph. fr. 295. 1; Mnesim. fr. 4. 49; and cf. _Birds_, 234–8; Dunbar on Ar. _Av._ 297.

9. δασύπους: 'a shaggy-foot', i.e. 'a hare' (in banquet catalogues and the like at e.g. Telecl. fr. 34. 2; Ar. _Ach._ 1110; Eup. fr. 174. 2; Ephipp. fr. 15. 9; Archestr. fr. 57. 1–2 with Olson–Sens ad loc.; cf. **G13**. 6 (where the word used is λαγώς)).   εἰσέλθηι: see 6–7 n.

10. ὡς μικρολόγος εἶ: 'How stingy you are!'; an ironic response to the contrast between Speaker A's specific requests (4–9) and his initial insistence on frugality (1–4), to which he returns in σὺ κτλ. But perhaps the adjective (literally 'small-talking') represents instead (or in addition) a sarcastic reference to the young man's constant resort to diminutives.   δέ γε is common in retorts (Denniston 152–4).

11. πάντως: 'in any case, at all events', i.e. 'whether you buy any of these things or not'.   πότερ(α) ἔπεμψέ τις;: Fresh meat spoiled rapidly, and it was therefore common practice to send portions of a sacrificial animal to friends, relatives, and others one wanted to influence or impress (Ar. _Ach._ 1049–50; Men. _Sam._ 403–4; Thphr. _Char._ 15. 5 with Diggle ad loc.; 17. 2).

12–13. Corone ('Crow') is elsewhere a prostitute's name (Philetaer. fr. 9. 6; Men. _Kol._ fr. 4. 1; Macho 435 with Gow ad loc.), and ἡ γυνή must be not 'my wife' but 'the lady of the house' in front of which the action is taking place and where the feast will occur.

G6. Seafood was a delicacy, and the comic fragments are full of complaints about the absurdly high prices and bad behaviour of fishmongers (e.g. **J6–J7** (the latter very similar to this passage); **J8**; Ar. fr. 402. 8–10; Antiph. frr. 159; 164; 217; Alex. fr. 204; Xenarch. fr. 7. 3–17). Arnott suggests that this fragment may be from an opening monologue; **G18** is from the same play and most likely represents the settling-up of accounts for the shopping expedition referred to obliquely here.

Preserved at Athenaeus 6. 224f–5a, in a collection of comic passages having to do with fishmongers that also includes **J7–J8**.
Iambic trimeter.

1–4. For generals, see **E4**. 4 n.

1–2. τὰς ὀφρῦς ... | ἀνεσπακότας: 'with their eyebrows drawn up', sc. in pride; cf. 6–7; and see **F9**. 3 n.   δεινὸν ... ποεῖν: 'they're behaving terribly'.

3. οὐ πάνυ τι θαυμάζω: 'I'm not particularly surprised'.   For the delayed position of δέ after the negative οὐ, see Denniston 186–7.

4. μεῖζόν τι τῶν ἄλλων φρονεῖν: see **F3**. 1 n.

5. τοὺς κάκιστ(α) ἀπολουμένους: literally 'who are going to perish most foully', i.e '—goddamn them!—the bastards!' *vel sim.* (e.g. Pherecr. fr. 22. 1; Ar. *Ach.* 865). Colloquial (Stevens 15); cf. **I2**. 1–2 n.

6. κάτω βλέποντας: i.e. rudely refusing to meet anyone's eyes or acknowledge their presence; cf. **A6**. 2 n.; **J7**. 4–10 (if anyone asks a fishmonger about his merchandise, 'he begins by staring at the ground in silence, as if he weren't paying attention and hadn't even heard'); Ar. *Nu.* 362 (of Socrates).

6–7. τὰς δ(ὲ) ὀφρῦς | κτλ.: see 1–2 n.

7. ἀποπνίγομαι: 'I'm choked', sc. with anger, as at D. 19. 199.

8–10.   The joke is that, when someone asks the price of the two mullets and learns that the fishmonger wants 10 obols, he offers 8 instead, and the fishmonger responds as if he had intended to sell them for 10 obols *apiece* but is willing to settle for 16 for the pair. For similar chicanery, see Diph. fr. 67. 9–14, where a fishmonger specifies a price in obols, but then insists on being paid in Aeginetan coins (which were heavier than Athenian)— and gives change in Athenian money.

8. πόσου: 'for how much?'; cf. 11 τοσουδί, 'So much!', i.e. 'That's the price!' τοὺς κεστρέας: 'the grey mullets' (in banquet catalogues and the like at e.g. Ar. *Nu.* 339; Philyll. fr. 12. 3; Antiph. fr. 130. 1); see *Fishes*, 108–10; Olson–Sens on Archestr. fr. 43. 1, and cf. **J13**. 8 with n.

9. βαρύ: '(that's) hard to bear, painful', i.e. 'Ouch!'

11. ὦ τᾶν: 'my good sir'. An ostensibly polite but generally impatient colloquial form of address; see Stevens 42–3; Olson on Ar. *Pax* 721–2. λαβέ: 'take (the money)!'   τοσουδί: see 8 n.   παράτρεχε: 'Run along!', i.e. 'Piss off!', sc. 'if you won't meet my price'.

12.   With his inset narrative complete, the speaker returns to the point he made at the end of 7.

G7. Cooks (see **C9–C10** n.) were independent contractors, who could be found in a special section of the Agora, the μαγειρεῖα (Poll. ix. 48, citing

Antiph. fr. 201), and seem generally to have provided their own assistants (cf. **C9** with introductory n.; **G9**) and equipment (cf. **G9**; Philem. Jun. fr. 1. 6–7 'a man's not a cook because he comes to someone's house with a soup-ladle and a butcher's knife'; for cooks renting equipment, see **G15**. 3–6 with 3 n.; cf. Men. *Sam.* 290–1). For a cook's description of how he seeks out or avoids different sorts of customers, see Diph. fr. 42.

The speaker may well be the title-character of the play, who intends to offer sacrifice (and therefore host a dinner party) to celebrate his good fortune, and who comes on stage with the man (note the deictic **οὑτοσί** in 9) he has hired to do the butchering and cooking, as in **D3**.

Preserved at Athenaeus 14. 661f–2b (manuscript A only), in a collection of literary references to cooks (the majority from comedy) that also includes **D3**; **G10**.

Iambic trimeter.

1.   **ἀναλαβών:** 'in the course of acquiring', i.e. 'hiring'.

2–3.   **τὰ ... | ... ἔλεγον:** 'all the abusive remarks the cooks were making about everyone competing with them for work'. A catalogue of the slanders offered—most of them having to do with proficiency in evaluating and seasoning food—follows in 3 ὁ μὲν–9 φέρων.

3–5.   Skill in seasoning only becomes an issue in the third charge (5–6 with n.), and the first two have to do instead with alleged deficiencies in evaluating raw culinary materials: the first man cannot recognize the smell of bad fish and is accordingly likely to poison anyone who hires him (cf. Antiph. fr. 159. 7–10, where a blind man is tricked into buying rotten fish, although the smell convinces him to throw them away once he gets home), and the second cannot taste the difference between good ingredients and bad.

3.   **ὡς** is to be taken with an implied verb of speaking; '(they said) of one fellow that . . . '

4–5.   **κριτικήν:** 'discriminating, sensitive'.   **τὸ (ὄ)ψον:** see **E31**. 9–10 n.
ὅτι <τὸ> στόμα | πονηρόν: sc. πρὸς τοὔψον.

5–6.   **τὴν γλῶτταν κτλ.:** 'he fouled his tongue unto unseemly desires for seasonings', i.e. 'he ruined his tastebuds, so that he prefers overly heavy seasonings'. Two alternative specific descriptions of this failing, followed by four nasty characterizations of other sorts, are offered in 7–8.

7.   'he uses too much salt (or) too much vinegar (or) he tends to nibble on the food he's preparing (or) to burn things'; see 5–6 n. For salt used for seasoning, see **B32**. 10 with n. Vinegar is used to add tang to stewing sauces, dipping sauces, and the like at Sotad. Com. fr. 1. 18–19; Timocl. fr. 3; Archestr. frr. 23. 6; 24. 8; 60. 8, and is sprinkled over roasted fish at Antiph.

fr. 216. 12–13; Archestr. frr. 37. 3–4; 38. 8; 46. 14; Dorion ap. Ath. 7. 309f. For thievish cooks, see **C9** introductory n.

8.   *οὐ φέρων*: 'he's unable to endure'.

8–9.   *ἐκ τοῦ πυρὸς* | *εἰς τὰς μαχαίρας*: i.e. 'from one terrible thing to another'; echoed in 10. The expression is clearly proverbial, here in reference to the fact that each time the speaker rejected a cook as unsuitable, the next one was said by his competitors to be even worse. But the image—like its colloquial English equivalent 'out of the frying pan into the fire'—is particularly apt for an encounter with cooks, who take a professional interest in cook-fires (see **G12**. 4–5 n.) and butcher's knives (see introductory n.; **J17**. 2 n.).

9.   *ὧν*: 'of which (men)', referring to the cooks (2).

10.   *διὰ τῶν μαχαιρῶν κτλ.*: i.e. 'has made it out alive' (cf. 8–9 n.), having somehow avoided the ruinous slanders of his colleagues and been hired.

G8. A cook boasts about the brilliance of his training and his ability to please his audience.

Preserved at Athenaeus (1) 4. 169d, in a collection of comic references to cooking utensils that also includes **G9**. In addition, Pollux x. 108, probably referring to this passage, says that the word *πατάνια* (a variant form of *βατάνια*; see 3–4 n.) was found in Alexis' *Asclepiocleides*; and Photius β 93 cites the word *βατάνια* from Alexis, although without naming the play. Alexis fr. 115. 21–3 (from *Crateia or The Pharmacist*; quoted at Athenaeus 3. 107d) is almost identical to 2 *ὥστε*–4; see 3–4 n.

Iambic trimeter.

1.   *οὕτως* (correlative with *ὥστε* in 2) is to be taken with *εὐφυῶς*, 'so skilfully'.   *ὀψοποιεῖν*: 'to prepare specialty dishes' *vel sim.*; see **E31**. 9–10 n.; and cf. **G11**. 2.

2.   *περὶ <τὴν> Σικελίαν*: Sicily is repeatedly referred to in the late fifth and fourth centuries as the place of origin of an innovative style of cooking that emphasized elaborate sauces and seasoning (e.g. Cratin. Jun. fr. 1; Anaxipp. fr. 1. 1–3, cf. 19–20 (another 'Middle Comic' cook who claims to have Sicilian training); Epicr. fr. 6. 2–3; Pl. *R*. 404d–e); cf. **G3** introductory n.; **G11**. 5–6 n.; Olson–Sens, *Archestratos*, pp. xxxvi–xxxix.

2–4.   *ὥστε κτλ.*: For similarly outrageous claims by comic cooks, see **G11**. 14–26; Aristophon fr. 9. 8–10 and Alex. fr. 178. 4–6 (the food is so delicious that anyone who tastes it will eat his own fingers, sc. to get at the sauce and spices that cling to them; cf. **G16**. 11 n.); Hegesipp. Com. fr. 1. 11–16 (one smell of his food at a funeral dinner makes weeping guests burst into laughter), 22–7 (anyone who comes to the door and catches a smell of the food will stand there mute, riveted to the spot, until a friend pinches his nostrils closed and drags him away).

3–4. εἰς τὰ βατάνι(α) ἐμβάλλειν … | … τοὺς ὀδόντας: 'to chew on the casserole-dishes', in which food was both cooked and served (cf. **G16.** 11 n.). A βατάνη/πατάνη is a broad, flat casserole-dish used for stewing, braising, frying, and the like; Attic comedy consistently uses the diminutives βατάνιον/πατάνιον; cf. ὀβελίσκος for ὀβελός at **G9.** 1; λεβήτιον for λέβης at **G9.** 5. The word (in the form πατάνη) was known to both Epicharmus (fr. 216) and Sophron (fr. 12), and seems to have been of Sicilian origin, making it particularly appropriate here (cf. 1–2); in Alex. fr. 115. 22 (see introductory n.), where the speaker does not claim to have studied in Sicily, he uses the metrically equivalent λοπάδι(α) (diminutive of λοπάς, for which see **G4.** 12 n.).

G9. The speaker is a μάγειρος giving orders to his slave-assistant as the two of them gather their equipment for a job; cf. **G7** introductory n.; Men. *Asp.* 222. The list of implements makes it clear that sacrificial meat (appropriately seasoned and sauced) will be the main item on the menu.

Preserved at Athenaeus 4. 169b–c, as the first in the collection of comic references to cooking utensils that also includes **G8**.

Iambic trimeter.

1. ζωμήρυσιν: 'a broth-ladle' (< ζωμός + ἀρύω ('draw liquid')); see 2 n.; **B33.** 8 n. (on meat broth). οἶσ(ε) ('bring!') is equivalent to φέρ(ε) in sense but not in metrical value, hence its use here; see Olson on Ar. *Ach.* 1099–1100. ὀβελίσκους: 'little spits', for roasting the σπλάγχνα ('entrails', i.e. the liver, kidneys, etc.) after the animal is killed (see van Straten plates 130–40) and then, after that, minced portions of the meat (see **D3.** 29 n.).

2. κρεάγραν: 'a meat-hook' (< κρέας + ἀγρέω ('seize')), for removing meat from the stewing-pot (see 5 n.), leaving the broth (cf. 1 n.); cf. Ar. *V.* 1155–6. θυείαν: 'a mortar', for grinding herbs to produce seasonings and sauces (see 3 n., 5 n.), and for culinary mixing and mashing generally (cf. **A9** n.; Diph. fr. 43. 5; Olson on Ar. *Pax* 228–9). Included in catalogues of cooking equipment and the like at e.g. Ar. fr. 7; Theopomp. Com. fr. 54; Axionic. fr. 7. 2. τυρόκνηστιν παιδικήν: 'a small cheese-grater' (< τυρός + κνάω), with the cheese to be melted over the roasting meat (cf. 6 with n.; **G11.** 5–6 with n.). Included in catalogues of cooking equipment and the like at e.g. Ar. *V.* 938; fr. 7.

3. στελεόν: 'an axe handle', presumably to be fitted with a head and used to kill the animal. σκαφίδας τρεῖς: 'three little bowls' or 'troughs' (diminutive < σκάφη; referred to as cooks' equipment at e.g. Alex. fr. 179.

8 with Arnott ad loc.; Philem. fr. 12), here most likely for mixing sauces (see 2 with n., 5 n.).   δορίδα: 'a flaying knife', for removing the animal's hide.   κοπίδας τέτταρας: 'four cleavers' (cf. **E14**. 6; Ar. fr. 143), for dismembering the animal after it has been flayed. Why more than two are needed is unclear; perhaps the animal is a large one and many men will work simultaneously at butchering it.

4. οὐ μή + interrogative future indicative οἴσεις is equivalent to an urgent imperative; 'won't you fetch?', i.e. 'hurry up and fetch!'; cf. Goodwin § 299; Barrett on E. *Hipp.* 212–14.   θεοῖσιν ἐχθρὲ σύ: 'you bastard' *vel sim.* A colloquial form of abuse (e.g. Ar. *Ach.* 934; *Ra.* 936; Men. *Pk.* 268).

5. τὸ λεβήτιον: 'the little cauldron' (diminutive < λέβης), in which a portion of the meat will be stewed; see 2 n., and cf. Men. *Dysc.* 472–5. τὰ (ἐ)κ τοῦ λίτρου: literally '(and) the things from the soda ash', i.e. 'from where the soda ash' (included in a catalogue of spices at Antiph. fr. 140. 2; added to the water in which cabbage is boiled to make it more tender at Thphr. *CP* ii. 5. 3) 'is sold', and thus 'from the spice market'; cf. 2 n.; **J1** introductory n.   πάλιν ὑστερεῖς;: 'Are you running behind again?' Comic slaves are routinely accused of inattentiveness and sloth; see **B32**. 8; Olson on Ar. *Pax* 255–6.

6. τὴν κύβηλιν τὴν ἀγωνιστηρίαν: 'the cheese-grater' (?; thus Poll. x. 104; cf. Cratin. fr. 352; Philem. fr. 12) 'suited for contests', i.e. 'the best cheese-grater', although the adjective may well be corrupt, and why a second such tool is needed (cf. 2 with n.) is unclear; cf. 3 n.

G10. A man planning a dinner party (Speaker A) gives orders to a cook (Speaker B) he hired to prepare it (cf. **G7** introductory n.). The cook has worked for Speaker A on previous occasions (cf. 1 ὥσπερ ἄλλοτε), and Speaker A finally grows exasperated with the man's endless questions (8), which presumably cover matters they have gone over in the past, and are in any case decisions the cook rather than the customer ought to make.

Preserved at Athenaeus (1) 7. 295d, in a collection of literary references (most from comedy) to the γλαῦκος (see 1 n.), with Speaker A's final remark omitted; and (2) 14. 662b–c (manuscript A only), immediately after **G7** (where see introductory n.), with the passage identified as an example of the typical σοφία ('cleverness') of cooks.

Iambic trimeter.

1. οὐκοῦν: 'so then'; moving on to the next point (Denniston 434–5), here how the various items on the menu are to be prepared.   τὸ ... γλαυκίδιον: like γλαυκίσκος in **G11**. 21, diminutive < γλαῦκος, an unidentified shark (in banquet catalogues and the like at e.g. Cratin. fr. 336;

Anaxandr. fr. 31. 2; Antiph. fr. 77. 2); see *Fishes*, 48; Olson–Sens on Archestr. fr. 21. 1.

2. **ἕψειν ἐν ἅλμηι:** 'to stew (it) in brine sauce'; cf. 4–5; **G4**. 18–19 n. (on the verb); **G12**. 8–9 n. (on stewing fish in brine). **τὸ … λαβράκιον:** diminutive < λάβραξ, 'sea bass' (in banquet catalogues and the like at e.g. Ar. fr. 380. 1; Eub. fr. 43. 3; Amphis fr. 35. 2–3); see *Fishes*, 140–2; Olson–Sens on Archestr. fr. 46. 2.

3. **ὀπτᾶν:** sc. φημί (cf. 2), as again with ζέσαι in 4. For the verb, see **G4**. 18–19 n. **τὸν γαλεόν:** 'the thresher shark' (in banquet catalogues and the like at e.g. Ar. fr. 333. 3; Ephipp. fr. 12. 1; Mnesim. fr. 4. 32); see *Fishes*, 12–13, 39–42; Olson–Sens on Archestr. fr. 22. 1–2. **ὑποτρίμματι:** like the simple τρῖμμα, a generic term for a sauce or paste created by grinding herbs, spices, or the like in a mortar (see **G9**. 2 n.), and intended for dipping (see **G12**. 10 n.) as much as for adding flavour to anything cooked or served in it. Cf. **B33**. 9; Ar. fr. 128. 2; Nicostr. Com. fr. 1. 3.

4. **τὸ … ἐγχέλειον:** like ἐγχελύδιον in **G5**. 6, a diminutive < ἔγχελυς, 'eel' (in banquet catalogues and the like at e.g. **J8**. 7; Call. Com. fr. 6. 2; Pherecr. fr. 50. 2–3; Theophil. fr. 4. 2; cf. 5 n.); see *Fishes*, 58–61; Olson–Sens on Archestr. fr. 10. 1–2.

4–5. **ἅλες ὀρίγανον | ὕδωρ:** i.e. 'a brine sauce' (see **G12**. 8–9 n.) 'flavoured with marjoram'. For marjoram (a common spice), see Olson–Sens on Archestr. fr. 36. 6; García Soler 356–7.

5. **ὁ γόγγρος:** 'the conger eel' (in banquet catalogues and the like at e.g. **G11**. 23; **G18**. 15; Antiph. fr. 127. 3; Eriph. fr. 3. 3); see *Fishes*, 49–50; Olson–Sens on Archestr. fr. 19. 1. **ἡ βατίς:** an unidentified ray or skate (in banquet catalogues and the like at e.g. Call. Com. fr. 6. 1; Eup. fr. 174. 2; Ephipp. fr. 22. 2); see *Fishes*, 26–8; Olson–Sens on Archestr. fr. 50. 1. **χλόη:** 'green herbs'; also used to produce a sauce for stewing fish at Sotad. Com. fr. 1. 30–3.

6. **θύννου τέμαχος:** 'a slice of tuna, a tuna steak'; see **C9**. 10 n. (on fish steaks); **G4**. 5 n. (on tuna); and cf. **G13**. 2. **ὀπτήσεις** is equivalent to an imperative; cf. **G3**. 3 n.

6–7. **κρέας | ἐρίφειον:** i.e. a haunch of the animal, as at Xenoph. fr. B 6. 1; Ar. fr. 449. For eating kid, see **C6**. 6; **G16**. 9; García Soler 222.

7. **θάτερον:** sc. κρέας, 'the other (meat)', sc. besides the kid (6–7). **τὰ (ἐ)ναντία:** 'the opposite', i.e. 'roasted'; cf. **G4**. 18–19 n.

8. **σεσάχθω:** 'let it have been stuffed' (perfect passive imperative < σάττω), so as to produce a sausage or haggis, as was more often done with stomachs or sow's wombs; cf. **G13**. 6 (hare-stomach sausage); and see Olson–Sens on Archestr. fr. 60. 7–8. For eating spleen (σπλήν), cf. Ar. fr. 520. 6. **νῆστις:** 'the jejunum' (a portion of the small intestine supposedly always

found empty, hence its name (literally 'fasting')), which ought also presumably to be stuffed, as at **G13**. 5.   **ἀπολεῖ μ(ε) οὑτοσί:** 'This guy will
be the death of me!' A colloquial expression of exasperation (cf. Ar. *Th.* 2;
Alex. fr. 177. 15; Men. *Mis.* 18; cf. **F16.** 1), addressed to the world at large
(i.e. to the audience in the theatre).

G11. A soliloquy by a self-congratulatory cook who has just prepared a
brilliant meal. Athenaeus preserves another fragment of a cook's speech at 7.
291d–f and attributes it to Philemo Junior (fr. 1), and Schweighäuser argued
that Philem. fr. 82 was probably part of the same speech and that *The Soldier*
ought therefore to be assigned to the younger Philemo rather than his father.
Philemo Junior was victorious six times at the City Dionysia (test. 2), but
only three fragments attributed specifically to him survive; and some of the
quotations assigned simply to 'Philemo' in ancient sources (and thus in
modern editions) are almost certainly his. Philem. fr. 82 and Philem. Jun. fr. 1
might thus easily belong to the same play (see 8 n.); but cooks' speeches are
so common that Schweighäuser's suggestion should be treated as merely an
interesting hypothesis. Line 20 suggests that the action was set somewhere
other than in Athens.

Lines 1–24 are preserved at Athenaeus 7. 288d–9a, in what begins as
a collection of literary references to eels (see 23 with n.) but turns into a
discussion of braggarts and especially braggart comic cooks that also includes
G12. (Athenaeus returns to eels at 7. 293e.) Lines 25–6 are preserved at
Athenaeus 7. 290a–b, after a digression on the boastful Syracusan physician
Menecrates, but are identified as having been spoken by 'the aforementioned
cook' and must belong to the same speech. There may nonetheless be a gap in
the text; see 25–6 n.

Iambic trimeter.

1–2. A parody of E. *Med.* 57–8 ὥσθ' ἵμερός μ' ὑπῆλθε γῆι τε κοὐρανῶι |
λέξαι μολούσηι δεῦρο δεσποίνης τύχας. For **γῆι τε κοὐρανῶι | λέξαι,**
cf. also **F16.** 9–10.

1. **ὡς** is exclamatory; 'what a desire . . .!'

2. **τὸ (ὄ)ψον ὡς ἐσκεύασα:** see **E31.** 9–10 n. (on fish as ὄψον); **F6.** 16–17 n.
(for the prolepsis); and cf. **G8.** 1.

3–4. **εὐημερεῖν | ἐν ἅπασιν:** 'to be successful in everything'.

4–5. **ἁπαλὸς κτλ.:** 'as tender as he was when I got him, that's how (tender) I've
served him'; cf. 7 with n.; **G12.** 8–9 with n. For παρατίθημι, see **G4.** 16 n.

5–6. **οὐ πεφαρμακευμένον | κτλ.:** 'not dosed with cheese or buried in herbs'.
Probably intended as implicit criticism of the Sicilian style of cooking;
cf. **G8.** 2 n.; Archestr. fr. 46. 13–15 (of Syracusan and Italian chefs) 'They
don't know how to prepare top-quality fish, but completely ruin them by

covering everything they cook with cheese and sprinkling it with liquid vinegar and silphium-flavoured broth'.

7.   The line repeats the boast in 4–5, but this time in order to introduce a description of the speaker's cooking technique (8–9) rather than his seasoning style (5–6).   **κ(αὶ ὀ)πτὸς ὤν** ('also when it was fried') is echoed in 9 ὀπτῶν τὸν ἰχθύν, as the speaker closes this portion of his remarks and moves on to his next subject.

8.   Cf. the orders a cook gives his assistants at Philem. Jun. fr. 1. 1–5 (see introductory n.): 'For the things that need to be roasted, just make the fire neither too high—because a fire of that sort doesn't roast something, it stews it—nor too hot—for this type, on the other hand, burns up whatever it touches and doesn't penetrate the meat!'   **ἔδωκα**: sc. 'to the fish' (which returns, however, in the accusative in 9).

9.   **ὀπτῶν τὸν ἰχθύν**: see 7 n.   **οὐδὲ πιστευθήσομαι** ('and I won't be believed') must originally have been followed by a line or lines containing words to the effect 'when I describe how the guests reacted to it'.

10–11.   'It was like when a bird snatches something too big to swallow at a gulp' (**B33**. 5 n.).

12.   **ἐσπούδακεν**: 'has done its best', i.e. 'has tried and failed'.

14–15.   **τὴν ἡδονὴν ... | τῆς λοπάδος**: 'the pleasure provided by the casserole-dish' (for which, see **G4**. 12 n.).

15.   **ἀνεπήδησε**: sc. from the couch on which he was reclining (see **A13**. 14 n.).   **κα(ὶ ἔ)φευγεν κύκλωι**: sc. around the inside of the circle of couches (see **G12**. 12 n.); an echo of 11 περιτρέχει κύκλωι. That the guest who has got hold of the casserole-dish behaves thus reflects his inability to swallow everything in it immediately, as he would like to do, a point that does not need to be made explicitly here since it was spelled out in the preceding description of the bird (11 τοῦ καταπιεῖν μεῖζόν τι, 12 καταπιεῖν δ' ἐσπούδακεν).

16.   **κατὰ πόδας**: 'in accord with his feet', i.e. 'in his tracks, close behind him'.

17.   **ἐξῆν ὀλολύζειν**: sc. μοι, 'I was able, had an occasion to give a cry of joy' (sc. at the success of his cooking; cf. 3–4); cf. Olson on Ar. *Pax* 96–7. For the postponement of **γάρ**, see Denniston 95–6.

17–18.   **οἱ δὲ πάντα** seems a bit illogical after **οἱ μὲν ἥρπασάν τι**, but presumably reflects the extreme compression of the narrative: as a general mêlée breaks out, everyone grabs whatever he can from the tables. In any case, the third element completes the set, 'something, nothing, everything'. ἥρπασαν recalls ἁρπάσηι in 10.

18.   **καίτοι**: 'but'; used here 'by a speaker in pulling himself up abruptly' (Denniston 557).   **παρέλαβον**: sc. from the man who was giving the party and had done the marketing, as in **G10**.

19. **ποταμίους ἐσθίοντας βόρβορον**: 'river-fish that eat muck', i.e. 'bottom-feeders', whose nasty diet affects the taste of their flesh.

20. **σκάρον**: 'a parrot wrasse'; see **A2**. 3 with n.

21. **γλαυκίσκον**: see **G10**. 1 n.　　**ὦ Ζεῦ σῶτερ**: The oath serves to underline the extraordinary quality of the γλαυκίσκος and the wonders the speaker might have been able to accomplish by cooking it (24). For the cult of Zeus the Saviour, see **I4**. 2 n.　　The **κάπρος** (literally 'boar') is an unidentified freshwater fish (despite the implication of the contrast with 19); see *Fishes*, 101–2; Andrews, *TAPA* 79 (1948), 232–53; Olson–Sens on Archestr. fr. 16. 2.

22–4.　Why Sicyon (a city on the Peloponnesian side of the eastern end of the Gulf of Corinth) is singled out for the epithet **φίλης** is unclear. Perhaps the point is simply that it furnishes good congers (22–3).　　For the idea of Poseidon carrying a conger eel (**γόγγρος**; see **G10**. 5 n.; similarly associated with Sicyon at Archestr. fr. 19. 1) to heaven for the gods to eat, cf. Archestr. fr. 5. 6–7, where Hermes is imagined visiting Lesbian Eresus to buy high-quality barley-groats for the Olympians' meals. The image of the gods dining on congers (22–3) sets up the speaker's assertion in 24 that any mortal who ate one he cooked would likewise become immortal.

25–6.　The lines have the same boastful tone as 1–24, but the thought does not follow neatly on the theoretical discussion in 20–4, and either the speaker has moved abruptly on to a new—if equally absurd—way of praising his own culinary abilities, or Athenaeus or his source omitted part of the text.

26.　**<μόνον>** is adverbial, 'only, merely'.

G12. A cook's description of his fast thinking in an emergency and its likely long-term professional benefits. Perhaps a soliloquy, like **G11**.

Preserved at Athenaeus 7. 292e–f, in a collection of literary references to braggarts and especially braggart comic cooks that also includes **G11** (where see introductory n.).

Iambic trimeter.

1–2.　**πρῶτον** is adverbial, 'first of all'.　　**ὠμῶν κειμένων | τῶν ἰχθύων**: 'while the fish were still lying there uncooked' (genitive absolute), i.e. 'before I had managed to get the main course under way'; cf. 3, 8–9. **οἱ κεκλημένοι**: 'the guests'; see **D3**. 6 n.

3.　Orders directed to the household's slaves by anonymous members of the company, who expect the meal to begin immediately.　　**δίδου κατὰ χειρός**: sc. ὕδωρ, as also at **G16**. 2. For κατὰ χειρός, see Slater, *Phoenix*, 43 (1989), 100–11, esp. 106–9. Slaves use a pitcher and basin to pour washing-water over diners' hands before meals already in Homer (e.g. *Od.* 1. 136–8);

cf. **B33**. 2; **H1**. 3 (before a symposium); Ar. *V.* 1216; fr. 516; Alex. fr. 263. 2. *τὸ (ὄ)ψον οἰχήσει λαβών*: 'Take the fish and get out of here!', i.e. 'Get the fish over to the cook and on the fire immediately!'; see **G3**. 3 n.

4–5. The speaker apparently intended to fry (*ὀπτάω*) the fish slowly over the coals. But now he is forced to move more rapidly than he had anticipated, and he displays his cleverness by sprinkling (*ἔρραν(α)* < *ῥαίνω*) oil on the coals, so as to produce a quick flame over which he can lightly stew (*ἕψω*) it (8–9) instead.   *πάντα* is adverbial, 'entirely, thoroughly' *vel sim.*

6. *ἐν ὧι*: sc. *χρόνωι*, 'while'.

6–7. *τὸ λάχανον αἵ τε τῶν παροψίδων* | *... δριμύτητες*: 'the vegetables (a collective singular; see **A1**. 3 n.) and the pungencies of the side-dishes', i.e. 'the pungent side-dishes', such as purse-tassel bulbs (see **G4**. 6 n.), silphium stalks (see **D1**. 4 n.), cheese (see **C6**. 7–9 n.), and olives (see **G16**. 3 n.), most of which were served cold (e.g. **G16**. 3–5; Nicostr. Com. fr. 1; Archestr. frr. 8–9 with Olson–Sens ad loc.; cf. **B39**. 2 with n.).

7. *τὸν ἄνδρα ... μου*: i.e. the speaker's employer, the host of the party.

8. *ἀποδίδωμ(ι)*: 'I deliver, hand over', sc. 'to him'.

8–9. *ἔχοντα τοὺς* | *χυμοὺς κτλ.*: 'having his juices in him'—i.e. 'as moist as when I got him'; cf. **G11**. 4–5, 7—'and a perfect brine sauce'. For stewing fish in brine sauce, in which diners could then dip bits of the meat (10 with n.), see e.g. **G10**. 1–2, 4–5; Ar. fr. 426; Antiph. fr. 221. 1–2; Sotad. Com. fr. 1. 9; Matro fr. 1. 77 with Olson–Sens ad loc.

10. For 'dipping' individual mouthfuls of food in cooking liquid or other sauces specifically produced for this purpose, see 8–9 n.; **B4**. 6 n.; **B33**. 9–10; **G10**. 4–5 n.; Cratin. fr. 150. 3–4 (brine sauce, vinegar-brine sauce, and garlic-brine sauce); Ar. fr. 158 (vinegar and dry salt); Archestr. fr. 23. 5–6 (marjoram and vinegar sauce) with Olson–Sens ad loc.   *πᾶς ἐλεύθερος*: in contrast to the slaves doing the serving; cf. 3 with n.; **C7** with introductory n. But the reference to the diners' social status is sufficiently gratuitous that it is tempting to think that this is a parody of a well-known tragic line, with *ἐμβάψαιτο* taking the place of some more elevated verb.

11. *ἐλαιδίου κοτύλης ... παραναλωμένης*: genitive absolute, 'with a single cup of olive oil wasted' (< *παραναλίσκω*), i.e. 'at the cost of a single cup of olive oil'.

12. *σέσωκ(α) ἐμοὶ κτλ.*: i.e. he has avoided getting a reputation for making a mess of things (cf. **G7**. 1–8 with nn.) and has thus saved the future commissions he might have lost, had he not thought and acted so quickly. *τρίκλινα*: A *τρίκλινον* is properly 'a room with three couches', i.e. with couches along three walls (for actual dining-rooms, see Dunbabin, in I. Nielsen and H. S. Nielsen (eds.), *Meals in a Social Context* (Aarhus

Studies in Mediterranean Antiquity: Aarhus and Oxford, 1998), 82–9),
and thus by metonymy 'a dinner party', as at Anaxandr. fr. 72. 1.
ἴσως modifies πεντήκοντ(α), 'perhaps fifty'.

G13. Part of an exotic banquet catalogue (mostly land-animals rather than
fish, discussion of which perhaps preceded; note 1 πρὸς τούτοισιν δέ, 'and in
addition to these things', which makes it clear that the fragment comes from
somewhere well into the speech; and cf. **G10**); perhaps spoken by a cook
advertising the menu he has planned or can produce if hired.

Preserved at Athenaeus 7. 330c, where the fragment caps the long
discussion of fish that takes up virtually the whole of Book 7.

Anapaestic dimeter; cf. **C6** introductory n.

1. παρέσται: see **H4.** 1 n.
2. θύννου τέμαχος: cf. **G10.** 6 with n.   κρέα δελφακίων: 'chunks of
   pork'; cf. **C9.** 6 n.; **G10.** 6–7. For eating pork, cf. **D1.** 9 n.; Ar. *Ach.* 795–6
   with Olson ad loc.; Pl. Com. fr. 27. 2–3 (of pigs) τὰ ... κρέα | ἥδιστ'
   ἔχουσιν ('they have the sweetest meat'); Alex. fr. 194; Olson on Ar. *Pax*
   24–5.
3–6. χορδαί ('sausages', also referred to as χόλικες, φύσκαι, and ἀλλᾶντες,
   although there must have been differences among these; cf. **B34.** 9) were
   made of intestinal casings stuffed with minced meat, blood, fat, spices, and
   the like (Ar. *Eq.* 160–1, 208, 213–16; *Pl.* 1168–9). Cf. Frost, *GRBS* 40 (1999),
   241–52.
4. ὄρχεις: 'testicles'. For eating testicles, see also Philippid. fr. 5.
5. νῆστις: see **G10.** 8 n.
6. κρανία ... ἀρνῶν: for eating goats' heads, cf. **I7.** 23–5 n.   γαστὴρ ...
   λαγώ: '(a sausage made of) a hare's stomach' (λαγώ is genitive singular of
   λαγώς). For eating hare, see **G5.** 9 n.
7. πνεύμων: 'a lung'; included in a catalogue of edible offal at Eub. fr. 23.

G14. Dinner parties were either organized as group efforts, with everyone
who attended (or at least everyone who was entitled to attend!; cf. **D12.** 6–9;
G15 with n.) making a cash contribution (4 συμβολαί; cf. **G15.** 2; Phryn. Com.
fr. 60; Men. fr. *673. 2; Dromo fr. 1. 5; Arnott on Alex. fr. 15) in advance, or
were paid for by one individual, who invited the other members of the party
to dine at his expense (cf. **D3**; **H20**), in which case the meal could be
described as ἀσύμβολον (as in **G15.** 2). The speaker is a parasite (see 1 n.;
A13 introductory n.).

Preserved at Athenaeus 6. 239a, as part of an extended discussion of the
history of the institution of parasitism that also includes **A13**; **C11**; **F11**.

Iambic trimeter.

1. **πρῶτος εὑρών:** The theme of the 'first inventor' of various institutions is common in comedy (e.g. Anaxandr. fr. 31; Alex. fr. 152; Men. fr. 18) and elsewhere; see Arnott on Alex. fr. 27. 1–2, and cf. **G15**; **I2**. 1–5.   **τ(ὰ) ἀλλότρια δειπνεῖν** ('to dine on someone else's food') and minor variants thereof are the standard comic shorthand description of the parasite's way of life (also Antiph. fr. 252. 2; Alex. fr. 213. 3; Nicol. Com. fr. 1. 16, 42; Timocl. fr. 31. 2–3; cf. **F13**. 3 with n.).

2. **δημοτικός:** 'well disposed towards the δῆμος', i.e. 'towards average people', who are too poor to pay for fine food, at least on an everyday basis. Cf. the very similar use of the adjective at Ar. *Nu.* 205; *Ec.* 411, 631; Philem. fr. 3. 3.

3–4. **ὅστις κτλ.** is a conditional relative clause, equivalent to 'If anyone . . . ' (Goodwin § 520–1).

4. **συμβολὰς ἐπράξατο:** 'assesses him συμβολαί' (see introductory n.; for πράττομαι in this sense, e.g. **G18**. 10; Ar. *Ach.* 1211; *Ra.* 561; Alex. fr. 265. 3), i.e. 'fails to treat him as a guest' (a gnomic aorist; see Goodwin § 154–5).

5. = adesp. tr. fr. 155. Anyone forced into exile from classical Athens on terms such as these would almost by definition be an enemy of the people rather than their friend (contrast 1–2). But as Hunter notes, the idea that this man will be forced to abandon his property 'would be of particular importance to a parasite, who would like the exile to leave behind all the supplies in his house' (sc. so that the parasite can consume them without interference).

G15. The parasite Chairephon (*PA* 15189) is mentioned repeatedly in late fourth- and third-century sources (e.g. Antiph. fr. 197. 3–4; Alex. fr. 213; Men. fr. 55; Nicostr. Com. fr. 26. 3 (apparently a character in the play); Matro fr. 1. 9 with Olson–Sens ad loc.; Macho 10–24).

Preserved at Athenaeus 4. 164f–5a, as part of one guest's denunciation of another who supposedly outdoes even Chairephon in going from one house to the next seeking out places where 'extraordinary dinners are being prepared'.

Iambic trimeter.

1–2. **ἀεί . . . τιν(α) εὑρίσκει τέχνην | καινήν:** see **G14**. 1 n.; and cf. Antiph. fr. 253 (of a parasite's existence; corrupt) 'What a wonderful life, in which I'm always obliged to find a new way to give my jaws something to chew!' **τὰ δείπν(α) ἀσύμβολα:** see **G14** introductory n.

3. For **ὁ κέραμος** ('the pottery', i.e. 'the cooking vessels') as a section of the Agora, see Diph. fr. 42. 28–31 (apparently identical with the place where cooks were hired; see **G7** introductory n.); and cf. **J1** introductory n.

μισθώσιμος: 'leased, rented out', by individuals too poor even to own their pots (contrast **G9**).

4.   *εὐθὺς ἐξ ἑωθινοῦ*: 'straightaway from dawn' (when the working-day began; e.g. Ar. *Av.* 488–92; *Pl.* 1120–2; Alex. fr. 78. 5; contrast **F11**. 8 with n.), i.e. 'first thing in the morning'.

5.   *μισθούμενον*: 'something being rented' (passive), sc. by a cook for a job he has got; scarcely 'someone hiring (a cook)' (middle; thus Arnott), since in that case there would be no reason to ask who was hosting the party (6–7).

6–7.   *τοῦ μαγείρου πυθόμενος | τὸν ἑστιῶντα*: 'after learning from the cook who is giving the dinner'.

7–8.   *τῆς θύρας χασμωμένης | ἂν ἐπιλάβηται*: 'if he catches the door' (sc. of the house where the meal is being held) 'yawning open'. *χασμάομαι* is not used elsewhere of an inanimate object, and serves to represent the open door as a sign of the carelessness (cf. Ar. *Eq.* 824) that makes the host an easy target.

8.   *πρῶτος εἰσελήλυθεν*: cf. **C11**. 2.

G16. The speaker is a glutton and most likely a parasite (see 1 n.; **A13** introductory n.), who somehow infiltrated a dinner party at which an extraordinary main dish (5–9) was served.

Preserved at Athenaeus 2. 59f–60b (manuscripts CE only), immediately after **F6** at the end of a collection of literary references to κολοκύνται ('gourds')—to which this fragment does not belong, unless something has been omitted from the text by the epitomator.

Iambic trimeter.

1.   *ἔλαθον γενόμενος*: 'I was there unnoticed', the implication being that the speaker was not invited but managed to join the party none the less, like Chairephon in **G15**.   *οὗ τὸ πρᾶγμ' ἠβούλετο* is difficult but is apparently to be taken 'where (the host) wished the affair' (i.e. the dinner party) 'to happen', with *γενέσθαι* to be supplied from *γενόμενος* in the first half of the line.

2.   *κατὰ χειρὸς ἐδόθη*: sc. ὕδωρ; see **G12**. 3 n.   *τὴν τράπεζαν ἧκ(ε) ἔχων*: sc. ὁ οἰκέτης. Meals were served on light, low tables, which were brought into the dining room already loaded with food (e.g. Eub. fr. 111. 3; Alex. fr. 89; cf. **A14** introductory n.; **E3**. 11; **G5**. 6), set before the individual couches (cf. 11–13, which make it clear that this table belonged to the speaker and his couch-mate alone), and carried out again at the end of the meal (see **H1**. 2 n.).

3.   *οὐ τυρὸς οὐδ(ε) ἐλαῶν γένη*: simple, inexpensive food of the sort peasants might eat; cf. **C6**. 7–9; **G1** with n.; Antiph. fr. 181. For different 'types of olives', see Olson–Sens on Archestr. fr. 8.

4–5. **παρέχουσαι κνῖσαν . . . πίονα:** 'supplying a rich smell', sc. and nothing
else. But the noun is elsewhere used specifically of the smell of roasting
meat (e.g. Ar. *Ach.* 1045; *Pax* 1050; Ephipp. fr. 3. 2; H. *Od.* 17. 270; E. *Alc.*
1156), which is not a **παροψίς** (see **G12**. 6–7 n.); so perhaps the point is that
the appetizers come to the table accompanied by the smell of the main
course (which is still being prepared) and are thus a great let-down.
καὶ λῆρος: 'and (similar) nonsense, rubbish'; cf. Olson–Sens on Archestr.
fr. 25. 1.

6. **ὑπερηφάνως:** 'magnificently, splendidly' *vel sim.*   **τῶν Ὡρῶν** is
dependent on **ὄζουσα** ('smelling of . . .'). The Seasons were goddesses of
natural growth, beauty, and fertility (see **B35**; Olson on Ar. *Pax* 456–7;
Gantz 53–4), and are referred to here as the givers of every sort of food in
its time. Cf. 7 n.

7. 'the half-sphere of the entire celestial vault' (explained in 8–10); in
apposition to λοπάς in 6. For πόλος in this sense, see e.g. Ar. *Av.* 179;
E. *Ion* 1154. For the Seasons (6 n.) as resident in 'heaven', see H. *Il.* 5.
749–50 = 8. 393–4.

8. 'for all the lovely things there' (i.e. in the sky) 'were in it' (i.e. the λοπάς).

9. **ἰχθῦς** alludes to the zodiacal sign Pisces; **σκορπίος** ('a bullhead'; see **G4**.
22 n.) to Scorpio; and **ἔριφοι** (see **G10**. 6–7 n.) to the non-zodiacal constel-
lation the Kids. For the zodiac, knowledge of which apparently reached
Greece in the sixth or fifth century, see also Sosip. fr. 1. 25–34 (a boastful
cook insists that his art requires knowledge of numerous aspects of
astronomy, including zodiacal signs, to ensure that foods are served in the
proper season).   **διέτρεχε:** 'was stretched out between' + genitive;
cf. Diph. fr. 120 (probably from a very similar passage) ὠιῶν δ' ἐν αὐτῆι
διέτρεχεν νεοττία.

10. **ὑπέφαινεν:** 'suggested'; the subject is **ὠιῶν ἡμίτομα**, 'sliced halves of
(hard-boiled) eggs'. For hard-boiled eggs eaten at dinner, see also Alex.
fr. 178. 10; and cf. **H4**. 4 n. (eggs eaten at symposia).

11. **ἐπεβάλομεν τὰς χεῖρας:** The Greeks did not normally use silverware or
individual plates, but ate with their hands (cf. **C12**; **G8**. 2–4 n.) from the
vessels in which the food was cooked and served (see **G8**. 3–4 n.; and
cf. **G17**. 4–5), although Hippolochus (ap. Ath. 4. 129c) mentions the
presence of spoons (μύστρια; see **J2**. 3 n.) at an extraordinarily
luxurious banquet given at the end of the fourth century. Handwashing
was therefore necessary not just before dinner (**G12**. 3 n.) but after it as
well (**H1**. 3).   **ὁ μὲν κτλ.:** i.e. the man with whom the speaker shared a
couch (which held two men lying next to one another on their left sides)
and a table (2 with n.).

12. **ἅμα καὶ διανεύων:** 'and simultaneously nodding his head (at me)', sc. in a friendly, animated fashion, as if the point of the party was to enjoy the company rather than to gobble down the food as aggressively as possible. Cf. **H9**. 8–10.   ἠσχολεῖτ(αι): 'was busy', with the participles defining what the subject was busy doing.

13. ἐπ(ὶ) ἐμὲ κατήντα: 'came down to me, devolved on me'.   τὸ πέρας is adverbial, 'to conclude, to cut a long story short'.   ἀνῆκ(α) is < ἀνίημι, 'leave off, relax'.

14. ὀρύττων 'digging (into)'.   ἀποδέδειχα κόσκινον: 'I had turned (it) into a sieve' (for which, see **J2**. 4 n.).

G17. A description of a mock-heroic challenge issued at a dinner party by the glutton Phoenicides (also mentioned at Antiph. frr. 50. 3; 188. 4).

Preserved at Athenaeus 8. 343b (manuscript A only), in a long collection of literary references (many from comedy) to ὀψοφάγοι.

Iambic trimeter.

1. ἐν πλήθει νέων: i.e. on one of the tables about which the company was reclining for dinner (see **G16**. 2 n.). But the words could also describe a group assembled in a wrestling school or the like (cf. **J12**), and the rest of the fragment plays on this ambiguity.

2. μεστὴν . . . Νηρείων τέκνων: 'full of the children of Nereus' (the Old Man of the Sea; cf. Alex. fr. 115. 1 with Arnott ad loc.; Hes. *Th.* 233–6 with West ad loc.), i.e. fish, shellfish, and the like. But there was also a well-known Chian cook named (or nicknamed) Nereus (Euphro fr. 1. 6; apparently the title character in plays by Anaxandrides (frr. 31–2) and Anaxilas (fr. 23)), which may be part of the joke.   ζέουσαν: 'boiling', and thus too hot for any normal person to eat from, setting up the challenge in 4–7.

3. ὀργῆι . . . ἠρεθισμένας: 'although they were stirred up with passion' (sc. for grabbing food; a more traditional hero would be eager for a fight). Cf. **C12**. 1–2, and the description of Corydos (6 n.) at Cratin. Jun. fr. 8. 4–5: 'he has a hand that is powerful, brazen, tireless, far stronger than fire itself'.

4. ἐκ κοινοῦ: 'in common, from a communal (cookpot)'; cf. **G16**. 11 n.

6. Three well-known late fourth-century gluttons. Corydos ('Lark'; his real name was Eucrates, *PAA* 437510) is mentioned also at Cratin. Jun. fr. 8; Alex. frr. 48. 2; 188. 3; 229. 1; Timocl. fr. 10. 4; Macho 1–5, where see Gow's n. For Phyromachus, see **F10**. 15–16 n. Neilus (*PAA* 705855) is mentioned also at Timocl. fr. 10. 4 (along with Corydos).   Νείλου βία: a mock-Homeric periphrasis (e.g. *Il.* 3. 105 Πριάμοιο βίην).

7. ἴτω πρὸς ἡμᾶς: 'Let him come face-to-face with us, confront us!' The use of the first-person plural for singular ἐμέ is a high-style affectation.   τάχ(α) ('perhaps') has a menacing tone; 'I rather suspect, I wouldn't be surprised if . . .'

G18. Athenaeus identifies Speaker A as συμβολάς τις ἀπαιτούμενος
('someone being asked to pay his share of the expenses', sc. for a dinner party
or symposium; see **G14** introductory n.), i.e. as he and Speaker B (who did
the purchasing) settle up accounts afterwards, the party having cost more
than anyone anticipated. Speaker A repeatedly expresses suspicion of Speaker
B (esp. 1–2), but his protests about prices are purely *pro forma* (esp. 13–14);
he knows that he and his companions asked for and consumed everything on
the list, and the problem is simply that, now that the fun is over, he is unhappy
about having to pay so much for what he none the less admits was a very
good time. Theophil. fr. 8, in which someone adds up the amount of food
consumed by an athlete, is similar. **G6** (where see introductory n.) is from the
same play.

Preserved at Athenaeus 3. 117e–18a (manuscript A only), in a collection of
literary references to saltfish (for which, see **D1**. 5 n.).

Iambic trimeter.

1.   **ἐὰν μὴ κτλ.:** 'unless you give me all the items individually', i.e. 'explain
them to me one by one'.
2.   One drachma contained 6 obols; 1 obol contained 8 **χαλκοῦς** ('coppers');
and 'a twelfth part of a χαλκοῦς' is thus an exceedingly small amount of
money.
3.   **ἀβάκιον ψῆφον:** Either A or B could speak these words, which must in any
case be orders addressed to the central stage-door, from which a mute slave
emerges carrying the items requested, which he hands to Speaker A. An
ἄβαξ (diminutive ἀβάκιον; cf. English 'abacus') was a ruled counting-
board on which pebbles (ψῆφοι) could be moved from one column to
another to perform simple mathematical functions (here addition,
although some counting-boards could handle multiplication and division
as well); cf. Ar. *V*. 656; Lang, *Hesperia*, 26 (1957), 275–82.
4–9.   The foods listed are all cold appetizers (for shellfish as appetizers, see
Alex. fr. 115. 1–4; Olson–Sens on Archestr. fr. 7) and relatively inexpensive;
contrast 15–16 with n. Line 7 implies that the items are mentioned in the
order they were served; but each is also more expensive than the next,
and Speaker A accordingly grows more and more unhappy as the scene
progresses.
4.   Exactly what **ὠμοτάριχος** ('raw saltfish'; also mentioned at Matro fr. 1.
17) was is unclear. For saltfish in general, see **D1**. 5 n.   **πέντε χαλκῶν:**
'for five coppers' (see 2 n.; genitive of price, as in 5, 6, 9, etc.).
5–6.   **μῦς:** 'mussels' (in banquet catalogues and the like at e.g. **A3**. 5; Philyll.
fr. 12. 2; Anaxandr. fr. 42. 61); see *Fishes*, 166–7; Olson–Sens on Archestr.
fr. 7. 1.   **οὐδὲν ἀσεβεῖς οὐδέπω:** i.e. 'you're not trying to cheat me yet'.

Religious language, like ἀγνεύεις ἔτι ('you're still keeping yourself pure'). τῶν ἐχίνων ὀβολός: 'An obol for the sea-urchins' (in banquet catalogues and the like at e.g. Alex. fr. 115. 3; Posidipp. fr. 15. 2); see *Fishes*, 70–3; Olson–Sens on Matro fr. 1. 18.

7. ἡ ῥάφανος: 'the cabbage', which was thought to prevent hangovers (Nicoch. fr. 18; Anaxandr. fr. 59; Eub. fr. 124; Alex. fr. 287) and was therefore an important part of the menu at a party where serious drinking was anticipated (cf. 18–19).   ἦν ἐβοᾶτε 'which you kept shouting for', sc. by crying 'Cabbage! (More) cabbage!'

9. γάρ is assentient (Denniston 87–8), 'it's true' (sc. that it was expensive; cf. 8), 'so . . .'   τὸ κύβιον: 'the cubed saltfish' (cf. 4 n.); also mentioned at Posidipp. fr. 17.

10 is incurably corrupt. οὐκ ἐπράξατ(ο) οὐδὲ ἕν; is 'Didn't he charge you anything?' (see **G14**. 4 n.), and the reference to λάχανα in 11–12 suggests that † ονεῖλκε χειρῶν γε † conceals the name of a herb such as coriander (Anaxandr. fr. 51. 2), which was eaten with saltfish (9 with n.) and was sometimes thrown in by the vendor (cf. Ar. *V.* 496), although in this case it was not. But Speaker B ought then to provide a separate price for the item, whereas 13 implies that it was included in (and contributed to) the high price of the κύβιον. Desrousseaux's ingenious ὅ γ' εἷλκε ('(Which is) what it weighed!', the point being that the κύβιον literally cost its weight in silver) may be right. But if so, it leaves too little space to get the sense needed out of what remains in the text, and a line must have dropped out.

11. οἶσθας: a hybrid form (elsewhere in comedy at e.g. **H17**. 5; Cratin. fr. 112; Men. *Epitr.* 481) produced via confusion of οἶδας and οἶσθα. See Arnott, in Willi (2002), 203–4.   ὦ μακάριε: a polite but exasperated form of address, as at Men. *Dysc.* 103; Diph. fr. 4. 1; adesp. com. fr. 1017. 64.

12. τρωξαλλίδες: probably 'crickets'; see Davies and Kathirithamby 147–8; Beavis 78–80.

14. ὁ ταριχοπώλης ἐστίν: sc. 'who's responsible for this'. For saltfish-vendors, see also Nicostr. Com. fr. 5. 3–4; Pl. *Chrm.* 163b; Thphr. *Char.* 6. 9; and cf. **J2** introductory n.

15–16. The lines describe the main items on the menu (contrast 4–9 with n.). The conger eel (see **G10**. 5 n.) in particular is more expensive than everything that has preceded it combined—but apparently no more expensive than it ought to be, given Speaker A's calm reaction (οὐχὶ πολλοῦ, 'That's not much') after he learns what it cost.   τὸν ὀπτὸν ἰχθύν: for purchasing meat already roasted or fried (which would raise the price, as apparently here), cf. Alex. fr. 27. 7 (liver); Philem. fr. 83 (fish). παπαῖ: 'Damn!'; a colloquial expression of surprise and grief (e.g. Ar. *Lys.* 215; Anaxipp. fr. *1. 22); see López Eire 89; Labiano Ilundain 276–8.

17.   **ἀνῆκεν:** sc. '(the price of) the baked/fried fish' (as subject).

18.   **προσέλαβον:** 'I bought in addition', sc. 'to what I purchased beforehand, which was now gone'.

19.   **χοᾶς τρεῖς, δέκ(α) ὀβολῶν ὁ χοῦς:** 'three *choes*, at ten obols a *chous*'. A *chous* (literally 'pitcher' (**B4**. 3 n.); = 12 *kotyloi*) contained about 3.2 litres, making this a substantial quantity of (quite expensive) wine; contrast **J10**. 4–5.

Section H

Wine and Symposia

H1. Plato Comicus fr. 71, from *Spartans or Poets* (V/IV)

(*A*.) ἄνδρες δεδειπνήκασιν ἤδη; (*B*.) σχεδὸν ἅπαντες. (*A*.) εὖ γε·
τί οὐ τρέχων <σὺ> τὰς τραπέζας ἐκφέρεις; ἐγὼ δὲ
νίπτρον παραχέων ἔρχομαι. (*B*.) κἀγὼ δὲ παρακορήσων.
(*A*.) σπονδὰς δ’ ἔπειτα παραχέας τὸν κότταβον παροίσω.
τῆι παιδὶ τοὺς αὐλοὺς ἐχρῆν ἤδη πρὸ χειρὸς εἶναι   5
καὶ προαναφυσᾶν. τὸ μύρον ἤδη παραχέω βαδίζων
Αἰγύπτιον κἀιτ’ ἴρινον· στέφανον δ’ ἔπειθ’ ἑκάστωι
δώσω φέρων τῶν ξυμποτῶν. νεοκρᾶτά τις ποείτω.
(*B*.) καὶ δὴ κέκραται. (*A*.) τὸν λιβανωτὸν ἐπιτιθεὶς † εἶπε
  *   *   *
σπονδὴ μὲν ἤδη γέγονε καὶ πίνοντές εἰσι πόρρω,   10
καὶ σκύλιον ἧισται, κότταβος δ’ ἐξοίχεται θύραζε.
αὐλοὺς δ’ ἔχουσά τις κορίσκη Καρικὸν μέλος <τι>
μελίζεται τοῖς συμπόταις, κἄλλην τρίγωνον εἶδον
ἔχουσαν, εἶτ’ ἦιδεν πρὸς αὐτὸ μέλος Ἰωνικόν τι

2 <σὺ> Musurus   3 νίπτρον Casaubon: λίτρον Ath.^A   παραχέων ἔρχομαι Hermann:
παραχέων εἰσέρχομαι Ath.^A: παρέχων εἰσέρχομαι Jacobs   5 πρὸ χειρὸς Hermann:
προχείρους Ath.^A   6 προαναφυσᾶν Cobet: προσαναφυσᾶν Ath.^A   παραχέω βαδίζων
Kaibel: παραχέων βαδίζων Ath.^A: παραχέων βαδίζω Bergk   10 μὲν Schweighäuser: με Ath.^A
εἰσι Porson: ἤδη Ath.^A   12 <τι> Hermann   13 κἄλλην Schweighäuser: καλὴν Ath.^A
14 αὐτὸ] αὐτὸν West

H2. Nicostratus Comicus fr. 27, from *Falsely Tattooed* (IV)

              καὶ σὺ μὲν
τὴν δευτέραν τράπεζαν εὐτρεπῆ πόει,
κόσμησον αὐτὴν παντοδαποῖς τραγήμασιν,
μύρον στεφάνους λιβανωτὸν αὐλητρίδα λαβέ.

H3. Clearchus Comicus fr. 4, from *Pandrosus* (IV)

(Α.) λάβ᾽ ὕδωρ κατὰ χειρός. (Β.) μηδαμῶς· καλῶς ἔχει.
(Α.) λάβ᾽ ὦγάθ᾽· οὐδὲν χεῖρον. <ἡ> παῖς, ἐπιτίθει
ἐπὶ τὴν τράπεζαν κάρυα καὶ τραγήματα

2 <ἡ> Dobree

H4. Ephippus fr. 8, from *Ephebes* (IV)

χόνδρος μετὰ ταῦτ᾽ εἰσῆλθε, μύρον Αἰγύπτιον,
Φοινικικοῦ βῖκός τις ὑπανεῴγνυτο,
ἴτρια τραγήμαθ᾽ ἧκε, πυραμοῦς ἄμης
ᾠῶν ἑκατόμβη. πάντα ταῦτ᾽ ἐχναύομεν.
ἐμασώμεθ᾽ οὕτως ἀνδρικῶς ὅσ᾽ εἴχομεν·   5
καὶ γὰρ παραμασύντας τινὰς παραβόσκομεν

1 ταῦτ᾽ εἰσῆλθε Jacobs: τ᾽ εἰσῆλθεν Ath. (1)^A   2 Φοινικικοῦ Casaubon: φοινικίνου Ath.
(2)^CE: φοινικου Ath. (1)^A   3 τραγήμαθ᾽ ἧκε Porson: τραγήματα θῆκε Ath. (1)^A: τραγήματα
Ath. (3)^CE

H5. Diphilus fr. 70, from *Sappho* (IV/III)

Ἀρχίλοχε, δέξαι τήνδε τὴν μετανιπτρίδα
μεστὴν Διὸς σωτῆρος, Ἀγαθοῦ Δαίμονος

H6. Antiphanes fr. 172. 1–4, from *Women Who Looked Like Each Other* or
Men Who Looked Like Each Other (IV)

ὡς δ᾽ ἐδείπνησαν (συνάψαι βούλομαι γὰρ τἀν μέσωι)
καὶ Διὸς σωτῆρος ἧλθε Θηρίκλειον ὄργανον,
τῆς τρυφερᾶς ἀπὸ Λέσβου σεμνογόνου σταγόνος
πλῆρες, ἀφρίζον, ἕκαστος δεξιτερᾶι δ᾽ ἔλαβεν

3 σεμνογόνου Kaibel: σεμνοπόνου Ath.^ACE: σεμνοπότου Casaubon

H7. Philyllius fr. 23, from an unidentified play (V/IV)

                    παρέξω Λέσβιον
Χῖον σαπρὸν Θάσιον ∪ – × Βίβλινον,
Μενδαῖον, ὥστε μηδένα κραιπαλᾶν

1 <οἶνον> παρέξω Kock

H8. Hermippus fr. *77, perhaps from *Porters* (late 430s/early 420s BC)

† Μενδαίω μὲν ἐνουροῦσι καὶ † θεοὶ αὐτοὶ
στρώμασιν ἐν μαλακοῖς. Μάγνητα δὲ μειλιχόδωρον
καὶ Θάσιον, τῶι δὴ μήλων ἐπιδέδρομεν ὀδμή,
τοῦτον ἐγὼ κρίνω πολὺ πάντων εἶναι ἄριστον
τῶν ἄλλων οἴνων μετ' ἀμύμονα Χῖον ἄλυπον.   5
ἔστι δέ τις οἶνος, τὸν δὴ σαπρίαν καλέουσιν,
οὗ καὶ ἀπὸ στόματος στάμνων ὑπανοιγομενάων
ὄζει ἴων, ὄζει δὲ ῥόδων, ὄζει δ' ὑακίνθου
ὀδμὴ θεσπεσία, κατὰ πᾶν δ' ἔχει ὑψερεφὲς δῶ,
ἀμβροσία καὶ νέκταρ ὁμοῦ. τοῦτ' ἔστι τὸ νέκταρ,   10
τούτου χρὴ παρέχειν πίνειν ἐν δαιτὶ θαλείηι
τοῖσιν ἐμοῖσι φίλοις, τοῖς δ' ἐχθροῖς ἐκ Πεπαρήθου

1 sic Ath.^C: Μενδαίω δὲ μὲν ἐνορούσι καὶ Ath.^E: Μενδαῖον μέν, <ἐφ' ὧι> καὶ ἐνουροῦσιν Bergk:
Μενδαῖον, <τοῦ> μὲν καὶ ἐνουροῦσιν Hermann   2 μειλιχόδωρον Musurus: μειλιχο^δρ' Ath.^CE
6 τὸν Dindorf: ὃν Ath.^CE   7 ὑπανοιγομενάων Casaubon: ἀνοιγομένων Ath.^CE
9 ὀδμὴ Dindorf (cf. 3): ὀσμὴ Ath.^CE   10 τὸ νέκταρ] τὸ πῶμα Meineke: τὸ νᾶμα Kock
11 χρὴ παρέχειν Musurus: χρὴ παρέχειν ἀεὶ Ath.^CE: ἀεὶ παρέχειν Bothe   δαιτὶ θαλείηι Dindorf:
τῇ θαλεία Ath.^CE

H9. Alexis fr. 9, from *Aesop* (IV/III)

(Α.) κομψόν γε τοῦτ' ἐστὶν παρ' ὑμῖν, ὦ Σόλων,
ἐν ταῖς Ἀθήναις, δεξιῶς θ' εὑρημένον.
(Σο.) τὸ ποῖον; (Α.) ἐν τοῖς συμποσίοις οὐ πίνετε
ἄκρατον. (Σο.) οὐ γὰρ ῥάιδιον· πωλοῦσι γὰρ
ἐν ταῖς ἁμάξαις εὐθέως κεκραμένον,   5
οὐχ ἵνα τι κερδαίνωσι, τῶν δ' ὠνουμένων
προνοούμενοι τοῦ τὰς κεφαλὰς ὑγιεῖς ἔχειν
ἐκ κραιπάλης. τοῦτ' ἔσθ', ὁρᾶις, Ἑλληνικὸς
πότος, μετρίοισι χρωμένους ποτηρίοις
λαλεῖν τι καὶ ληρεῖν πρὸς αὑτοὺς ἡδέως·   10
τὸ μὲν γὰρ ἕτερον λουτρόν ἐστιν, οὐ πότος,
ψυκτῆρι πίνειν καὶ κάδοις. (Α.) θάνατος μὲν οὖν.

3 πίνετε Musurus: πίνεται Ath.^A: πίνετ' Ath.^CE

H10. Pherecrates fr. 76, from *Corianno* (V)

(Α.) ἄποτος, ὦ Γλύκη.

(Γλ.) ὑδαρῆ 'νέχεέν σοι; (Α.) παντάπασι μὲν οὖν ὕδωρ.
(Γλ.) τί ἠργάσω; πῶς ὦ κατάρατε <δ'> ἐνέχεας;
(Β.) δύ' ὕδατος, ὦ μάμμη— (Γλ.) τί δ' οἴνου; (Β.) τέτταρας.
(Γλ.) ἔρρ' ἐς κόρακας. βατράχοισιν οἰνοχοεῖν σ' ἔδει.   5

1–2 σοι om. Ath.^{CE}   1 ἄποτος Meineke: ἄποτες Ath.^A   2 ὑδαρῆ 'νέχεέν Erfurdt:
ὑδαρην ἐνέχεεν Ath.^A   3 <δ'> Meineke

H11. Anaxandrides fr. 1, from *Rustics* (IV)

(Α.) τίνα δὴ παρεσκευασμένοι

πίνειν τρόπον νῦν ἐστε; λέγετε. (Β.) τίνα τρόπον
ἡμεῖς; τοιοῦτον οἷον ἂν καὶ σοὶ δοκῆι.
(Α.) βούλεσθε δήπου τὸν ἐπιδέξι', ὦ πάτερ,
λέγειν ἐπὶ τῶι πίνοντι; (Β.) τὸν ἐπιδέξια   5
λέγειν; Ἄπολλον, ὥσπερ ἐπὶ τεθνηκότι;

2 νῦν ἐστε Meineke: ἐστὲ νῦνὶ Ath.^A   6 ὥσπερ ἐπὶ Schweighäuser: ὡσπερεὶ Ath.^A

H12. Alexis fr. 21, from *The Man Who Was Mutilated* (IV/III)

οὐ συμποσίαρχος ἦν γάρ, ἀλλὰ δήμιος
ὁ Χαιρέας, κυάθους προπίνων εἴκοσιν

H13. Antiphanes fr. 57, from *The Birth of Aphrodite* (IV)

(Α.) τονδὶ λέγω, σὺ δ' οὐ συνιεῖς; κότταβος
τὸ λυχνεῖόν ἐστι. πρόσεχε τὸν νοῦν· ὠιὰ μὲν
× – ∪ – × πέντε νικητήριον.
(Β.) περὶ τοῦ; γελοῖον. κοτταβιεῖτε τίνα τρόπον;
(Α.) ἐγὼ διδάξω· καθ' ὅσον ἂν τὸν κότταβον   5
ἀφεὶς ἐπὶ τὴν πλάστιγγα ποιήσηι πεσεῖν—
(Β.) πλάστιγγα; ποίαν; (Β.) τοῦτο τοὐπικείμενον
ἄνω τὸ μικρόν. (Β.) τὸ πινακίσκιον λέγεις;
(Α.) τοῦτ' ἔστι πλάστιγξ, οὗτος ὁ κρατῶν γίγνεται.
(Β.) πῶς δ' εἴσεταί τις τοῦτ'; (Α.) ἐὰν θίγηι μόνον   10
αὐτῆς, ἐπὶ τὸν μάνην πεσεῖται καὶ ψόφος
ἔσται πάνυ πολύς. (Β.) πρὸς θεῶν, τῶι κοττάβωι
πρόσεστι καὶ Μάνης τις ὥσπερ οἰκέτης;

*   *   *

ὧι δεῖ λαβὼν τὸ ποτήριον δεῖξον νόμωι.
(Α.) αὐλητικῶς δεῖ καρκινοῦν τοὺς δακτύλους   15
οἶνόν τε μικρὸν ἐγχέαι καὶ μὴ πολύν·
ἔπειτ' ἀφήσεις. (Β.) τίνα τρόπον; (Α.) δεῦρο βλέπε·
τοιοῦτον. (Β.) <ὦ> Πόσειδον, ὡς ὑψοῦ σφόδρα.
(Α.) οὕτω ποήσεις. (Β.) ἀλλ' ἐγὼ μὲν σφενδόνηι
οὐκ ἂν ἐφικοίμην αὐτόσ'. (Α.) ἀλλὰ μάνθανε   20

5 διδάξω Ath. (1)^ACE: ἐπιδείξω Ath. (3)^A   10 θίγηι Jacobs: τύχηι vel sim. Ath.
(1)^ACE, (3)^A Σ Luc.   18 <ὦ> Musurus

H14. Plato Comicus fr. 46, from *Zeus Abused* (V/IV)

(Α.) πρὸς κότταβον παίζειν, ἕως ἂν σφῶιν ἐγὼ
τὸ δεῖπνον ἔνδον σκευάσω. (Ηρ.) πάνυ βούλομαι.
ἀγὼν ἐμός ἐστ'. (Α.) ἀλλ' ἐς θυείαν παιστέον.
(Ηρ.) φέρε τὴν θυείαν, αἶρ' ὕδωρ, ποτήρια
παράθετε. παίζωμεν δὲ περὶ φιλημάτων.   5
(Α.) <   > ἀγεννῶς οὐκ ἐῶ
παίζειν. τίθημι κοττάβεια σφῶιν ἐγὼ
ταυδί τε ᾽ὰς κρηπῖδας, ἃς αὕτη φορεῖ,
καὶ τὸν κότυλον τὸν σόν. (Ηρ.) βαβαιάξ· οὑτοσὶ
μείζων ἀγὼν τῆς Ἰσθμιάδος ἐπέρχεται   10

2 ἔνδον Dindorf: ὃν ἐν Ath.^A   3 ἀγὼν ἐμός ἐστ' Kaibel: αλλα νεμος εστ Ath.^A   8 τε
Elmsley: γε Ath.^A   9 οὑτοσὶ Casaubon: ουτοισι Ath.^A   10 μείζων ἀγὼν τῆς
Casaubon: μιζωνι αγωνιστὴς Ath.^A

H15. Antiphanes fr. 85, from *Men Who Were Twice as Big* (IV)

(Α.) τί οὖν ἐνέσται τοῖς θεοῖσιν; (Β.) οὐδὲ ἕν,
ἂν μὴ κεράσηι τις. (Α.) ἴσχε, τὸν ὠιδὸν λάμβανε.
ἔπειτα μηδὲν τῶν ἀπηρχαιωμένων
τούτων περάνηις, τὸν Τελαμῶνα, μηδὲ τὸν
Παιῶνα, μηδ' Ἁρμόδιον   5

H16. Aristophanes fr. 444, from *Storks* (390s BC?)

ὁ μὲν ἦιδεν Ἀδμήτου λόγον πρὸς μυρρίνην,
ὁ δ' αὐτὸν ἠνάγκαζεν Ἁρμοδίου μέλος

H17. Philemo fr. 45, from *The Seducer* (IV/III)

(Α.) ἔδει παρεῖναι, Παρμένων, αὐλητρίδ᾽ ἢ
ναβλᾶν τιν᾽. (Πα.) ὁ δὲ ναβλᾶς τί ἐστιν; – ∪ –
(Α.) × – ∪ – οὐκ οἶδας, ἐμβρόντητε σύ;
(Πα.) μὰ Δία. (Α.) τί φήις; οὐκ οἶσθα ναβλᾶν; οὐδὲν οὖν
οἶσθας ἀγαθὸν σύ <γ᾽>· οὐδὲ σαμβυκίστριαν;   5

H18. Eubulus fr. *93, probably from *Semele or Dionysus* (IV)

τρεῖς γὰρ μόνους κρατῆρας ἐγκεραννύω
τοῖς εὖ φρονοῦσι· τὸν μὲν ὑγιείας ἕνα,
ὃν πρῶτον ἐκπίνουσι, τὸν δὲ δεύτερον
ἔρωτος ἡδονῆς τε, τὸν τρίτον δ᾽ ὕπνου,
ὃν ἐκπιόντες οἱ σοφοὶ κεκλημένοι   5
οἴκαδε βαδίζουσ᾽. ὁ δὲ τέταρτος οὐκέτι
ἡμέτερός ἐστ᾽, ἀλλ᾽ ὕβρεος· ὁ δὲ πέμπτος βοῆς·
ἕκτος δὲ κώμων· ἕβδομος δ᾽ ὑπωπίων·
<ὁ δ᾽> ὄγδοος κλητῆρος· ὁ δ᾽ ἔνατος χολῆς·
δέκατος δὲ μανίας, ὥστε καὶ βάλλειν ποεῖ   10
          *   *   *
πολὺς γὰρ εἰς ἓν μικρὸν ἀγγεῖον χυθεὶς
ὑποσκελίζει ῥᾶιστα τοὺς πεπωκότας

   9 <ὁ δ᾽> Casaubon   inter 10 et 11 lac. indic. Kassel

H19. Alexis fr. 160, from *Odysseus Weaving* (IV/III)

             (Α.) φιλεῖ γὰρ ἡ μακρὰ συνουσία
καὶ τὰ συμπόσια τὰ πολλὰ καὶ καθ᾽ ἡμέραν ποεῖν
σκῶψιν, ἡ σκῶψις δὲ λυπεῖ πλεῖον ἢ τέρπει πολύ.
τοῦ κακῶς λέγειν γὰρ ἀρχὴ γίγνετ᾽. ἂν δ᾽ εἴπηις ἅπαξ,
εὐθὺς ἀντήκουσας· ἤδη λοιδορεῖσθαι λείπεται,   5
εἶτα τύπτεσθαι δέδεικται καὶ παροινεῖν. (Β.) ταῦτα γὰρ
κατὰ φύσιν πέφυκεν οὕτως· καὶ τί μάντεως ἔδει;

   4 ἂν] ἂν Valckenaer   7 τί μάντεως Canter: τιμᾶν τέως Ath.ᴬ: vers. om. Ath.ᶜᴱ

H20. Pherecrates fr. 162, from *Cheiron* (V)

μηδὲ σύ γ᾽ ἄνδρα φίλον καλέσας ἐπὶ δαῖτα θάλειαν
ἄχθου ὁρῶν παρεόντα· κακὸς γὰρ ἀνὴρ τόδε ῥέζει.

ἀλλὰ μάλ᾽ εὔκηλος τέρπου φρένα τέρπε τ᾽ ἐκεῖνον
          *   *   *

ἡμῶν δ᾽ ἤν τινά τις καλέσηι θύων ἐπὶ δεῖπνον,
ἀχθόμεθ᾽ ἢν ἔλθηι καὶ ὑποβλέπομεν παρεόντα   5
χὥττι τάχιστα θύραζ᾽ ἐξελθεῖν βουλόμεθ᾽ αὐτόν.
εἶτα γνούς πως τοῦθ᾽ ὑποδεῖται, κἆιτά τις εἶπε
τῶν ξυμπινόντων "ἤδη σύ; τί οὐχ ὑποπίνεις;
οὐχ ὑπολύσεις αὐτόν;" ὁ δ᾽ ἄχθεται αὐτὸς ὁ θύων
τῶι κατακωλύοντι καὶ εὐθὺς ἔλεξ᾽ ἐλεγεῖα·   10
"μηδένα μήτ᾽ ἀέκοντα μένειν κατέρυκε παρ᾽ ἡμῖν
μήθ᾽ εὕδοντ᾽ ἐπέγειρε, Σιμωνίδη." οὐ γὰρ ἐπ᾽ οἴνοις
τοιαυτὶ λέγομεν δειπνίζοντες φίλον ἄνδρα;

6 θύραζ᾽ Cobet: θύρας Ath.ᴬ   7 ὑποδεῖται Musurus: ὑποδειταν Ath.ᴬ   11 ἀέκοντα
. . . κατέρυκε Theognis: ἄκοντα . . . κατερύκει Ath.ᴬ

COMMENTARY

H1–H20. For drinking and drinking parties (a particularly common theme in 'Middle Comedy') and their significance, see in general Lissarrague; O. Murray (ed.), *Sympotica: A Symposium on the Symposion* (Oxford and New York, 1990); E. L. Bowie, in O. Murray and M. Tecusan (eds.), *In Vino Veritas* (London, 1995), 113–25 (on wine and drinking in 'Old Comedy'); Davidson 36–69; A. M. Bowie, *JHS* 117 (1997), 1–21 (on the symposium in Aristophanes); Pütz; and cf. **C7**; **C8**. 4–5; **E7**.

H1. Two (or perhaps three) slaves are discussing their responsibilities in regard to a banquet taking place offstage which is about to enter the symposium phase. Cf. **H17**. Speaker A is in charge, while Speaker B (who has just returned from the dining room) is his subordinate. Both men exit at some point after 9; after they return, one of them reports on the progress of the drinking party. Lines 1–9 are connected to 10–14 in Athenaeus by the words εἶτ' ἐπάγει ('then [the poet] continues'), and it is impossible to know how much is missing from the text.

Preserved at Athenaeus 15. 665b–d (manuscript A only), as part of the introduction to the long discussion of items associated with symposia that makes up the bulk of what is preserved of Book 15 and also includes **H2**; **H13–H14**.

Iambic tetrameter catalectic.

1. **δεδειπνήκασιν ἤδη;**: 'have they finished dinner now?' For this use of ἤδη, cf. 6, 10.   **εὖ γε**: sc. ποιήσαντες (e.g. Ar. *Pax* 285), 'Good for them!, Bravo!'
2. **τί οὐ ... ἐκφέρεις;** is a passionate exhortation equivalent to an imperative (Gildersleeve § 198).   **τὰς τραπέζας**: i.e. those on which the dinner was served (**G16**. 2 n.), which are now to be cleared from the dining room (e.g. Philyll. fr. 3. 1–2; Antiph. fr. 280; Dromo fr. 2. 2) and brought back, loaded with symposium-goods, as the 'second tables' (cf. **H2**; **H4**; Pherecr. fr. 73. 3; Anaxandr. fr. 2; Olson on Ar. *Pax* 771–2).
3. **νίπτρον**: 'washing-water' (cognate with νίζω) to clean the guests' hands after dinner (cf. **G12**. 3 n.; **G16**. 11 n.), as at **H3**. 1–2; Philyll. fr. 3. 3; Antiph. fr. 280; Dromo fr. 2. 2–3; Achae. *TrGF* 20 F 17. 4–5.   **παραχέων** is a future (not present) active participle, 'in order to pour ... for them'. Cf. 6. **παρακορήσων**: sc. ἔρχομαι, 'I'll (go) to sweep up', since bones, stems, shells, and the like were routinely thrown on the floor during meals. Cf. Eup. fr. 167; Philyll. fr. 3. 2 (in a catalogue of tasks from a discussion

apparently very similar to this one); Matro fr. 1. 18–20 with Olson–Sens on 19–20; Olson on Ar. *Pax* 58–9.

4. σπονδὰς ... παραχέας: 'after pouring libations for (the guests)' (cf. 3, 6), sc. into their cups, so that they can empty them onto the floor before the drinking begins; cf. 10; Antiph. fr. 150. 3; Alex. fr. 252. 2–3; Men. fr. 209. 2. τὸν κότταβον: a drinking game (see **H13–H14** with **H13** introductory n.), with the word used by extension here of the equipment required for it, as also in 11; **H13**. 1–2.

5–6. τῆι παιδί: 'the slave-girl', who is to provide musical entertainment; referred to again in 12–13 (see 12–14 n.). For αὐλός-girls and the like at symposia, e.g. **H2**. 4; **H18**. 4 n.; Ar. *V.* 1368–9; Metag. fr. 4; Antiph. fr. 224. 1–2; Amphis fr. 9. 4.   The use of the imperfect ἐχρῆν indicates that, although the αὐλούς ought by now to be ready at hand (πρὸ χειρὸς εἶναι) for the musician, and although she ought even to be practising her playing (καὶ προαναφυσᾶν, with τὴν παῖδα to be supplied as the subject of the infinitive), none of this has been done—which is to say that Speaker B is being given an indirect order to get these matters taken care of; cf. 8 n.; **B32**. 8 n. For the αὐλός (a reed-instrument routinely played in pairs, as here, with the aid of a halter (φορβειά)), see *AGM* 81–107; Bundrick 34–42; and cf. **H13**. 15 (referring to how the musician's hands must be curled around the instrument).   τὸ μύρον: 'the perfume', with which the guests will anoint themselves; see Olson–Sens on Archestr. fr. 60. 3; Pütz 264–78. Included in catalogues of symposium-goods and the like at e.g. **II2**. 4; **H4**. 1; Ar. *Ach.* 1091; Philyll. fr. 3. 3; Amphis fr. 9. 4; cf. **C3**. 5–6. ἤδη: 'now' (cf. 1 n.), i.e. after the jobs described in 4 are done. παραχέω is future (not present); cf. 3.

7. Αἰγύπτιον κα(ὶ ε)ἶτ(α) ἴρινον: '(first) the Egyptian variety'—also referred to at **H4**. 1; Dexicr. fr. 1 (mentioned along with getting drunk and 'drinking snow', for which see Stratt. fr. 60)—'and then the type scented with iris root' (also mentioned at Cephisod. fr. 3. 2; Alex. fr. 63. 8; Matro fr. 1. 106 with Olson–Sens ad loc.).   στέφανον: for wearing garlands of flowers at symposia, e.g. **H2**. 4; Cratin. fr. 105; Pherecr. fr. 134; Ar. *Ach.* 1091; *Ec.* 131–2; Antiph. fr. 238. 2; and cf. **E6** n. (on wearing ribbons).

8. νεοκρᾶτά τις ποιείτω: sc. οἶνον, 'Let someone produce some newly mixed (wine)!', i.e. 'mix up a fresh batch of wine' with water in a *kratêr*; cf. **H9** introductory n.; **H18**; Richter–Milne 6–8. Orders to anonymous slaves within the house are often expressed thus (cf. **C8**. 7–8 with n.). But the words are probably intended for Speaker B (who has in any case anticipated them (9)); cf. 5–6 n.

9. καὶ δή: 'indeed!, in fact!', with -κρᾶτα (cognate with κεράννυμι) in the command in 8 echoed in κέκραται (see Denniston 251–2).   τὸν

λιβανωτόν: 'the frankincense', which is to be placed upon (*ἐπιτιθείς*) a brazier and burned (e.g. Alex. fr. 252. 3 with Arnott ad loc.; Nicostr. Com. fr. 27. 4; Archestr. fr. 60. 4–5 with Olson–Sens ad loc.; cf. **A20**. 12 with n.; **D1**. 13 with n.; **H2**. 4; **J1**. 3 with n.).

10.   *πίνοντές εἰσι πόρρω*: 'they're far on drinking, well into their drinking'; cf. Pl. *Smp*. 176d *πόρρω . . . πιεῖν*.

11.   *σκόλιον ᾖσται*: 'a *skolion* has been sung' (< *ᾄδω* = *ἀείδω*). *Skolia* were traditional, generally moralizing or patriotic songs commonly sung at symposia (esp. Ar. *V*. 1222–49); cf. **D13**. 1–2 n.; **H15–H16** with nn. The surviving examples are collected at *PMG* 884–917.   *κότταβος ἐξοίχεται θύραζε*: 'the *cottabus*(-equipment; see 4 n.) is gone away outside', i.e. 'has been removed from the room' by a slave, the game being over.

12–14.   Entertainment was routinely provided at symposia by hired slave-women who danced, played instruments, and provided sexual services for the guests (perhaps for an additional fee); cf. 5 n.; **H17**; Olson–Sens on Matro frr. 1. 121; 6. 2.

12–13.   *αὐλούς*: see 5–6 n.   *Καρικὸν μέλος <τι> | μελίζεται*: 'is playing some Carian song'; cf. 14. 'Carian pipe-songs' are also mentioned at Ar. *Ra*. 1302 (allegedly incorporated by Euripides into his lyrics, and clearly disreputable), where see Dover's n.

13.   *τρίγωνον*: a type of lyre also mentioned at Pherecr. fr. 47; Ar. fr. 255; Eup. frr. 88. 2; 148. 4. See *AGM* 72.

14.   *πρὸς αὐτό*: 'to its accompaniment, along with it' (LSJ s. *πρός* C. III. 6; cf. **H16**. 1).   *μέλος Ἰωνικόν τι*: i.e. something luxuriant and sensual; cf. Ar. *Ec*. 882–3, where a randy old woman asks the Muses to come to her 'after inventing *μελύδριόν . . . τι τῶν Ἰωνικῶν*', with Ussher ad loc.; Austin–Olson on Ar. *Th*. 163.

H2. Orders to a slave at the beginning of a symposium. Alex. fr. 252 is similar; and cf. **H1**.

Preserved at Athenaeus 15. 685c–d, near the end of a long discussion of the literary evidence for wreaths and their uses; cf. **H1** introductory n.

Iambic trimeter.

2.   *τὴν δευτέραν τράπεζαν*: see **H1**. 2 n. For the term 'second table(s)', e.g. Antiph. fr. 172. 5; Philox. Leuc. *PMG* 836(e). 3; Matro fr. 1. 111 with Olson–Sens ad loc.   What *εὐτρεπῆ πόει* means is made clear in 3.

3.   *τραγήμασιν*: 'dainties' (cognate with *τρώγω*) such as nuts, beans, cakes, hard-boiled eggs, and roast thrushes (e.g. **D1**. 20–1; **H3**. 3; **H4**. 3–4; Pherecr. fr. 158; Philyll. fr. 18; Ephipp. frr. 13; 24; Antiph. frr. 138; 273; Alex. fr. 168), which symposiasts snacked on as they drank their wine.

4. The nouns are all objects of **λαβέ**. For **μύρον** ('perfume'), see **H1**. 6 n.; for **στεφάνους** ('garlands'), see **H1**. 7 n.; for **λιβανωτόν** ('frankincense'), see **H1**. 9 n.; for the **αὐλητρίδα** ('pipe-girl'), see **H1**. 5 n., 12–14 n.

H3. Part of a symposium-education scene, in which a man with no experience of drinking parties (Speaker B) is entertained by another (Speaker A); cf. **A14** with introductory n.; **H11**; **H13–H14**; **H17**.

Preserved at Athenaeus 14. 642b–c, as part of a long discussion of the literary evidence (most of it from comedy) for 'second tables' (see **H2**. 2 n.) and the food served on them that also includes **H4**.

Iambic trimeter.

1. For hand-washing at the beginning of the symposium, see **H1**. 3 n. **καλῶς ἔχει**: 'it's fine', i.e. 'No, thanks'; cf. Antiph. fr. 163. 2; Men. *Dysc.* 829; *Pk.* 516–17.

2. **ὦ (ἀ)γαθ(έ)** ('my good sir') generally has an exasperated tone (e.g. Ar. *Eq.* 188; *Nu.* 675; Metag. fr. 2. 1; Anaxandr. fr. 4. 1). **οὐδὲν χεῖρον**: i.e. 'there's no damage done!', sc. by having one's hands washed. The nominative <ἡ> **παῖς** functions like a vocative ('Slave-girl!'); cf. Ar. *Ra.* 40 with Dover ad loc., 271; Amips. fr. 2. 1; Gildersleeve § 13.

3. **κάρυα**: 'nuts' (a generic term), included in catalogues of symposium goods and the like at e.g. Philyll. fr. 24; Anaxandr. fr. 42. 45. **καὶ τραγήματα**: 'and (other) dainties'; see **H2**. 3 n.

H4. A report of events at a symposium, delivered by one of the participants.

Preserved entire at Athenaeus (1) 14. 642e (manuscript A only), in a collection of literary references to 'second tables' that also includes **H3** (where see introductory n.). In addition, 2 is quoted at Athenaeus (2) 1. 29d (manuscripts CE only), as part of a long discussion of different local varieties of wine; and 3–4 are quoted at Athenaeus (3) 2. 58a (manuscripts CE only), in a collection of literary references to eggs.

Iambic trimeter.

1. **χόνδρος**: a pudding made of wheat or barley cooked in water or milk; often included in catalogues of dainties (e.g. Anaxandr. fr. 42. 45; Antiph. fr. 273. 2; Matro fr. 1. 102 with Olson–Sens ad loc.; cf. **C3**. 4–5 with n.). **εἰσῆλθε**: The dish is described as if it entered the room under its own power, as at e.g. 3; **C10**. 2; **G13**. 1; **H6**. 2; Eub. fr. 36. 1; adesp. com. fr. 1064. 20–2. **μύρον Αἰγύπτιον**: see **H1**. 6 n., 7 n.

2. **Φοινικικοῦ βῖκός τις**: 'a transport jar' (see Olson–Sens on Archestr. fr. 39. 1–2) '(full) of Phoenician (wine)' (also referred to at Ephipp. fr. 24. 2, although in both places one might print instead *φοινικίνου*, 'date (wine)', which Athenaeus (1) actually has here). For Phoenician wine, see also

Archestr. fr. 59. 5, 13 (allegedly of very high quality).   *ὑπανεώιγνυτο*: 'had been tapped' (< *ὑπανοίγνυμι*), as at **H8**. 7.

3.   *ἴτρια*: cakes made of wheat-paste, cheese, milk, and honey (see Olson on Ar. *Ach.* 1092); apparently referred to as symposium-dainties also at Archipp. fr. 11.   *τραγήματ(α) ἦκε*: see 1 n.; **H2**. 3 n.   *πυραμοῦς*: a type of cake said at Plu. *Mor.* 747a to have been given as a prize to boys who danced at symposia, and according to *EM*, p. 533. 21–3, to winners at *cottabus* (cf. **H13**. 2–3; **H14**. 5–9). Cf. Iatrocles *On Cakes* ap. Ath. 14. 647b–c; Austin–Olson on Ar. *Th.* 94.   *ἄμης*: a milk-cake (thus *Σ*RVΘNBarbRs Ar. *Pl.* 999), also referred to as symposium food at **C7**. 5; Alex. fr. 168. 5; Amphis fr. 9. 3.

4.   *ᾠῶν ἑκατόμβη*: i.e. 'a massive quantity of eggs'; cf. Anaxandr. fr. 42. 29 *πουλυπόδων ἑκατόμβην* ('a hecatomb of octopuses'). For hard-boiled eggs eaten at symposia, e.g. Ephipp. fr. 24. 3; Amphis fr. 9. 3; Philippid. fr. 20. 1; and cf. **G16**. 10 (eggs eaten at dinner parties); **H13**. 2–3 (eggs offered as *cottabus*-prizes).   *ἐχναύομεν*: 'we were nibbling on' (but see 5–6, where the situation is represented somewhat differently).

5.   *ἐμασώμεθ(α) ... ἀνδρικῶς*: 'we were chewing vigorously'.

6.   *καὶ γάρ* ('for in fact'; see Denniston 108–9) marks what follows as an explanation of why the invited guests were eating as aggressively as they could: they were also feeding some *παραμασύντας*, 'fellow-chewers' (cognate with *μασάομαι*; attested elsewhere only at Alex. fr. 224. 8, where see Arnott's n.), a comic variant of *παράσιτος*, with the point made clear via the repetition of the prefix in *παραβόσκομεν*. For *βόσκω*, see **E29**. 4 n.

H5. After their hands had been washed (see **H1**. 3 n.) but before the regular drinking began, symposiasts were offered a taste of unmixed wine from a *μετανιπτρίς* (literally 'after-washing (cup)') dedicated to the *Ἀγαθὸς Δαίμων* ('Good Divinity'; e.g. Antiph. fr. 135; Nicostr. Com. fr. 19). But reference is also made to *μετανιπτρίδες* dedicated to *Ζεὺς σωτήρ* (for whose cult, see **I4**. 2 n.), who is seemingly confounded in this fragment with the 'Good Divinity' (cf. **H6**; Eriph. fr. 4; Xenarch. fr. 2 (where the two cups appear to be distinguished)), as well as to Health (e.g. Call. Com. fr. 9; Philetaer. fr. 1; Nicostr. Com. frr. 3; 18. 2), to whom the first mixing-bowl of wine is said to be dedicated at **H18**. 2–3 (although the word does not seem to be treated as a divine name there). The details of the matter are thus confused, but the contents of the initial cup were in any case unusual, for most wine was drunk mixed; see **H9–H10** with nn.

Nothing is known of the plot of Diphilus' *Sappho* beyond the fact that Archilochus and Hipponax were represented as Sappho's lovers (*ἐρασταί*; fr. 71) and thus presumably as rivals; cf. Men. *Leucad.* fr. 1 (Sappho's love for Phaon); Hermesian. fr. 7. 47–55, p. 99 Powell (Alcaeus and Anacreon as Sappho's lovers). As iambic poets, they must have had many choice things to say about one another, and perhaps about Sappho (apparently represented as heterosexual, and most likely as a courtesan) as well. Plays entitled *Sappho* were also written by Amipsias (fr. 15), Ephippus (fr. 20), Antiphanes (see **E7**), Amphis (fr. 32), and Timocles (fr. 32), although we know nothing significant about any of them; and Sappho and Alcaeus appear together on at least one and perhaps two fourth-century *phlyax*-vases (Trendall #19, *62; cf. Bundrick 99–102).

Preserved at Athenaeus 11. 486f–7a, in a collection of literary references (all from comedy) to the cup called μετανιπτρίς or μετάνιπτρον.

Iambic trimeter.

H6. A fragment of a report on the drinking of a cup dedicated to Zeus the Saviour (see **H5** introductory n.) at a symposium conducted off stage. Eubulus fr. 56 (preserved in the same section of Athenaeus) is similar.

Preserved at Athenaeus 11. 471c, in a collection of literary references (most from comedy) to the deep *kylix* ('wine-cup') that Athenaeus 11. 470f suggests was called a *Therikleios* after the Corinthian potter (probably resident in Athens) who invented the shape. But the 'Thericleian' vessels mentioned in our sources are of many different sizes, and not all are drinking cups (Alex. fr. 124. 1; Dionys. Com. fr. 5. 1–3; Theophil. frr. 2. 1–2; 10; Dioxipp. fr. 5), and most likely the adjective was originally applied to anything Thericles made and only later restricted to a particular type of vessel; see Arnott on Alex. fr. 5. 1.

Two additional verses (εἶτ' ἐπεισῆγεν χορείαν ἢ τράπεζαν δευτέραν | καὶ παρέθηκε γέμουσαν πέμμασι παντοδαποῖς) from Antiphanes' *Peers* preserved at Athenaeus 14. 642a are printed by K–A as Antiphanes fr. 172. 5–6. The first of these verses is a trochaic tetrameter catalectic, the second D – D, and there can be little doubt that they are from the same song as 1–4 (see below). But ἕκαστος in 4 means 'each (guest)', whereas the subject of the verbs in K–A's 5–6 is probably a slave, and those verses are better treated as a separate fragment.

Lines 1–2 are trochaic tetrameter catalectic, 3–4 dactylo-epitrite (D – D).

1. **συνάψαι ... τὰ (ἐ)ν μέσωι:** 'to abridge, give a summary account of what went on in the meantime', i.e. between whatever event was referred to in the lost verses that preceded this one, and the end of dinner and beginning of the symposium.
2. **Διὸς σωτῆρος:** here again seemingly confounded with the 'Good Divinity'; see **H5** introductory n.   **Θηρίκλειον ὄργανον:** 'a Thericleian instrument', i.e. 'a Thericleian cup'.   **ἦλθε:** see **H4.** 1 n.

3–4. **πλῆρες κτλ.:** 'full of the luxurious, nobly born drop from Lesbos', i.e. of Lesbian wine (for which, see **F18**. 2 n.). Dithyrambic style (cf. **C4**. 1 n.) and perhaps a parody specifically of Philoxenus of Leucas' dactylo-epitrite *Dinner-Party* (*PMG* 836; cf. **G4** introductory n.).

4. **ἕκαστος κτλ.:** sc. to make a toast; see **H11** introductory n.

H7. A catalogue of the most famous wines of antiquity, which the speaker proposes to offer his guests. See in general Dalby, in *Rivals*, 397–405. For Lesbian wine, e.g. **F18**. 2; Eub. fr. 121. 2; Ephipp. fr. 28; Antiph. fr. 172. 3; cf. Olson–Sens on Archestr. fr. 59. 4. For Chian wine, e.g. **H8**. 5; Ar. *Ec.* 1139; Anaxil. fr. 18. 5. For Thasian wine, e.g. **H8**. 3–5; Ar. *Lys.* 196; *Ec.* 1118–22; Epilyc. fr. 7; Antiph. fr. 138. 1. For Mendaean wine, e.g. **B3**. 1–2; **H8**. 1–2; Eub. fr. 123. 4; cf. Papadopoulos and Papalas, *Hesperia*, 68 (1999), 161–88. Bibline wine (first mentioned at Hes. *Op.* 589) was apparently called after the variety of grape used to produce it rather than the place the wine came from; see Olson–Sens on Archestr. fr. 59. 5.

Preserved at Athenaeus 1. 31a (manuscripts CE only), in a long collection of passages (most from comedy) that refer to various local wines, and that also includes **H8**.

Iambic trimeter.

2. **σαπρόν:** properly 'rotten' (cognate with σήπομαι; cf. **J6**. 6), but when used of wine 'old and delicious', as at e.g. Ar. *Pax* 554; Eup. fr. 478; cf. **H8**. 6.

3. **ὥστε μηδένα κραιπαλᾶν:** 'to keep anyone from getting a hangover', the idea being that expensive wine is less likely to have this effect; cf. **H8**. 5 n. For hangovers, see **G18**. 7 n.; Alex. fr. 257; Clearch. Com. fr. 3.

H8. An evaluative discussion of a number of fine wines (cf. **H7**)—all of which pale in comparison to the variety described in 6–12, which only the most favoured gods are allowed to drink. The emphasis throughout is on bouquet (3, 7–10), and the language is heavily epicizing. Athenaeus reports that the speaker is Dionysus, the god of wine himself, who is accordingly able to report on the Olympians' habits in 1–2, 6, 9. Meineke and Bergk assigned the fragment to *Porters* on account of its similarity to **D1** (where see introductory n.).

Preserved at Athenaeus 1. 29e–f (manuscripts CE only), in the same collection of passages as **H7** (where see introductory n.).

Dactylic hexameter.

1–2. Line 1 is too corrupt to be restored with any confidence, and it is accordingly unclear whether the point is that the gods get so drunk on Mendaean wine (for which, see **H7** introductory n.) that they piss on the couches on which they recline, or that Mendaean wine is actually divine urine (and thus delicious (cf. **A2**. 3)? or revolting?).

1. **θεοὶ αὐτοί** is always found in this position in the line in Homer (e.g. *Il.* 9. 497 καὶ θεοὶ αὐτοί |; *Od.* 1. 384; 11. 139).

2. **στρώμασιν ἐν μαλακοῖς**: cf. H. *Od.* 3. 38 | κώεσιν ἐν μαλακοῖσιν (of the Pylians at a feast). στρώματα (cognate with στόρνυμι, 'strew') are the rugs, blankets, and fabrics that were spread out on couches to make them both more comfortable and more beautiful; included in catalogues of symposium-goods and the like at e.g. Ar. *Ach.* 1090; Anaxandr. fr. 42. 7; Antiph. fr. 213.   **μειλιχόδωρον**: 'that gives gentle gifts', i.e. that produces a mild intoxication rather than simply knocking the drinker unconscious; cf. 5 with n., and contrast 1–2. A very rare word, first attested here; cf. ἠπιόδωρος at H. *Il.* 6. 251. Nothing else is known of Magnesian wine.

3. **καὶ Θάσιον**: for Thasian wine, see **H7** introductory n.   **ἐπιδέδρομεν ὀδμή**: cf. H. *Od.* 6. 45 ἐπιδέδρομεν αἴγλη |; 20. 357 ἐπιδέδρομεν ἀχλύς |. ὀδμή (the older form of the word, for which Attic uses ὀσμή; probably to be restored in 9) appears at line-end at H. *Il.* 14. 415; *Od.* 4. 442; 5. 59.

4. Forms of **εἶναι ἄριστ-** are common at line-end in Homer (e.g. *Il.* 8. 229; 9. 103; *Od.* 5. 360; 8. 383).

5. Modelled on H. *Il.* 2. 674 (Nireus was the finest man at Troy τῶν ἄλλων Δαναῶν μετ᾽ ἀμύμονα Πηλείωνα; from the Catalogue of Ships, cf. **D1**. 1 n.). For Chian wine, see **H7** introductory n. The point of **ἄλυπον** is that Chian does not cause hangovers; cf. **H7**. 3 n.; Dodds on E. *Ba.* 421–3.

6. **ἔστι δέ τις** occurs at the head of the line at H. *Il.* 2. 811; 11. 711, 722; *Od.* 3. 293 (all of geographical features), as well as at Matro fr. 7. 4 (epic parody). Here the words introduce an important new element into the discussion, as at Ar. *Th.* 31 (see Austin–Olson ad loc.).   The adjective **σαπρίας** (cognate with σαπρός; see **H7**. 2 n.) is not attested elsewhere; but cf. **B34**. 6 οἴνωι καπνίαι with n.   The subject of **καλέουσι(ν)** is not specified but is most likely the gods (cf. 1–2), whose house on Olympus is referred to in 9. The word occurs at line-end in similar formulations at e.g. H. *Il.* 5. 306; 22. 506; *Od.* 5. 273. For the epic idea that the gods have their own language, or at least their own names for people and things, taken over in comedy, see **A3**. 10–11 n.

7–9. **οὗ καὶ ἀπὸ στόματος . . . | ὄζει ἴων κτλ.**: 'from whose mouth comes a divine scent of violets, of roses, of hyacinth', as if the wine itself were a particularly sweet-breathed being, although the mouth in question is really that of the jar.   **στάμνων ὑπανοιγομενάων**: 'when the jars are tapped' (genitive absolute). For στάμνος used of wine-jars, e.g. Ar. *Lys.* 199; fr. 546; and cf. Arnott on Alex. fr. 179. 10. For the verb, see **H4**. 2 n.

Cf. H. *Od.* 9. 210–11 (Odysseus' description of the bouquet of Maron's wine when it was mixed) ὀδμὴ δ' ἡδεῖα ἀπὸ κρητῆρος ὀδώδει, | θεσπεσίη. For Dindorf's ὀδμή in place of Athenaeus' Attic ὀσμή, see 3 n. **θεσπεσία** is Homeric vocabulary (e.g. *Il.* 8. 159; 16. 295; *Od.* 12. 314). **ὑψερεφὲς δῶ** (see 6 n.) is a Homeric phrase, found at line-end at *Od.* 10. 111; 15. 424, 432.

10.   **ἀμβροσία καὶ νέκταρ ὁμοῦ:** 'ambrosia and nectar all in one'. Probably an echo of H. *Od.* 9. 359 (Polyphemus' response to his first taste of Maron's wine; cf. 9 n.; Ar. *Ach.* 196) ἀλλὰ τόδ' ἀμβροσίης καὶ νέκταρός ἐστιν ἀπορρώξ.   **τὸ νέκταρ** seems awkward after **νέκταρ** in the first half of the line, hence the emendations recorded in the apparatus.

11–12.   **τούτου χρὴ παρέχειν πίνειν κτλ.:** supply με as subject of the infinitive, 'a portion of this is what I must supply my friends to drink'.   **ἐν δαιτὶ θαλείηι** appears at line-end at H. *Od.* 8. 76 θεῶν ἐν δαιτὶ θαλείηι (the setting of the quarrel between Odysseus and Achilleus that is the subject of Phemius' first song). Cf. **H20.** 1 ἐπὶ δαῖτα θάλειαν | (epic parody) with n.   **ἐκ Πεπαρήθου:** '(wine) from Peparethus' (an island off the coast of Thessaly); referred to also at Ar. fr. 334, along with Pramnian, Chian, and Thasian. That the words are reserved for the end of the line suggests that they are intended as a joke and that this is a particularly poor local variety (cf. **B29.** 3 n.). But perhaps the point is instead that even Dionysus' enemies (sc. among the gods) get excellent wine to drink.

H9.   Wine was regularly mixed with water (see also **B3.** 3; **H10; J10**), although more out of fear of a hangover or getting too drunk too fast than as a result of any broad cultural taboo; cf. Olson on Ar. *Ach.* 73–5.

The second speaker is the Athenian lawgiver Solon (*PA* 12806; early sixth century BC), who also appeared on stage in Cratinus' *Cheirons* (fr. 246) and most likely in Eupolis' *Demes* (test. i), and who is similarly addressed as a cultural innovator in Philemon's *Brothers* (fr. 3), although he probably did not appear on stage in that play. For other mentions of Solon in comedy, see Cratin. fr. 300; Ar. *Nu.* 1187–91; *Av.* 1660–6; Alex. fr. 131. 1–2. Speaker A might be the title-character Aesop; but 8–10 suggest that Solon's interlocutor is not Greek, and he is more likely Croesus, in whose court Solon and Aesop were said to have met (Plu. *Sol.* 28. 1).

Preserved at Athenaeus 10. 431d–f, in a long discussion of literary references to drinking, wine, and the like that also includes **H10; H12.**

Iambic trimeter.

1–2.   **παρ(ὰ) ὑμῖν . . . | ἐν ταῖς Ἀθήναις** suggests (but does not prove) that the action of the play was set somewhere other than Athens; see introductory n.

3.   τὸ ποῖον;: 'What sort of thing?', i.e. 'Which thing in particular (are you referring to)?'

4.   ἄκρατον: 'unmixed, undiluted (wine)' (cognate with κεράννυμι). οὐ γὰρ ῥᾴδιον: '(Yes,) because it's not very easy', sc. 'to drink wine that's *not* watered'; see Denniston 73–4; and cf. **H19**. 6.

4–6.   πωλοῦσι γὰρ | κτλ.: For other complaints about wine-merchants and bartenders watering wine (treated ironically here, since to the extent that this occurred in real life, it was done precisely ἵνα τι κερδαίνωσι), see **J11**; Ar. *Th*. 348; *Pl*. 436; Thphr. *Char*. 30. 5; Hegesander of Delphi fr. 22 (*FHG* iv. 417) ap. Ath. 10. 431d.

5.   ἐν ταῖς ἁμάξαις: literally 'in the wagons'. But according to Pollux vii. 192, γλεῦκος (unfermented grape-must) was brought for sale to the Agora in wagons (ἐφ' ἁμαξῶν), and 'the wagons' must be another way of designating the section of the marketplace where wine and related commodities were sold; see **J1** introductory n.   εὐθέως κεκραμένον: 'mixed at that very moment', i.e. 'already mixed'.

6–8.   προνοούμενοι takes two genitives, the second of which expresses purpose (see KG ii. 40–1); 'looking out for the buyers, so that they have heads that are healthy after an all-night drinking-bout'.

8.   For κραιπάλη in the sense 'all-night drinking-bout', cf. Ar. *Ach*. 277; *V*. 1255; contrast **H7**. 3 with n.   τοῦτ(ό) ἐστ(ι) marks a slight change of subject, indicated in part by the condescending interjection ὁρᾷς (e.g. Ar. *Nu*. 355; Anaxandr. fr. 18. 4; Amphis fr. 38. 1): Solon is no longer discussing what the Athenians in particular drink, but how Greeks generally believe drinking ought to proceed.

9.   πότος: '(way of) drinking'.

10.   'to have some conversation and pleasant banter with one another'; cf. **G16**. 12 n.; Metag. fr. 3. The use of ληρέω indicates that the talk is inconsequential even if enjoyable.

11.   τὸ ... ἕτερον: 'the other thing', i.e. to drink immoderately (contrast 9–10); given specific content in 12.   λουτρόν ἐστιν: cf. the very similar use of βαπτίζω at Pl. *Smp*. 176b.

12.   ψυκτῆρι πίνειν καὶ κάδοις: 'to drink with', i.e. 'from a wine-cooling vessel and wine-buckets', oversize vessels intended for mixing or storage; in apposition to τὸ ... ἕτερον in 11. For drinking from a ψυκτήρ, cf. Men. fr. 401. 2–3; Pl. *Smp*. 213e–14a. For κάδοι in catalogues of symposium equipment and the like, e.g. Antiph. frr. 112. 1; 113. 4; Epig. fr. 6. 1; and cf. **B4**. 4 with n.   μὲν οὖν indicates that Speaker A considers Solon's characterization of overly heavy drinking as a 'bath' (11) correct but inadequate, and he therefore substitutes a stronger image of his own (Denniston 475–6); cf. **H10**. 2; **H12**. 1 with n.

H10. Two women (Speaker A and Glyce) are drinking privately (rather than in a symposium) in the presence of a third character (Speaker B), who calls Glyce 'Mummy' (4 with n.) but acts and is treated like a slave. Athenaeus reports that the title-character Corianno (*PAA* 582037) was a prostitute (13. 567c = *Corianno* test. ii; the name is not otherwise attested in Athens), and she may be Speaker A. That women generally are heavy drinkers is a comic trope (e.g. **C2** with **C2.** 18 n.; **J10**; Ar. *Lys.* 193–208; *Pl.* 644–5; Eub. fr. 42; Antiph. fr. 58; Alex. fr. 172. 1–2 with Arnott ad loc.; Xenarch. fr. 6; Men. *Dysc.* 858). Here the wine is mixed cup by cup rather than in a *kratêr*, as also in **J10**.

For other comic references to acceptable proportions of wine to water (all much weaker than what Glyce and Speaker A call for), e.g. **B3.** 3 (one part to three) with n.; Alex. fr. 228. 2 (one to four) with Arnott ad loc.; Anaxil. fr. 23 (one to three).

Preserved at Athenaeus 10. 430e, in the same collection of texts as **H9** (where see introductory n.); **H12**.

Iambic trimeter.

1. **Γλύκη**: a common name (ten additional fifth- and fourth-century examples in *LGPN* ii s.v., including Ar. *Ec.* 43).
2. **(ἐ)νέχεέν σοι;**: 'did she pour it into (your cup) for you?'; the subject of the verb is Speaker B.   **παντάπασι** is adverbial, 'entirely, altogether'. **μὲν οὖν**: see **H9.** 12 n.
3. Addressed to Speaker B.   **ὦ κατάρατε**: see **D14.** 8 n.
4. Four parts of wine to two of water is by Greek standards a strong mixture (see introductory n.), and the humour depends on the shared disgust of Speaker A and Glyce at the fact that the mixture is not . . . even stronger (5).   **ὦ μάμμη** is simply a familiar form of address for an older woman, like ὦ πάτερ for an older man (**H11.** 4 n.); cf. Men. *Asp.* 495–6.
5. **ἔρρ(ε) ἐς κόρακας**: literally 'Wander off to the ravens!' (who are commonly represented as feeding on unburied bodies), i.e. 'Goddamn you to hell!' *vel sim.*; see *Birds*, 159–64; Olson on Ar. *Pax* 19. Colloquial (Ar. *Pl.* 604; Amips. fr. 23; see Stevens 12–13).   **βατράχοισιν οἰνοχοεῖν σ(ε) ἔδει**: because frogs *like* water; cf. **F11.** 3. For ἔδει used of unfulfilled obligation, **B32.** 8 n.

H11. Speaker B is an unsophisticated older man being introduced to the 'good life' of parties and drinking by Speaker A, who may or may not be his son (see 4 with n.); cf. **H3** introductory n.; **H13**, and the plot of Aristophanes' *Wasps*. Speaker B represents a group, doubtless the eponymous Rustics, and is probably also the speaker in Anaxandr. fr. 2 (who expresses astonishment at the quantity of food served on the 'second tables' at a symposium), as well as Speaker B in Anaxandr. fr. 3 (who confesses that he and his friends were not just 'overcome' but 'thrown' by the immense cups of wine they drank).

Symposium drinking was highly ritualized behaviour, hence Speaker A's suggestion in 1–2 that they might proceed in a number of ways. (Speaker B, of course, has no idea what Speaker A is talking about.) The suggestion in 4–5 appears to refer to use of the φιλοτησία κύλιξ ('loving cup'), which was passed about the company from left to right, with each man taking it in his right hand (cf. **H6**. 4) and drinking from it, handing it to the next, and speaking in that man's praise while he drank in turn; cf. Alex. fr. 55 'toast this man, in order that he might toast another'; Olson on Ar. *Ach.* 983. For toasting at symposia, see also **F2**. 1 n.; **H12**.

Preserved at Athenaeus 11. 463f–4a (manuscript A only), in support of the claim made by the late fifth-century Athenian politician and intellectual Critias (*PAA* 585315) in his *Constitution of the Lacedaimonians* (88 B 33) that the Athenians 'drink from small cups from left to right' (ἐκ μικρῶν ἐπιδέξια; cf. **H9**. 9).

Iambic trimeter.

1–2. τίνα δὴ παρεσκευασμένοι πίνειν τρόπον νῦν ἐστε;: cf. Pl. *Smp.* 176a σκοπεῖσθε οὖν, τίνι τρόπῳ ἂν ὡς ῥᾷστα πίνοιμεν.

2. λέγετε betrays the speaker's impatience; cf. **C13**. 1 n.

4. δήπου ('I suppose, presumably'; see Denniston 267) adds a tone of tentativeness and thus politeness to the question.

4–5. τὸν ἐπιδέξι(α) (sc. ἄνδρα) | λέγειν ἐπὶ τῶι πίνοντι: literally 'that the (man) from left to right speak in honour of the one who is drinking', i.e. 'that moving counterclockwise each man speak . . . '. For ἐπιδέξια, see **F2**. 1 n.   ὦ πάτερ is an ingratiating form of address when directed to an older man (**E7**. 13; Ar. *Eq.* 725, 1215; *V.* 556; Men. *Dysc.* 171; Diph. fr. 17. 5; cf. **H10**. 4 n.; **I8**. 14–15 with n.) and does not prove that Speaker A is Speaker B's son (note esp. Men. *Dysc.* 493–4).

6. Ἄπολλον: see **B12**. 1 n.   ὥσπερ ἐπὶ τεθνηκότι: apparently an allusion to the περίδειπνον, an ill-attested funerary rite in which the individual being buried was eulogized (esp. *Suda* ο 874; also mentioned at Men. *Asp.* 233; fr. 270. 4; Anaxipp. fr. 1. 42; Hegesipp. Com. fr. 1. 11; D. 18. 288).

H12. The job of the symposiarch (mentioned also at X. *An.* vi. 1. 30; cf. Pl. *Smp.* 213e) was not just to set the toasts (cf. **H11**), as in this fragment, but to control each guest's drinking, set the general pace of the party, and determine when songs were to be sung, stories told, and the like; see Plu. *Mor.* 620a–2b; Dover, *Symposium*, p. 11. Chaireas (2) is otherwise unknown and is most likely either a character in the play or an invented member of the offstage drinking party about which the speaker is reporting.

Preserved at Athenaeus 10. 431c, in the middle of a collection of literary references (including **H9–H10**) to mixing wine and water, to which this fragment (like Men. fr. 2, which immediately precedes it) does not obviously belong.

Iambic trimeter.

1. δήμιος: sc. δοῦλος, 'a state (slave)', i.e. 'a public executioner', the point being that Chaireas made the company drink far too much (2). For the equation of drinking to excess with death, cf. **H9**. 12. For the δήμιος δοῦλος (who worked under the supervision of the Eleven), see Ar. *Ec.* 81; Diph. fr. 31. 11; Lys. 13. 56; Pl. *R.* 439e; *Lg.* 872b–c; [Arist.] *Ath.* 45. 1; and cf. **I11**. 13 with n.

2. κυάθους προπίνων εἴκοσιν: 'proposing toasts totalling twenty cups'

H13. Speaker B knows nothing of symposium customs, or at least of *cottabus* (see below), and Speaker A is undertaking to teach him or her; cf. **H5** introductory n.; Nesselrath 234 (who suggests that Speaker B may be Aphrodite herself, who has just emerged from the sea and is thus a social naive). The plural **κοτταβεῖτε** in 4 shows that the group includes other characters as well.

Cottabus was a symposium game that involved flipping small quantities of wine or wine-lees (the λάταξ or λάταγες) from one's cup at a target set up in the middle of the circle of couches. In the variant of the game known as κότταβος κατακτός and described in this fragment (contrast **H14**), a rod resembling a lampstand was set up (1–2) and a disk (the πλάστιγξ) balanced on top of it (7–9); the object was to toss one's λάταγες in the air in such a way that they knocked the πλάστιγξ down onto a mysterious object known as the μάνης, producing a noise (5–6, 10–12). See Bieber fig. 538; Lissarrague 80–6; Olson on Ar. *Pax* 343/4; Campagner, *QUCC* 72 (2002), 111–27; Pütz 221–7.

Preserved entire at Athenaeus (1) 15. 666f–7b, as part of an extensive collection of literary references to *cottabus* that also includes **H14**, with 1–13 and 14–20 separated by the words καὶ μετ' ὀλίγα ('and a few verses later'). In addition, 2–3 are referred to (but not quoted) at Athenaeus (2) 15. 667d ('that a prize was set for the one who threw the *cottabus* well has been said before this by Antiphanes; for [the prizes] are eggs and cakes (πεμμάτια) and τραγήματα'); 5–13 are quoted at Athenaeus (3) 11. 487d (manuscript A only), in a short collection of literary references to the μάνης; 5–11 are quoted in a *scholium* to Luc. *Lexiph.* 3 (apparently drawn from Athenaeus, but from a different manuscript tradition than the one preserved for us), in a gloss on the phrase λαταγεῖν κοττάβους; and the word πινακίσκιον in 8 is cited from this play at Pollux x. 84.

Iambic trimeter.

1.   **τονδὶ λέγω**: 'I'm talking about *this*', with a gesture towards the object in question, about which Speaker B has exhibited unexpected ignorance. For the use of λέγω, cf. 8 'Are you talking about τὸ πινακίσκιον?'

1–2.   **κότταβος Ι τὸ λυχνεῖόν ἐστι**: 'the lampstand is a *cottabus*', i.e. 'the thing that looks to you like a lampstand is actually basic equipment for a game of *cottabus*'; cf. 4 with n., 6 with n., 8 (where Speaker B identifies the πλάστιγξ as a πινακίσκιον); **H1**. 4 with n.

2.   **πρόσεχε τὸν νοῦν**: 'Pay attention!' (as Speaker B has apparently not been doing up to this point). For the idiom, e.g. **B1**. 2–3; **C18**. 30; **F7**. 3 with n.; **J7**. 9 (supply τὸν νοῦν); Pherecr. fr. 84. 1; Ar. *Th*. 25.

2–3.   **ᾠὰ Ι × – ∪ – × πέντε νικητήριον**: 'eggs (and) five (?) as a prize'; cf. **H4**. 4 n. (on hard-boiled eggs as symposium-dainties); **H14**. 5–9 (kisses, shoes, and a cup as *cottabus*-prizes); Eub. fr. 2. 3–4 'I shall set as a νικητήριον three ribbons, five apples, and nine kisses' (for the best or most vigorous dancer at an all-night women's celebration). Casaubon compared the comment at Ath. (2) and suggested printing ᾠὰ μὲν Ι <καὶ πέμμα καὶ τράγημα> νικητήριον, with πέντε to be explained as a corruption of πέμμα.

4.   **περὶ τοῦ;**: '(As a prize) for what?'

5–6.   **κατ(ὰ) ὅσον κτλ.**: 'to the extent that someone ... '; the sentence is completed in the second half of 9.   **τὸν κότταβον Ι ἀφείς**: 'when he lets go of', i.e. 'throws the *cottabus*' (for this use of ἀφίημι, cf. 17). But here the noun refers to the λάταγες; contrast 1–2 with n.

6.   **ποιήσηι πεσεῖν**: 'causes it (i.e. the πλάστιγξ) to fall'.

8.   **τὸ πινακίσκιον λέγεις;**: 'Are you talking about the little platter?'; see 1 n., 1–2 n.

9.   **οὗτος ὁ κρατῶν γίγνεται**: 'this fellow is the winner' (completing the thought in 5–6, after Speaker B's interruptions and Speaker A's responses in 7–9 πλάστιγξ).

10–11.   **τοῦτ(ο)**: i.e. whether the κότταβος (here the wine that has been thrown; cf. 5–6 n.), which is the subject of θίγηι in the answer that follows, has made the πλάστιγξ (= αὐτῆς) fall, and thus who is the winner of the game.

13.   **Μάνης**: a common Phrygian personal name used routinely as a slave-name in comedy (e.g. Pherecr. fr. 10. 1; Ar. *Pax* 1146; *Lys*. 908; Amips. fr. 2. 1; Mnesim. fr. 4. 2; cf. **D1**. 18 n.), hence the joke: the μάνης works for the *cottabus*-game just like a domestic slave works for his master.

14–19.   The explanation of the *cottabus*-equipment is complete and the discussion has moved on to matters of technique. It is impossible to know how much is missing from the text.

14.   'Take the cup and show (me) how!'

15. 'You have to curl your fingers up like a crab's claws, as if you were playing the αὐλός', in preparation for the flip of the wrist (ἀγκύλη) emphasized elsewhere in descriptions of the game (esp. Pl. Com. fr. 47; cf. A. fr. 179. 3–4; Cratin. fr. 299. 3–4). For the αὐλός, see **H1**. 5 n.

17. ἀφήσεις is equivalent in sense to an imperative; see **G3**. 3 n. For the verb, see 5–6 n.

18. τοιοῦτον: 'Like this!'; Speaker A offers a demonstration.

19. οὕτω ποήσεις: sc. 'if you follow my instructions and example'.

19–20. ἐγὼ μὲν σφενδόνηι | οὐκ ἂν ἐφικοίμην αὐτόσ(ε): 'I wouldn't reach there' (i.e. so high in the air with my throw; cf. 18) 'with a sling!' For slings and slingers (a common type of light-armed troops), see W. K. Pritchett, *The Greek State at War*, v (Berkeley, Los Angeles, and Oxford, 1991), 1–67.

20. For ἀλλά ('Come on!' *vel sim.*) introducing an imperative, see Denniston 13–14.   μάνθανε: 'be learning!', i.e. 'practise!' Speaker B's clumsy efforts at the game doubtless made up the next section of the scene.

H14. The game referred to here is κότταβος ἐν λεκάνηι or δι' ὀξυβάφων (contrast **H13** with introductory n.), in which a basin (λεκάνη, although in this case Speaker A insists that a mortar must be used instead (3)) was filled with water (4), and a number of smaller vessels (ὀξύβαφα; see **B4**. 6 n.) floated in it. The goal was to sink as many of these as one could with the λάταγες thrown from one's drinking cup (cf. 4–5). See Pütz 227–31.

Three characters are on stage. Athenaeus' comments at 15. 667b, where he quotes Pl. Com. fr. 47 (also from *Zeus Abused*), show that the second speaker is Heracles. Speaker A appears to be a brothel-owner or pimp, who is for some reason making matters more difficult than they would seem to need to be, by offering a mortar instead of a basin (3) and rejecting Heracles' initial proposal for prizes (6–10). The third character is a woman (8) dressed in fancy clothes belonging to Speaker A (7–8) and whom Heracles would like to kiss (5), and is presumably a prostitute. For Heracles in comedy, and in particular his role as archetypal glutton, see **A1** introductory n.

Preserved at Athenaeus 15. 666d–e (manuscript A only), in a collection of literary references to *cottabus* that also includes **H13**.

Iambic trimeter.

1. σφῶιν: 'for the two of you', i.e. Heracles and the girl, as again in 7.

3. ἀγὼν ἐμός ἐστ(ι): 'The contest's mine!', i.e. 'I'm sure to win!' ἀλλ(ὰ) ἐς θυείαν παιστέον: cf. Amips. fr. 2. 2, where a foot-washing basin is apparently to be used for playing *cottabus*. For mortars, see **G9**. 2 n.

4–5. Speaker A is going to be occupied with making dinner (1–2), and these orders are presumably addressed to a pair of mute slaves first referred to individually and then collectively.

4.   **αἶρ(ε) ὕδωρ**: 'draw water!' (cf. Ar. *Ra.* 1339a), sc. 'and bring it here!'

5.   **παίζωμεν κτλ.**: for *cottabus*-prizes, see **H13**. 2–3 n.

6.   **ἀγεννῶς**: 'in a coarse, sordid fashion', i.e. for such insignificant prizes.

7.   **κοττάβεια**: 'as *cottabus*-prizes'; cf. **H4**. 3 n.; **H13**. 2–3 with n.

8.   **κρηπῖδας**: 'platform shoes' of some sort (see LSJ Supplement s.v. I. 1. a, correcting the main entry), presumably intended to make the girl appear taller and thus more attractive; cf. **I7**. 7–8 n. That she will have to take them off, if Heracles wins the contest, perhaps suggests that he will eventually be allowed to have sex with her as well.

9.   **βαβαιάξ**: 'Damn!' An intensified form of βαβαί (**I9**. 2), which serves as a colloquial expression of shock, surprise, or the like; cf. Ar. *Ach.* 64; *Lys.* 312; López Eire 90; Labiano Ilundain 105–10.

9–10.   **οὑτοσὶ | κτλ.**: 'this contest that's coming up is bigger than the Isthmian one!', referring to the Isthmian Games, celebrated at Corinth in honour of Poseidon every other year.

H15. For *skolia* sung at symposia, see **H1**. 11 n.

Preserved at Athenaeus 11. 503d–e, in support of the claim by the late first-century BC grammarian Tryphon (fr. 115 Velsen) that the cup used when *skolia* were sung was called an ὠιδός (cognate with ἀείδω, 'sing').

Iambic trimeter.

1.   **τί . . . ἐνέσται τοῖς θεοῖσιν;**: 'What'll be in it for the gods?' The characters seem to be participating in an aggressively 'modern' symposium, in which the old libations are no longer poured (see **H5** introductory n.) or the old songs sung (3–5; cf. **D13**. 1–2 n.). But θεοῖσιν is odd, and Antiphanes may have written something like Kock's τοῖς σκύφοισιν ('What will be in our drinking cups?'; cf. **A11** n.), to which Speaker B's 'Nothing—unless some-one mixes up (some wine)!' in 2 would be an appropriately witty response.

2.   **ἴσχε**: 'Hold on!, Wait!'   **τὸν ὠιδόν**: see introductory n.

3.   **ἀπηρχαιωμένων**: 'antiquated, old-fashioned' (< ἀπαρχαιόομαι).

4.   **περάνηις**: 'proceed through', i.e. 'recite', as at Ar. *Ra.* 1170; Antiph. fr. 1. 6 τραγωιδίαν περαίνω Σοφοκλέους ('I'm reciting a tragedy of Sophocles').   **τὸν Τελαμῶνα**: Athenaeus 15. 695c preserves a *skolion* that praises Telamon, father of Salaminian Ajax (see **C11**. 7 n.): 'They say that Telamon went to Troy as first man of the Danaans after Achilleus, and Ajax as second' (*PMG* 899; cf. *PMG* 898). For Telamon-*skolia* sung at symposia, see also Ar. *Lys.* 1236–7; Theopomp. Com. fr. 65.

4–5.   **τὸν | Παιῶνα**: for singing paeans (hymns in honour of Paian, a god often associated with Apollo; see Olson on Ar. *Ach.* 1212) at dinner parties and symposia, see Alcm. *PMG* 98; Antiph. fr. 3. 1; Pl. *Smp.* 176a with Dover ad loc.

5. **Ἁρμόδιον:** Harmodius of Aphidnae (*PAA* 203425) and his lover Aristo-
    geiton assassinated Hipparchus son of Peisistratus in 514 and were
    remembered (inaccurately) as having freed Athens from the tyrants and
    establishing a democracy; see Th. i. 20. 2; vi. 53. 3–59; Olson on Ar. *Ach.*
    978–9. For other comic references to Harmodius-*skolia*, see **H16**. 2 with n.;
    Ar. *V.* 1225–6 (sung at a symposium); *Lys.* 631–2 (cf. *PMG* 893. 1 = 895. 1);
    Antiph. fr. 3. 1 (sung at a symposium).

H16. That the *skolia* a man chose to sing (see **H15** introductory n.) might
have political or social significance, and that in certain company some *skolia*
might be acceptable and others not, is also apparent from Ar. *Lys.* 1236–8,
where the Spartans sing of Telamon (see **H15**. 4 n.) when they 'ought to have'
sung of Cleitagoras, but the Athenians magnanimously ignore the gaffe.
Cf. also Cratin. fr. 254 'to sing of Cleitagoras whenever someone pipes the
Admetus-song'.
  Preserved in a *scholium* on Ar. *V.* 1238, in a gloss on the words Ἀδμήτου
λόγον.
  Iambic trimeter.

1. The *skolion* to which **Ἀδμήτου λόγον** refers is quoted in full in the note
    that preserves these verses (on a passage where Aristophanes' character
    recites only the first line), as well as at Athenaeus 15. 695c, and urges the
    listener to 'learn the saying of Admetus ..., and love τοὺς ἀγαθούς
    but keep away from cowards, recognizing that there is little thanks from
    cowards' (*PMG* 749 ~ 897). The mention of οἱ ἀγαθοί suggests an aristo-
    cratic perspective, which stands in contrast to the democratic perspective
    implicit in the 'Harmodius song' (see **H15**. 5 n.) and may explain why the
    second man (referred to in 2) kept insisting that the latter song be sung
    instead. Admetus was a great friend of the gods and the husband of the
    eponymous Alcestis in Euripides' play; see Pl. *Smp.* 179b–c; [Apollod.] *Bib.*
    i. 9. 14–15; Scodel, *HSCP* 83 (1979), 51–62, esp. 51–4; Gantz 195–6; and
    cf. **I2**. 11.   **πρὸς μυρρίνην:** 'to the accompaniment of a laurel branch'
    (for this use of πρός, see **F2**. 2 n.), i.e. 'while holding a laurel branch', as at
    Ar. *Nu.* 1364 (where lyric poetry is being recited at a symposium; cf. **D13**.
    1–2 n.).
2. **Ἁρμοδίου μέλος:** Four Harmodius-*skolia* (*PMG* 893–6) are preserved at
    Ath. 15. 695a–b, and three of the four refer to killing the tyrant or making
    Athens a place of equality under the law; see 1 n.; **H15**. 5 n.

H17. Part of either a 'symposium-education' scene (cf. **H13** introductory n.)
or a servile symposium-preparation scene (cf. **H1**, and see 1 n.). In either
case, Parmenon knows what a female pipe-player (**αὐλητρίς**) is, but is

unacquainted with more exotic instruments and thus with the women who play them; Speaker A hyperbolically denounces his ignorance before, presumably, going on to enlighten him. For female symposium-entertainers, see **H1**. 5 n., 12–14 n.

Preserved at Athenaeus 4. 175d, in a brief collection of literary references to the stringed instrument known as the **ναβλᾶς** (also Sopat. frr. 10; 15) designed to show that, despite Aristoxenus' claim (fr. 95 Wehrli) to the contrary, string and percussion instruments are not universally superior to wind instruments. For the ναβλᾶς (a Phoenician harp of some sort), see *AGM* 77.

Iambic trimeter.

1.   **ἔδει**: see **B32**. 8 n.   **Παρμένων** is a common comic slave-name (e.g. Ar. *Ec.* 868; Men. *Sam.* 61); see Fragiadakis 364–5.

3.   **ἐμβρόντητε σύ**: literally 'thunderstruck one', i.e. 'witless one, fool' *vel sim.*; cf. Ar. *Ec.* 793; Men. *Georg.* fr. 4. 1; *Pk.* 523.

3–5.   For the alternative forms **οἶδας, οἶσθα**, and **οἶσθας**, see **G18**. 11 n.

5.   **σαμβυκίστριαν**: 'a female σαμβύκη-player'. For the σαμβύκη (a type of harp), see **D13**. 4 n.

H18. Athenaeus reports that the speaker is Dionysus, and Grotius assigned the fragment on that basis to *Semele or Dionysus*, a play that probably dealt with the birth of the god and the establishment of human customs having to do with wine and symposia. Cf. **G14**. 1 n. The theme of the descent of the symposium into chaos as more and more wine is drunk was commonplace; cf. **A15**; **C11**. 3–7 with nn.; **H19** with introductory n.; adesp. com. fr. 101. 10–11; Anacharsis fr. A27 Kindstrand ap. Stob. iii. 18. 25 'When a bowl of wine is mixed up on the hearth, the first that is drunk belongs to health (ὑγιείας), the second to pleasure (ἡδονῆς), the third to *hybris*, the fourth to madness (μανίας)'; Panyas. fr. 17. Here the mixing-bowls (for which, see **H1**. 8 n.) are divided into symmetrical sets of three, two, three, and two.

Preserved at Athenaeus 2. 36b–c (manuscripts CE only), immediately before **A15** in a collection of literary references to the benefits and dangers of wine. Lines 11–12 (where see n.) do not effectively sum up the sense of 1–10; after δέκατος (κρατήρ) in 10, οἶνος is not easily supplied with πολὺς . . . χυθείς in 11; and the athletic imagery in 12 finds no echo in what precedes it. Kassel was therefore most likely right to suggest that something has fallen out of the text between 10 and 11, although what is missing might well be another lemma assigning 11–12 to a different play or poet.

Iambic trimeter.

2–3.   **τὸν μὲν ὑγιείας ἕνα, | ὃν πρῶτον ἐκπίνουσι**: see **H5** introductory n. For the idea that wine is (or can be) good for one, see adesp. com. fr. 101. 4–8 (supposedly citing the medical author Mnesitheus); E. *Ba.* 280–3.

4. **ἔρωτος ἡδονῆς τε**: an oblique reference to the availability of female musicians and other entertainers with whom symposiasts might have sex; see **H1**. 5 n.   **ὕπνου**: 5–6 are most naturally taken to imply that the sleep in question is to take place in the drinker's own house. But guests at symposia also frequently dropped off during the party; cf. **H20**. 12.

5–6. **ὃν ἐκπιόντες κτλ.** constructs a firm verbal boundary between the first three bowls of wine (good) and the many increasingly dangerous bowls that follow.   **οἱ σοφοὶ κεκλημένοι**: 'wise guests' (see **D3**. 6 n.).

7. **ἡμέτερος**: 'mine'; the use of the first-person plural for singular is a mark of elevated style, which perhaps reflects the fact that the speaker is a divinity.   'Abuse' (**ὕβρεος**) and 'shouting' (**βοῆς**) represent the breakdown of good order within the symposium, as unpleasant words lead to loud quarrels (cf. **H19**. 3–6); contrast 8–9, where the party (or what is left of it) has moved out into the street.

8. **κώμων**: 'revelling bands', i.e. groups of men, sometimes accompanied by pipe-girls, who left the house where a symposium was held to wander the streets, looking for excitement or trouble. See Pütz 156–7, 181–9. **ὑπωπίων**: 'black eyes', sc. from the fights that break out as the κῶμος (above) tries to force its way into a house (cf. **C11**. 5–6) or meets up with another group of revellers. Cf. **J8**. 3–4 with introductory n.; Ar. *Ach.* 551 with Olson ad loc.; E. *Cyc.* 534 'the κῶμος is closely associated with fistfights and abusive quarrelling'.

9. **κλητῆρος**: 'a summoner', and thus by extension 'a lawsuit', when someone the group assaults is seriously hurt.

9–10. The ninth bowl belongs to **χολῆς** ('bile') because an excess of bile was thought to produce **μανίας** ('madness'), to which the tenth bowl belongs; cf. Ar. *Pax* 66 with Olson ad loc.

10. **καὶ βάλλειν**: 'even to start throwing stones', as happened in drunken streetfights (e.g. Ar. *Ach.* 1168–73; *V.* 1253–4; Alex. fr. 112; Lys. 3. 8), but also as mentally disturbed individuals sometimes did at random (e.g. [Pl.] *Alc. 2* 139d), lending more point to the image.

11–12. The lines sound like an explanation of why using a small cup is no guarantee against drunkenness.

11. **πολὺς . . . χυθείς** modifies an implied οἶνος. But a 'great deal' of wine cannot be poured **εἰς ἓν μικρὸν ἀγγεῖον** at one time, and the point must be that the drinker's cup is filled again and again, with ἓν μικρόν added for the sake of the contrast with πολύς.

12. **ὑποσκελίζει**: 'trips up'. A technical term from wrestling (Pl. *Euthd.* 278b; Poll. iii. 155); cf. E. *Cyc.* 678 'wine is dangerous and difficult to wrestle with'.

H19. For the theme of the descent of the symposium into arguments and uproar, see **H18** introductory n.; Ar. *V.* 1224–48, 1308–21 (where two guests exchange rude remarks, initially to the applause of the rest of the company) with MacDowell on 1308–13; adesp. eleg. fr. 27. 3–6 (fourth century?); Rosen, *Pallas*, 61 (2003), 131–5 (arguing that mutual abuse and mockery were a regular feature of symposia). Webster (1970), 57, suggested that the plot of *Odysseus Weaving* was an inversion of the story of the *Odyssey*, with Odysseus taking Penelope's part in producing Laertes' shroud; see Arnott, *Alexis*, pp. 465–6.

Preserved at Athenaeus 10. 421a–b, in support of the speaker's assertion that 'an inexpensive dinner produces no acts of outrage or personal abuse'.

Trochaic tetrameter catalectic.

1.   ἡ μακρὰ συνουσία: 'extended socializing', at dinner parties in particular.
2.   κατ(ὰ) ἡμέραν: 'on a daily basis'; modifying τὰ συμπόσια.
3–7.   For the idea, cf. **H18**. 7.
3.   σκῶψιν: 'mockery', implicitly presented as an innocent (if ultimately destructive) pleasure; cf. **J13** with nn.   πολύ is to be taken with πλεῖον, 'much more' (adverbial).
4–5.   τοῦ κακῶς λέγειν γὰρ ἀρχὴ γίγνετ(αι): 'For (σκῶψις) is the beginning of verbal abuse'. The idea is unpacked in the line-and-a-half that follows: one mocking remark leads to another in reply, and suddenly the two parties are actively exchanging insults. For the expression κακῶς λέγω ('speak ill of, abuse'), e.g. **I2**. 3; Ar. *Th.* 85; Antiph. fr. 94. 3–4.
4.   ἂν ... ἅπαξ: 'if once ... ', i.e. 'as soon as ... the minute ... '. An Attic colloquialism; see Olson on Ar. *Ach.* 307–8.
5–6.   ἀντήκουσας is a gnomic aorist (Goodwin § 154–5).   ἤδη λοιδορεῖσθαι κτλ.: literally 'now it is lacking to abuse another, and then it has been shown forth to be struck and to be drunk', i.e. 'trading abuse is the inevitable next step; and then one sees people striking one another and acting like drunken boors'. δέδεικται + infinitive is not used this way elsewhere, but the sense is clear. For παροινέω, see **C11**. 4 n.
6.   γάρ marks Speaker B's assent to Speaker A's argument; '(Yes,) for ... '; cf. **H9**. 4 with n.
7.   πέφυκεν is by this period little more than a metrically convenient synonym of ἐστι; κατὰ φύσιν is therefore needed to produce the sense 'naturally', and is not pleonastic.   τί μάντεως ἔδει;: 'what need was there of a seer?', sc. 'to tell us this'. μάντεως ἔδει is most likely proverbial (cf. S. *OT* 393–4; [E.] *Rh.* 952; Pl. *Smp.* 206b); in any case, no one has actually brought in a prophet.

H20. Advice about how to treat guests at dinner parties (1–3) of a sort that might easily have been offered by the title-character Cheiron the centaur, followed by a denunciation of the bad behaviour at symposia (esp. 8) typical of the group to which the speaker belongs (4–13). Pherecr. fr. 159 (also from *Cheiron*) appears to parody the discussion that takes place between Odysseus and Achilleus over dinner at H. *Il.* 9. 222–429, and may provide the context for these remarks; cf. **D1–D4** n. (on the reception of Homer in comedy). **D14** is from the same play, but is more difficult to integrate with the other fragments. After quoting 1–3, Athenaeus identifies 4–13 as τὰ ... ἑξῆς αὐτῶν, ἅπερ πάντα ἐκ τῶν εἰς Ἡσίοδον ἀναφερομένων μεγάλων Ἠοιῶν καὶ μεγάλων Ἔργων πεπαρῴδηται ('the verses that come after these, which are all a parody of the *Great Eoiai* and *Great Works* attributed to Hesiod'). μεγάλων Ἠοιῶν καὶ ought probably to be expelled from the text (thus Merkelbach–West, p. 146). But the more substantial problem is that 1–3 are full of epic language and formulae, whereas 4–13 are not; it is tempting to think that Athenaeus (or the textual tradition of the *Deipnosophists*) has somehow got things backwards and that the first three verses rather than the final ten are adapted from a passage in Hesiod. For echoes of Hesiod in comedy, see **C1** introductory n.

In the scene imagined in 4–13, a number of men are drinking together (7–8) but only one is regarded with hostility by the host, who has invited him to the party in the expectation that he will not attend (4–5). The most likely explanation is that the man is a dependent of some sort, and the repeated reference to him as a φίλος (1, 13) thus represents a pointed attempt to insist that he ought to be treated as such, despite his inferior social status, at least at dinner or a symposium.

Preserved at Athenaeus 9. 364a–c (manuscript A only), in a wandering discussion of sacrifice and feasts, as evidence of the deplorable state of modern manners.

Dactylic hexameter.

1. For the sentiment, cf. Hes. *Op.* 342 τὸν φιλέοντ᾽ ἐπὶ δαῖτα καλεῖν, τὸν δ᾽ ἐχθρὸν ἐᾶσαι ('Invite your friend to a meal, but ignore your enemy') with West on 353.   **μηδὲ σύ γ᾽** is found at the head of the line at H. *Il.* 10. 237.   **δαῖτα θάλειαν**: cf. **H8.** 11 δαῖτι θαλείῃ | (Homeric parody) with n.; H. *Il.* 7. 475; *Od.* 3. 420.
2. **παρεόντα** is found in the same position in the line at H. *Od.* 15. 74 χρὴ ξεῖνον παρεόντα φιλεῖν, ἐθέλοντα δὲ πέμπειν ('One should treat the stranger kindly when he's present, and send him off when he wants to go'). **τόδε ῥέζει:** cf. τάδε ῥέζει at line-end at H. *Od.* 22. 158.
3. **ἀλλὰ μάλ᾽ εὔκηλος** is found in this position in the line at H. *Il.* 1. 554. εὔκηλος is 'at your ease'.

4–6 echo 1–2 (**καλέσηι ... ἐπὶ δεῖπνον** ~ καλέσας ἐπὶ δαῖτα θάλειαν; **ἀχθόμεθ(α) ... καὶ ὑποβλέπομεν παρεόντα** ~ ἄχθου ὁρῶν παρεόντα), while describing behaviour diametrically opposed to that recommended there.

5. **ὑποβλέπομεν**: 'we give him a narrow glance', i.e. 'a dirty look'; see Austin–Olson on Ar. *Th.* 396.

7–9. The host's feelings are not obvious to everyone—even the unwanted guest takes a while to make sense of them (**γνούς πως τοῦτ(ο)**)—and the individual who speaks up in 8–9 misunderstands the situation entirely, in that he interprets the other man's preparations to leave as evidence of a lack of sociability and does his best to make him stay. **εἶτα ... κα(ὶ ε)ἶτα**: see **D6**. 16 n.   **εἶπε**, like ἔλεξ(ε) in 10, is a gnomic aorist (Goodwin § 154–5).   **ὑποδεῖται**: 'he puts on his shoes/sandals' (which were taken off when one entered a house; cf. Ar. *Eq.* 888–9; *V.* 103; Eub. fr. 29; Dunbar on Ar. *Av.* 492); contrast 9 with n.   **ἤδη σύ;**: '(Are) you already (leaving)?'   **ὑποπίνεις**: properly 'drink a little'; but the verb is commonly used to refer to excessive drinking ('get good and drunk'), as at Alex. fr. 287. 1, where see Arnott's n.   **οὐχ ὑπολύσεις αὐτόν;**: 'Take off his shoes!' (cf. 7 n.; **B32**. 10 n.); addressed to a slave.

10–12. For lyric and elegiac poetry recited at symposia (a custom that here provides the host an opportunity discreetly to signal his lack of interest in having his guest linger in the house any longer), see **D13** introductory n.

11–12. A slightly adapted quotation of Theognis 467, 469 μηδένα τῶνδ' ἀέκοντα μένειν κατέρυκε παρ' ἡμῖν | μηδ' εὕδοντ' ἐπέγειρε Σιμωνίδη, with 468 μηδὲ θύραζε κέλευ' οὐκ ἐθέλοντ' ἰέναι ('and do not urge him to go away when he deosn't want to'; cf. 6) pointedly omitted. For another allusion to Theognis in comedy, see Theophil. fr. 6 (~ Thgn. 457–60).

12. **μήθ' εὕδοντ' ἐπέγειρε**: cf. **H18**. 4 n.   **ἐπ(ὶ) οἴνοις**: 'over our wine', i.e. 'while we are drinking'.

13. **φίλον ἄνδρα**: an echo of 1 that serves to bring the discussion to a close.

Section I

Women

I1. [Susarion] fr. 1, an ancient forgery (date uncertain)

ἀκούετε λεώι· Σουσαρίων λέγει τάδε,
υἱὸς Φιλίνου Μεγαρόθεν Τριποδίσκιος.
κακὸν γυναῖκες· ἀλλ' ὅμως, ὦ δημόται,
οὐκ ἔστιν οἰκεῖν οἰκίαν ἄνευ κακοῦ
        *   *   *

καὶ γὰρ τὸ γῆμαι καὶ τὸ μὴ γῆμαι κακόν   5

   1 λεώι Tzetzes: λέως vel λεώς Stob.^SMA Joh.Diac. Σ D.T.: λέξιν Anon.Cram.   2 om.
Stob. Joh.Diac. Anon.Cram. Diomed.: damn. Nauck   4 οἰκεῖν Stob.^SMA Ammon.
Σ D.T. Anon.Cram. Σ Ar. S (2): εὑρεῖν S (1) Joh.Diac. Tzetz. Σ Tzetz. Diomed.   5 damn.
Hense

I2. Eubulus fr. 115, from *Chrysilla* (IV)

                  0κακὸς
κακῶς ἀπόλοιθ' ὅστις γυναῖκα δεύτερος
ἔγημε· τὸν γὰρ πρῶτον οὐκ ἐρῶ κακῶς.
ὁ μὲν γὰρ ἦν ἄπειρος, οἶμαι, τοῦ κακοῦ,
ὁ δ' οἷον ἦν γυνὴ κακὸν πεπυσμένος   5
       *   *   *

ὦ Ζεῦ πολυτίμητ', εἶτ' ἐγὼ κακῶς ποτε
ἐρῶ γυναῖκας; νὴ Δί' ἀπολοίμην ἄρα,
πάντων ἄριστον κτημάτων. εἰ δ' ἐγένετο
κακὴ γυνὴ Μήδεια, Πηνελόπη δέ <γε>
μέγα πρᾶγμ'· ἐρεῖ τις ὡς Κλυταιμήστρα κακή·   10
Ἄλκηστιν ἀντέθηκα χρηστήν· ἀλλ' ἴσως
Φαίδραν ἐρεῖ κακῶς τις· ἀλλὰ νὴ Δία
χρηστή—τίς ἦν μέντοι; τίς; οἴμοι δείλαιος,
ταχέως γέ μ' αἱ χρησταὶ γυναῖκες ἐπέλιπον,
τῶν δ' αὖ πονηρῶν ἔτι λέγειν πολλὰς ἔχω   15

2 δεύτερος Meineke: δεύτερον Ath.^AE: δευτέραν Ath.^C   5 πεπυσμένος Porson: πεπεισμένος Ath.^ACE   6 κακῶς ποτε Morelius: ποτε κακῶς Ath.^ACE   9 <γε> Cobet

I3. Menander fr. 236, from *The Misogynist* (IV/III)

(Σι.) πρὸς τὸ πρᾶγμ' ἔχω
κακῶς. (Β.) ἐπαριστέρως γὰρ αὐτὸ λαμβάνεις·
τὰ δυσχερῆ γὰρ καὶ τὰ λυπήσοντά σε
ὁρᾷς ἐν αὐτῶι, τὰ δ' ἀγάθ' οὐκ ἐπιβλέπεις.
εὕροις δ' ἂν οὐθὲν τῶν ἁπάντων, Σιμύλε,   5
ἀγαθόν, ὅτωι τι μὴ πρόσεστι καὶ κακόν.
γυνὴ πολυτελής ἐστ' ὀχληρόν, οὐδ' ἐᾶι
ζῆν τὸν λαβόνθ' ὡς βούλετ'· ἀλλ' ἔν ἐστί τι
ἀγαθὸν ἀπ' αὐτῆς, παῖδες· ἐλθόντ' εἰς νόσον
τὸν ἔχονθ' ἑαυτὴν ἐθεράπευσεν ἐπιμελῶς,   10
ἀτυχοῦντι συμπαρέμεινεν, ἀποθανόντα τε
ἔθαψε, περιέστειλεν οἰκείως. ὅρα
εἰς ταῦθ', ὅταν λυπῆι τι τῶν καθ' ἡμέραν·
οὕτω γὰρ οἴσεις πᾶν τὸ πρᾶγμ'. ἂν δ' ἐκλέγηι
ἀεὶ τὸ λυποῦν, μηδὲν ἀντιπαρατιθεὶς   15
τῶν προσδοκωμένων, ὀδυνήσηι διὰ τέλους

3 γὰρ Stob. (1)^SMA: τε Clem.^L   λυπήσοντά Stob. (1)^SMA: λυπήσαντά Clem.^L   4 τὰ δὲ ἀγαθὰ Clem.^L: τἀγαθὰ δ' Stob. (1)^SMA   οὐκ ἐπιβλέπεις Clem.^L: οὐκέτι βλέπεις Stob. (1)^SMA   5 Σιμύλε Stob. (1)^SMA: ὦ Δημέα Stob. (2)^SMA: Δημέα Grotius: Δημύλε Meineke   6 ὅτωι τι Grotius: ὅπου τι Stob. (1)^SMA: ἐν ὧι τι Stob. (2)^SM: ἐν ὥτινι Stob. (2)^A   7 πολυτελής] -ές Bothe   8 τι Voss: τοι Stob. (3)^SMA   14 ἂν δ' ἐκλέγηι Meineke: ἂν ἐκλέγηι vel ἐκλέγη Stob. (4)^SMA: ἂν δὲ λέγηις Stob. (3)^SMA   16 sic Stob. (4)^SMA: προσλεγομένων οὐ δυνήσηι Stob. (3)^SMA

I4. Menander fr. 804, from an unidentified play (IV/III)

καὶ τοῦτον ἡμᾶς τὸν τρόπον γαμεῖν ἔδει
ἅπαντας, ὦ Ζεῦ σῶτερ, ὡς ὠνήμεθα·
οὐκ ἐξετάζειν μὲν τὰ μηθὲν χρήσιμα,
τίς ἦν ὁ πάππος ἧς γαμεῖ, τήθη δὲ τίς,
τὸν δὲ τρόπον αὐτῆς τῆς γαμουμένης, μεθ' ἧς   5
βιώσεται, μήτ' ἐξετάσαι μήτ' εἰσιδεῖν·
οὐδ' ἐπὶ τράπεζαν μὲν φέρειν τὴν προῖχ', ἵνα
εἰ τἀργύριον καλόν ἐστι δοκιμαστὴς ἴδηι,
ὃ πέντε μῆνας ἔνδον οὐ γενήσεται,
τῆς διὰ βίου δ' ἔνδον καθεδουμένης ἀεὶ   10

μὴ δοκιμάσασθαι μηδέν, ἀλλ᾽ εἰκῆι λαβεῖν
ἀγνώμον᾽ ὀργίλην χαλεπήν, ἐὰν τύχηι
λάλον. περιάξω τὴν ἐμαυτοῦ θυγατέρα
τὴν πόλιν ὅλην· οἱ βουλόμενοι ταύτην λαβεῖν
λαλεῖτε, προσκοπεῖσθε πηλίκον κακὸν   15
λήψεσθ᾽· ἀνάγκη γὰρ γυναῖκ᾽ εἶναι κακόν,
ἀλλ᾽ εὐτυχής ἐσθ᾽ ὁ μετριώτατον λαβών

2 ὠνήμεθα] ὠνήμεθ᾽ ἄν Meineke: ὠνούμεθα Hirschig   4 τήθη Brunck: τιθῆ (i.e. τιτθὴ)
Stob.ᴿᴹᴬ   6 εἰσιδεῖν Meineke: ἰδεῖν Stob.ᴿᴹᴬ: ἐξετάζειν μήτ᾽ ἰδεῖν Bentley   7 οὐδ᾽ C. F.
Hermann: ἀλλ᾽ Stob.ᴿᴹᴬ

I5. Menander fr. 815, from an unidentified play (IV/III)

τοὺς τῆς γαμετῆς ὅρους ὑπερβαίνεις, γύναι,
τὴν αὐλίαν· πέρας γὰρ αὔλειος θύρα
ἐλευθέραι γυναικὶ νενόμιστ᾽ οἰκίας.
τὸ δ᾽ ἐπιδιώκειν εἴς τε τὴν ὁδὸν τρέχειν
ἔτι λοιδορουμένην, κυνός ἐστ᾽ ἔργον, Ῥόδη   5

2 τὴν αὐλίαν Gesner: διὰ τὴν αὐλὰν λίαν Stob.ᴿᴹᴬ: διὰ τὴν λαλιάν Nauck   5 Ῥόδη Gesner:
ῥώδη Stob.ᴿᴹᴬ

I6. Plato Comicus fr. 188, from *Phaon* (391 ʙᴄ)

εἶέν, γυναῖκες, <ἴστ᾽ ἄρ᾽> ὡς ὑμῖν πάλαι
οἶνον γενέσθαι τὴν ἄνοιαν εὔχομαι.
ὑμῖν γὰρ οὐδέν, καθάπερ ἡ παροιμία,
ἐν τῶι καπήλου νοῦς ἐνεῖναί μοι δοκεῖ.
εἰ γὰρ Φάωνα δεῖσθ᾽ ἰδεῖν, προτέλεια δεῖ   5
ὑμᾶς ποῆσαι πολλὰ πρότερον τοιαδί·
πρῶτα μὲν ἐμοὶ γὰρ Κουροτρόφωι προθύεται
πλακοῦς ἐνόρχης ἄμυλος ἐγκύμων κίχλαι
ἑκκαίδεχ᾽ ὁλόκληροι μέλιτι μεμιγμέναι
λαγῶια δώδεκ᾽ ἐπισέληνα. τἆλλα δὲ   10
ἤδη † ταῦτ᾽ εὐτελέστατα· † ἄκουε δή.
βολβῶν μὲν Ὀρθάννηι τρί᾽ ἡμίεκτεα,
Κονισάλωι δὲ καὶ παραστάταιν δυοῖν
μύρτων πινακίσκος χειρὶ παρατετιλμένων·
λύχνων γὰρ ὀσμὰς οὐ φιλοῦσι δαίμονες.   15
† πύργης τετάρτης † Κυσί τε καὶ Κυνηγέταις,
Λόρδωνι δραχμή, Κυβδάσωι τριώβολον,

ἥρωι Κέλητι δέρμα καὶ θυλήματα.
ταῦτ᾽ ἐστι τἀναλώματ᾽. εἰ μὲν οὖν τάδε
προσοίσετ᾽, εἰσέλθοιτ᾽ ἄν· εἰ δὲ μή, μάτην　　　　　　　　20
ἔξεστιν ὑμῖν διὰ κενῆς βινητιᾶν

1 <ἴστ᾽ ἄρ᾽> Kaibel: <προσέχεθ᾽,> Blaydes　　　4 καπήλου Casaubon: καπήλωι Ath.ᴬ
9 μεμιγμέναι Heringa: διαμεμιγμέναι Ath.ᴬ　　　16 πυροῦ τετάρτη Daléchamp
17 Λόρδωνι Casaubon: δορδωνι Ath.ᴬ

I7. Alexis fr. 103, from *Isostasion* (IV/III)

πρῶτα μὲν γὰρ πρὸς τὸ κέρδος καὶ τὸ συλᾶν τοὺς πέλας
πάντα τἀλλ᾽ αὐταῖς πάρεργα γίγνεται, ῥάπτουσι δὲ
πᾶσιν ἐπιβουλάς. ἐπειδὰν δ᾽ εὐπορήσωσίν ποτε,
ἀνέλαβον καινὰς ἑταίρας, πρωτοπείρους τῆς τέχνης·
εὐθὺς ἀναπλάττουσι ταύτας, ὥστε μήτε τοὺς τρόπους　　　5
μήτε τὰς ὄψεις ὁμοίας διατελεῖν οὔσας ἔτι.
τυγχάνει μικρά τις οὖσα· φελλὸς ἐν ταῖς βαυκίσιν
ἐγκεκάττυται. μακρά τις· διάβαθρον λεπτὸν φορεῖ
τήν τε κεφαλὴν ἐπὶ τὸν ὦμον καταβαλοῦσ᾽ ἐξέρχεται·
τοῦτο τοῦ μήκους ἀφεῖλεν. οὐκ ἔχει τις ἰσχία·　　　10
ὑπενέδυσ᾽ ἐρραμμέν᾽ αὐτήν, ὥστε τὴν εὐπυγίαν
ἀναβοᾶν τοὺς εἰσιδόντας. κοιλίαν ἁδρὰν ἔχει·
στηθί᾽ ἔστ᾽ αὐταῖσι τούτων ὧν ἔχουσ᾽ οἱ κωμικοί·
ὀρθὰ προσθεῖσαι τοιαῦτα τοὔνδυτον τῆς κοιλίας
ὡσπερεὶ κοντοῖσι τούτοις εἰς τὸ πρόσθ᾽ ἀπήγαγον.　　　15
τὰς ὀφρῦς πυρρὰς ἔχει τις· ζωγραφοῦσιν ἀσβόλωι.
συμβέβηκ᾽ εἶναι μέλαιναν· κατέπλασεν ψιμυθίωι.
λευκόχρως λίαν τις ἐστίν· παιδέρωτ᾽ ἐντρίβεται.
καλὸν ἔχει τοῦ σώματός τι· τοῦτο γυμνὸν δείκνυται.
εὐφυεῖς ὀδόντας ἔσχεν· ἐξ ἀνάγκης δεῖ γελᾶν,　　　20
ἵνα θεωρῶσ᾽ οἱ παρόντες τὸ στόμ᾽ ὡς κομψὸν φορεῖ.
ἂν δὲ μὴ χαίρηι γελῶσα, διατελεῖ τὴν ἡμέραν
ἔνδον, ὥσπερ τοῖς μαγείροις ἃ παράκειθ᾽ ἑκάστοτε,
ἡνίκ᾽ ἂν πωλῶσιν αἰγῶν κρανία, ξυλήφιον
μυρρίνης ἔχουσα λεπτὸν ὀρθὸν ἐν τοῖς χείλεσιν·　　　25
ὥστε τῶι χρόνωι σέσηρεν, ἄν τε βούλητ᾽ ἄν τε μή

1–6 contrax. Ath.ᶜᴱ　　　1 πρὸς Ath.ᴬ: ἐς Clem.ᴾ　　　2 τ᾽ ἄλλ᾽ Ath.ᴬ: τὰ ἄλλα ἔργα
Clem.ᴾ　　　4 καινὰς Musurus: κενὰς Ath.ᴬ　　　7 βαυκίσιν Ath.ᴬᶜᴱ: βλαύτισιν Clem.ᴾ
8 ἐγκεκάττυται Ath.ᴬᶜᴱ: ἐνεγκάττυται (at in ras.) Clem.ᴾ　　　9 καταβαλοῦσ᾽ Ath.ᴬᶜᴱ:
καταβάλλουσα Clem.ᴾ　　　12 εἰσιδόντας Sylburg: εἰσιόντας Clem.ᴾ: ἰδόντας Ath.ᴬᶜᴱ

13–15 om. Ath.^{CE}   13 στηθί’ ἔστ’ αὐταῖσι] τιτθίαις ταύταισιν Clem.^P   15 ἀπήγαγον
Ath.^A: ἀπήγαγεν Clem.^P   19 τοῦτο Clem.^P: ταυτο Ath.^A: τοῦτ’ αὐτὸ Ath.^{CE}   δείκνυται
Ath.^{ACE}: δεικνύει Clem.^P   21 θεωρῶσιν Clem.^P: θεωροῖεν Ath.^{ACE}   ὡς Ath.^{ACE}: ὡς ὅτι
Clem.^P   22 διατελεῖ Clem.^P: διὰ τέλους Ath.^{ACE}   26 σέσηρεν Clem.^P: σεσηρέναι
Ath.^{ACE}   βούλητ’ Ath.^C: βούλετ’ Clem.^P: βούλωνται Ath.^{AE′}

I8.   Xenarchus fr. 4, from *The Pentathlete* (IV)

δεινά, δεινὰ κοὐκ ἀνασχετὰ
ἐν τῆι πόλει πράττουσιν οἱ νεώτεροι.
ὅπου γὰρ οὐσῶν μειράκων μάλ’ εὐπρεπῶν
ἐπὶ τοῖσι πορνείοισιν, ἃς ἔξεσθ’ ὁρᾶν
εἰληθερούσας, στέρν’ ἀπημφιεσμένας,   5
γυμνὰς ἐφεξῆς τ’ ἐπὶ κέρως τεταγμένας·
ὧν ἔστιν ἐκλεξάμενον ἧι τις ἥδεται,
λεπτῆι, παχείαι, στρογγύληι, μακρᾶι, ῥικνῆι,
νέαι, παλαιᾶι, μεσοκόπωι, πεπαιτέραι,
μὴ κλίμακα στησάμενον εἰσβῆναι λάθραι   10
μηδὲ δι’ ὀπῆς κάτωθεν εἰσδῦναι στέγης
μηδ’ ἐν ἀχύροισιν εἰσενεχθῆναι τέχνηι.
αὐταὶ βιάζονται γὰρ εἰσέλκουσί τε
τοὺς μὲν γέροντας ὄντας ἐπικαλούμεναι
πατρίδια, τοὺς δ’ ἀπφάρια, τοὺς νεωτέρους.   15
καὶ τῶνδ’ ἑκάστην ἔστιν ἀδεῶς, εὐτελῶς,
μεθ’ ἡμέραν, πρὸς ἑσπέραν, πάντας τρόπους·
ἃς δ’ οὔτ’ ἰδεῖν ἔστ’, οὔθ’ ὁρῶντ’ ἰδεῖν σαφῶς,
αἰεὶ δὲ τετραμαίνοντα καὶ φοβούμενον
[δεδιότα, ἐν τῆι χειρὶ τὴν ψυχὴν ἔχοντα]   20
       *   *   *

ἃς πῶς ποτ’, ὦ δέσποινα ποντία Κύπρι,
βινεῖν δύνανται, τῶν Δρακοντείων νόμων
ὁπόταν ἀναμνησθῶσι προσκινούμενοι;

5 στέρν’ ἀπημφιεσμένας Tyrwhitt: στέρμνατ’ ημ- Ath.^A: στέρνα τ’ ἠμ- Ath.^{CE}   6 ἐπὶ κέρως
Musurus: επικαιρως Ath.^A: ἐπικαίρους Ath.^{CE}   10 κλίμακα στησάμενον Meineke: καὶ
μακαιτησ- Ath.^A: om. Ath.^{CE}   11 εἰσδῦναι Dobree: ἐκδῦναι vel sim. Ath.^{ACE}   post 15
defic. Ath.^{CE}   19 τετραμαίνοντα Kassel–Austin: τετραμένοντε Ath.^A: om. Ath.^{CE}
20 del. Meineke   post 20 lac. indic. Kock

I9. Timocles fr. 24, from *Men from Marathon* (IV)

ὅσον τὸ μεταξὺ μετὰ κορίσκης ἢ μετὰ
χαμαιτύπης τὴν νύκτα κοιμᾶσθαι. βαβαί,
ἡ στιφρότης, τὸ χρῶμα, πνεῦμα, δαίμονες.
τὸ μὴ σφόδρ᾽ εἶναι πάνθ᾽ ἕτοιμα, δεῖν δέ τι
ἀγωνιᾶσαι καὶ ῥαπισθῆναί τε καὶ   5
πληγὰς λαβεῖν ἁπαλαῖσι χερσίν· ἡδύ γε
νὴ τὸν Δία τὸν μέγιστον

1 ὅσον Jacobs: θεὸν Ath.ᴬ   3 τὸ χρῶμα, πνεῦμα] τὸ χρῶμα, πνεῦμ᾽, ὦ Gulick: τὸ χρῶμα,
<τὸ> πνεῦμα Jacobs: ὁ χρώς, τὸ πνεῦμα Wilamowitz   5 τε Jacobs: γε Ath.ᴬ

I10. Epicrates fr. 8, from *The Chorus* (IV)

τελέως μ᾽ ὑπῆλθεν ἡ κατάρατος μαστροπός,
ἐπομνύουσα τὰν Κόραν, τὰν Ἄρτεμιν,
τὰν Φερρέφατταν, ὡς δάμαλις, ὡς παρθένος,
ὡς πῶλος ἀδμής· ἡ δ᾽ ἄρ᾽ ἦν μυωνιὰ
<ὅλη>   5

1 τελέως μ᾽ Meineke: τελείως δέ με Ael.ᵛ: τελείως δεῦμε Ael.ᴸ   5 <ὅλη> Meineke
ex Aeliani verbis

I11. Phoenicides fr. 4, from an unidentified play (III)

μὰ τὴν Ἀφροδίτην οὐκ ἂν ὑπομείναιμ᾽ ἔτι,
Πυθιάς, ἑταιρεῖν. χαιρέτω· μή μοι λέγε·
ἀπέτυχον· οὐδὲν πρὸς ἐμέ· καταλῦσαι ᾽θέλω.
εὐθὺς ἐπιχειρήσασα φίλον ἔσχον τινὰ
στρατιωτικόν· διαπαντὸς οὗτος τὰς μάχας   5
ἔλεγεν, ἐδείκνυ᾽ ἅμα λέγων τὰ τραύματα,
εἰσέφερε δ᾽ οὐδέν. δωρεὰν ἔφη τινὰ
παρὰ τοῦ βασιλέως λαμβάνειν, καὶ ταῦτ᾽ ἀεὶ
ἔλεγεν· διὰ ταύτην ἣν λέγω τὴν δωρεὰν
ἐνιαυτὸν ἔσχε μ᾽ ὁ κακοδαίμων δωρεάν.   10
ἀφῆκα τοῦτον, λαμβάνω δ᾽ ἄλλον τινά,
ἰατρόν. οὗτος εἰσάγων πολλούς τινας
ἔτεμν᾽ ἔκαε· πτωχὸς ἦν καὶ δήμιος.
δεινότερος οὗτος θατέρου μοι κατεφάνη·
ὁ μὲν διήγημ᾽ ἔλεγεν, ὁ δ᾽ ἐποίει νεκρούς.   15
τρίτωι συνέζευξ᾽ ἡ Τύχη με φιλοσόφωι,

πώγων᾽ ἔχοντι καὶ τρίβωνα καὶ λόγον.
εἰς προὖπτον ἦλθον ἐμπεσοῦσα δὴ κακόν·
οὐδὲν ἐδίδου γάρ. † ταῦτ᾽ ἀλλ᾽ ἂν αἰτῶντι † ἔφη
οὐκ ἀγαθὸν εἶναι τἀργύριον. ἔστω κακόν,   20
διὰ τοῦτο δός μοι, ῥῖψον· οὐκ ἐπείθετο

4 ἔσχον Stob.ᴸ: ἔχον Stob.ᴹᵈ: εἶχον Stob.ᴬ   6 ἐδείκνυ <δ᾽> Grotius   9 λέγω] λέγει
Nauck: ἔλεγε Meineke   11 δ᾽ Stob.ᴸ: om. Stob.ᴹᵈᴬ   18 ἦλθον] ἔλαθον Herwerden
19 sic Stob.ᴸ: ταῦτάλαν αὐτῶ τι Stob.ᴹᵈ: τάλαν αἰτῶ τι Stob.ᴬ: εἴ τι δ᾽ αἰτοίην Grotius

I12. Epicrates fr. 3, from *Antilais* (IV)

αὐτὴ δὲ Λαῒς ἀργός ἐστι καὶ πότις,
τὸ καθ᾽ ἡμέραν ὁρῶσα πίνειν κἀσθίειν
μόνον· πεπονθέναι δὲ ταῦτά μοι δοκεῖ
τοῖς ἀετοῖς. οὗτοι γὰρ ὅταν ὦσιν νέοι
ἐκ τῶν ὀρῶν πρόβατ᾽ ἐσθίουσι καὶ λαγὼς   5
μετέωρ᾽ ἀναρπάζοντες ὑπὸ τῆς ἰσχύος·
ὅταν δὲ γηράσκωσιν ἤδη, τότε ∪×
ἐπὶ τοὺς νεὼς ἵζουσι πεινῶντες κακῶς·
κἄπειτα τοῦτ᾽ εἶναι νομίζεται τέρας.
καὶ Λαῒς ὀρθῶς <νῦν> νομίζοιτ᾽ ἂν τέρας.   10
αὕτη γὰρ οὖν ὁπότ᾽ ἦν νεοττὸς καὶ νέα,
ὑπὸ τῶν στατήρων ἦν ἀπηγριωμένη,
εἶδες δ᾽ ἂν αὐτῆς Φαρνάβαζον θᾶττον ἄν·
ἐπεὶ δὲ δόλιχον τοῖς ἔτεσιν ἤδη τρέχει
τὰς ἁρμονίας τε διαχαλᾷ τοῦ σώματος,   15
ἰδεῖν μὲν αὐτὴν ῥᾷόν ἐστιν ἢ πτύσαι·
ἐξέρχεταί τε πανταχόσ᾽ ἤδη πιομένη,
δέχεται δὲ καὶ στατῆρα καὶ τριώβολον,
προσίεται δὲ καὶ γέροντα καὶ νέον·
οὕτω δὲ τιθασὸς γέγονεν ὥστ᾽, ὦ φίλταται,   20
τἀργύριον ἐκ τῆς χειρὸς ἤδη λαμβάνει

6 ὑπὸ Scaliger: ἀπὸ Ath.ᴬᶜᴱ   10 <νῦν> Meineke   16 ἢ Herwerden: καὶ Ath.ᴬᶜᴱ
20 φίλταται Ath.ᴬ: φίλτατε Ath.ᶜ: φίλταᵀ Ath.ᴱ

COMMENTARY

I1–I12. As the material collected in this section makes clear, comedy tends to present women in a limited set of roles, the most significant of which are wives and daughters, on the one hand (**I1–I5**), and prostitutes of various types, on the other (**I7–I12**). See also **A8** (personified female virtues); **A20** (a sorceress); **B1–B3** (a difficult wife); **B27–B29** (personified female cities); **C1** (an unhappy wife); **C2** (personified argumentative, drunken female cities); **C4–C5** (the sorceress Circe); **C15** (a young man's marital problems); **C16–C17** (a difficult wife); **C18** (problems involving a proposed marriage); **D7** (paratragic prostitutes/hags); **D13** (adulterers' songs); **D14** (a courtesan abused by a series of lovers); **E6** (an attack on a politician's mother); **E8** (courtesans as deceivers); **E13** (the 'shameless' Aspasia); **E26–E27** (Alcibiades' adulteries); **F14** (a Cynic philosopher's odd treatment of his wife and daughter); **F18** (enjoying oneself with a prostitute and wine as the best thing in life); **H10** (hard-drinking women); **J10** (an attempt at seduction and a drunken nurse).

For the social and legal status of women in Athenian society, see in general D. M. Schaps, *Economic Rights of Women in Ancient Greece* (Edinburgh, 1979); Gould, *JHS* 100 (1980), 38–59; Cohen 35–170; V. Hunter, *Policing Athens* (Princeton, 1994), 9–42; R. Omitowoju, *Rape and the Politics of Consent in Classical Athens* (Cambridge, 2002); S. Lewis, *The Athenian Woman: An Iconographic Handbook* (London and New York, 2002); Johnstone, *CA* 22 (2002), 247–74; P. Brulé, *Women of Ancient Greece* (Edinburgh, 2003), 114–85. For the treatment and position of women in comedy in particular, see Fantham, *Phoenix*, 29 (1975), 44–74 (on 'New Comedy'); Henderson, *TAPA* 117 (1987), 105–29 (on older women in 'Old Comedy'), and in *Rivals*, 135–50 (on women in the 'Old Comic' poet Pherecrates, with a checklist of likely speaking parts for women in 'Old Comedy' down to *c.*380 BC); L. K. Taaffe, *Aristophanes and Women* (London and New York, 1993); L. McClure, *Spoken Like a Woman* (Princeton, 1999), 3–31, 205–59.

I1. Were these verses authentic, they would represent all that survives of the work of Susarion, whom the Marmor Parium (*FGrHist* 239 A 39 = Susar. test 1; mid-third c. BC, drawing on earlier materials), followed by a number of late sources, identifies as the εὑρετής ('inventor') of comedy and associates with the Attic deme Icarius, from which Thespis, the alleged originator of tragedy, was also supposed to have come (*Suda* θ 282 = *TrGF* 1 T 1). But even if Susarion was a real person, there is no reason to believe that any of his poetry was preserved, and the fragment appears instead to be the end-product of an

extended process of forgery, counter-forgery, and textual corruption, driven
in part by ancient disputes over the history of the comic genre. It is impossible
to say how old any portion of the fragment is; the first witness (Stobaeus)
dates probably to the early fifth century AD.

Line 5 is preserved only in Stobaeus and, by identifying both marrying
and staying single as evils, sits uneasily with 3–4, which assume that a man
will take a wife even if she makes him unhappy. Hense was therefore almost
certainly correct to suggest that a lemma assigning 5 to another author has
fallen out of the text of Stobaeus and that the verse ought to be separated
from the rest of the fragment and printed among the adespota. Line 2 is
missing from the version of the text preserved in Stobaeus, Diomedes, and the
Anonymous Crameri, and conflicts with 3, in which Susarion addresses his
fellow demesmen, implicitly identifying himself as Athenian. The verse may
thus have been added by someone concerned to bolster the Megarian claim
to have invented comedy (Arist. *Po.* 1448ᵃ31–2 = com. dor. test. 6; see Introduction, pp. 3–5); that it is ignored in the discussion of the origin of the genre
in Aristotle's *Poetics* is an argument from silence, but none the less suggests
that the rewriting occurred no earlier than the Hellenistic period. The fragment thus most likely originally consisted of only three verses (1, 3–4).

Whether Susarion (dated by the Marmor Parium (*FGrHist* 239 A 39 =
Susar. test. 1) to between 582/1 and 561/0) was a real person is unclear, and all
that can really be said is that in the Hellenistic period he was remembered as
having been associated with the early history of comedy in Athens (although
not by Aristotle). The name is not Athenian, and if Susarion was in fact
thought to have been from Megara, the initial version of the fragment may
represent a deliberate Athenian attempt to claim the origin of comedy, to
which the addition of 2 is a pointed response. The misogynist announcement
in 3–4, at any rate, was certainly intended by the fragment's various authors
and redactors to articulate their perception of one of the genre's most basic
themes and concerns. See *DTC* 280–4; Breitholtz 74–82; Kerkhof 38–50.

Lines 1, 3–4 are preserved at *Anon. Crameri* i. 21, and at Diomedes, *de
Poem.* p. 488. 27 (both accounts of the early history of comedy, the former
closely related to the *scholium* on Dionysius Thrax cited below). Lines 1,
3–5 (the same form of the fragment as in the sources cited above, but with
5 accidentally added) are preserved at Stobaeus iv. 22ᶜ. 68–9, under the
heading 'That the character of those joined together renders marriage beneficial to some, but unfortunate for others'. Lines 1–4 (the revised form of the
fragment, with 2 added) are preserved at John the Deacon, *On Hermogenes'
on Invention*, p. 149. 29; Tzetzes, *Prooemion* i. 83; a *scholium* on Tzetzes' *On
Prosody* 81; and a *scholium* on Dionysius Thrax (all accounts of the early
history of comedy, = Susar. test. 7–9). In addition, 3–4 alone are preserved in a

scholium on Ar. *Lys.* 1038 (whence *Suda* (1) ο 969; (2) τ 829); and 4 alone is preserved at Ammonius, *On Aristotle's de Interpretatione* 7.

Iambic trimeter.

1. **ἀκούετε λεώι** ('Listen, people!'; λεώι is nominative/vocative of Attic λεώς = common λαός) is a traditional formula used to introduce public proclamations in Athens; cf. Ar. *Ach.* 1000; *Pax* 551; *Av.* 448.
2. Tripodiscus was a village belonging to Megara (Th. iv. 70. 1; Paus. i. 43. 7–8), and the adjective **Τριποδίσκιος** is used in the same way an Athenian would use a demotic.

3–4. For the sentiment, cf. I4. 16–17; Ar. *Lys.* 1038–9; Men. fr. 801.

4. **οἰκεῖν οἰκίαν**: 'to have a household'.

5. For the sentiment, cf. Hes. *Th.* 600–13.

I2. Lines 1–5 are a furious denunciation of women and specifically of wives, and are clearly pronounced by a married man. Aristophon fr. 6 is very similar and is most likely modelled on these verses (see **B42** introductory n.); cf. Men. fr. 119 'Damn to hell whoever was the first man to marry—and the second, and the third, and the fourth, and the one after him!' Lines 6–15 (treated as a separate fragment by Kock), on the other hand, begin not just with a refusal to condemn women, but with the expression of a positive desire to defend them—although the effort ends in failure (13–15). Lines 6–15 are separated from 1–5 in Athenaeus by the words καὶ προελθών φησιν ('and further on [the poet] says'), and although it is impossible to know how much is missing from the text, 6–15 probably belong to a second speaker and represent a response to 1–5. Chrysilla appears to be a prostitute's name at Telecl. fr. 18, as presumably in this play; perhaps the first speaker sought at least temporary refuge from his domestic troubles in her house. See J. L. Sanchis Llopis, in *Aurea Saecula ii* (1990), 725–31.

Preserved at Athenaeus 13. 559b–c, in a collection of passages (all but one from comedy) that condemn wives and marriage and are quoted by a character described as ψέγων τὸ τῆς γαμετῆς ὄνομα ('finding fault with the very name "wife"').

Iambic trimeter.

1–2. **κακὸς | κακῶς ἀπόλοιτ(ο)**: 'Might the villain die the death he deserves!', i.e. 'Damn the bastard!' (a colloquial curse; cf. **G6**. 5 n.; Olson on Ar. *Ach.* 778–9), sc. because his seeming endorsement of the practice converted one individual's terrible mistake (see 4) into a custom, dooming everyone who came after him.

2–3. **γυναῖκα . . . | ἔγημε**: a common pleonasm (e.g. Ar. *Th.* 412; Antiph. fr. 58. 2).

3.   *ἐρῶ κακῶς*: for the idiom, cf. 6–7, 12; and see **H19**. 4–5 n.
5.   *οἷον ἦν γυνὴ κακὸν πεπυσμένος*: 'having heard what sort of trouble a wife
      is . . . '; words to the effect of 'should have refused to have anything to do
      with one' must have followed.
6.   *ὦ Ζεῦ πολυτίμητ(ε)*: used to express shock or indignation at e.g.
      Pherecr. fr. 166. 1; Ar. *Eq.* 1390; *Av.* 667; fr. 336. 1; Men. *Mis.* 685; fr. 457.
      The adjective is common in invocations of all sorts; cf. **J22**. 2 n.; Olson on
      Ar. *Ach.* 759.
7–8.   *ἀπολοίμην*: sc. 'if I condemn them', with *πάντων ἄριστον κτημάτων* in
      apposition to the implied 'them'.
9–12.   The exempla put forward by the speaker and his imaginary opponent
      are all drawn from literature, and in particular from the *Odyssey* (where
      Penelope and Clytaemestra are already an opposed pair (esp. 24. 192–202))
      and Euripidean tragedy; cf. **D1–D4** n.; **D11–D12** n.
9.   For Medea, see Gantz 358–73.   For the strongly adversative use of
      δέ <γε>, as the speaker counters his imaginary interlocutor's point, see
      Denniston 155.
10.   *μέγα πρᾶγμ(α)*: 'a big deal, something special' (Men. *Sam.* 390; Timo
      SH 808. 4; D. 35. 15), i.e. 'someone equally prominent (but good)'.
11–12.   For Alcestis, see **H16**. 1 n. For Theseus' wife Phaedra as a symbol of
      wifely depravity (cf. E. frr. 430; 440 (both from the lost first *Hippolytus*);
      Gantz 285–8), and Penelope as a symbol of wifely virtue, see also Ar. *Th.*
      547–8 with Austin–Olson ad loc., and cf. Ar. *Ra.* 1043 ('Aeschylus' attack-
      ing 'Euripides') 'I didn't write about whores like Melanippe and Phaedra'.
12–15.   Cf. Ar. *Th.* 549–50, where Inlaw responds to the complaint that
      Euripides' tragedies feature countless Melanippes and Phaedras, but no
      Penelopes: 'I know the reason; you couldn't name a single Penelope among
      today's women—they're all Phaedras!'
13.   For *μέντοι* in impatient questions, as the speaker ransacks his brain for
      an elusive answer, see Ar. *Nu.* 787; *Th.* 630; Denniston 402–3.   *οἴμοι
      δείλαιος*: 'Alas, miserable (me)!', equivalent to an exasperated 'Damn!' *vel
      sim.*; common in Aristophanes (e.g. *Eq.* 139; *Nu.* 1473; *Av.* 990, all in the
      same position in the line, with the second syllable in *δείλαιος* scanned
      short via 'internal correption', as here) and probably colloquial.
14.   *μ(ε) . . . ἐπέλιπον*: 'failed me, ran out for me'.

I3. A fragment of a conversation between the newly married Simylus, who
is presumably the eponymous misogynist, and an (older? in any case wiser)
friend, who concedes that marriage brings trouble and aggravation on a
day-to-day basis, but defends the institution as ultimately to an individual
man's great benefit.

Lines 1–4 are preserved at Clement of Alexandria, *Stromateis* ii. 141. 1, in a discussion of why marriage is necessary, with 1–2 separated from 3–4 by the words εἶτ' ἐπιφέρει ('then he continues'); 3–6 are preserved at Stobaeus (1) iv. 44. 37, under the heading 'That, being human and obliged to live in accord with virtue, one must bear what befalls one nobly'; and 5–6 are preserved at Stobaeus (2) iv. 41. 10, under the heading 'That human good fortune is insecure, since one's luck changes easily'. Lines 7–16 are preserved at Stobaeus (3) iv. 22ᶜ. 71, under the heading 'That the character of those joined together renders marriage beneficial to some, but unfortunate for others'; and 14–16 are preserved at Stobaeus (4) iv. 44. 35, under the same heading as Stobaeus (1). The verses are attributed to Menander's *Misogynist* only at Stobaeus (1) and (4), and elsewhere simply to Menander. But the overlaps among the quotations allow all sixteen lines to be assigned to the play, while leaving open the possibility that something is missing between 6 and 7.

Iambic trimeter.

1–2. πρὸς τὸ πρᾶγμ(α) ἔχω | κακῶς: 'I don't feel good about the business' (for the construction, cf. Antiph. fr. 138. 2; Theophil. fr. 4. 3), i.e. about the fact that he has got married and anticipates being miserable, because his wife is spending his money and restricting his freedom to do as he pleases (7–8, cf. 13).

2. ἐπαριστέρως: 'left-handedly', i.e. 'the wrong way around'; cf. **F16**. 7 n.

3–4. τὰ λυπήσοντά σε | ὁρᾷς: cf. the echoes in 12–16 with n.

5–6. A gnomic statement, which sets the debate in more positive terms than might have been anticipated from 3–4, by casting a wife not as a trouble with positive aspects, but as a good that—like all goods—inevitably brings some evil with it.

5. οὐθέν: see **D3**. 9 n.   Δημέα (Stob. (2), as emended by Grotius) is a common name (sixty-nine examples in *LGPN* ii, including one of the characters in Menander's *Samia*), whereas Σιμύλε (Stob. (1)) is considerably rarer (eleven examples in *LGPN* ii) and ought to be printed as the *lectio difficilior*.

7–12. The lines apply the general view of the world spelled out in 5–6 to the matter of a wife, not only by showing that marriage brings advantages as well as disadvantages, but by stressing that over the long term human life is not simply a matter of 'doing as one pleases' (cf. 8) and that one must take forethought for troubles to come.

7. γυνὴ πολυτελής: for women's extravagance, cf. **A19**. 4.

8. τὸν λαβόντα: 'the man who married her'; cf. 10 τὸν ἔχοντ(α) ἑαυτήν; **I4**. 4.

8–9. What follows makes it clear that the speaker does not mean that a wife is the source of only one good thing for a man, and **ἕν ἐστί τι | ἀγαθὸν ἀπ' αὐτῆς, παῖδες** must instead mean something like '[Here's] one good thing that comes from her: children', with further additions made to the list in what follows. But Hense argued that παῖδες was an interpolation (presumably a superlinear gloss that drove out the less interesting word (e.g. δῆλον) that stood beneath it).

10. **τὸν ἔχοντ(α) ἑαυτήν:** i.e. 'her husband'.

10–12. **ἐθεράπευσεν, συμπαρέμεινεν, ἔθαψε, περιέστειλεν:** gnomic aorists (Goodwin § 154–5).

12. **περιέστειλεν οἰκείως:** 'she wraps him properly', i.e. in his funeral clothes; see R. Garland, *The Greek Way of Death* (Ithaca, NY, 1985), 24–6.

12–16. **ὅρα | κτλ.:** applying the lesson in 5–6 and the specific application of it in 7–12 to Simylus' situation, first in a positive (12–14) and then in a negative (14–16) way, each time with an echo of 3–4 τὰ λυπήσοντά σε | ὁρᾶις.

14. **οἴσεις:** sc. εὖ.   **πᾶν τὸ πρᾶγμ(α):** an echo of Simylus' τὸ πρᾶγμ(α) in 1.   **ἐκλέγηι:** 'you pick out for yourself, pay exclusive attention to'.

16. **τῶν προσδοκωμένων:** 'the anticipated (benefits)', as defined in 8–12.   **διὰ τέλους:** 'always, constantly' (LSJ s. τέλος II. 2. c).

I4. The speaker criticizes what he presents as the normal calculations made by a man preparing to marry (the distinction of the woman's family and the size of the dowry), and proposes to dispose of his own daughter in what he treats as a more rational fashion—while conceding that whoever takes her will inevitably be sorry none the less, although perhaps less sorry than he might have been, had he acted otherwise (14–16). The speaker's willingness to expose his daughter to endless, inevitably degrading public scrutiny (13–15) is striking (cf. the even more eccentric behaviour of the Cynic philosopher Crates of Thebes described in **F14**. 3–4), and it is tempting to think that he and his family lack exactly those qualities he argues ought to be disregarded, i.e. a fine pedigree and wealth—and also that she must have an exceptionally accommodating disposition.

Preserved at Stobaeus iv. 22^f. 119, under the heading 'That in marriage one ought to consider not noble birth or wealth but (the woman's) character'.

Iambic trimeter.

2.   ὦ Ζεῦ σῶτερ: appropriately invoked in a discussion of a fraught situation which might lead to ruin; cf. **G11**. 21. For the cult of Zeus the Saviour (invoked or referred to in Menander also at *Dysc.* 690; *Epitr.* 907; *Kith.* POxy. lxviii 4642 col. ii. 6 with Nünlist ad loc.; *Pk.* 759; *Sam.* 310; fr. 420. 7), see **H5** introductory n.; Ar. *Pl.* 1171–84; Diph. fr. 42. 24–5; adesp. com.

fr. 1017. 107; Garland, *ABSA* 79 (1984), 108; Austin–Olson on Ar. *Th.* 1009.
ὡς ὠνήμεθα: 'in order that we profit' (aorist middle < ὀνίνημι), sc. 'from our choices', as has often not happened in the past (Goodwin § 333).

3. οὐκ ἐξετάζειν: sc. ἡμᾶς ἔδει (cf. 1), as again in 7.   μηθέν (= μηδέν; see **D3**. 9 n.) is adverbial, 'not at all'.

4. 'who the grandfather of the woman one is going to marry was, and who her grandmother (was)'. One important reason for engaging in such enquiries would in fact be to ensure that the family was of citizen status.

7. τράπεζαν: 'a money-changer's table' (LSJ s. τράπεζα II). For money-changers, see 8 n.; Antiph. fr. 157. 11–12 'there's no more loathsome group than this' (since their profit came from paying slightly less for the money they accepted than it was worth).   φέρειν: see 3 n.   τὴν προῖκ(α): The dowry (usefully conceived as a form of ante-mortem inheritance) was an important part of any marriage agreement (see Men. *Dysc.* 842–4 with Handley ad loc.; *Mis.* 974–6; *Sam.* 726–7; adesp. com. fr. 1098. 4–6; Harrison i. 45–60, esp. 49–50) and served—as the angry protests of numerous male characters in comedy (e.g. Anaxandr. fr. 53. 4–6; Antiph. fr. 270; Alex. fr. 150 with Arnott's introductory n.; Men. frr. 802; 805; cf. **15** introductory n.) make clear—as a means of protecting the bride's interests. In the event of a divorce, her husband was required to return her dowry; he therefore had a substantial interest in keeping her happy and, if she insisted, in allowing her input into their affairs, particularly since it might be the dowry money that allowed the household to be set up in the first place (9 n.). See Foxhall, *CQ* ns 39 (1989), 22–44 (on the social function of the dowry); Cohn-Haft, *JHS* 115 (1995), 11–13 (on a woman's right to seek a divorce); Ingalls, *Phoenix*, 56 (2002), 246–54. The position of an heiress (**C16**. 1 n.) was similar.

8–11. The contrast is set up in chiastic (A–B–B′–A′) style and is reinforced with specific verbal echoes: a δοκιμαστής examines money which is not fated to remain ἔνδον ('within (the house)') for more than a few months, whereas the woman who will remain ἔνδον ('within (her husband's house)') for her entire life (although cf. **15**) is not scrutinized (δοκιμάσασθαι) at all.

8. δοκιμαστής: 'the tester', i.e. the money-changer himself (since assaying coins was a basic part of the business), called after the specific service he provides the groom or the groom's family.

9. What the dowry is spent on is left unspecified. But this is clearly intended to be a typical case, making it more likely that the money is to be imagined as having been used to set up housekeeping than as simply dissipated by the husband.   πέντε is here a small round number ('a few'), as at Antiph. fr. 203. 4. Cf. Headlam on Herod. 3. 23.

10.   All Athenian women must have gone out of the house from time to time to attend festivals and funerals, or to visit family and friends, and poorer women probably went out constantly to fetch water, visit the market, or work (Brock, *CQ* NS 44 (1994), 336–46). But this verse describes the ideal case: a genuinely 'good' woman never steps outside the courtyard door of her house, but remains sitting (**καθεδουμένης** < καθέζομαι) quietly within. Cf. **A19**. 4–5; **I5** with nn.; **I8**. 18 with n.; Headlam on Herod. 1. 37; Cohen 146–67.   **διὰ βίου**: 'through her entire life', as at Bato fr. 1. 2.

11.   **εἰκῆι**: 'at random', because no questions were asked about his potential bride's character.

12.   **ἀγνώμον(α) ὀργίλην χαλεπήν**: '(someone) thoughtless, hot-tempered, (or) difficult'. For the proverbially bad temper of women, e.g. Alex. fr. 150. 5–8; Men. fr. 636.   **ἐὰν τύχηι**: literally 'if it should happen', i.e. 'perhaps'.

13.   **λάλον**: 'talkative' (a two-termination adjective), a trait for which women are criticized constantly in comedy (e.g. **A19**. 4; Ar. *Ec.* 120; Antiph. fr. 247; Alex. fr. 96; Xenarch. fr. 14; Philem. fr. 154).

14.   **ταύτην λαβεῖν**: sc. as a wife, as in 11; cf. **I3**. 8.

15.   **λαλεῖτε**: 'talk (to her)!'

16–17.   **ἀνάγκη γὰρ κτλ.**: For the sentiment (gnomic), cf. **I1**. 3–4 n.; Men. fr. 797 'You need to know, if you've decided to marry, that you'll acquire a great good if you get a small evil'.

I5. The speaker has emerged from his house, pursued by his wife Rhode (4–5), who is intent on continuing a quarrel that began within, and who is most likely an heiress (**C16**. 1 n.) or a richly dowered and thus self-confident wife of the sort complained about in the passages cited in **I4**. 7 n. For the ideal (invoked in vain here) of the 'good wife' who is never seen outside her courtyard, see **I4**. 10 n.

   Preserved at Stobaeus iv. 23. 11, under the heading 'Marital precepts'.
   Iambic trimeter.

1–2.   **τὴν αὐλίαν**: i.e. the **αὔλειος θύρα** (as at the end of 2), which led from the walled courtyard that surrounded the house into the street (cf. 4); to be distinguished from the door of the house itself. In apposition to **τοὺς τῆς γαμετῆς ὅρους**.

3.   The implicit point of **ἐλευθέραι γυναικί** is that errands that involve going out of the courtyard into the street can be done by slaves, of whom a normal household is assumed to have at least one. Cf. **A13**. 8–10 n.   **νενόμισται** represents an explicit appeal to social convention (νόμος).   **οἰκίας**: to be taken with **πέρας** ('limit'; in apposition to αὔλειος θύρα) in 2.

5. **κυνός ἐστ(ι) ἔργον**: '(this) is what a dog does', sc. when it chases someone, barking. For dogs (common domestic animals) generally, see Olson on Ar. *Pax* 24–5. For calling someone a 'dog' by way of insult, see Graver, *CA* 14 (1995), 43–53; Steiner, *JHS* 121 (2001), 154–8.   **Ῥόδη** (a common woman's name in Athens; eleven additional examples in *LGPN* ii, including Philem. fr. 87) is also the name of a wife who appears on stage in Men. fr. 188. 6 (from *The Priestess*, to which Clericus suggested this fragment might belong as well).

16. Plato's *Phaon* may have been a version of a story also told by Cratinus (fr. 370 ap. Ath. 2. 69d), according to whom 'Aphrodite fell in love with Phaon and hid him in some beautiful lettuce' (Φάωνος ἐρασθεῖσαν τὴν Ἀφροδίτην ἐν καλαῖς θριδακίναις αὐτὸν ἀποκρύψαι; cf. Eub. fr. 13 and Call. fr. 478, where the same story is told of Adonis). Cf. Marsyas *FGrHist* 135–6 F 9 (cited in the same section of Athenaeus), who claims that Phaon was hidden in green wheat; Ael. *VH* 12. 18, who adds that he was 'the fairest of human beings'. But this fragment suggests that in Plato's play Phaon was the darling of mortal women as well as of Aphrodite; and fr. 189 (= **G4**) presents a character—probably Phaon himself—consulting a cookbook about aphrodisiacs in the hope of keeping up with the immense demands being made upon him. For the date of the play, see test. ii. Antiphanes also wrote a *Phaon* (fr. 213), about which nothing is known; cf. Sapph. fr. 211a–b (a collection of sources on Sappho and Phaon); M. Williamson, *Sappho's Immortal Daughters* (Cambridge, Mass., and London, 1995), 8–11.

The speaker is a deity (7) who calls herself Κουροτρόφος ('Rearer of Children') and may be Aphrodite herself (thus Meineke) but is more likely the independent deity referred to at Ar. *Th.* 300 and offered sacrifice at *IG* II² 1358 col. II. 6, 14, 31, 46; *SEG* xxi 527. 12, 85 (thus Wilamowitz). The women to whom she is speaking are presumably the chorus, who want not just to see Phaon (5) but to 'enter in' somewhere (19–20); the action probably takes place before a temple of Aphrodite, in which Phaon (as the goddess' favourite) is resident and from which, if he is Speaker A in **G4**, he eventually emerges with his book-roll.

Preserved at Athenaeus 10. 441e–2a (manuscript A only), at the end of a collection of comic references to women's fondness for wine (see **H10** introductory n.). The speaker in Athenaeus characterizes Plato as διηγούμενος ὅσα διὰ τὸν οἶνον συμβαίνει ταῖς γυναιξί ('describing the things that happen to women on account of wine'), apparently because he takes 1–4 to mean that they only want sex so desperately when they are drunk. But the focus is actually on women's lust, for which see e.g. Anaxandr. fr. 61; Theophil. fr. 6; Apollod. Car. fr. 6.

Iambic trimeter.

1–6. The argument is complicated and obscure, but appears to proceed as follows. If the speaker got her wish and the women's ἄνοια became wine (1–2), their νοῦς (i.e. their transformed ἄνοια) would belong ἐν τῶι καπήλου ('in the bartender's place, the wineshop'; cf. **J10–J11** with nn.) (3–4). But that has not happened, as is proven by the fact that they hope to get access to Phaon without making the necessary preliminary offerings (5–6)—which is no more likely than that one would be allowed to drink wine in a bar without paying for it first, and so shows a lack of 'wineshop thinking'. The speaker has thus not got her wish, and the women are behaving as foolishly as ever; and there is (despite Athenaeus) no direct allusion to women's bibulousness.

1. εἰέν: 'alright'; cf. **C2.** 9 n.

3–4. Cf. Ar. *Lys.* 426–7 (to an inattentive slave) 'Where are *you* looking, doing nothing except keeping an eye out for a wineshop?'

5. προτέλεια: 'preliminary sacrifices' carried out before the main ritual begins; cf. 7 προθύεται.

6. πρότερον is adverbial, 'first'.

8–9. πλακοῦς ἐνόρχης, ἄμυλος ἐγκύμων, κίχλαι | ἐκκαίδεχ᾽ ὁλόκληροι: 'an uncastrated cake, a pregnant wheat-paste cake, sixteen perfect thrushes'; a parody of language commonly used to describe animal victims in sacrificial calendars and the like (e.g. *IG* II² 1356; 1358). πλακοῦς (sc. ἄρτος) is a generic term for unleavened baked cakes; see Olson–Sens on Archestr. fr. 60. 15 and Matro fr. 1. 116–17. For ἄμυλοι (which also contained cheese, milk, and honey), see Olson–Sens on Matro fr. 1. 4–5. For thrushes, see **B34.** 10 n. For ὁλόκληρος, cf. Anaxandr. fr. 40. 10; *SEG* xxv 687. 1 (of a sacrificial animal).   μέλιτι μεμιγμέναι is most likely to be taken 'glazed with honey' or 'in a honey sauce'; cf. Ar. *Ach.* 1040 (honey poured over a sausage hot from the fire). But perhaps the thrushes are simply to be served at the same time as the honey (in banquet catalogues and the like at e.g. Anaxandr. fr. 42. 44; Antiph. frr. 273. 2; 295. 1). For honey, see **J6.** 5–6 n.

10. ἐπισέληνα: probably 'moon-shaped'. The adjective is properly applied to a type of sacrificial cake (see Hsch. ε 5154) and is here used—absurdly—of portions of hare-meat (λαγῶια; see **G5.** 9 n.).

11. Whatever is concealed in Athenaeus' unmetrical ταῦτ᾽ εὐτελέστατα (the problem might easily involve ἤδη as well), it must mark a change in the character of the catalogue, for what follows in 12–18 is a list of less substantial and less expensive items dedicated to subsidiary deities, and is suddenly full of crude sexual allusions and double entendres.

12. βολβῶν: see H4. 10 n. Ὀρθάννηι: an ithyphallic fertility deity (Ar. fr. 325 ap. Phot. α 3404 with K–A ad loc.; Str. 13. 588) who was the title-character in a play by Eubulus (frr. 75–9; see Hunter's introductory n.). The name is cognate with ὀρθός ('upright, erect'). A μέδιμνος (a dry measure equal to about 40 litres) contained six ἑκτεῖς, and τρί(α) ἡμιέκτεα ('three half-*hekteis*') is thus equivalent to one-quarter of a μέδιμνος.

13. Κονισάλωι . . . καὶ παραστάταιν δυοῖν: Conisalus was another ithyphallic fertility deity (Ar. *Lys.* 982; fr. 325 ap. Phot. α 3404 with K–A ad loc.; Str. 13. 588) and the title-character in a play by Timocles (fr. 22). He is imagined here as a deity flanked by twin attendants. But Athenaeus 9. 395f notes that the word παραστάται was also used of the testicles, and the joke is that Conisalus' name stands in for his most prominent physical feature: an erect penis.

14–15. μύρτων πινακίσκος: 'a little platter of myrtle-berries (< μύρτος)'. But the specification that the berries be 'plucked by hand' is odd, and the explanation in 15 that this must be done because 'the deities dislike the smell of lamps' makes it clear that there is word-play on μύρτον ('clitoris', and by extension 'female genital region' generally) and thus a reference to the partial pubic depilation accomplished either by plucking (τίλλω) or singeing with fire that was practised by fashionable Athenian women; cf. M. F. Kilmer, *JHS* 102 (1982), 104–12; and *Greek Erotica on Attic Red-Figure Vases* (London, 1993), 133–69, esp. 133–41; Austin–Olson on Ar. *Th.* 216–17.

16. Κυσί τε καὶ Κυνηγέταις: IG II² 4962. 9–10 (a list of preliminary sacrifices to deities associated with Asclepius; early fourth century) describes offerings made to divine Hounds and Huntsmen (Κυσὶν πόπανα τρία· Κυνηγέταις πόπανα τρί (sic)), and Hesychius κ 4763 reports that κύων could be used to mean 'penis' (τὸ ἀνδρεῖον μόριον; cf. Ar. *Lys.* 158). But the obscurity of these figures and the corruption in the first half of the line make it impossible to know exactly what the joke was.

17–18. Λόρδωνι . . ., Κυβδάσωι . . ., | ἥρωι Κέλητι: invented names that recall the terms for three sexual positions, in which the woman, respectively, threw her head back and her pelvis forward (λορδόω; cf. Ar. *Ec.* 10; Mnesim. fr. 4. 55); bent over forward 'doggy style' (κύβδα; cf. Ar. *Th.* 489; Macho 308); and sat astride the man (κελητίζω; cf. Ar. *V.* 501; *Th.* 153; Macho 171). Athenaeus' δορδωνι is in origin a majuscule error, Λ having been mistaken for Δ. τριώβολον: i.e. a half-drachma; perhaps an allusion to a standard prostitute's fee (see I12. 18 n.).

18. δέρμα καὶ θυλήματα: 'a hide and sacrificial barley-cakes'. The hide of a sacrificial animal was given to the god or his priest, which in practice amounted to the same thing (e.g. Ar. *Th.* 758; *IG* I³ 35. 9–12; II² 1356. 5–6, etc.; D. Gill, *Greek Cult Tables* (New York and London, 1991), 15–19). But here there may be an allusion to dildoes (ὄλισβοι), which were made of leather (Ar. *Lys.* 110 with Henderson ad loc.; Herod. 6. 18–19). For θυλήματα, see Telecl. fr. 35; Pherecr. fr. 28. 6; Ar. *Pax* 1040 with Olson ad loc.

19–21.   Resuming the argument in 5–6 after the catalogue of offerings in 7–18, but with an explicit threat about the consequences of non-compliance appended in 20–1.

19.   ταῦτ(α) ἐστι τ(ὰ) ἀναλώματ(α): 'this is what you must spend'.

20–1.   διὰ κενῆς (sc. χειρός) merely reinforces μάτην, literally 'in vain (and) with an empty (hand)'. Cf. Ar. *V.* 929 διὰ κενῆς ἄλλως.

21.   βινητιᾶν: 'to want to be fucked' (desiderative < βινέω, for which see **B29.** 3 n.), as at Ar. *Lys.* 715. For the passive sense (= βινεῖσθαι ἐπιθυμεῖν rather than βινεῖν ἐπιθυμεῖν, as one would expect), see Sandbach on Men. *Dysc.* 462.

I7–I12. For prostitution (practised by boys and men, as well as by women) in Athens, see Davidson 78–91; D. Hamel, *Trying Neaira* (New Haven, 2003), 4–16; P. Brulé, *Women of Ancient Greece* (Edinburgh, 2003), 186–220; and cf. **H14** with introductory n.

I7. The individuals referred to in 1–6 (the real subject of the attack) are not common prostitutes like those described in 7–26 and **I8.** 3–9, 13–17, but courtesans like Lais (**I12**) and the speaker of **I11**, who extract enough money from their clients over the years to allow them to set up their own brothels, like Nicarete in D. 59. 18–19 (although she appears to have been running an extremely high-class operation). Cf. **D14** (where the business has not, however, gone as smoothly as it was supposed to); **H5** introductory n.; **I11** introductory n.; and contrast the situation referred to in **J9**, where a male pimp runs a stable of women. Isostasion is probably a prostitute's name ('Equal in weight (to gold)' *vel sim.*), and Webster suggested that this fragment might be part of a father's or paedagogue's warning to a young man who had fallen in love with her.

Preserved complete at Athenaeus (1) 13. 568a–d, in a long collection of comic references to prostitutes *et sim.* that also includes **E27**; **I8**; **I9**; **I12**. In addition, 1–2 γίγνεται, 7–26 are preserved at Clement of Alexandria, *Paid.* iii. 8. 1, in an attack on female luxury, with the omission of 2 ῥάπτουσι–6 serving to disguise the fact that the passage does not refer to ordinary women.

Trochaic tetrameter catalectic.

1.   πρός + accusative: 'in comparison to'.   τοὺς πέλας: i.e. their lovers/customers.

2.   πάντα τἆλλ(α) αὐταῖς πάρεργα γίγνεται: 'everything else is of secondary importance for them'.

2–3.   ῥάπτουσι . . . | πᾶσιν ἐπιβουλάς: 'they stitch together plots against everyone', sc. so as to extract as much money as possible from the men with whom they spend their time; cf. I12. 11–13. 'Weaving' or 'stitching plots' is a banal image; cf. Ar. *Lys.* 630; S. *OT* 387; Taillardat § 419–20.

4.   ἀνέλαβον: 'they take up, accept (into their houses)', presumably after buying them from slave-dealers, since the women are not treated like free agents (esp. 22–6). A gnomic aorist, like e.g. ἀφεῖλεν in 10, ὑπενέδυσ(ε) in 11, and ἀπήγαγον in 15.   πρωτοπείρους τῆς τέχνης: 'novices in the craft'; in contrast to the woman running the house, who has already put in her time as a prostitute.

5–6.   These lines announce the theme of the rest of what is preserved of the speech (7–26).   ἀναπλάττουσι: 'they reshape, rework'.   μήτε τοὺς τρόπους | μήτε τὰς ὄψεις: The emphasis in what follows, however, is almost entirely on the women's appearance.   ὁμοίας διατελεῖν οὔσας ἔτι: 'continue still to be the same', i.e. 'remain the same'; cf. 22–3 with n.

7–20.   τυγχάνει μικρά τις οὖσα etc. function like conditional clauses; see D5. 13–16 n.

7–8.   μικρά: '(too) short'; contrast μακρά '(too) tall' (cf. I8. 8, where the adjective is used in a more neutral fashion).   φελλὸς ἐν ταῖς βαυκίσιν | ἐγκεκάττυται: 'cork has been attached to the soles of her shoes'; cf. H14. 8 n.; X. *Oec.* 10. 2, where Ischomachus' wife, as part of a misguided attempt to appear more attractive, covers her face with white lead (see 17 n.) and wears ὑποδήματα . . . ὑψηλά, ὅπως μείζων δοκοίη εἶναι ἢ ἐπεφύκει ('high shoes, in order to seem taller than she was naturally'). Pollux vii. 94 describes βαυκίδες as 'expensive yellow shoes'; cf. Ar. fr. 355 (worn by Ionian women and thus presumably luxurious). For the simplex καττύω ('put a sole on a shoe or sandal') and its cognates, see Olson on *Ach.* 299–302.

8.   διάβαθρον λεπτόν: 'a thin(-soled) shoe'; it is unclear exactly what type of shoe or sandal a διάβαθρον (in a list of items for sale in a cobbler's shop at Herod. 7. 61) is.

9.   ἐξέρχεται: sc. from the brothel into the street, where she stands, soliciting customers; cf. I8. 5 n., 13 n.; contrast 22–3 with n.

10.   τοῦτο τοῦ μήκους ἀφεῖλεν: 'this reduces (see 4 n.) her height'.   ἰσχία: 'hips', i.e. 'arse' (cf. 11). For a small arse as unattractive, see Semon. fr. 7. 76, where one of the ugly Monkey-Woman's faults is that she 'has no arse and is all legs' (ἄπυγος, αὐτόκωλος).

11.   ὑπενέδυσ(ε) ἐρραμμέν(α) αὐτήν: '(the woman running the brothel; cf. 17) secretly puts a pad on her', sc. beneath her clothes, where an

unsuspecting customer will not see it until it is too late. ἐρραμμέν(α) (literally 'stitched things') is < ῥάπτω.

11–12. τὴν εὐπυγίαν | ἀναβοᾶν: 'loudly comment on what a fine rear end she has'. For outspoken appreciation of a sexually desirable individual's arse, cf. Ar. *Lys.* 1148 (where the speaker uses the crude πρωκτός (literally 'arse-hole') rather than the inoffensive πυγή (for which, see *Maculate Muse*, § 450)); J12. 4–6 (older men admiring a gorgeous boy). For audience reaction as the key point for all these preparations, cf. 21.

12. κοιλίαν ἁδρὰν ἔχει: 'she has a thick belly', i.e. 'is fat'.

13–15. 'They have some of the chest-pieces that (ὧν for ἅ, via attraction of the relative) belong to the comic actors, and by attaching such things at a right angle' (sc. so that they stick straight out from the girl's chest), 'they move her clothing forward away from her belly with these as if with poles.' The reference is to the 'falsies' used to make male actors look like women.

16. ζωγραφοῦσιν ἀσβόλωι: 'they draw them in with soot'.

17. συμβέβηκ(ε) is impersonal, 'it's happened that . . . ', i.e. 'it's the case that . . .' εἶναι μέλαιναν: for a dark complexion on a woman as unattractive, cf. Diph. fr. 91. 3. Contrast the common use of λευκός and its compounds to describe beautiful women and boys (cf. **B3**. 3 n.). The subject of κατέπλασεν in the woman who owns the house; cf. 11. ψιμυθίωι: 'white lead', referred to as a cosmetic also at e.g. Ar. *Ec.* 878; Eub. fr. 97. 1; Lys. 1. 14; X. *Oec.* 10. 2 (cf. 7–8 n.).

18. παιδέρωτ(α) ἐντρίβεται: 'she rubs rouge on herself'. Dioscorides 3. 17 reports that παιδέρως was made from acanthus root.

19–26. Unlike in 7–18, what is described here is an attempt to improve a good natural feature rather than the means of disguising a bad one.

19. δείκνυται: probably passive (with τοῦτο as subject) rather than middle (with τοῦτο as object and the woman as subject, as in 18). For the idea, cf. I8. 5.

20. εὐφυεῖς: i.e. 'straight and well-spaced'. ἐξ ἀνάγκης: 'of necessity', i.e. 'like it or not'; setting up 22–6 (cf. 26 ἄν τε βούλητ(αι) ἄν τε μή).

21. τὸ στόμ(α) ὡς κομψὸν φορεῖ: 'what a lovely mouth she has' (prolepsis). Cf. 11–12 with n.

22–3. διατελεῖ . . . | ἔνδον: 'she'll remain inside' (for the verb, see 6 n.), sc. because her appearance is not yet likely to attract customers; contrast 9 with n.

23–5. ὥσπερ κτλ. offers a proleptic description of the type of 'thin peg of laurel' the woman is made to keep between her lips: it resembles the bits of wood butchers jam between the teeth of goats' heads (sc. to allow customers to inspect the tongue and thus judge the health of the animal;

cf. Ar. *Eq.* 375–81 with Sommerstein on 376). For eating goats' heads, see **G13**. 5.

26. τῶι χρόνωι: 'in time, eventually'.   σέσηρεν is < σαίρω, 'show one's teeth, grin'.

I8. A moralizing speech by an older man. For an explanation of the insistence of young men on engaging in the dangerous behaviour he describes (esp. 19–23), see **I9**; and cf. Cohen 168–70. For the idea that prostitution supplies a necessary outlet for the sexual energies of young men, who would otherwise try to seduce free citizen-women, cf. **F18**. 5–6; Philem. fr. 3. 5–9. For the style of prostitution described in 3–9, 13–17, see **I7** introductory n.

Eubulus fr. 67 (~ Eub. fr. 82; both passages are quoted by Athenaeus just before this one) is very similar, and 6 (where see n.) is actually identical to Eub. frr. 67. 4 = 82. 3. One poet certainly took the lines over from the other; but who borrowed from whom is impossible to say. Cf. **B42** introductory n.

Preserved at Athenaeus 13. 569a–d, in the same collection of texts as **I7** (where see introductory n.); **I9**; **I12**.

Iambic trimeter.

1.   The repetition of δεινά marks the speaker's depth of feeling; cf. E. *Hec.* 1097.

3–4. ὅπου γὰρ κτλ. explains why the behaviour of Athens' young men is supposed to be so terrible: 'for (they live in a place) where one can see very good-looking girls at the brothels'. The construction is colloquial: after the initial ellipse, the genitive absolute introduces a relative clause that contains what, in a more formal style, would be the main verb.

4–5. ἃς ἔξεστ(ι) ὁρᾶν | κτλ.: contrast 18 (of citizen-women).

5.   εἰληθερούσας: 'basking in the sun', i.e. 'out in the street'; cf. 13 (prostitutes drag men 'in' off the street); **I7**. 9 n.; Eub. fr. 67. 3 (a customer can examine prostitutes πρὸς τὸν ἥλιον ('in the sunlight')).   στέρν(α) ἀπημφιεσμένας: 'undressed as regards their chests', i.e. 'with their breasts bare'; cf. **I7**. 19.

6.   γυμνάς: 'half-dressed' (not 'naked', as at Philem. fr. 3. 10 (also of prostitutes standing outside a brothel), since the mention of bare breasts in 5 would then be pointless), i.e. 'wearing no *himatia*', which served to cover up a respectable woman's body. Cf. **J8**. 4 (where it is probably only the outer robe that is stolen); Eub. frr. 67. 4–5 = 82. 3–4 (also of prostitutes) γυμνὰς . . . | ἐν λεπτοπήνοις ὑμέσιν ('half-dressed in thin, sheer garments').   ἐφεξῆς . . . ἐπὶ κέρως τεταγμένας: 'lined up one after another in a column', like soldiers preparing for battle. The description of the women standing in line sets up the scene imagined in 7–9, as a potential customer inspects them one by one. κέρως is the Attic equivalent of common κέρας.

7.   Literally 'of whom after selecting (the one) with whom he is pleased, it is possible for a man . . . ', sc. 'to go straight to bed with her'. But the speaker fails to complete the thought, since what he means is obvious, as again in 16–17.

8–9.   Unlike in **I7**. 7–18, where the assumption is that every prostitute's body must be made to conform to an ideal shape and size in order for her to appeal to customers, the emphasis here is on the fact that the women all look different, so that part of the appeal of a brothel is that a man can select the body-type (8) and age (9) he prefers.

8.   **στρογγύληι**: literally 'round', and thus perhaps 'short and solid' (in contrast to the two adjectives that follow).   **ῥικνῆι**: 'withered up (with age)' (cf. the final adjective in 9), or perhaps 'emaciated'.

9.   **μεσοκόπωι**: 'in the middle', i.e. 'middle-aged', as at Cratin. fr. 473. **πεπαιτέραι**: 'very ripe' (comparative < πέπων), i.e. 'very old', as at Ar. *Ec*. 895–6 (an old woman contrasts πέπειροι like herself with νέαι in a specifically sexual context).

10–12 recall popular tales of romantic intrigue of a sort alluded to also at Ar. *Th*. 499–516.

10.   **μὴ κτλ.**: 'without having to . . .'   **εἰσβῆναι**: sc. to a citizen-girl's house (as also with εἰσδῦναι in 11 and εἰσενεχθῆναι in 12). For the idea, cf. **C11**. 5–6.

11.   **δι(ὰ) ὀπῆς κάτωθεν . . . στέγης**: '(by going) through a peep-hole beneath the roof', in implicit contrast to entering through a window (10). For the idea, cf. Sannyr. fr. 8. 1 'What could I turn into, to get into this peep-hole?' (from *Danae*; probably Zeus trying to discover a means of access to the princess's chamber). For peep-holes (ὀπαί; cognate with ὄψομαι, ὄπωπα), see also Ar. *V*. 317/b, 352; fr. 10 with K–A ad loc.

12.   **ἐν ἀχύροισιν**: 'in (a basket full of) bran' (for which, see **G1**. 1–2 n.), most likely intended for animal fodder (cf. Ar. *V*. 1309–10; Philem. fr. 158). **τέχνηι**: 'as a trick', i.e. 'craftily'.

13.   **αὗταί**: i.e. the prostitutes, who not only do not need to be approached by means of elaborate devices (contrast 10–12), but are themselves the aggressors.   **εἰσέλκουσι**: see 5 n.

14–15.   **ἐπικαλούμεναι Ι πατρίδια**: 'calling them "daddykins"' (an affectionate diminutive < πατήρ); cf. **H11**. 4 n.

15.   **τοὺς δ(ὲ) ἀπφάρια, τοὺς νεωτέρους**: '(calling) others, those who are younger, "sweet brother"' (an affectionate diminutive < ἄπφα, which the lexicographers identify as an endearing name used between brothers and sisters; cf. Men. fr. 652).

16. ἔστιν: 'one can', sc. 'have sex with'. But the speaker again (cf. 7 n.) fails to express himself explicitly.   ἀδεῶς sets up 19–23 (esp. 19). εὐτελῶς: The idea is left undeveloped in what is preserved of the fragment; but cf. Eub. frr. 67. 7 = 82. 7 μικροῦ πρίασθαι κέρματος τὴν ἡδονήν ('to buy your pleasure for a small copper coin'; also of prostitutes); Philem. fr. 3. 12–13 (on the glories of organized prostitution) 'The door (to the brothel) is open; one obol (is the price). Leap in!'

17. πάντας τρόπους: cf. I6. 17–18 n.; I9, esp. 4–6; Philem. fr. 3. 15 (see 16 n.) 'Have the girl you want, and in the way you want her!'

18. The line refers to citizen-girls, who are (at least ideally; see I4. 10 n.) kept entirely out of men's sight (ἃς δ(ὲ) οὔτ(ε) ἰδεῖν ἐστ(ι)) and can there- fore only be visited (and seen) under cover of darkness (οὔτ(ε) ὁρῶντ(α) ἰδεῖν σαφῶς).

19. τετραμαίνοντα: 'trembling' (equivalent to τρέμοντα), sc. when they reflect on the penalties for adultery (see 22 n.).

20. ἐν τῆι χειρὶ τὴν ψυχὴν ἔχοντα: 'having one's soul in one's hand', i.e. risking one's life, appears to be a Hebrew idiom (e.g. *ISam.* 19. 5) rather than a Greek one, and Casaubon—presumably objecting as well to the hiatus δεδιότα, ἐν—accordingly expelled this verse as a late addition to the text. There must in any case be a small lacuna before 21.

21. The line echoes E. *Hipp.* 415–16 (Phaedra's baffled question about married women who conduct secret love affairs) αἳ πῶς ποτ', ὦ δέσποινα ποντία Κύπρι, | βλέπουσιν ἐς πρόσωπα τῶν ξυνευ- νετῶν; 'Cypris' is Aphrodite (see Olson on Ar. *Ach.* 988–9), who is appropriately invoked both in Euripides and here as the goddess of physical love.

22. The crude verb βινεῖν (**B29**. 3 n.) stands in sharp contrast to the lack of explicit sexual reference that characterizes much of what survives of this speech (see 7 n., 16 n.), and marks this as its emotional and rhetorical climax.   τῶν Δρακοντείων νόμων: Pausanias ix. 36. 8 reports that the late seventh-century Athenian lawgiver Draco (*PAA* 374190) established the principle that the vengeance taken on a μοιχός (a man who had unsanctioned consenting sex with a free woman belonging to another household; cf. **D13**. 3–4; **E27**) should not be subject to legal oversight by the state, and individuals caught in the act by the woman's κύριος could still be executed on the spot in the classical period (Lys. 1. 49). Sex with a prostitute, on the other hand, was specifically excluded from the definition of μοιχεία (D. 59. 67). See Harrison i. 32–7.

23. προσκινούμενοι: 'as they move in coordination with (their partners)', as at Ar. *Lys.* 227–8 (cf. *Ec.* 256–7).

I9. This fragment (most likely spoken by a young man who has just experienced the situation he describes) amounts to a response to the arguments put forward in **I8**: whatever the risks (see **I8**. 22 n.), indulging in μοιχεία by sleeping with a free citizen-girl—and particularly, it seems, with someone with little or no experience in bed (4)—is far more enjoyable than having sex with a prostitute.

Preserved at Athenaeus 13. 570f–1a (manuscript A only), as the last in the collection of texts that also includes **I7** (where see introductory n.); **I8**; **I12**.

Iambic trimeter.

1–2. ὅσον τὸ μεταξὺ … | … τὴν νύκτα κοιμᾶσθαι is exclamatory; 'How great the difference between spending the night . . .!'
1. κορίσκης: 'a nice little girl' (affectionate diminutive < κόρη), i.e. 'a nice free girl' (with whom no one ought to be sleeping; see **I8**. 22 n.).
2. χαμαιτύπης: 'a common prostitute', as at Men. *Sam.* 348.   βαβαί (see **H14**. 9 n.), like the oath at the end of 3, expresses the speaker's own astonishment at the truth of the observation he has just made.
3. Exclamatory nominatives.   ἡ στιφρότης: 'the firmness (of her flesh)!'; the cognate adjective στιφρός is used of young girls' bodies at Ar. fr. 148. 3 and most likely Men. fr. 343.   A definite article would seem to be expected with πνεῦμα, as with the nouns that precede it, hence the conjectures listed in the apparatus. But the grammatical function of the word is clear from the first half of the verse, and the omission is most likely colloquial.   δαίμονες: 'ye gods!'; see 2 n.
4–6. Up to χερσίν is a single long exclamatory nominative governed by τό at the beginning of 4.
4. τὸ μὴ σφόδρ(α) εἶναι πάνθ' ἕτοιμα: 'that everything is not all too ready!', i.e. that the girl is not immediately prepared to do whatever her lover wants, as a prostitute would be (see **I8**. 17 with n.; and cf. the description of common prostitutes at Philem. fr. 3. 9 as κατεσκευασμένας ('in a state of readiness')).
4–5. τι is an internal accusative with ἀγωνιᾶσαι, 'to have a bit of a struggle'.
5–6. ῥαπισθῆναί τε καὶ | πληγὰς λαβεῖν (= πληγῆναι): 'to be both slapped and punched'—which the speaker regards as part of the fun of the encounter.
6. ἁπαλαῖσι χερσίν: instrumental dative. The softness of the girl's hands means that the blows she delivers do no damage. But the adjective also has erotic undertones, as at Alex. fr. 49. 2–3; cf. **B3**. 3 n.
6–7. τὸν μέγιστον: a gratuitous qualification of τὸν Δία, the effect of which is to add force to ἡδύ γε: what the speaker is describing is no minor pleasure.

I10. A complaint by a disappointed μοιχός, who had been led to expect an experience like that described in **I9**, but instead found himself in bed with someone too sexually experienced or aggressive for his tastes.

Preserved at Aelian, *On Animals* 12. 10, along with Cratin. fr. 58 and Philem. fr. 65, as evidence of the reputation of the female mouse for lechery. After quoting the fragment, Aelian provides a gloss on the final sentence, saying that Epicrates wished to offer a hyberbolic characterization of the girl as extremely lecherous by calling her μυωνιὰν ὅλην; and Meineke on this basis proposed the supplement <ὅλη> in 5.

Iambic trimeter.

1. **τελέως μ(ε) ὑπῆλθεν**: 'deceived (LSJ s. ὑπέρχομαι III. 2) me completely'. **κατάρατος**: see **D14**. 8 n.   A **μαστροπός** ('go-between') is someone (normally a woman) who tries to make one party in a potential sexual relationship attractive to the other (e.g. Ar. *Th.* 558; Epicr. fr. 8. 1; Theophil. fr. 11. 4; X. *Smp.* 4. 57–60), presumably in the hope of extracting money from one of the lovers at some point; Xenophon's Socrates, at any rate, claims that a considerable income could be generated this way (*Smp.* 3. 10).

2–3. The μαστροπός uses the Doric form of the feminine accusative singular definite article **τάν** and invokes the goddess generally referred to today as Persephone as both **Κόρα** ('the Daughter'; a Doric form of Κόρη) and **Φερρέφαττα** (the normal Attic form of the name in the classical period; see Ar. *Th.* 287 with Austin–Olson ad loc.). The most straight-forward explanation of the mix of dialects would seem to be that she is a Doric-speaker attempting to appeal to an Athenian; cf. **F6** introductory n. (also a play by Epicrates). That the divinities by whom the go-between swears are virginal females is part of her strategy of persuasion, for this is how she represents the girl on whose behalf she is acting (3–4).

3–4. The repeated **ὡς** is dependent on ἐπομνύουσα in 2, 'swearing that (the girl was) . . .'   **δάμαλις** ('a heifer') may be an allusion to A. *Supp.* 351 (the chorus of Danaids describe themselves as 'like a heifer pursued by a wolf'; cf. **D7** introductory n.), as **πῶλος ἀδμής** ('an unbroken filly') certainly is to H. *Od.* 6. 109, 228 παρθένος ἀδμής (of Nausicaa). Both are in any case elevated poetic images glossed by the more straightforward **παρθένος** (here specifically 'virgin' rather than simply 'unmarried girl').

4. **ἄρ(α)**: 'expressing the surprise attendant upon disillusionment' (Denniston 35–6).

4–5. **μυωνιὰ | <ὅλη>**: 'an utter (LSJ s. ὅλος I. 3) mouse-nest', although whether this means that the girl was as sexually active as a female mouse (as Aelian would have it), or the word has some crude physical sense (e.g.

that she was constantly being penetrated from different directions) is
unclear.

I11. The speaker is a courtesan (ἑταίρα; see 2; **I7** introductory n.), a
stock 'Middle' and 'New Comic' character; cf. **C7–C13** n. (on other stock
characters); **E7**; **I12**; M. M. Henry, *Menander's Courtesans and the Greek
Comic Tradition* (Studien zur klassischen Philologie 20: Frankfurt am Main,
1985), esp. 32–48. Her lovers—all of whom have turned out to be selfish or
insolvent, driving her to consider abandoning her profession—are also
standard types. For the soldier (4–10), see **C13** introductory n. For the doctor
(11–15), see **F6**. 27–9 n. For the philosopher (16–21), see **F1–F19**. **D14** is
similar; and cf. Apollod. Car. fr. 8.

Preserved at Stobaeus iii. 6. 13, under the heading 'On licentiousness'.
Iambic trimeter.

1.   **μὰ τὴν Ἀφροδίτην:** an appropriate oath for a courtesan.
2.   **Πυθιάς** might be either a slave-girl (as in Terence's *Eunuch*) or another
courtesan (as at Asclep. *AP* v. 164. 2 = *HE* 867; Posidipp. 130. 1; Luc.
D.Meretr. 12). The name is borne by what are presumably free citizen-
women at e.g. *IG* II² 1514. 11; 1515. 5 (dedicants at Brauron).
ἑταιρεῖν: 'to work as a courtesan'.   **χαιρέτω:** 'to hell with it!'
Colloquial; cf. Ar. *Ach.* 200 with Olson ad loc.; Barrett on E. *Hipp.* 113;
Stevens 26.   **μή μοι λέγε:** 'don't talk to me (about it)!'
3.   'I failed (at it); it's not for me; I want to bring it to an end.'
4.   **εὐθύς** is adverbial; cf. **A12**. 4.   **ἐπιχειρήσασα:** 'when I undertook
(this trade)'.
5–6.   Cf. Ter. *Eun.* 482–3 (part of a description of a desirable lover offered to
a courtesan) *neque pugnas narrat neque cicatrices suas | ostentat.*
διαπαντός ('constantly, continually') is equivalent to διὰ παντὸς (τοῦ
χρόνου).   **ἐδείκνυ(ε) κτλ.:** i.e. so as to lend credibility to his stories
(which—at least on the one point that mattered—none the less turned out
to be false; cf. 7–10).
7.   **εἰσέφερε:** sc. into the speaker's house, where he was being entertained;
cf. the similar use of εἰσάγων in 12.   **δωρεάν . . . τινα:** 'a gift, grant of
some sort'; LSJ's 'fief' is too precise.
8.   **τοῦ βασιλέως:** Exactly which king is in question is unclear; but the soldier
(who is supposed to have fought as a mercenary commander, hence
the battle-stories and wounds mentioned in 5–6) was lying in any
case.   **ταῦτ(α)** refers back vaguely to the claim δωρεάν τινα παρὰ
τοῦ βασιλέως λαμβάνω described in indirect discourse in the preceding
clause.
10.   **ἐνιαυτόν** is accusative of extent of time, 'for a year'.   **δωρεάν** (an

ironic echo of the word in the same position in the line in 9) is here 'as a gift' (in apposition to $\mu(\epsilon)$), i.e. 'for free'.

11. $\lambda\alpha\mu\beta\acute{\alpha}\nu\omega$ is a vivid, 'historic' present (Goodwin § 33).

12. $\epsilon\acute{\iota}\sigma\acute{\alpha}\gamma\omega\nu$: see 7 n. $\pi o\lambda\lambda o\acute{\upsilon}s$ $\tau\iota\nu\alpha s$: 'quite a few'; for this seemingly pleonastic use of $\tau\iota s$ after another pronominal adjective (more often $o\acute{\upsilon}$ $\pi o\lambda\lambda o\acute{\iota}$ or $\dot{o}\lambda\acute{\iota}\gamma o\iota$ (e.g. Th. ii. 17. 1, 79. 4) than $\pi o\lambda\lambda o\acute{\iota}$), see LSJ s.v. A. II. 2; G. L. Cooper, *Attic Greek Prose Syntax*, i (Ann Arbor, 1998), 550 (51. 16. 4).

13. $\check{\epsilon}\tau\epsilon\mu\nu(\epsilon)$ $\check{\epsilon}\kappa\alpha\epsilon$: 'performed surgery on them (or) cauterized them' (two basic—and very painful and dangerous—medical procedures; cf. A. *Ag.* 849; Pl. *Grg.* 456b with Dodds ad loc.). $\pi\tau\omega\chi\grave{o}s$ $\mathring{\eta}\nu$ $\kappa\alpha\grave{\iota}$ $\delta\acute{\eta}\mu\iota os$: The complaints are closely related: the doctor made no money because he killed his patients (cf. 16). For the $\delta\acute{\eta}\mu\iota os$ $\delta o\hat{\upsilon}\lambda os$ ('public executioner'), see H12. 1 n.; LSJ s. $\delta\acute{\eta}\mu\iota os$ II. 2 misses the joke.

14–15. The speaker's description of her realization that she was even worse off with the doctor than with the soldier implies that she got rid of the latter, and thus takes the place of a more straightforward remark like $\mathring{\alpha}\phi\hat{\eta}\kappa\alpha$ $\tau o\hat{\upsilon}\tau o\nu$ in 11.

15. $\delta\iota\acute{\eta}\gamma\eta\mu(\alpha)$: 'a tall-tale'.

16. $T\acute{\upsilon}\chi\eta$ ought probably to be capitalized, as at C18. 7.

17. For a beard ($\pi\acute{\omega}\gamma\omega\nu$) as typical of a philosopher, see Ephipp. fr. 14. 7. For the $\tau\rho\acute{\iota}\beta\omega\nu$, see F4 introductory n. $\kappa\alpha\grave{\iota}$ $\lambda\acute{o}\gamma o\nu$: 'and an argument to make'; a surprise after the previous two nouns, which serves to set up 19–21.

18. 'I got into manifest trouble; indeed, I fell right into it.'

19. The line is incurably corrupt; but the sense must have been something like 'and when I asked him to give me something . . .'.

20. $\check{\epsilon}\sigma\tau\omega$ $\kappa\alpha\kappa\acute{o}\nu$: 'Let it be bad!', i.e. 'Let's assume it's bad—, Granted it's bad—'.

21. $\delta\iota\grave{\alpha}$ $\tau o\hat{\upsilon}\tau o$: 'on this account', i.e. 'if this is true . . .' $\hat{\rho}\hat{\imath}\psi o\nu$: 'throw (it to me)!'

I12. Lais was a famous courtesan (see I7 introductory n.), who was born in Sicily probably in the late 420s, but was captured by the Athenians when they invaded the island (Timae. FGrHist 566 F 24 ap. Ath. 13. 588c; Paus. ii. 2. 5; Plu. *Nic.* 15. 4) and sold in Corinth (cf. Stratt. fr. 27; Anaxandr. fr. 9. 1–2); see Sommerstein on Ar. *Pl.* 179. She is referred to elsewhere in comedy at Philetaer. fr. 9. 4, where the speaker claims that she 'died while being fucked', an idea that fits neatly with the image presented of her here (see below), and at Pl. Com. fr. 196. The speaker criticizes Lais not for her venal savagery but for her lack of it (esp. 18), while praising her more mercenary behaviour in her youth (12); most likely the denunciation is made by another courtesan, who views the aged Lais as having betrayed the profession and is perhaps arguing that she ought to be replaced by the eponymous 'Antilais'. The speaker is addressing a number of women (20), probably other courtesans. Cephisodorus also wrote an *Antilais*, of which only the title is preserved.

The charge the speaker brings against Lais in 1–3 is that she has grown lazy and is interested only in eating and (especially) drinking. The alleged proof of this is that she no longer keeps every minute of her schedule full of paying customers (13), but goes out constantly to parties to drink (16–17). Nor is Lais as concerned with making money as she once was (contrast 12 with 18), or as choosy about her clientele; this is all described as a sad decline from savagery (12) to tameness (20–1). In sum, she has lost her sense of herself and of what she does, and she is accordingly presented in 3–8 as resembling eagles who when they are young hunt down food in the mountains, but after they grow old sit hungrily on top of temples (sc. in the hope of snatching an easy meal from the altar; see 7–8 n.). The problem with this argument is that, by the speaker's own admission, the eagles' behaviour has nothing to do with laziness or greed; they need to eat, and when the strength of their youth (6) disappears, they can no longer provide for themselves as they once could. So too in Lais' case, nothing except the hostile initial characterization suggests that she has grown unwilling to work or addicted to symposia. Instead, she too has grown old and, as a result, less attractive than she once was (14–15), and she now has little choice but to accept whatever invitations to men's parties she can get, no matter how little they pay or how mean the company (17–19). Indeed, once the misleading rhetoric is stripped away, this speech can be read as an unintentionally poignant description of the difficult situation of an ageing courtesan who has not accumulated large amounts of money over the years, perhaps in part because she declined to entertain a constant stream of customers when she was younger (13), reserving herself for those who paid the most (contrast **I7** with introductory n.), and who must therefore work harder as she grows old, accepting as lovers men with whom she would have refused to associate when she was younger (18–19)—and being abused as a result.

Preserved at Athenaeus 13. 570b–d, in the same collection of texts as **I7** (where see introductory n.); **I8–I9**.

Iambic trimeter.

1. **πότις**: 'a drunk' (feminine of πότης).
2. **τὸ κατ(ὰ) ἡμέραν** is adverbial, 'on an everyday basis'.   **ὁρῶσα**: 'looking to, intent on' + infinitive of the activity the individual is eager for; cf. Ar. *Ach.* 376 βλέπουσιν ... δάκνειν with Olson ad loc.

3.   μόνον is adverbial, 'only'.

4–6.   The point of this part of the comparison is left undeveloped in 11–13, but must be that Lais (the greatest of courtesans) in her youth captured and consumed helpless men just as young eagles (the greatest and most powerful of birds) capture and consume flock-animals and hares. Cf. the lengthy denunciation of courtesans as man-eating monsters in Anaxil. fr. 22.

5.   ἐκ τῶν ὀρῶν identifies the source of the animals the young eagles seize and eat, setting up the contrast with the implicitly urban setting of the action in 7–8.

6.   ὑπὸ τῆς ἰσχύος: 'with their strength'.

7–8.   Kites (ἴκτινοι) are occasionally said to steal sacrificial meat from altars (Ar. *Pax* 1099–1101 with Olson ad loc.; *Av.* 865 with Dunbar ad loc.), which must be what the hungry eagles are waiting to do here: like Lais in her dotage (1–3, 16–18), they no longer work for their food, but prefer to go to someone else's house (in their case, a god's) to eat at his expense.

8.   κακῶς intensifies the negative sense implicit in πεινῶντες, 'being terribly hungry'; cf. Ar. *Ach.* 734 with Olson ad loc.

9–10.   τοῦτ(ο): i.e. the fact that they sit on the temple roofs (8); for oracular signs associated with the movements of eagles, see *Birds*, 7–8. This is a new point, which bears only an incidental relationship to the contrast developed in 4–8 and used in 11–16 to make sense of the history of Lais' career. It none the less serves as the basis for the speaker's transition to talking about her, with νομίζεται τέρας echoed in νομίζοιτ(ο) ἂν τέρας, although Lais is 'a marvel' only because of the extent to which her fortunes have declined (11–21).

11.   νεοττός: 'a nestling, chick' (glossed by καὶ νέα); the term serves as an explicit marker of the analogical relationship being established between Lais' career and the eagles', despite the fact that the latter are first described at the height of their youthful power (4–6) rather than as hatchlings.

12.   τῶν στατήρων: a generic term for large coins of the standard local weight, whatever that might be, with smaller coins in the series consisting of 'thirds' (τρίται), 'sixths' (ἕκται), and so forth. This was a primarily Eastern Mediterranean system (cf. B29. 1) and different from the system of drachmas and obols used in Athens (cf. 18 with n.); see Kraay 313–17. The basic point is that the young Lais was interested in (and her services available only in return for) the largest amount of money possible. ἀπηγριωμένη ('driven wild') sets up τιθασός in 20 and exploits an idea hinted at but left largely undeveloped in 4–8; see 20–1 n.

13.   εἶδες ... ἄν: i.e. 'would have had an audience with', and thus in Lais' case 'had sex with', as also in 16.   Φαρνάβαζον: a Persian satrap in

Asia Minor from the late 410s until around 390, when he returned to Susa and married one of the Great King's daughters; he seems to have died in the late 370s. Gaining a personal audience with Persian high officials was notoriously difficult; see M. C. Miller, *Athens and Persia in the Fifth Century* BC (Cambridge, 1997), 125–6.

14.   δόλιχον τοῖς ἔτεσιν . . . τρέχει: 'she is running the long-distance race in years', i.e. 'is growing old, is in decline'. A stade (the length, whatever it might be, of the stadium where games were held) was generally about 200 yards, and the δόλιχος-race (the longest event, run back and forth within the stadium rather than outside it) could range anywhere from 7 stades (somewhat less than a mile) to 24 (somewhat less than 3 miles). See Gardiner 128–43, esp. 136–40; H. A. Harris, *Greek Athletes and Athletics* (London, 1964), 64–77, esp. 73.

15.   'and is loosening the joinings of her body', i.e. 'is losing her figure'.

16.   πτύσαι: 'to spit'. An ugly image that effectively communicates the speaker's contempt for Lais.

17–19.   The lines give specific content to the complaint voiced in 16.

17.   ἐξέρχεται . . . πανταχόσ(ε) . . . πιομένη: 'she goes out everywhere to drink', i.e. 'she attends any symposium to which she is invited'; returning to the complaint in 1–3.

18.   A *triobol* (half a drachma) is a proverbially small amount (e.g. Ar. *Pl.* 125; Nicophon fr. 20. 3) and appears to be a common prostitute's fee at Antiph. fr. 293. 3 (cf. **16**. 17 n.); and **καὶ στατῆρα καὶ τριώβολον** means simply 'any coin of any size' (cf. 19 with n.; for the *statêr*, see 12 n.), i.e. 'whatever anyone will pay'.

19.   προσίεται: 'she admits to her company' (< προσίημι), i.e. 'has sex with'.   καὶ γέροντα καὶ νέον: i.e. 'anyone of any age'; cf. 18 n.

20–1.   That Lais has grown tame enough to take . . . money (a surprise for 'bread' or the like; cf. Diph. fr. 91. 2) from someone's hand proves that she is no longer 'wild', as she was in her youth (11–12), and assimilates her to the eagles in a way left only implicit in the description of them in 4–8. When they were young, they lived in the mountains and got their own food (4–6); now that they are old, they hang about the cities of men and expect to be fed (7–8), much like the allegedly greedy, lazy courtesan they represent.

Section J

Aspects of Daily Life

J1. Eupolis fr. 327, from an unidentified play (V)

οὗ τὰ βίβλι’ ὤνια

*   *   *

περιῆλθον εἰς τὰ σκόροδα καὶ τὰ κρόμμυα
καὶ τὸν λιβανωτόν, κεὐθὺ τῶν ἀρωμάτων,
καὶ περὶ τὰ γέλγη

4 (cf. 1) καὶ περὶ τὰ γέλγη χοὗ τὰ βίβλι’ ὤνια Bergk

J2. Nicophon fr. 10, from *Men Who Live from Hand to Mouth* (V/IV)

μεμβραδοπώλαις, ἀνθρακοπώλαις,
ἰσχαδοπώλαις, διφθεροπώλαις,
ἀλφιτοπώλαις, μυστριοπώλαις,
βιβλιοπώλαις, κοσκινοπώλαις,
ἐγκριδοπώλαις, σπερματοπώλαις   5

1 ἀνθρακοπώλαις Meineke: ἀκρατοπώλαις Ath.ACE

J3. Nicophon fr. 6, from *Men Who Live from Hand to Mouth* (V/IV)

ἐγὼ μὲν ἄρτους μᾶζαν ἀθάρην ἄλφιτα
κόλλικας ὀβελίαν μελιτοῦτταν ἐπιχύτους
πτισάνην πλακοῦντας δενδαλίας ταγηνίας

J4. Menander fr. 150, from *The Ephesian* (IV/III)

ἐγὼ μὲν ἤδη μοι δοκῶ, νὴ τοὺς θεούς,
ἐν τοῖς κύκλοις ἐμαυτὸν ἐκδεδυκότα
ὁρᾶν κύκλωι τρέχοντα καὶ πωλούμενον

1 ἤδη Harp.N: οὖν ἤδη Harp.QPM: οὖν δὴ Harp.K

J5. Aristophanes fr. 680, from an unidentified play (V/IV)

κοπρολογεῖ κόφινον λαβών

J6. Antiphanes fr. 123, from *The Man from Mt Cnoethideus or Potbelly* (IV)

ἄτοπά γε κηρύττουσιν ἐν τοῖς ἰχθύσι
κηρύγμαθ', οὗ καὶ νῦν τις ἐκεκράγει μέγα
μέλιτος γλυκυτέρας μεμβράδας φάσκων ἔχειν.
εἰ τοῦτο τοιοῦτ' ἐστίν, οὐδὲν κωλύει
τοὺς μελιτοπώλας αὖ λέγειν βοᾶν θ' ὅτι   5
πωλοῦσι τὸ μέλι σαπρότερον τῶν μεμβράδων

1–2 ἄτοπά γε . . . | κηρύγμαθ', οὗ Meineke: ατοπόν τε . . . κήρυγμα, οὗ Ath.ᴬ: om. Ath.ᶜᴱ: ἄτοπόν γε . . . | κήρυγμ', ὅπου Porson

J7. Amphis fr. 30, from *The Vagabond Acrobat* (IV)

πρὸς τοὺς στρατηγοὺς ῥᾶϊόν ἐστιν μυρίαις
μοίραις προσελθόντ' ἀξιωθῆναι λόγου
λαβεῖν τ' ἀπόκρισιν <ὧν> ἂν ἐπερωτᾶι τις ἢ
πρὸς τοὺς καταράτους ἰχθυοπώλας ἐν ἀγοράι.
οὓς ἂν ἐπερωτήσηι τις ἀναλαβών τι τῶν   5
παρακειμένων, ἔκυψεν ὥσπερ Τήλεφος
πρῶτον σιωπῆι (καὶ δικαίως τοῦτό γε·
ἅπαντες ἀνδροφόνοι γάρ εἰσιν ἑνὶ λόγωι),
ὡσεὶ δὲ προσέχων οὐδὲν οὐδ' ἀκηκοὼς
ἔκρουσε πουλύπουν τιν'· ὁ δ' ἐπρήσθη ∪×   10
×–∪–× καὶ τότ' οὐ λαλῶν ὅλα
τὰ ῥήματ', ἀλλὰ συλλαβὴν ἀφελὼν "τάρων
βολῶν γένοιτ' ἄν." "ἡ δὲ κέστρα;" "κτὼ βολῶν."
τοιαῦτ' ἀκοῦσαι δεῖ τὸν ὀψωνοῦντά τι

3 <ὧν> Porson   5–14 om. Ath.ᶜᴱ   5 ἂν Musurus: ἐὰν Ath.ᴬ   ἀναλαβών Kock: λαβών Ath.ᴬ   9 δὲ προσέχων Dindorf: προσέχων δ' Ath.ᴬ: τε προσέχων Meineke 12 τάρων Musurus: τεττάρων Ath.ᴬ   13 βολῶνˡ Schweighäuser: ὀβολῶν Ath.ᴬ   κτὼ Meineke: ὀκτὼ Ath.ᴬ

J8. Alexis fr. 78, from *The Heiress* (IV/III)

ὅστις ἀγοράζει πτωχὸς ὢν ὄψον πολὺ
ἀπορούμενός τε τἆλλα πρὸς τοῦτ' εὐπορεῖ,
τῆς νυκτὸς οὗτος τοὺς ἀπαντῶντας ποεῖ

γυμνοὺς ἅπαντας. εἶτ᾽ ἐπάν τις ἐκδυθῆι,
τηρεῖν ἕωθεν εὐθὺς ἐν τοῖς ἰχθύσιν·   5
ὃν ἂν δ᾽ ἴδηι πρῶτον πένητα καὶ νέον
παρὰ Μικίωνος ἐγχέλεις ὠνούμενον,
ἀπάγειν λαβόμενον εἰς τὸ δεσμωτήριον

6 ἂν δ᾽ Dindorf: δ᾽ ἂν Ath.^ACE

J9. Diphilus fr. 87, from an unidentified play (IV/III)

οὐκ ἔστιν οὐδὲν τεχνίον ἐξωλέστερον
τοῦ πορνοβοσκοῦ – ∪ – × – ∪ ×
κατὰ τὴν ὁδὸν πωλεῖν περιπατῶν βούλομαι
ῥόδα ῥαφανῖδας θερμοκυάμους στέμφυλα,
ἁπλῶς ἅπαντα μᾶλλον ἢ ταύτας τρέφειν   5

2 τοῦ πορνοβοσκοῦ del. Jacobs: τοῦ πορνοβοσκεῖν Meineke   5 ἁπλῶς Jacobs: ἄλλως Ath.^CE

J10. Eubulus fr. 80, from *Pamphilus* (IV)

ἐγὼ δέ, καὶ γὰρ ἔτυχεν ὂν κατ᾽ ἀντικρὺ
τῆς οἰκίας καινὸν καπηλεῖον μέγα,
ἐνταῦθ᾽ ἐπετήρουν τὴν τροφὸν τῆς παρθένου,
κεράσαι κελεύσας τὸν κάπηλόν μοι χοᾶ
ὀβολοῦ, παραθεῖναί θ᾽ ὡς μέγιστον κάνθαρον   5
     *   *   *

ὁ δὲ κάνθαρος πάλαι κενός· ὡς ξηραίνεται
     *   *   *

ἅμα δὲ λαβοῦσ᾽ ἠφάνικε πηλίκον τινὰ
οἴεσθε μέγεθος † ἀρεσιαν † μέγαν πάνυ
καὶ ξηρὸν ἐποίησ᾽ εὐθέως τὸν κάνθαρον

6 πάλαι Pursanus: πάλαι δὴ Ath.^A: πάλιν ἦν Kaibel   κενός Musurus: καινός Ath.^A   ὡς ξηραίνεται del. Kaibel

J11. Nicostratus Comicus fr. 22, from *Countrymen* (IV)

     ὁ κάπηλος γὰρ οὐκ τῶν γειτόνων
ἄν τ᾽ οἶνον ἄν τε φανὸν ἀποδῶταί τινι
ἄν τ᾽ ὄξος, ἀπέπεμψ᾽ ὁ κατάρατος δοὺς ὕδωρ

2 τε φανὸν Ath.^B: στέφανον Ath.^A

J12. Damoxenus fr. 3, from an unidentified play (III)

νεανίας τις ἐσφαίριζεν εἰς
ἐτῶν ἴσως × – ∪ ἑπτακαίδεκα,
Κῶιος· θεοὺς γὰρ φαίνεθ᾽ ἡ νῆσος φέρειν.
ὃς ἐπεί ποτ᾽ ἐμβλέψειε τοῖς καθημένοις
ἢ λαμβάνων τὴν σφαῖραν ἢ διδούς, ἅμα   5
πάντες ἐβοῶμεν – ∪ – × – ∪ ×
ἡ δ᾽ εὐρυθμία τό τ᾽ ἦθος ἡ τάξις θ᾽ ὅση
ἐν τῶι τι πράττειν ἢ λέγειν ἐφαίνετο.
πέρας ἐστὶ κάλλους, ἄνδρες, οὔτ᾽ ἀκήκοα
ἔμπροσθεν οὔθ᾽ ἑόρακα τοιαύτην χάριν.   10
κακὸν ἄν τι μεῖζον ἔλαβον, εἰ πλείω χρόνον
ἔμεινα· καὶ νῦν δ᾽ οὐχ ὑγιαίνειν μοι δοκῶ

2 <ἐκκαίδεκ᾽ ἢ> Porson: <γενόμενος> Schweighäuser: <εἰ θνητός> Kock   7 τό τ᾽
Musurus: τὸ δὲ Ath.CE   ἡ τάξις θ᾽ Porson: ἡ δὲ τάξις Ath.CE   8 πράττειν ἢ λέγειν
Casaubon: λέγειν ἢ πράττειν Ath.CE   9 πέρας ἐστὶ Casaubon: πέρας ἔτι Ath.E: πέρας ἔτι
Ath.C: πέρας τι Porson

J13. Anaxandrides fr. 35, from *Odysseus* (IV)

ὑμεῖς γὰρ ἀλλήλους ἀεὶ χλευάζετ᾽, οἶδ᾽ ἀκριβῶς.
ἂν μὲν γὰρ ἦι τις εὐπρεπής, Ἱερὸν Γάμον καλεῖτε·
ἐὰν δὲ μικρὸν παντελῶς ἀνθρώπιον, Σταλαγμόν.
λαμπρός τις ἐξελήλυθ᾽ – ×Ὄλολυς οὗτός ἐστι·
λιπαρὸς περιπατεῖ Δημοκλῆς, Ζωμὸς κατωνόμασται·   5
χαίρει τις αὐχμῶν ἢ ῥυπῶν, Κονιορτὸς ἀναπέφηνεν·
ὄπισθεν ἀκολουθεῖ κόλαξ τωι, Λέμβος ἐπικέκληται·
τὰ πόλλ᾽ ἄδειπνος περιπατεῖ, Κεστρῖνός ἐστι Νῆστις.
εἰς τοὺς καλοὺς δ᾽ ἄν τις βλέπηι, καινὸς Θεατροποιός·
ὑφείλετ᾽ ἄρνα ποιμένος παίζων, Ἀτρεὺς ἐκλήθη·   10
ἐὰν δὲ κριόν, Φρῖξος· ἂν δὲ κωιδάριον, Ἰάσων

2 ἂν Eust.: ἐὰν Ath.ACE   11 ἂν Dindorf: ἐὰν Ath.ACE

J14. Phrynichus Comicus fr. 3, from *Epialtes* or *Ephialtes* (V)

ἔστιν δ᾽ αὐτούς γε φυλάττεσθαι τῶν νῦν χαλεπώτατον ἔργον.
ἔχουσι γάρ τι κέντρον ἐν τοῖς δακτύλοις,
μισάνθρωπον ἄνθος ἥβης·
εἶθ᾽ ἡδυλογοῦσιν ἅπασιν ἀεὶ κατὰ τὴν ἀγορὰν περιόντες.

ἐπὶ τοῖς <δὲ> βάθροις ὅταν ὦσιν, ἐκεῖ τούτοις οἷς ἡδυλογοῦσι   5
μεγάλας ἀμυχὰς καταμύξαντες καὶ συγκύψαντες ἅπαντες
γελῶσι

5 <δὲ> Meineke   6 συγκύψαντες G. H. Schaefer: συγκρύψαντες Ath.ᴬ   ἅπαντες]
ἅπαντας Seidler

J15. Plato Comicus fr. 168, from *The Alliance* (V/IV)

εἴξασιν γὰρ τοῖς παιδαρίοις τούτοις, οἳ ἑκάστοτε γραμμὴν
ἐν ταῖσιν ὁδοῖς διαγράψαντες, διανειμάμενοι δίχ᾽ ἑαυτούς,
ἑστᾶσ᾽ αὐτῶν οἱ μὲν ἐκεῖθεν τῆς γραμμῆς, οἱ δ᾽ αὖ ἐκεῖθεν·
εἷς δ᾽ ἀμφοτέρων ὄστρακον αὐτοῖσιν ἀνίησ᾽ εἰς μέσον ἑστώς,
κἂν μὲν πίπτῃσι τὰ λεύκ᾽ ἐπάνω, φεύγειν ταχὺ τοὺς ἑτέρους δεῖ,   5
τοὺς δὲ διώκειν

J16. Strattis fr. 48, from *Phoenician Women* (V/IV)

εἶθ᾽ ἥλιος μὲν πείθεται τοῖς παιδίοις
ὅταν λέγωσιν "ἔξεχ᾽ ὦ φίλ᾽ ἥλιε"

J17. Plato Comicus fr. 98, from *The Little Child* (V/IV)

φέρε τοῦτ᾽ ἐμοί,
δεῖξον τὸ κανοῦν μοι δεῦρο. πῆι μάχαιρ᾽ ἔνι;

J18. Adespota comica fr. *142 (undated)

τίς ὧδε μῶρος καὶ λίαν ἀνειμένως
εὔπιστος ἀνδρῶν ὅστις ἐλπίζει θεοὺς
ὀστῶν ἀσάρκων καὶ χολῆς πυρουμένης,
ἃ καὶ κυσὶν πεινῶσιν οὐχὶ βρώσιμα,
χαίρειν ἅπαντας καὶ γέρας λαχεῖν τόδε;   5

1 ἀνειμένως Grotius: ἀνείμενος Clem.ᴸ   5 ἅπαντας Porph. Cyrill.: ἅπαντα Clem.ᴸ

J19. Eupolis fr. 88, from *Dyers* (410s BC?)

ὃς καλῶς μὲν τυμπανίζεις
καὶ διαψάλλεις τριγώνοις
κἀπικινεῖ ταῖς κοχώναις
κἀνατείνεις τὼ σκέλη

1 ὅς Ath.^{ACE}: οἷς Erot.   τυμπανίζεις Erot.: τυμπανίζει Ath.^{ACE}   2 διαψάλλεις
Deubner: διαψάλλει Ath.^{ACE}   3 κἀπικινεῖ Cobet: κἀπικινεῖς Erot.   4 Fritzsche:
καὶ πείθεις ἄνω Erot.

J20. Pherecrates fr. 43, from *The Teacher of Slaves* (V)

(A.) κίθαρος γεγενῆσθαι κἀγοράζειν κίθαρος ὤν.
(B.) ἀγαθόν γ' ὁ κίθαρος καὶ πρὸς Ἀπόλλωνος πάνυ.
(A.) ἐκεῖνο θράττει μ', ὅτι λέγουσιν, ὦ 'γαθή·
"ἔνεστιν ἐν κιθάρωι τι κακόν"

2 ἀγαθόν Schweighäuser: ὡς ἀγαθόν Ath.^{ACE}

J21. Philemo fr. 101, from an unidentified play (IV/III)

ὅταν <δὲ> παρατηροῦντ' ἴδω τίς ἔπταρεν,
ἢ τίς ἐλάλησεν, ἢ τίς ἐστιν ὁ προσιὼν
σκοποῦντα, πωλῶ τοῦτον εὐθὺς ἐν ἀγορᾶι.
αὑτῶι βαδίζει καὶ λαλεῖ καὶ πτάρνυται
ἕκαστος ἡμῶν, οὐχὶ τοῖς ἐν τῆι πόλει.   5
τὰ πράγμαθ' ὡς πέφυκεν, οὕτως γίγνεται

1 <δὲ> παρατηροῦντ' ἴδω Grotius: ἴδω παρατηροῦντα Clem.^L Theodoret. An.Ox.
2 προσιὼν Theodoret. An.Ox.: προϊὼν Clem.^L   3 πωλῶ Sylburg: πώλωι Clem.^L: ἀπολῶ
Theodoret. An.Ox.   6 γίγνεται Theodoret.: γίνεσθαι Clem.^L

J22. Menander fr. 106, from *The Superstitious Man* (IV/III)

                                        (A.) ἀγαθόν τι μοι
γένοιτο – ∪ ὦ πολυτίμητοι θεοί,
ὑποδούμενος τὸν ἱμάντα <γὰρ> τῆς δεξιᾶς
ἐμβάδος ἀπέρρηξ'. (B.) εἰκότως, ὦ φλήναφε·
σαπρὸς γὰρ ἦν, σὺ δὲ μικρολόγος <τις> οὐ θέλων   5
καινὰς πρίασθαι

1–2 ἀγαθόν τι γίνοιτ', ὦ πολυτίμητοι θεοί uno verso Raeder   3 <γὰρ> Meineke
4 ἀπέρρηξ' Meineke: διέρρηξα Clem.^L   5 <τις> Sandbach: <ἄρ'> Meineke: <ἦσθ'>
Borgogno   οὐ θέλων Grotius: οὐκ ἐθέλων Clem.^L

COMMENTARY

J1. For ancient testimonia regarding the areas in and around the Athenian Agora devoted to particular commodities (after which they were routinely called), see below; **G15.** 3–4 n.; **H9.** 5 n.; **J2.** 5 n.; **J6.** 1 with n.; Pherecr. fr. 13; R. E. Wycherley, *Agora*, iii (Princeton, 1957), 193–201 (test. 632–68); Arnott on Alex. fr. 47. 8.

Preserved entire at Pollux ix. 47, where 1 is initially cited (misleadingly) as evidence that βιβλιοθῆκαι ('book collections', i.e. 'libraries') were among the regular public spaces in a city, after which Pollux notes that the Athenians routinely called other places after the goods sold in them and offers 2–4 as proof of this assertion. Pollux attributes both 1 and 2–4 simply to 'Eupolis'; that the verses are from the same speech—or even the same play—may be true but is only a conjecture. In addition, 2–3 are quoted at Phot. p. 589. 13 = *Suda* τ 845, in a gloss on τοὖψον ('the place where ὄψον is sold'); 2 is quoted in a *scholium* on Ar. *Ra.* 1068, as part of a gloss on τοὺς ἰχθῦς ('the place where fish are sold'); and 3 is quoted in a *scholium* on Ar. *Pax* 1158, as part of a gloss on τ(ὰ) ἀρώματα, although there the word means 'the ploughlands' (ἄρωμα (B)).

1. **οὗ τὰ βίβλι(α) ὤνια:** for the expression, cf. Ar. *Eq.* 1247 οὗ τὸ τάριχος ὤνιον ('where the saltfish is for sale'). For other references to 'book-sellers' or 'the books' (i.e. 'the book-market') in Athens, see **J2.** 4 with n.; Ar. *Av.* 1288–9 (which makes it clear that these were primarily copying-shops, which took on related business of all sorts); Pl. *Ap.* 26d–e.

2–3. That the garlic market (**τὰ σκόροδα**) and the onion market (**τὰ κρόμμυα**) were located next to one another is likely enough, since the same merchants may have sold both (cf. Ar. *Eq.* 600 (the purchase of onions and garlic mentioned together)). But the juxtaposition of these two areas with the much more sweet-smelling frankincense market (**τὸν λιβανωτόν**; for frankincense, see **H1.** 9 n.) and spice market (**τῶν ἀρωμάτων**) is also a nice literary touch, if nothing else. For onion-vendors, see also Ar. *Pl.* 167. For the spice market, see also **G9.** 5 with n.   **εὐθύ** + genitive: 'straight toward'.

4. **τὰ γέλγη:** glossed ὁ ῥῶπος ('the petty goods, cheap goods') at Hsch. γ 292 ~ Phot. γ 55; but exactly what items are in question is unclear (although see Diph. fr. 55. 5 (a collection of household equipment of every sort referred to as ῥῶπος); A. fr. 263. 4 (goods exported by sea called ῥῶπος); D. 34. 9 (a load of unsaleable merchandise described as ῥῶπος by a hostile speaker)).

J2. The individuals referred to in this fragment are most likely the eponymous men 'who live from hand to mouth' or their peers; and although the list is perhaps skewed to stress how tiny the economic niches occupied by some individuals were, it still suggests an extraordinary degree of specialization among small-scale marketplace vendors. Contrast **J3** with introductory n.

Preserved at Athenaeus 3. 126e–f, in a discussion of the word μύστρον (for which, see 3 n.).

Anapaestic dimeter; see **C6** introductory n.

1. **μεμβραδοπώλαις:** μεμβράδες (also called βεμβράδες) were small, inexpensive fish (esp. Alex. frr. 200 with Arnott on v. 3; 260); see *Fishes*, 32; García Soler 160–2. For comic μεμβραδοπῶλαι, see also **J6**; Ar. *V.* 493–5. **ἀνθρακοπώλαις:** for charcoal (ἄνθραξ), the household and industrial fuel of choice in Athens, and the charcoal-trade, see Olson, *Hesperia*, 60 (1991), 411–20. For another comic reference to a charcoal-seller, see Philyll. fr. 13 (in a list of typical occupations, along with sieve-maker, barber, and gardener).
2. **ἰσχαδοπώλαις:** Dried figs (ἰσχάδες) were a simple, common food (e.g. **G1**. 4; Ar. *Pl.* 191; Alex. fr. 167. 15; Timocl. fr. 38. 1); cf. García Soler 111–15, esp. 115. For a female dried fig-vendor in the Agora, see Ar. *Lys.* 564. **διφθεροπώλαις:** A διφθέρα is a rough leather garment worn by peasant farmers, shepherds, slaves, and the like (Ar. *Nu.* 72; *V.* 444; *Ec.* 80; Men. *Dysc.* 415; *Epitr.* 229–30); see Stone 166–7.
3. **ἀλφιτοπώλαις:** ἄλφιτα are 'rough-milled barley groats' (as opposed to ἄλευρα, '(wheat-)flour'); a basic commodity (e.g. Ar. *V.* 300–1; *Th.* 418–20; Men. fr. 218. 2–3). See **B32**. 6 n.; **F10**. 17 n.; **J3**. 1; Olson–Sens on Archestr. fr. 5. 7.   **μυστριοπώλαις:** A μύστριον (diminutive < μύστρον) is a 'small spoon'; perhaps intended for measuring or stirring rather than eating, since utensils were rarely used at meals (see **G16**. 11 n.).
4. **βιβλιοπώλαις:** see **J1**. 1 n. 'Book-sellers' are also mentioned at Aristomen. fr. 9; Theopomp. Com. fr. 79; Cratin. Jun. fr. 11.   **κοσκινοπώλαις:** for sieves (κόσκινα), which were made of basketry rather than terracotta and were used primarily for sifting flour and grain, see Amyx 259–61; and cf. **G16**. 13–14. For a comic reference to a sieve-maker (κοσκινοποιός), see Philyll. fr. 13 (in a list of typical occupations; see 1 n.).
5. **ἐγκριδοπώλαις:** An ἐγκρίς (also mentioned at Epich. fr. 46; Pherecr. fr. 99; Ar. fr. 269 (corrupt, but apparently referring to the occupation of ἐγκριδοπώλης)) is described at Athenaeus 14. 645e (cf. Hsch. ε 261) as 'a small cake fried in olive oil and then treated with honey'. **σπερματοπώλαις:** Most likely the seeds (σπέρματα) in question are those used for culinary purposes, such as sesame (see Moer. σ 26, which implies

that a section in the Agora was called τὰ σήσαμα ('the place where the sesame is sold'; see **J1** introductory n); García Soler 359), poppy (see García Soler 343–4), mustard (see García Soler 345–6), and cumin (see Olson–Sens on Archestr. fr. 24. 3; García Soler 352–3).

J3. Meineke argued that the speaker (who offers a catalogue of grain-products of all sorts) must be one of the eponymous men 'who live from hand to mouth', and Kock suggested that he is listing the items he has for sale, like the Boeotian at Ar. *Ach.* 874–6, 878–80. If so, he operates on a much larger scale than e.g. the simple ἐγκρίδες-vendor mentioned in **J2.** 3, since his stock includes not just baked and unbaked cakes of many kinds, but also wheat gruel, barley gruel, and barley meal.

Preserved at Athenaeus 14. 645b–c, in a discussion of the cake called ἐπίχυτος (2 with n.), about which Athenaeus appears to know nothing more than that a certain Pamphilus identified it with the almost equally obscure ἀττανίτης.

Iambic trimeter.

1. For **ἄρτος** ('wheat bread') and **μᾶζα** ('barley-cake'), see **B33.** 4–6 n. **ἀθάρη** (mentioned elsewhere in comedy at e.g. Pherecr. fr. 113. 3; Ar. *Pl.* 673; Anaxandr. fr. 42. 42) is 'wheat gruel' (Hsch. α 1533, 1535; Phot. α 471). For **ἄλφιτα** ('barley groats'), see **J2.** 3 n.
2. **κόλλικες** are baked barley loaves (see Olson on Ar. *Ach.* 872–3); **ὀβελίας** (sc. ἄρτος) is 'spit-bread' (Ar. fr. 105); a **μελιτοῦττα** is a 'honey-cake' of a sort often used in offerings (e.g. Ar. *Av.* 567; *Lys.* 601); and **ἐπίχυτοι** are cakes that have been 'poured over' (cognate with ἐπιχέω) something, perhaps a mould or a filling.
3. **πτισάνη** is 'barley gruel'; see Arnott on Alex. fr. 146. 2–3. For **πλακοῦντες** ('unbaked cakes'), see **B33.** 13 n. **δενδαλίαι** are a type of barley-cake (Hsch. δ 621 ~ Phot. δ 181). **ταγηνίαι** (referred to elsewhere in comedy at Magnes fr. 2. 1; Cratin. fr. 130 (both ap. Ath. 14. 646e)) are 'fried cakes' (cognate with τάγηνον, 'frying pan'; see **G4.** 12 n.).

J4. According to Harpocration (citing this fragment), **κύκλοι** was a term for 'the places where people are sold. They got this name from the fact that the buyers stood around in a circle'; cf. Hsch. κ 4478 'κύκλος: . . . a place in the Agora, where vessels and bodies are sold'; Poll. vii. 11 'The term κύκλοι is used in New Comedy for the places where slaves are sold, and perhaps also other goods'; x. 18 (citing Alex. fr. 104). The speaker is thus presumably a slave who has done something he knows will offend his master so badly that he will be sold in short order (thus Meineke; cf. **J21.** 3 with n.) or, less likely, a free man who has committed a terrible crime (thus Kock). For slaves (on

whose plight the original audience probably wasted little sympathy), see
C7–C8 n.

Preserved at Harpocration *K* 91, in a gloss on the word κύκλοι (2).

Iambic trimeter.

1.   μοι δοκῶ: 'I think'; cf. **J12.** 12 with n.

2–3.   ἐκδεδυκότα: 'stripped'; like **κύκλωι τρέχοντα** ('running in a circle',
which would give everyone gathered around an equal view of the individual being sold, as well as assuring that he was not crippled or the like),
a way of ensuring that the potential buyer knew exactly what he was
getting.

J5. Entrepreneurs (or their slaves) known as κοπρολόγοι went door-to-
door in Athens carrying baskets and collecting dung (κόπρος), which they
then transported out into the countryside, dumped, and most likely sold
eventually as fertilizer; cf. Ar. *Pax* 9 with Olson ad loc.; *Ec.* 316–17; Owens, *CQ*
NS 33 (1983), 44–50; Ault, *Hesperia*, 68 (1999), 550–9.

Preserved at Pollux vii. 134, in a catalogue of words cognate with φέρω
and related terms.

Iambic trimeter.

κόφινον: a basket of some sort; cf. Ar. *Av.* 1310; fr. 363; *AB* p. 102. 1.

J6. For vendors advertising their wares, cf. Ar. *Ach.* 34–5 (where the reference
is probably to itinerant street-merchants like those referred to in **J9**). For the
generally bad reputation of fishmongers in comedy, see **G6** introductory n.;
J7. Photius reports that Cnoethideus (from which the title-character of the
play hailed) was 'a mountain in Attica' (κ 825); the name is otherwise
unknown.

Preserved at Athenaeus 7. 287e, in a collection of literary references (most
from comedy) to the fish known as βεμβράς/μεμβράς.

Iambic trimeter.

1–2.   ἄτοπα … κηρύττουσιν … | κηρύγματ(α) might be either a real claim
that numerous odd announcements are being made **ἐν τοῖς ἰχθύσι** ('in the
fish-market'; see **J1** introductory n.; **J8.** 5), with other examples appended
but omitted by Athenaeus or his source, or (more likely) a generalization
that introduces the only instance of this sort of thing the speaker has or is
interested in.

2–3.   For **μεμβράδες** and μεμβραδοπῶλαι, see **J2.** 1 n.   **οὗ:** 'where'.
The perfect **κέκραγα** frequently stands in for the rare present κράζω
('shriek, cry'), and the pluperfect **ἐκεκράγει** is thus equivalent to an
imperfect.   **μέγα** is adverbial, 'loudly'.   **μέλιτος γλυκυτέρας:** for

the image (a commonplace in a world where refined sugar was unknown), see Taillardat § 739. For honey and honey-production, see 5–6 n.

4.   εἰ τοῦτο τοιοῦτ(ο) ἐστίν: 'if that's how it is, if that's true'.

5–6.   Honey was one of Attica's most famous products (e.g. Ar. *Th.* 1192; Antiph. fr. 177. 1–3; Phoenicid. fr. 2. 1; Archestr. fr. 60. 16–18 with Olson–Sens ad loc.; for bee-keeping, see Jones, Graham, and Sackett, *ABSA* 68 (1973), 397–412; Jones, *Archaeology,* 29. 2 (April 1976), 80–91; Anderson-Stojanovic and Jones, *Hesperia,* 71 (2002), 345–76), and honey-vendors are referred to in comedy also at Ar. *Eq.* 853.   αὖ: 'on the other hand, for their part'.   σαπρότερον τῶν μεμβράδων: for the implicit charge that fishmongers routinely sell fish that is too old to be eaten, see also **G7.** 3–5 n.; Antiph. fr. 217. 4; Xenarch. fr. 7. 4–17. For σαπρός ('rotten', but also 'old (and sweet)', with the ambiguity lending more point to the joke), see **H7.** 2 n.

J7.   For Agora-vendors characterized as vile and contemptible figures, see also Ar. *Eq.* 128–93, esp. 180–1. Ar. fr. 706 ('having a normal city-dialect, one that's neither dainty and effeminate, nor servile and rustic') makes it clear that there were subdialects of Attic Greek and that the way a man spoke was taken to indicate something important about his social or socioeconomic status; cf. **E24** introductory n. The speaker of this fragment can at least imagine getting an audience with the city's generals (1–3), and is thus unlikely to be poor; and part of what infuriates him about the fishmonger is his clipped style of talking, which was presumably typical of uneducated urban residents but is here implicitly characterized as another aspect of the man's calculated contempt for someone he ought to recognize as a social superior. For fishmongers, see **G6** introductory n.; **J6**; Diph. fr. 67 (where the fishmonger is not only a sharp dealer but has a tattoo on his forehead that identifies him as a freed slave). For wandering acrobats (πλάνοι) like the title-character, see Athenaeus 14. 615e–16b, citing Dionys. Com. fr. 4; Nicostr. Com. fr. 25; Theognet. fr. 2.

Preserved at Athenaeus 6. 224d–e, immediately before **G6** (where see introductory n.).

Iambic trimeter.

1–4.   For the comparison of the haughtiness of the city's fishmongers with that of its generals, to the advantage of the latter, see **G6.** 1–6 with nn.

1–2.   μυρίαις | μοίραις: dative of degree of difference with ῥᾷον, 'a million degrees easier'.

2.   ἀξιωθῆναι λόγου: 'to be thought worthy of an audience' (which, as 3 makes clear, is a separate matter from getting an answer to one's questions).

3. **<ὧν>** = τούτων ἅ, with the genitive dependent on an implied τι and the relative attracted into the case of its antecedent; '(regarding any) of (the things) which'.

4. **καταράτους**: see **D14**. 8 n.   **ἐν ἀγορᾶι**: As the name of a well-known place, ἀγορά ('the city's central marketplace, the Agora') can take a definite article (e.g. **J14**. 4) but does not require one (also **J21**. 3).

5–6. **τι τῶν | παρακειμένων**: i.e. one of the fish the man is—supposedly— trying to sell; to be taken with both **ἐπερωτήσηι** ('asks him about . . .') and **ἀναλαβών**.   **ἔκυψεν**: 'he looks down at the ground'; cf. **G6**. 6 with n. A gnomic aorist (Goodwin § 154–5), like ἔκρουσε and ἐπρήσθη in 10. The singular often replaces the plural when a specific example is offered of behaviour previously described in general terms (KG i. 87; cf. **B45**. 5–10). **ὥσπερ Τήλεφος**: see **D5**. 10 n. The reference must be to the *Mysians* of either Aeschylus (frr. *143–5) or Sophocles (frr. 409–18), in which Telephus, having murdered his maternal uncles (Hyg. *fab.* 244. 2), fled to Mysia, and upon his arrival there, as a polluted murderer (cf. 8 n.), 'ate without speaking, only nodding his head in response to those who asked him questions' (Alex. fr. 183. 3–4; cf. Arist. *Po.* 1460ª32).

7. **πρῶτον** is adverbial, 'at first'.

8. **ἅπαντες ἀνδροφόνοι γάρ εἰσιν**: an allusion to what Orestes at A. *Eu.* 448 calls the 'established custom' (νόμος) that a murderer must remain silent until purified; see also E. *HF* 1219; *IT* 951; *Or.* 75; fr. 1008 'Why are you silent? You didn't commit a murder, did you?' But all the speaker really means is that the fishmongers are 'dirty bastards' or the like, as at Men. *Dysc.* 481; Philippid. fr. 5. 3; Euphr. fr. 9. 10.   **ἐνὶ λόγωι**: 'in a word, to put it simply'.

9. **προσέχων οὐδέν**: 'paying no attention' (LSJ s. προσέχω I. 4; cf. **H12**. 2 n.).

10. **ἔκρουσε πουλύπουν τιν(α)**: 'he beats an octopus', i.e. to make it soft enough to be eaten (cf. Ar. fr. 197; Eub. fr. dub. 148. 7 = Ephipp. fr. 3. 10). For the aorist, see 6 n. For octopus (a delicacy), see *Fishes*, 204–8; Olson– Sens on Archestr. fr. 54. 1; García Soler 140–1.   **ὁ δ(έ)** ought to be the customer (not the octopus, as Kusses and Marx argued), and **ἐπρήσθη** (aorist passive < πρήθω, which supplies principal parts for the defective verb πίμπρημι) must therefore mean 'is inflamed (with anger)', sc. at the haughty way he is being treated. (For the image, see Taillardat § 348–52; for the aorist, see 6 n.). But what the customer says has been lost, and when the text resumes in 11, the fishmonger is again the subject.

11. **λαλῶν**: here 'pronouncing'.

12. **συλλαβὴν ἀφελών**: 'removing a syllable'.

12–13. **(τετ)τάρων | (ὀ)βολῶν . . . (ὀ)κτὼ (ὀ)βολῶν**: The fishmonger drops the first syllable of many of his words (although the majority of these omissions were 'corrected' by Athenaeus or his source, rendering the text unmetrical, and have been restored by modern editors). He thus marks himself as being of a less elevated social status than his customer, who treats this as a deliberate—and deliberately hostile—linguistic choice.

13.   ἡ δὲ κέστρα;: 'And the spet?' The spet (called σφύραινα in most dialects; see Strattis fr. 29; Antiph. fr. 97; Speusipp. fr. 20 Tarán ap. Ath. 6. 323a–b) resembles a pike; see *Fishes*, 108, 256–7.

J8. Athens had no police force, and the city's streets were accordingly quite dangerous after dark; cf. 3–4 n.; **A13**. 8–10 n.; **H18**. 8 n.; Ar. *Ach.* 1161–8.

Preserved at Athenaeus 6. 227d–e, in a collection of comic passages having to do with fishmongers that also includes **G5**; **J7**. Diph. fr. 31 (preserved immediately after this fragment) is similar.

Iambic trimeter.

1–2 are arranged in chiastic order: '(A) whoever buys large quantities of fish, (B) although he's poor, and who (B′), although he's short of money for everything else, (A′) has plenty of money for this'.   For ὄψον in the specific sense 'fish', see **E31**. 9–10 n.

3–4.   τῆς νυκτὸς . . . τοὺς ἀπαντῶντας ποεῖ | γυμνοὺς ἅπαντας: i.e. 'works as a λωποδύτης', a type of mugger who specialized in stripping his victims of their cloaks; cf. Ar. *Av.* 496–8 with Dunbar ad loc.; Austin–Olson on Ar. *Th.* 816–18. For the sense of γυμνός, see **I8**. 6 n.   ἐπάν τις ἐκδυθῆι sums up the content of the preceding clause from the victim's perspective.

5.   τηρεῖν: The infinitive functions as an imperative (Goodwin § 784. 2), as often in official language, which is imitated here; cf. 8.   ἔωθεν εὐθύς: i.e. first thing in the morning (see **G15**. 4), as soon as the sun comes up (contrast 3 τῆς νυκτός).   ἐν τοῖς ἰχθύσιν: see **J6**. 1 n.

7.   Μικίωνος: *PAA* 652905; otherwise unknown.   ἐγχέλεις: for eels as a delicacy, see **G10**. 4 n.

8   'let him arrest him and take him off to jail', sc. to await trial. For the imperatival infinitive, see 5 n. For Athenian jails and imprisonment, see J. M. Camp, *The Athenian Agora* (London, 1986), 113–16; Hunter, *Phoenix*, 51 (1997), 296–326; D. S. Allen, *The World of Prometheus* (Princeton, 2002), 226–30.

J9. Many goods were sold outside the Agora, and Athens' streets were full of itinerant bread-vendors (e.g. Ar. *V.* 1388–91; fr. 129), porridge-vendors (e.g. Ar. *Pl.* 427), and the like; see 3–4 with nn.; **J6** introductory n.

Probably the beginning of a soliloquy. The speaker has little sympathy for pimps (1–2); cf. the hostile attitude expressed at Myrtil. fr. 5; Ar. *Pax* 848–9;

and see **H14** introductory n.; Hunter on Eubulus' *The Pimp* (p. 179). But what disgusts him more is the women they are forced to manage (3–5). For prostitutes and prostitution, see **I7–I12** with nn.

Preserved at Athenaeus 2. 55d–e (manuscripts CE only), in a collection of literary references to lupines (see 3 n.).

Iambic trimeter.

1. **τεχνίον** (diminutive < *τέχνη*) does not necessarily have a deprecatory sense and may simply be a colloquial Attic form, as at Antid. fr. 2. 4 (where a parasite describes his own 'trade' this way).

2. **τοῦ πορνοβοσκοῦ** is metrical but unnecessary for the sense; 1, 3–5 read smoothly without it; and Jacobs may have been right to expel the words as an intrusive explanatory gloss.

4. **ῥόδα:** for selling roses (commonly used in garlands, as at e.g. Cratin. fr. 105. 1–2; Ar. *Eq.* 966), see also Eub. fr. 74. 1–3.   **ῥαφανῖδας:** for buying and selling radishes (simple, inexpensive food; cf. García Soler 46–7), see also Amphis fr. 26.   **θερμοκυάμους:** 'lupine beans', i.e. 'lupine seeds'; the word is not attested elsewhere. For lupine seeds (coarse, unappealing food that required extended soaking to be made palatable), see Arnott on Alex. fr. 167. 11; García Soler 70.   **στέμφυλα:** 'olive pomace', i.e. the residue left after green olives are squeezed for oil; referred to as a typical rural product at Ar. *Eq.* 806; *Nu.* 45.

5. **ἁπλῶς ἅπαντα:** 'simply everything', i.e. 'absolutely anything'. **ταύτας:** i.e. prostitutes.   For **τρέφειν** used in a similar way, see Antiph. fr. 2. 1 (of a man 'keeping' a courtesan, as if she were a domestic animal).

J10–J11. For bars (*καπηλεῖα*), where average citizens did most of their drinking (in contrast to the aristocratic symposium), see Ar. *Pl.* 435–6 (with a complaint about always being cheated there); Antiph. fr. 25; Lys. 1. 24; Davidson 53–61.

J10. Pamphilus is a common name (at least forty-five fifth- and fourth-century examples in *LGPN* ii) and in comedy 'seems always to belong to a young man . . ., who very often is in both love and trouble' (Hunter, *Eubulus*, p. 172; cf. esp. Philippid. fr. 27). The speaker is a man (note 4 *κελεύσας*), who is reporting to a group of people (note 8 *οἴεσθε*) on his attempt to get access to a respectable girl through her nurse (3), and he is thus most likely the title-character. He assumes that the old woman will be a heavy drinker (4–5 with nn.; cf. **H10** introductory n.), and she meets—and perhaps exceeds—his expectations (6–9). Line 6 is connected to 1–5 by the words *καὶ πάλιν* ('and again'), while 7–9 are connected to 6 by the words *καὶ ἔτι* ('and furthermore'); and Athenaeus or his source appears to have quoted selectively from the passage, preserving only those portions of the speech that mentioned the κάνθαρος (see below), and breaking off immediately afterwards. How much has been lost between 5 and 6, and 6 and 7, is impossible to say; but the speaker was presumably interested neither in the nurse's drinking (reference to which has been added to amuse the audience in the theatre) nor in the vessel she used, but in how she could help him make contact with the girl in her charge; and what was for him the crucial part of the encounter has thus been omitted.

Preserved at Athenaeus 11. 473e–f (manuscript A only), as the first in a collection of literary references (the great majority from comedy) to the drinking vessel known as a κάνθαρος (for which, see 5 n.).

Iambic trimeter.

1.   **καὶ γάρ**: 'for in fact'; see **H4**. 6 n.
1–2.   **κατ(ὰ) ἀντικρὺ | τῆς οἰκίας**: 'right opposite the house' (in which the girl lived).
3.   **ἐπετήρουν**: 'I was keeping an eye out for'.
4.   **κεράσαι**: for mixing wine (sc. with water), see **B3**. 3 n.; **H10** introductory n. For another reference to a bartender mixing wine for his customers, see Antiph. fr. 25.
4–5.   **χοᾶ | ὀβολοῦ**: 'a *chous* for an obol' (genitive of price). This would appear to be a very large quantity of very cheap wine (contrast **G18**. 19, where wine for a fancy dinner party is purchased for 10 obols per *chous*), although the water that is mixed in is perhaps included in the measure, so that the speaker bought only a half or a third of a *chous* of wine. But even then his interest was clearly in the quantity rather than the quality of what he was going to offer his guest.
5.   **ὡς μέγιστον κάνθαρον**: 'a *kantharos*, as big as possible', i.e. 'the biggest *kantharos* he had'. A *kantharos* is a large, deep-bellied cup suited to heavy drinking; cf. Alex. fr. 120. 1–2 with Arnott ad loc.; Epigen. fr. 4. 1–2; Xenarch. fr. 10 (all preserved in the same section of Athenaeus as this fragment); Richter–Milne 25–6 and figs. 167–9.
6.   The nurse has entered the bar and begun to drink; if the text printed here is correct (see below), this is more likely her complaint (reported in direct speech by the narrator) than the narrator's own comment on the action (employing a vivid 'historic present', as he does not do elsewhere). **ὁ δὲ κάνθαρος πάλαι κενός**: sc. ἐστι, and see **D12**. 2 n. Athenaeus has πάλαι δὴ κενός (unmetrical), which Kaibel corrected to πάλιν ἦν κενός ('the *kantharos* was once again empty'); but Pursanus' πάλαι κενός (with δή expelled from the text) is closer to the paradosis, which probably represents

a deliberate correction after ΠΑΛΑΙΑΙ was written for ΠΑΛΑΙ (dittography) and then misread as ΠΑΛΑΙΔΙ.   ὡς ξηραίνεται either introduces a simile omitted by Athenaeus or his source ('as X is dried up, (so is my cup)') or is exclamatory ('How dried up (my *kantharos*) is!'; cf. 9); but the care that has been taken in 1–5 and 7–9 to quote complete sentences rather than single verses in isolation argues for the latter. Kaibel expelled the words as an explanatory gloss on the first half of the line; it is difficult to see why such a note would have been needed.

7–9. The narrator offers a further report on the behaviour of the nurse, who continued to drink wine (and consume anything else she could get her hands on) at an astonishing pace.

7–8. **ἅμα . . . λαβοῦσ(α) ἠφάνικε:** 'as soon as she had got it, she had made it disappear', i.e. most likely 'had gobbled it down'; but see below. **πηλίκον τινὰ | οἴεσθε μέγεθος;:** 'how large as regards size do you think?', i.e. 'remarkably large'. For an interrogative adjective or adverb + οἴομαι used as a colloquial intensifier, cf. Ar. *Ra.* 54 with Dover ad loc. But **μέγαν πάνυ** seems flat and pointless, and the words ought perhaps to be expelled as an intrusive gloss. What is concealed in the corrupt portion of the line is in any case obscure, as is therefore also the specific sense of ἠφάνικε.

J11. For complaints about bartenders and the like diluting the wine they sell, see **H9.** 4–6 n. For torches (2; got at a καπηλεῖον at Lys. 1. 24), which seem to have consisted of a bundle of split wood, perhaps with a core of vegetable matter soaked in pitch, see Austin–Olson on Ar. *Th.* 101–3.

Preserved at Athenaeus 15. 700b (manuscript A only), in a discussion of torches.

Iambic trimeter.

1. **ὁ κάπηλος . . . ὁ (ἐ)κ τῶν γειτόνων:** i.e. 'my neighbourhood bartender'; cf. Ar. *Pl.* 435 ἡ καπηλὶς ἡ (ἐ)κ τῶν γειτόνων.

3. Vinegar (**ὄξος**) is merely wine in which the alcohol has been converted into acetic acid via exposure to the air and thus bacteria, and it is therefore not surprisingly sold in a bar.   **ἀπέπεμψ(ε)** (a gnomic aorist) **δοὺς ὕδωρ:** because not only are the wine and the vinegar watered, but the torch is made of wet (green) wood; cf. Men. fr. 60; Diph. fr. 6 (both 'This torch is full of water').   **κατάρατος:** see **D14.** 8 n.

J12. The speaker describes a scene in which a group of older men are sitting (4) together, watching boys play a ball-game and admiring not just the skill but the physical beauty of one of them in particular. The setting is almost certainly a *palaestra* ('wrestling school'), where the young men have gone to work out and a number of adult males have gathered to watch them, talk with one another, and perhaps fall in love or strike up a conversation with someone who catches their eye; cf. **B3**; **B29**. 3 n. (on pederasty); **C11**. 7; **J13**. 9. The setting and initial action in Plato's *Charmides* are very similar; and cf. **F6**. 9–11; Ar. *V.* 1025 ~ *Pax* 762–3 ('the poet' claims that he—unlike his rival Eupolis—did not use his success in the theatre to help him pick up boys in the wrestling-schools) with Olson ad loc.; Aeschin. 1. 135; Hubbard, *Arethusa*, 35 (2002), 255–96. The game the boys are playing is probably φαινίνδα (perhaps cognate with φαίνω; for the ending -ίνδα, cf. ὀστρακίνδα (**J15** introductory n.)), which is referred to by name in Antiph. fr. 278 and is called ἐφετίνδα at Cratin. fr. 465, and which Poll. ix. 105 says involved pretending to throw the ball to one person but actually throwing it to another. According to Athenaeus (1. 14f), Antiph. fr. 231 is a description of someone playing the game, which appears to have elements of our 'Keep-Away': 'After he got the ball, he was laughing as he offered it to one person and simultaneously escaped another, and knocked it away from someone else, and made someone else stand up, with shrill cries (half a line is missing) "Outside! Long! Beside him! Over him! Down! Up! Short!" (the end of the fragment is corrupt)'. See Gardiner 233.

Preserved at Athenaeus 1. 15b–c (manuscripts CE only), as part of a discussion of ball-games that also includes Antiph. frr. 231; 277; 278 (above), as evidence that εὐρυθμία (7) was an important aspect of the sport.

Iambic trimeter.

1. **νεανίας τις . . . εἷς**: 'one particular boy', i.e. out of the group that must have been referred to in the preceding lines.
2. **ἐτῶν ἴσως . . . ἐπτακαίδεκα**: 'perhaps 17 years old', the age the Greeks regarded as the peak of youthful beauty.
3. **θεοὺς γὰρ κτλ.** does not explain how the speaker knew the boy he saw was from Cos, but is instead a conclusion drawn from the truth of that fact: if he was Coan, the island must produce gods. See Denniston 61–2.
4–6. Compare Socrates' description at Pl. *Chrm.* 155c of the extraordinary effect the gaze of the beautiful Charmides had upon him; and **I6**. 11–12 (onlookers cry out at the sight of a particularly fine arse on a prostitute).
5. **ἢ λαμβάνων τὴν σφαῖραν ἢ διδούς**: cf. Antiph. fr. 231. 1–2 (of someone playing φαινίνδα) σφαῖραν λαβὼν | τῶι μὲν διδοὺς ἔχαιρε.
7. **ἡ . . . εὐρυθμία τό τ(ε) ἦθος ἡ τάξις τ(ε)**: 'his grace, his manner, and the way he held himself'.   **ὅση** ('how great!', i.e. 'how marvellous!'; prolepsis) agrees in gender with the noun to which it is closest, but is to be taken with all three.
8. **ἐν τῶι τι πράττειν ἢ λέγειν**: 'in whatever he said or did' (a compound

articular infinitive with an internal accusative object, to be taken with both verbs); picked up by **οὔτ(ε) ἀκήκοα Ι . . . οὔτ(ε) ἑόρακα** in 9–10.

9. **πέρας ἐστὶ κάλλους**: '(He) is the height, the *ne plus ultra* of beauty'. For this use of πέρας, cf. Hegesipp. Com. fr. 1. 4 τὸ πέρας τῆς μαγειρικῆς ('the height of the cook's art').

11. **κακὸν ἄν τι μεῖζον ἔλαβον**: 'I would have sustained more damage', i.e. 'been even more thoroughly smitten' (cf. 12).

12. **καὶ νῦν δ(έ)**: 'and even now', i.e. despite having not stayed as long as he might otherwise have wished.   **οὐχ ὑγιαίνειν μοι δοκῶ**: 'I don't think I'm entirely healthy', i.e. 'entirely in my right mind'. For ὑγιαίνω in this sense, e.g. Ar. *Nu.* 1275; *Av.* 1214; Alex. fr. 264. 1; adesp. com. fr. 859. 2. μοι δοκῶ is colloquial; see Austin–Olson on Ar. *Th.* 508.

J13. Athenaeus' introduction to this fragment makes it clear that the 'you' to whom the remarks are addressed is the Athenians. The speaker is thus perhaps the title-character Odysseus, who has made his way to the city in the course of his wanderings and been struck by its odd ways; cf. **D1–D4** with nn. (on the reception of Homer in comedy). For other references to Athenian nicknames, see **C11**. 2–7 with 5 n.; Ar. *Av.* 1290–9; Anaxandr. fr. 46; Antiph. frr. 20; 193. 10–11; Alex. frr. 173; 183. 1–2; Aristophon fr. 5. 1–3.

Preserved entire at Athenaeus 6. 242d–f (whence Eustathius p. 1642. 60 has got 1–3, 5–8, 10–11), in the course of a long discussion of parasites that also includes **A13** (where see introductory n.), as an aside (sparked by the quotation of Alex. fr. 173) on the Athenians' use of derisive nicknames. In addition, 8 (where see n.) is quoted at Athenaeus 7. 307e–f, in a collection of literary references to various types of mullet.

Iambic tetrameter catalectic.

1. **χλευάζετ(ε)**: 'you mock, jeer at', describing a rough, hostile style of humour (cf. 10 n.), as at Ar. *Ra.* 375.

2–11. In 2–6, a man's personal appearance is the basis on which he is awarded a nickname, whereas in 7–12 it is his behaviour; and within these groups, many of the descriptions fall into opposed pairs (2–3 a handsome man and a very short one, 5–6 the well-oiled Democles and someone who refuses to bathe or oil himself, 7–8 a parasite who has a patron to follow about and one who can never find anything to eat; perhaps also 4 (where see n.), if this is the remains of two verses, the first of which described someone very bold, the second someone very 'womanly').

2. **Ἱερὸν Γάμον**: a reference to the obscure Athenian festival celebrating the marriage of Zeus and Hera mentioned at Phot. ι 57 (cf. Men. fr. 225. 2; Parke 104), the point being that the man in question is good-looking (**εὐπρεπής**) enough to attract a goddess.

3. μικρὸν παντελῶς ἀνθρώπιον: 'an altogether tiny little fellow', i.e. 'a midget'.   Σταλαγμόν: 'Drop'.

4–8. The initial proposition in each line functions like an 'if'-clause; see **D5.** 13–16 n.

4. Ὄλολυς (cognate with ὀλολύζω) is defined by Photius (citing Men. fr. 109 and Theopomp. Com. fr. 62) as meaning (1) 'effeminate and super-stitious and womanish' (p. 329. 18–19) and (2) 'superstitious' (p. 329. 21–2); and the reason why someone who goes out in public λαμπρός ('shining, glistening') is called this may have been given in an accusative of respect (e.g. Richards's ὄψιν) that filled the gap in the middle of the verse (as printed here). But what we have in 4 might easily be instead the beginning of one line and the end of another, in which case λαμπρός might mean something like 'vigorous, bustling' (as at Ar. *Eq.* 430 ἔξειμι … λαμπρός), in contrast to the retiring behaviour displayed by the man dubbed Ὄλολυς.

5. λιπαρός: 'covered with (too much) oil'; cf. 6 n.   Δημοκλῆς (*PAA* 315565) cannot be identified, although the original audience must have known who was being referred to; the name is common (at least forty-one other fifth- and fourth-century examples in *LGPN* ii).   Ζωμὸς κατωνόμασται: 'he's been dubbed "Meat-Broth"', sc. because he has a greasy sheen or appears eager to attend a dinner-party; cf. **C11.** 2–3 with n.

6. χαίρει … αὐχμῶν ἢ ῥυπῶν: 'likes being dry' (i.e. going unoiled) 'or being dirty', and thus 'refuses to bathe', since one oiled oneself immediately after bathing (esp. Ar. *Pl.* 615–16 λουσάμενος | λιπαρὸς χωρῶν ἐκ βαλανείου).   Κονιορτός: 'Dustcloud'; used by Demosthenes as a nickname for Euctemon of Lousia (*PAA* 438275) at 21. 103, 139; and cf. **F11.** 7–8.

7. Λέμβος: 'Dinghy, Skiff', referring to a ship's boat of the sort that was tied to the rear of a larger merchant vessel (cf. Anaxandr. fr. 12. 1; D. 32. 6; 34. 10; Casson 162), just as the parasite tags along behind the man he expects will furnish him with dinner (as in **G15**).

8. τὰ πόλλ(α) is adverbial, 'for the most part, generally'; cf. Eup. fr. 172. 4. Κεστρῖνος … Νῆστις: 'Fasting Mullet'. The mullet (more often called κεστρεύς; see **G6.** 8 n.) was thought to eat no flesh (Arist. *HA* 591ª18–22) and to go without food for long periods of time and then gorge itself (Arist. *HA* 591ᵇ1–3); and the name of the fish was used routinely in com-edy to refer to hungry human beings (e.g. Ar. fr. 159; Amips. fr. 1. 2–3; Antiph. fr. 136, all collected at Ath. 7. 307d–8a, along with this verse).

9. εἰς τοὺς καλοὺς δ' ἄν τις βλέπηι: i.e. with pederastic interest; cf. **J12**. But what follows ('(he is called) "The New Theatre-maker"', implying the existence of another man known by the name) is obscure, unless

Θεατροποιός (attested nowhere else) means 'Stage-Producer', so that the individual who gets the nickname is imagined to resemble someone recruiting attractive young men for a dithyrambic or dramatic chorus. Schweighäuser (comparing **C11**. 7) proposed emending **καινός** to Καπνός, in which case the man receives two nicknames ('Smoke (and) Theatre-maker'). But everyone else gets only one, which counts against the suggestion, and the final word remains a problem in any case.

10.   **παίζων**: 'as a joke'—but a nasty one, intended to provoke laughter in others rather than the victim; cf. 1 n.; **H19** introductory n.; **J14** introductory n.   **Ἀτρεὺς ἐκλήθη**: a reference to the golden lamb that belonged to Atreus and was stolen by his brother Thyestes (see Gantz 545– 7; Olson on Ar. *Ach.* 432–4), after whom the thief ought really to be called.

11.   The sudden increase in the pace of the catalogue in this verse (two men and their nicknames described rather than one, as in 2–9) probably indicates that it is coming to a close.   **ἐὰν δὲ κριόν, Φρῖξος**: sc. ὑφείλετ(ο) (cf. 10) in the first clause, as again in the second half of the line. For Phrixus son of Athamas, who fled his wicked stepmother on the back of a flying golden ram that took him to Colchis (cf. below), see Gantz 176–80, 183–4.   **ἂν δὲ κωιδάριον, Ἰάσων**: When Phrixus arrived in Colchis, he sacrificed the golden ram (see above), and it was this fleece (κώιδιον; diminutive κωιδάριον) that Jason stole with Medea's assistance; see Gantz 358–61.

J14. For men gathering in informal groups to talk, see 5 n.; **J12**. The irony of the complaint registered here is that the speaker, who must be an old man, can have no idea what the city's young men say to one another in private, and simply assumes that the laughter he hears when they form groups (7) is directed against him and his peers and proves that the graceful public behaviour to which he also attests (4) is a sham. For hostile humour of the sort the speaker assumes the young men express against their elders, see **J13**. 1 n., 10 n.

Preserved at Athenaeus 4. 165b–c, in response to a question about the source of the word ἡδυλογία (see 5 with n.).

Lines 1 and 4–6 are anapaestic tetrameter catalectic; 2 and 7 are iambic trimeter; and 3 is – – ith.

1.   **αὐτοὺς ... φυλάττεσθαι**: 'to be on our guard, protect ourselves against them' (referring to the city's young men).   **τῶν νῦν** is to be taken with **χαλεπώτατον ἔργον**, 'the most difficult task we have nowadays'.

2.   **τι κέντρον ἐν τοῖς δακτύλοις**: 'a sort of sting in their fingers', as if they were wasps or bees (see 3 n.). The reference is to the middle (or little?) finger (σκίμαλλος), display of which had the same hostile sense in Athens

as it does today (see **C1**. 6; Ar. *Nu.* 652–4 with Olson on *Pax* 548–9), and which allegedly 'blooms' on the young men's hands (3). But in fact they behave quite well in public (4) and only become abusive in private (5–7), and the complaint is thus not that they literally give 'the finger' to their elders on a regular basis, but that their attitude is fundamentally contemptuous and any apparent public courtesy they display mere pretence. Line 6 takes the image in a different direction, by presenting the young men as tearing their enemies to shreds.

3.   **μισάνθρωπον**: setting up 6–7.   **ἄνθος ἥβης** (see 2 n.) echoes H. *Il.* 13. 484 καὶ δ᾽ ἔχει ἥβης ἄνθος, ὅ τε κράτος ἐστὶ μέγιστον (said of Aeneas by Idomeneus; cf. **D1–D4** n.), and is thus an elevated poetic flourish (as also at Ar. fr. 483) that simultaneously picks up the bee-imagery in 2.

4.   **περιόντες**: used of individuals 'going around' the Agora to do their marketing also at Pherecr. fr. 13; Pl. Com. fr. 211; cf. Ar. *Lys.* 558 περιέρχονται κατὰ τὴν ἀγοράν.

5.   **τοῖς . . . βάθροις**: most likely 'their seats' in the perfume-vendors' shops or the like; cf. Pherecr. fr. 70. 2–3; Ar. *Eq.* 1375–6; and the similar use of barbers' shops at Ar. *Av.* 1439–45 with Dunbar on 1440–1; *Pl.* 337–9; Eup. fr. 194; Men. *Sam.* 510–13. But perhaps the reference is instead to 'the steps' of a stoa (cf. Men. *Dysc.* 173; *Sam.* 511). In any case, the contrast is with walking around the Agora (4), where the young men are forced to mix with—and be civil to—individuals of all ages.   **τούτοις** is to be taken with γελῶσι in 7, 'they laugh at them'.

6.   **μεγάλας ἀμυχὰς καταμύξαντες**: 'after tearing deep rents, producing long scratches in them' (cf. 2–3 with 2 n.).   **συγκύψαντες**: 'after putting their heads together' in a conspiratorial fashion, as at Ar. *Eq.* 854; Hdt. iii. 82. 4.

J15. According to Pollux ix. 111, each of the two groups of boys playing the game (known as ὀστρακίνδα; for the name, cf. **J12** introductory n.) referred to in this fragment had one side of the potsherd assigned to it in advance. But Hermias (below) and Pollux ix. 112 agree that the boy who threw the sherd in the air cried out νὺξ ἢ ἡμέρα (thus Hermias; νὺξ ἡμέρα tantum Pollux), with 'night' standing for the interior side of the sherd (which was often covered with pitch, to make the vessel water-tight) and 'day' standing for the exterior side (referred to in 5 as τὰ λευκ(ά), 'the white parts'); and if this was not merely a verbal signal that the sherd was in the air, it may be that what the boy said was not 'Day or night!' but 'Day!' or 'Night!', indicating which side belonged to his team for this throw, and introducing another element of interest and excitement into the game. Touching the wall of one of the buildings along one's own side of the street presumably rendered one safe from capture, and Pollux reports that anyone who was caught was called ὄνος ('donkey'). For another children's game, see **J16**.

Political factionalism of some sort is being denounced, and **φεύγειν** (both 'flee' and 'be a defendant') and **διώκειν** (both 'chase' and 'prosecute') in 5–6 suggest a reference to politically motivated trials. Whether mention of an **ὄστρακον** in 4 is supposed to call to mind the institution of ostracism and thus the fate of Hyperbolus (see **E23–E25** with nn.; thus Bergk) is less clear. Alternatively, the title of the play may suggest that the reference is to the behaviour of the Greek cities as they form pointless alliances against one another (thus Körte).

Preserved at Hermias Alexandrinus, *On Plato's Phaedrus*, in a note on the phrase ὀστράκου μεταπεσόντος ἵεται φυγῆι (241b, 'when the potsherd falls on the other side, he is sent off in flight').

Anapaestic tetrameter catalectic.

2.   **διανειμάμενοι δίχ(α) ἑαυτούς**: '(and) after dividing themselves into two groups'.
3.   **αὐτῶν οἱ μὲν κτλ.**: 'some them on one side of the line, the rest on the other'.
4.   **ἀμφοτέρων** is to be taken with **εἰς μέσον ἑστώς**, 'standing between the two sides'; see LSJ s. μέσος III. 1. b.
5.   **πίπτηισι**: an epic form = common πίπτηι.   **τοὺς ἑτέρους**: i.e. those to whom the white (exterior) side does not belong.

J16. The point of the appeal is that, if the sun obeys children when they ask it to come out from behind a cloud, surely someone or something else ought to obey the speaker in the current situation. The game, which according to Pollux involved clapping one's hands as one cried **ἔξεχ᾽ ὦ φίλ᾽ ἥλιε** (= *PMG* 876(b)), is also referred to at Ar. fr. 404; provided one has sufficient patience, the incantation is almost a hundred per cent effective.

Preserved at Pollux ix. 123, in a discussion of children's games.

Iambic trimeter.

1.   **εἶθ᾽ ἥλιος μὲν κτλ.** is a parody of E. *Ph.* 546 εἶθ᾽ ἥλιος μὲν νύξ τε δουλεύει βροτοῖς; cf. **D11–D12** n.
2.   **ἔξεχ(ε)**: 'Come out!'

J17. Orders are being given (most likely to a slave) in preparation for a sacrifice. See also **A20** with nn.; **D3**. 21–2 n., 26 n.; and in general van Straten, esp. 31–43. **B38** is from the parabasis of the same play.

Preserved in a *scholium* on Ar. *Pax* 948 τὸ κανοῦν πάρεστ᾽ ὀλὰς ἔχον καὶ στέμμα καὶ μάχαιραν.

Iambic trimeter.

2. **τὸ κανοῦν**: 'the basket', a basic ritual implement used to transport the objects necessary for a sacrifice—above all else the knife—to the altar. Cf. J. Schelp, *Das Kanoun* (Beiträge zur Archäologie 8: Würzburg, 1975); Olson on Ar. *Ach.* 244. **δεῦρο** has quasi-verbal force, as often (Olson on Ar. *Ach.* 239–40); '(Get it) over here!' **πῆι μάχαιρ(α) ἔνι;**: 'Where's the knife in it?', i.e. 'I don't see the butcher's knife inside.' For the butcher's knife (used to slit the animal's throat and then dismember it), e.g. Ar. *Th.* 693–5; adesp. com. fr. 1072. 6; Olson on Ar. *Pax* 948–9.

J18. A cynical comment by someone who assumes that the gods see things more or less as human beings do. That the Olympians' portion of a sacrifice consists mostly of the parts of the animal that humans are unable (or unwilling) to eat is a commonplace already in Hesiod, who explains it as the consequence of Prometheus' deception of Zeus (*Th.* 535–57); cf. Pherecr. fr. 28; Eub. frr. 94 (corrupt); 127; Men. *Dysc.* 451–3; *Sam.* 399–402; fr. 224.

Preserved at Clement of Alexandria, *Stromateis* vii. 34. 3, in a discussion of sacrifice, as well as by Porphyry, *On Abstinence* ii. 58 (whence Cyrill. *c. Iul.* 9 p. 306F). Grotius converted the words that follow in Clement, καὶ χάριν τούτων τοῖς δρῶσιν ἐκτείνειν, into a sixth verse, τούτων τε τοῖσι δρῶσιν ἐκτίνειν χάριν.

Iambic trimeter.

1–2. **τίς ὧδε μῶρος . . . | . . . ἀνδρῶν ὅστις**: 'who's such a fool . . . that he . . .?' **λίαν ἀνειμένως | εὔπιστος**: 'so utterly credulous'. For λίαν adding a note of subjective disapproval, see **B4.** 2 n.
3. Genitive absolute, with the participle **πυρουμένης** to be taken with both nouns. **ὀστῶν ἀσάρκων**: i.e. the thighbones, which in this case have been completely stripped of flesh. **χολῆς**: for the gall bladder burned as part of the sacrifice, cf. S. *Ant.* 1010; Men. *Dysc.* 452.
4. Cf. Pherecr. fr. 28. 5 νέμεθ' ὥσπερ καὶ τοῖς κυσὶν ἡμῖν ('you give us a portion that's like what you offer dogs'; a god's complaint about sacrifice). **πεινῶσιν** adds a nice comic touch to the description: although dogs will eat almost anything, not even *hungry* dogs would (allegedly) eat the parts of the animal offered to the gods.
5. **γέρας λαχεῖν τόδε**: 'accept this as a portion of honour'.

J19. The plot of *Dyers*, to which **B42** also belongs, involved effeminate devotees (one of whom is addressed here) of the goddess Cotyto (test. ii), whose cult involved exotic instruments (1–2)—as well as, allegedly, sexual depravity (3–4). The play also contained an attack on Alcibiades, which a number of ancient sources report—improbably—led him to drown Eupolis (test. ii–vi). See Storey 94–111, esp. 98–107. For the arrival of new cults like that of Cotyto in late fifth- and fourth-century Athens, see **B35** introductory n.

Lines 1–2 are preserved at Athenaeus 4. 183f, in a discussion of the musical instrument known as a τρίγωνος (see 2 n.); and 1, 3–4 are preserved in Erotianus fr. 17 (p. 104. 1–3 Nachmanson; from a *scholium* on Hippocrates *Epid.* v. 7).

Iambic trimeter.

1. Given the aggressively hostile content of 3–4, **καλῶς** (to be taken with all four verbs) is certainly sarcastic.   **τυμπανίζεις**: 'you play the drum' or 'the tambourine', like the choruses of exotic Eastern maenads in Euripides' *Bacchae* (58–9) and Diogenes of Athens' *Semele* (*TrGF* 45 F 1. 1–4), Philocleon when he is initiated into the Corybantic rites in Aristophanes' *Wasps* (199), celebrants in various female-dominated cults in *Lysistrata* (3), and a priestess of Sabazius at D. 18. 284; see Orph. 212 F; *AGM* 124; Bundrick 48.

2. **διαψάλλεις**: 'you pluck all the notes' *vel sim.*; the mock-praise (cf. 1) continues.   **τριγώνοις**: exotic harps; see **D13**. 4 n.

3. **(ἐ)πικινεῖ ταῖς κοχώναις**: literally 'you move about with your perineums', i.e. 'you wiggle your arse', sc. suggestively. For κοχώνη, see Austin–Olson on Ar. *Th.* 246.

4. **ἀνατείνεις τὼ σκέλη**: sc. with high, balletic kicks; undignified behaviour which, not incidentally, exposes the dancer's arsehole to view—and thus potentially to penetration.

J20. Speaker A is a superstitious man (note the masculine participle ὤν), who is reporting a strange dream to Speaker B (a woman; note 3 ὦ (ἀ)γαθή), who attempts to convince him that the omen is a good one (thus Meineke). Cf. Ar. *V.* 42–53 (which makes it clear that by the late fifth century some individuals made a living interpreting dreams) with MacDowell on 53; Alex. fr. 274; Thphr. *Char.* 16. 11 with Diggle ad loc.

Preserved at Athenaeus 7. 305f–6a, in a collection of literary references to the fish known as the **κίθαρος** (unidentified; see *Fishes*, 114–15; Olson–Sens on Archestr. fr. 32. 1).

Iambic trimeter.

1. The preceding lines must have contained something to the effect of 'I thought that I . . .'

2. **πρὸς Ἀπόλλωνος πάνυ**: 'very closely connected to Apollo' (see LSJ s. πρός A. III), because the lyre (κίθαρις/κιθάρα or φόρμιγξ; see *AGM* 50–6; Bundrick 18–21, 25–6) was Apollo's instrument (cf. Ar. *Th.* 315 with Austin–Olson ad loc.), an argument also put forward by Apollodorus (*FGrHist* 244 F 109b ap. Ath. 7. 306a, shortly after this fragment is quoted).

3. ἐκεῖνο refers to what follows, i.e. to the fact 'that they say ...'. **θράττει**: 'troubles, disturbs', as in Cratin. fr. 331 θράττει με τὸ (ἐ)νύπνιον ('the dream disturbs me'). **(ἀ)γαθή** ('my good woman'; presumably colloquial), like masculine ἀγαθέ (see Olson on Ar. *Ach.* 296), is familiar but not necessarily friendly.

4. A punning allusion to a proverb referred to also at Ar. fr. 591. 60 ὁρᾶις ἄρ' ὡς ἐνῆν τι κἂν κιθ[ά]ρωι κακόν ('You see, then, that there's some trouble even in the *kitharos*'), the sense of which must be 'Although the situation seems happy' (with the lyre standing via synecdoche for the occasion on which it is played) 'there's trouble lurking'.

J21. A determined sceptic's denunciation of those who believe in supernatural signs of all sorts. For the beliefs referred to here, cf. Ar. *Av.* 719–21 (addressed to the audience) 'You consider everything that's decisive as regards prophecy "a bird" (i.e. "an omen"). A chance remark is a "bird" in your eyes; you call a sneeze a "bird", an unexpected encounter a "bird", a sound a "bird", a servant a "bird", a donkey a "bird"'; adesp. com. fr. 141; Theophrastus' Superstitious Man, who *inter alia* grows worried if a weasel crosses the road in front of him, or if he sees a snake in his house, or catches a glimpse of a corpse or of someone having an epileptic fit (*Char.* 16. 3–4, 9, 15); W. R. Halliday, *Greek Divination* (London, 1913), 172–83, 229–34.

Preserved at Clement of Alexandria, *Stromateis* vii. 25. 4, in a discussion of how chance occurrences are treated as significant or as the cause of troubles; and Theoderet. *Graec. aff. cur.* vi. 16 (drawing on Clement but offering a better text at 2 and 6). In addition, *An.Ox.* iv p. 250. 27, preserves 1–3 (and agrees systematically with the readings in Theoderet.).

Iambic trimeter.

1. **παρατηροῦντ(α) ... τίς ἔπταρεν:** 'keeping an eye out for who sneezed'; cf. 2–3. For sneezes as omens, e.g. Men. fr. 844. 9 (in a list of terrors that also includes dreams and the hooting of an owl); H. *Od.* 17. 541–7; X. *An.* iii. 2. 9; Arist. *HA* 492^{b}6–8; Philoch. *FGrHist* 328 F 192; Pease, *CP* 6 (1911), 429–43.

2–3. For chance remarks and encounters as omens, see introductory n. **ἢ τίς ἐστιν κτλ.:** for the construction, in which σκοποῦντα governs the question in the second half of 2, see 1 n. **πωλῶ τοῦτον εὐθὺς ἐν ἀγορᾶι** might be figurative (i.e. 'I treat him like a worthless slave'; cf. J4), with part of the point perhaps being that the view of the world inherent in such an attitude assumes that whatever a man does, he does for someone else (4–5). But the speaker could just as well be a slave-owner who refuses to be burdened with superstitious servants. For ἀγορά without the definite article, see J7. 4 n.

4–6.   Lines 4–5 offer the ground for the policy described in 1–3, with this ground then justified by the even more general view of things articulated in 6.

4.   **αὐτῶι**: 'for himself' (dative of advantage or disadvantage, like τοῖς ἐν τῆι πόλει in 5); the point is that the actions or choices in question are unable to exercise any supernatural effect over the situation of others (5). **βαδίζει καὶ λαλεῖ καὶ πτάρνυται** resumes the list of omens in 1–2, but in reverse order.

5.   **τοῖς ἐν τῆι πόλει**: i.e. 'for everyone else' (cf. 4 n.).

6.   **πέφυκεν**: 'are naturally', i.e. 'happen' *vel sim.* For the sentiment, e.g. adesp. com. fr. *883.

J22. Speaker A is perhaps the eponymous Superstitious Man. Speaker B is a sceptic, like the man who speaks **J21** (where see introductory n.).

Preserved at Clement of Alexandria, *Stromateis* vii. 24. 3, as an example of superstitious belief.

Iambic trimeter.

1–2.   **ἀγαθόν τι μοι | γένοιτο**: a spontaneous wish or prayer offered in response to an unexpected event that may portend something terrible. **πολυτίμητοι** ('much-honoured') is a common epithet of gods and heroes in comedy (e.g. **I2**. 6 with n.; Ar. *Ach.* 807; Eub. fr. 115. 6; Antiph. fr. 143. 2), but may be used deliberately here by the superstitious man, who shows the gods and everything associated with them an extraordinary degree of deference.

3.   **ὑποδούμενος**: 'as I was putting on my shoes' (< ὑποδέω); cf. **H20**. 7 with n.

3–4.   **τὸν ἱμάντα ... τῆς δεξιᾶς | ἐμβάδος**: 'the strap of my right shoe'. That the right shoe is involved is clearly taken to be significant; breaking the strap on one's left shoe might mean something entirely different. ἐμβάδες are rough men's leather shoes commonly worn by the poor; see Stone 223–5.   **φλήναφε**: 'babbler'; cf. **F19**. 1 φληναφῶν (of someone who insists on 'babbling' about philosophy).

5–6.   **σὺ δὲ κτλ.** offers a more pedestrian explanation of the supposed omen. **μικρολόγος <τις>**: 'a cheapskate'.   **καινάς**: sc. ἐμβάδας.

Epigraphic Evidence for the Chronology
of Attic Comedy

The most important sources for the chronology of the dramatic competitions at the City Dionysia and Lenaia in Athens are two fragmentary inscriptions, *IG* II² 2318 and 2325.[1] This appendix is an introduction to the evidence these inscriptions preserve about the comic contests and the poets who participated in them. The fundamental work on the topic was done by Capps over a century ago,[2] and readers concerned with the details of how the inscriptions have been reconstructed or wanting a more substantial treatment of how they can be used to illuminate one another are referred to his studies and to my own forthcoming re-examination of the topic (with a fresh text of the portions of the text discussed below prepared by Benjamin Millis).

A. The Inscriptions

(1) *IG* II² 2318 (conventionally referred to as the 'Fasti') consists of twelve fragments of a large inscription that covered a retaining wall or the like and recorded the results of the dithyrambic, tragic, and comic competitions at the City Dionysia on a year-by-year basis beginning around the end of the

---

[1] See in general *DFA* 101–20, 359–61; H. J. Mette, *Urkunden dramatischer Aufführungen in Griechenland* (Texte und Kommentare 8: Berlin and New York, 1977), although the latter is so ill-presented as to be difficult to use. A few additional details about the careers of Callias Comicus, Lysippus, Teleclides, Xenophilus, Anaxandrides, and perhaps Aristomenes can be extracted from the so-called 'Roman fragments' (*IG* XIV 1097 + 1098a + 1098, = L. Moretti, *Inscriptiones Graecae Urbis Romae* (Rome, 1968), nos. 216, 215, 218), which come from a large inscription that gave the agonistic history of the individual Athenian comic poets. But this material is so problematic and the addition it represents to our knowledge so limited, that I have chosen not to treat it here. For detailed discussion, see Capps, *CP* 1 (1906), 203–20; W. A. Dittmer, *The Fragments of Athenian Comic Didascaliae Found in Rome* (Leiden, 1923); *DFA* 120–2; Moretti (above) 184–92 (with photographs), who identifies several other tiny fragments of the inscription.

[2] Esp. E. Capps, *The Introduction of Comedy into the City Dionysia* (Decennial Publications of the University of Chicago: Chicago, 1903); *AJP* 28 (1907), 179–99; *Hesperia*, 12 (1943), 1–11 (announcing the discovery of fr. b² of *IG* II² 2318). See also Capps, *AJP* 20 (1899), 388–405 (separating material referring to the City Dionysia and the Lenaia festivals in *IG* II² 2325); *AJP* 21 (1900), 38–61, esp. 50–61 (on the careers of Cephisodorus, Aristomenes, Antiphanes, and Menander); *AJA* 4 (1900), 74–91; Camp, *Hesperia*, 40 (1971), 302–7 (announcing the discovery of a new fragment of the Didascaliae referring to competitions in the late 360s).

sixth century and continuing until at least 329/8. After the entry for 347/6
the inscriber's hand changes, and the records preserved on the remaining
fragments, for the contests in 343/2 and later, must represent additions to
the original monument, which can be confidently dated on that basis to the
mid-340s. Almost all the fragments were found on the north slope of the
Acropolis, and they are therefore unlikely to come from the same structure as
IG II² 2319–25 (the 'Didascaliae'; see below).

The heading of *IG* II² 2318, which probably extended across the entire
inscription, is partially preserved in frr. *a* and *b²*, and appears to have read
[ἀπὸ ... ⁹ ... , ἐφ' οὗ πρῶ]τον κῶμοι ἦσαν τῶ[ι Διονύ]σωι, τραγωιδοὶ
δ[ημοτελεῖς ...] ('from [the archonship of] ..., in whose year *kômoi* first
occurred for Dionysus. Publicly funded tragedians ... ').³ Entries appear in a
standard, multi-line form, with the eponymous archon's name, which gives
the date for the results that follow, in the first line, followed by: the name of
the victorious tribe in the boys' dithyramb (line 2) and of the victorious
choregus in that event (line 3); the name of the victorious tribe in the men's
dithyramb (line 4) and of the victorious *choregus* in that event (line 5); the
title 'of the comic poets' (line 6), followed by the name of the victorious
choregus in the comic competition (line 7) and of the victorious poet (line 8);
the title 'of the tragic poets' (line 9), followed by the name of the victorious
choregus in the tragic competition (line 10) and of the victorious poet (line
11); and (beginning around the middle of the fifth century) the name of the
individual who was victorious in the contest for best tragic actor. Perhaps
most important for our purposes, several fragments preserve portions of
two adjacent columns that contain archons' names. We have a complete list
of archons' names for this period, and so any annual entries that contain
them can be dated; and the fact that the entries are of a standard length means
that when we have archons' names in two adjacent columns, we can calculate
how many eleven- or twelve-item entries, and thus how many total lines the
column to the left contained. It is thus possible to show that the individual
columns in the inscription contained 141 lines (i.e. enough room for eleven
full twelve-line entries, plus nine lines from a partial twelfth entry, the rest of
which wrapped around to the next column) and that there were fifteen
columns (thirteen to accommodate the preserved fragments, plus two at the
beginning of the inscription that have perished completely). That knowledge
in turn can be combined with information provided by the preserved margins
of the individual stones that made up the inscription, which eliminates
numerous possible positions for fragments that lack archons' names, to

³ Thus Capps, *Hesperia*, 12 (1943), 9–10, who speculatively restored the rest of the heading
[... ἀγωνίσαντες ἐν ἄστει οἵδε νενικήκασιν].

determine the exact position of all the preserved portions of the inscription and thus the dates of the victories they record.

(2) *IG* II² 2319–25 (conventionally referred to collectively as the 'Didascaliae') are fragments of a series of inscriptions that decorated the interior sides of three walls and six architrave blocks of a hexagonal building.⁴ Almost all the fragments were found on the south slope of the Acropolis, making it likely that the building stood in the sacred precinct of Dionysus there. The inscriptions on the building's walls (*IG* II² 2319–24) offered a year-by-year record of the competitions at the City Dionysia and the Lenaia, with the poets listed in the order in which they placed, along with the titles of their plays, the names of their protagonists ('lead actors'), and (in cases where there was a separate actors' contest) the name of the protagonist who was victorious in the actors' contest. Unfortunately, these inscriptions are very badly damaged, and in the case of comedy we have only some fragments of the records from the City Dionysia in 312 and 311 (*IG* II² 2323a), the Lenaia in 289 and 288 (*IG* II² 2319. 54–66), and the City Dionysia from approximately the late 210s to the late 140s (*IG* II² 2323).

The inscriptions on the building's architrave blocks (*IG* II² 2325, conventionally referred to as the 'Victors' Lists') were divided into four sections: tragic poets victorious at the City Dionysia, followed by tragic actors victorious there; comic poets victorious at the City Dionysia, followed by comic actors victorious there; comic poets victorious at the Lenaia, followed by comic actors victorious there; and tragic poets victorious at the Lenaia, followed by tragic actors victorious there. Large portions of the comic Victors' Lists are preserved and are discussed in detail in §§ B–D, below. The information was presented in columns containing seventeen lines, with a few lines occasionally left blank at the foot of a column; individuals were listed in the order in which they achieved their first victory at the festival in question, with the name followed by the total number of times the poet or actor took the prize. This is thus a very different style of catalogue from the one partially preserved in the Fasti, and the conclusions it allows are generally broader but less precise than the specific but limited information contained there.

IG II² 3080 (on the outer face of the fragmentary architrave block whose inner face preserves fr. *q* of *IG* II² 2325) associates the building on which the Didascaliae were inscribed with a set of performances at the City Dionysia in the middle of the third century. Reisch accordingly argued that the man who erected the building must have been the *agonothetes* for that year, and suggested that the same individual was responsible for *IG* II² 2853, a

---

⁴ See the drawing at P. Ghiron-Bistagne, *Recherches sur les Acteurs dans la Grèce antique* (Paris, 1976), 27. The other three sides of the structure were left open.

fragmentary dedicatory inscription (also found on the south slope of the Acropolis) by an *agonothetes* that dates to 279/8. The records preserved in *IG* II² 2323 and 2325 none the less continue well after this date, and the later portions of the inscriptions must represent additions, although the fact that room was left for them suggests that an eventual expansion of the records was anticipated from the first.[5]

B. Evidence for the Fifth-Century Comic Poets and the Origins of the Comic Competitions

Much of what we know about the fifth-century chronology of comedy in Athens is drawn from the first three columns of the City Dionysia Victors' List (*IG* II² 2325. 39–70), although the very earliest history of the competitions remains obscure. As noted above, the Victors' List offers only a relative chronology of poets, and it is our great good fortune that the information it preserves can be supplemented and rendered more comprehensible by a few fixed City Dionysia dates known from other sources. In particular, the Fasti record victories by Magnes in 473/2 (*IG* II² 2318. 8); Euphronius in 459/8 (*IG* II² 2318. 48); Callias in 447/6 (*IG* II² 2318. 78); Hermippus in 436/5 (*IG* II² 2318 fr. *b*²); and Hermippus or Cantharus in 423/2 (*IG* II² 2318. 115). In addition, a hypothesis to Aristophanes' *Clouds* informs us that Cratinus was victorious at the City Dionysia in 424/3; a hypothesis to Aristophanes' *Peace* informs us that Eupolis was victorious in 422/1; a hypothesis to Aristophanes' *Birds* informs us that Amipsias was victorious in 415/14; and we know from Lysias 21. 4 that Cephisodorus was victorious in 403/2. This information allows us to attach a number of relatively firm dates to the information preserved in the City Dionysia Victors' List, and to arrive at a rough estimate for the date of the beginning of the comic competitions at the festival.

IG II² 2325. 39–70

col. I	col. II	col. III
[ΑΣΤΙΚΑΙ ΠΟΗΤΩΝ]	[ΤΗΛΕΚΛΕΙ]ΔΗΣ III	ΝΙΚΟΦΩ[Ν]
[ΚΩΜΙΚΩΝ]	. . . .⁹. . . . Σ I	ΘΕΟΠΟΜΠ[ΟΣ
[ΧΙΩΝΙΔΗΣ]	– – –	Κ[Η]ΦΙΣΟ[ΔΩΡΟΣ
– – –	– – –	[ΑΡΧ]Ι[ΠΠΟΣ
– – – I	ΦΕΡ[ΕΚΡΑΤΗΣ –]	– – –
. . . .⁹. . . . Σ I	ΕΡΜ[ΙΠΠΟΣ –]	– – –

⁵ See in general C. A. P. Ruck, *IG* II² 2323: *The List of the Victors in Comedies at the Dionysia* (Leiden, 1967), with further bibliography.

col. I	col. II	col. III
– – –	ΑΡΙ[ΣΤΟΦΑΝΗΣ –]	– – –
[ΜΑΓΝΗ]Σ ΔΙ	ΕΥ[ΠΟΛΙΣ –]	– – –
….⁷…Σ Ι	ΚΑ[ΝΘΑΡΟΣ –]	– – –
[ΑΛΚΙΜΕ]ΝΗ[Σ] Ι	ΦΡΥ[ΝΙΧΟΣ –]	– – –
…⁶…Σ Ι	ΑΜ[ΕΙΨΙΑΣ –]	– – –
[ΕΥΦΡΟΝ]ΙΟΣ Ι	ΠΛΑ[ΤΩΝ –]	– – –
[ΕΚΦΑΝ]ΤΙΔΗΣ ΙΙΙΙ	ΦΙΛ[ΥΛΛΙΟΣ –]	– – –
[ΚΡΑΤΙ]ΝΟΣ ΠΙ	ΛΥΚ[ΙΣ –]	– – –
[ΔΙΟΠ]ΕΙΘΗΣ ΙΙ	ΛΕΥ[ΚΩΝ –]	– – –
[ΚΡΑ]ΤΗΣ ΙΙΙ	vac.	– – –
[ΚΑΛΛΙΑ]Σ ΙΙ	vac.	– – –

Anon. περὶ κωμωιδίας III. 18 (= Magnes test. 2. 5) reports that the comic poet Magnes was victorious eleven times; and since we know that the comic competitions at the Lenaia did not begin until the mid-440s or so (see below) and Magnes does not appear in the preserved portion of the first column of the Victors' List for that festival, which takes us down into the early 420s (see below), all eleven of his triumphs must have been at the City Dionysia. This was obviously an extraordinary record, which made Magnes one of the great names of his generation (cf. Ar. *Eq.* 520–1), and he can be confidently restored as the sixth poet (with eleven victories) in col. I of the Victors' List and his initial victory dated to 473/2 or earlier on the basis of *IG* II² 2318. 8 (referred to above). That fact in turn allows us to make some progress towards determining when the comic competitions at the City Dionysia began.[6] The Victors' List has room for five victorious comic poets before Magnes. If his success in 473/2 was his first, therefore, and if there were no repeat winners before that, the comic competition could have begun at the City Dionysia as late as 478/7 (exactly five years earlier, with a new poet taking the prize each year). But those are both quite conservative assumptions, and the *Suda* (χ 318 = Chionid. test. 1) reports that Chionides—referred to by Aristotle at *Po.* 1448ª33–4 as one of the earliest Attic comic poets, along with Magnes— staged a comedy 'eight years before the Persian Wars'. On inclusive reckoning that is 487/6, which has become the generally accepted date for the origin of

---

[6] Tragic competitions at the festival probably began near the end of the 6th c., although this date (which depends on attempts to restore the lost first column or columns of *IG* II² 2318) is also conjectural.

the competition (and is also the basis for the restoration of Chionides' name in the first line of the list). The Victors' List is compatible with that date, on the assumption that some of the poets who appear on it won again before he had his initial success, pushing the beginning of the contest back one year for each such additional victory, but offers positive support for nothing more specific than a *terminus ante quem* of a decade or so later.

If we accept Magnes as the sixth poet in col. I of the City Dionysia Victors' List and date this entry no later than 473/2, as the Fasti require, [ΕΥΦΡΟ-Ν]ΙΟΣ, who appears at *IG* II² 2318. 48 as victorious at the City Dionysia in 459/8, can reasonably be restored four lines below him.[7] Even more important, the fact that this entry informs us that Euphronius took the prize only once allows us to date his appearance in the catalogue to precisely that year.[8] The initial victory of Ecphantides, whose name appears in the next line of the Victors' List, therefore, must have occurred no earlier than 458/7, but might easily have been a few years later, if Magnes or another poet listed above who had already taken the prize one or more times won again in the meantime. So too in the case of the poets whose names follow in the list, Cratinus' initial victory must have occurred no earlier than 457/6 (two years after Euphronius' victory), but probably came somewhat later; the otherwise obscure Diopeithes' initial victory must have occurred no earlier than 456/5 (three years after Euphronius' victory); and Crates' initial victory must have occurred no earlier than 455/4 (four years after Euphronius' victory). [ΚΑΛΛΙΑ]Σ, who appears in one of the preserved portions of the Fasti (*IG* II² 2318. 78) with a victory (not necessarily his first) in 447/6, can then be restored at the bottom of the column, with his initial victory occurring no earlier than 454/3 (five years after Euphronius' victory) but most likely somewhat later.[9]

Most of the upper portion of the second column of the City Dionysia Victors' List cannot be read. In what is preserved, however, Pherecrates is listed immediately before Hermippus; and since we know from fr. *b²* of the Fasti that Hermippus took the prize in 436/5, this tends to confirm Dobree's suggestion that anon. περὶ κωμωιδίας III. 29 (= Pherecr. test. 2a. 6) be emended[10] to put Pherecrates' initial victory in 438/7. There is space at the top

---

[7] There must, therefore, have been numerous victories during these years by poets who had already taken the prize once—and many of these additional victories were presumably by Magnes.

[8] Nothing else is known of Alcimenes, whose name is plausibly restored two lines above Euphronius, except that he was a comic poet (S α 1284 = test. 1).

[9] *IG* XIV 1097. 1, 5–6 shows that Callias was still active in the mid- to late 430s and perhaps even later, suggesting that the victory in 447/6 was in fact his first.

[10] From νικᾶι ἐπὶ θεάτρου to νικᾶι ἐπὶ Θεοδώρου.

of the column for the names of three other poets between Pherecrates and Teleclides. If there were no repeat winners during those years, Teleclides' initial victory must date to 442/1 (four years before 438/7, with a new poet taking the prize each year during the interval). But this is once again a quite unlikely assumption, and the date for Teleclides' initial victory ought probably to be pushed up a few years, allowing for some repeat victories, into the mid-440s, which is consistent with the date of 447/6 or earlier for Callias one position ahead of him at the bottom of the first column.

The names partially preserved in col. II of the City Dionysia Victors' List beneath *ΦΕΡ[ΕΚΡΑΤΗΣ]* and *ΕΡΜ[ΙΠΠΟΣ]* are of more immediate, obvious interest to modern students of Athenian comedy, but have also caused more trouble. Eupolis, almost an exact contemporary of Aristophanes, began competing in 430/29 (test. 2a. 6) and died most likely in 411 (see Appendix III). We know from a literary source that Eupolis was victorious at the Dionysia in 422/1 (see the beginning of this section), and the combination of information preserved in the *Suda* (ε 3657 = test. 1), which credits him with a total of seven victories, and in the catalogue of victors at the Lenaia (below), where he won three times, makes it clear that he had four City Dionysia victories (i.e. three in addition to the initial one that got his name into the inscription at this point). The name above Eupolis' in the City Dionysia Victors' List is most naturally restored *ΑΡΙ[ΣΤΟΦΑΝΗΣ]* (thus Kaibel); and since Aristophanes' *Banqueters* is known to have taken second place in 428/7 (*Banqueters* test. iv–vi; festival unknown), and since his *Clouds* took third at the City Dionysia in 424/3 (*Nu.* hyp. II. 1–2) and we know of no other City Dionysia performances this early in his career, the play with which Aristophanes took the prize the first time is likely to have been *Babylonians*, which was staged at the City Dionysia at 427/6.[11] This would mean that no new poet took the prize at the festival for almost a decade after Hermippus in 436/5 (unless his initial victory came earlier than that, making the interval even longer); and Wilhelm, noting that Aristophanes' name is also missing from the Lenaia Victors' List and that he presented *Babylonians* (like *Banqueters*, *Acharnians*, *Birds*, and *Lysistrata*) διὰ Καλλιστράτου ('with Callistratus as producer'), restored *ΑΡΙ[ΣΤΟΜΕΝΗΣ]* in the City Dionysia Victors' List instead, on the theory that the man responsible for

[11] Gilula, *CQ* NS 39 (1989), 336–7, rejects the assignment of *Babylonians* to the City Dionysia at Σ^REΓ Ar. *Ach.* 378 (= *Bab.* test. iv) on the ground that this might be an inference from *Ach.* 502–5. But 502–5 itself could not be clearer: unlike *Acharnians*, 'last year's comedy' (i.e. *Babylonians*) was staged not at the Lenaia but at a different festival, which a large number of non-Athenians attended (cf. Ar. *Pax* 45–6 with Olson ad loc.) and which must be the City Dionysia.

staging the play rather than the one who had written it was given official credit for a victory. In addition, Wilhelm restored *KA[ΛΛΙΣΤΡΑΤΟΣ]* in the line below *ΕΥ[ΠΟΛΙΣ]*, and four lines after that restored *ΦΙΛ[Ω-ΝΙΔΗΣ]* (another of Aristophanes' producers, for *Wasps*, *Amphiaraus* (Lenaia 414), and *Frogs*).¹² This reconstruction puts the prize awarded to *Babylonians* after Eupolis' first victory, allowing the latter to be pushed up as early as Eupolis' initial appearance at the festival (perhaps in 430/29), substantially reducing the gap between Hermippus and the poet who follows him in the list.

The most significant objection to Wilhelm's thesis is that the use of theatrical producers appears to have been unexceptional by the final quarter of the fifth century: Eupolis produced *Autolycus* διὰ Δημοστράτου in 421/20 (Ath. 5. 216d = test. 15); Plato Comicus used producers a number of times at the beginning of his career (test. 7); Anaxandrides apparently used one at least once near the end of his in the middle of the fourth century (*IG* XIV 1098. 9 = test. *5. 9 with supplement); and [Plu.] *Mor.* 839d reports that the fourth-century tragic poet Aphareus (*TrGF* 73 T 2) was twice victorious at the City Dionysia using Dionysius as producer and twice victorious at the Lenaia δι' ἑτέρων. Given how limited our evidence for the period is, this is a remarkably large number of examples and leaves no doubt that the practice of using theatrical producers was widespread in the classical period. There is none the less no certain instance of a man not known to have been a poet appearing in the Victors' Lists. Much more important, the fact that the names of poets rather than producers were recorded would seem to be proven by *IG* II² 2325. 12, where *[ΑΦΑ]ΡΕΥΣ* is listed as having been awarded the prize twice in the tragic competitions at the City Dionysia, although he used Dionysius as his producer (above). Despite Wilhelm, therefore, Aristophanes' name almost certainly belongs in the middle of col. II of the City Dionysia Victors' List; and in that case Eupolis' first victory at the festival must have come in 426/5, 425/4, or perhaps as late as 422/1, when his *Flatterers* took the prize ahead of Aristophanes' *Peace*.¹³

The section of *IG* II² 2325 that treats the fifth-century history of the Lenaia is less problematic.

---

¹² Thus *IG* II² (which none the less prints *ΑΡΙ[ΣΤΟΦΑΝΗΣ]* in 58). On Wilhelm's thesis, therefore, Aristophanes did not appear in the catalogue of City Dionysia victors at all, unless he took the prize in his own name late in his career (with the victory presumably recorded in the damaged final section of col. III).

¹³ As noted above, Cratinus was victorious at the City Dionysia in 424/3, and either Hermippus or Cantharus was victorious there in 423/2, excluding those dates for Eupolis' first victory.

IG II² 2325. 116–38

col. I	col. II
[ΛΗΝΑΙΚ]Α[Ι ΠΟΗ]ΤΩΝ	ΠΟ[ΛΙΟΧΟΣ] Ι
[ΚΩΜΙΚΩΝ]	ΜΕ[ΤΑΓΕΝΗ]Σ ΙΙ
[Ξ]ΕΝΟΦΙΛΟΣ Ι	ΘΕΟ[ΠΟΜΠ]ΟΣ ΙΙ
[Τ]ΗΛΕΚΛΕΙΔΗΣ ΙΙΙ	ΠΟΛ[ΥΖΗΛΟ]Σ ΙΙΙΙ
ΑΡΙΣΤΟΜΕΝΗΣ ΙΙ	ΝΙΚΟΦ[ΩΝ –]
ΚΡΑΤΙΝΟΣ ΙΙΙ	ΑΠΟ[ΛΛΟΦΑΝΗ]Σ Ι
ΦΕΡΕΚΡΑΤΗΣ ΙΙ	ΑΜ[ΕΙΨΙΑΣ –]
ΕΡΜΙΠΠΟΣ ΙΙΙΙ	Ν[ΙΚΟΧΑΡΗΣ? –]
ΦΡΥΝΙΧΟΣ ΙΙ	ΧΕΝΟ[Φ]ΩΝ Ι
ΜΥΡΤΙΛΟΣ Ι	ΦΙΛΥΛΛΙΟΣ Ι
[ΕΥ]ΠΟΛΙΣ ΙΙΙ	ΦΙΛΟΝΙΚΟΣ Ι
– – –	…⁷…Σ Ι

(five additional lines are lost)

Aristophanes (whose name is missing from the list but may have come next in col. I) is known from the Hellenistic hypotheses to his plays to have taken the prize at the Lenaia in 426/5 with *Acharnians* and in 425/4 with *Knights* (as well as with *Frogs* in 405). The initial victory by Eupolis recorded at the bottom of the preserved portion of col. I must accordingly have come sometime between 430/29 (his first appearance at either festival; see above) and 427/6 (the year before *Acharnians*). Eight poets credited with a total of twenty victories appear above Eupolis in col. I, the top of which is complete and thus dates back to the beginning of the competition at the festival. If Eupolis took the prize in 430/29 (the earliest possible date), and if all twenty of the triumphs credited to the poets whose names precede his occurred before that (i.e. if none of them was victorious again at the Lenaia after Eupolis and Aristophanes appeared on the scene), the comic competitions at the festival might have begun as early as 450/49 (twenty years earlier). If, on the other hand, Eupolis took the prize at the Lenaia for the first time in 427/6 (the latest possible date), and if none of the poets before him in the list was victorious there a second time until 424/3 (i.e. with all the repeat victories of the previous eight victors coming after Eupolis' initial victory; 426/5 and 425/4 must be excluded, since they belong to Aristophanes), the competition might have begun as late as 435/4 (eight years before 427/6, at one poet per year). More likely, at least half of the extra Lenaia victories of the pre-Eupolis poets should be assigned to the years before his first triumph, and the origins of the contest are generally placed in the mid- to late 440s on that basis.[14] There was a competition for tragic actors at the Lenaia from the very first (*IG* II² 2325. 247–82), and analogy suggests that there may also have been one for comic actors, although the preserved portions of the records date only to the middle of the fourth century (*IG* II² 2325. 190–8).

C. Evidence for the Early Fourth-Century Comic Poets

The Fasti record victories in the comic competitions at the City Dionysia by Araros (one of Aristophanes' sons, probably competing with one of his father's plays) in 388/7 (*IG* II² 2318. 196); Anaxandrides in 376/5 (*IG* II² 2318. 241); and Alexis in 348/7 (*IG* II² 2318. 278). In addition, the *Suda* dates Anaxandrides (α 1982 = test. 1) and Eubulus (ε 3386 = test. 1) to the Olympiad 376/2, and puts Antiphanes' birth in the Olympiad 408/4 (α 2735 = test. 1). No fragments of the fourth-century portions of the City Dionysia Victors' List are preserved. But Anaxandrides and Alexis appear in the expected order in col. III of the Lenaia Victors' List, along with a number of other 'Middle Comic' poets.

IG II² 2325. 140–52

col. III

ΦΙΛΙ[ΠΠΟΣ –] ΙΙ

ΧΟΡΗ[ΓΟΣ]

ΑΝΑΞΑ[ΝΔΡΙ]ΔΗΣ ΙΙΙ

ΦΙΛΕΤΑ[ΙΡΟ]Σ ΙΙ

---

[14] This date also sits easily with the fact that, according to *IG* XIV 1097 (one of the 'Roman fragments'), Xenophilus (the first victor at the Lenaia, according to the Victors' List) and Teleclides (the second victor there, according to the Victors' List) were both active already in the mid-440s. Assigning all twelve additional victories by the poets who took the prize for the first time before Eupolis won to the period after 425/4 is made particularly difficult by the fact that Cratinus must be given two of the three dates between 424/3 and 422/1, since he seems to have been dead or retired by the end of the 420s. In addition, even if the other five poets whose names followed Eupolis and Aristophanes in col. I won only one time apiece, and all the additional victories by Metagenes, Theopompus, and Polyzelus recorded in col. II occurred only after Amipsias' and Philyllius' first, Amipsias (who took the prize for the first time at the City Dionysia in 415/4 (see above) or perhaps a few years earlier) is then unlikely to have been victorious at the Lenaia before the mid-390s, and Philyllius (whose name comes only two lines after Amipsias in the City Dionysia Victors' List) is unlikely to have won before the late 390s.

col. III

ΕΥΒΟΥΛΟΣ ΙΙΙ

ΕΦΙΠΠΟΣ Ι –

[Α]ΝΤΙΦΑΝ[ΗΣ] ΙΙΙΙ

[Μ]ΝΗΣΙΜ[ΑΧΟΣ] Ι

ΝΑΥ[ΣΙΚΡΑΤ]ΗΣ ΙΙΙ

ΕΥΦΑΝΗ[Σ –]

ΑΛΕΞΙΣ ΙΙ –

[ΑΡ]ΙΣΤ[ΟΦΩΝ –]

– – –

– – –

– – –

– – –

[ΑΣΚΛΗΠΙΟΔΩ]ΡΟΣ? Ι

D. The Late Fourth-Century Comic Poets

The Fasti record victories in the comic competitions at the City Dionysia by Procleides in 333/2 (*IG* II² 2318. 327) and Theophilus in 330/29 (*IG* II² 2318. 354), and the Didascaliae inform us that Menander (whose name is restored on the basis of the title Ἡνίοχος) took fifth place there in 313/12 (*IG* II² 2323a. 36), and that Philippides, Nicostratus, Ameinias, and perhaps Theophilus competed in 312/11, with Philippides taking the prize (*IG* II² 2323a. 41, 43, 46, 49). We know from other sources that Timocles was active already by the mid-320s (see **E31** with introductory n.) and that Menander (342/1–292/1) staged his first play in 322/1 (anon. *de Com.* III. 58–9 = test. 3. 6–7); the *Suda* puts Philemo's *floruit* in the time of Alexander the Great and a little before Menander (φ 327 = test. 1), and calls Apollodorus of Gela a contemporary of Menander (α 3405 = test. 1); anon. *de Com.* III. 61 (= test. 1) says that Diphilus too was Menander's contemporary; and internal evidence shows that Philippides belongs to the very end of the century (cf. **E32** with introductory n.). No fragments of the City Dionysia Victors' List survive for this period; but all the information above fits neatly with col. IV of the Lenaia Victors' list, which probably begins in the late 340s or early 330s.

IG II² 2325. 153–67

col. IV

(one line is missing at the top)

ΔΙΟ[ΝΥΣΙ]ΟΣ   *I*

ΚΛΕ[ΑΡΧ]ΟΣ   –

ΑΘΗΝΟΚΛΗΣ   –

ΠΥΡ[ΡΝΗ]   *I*

ΑΛΚΗΝΩΡ   *I*

ΤΙΜΟΚΛΗΣ   *I*

ΠΡΟΚΛΕΙΔΗΣ   *I*

Μ[ΕΝ]ΛΝΔΡΟΣ   *I* –

Φ[Ι]ΛΗΜΩΝ   *III*

ΑΠΟΛΛΟΔΩΡΟ[Σ   –]

ΔΙΦΙΛΟΣ   *III*

ΦΙΛΙΠΠΙΔΗΣ   *II* –

ΝΙΚΟΣΤΡΑΤΟΣ   –

ΚΑΛΛΙΑΔΗΣ   *I*

ΑΜΕΙΝΙΑΣ   *I*

A comic actors' competition was added at the City Dionysia sometime between 330/*29*, when the Fasti break off with no mention of it, and 313/*12*, when *IG* II² 2323a. 38 records that Callippus the Younger took the prize; a portion of the actors' Victors' List for the third century is preserved at *IG* II² 2325. 88–115.

E. Evidence for the Third and Second Centuries

The lower portions of cols. V and VI of the City Dionysia Victors' List survive (*IG* II² 2325. 71–85, covering most of the third century and the first several decades of the second), as does much of cols. VI, VII, and VIII of the Lenaia Victors' List.[15] In addition, we know that Phoenicides? was victorious at the Lenaia probably in 290/*89* (*IG* II²2319. 56), and that Simylus, Diodorus (with two plays), and Phoenicides competed in 289/*8*, with Simylus taking the prize

---

[15] For this portion of the text (not in *IG* II²), see Peppas-Delmousou, *MDAI(A)* 92 (1977), 229–38.

(*IG* II² 2319. 59–61, 63, 65). But *IG* II² 2323 (the most important of the Didascaliae, covering the 210s–late 140s) makes it clear that the dramatic competitions gradually came to be dominated by revivals, and then to be held less and less often, until they finally vanish completely from our sight.

Conspectus Numerorum

A. Poets arranged in approximate chronological order

	Kassel–Austin	This Edition
[Susarion]	fr. 1	I1
Epicharmus	fr. 18	A1
	fr. 32	A13
	fr. 40	A3
	fr. 48	A2
	fr. 50	A5
	fr. 51	A4
	fr. 70	A9
	fr. 71	A10
	fr. 72	A11
	fr. 97	A6
	fr. 99	A7
	fr. 100	A8
	fr. 135	A12
	fr. 146	A15
	fr. 147	A14
	fr. 213	A17
	fr. 214	A16
[Epicharmus]	fr. 244	A18
	fr. 269	A19
Sophron	fr. 3	A21
	fr. 4. a	A20
Cratinus	fr. 17	D8
	fr. 40	B18
	fr. 41	B17
	fr. 42	B14
	fr. 43	B15
	fr. 45	B19
	fr. 47	B20
	Dionys. test. i	B13
	fr. 193	B1
	fr. 194	B2
	fr. *195	B3
	fr. 197	B5
	fr. 198	B12
	fr. 199	B4
	fr. 200	B10

	Kassel–Austin	This Edition
Cratinus *continued*	fr. *203	B11
	fr. 208	B6
	fr. 209	B7
	fr. 210	B9
	fr. 211	B8
	fr. 255	B46
	fr. 258	E12
	fr. *259	E13
	fr. 327	B16
	fr. 342	B41
	fr. 360	B37
Crates	fr. 16	B32
Callias Comicus	fr. 15	F3
Teleclides	fr. 1	B33
	fr. 41	F5
	fr. 44	E22
	fr. 45	E11
Pherecrates	fr. 43	J20
	fr. 76	H10
	fr. 102	B43
	fr. 137	B34
	fr. 155	D14
	fr. 162	H20
	fr. 164	E26
Hermippus	fr. *47	E14
	fr. 63	D1
	fr. *77	H8
Aristophanes	fr. 102	E20
	fr. 233	D2
	fr. *322	B31
	fr. 372	B22
	fr. 373	B23
	fr. 403	B25
	fr. 410	B26
	fr. 444	H16
	fr. 581	B35
	fr. 680	J5
Eupolis	fr. 13	B30
	fr. 88	J19
	fr. 89	B42
	fr. 102	E10
	fr. 148	D13
	fr. 172	B45
	fr. 193	E23
	fr. 219	E5
	fr. 245	B27
	fr. 246	B28
	fr. 247	B29

	Kassel–Austin	This Edition
Eupolis *continued*	fr. 261	A22
	fr. 262	E6
	fr. 316	E18
	fr. 327	J1
	fr. 331	E17
	fr. 384	E4
	fr. 386	F1
	fr. 392	B44
	fr. 395	F2
Phrynichus Comicus	fr. 3	J14
	fr. 19	B21
	fr. 32	D9
	fr. 61	E28
	fr. 62	E21
Amipsias	fr. *9	F4
Plato Comicus	fr. 46	H14
	fr. 71	H1
	fr. 96	B36
	fr. 98	J17
	fr. 99	B38
	fr. 115	E19
	fr. 168	J15
	fr. 183	E24
	fr. 188	I6
	fr. 189	G4
	fr. 201	E29
	fr. 202	E9
	fr. 203	E25
Philyllius	fr. 7	B24
	fr. 23	H7
Poliochus	fr. 2	G1
Metagenes	fr. 15	B39
Theopompus Comicus	fr. 16	F8
Nicophon	fr. 6	J3
	fr. 10	J2
Lysippus	fr. 4	B40
Strattis	fr. 48	J16
Nicostratus Comicus	fr. 22	J11
	fr. 27	H2
	fr. 30	E1
Anaxandrides	fr. 1	H11
	fr. 35	J13
Eubulus	fr. 26	D11
	fr. 63	G13
	fr. 72	G14
	fr. 80	J10

	Kassel–Austin	This Edition
Eubulus *continued*	fr. 89	C3
	fr. *93	H18
	fr. 106. 1–9	E30
	fr. 115	I2
	fr. 118	D4
	fr. 137	F13
Ephippus	fr. 8	H4
	fr. 15	G5
Antiphanes	fr. 57	H13
	fr. 75	C8
	fr. 85	H15
	fr. 123	J6
	fr. 131	C6
	fr. 172. 1–4	H6
	fr. 174	G2
	fr. 180	C10
	fr. 189	D6
	fr. 194	E7
	fr. 200	C13
	fr. 202	E3
	fr. 221	G10
	fr. 228	D10
Euphanes	fr. 1	G17
Alexis	fr. 9	H9
	fr. 15	G18
	fr. 16	G6
	fr. 21	H12
	fr. 24	G8
	fr. 25	F19
	fr. 78	J8
	fr. 103	I7
	fr. 140	G3
	fr. 160	H19
	fr. 223	F10
	fr. 259	G15
	fr. 263	G16
Aristophon	fr. 5	C11
	fr. 10	F11
	fr. 12	F12
Amphis	fr. 6	F7
	fr. 13	F9
	fr. 17	E2
	fr. 30	J7
Anaxilas	fr. 12	C4
	fr. 13	C5
Crobylus	fr. 8	C12

	Kassel–Austin	This Edition
Epicrates	fr. 3	I12
	fr. 5	C7
	fr. 8	I10
	fr. 10	F6
Heniochus	fr. 5	C2
Strato Comicus	fr. 1	D3
Xenarchus	fr. 4	I8
Dionysius Comicus	fr. 3	C9
Clearchus Comicus	fr. 4	H3
Philemo	fr. 45	H17
	fr. 82	G11
	fr. 95	C14
	fr. 101	J21
Timocles	fr. 4	E31
	fr. 6	D5
	fr. 24	I9
	fr. 27	D7
Menander	fr. 106	J22
	fr. 114	F14
	fr. 150	J4
	fr. 193	F15
	fr. 236	I3
	fr. 296	C16
	fr. 297	C17
	fr. 804	I4
	fr. 815	I5
Diphilus	fr. 70	H5
	fr. 74	D12
	fr. 87	J9
	fr. 101	E8
Philippides	fr. 25	E32
Anaxippus	fr. 6	G9
Posidippus Comicus	fr. 1	G7
Damoxenus	fr. 3	J12
Phoenicides	fr. 4	I11
Archedicus	fr. 2	G12
Hegesippus Comicus	fr. 2	F17
Theognetus	fr. 1	F16
Bato	fr. 3	F18
adespota comica	fr. 123	E27
	fr. *142	J18
	fr. 461	E16
	fr. 957	E15
	fr. 1062	C1
	fr. 1063. 1–34	C18
	fr. 1084	C15

B. Poets arranged alphabetically

	Kassel–Austin	This Edition
adespota comica	fr. 123	E27
	fr. *142	J18
	fr. 461	E16
	fr. 957	E15
	fr. 1062	C1
	fr. 1063. 1–34	C18
	fr. 1084	C15
Alexis	fr. 9	H9
	fr. 15	G18
	fr. 16	G6
	fr. 21	H12
	fr. 24	G8
	fr. 25	F19
	fr. 78	J8
	fr. 103	I7
	fr. 140	G3
	fr. 160	H19
	fr. 223	F10
	fr. 259	G15
	fr. 263	G16
Amipsias	fr. *9	F4
Amphis	fr. 6	F7
	fr. 13	F9
	fr. 17	E2
	fr. 30	J7
Anaxandrides	fr. 1	H11
	fr. 35	J13
Anaxilas	fr. 12	C4
	fr. 13	C5
Anaxippus	fr. 6	G9
Antiphanes	fr. 57	H13
	fr. 75	C8
	fr. 85	H15
	fr. 123	J6
	fr. 131	C6
	fr. 172. 1–4	H6
	fr. 174	G2
	fr. 180	C10
	fr. 189	D6
	fr. 194	E7
	fr. 200	C13
	fr. 202	E3
	fr. 221	G10
	fr. 228	D10
Archedicus	fr. 2	G12

	Kassel–Austin	This Edition
Aristophanes	fr. 102	E20
	fr. 233	D2
	fr. *322	B31
	fr. 372	B22
	fr. 373	B23
	fr. 403	B25
	fr. 410	B26
	fr. 444	H16
	fr. 581	B35
	fr. 680	J5
Aristophon	fr. 5	C11
	fr. 10	F11
	fr. 12	F12
Bato	fr. 3	F18
Callias Comicus	fr. 15	F3
Clearchus Comicus	fr. 4	H3
Crates	fr. 16	B32
Cratinus	fr. 17	D8
	fr. 40	B18
	fr. 41	B17
	fr. 42	B14
	fr. 43	B15
	fr. 45	B19
	fr. 47	B20
	Dionys. test. i	B13
	fr. 193	B1
	fr. 194	B2
	fr. *195	B3
	fr. 197	B5
	fr. 198	B12
	fr. 199	B4
	fr. 200	B10
	fr. *203	B11
	fr. 208	B6
	fr. 209	B7
	fr. 210	B9
	fr. 211	B8
	fr. 255	B46
	fr. 258	E12
	fr. *259	E13
	fr. 327	B16
	fr. 342	B41
	fr. 360	B37
Crobylus	fr. 8	C12
Damoxenus	fr. 3	J12
Dionysius Comicus	fr. 3	C9
Diphilus	fr. 70	H5

	Kassel–Austin	This Edition
Diphilus *continued*	fr. 74	D12
	fr. 87	J9
	fr. 101	E8
Ephippus	fr. 8	H4
	fr. 15	G5
Epicharmus	fr. 18	A1
	fr. 32	A13
	fr. 40	A3
	fr. 48	A2
	fr. 50	A5
	fr. 51	A4
	fr. 70	A9
	fr. 71	A10
	fr. 72	A11
	fr. 97	A6
	fr. 99	A7
	fr. 100	A8
	fr. 135	A12
	fr. 146	A15
	fr. 147	A14
	fr. 213	A17
	fr. 214	A16
[Epicharmus]	fr. 244	A18
	fr. 269	A19
Epicrates	fr. 3	I12
	fr. 5	C7
	fr. 8	I10
	fr. 10	F6
Eubulus	fr. 26	D11
	fr. 63	G13
	fr. 72	G14
	fr. 80	J10
	fr. 89	C3
	fr. *93	H18
	fr. 106. 1–9	E30
	fr. 115	I2
	fr. 118	D4
	fr. 137	F13
Euphanes	fr. 1	G17
Eupolis	fr. 13	B30
	fr. 88	J19
	fr. 89	B42
	fr. 102	E10
	fr. 148	D13
	fr. 172	B45
	fr. 193	E23
	fr. 219	E5
	fr. 245	B27

	Kassel–Austin	This Edition
Eupolis *continued*	fr. 246	B28
	fr. 247	B29
	fr. 261	A22
	fr. 262	E6
	fr. 316	E18
	fr. 327	J1
	fr. 331	E17
	fr. 384	E4
	fr. 386	F1
	fr. 392	B44
	fr. 395	F2
Hegesippus Comicus	fr. 2	F17
Heniochus	fr. 5	C2
Hermippus	fr. *47	E14
	fr. 63	D1
	fr. *77	H8
Lysippus	fr. 4	B40
Menander	fr. 106	J22
	fr. 114	F14
	fr. 150	J4
	fr. 193	F15
	fr. 236	I3
	fr. 296	C16
	fr. 297	C17
	fr. 804	I4
	fr. 815	I5
Metagenes	fr. 15	B39
Nicophon	fr. 6	J3
	fr. 10	J2
Nicostratus Comicus	fr. 22	J11
	fr. 27	H2
	fr. 30	E1
Pherecrates	fr. 43	J20
	fr. 76	H10
	fr. 102	B43
	fr. 137	B34
	fr. 155	D14
	fr. 162	H20
	fr. 164	E26
Philemo	fr. 45	H17
	fr. 82	G11
	fr. 95	C14
	fr. 101	J21
Philippides	fr. 25	E32
Philyllius	fr. 7	B24
	fr. 23	H7

	Kassel–Austin	This Edition
Phoenicides	fr. 4	I11
Phrynichus Comicus	fr. 3	J14
	fr. 19	B21
	fr. 32	D9
	fr. 61	E28
	fr. 62	E21
Plato Comicus	fr. 46	H14
	fr. 71	H1
	fr. 96	B36
	fr. 98	J17
	fr. 99	B38
	fr. 115	E19
	fr. 168	J15
	fr. 183	E24
	fr. 188	I6
	fr. 189	G4
	fr. 201	E29
	fr. 202	E9
	fr. 203	E25
Poliochus	fr. 2	G1
Posidippus Comicus	fr. 1	G7
Sophron	fr. 3	A21
	fr. 4. a	A20
Strato Comicus	fr. 1	D3
Strattis	fr. 48	J16
[Susarion]	fr. 1	I1
Teleclides	fr. 1	B33
	fr. 41	F5
	fr. 44	E22
	fr. 45	E11
Theognetus	fr. 1	F16
Theopompus Comicus	fr. 16	F8
Timocles	fr. 4	E31
	fr. 6	D5
	fr. 24	I9
	fr. 27	D7
Xenarchus	fr. 4	I8

The Poets

Alexis: Victorious at least once at the City Dionysia, in 347 (*IG* II² 2318. 278), and at least twice at the Lenaia, first probably in the late 350s (*IG* II² 2325. 150; just after Euphanes). According to the *Suda* (test. 1) he was from Thurii in Southern Italy and staged 245 plays. The *Suda* also claims that Alexis was Menander's paternal uncle, which may be a garbled version of the report in an anonymous essay on comedy (test. 2. 4–5) that Menander spent a considerable amount of time with and was trained by him. Of Alexis' comedies 342 fragments (including two *dubia* and one *spurium*) survive, along with 137 titles: *Ankylion, Agonis or The Brooch, Brothers, Goatherds, Aesop, The Prisoner-of-War, The Female Oiler, The Vine-Dresser, The Milk-Pail, Anteia, The Man Who Had a Cataract, The Chariot-Acrobat, The Man Who Was Mutilated, Archilochus, Asclepiocleides, The Instructor in Profligacy, Atalanta, The Girl from Attica, The Pipe-Girl, The Girl from Achaia, The Lock of Hair, The Girl from Bruttium, The Altar, Galateia, The Picture, Women in Power, The Ring, Demetrius or The Man Who Loved His Comrades, Women Sailing Across, Twins or Twin Sisters, Grieving Twice, Dorcis or The Girl Who Popped Her Lips, Dropides, The Man Who Was Moving In, The Goblet-Maker, Helen, The Rape of Helen, The Suitors of Helen, The Greek Girl, The Man from Epidaurus, The Heiress, The Letter, The Guardian, Seven Against Thebes, The Man Who Wished He Was from Eretria, She Went into the Well, Hesione, The Man Who Was Possessed by a God, Thesprotians, Thebans, Hired Labourers, Thrason, Iasis (perhaps The Girl from Iasos), Himilkon, The Knight, Isostasion, Calasiris (perhaps The Egyptian Garment), The Carthaginian, Men from Caunus, The Man Who Was Named in a Proclamation, The Citharode, Cleoboulina, The Girl From Cnidus, The Plasterer, The Female Barber, Crateia or the Pharmacist, The Steersman, Dice-Players, Cycnus, The Man from Cyprus, Lampas, The Cauldron, The Girl from Leucas or Runaways, Leuce, The Girl from Lemnos, Linus, Locrians, The Woman Who Ate Mandrake, Seers, Meropis, Midon, Milesians, Minos, The Miller, Odysseus Being Bathed, Odysseus Weaving, Wine, Olympiodorus, Olynthians, The Girl Who Looked Like Someone Else, Opora, Orestes, The Female Dancer, The Pancratiast, The Concubine, Pamphile, The All-Night Festival or Hired Workers, The Parasite, Pezonike, Poets, The Poetess, Polycleia, The Miserable Woman, The Man From Pontus, The Man Who Swept*

Everything Before Him, The Lead-Dancer, The Female Pythagorean, The Girl from Thermopylae (or perhaps *The Meeting at Pylae*), *The Pan of Coals, The Man from Sicyon, Sciron, The Libation-Bearer, The Soldier, Men Who Were Dying Together, Men Who Agree, Foster-Brothers, The Syracusan, The Storage-Containers, Men From Tarentum, The Wet-Nurse* or *The Wet-Nurses, The Loan-Shark* or *The Liar, The Wounded Man, Trophonius, Tyndareus, Sleep, The Supposititious Child, Phaedrus, Phaedon* or *Phaedrias, The Man Who Loved Athens, Philiscus, The Man Who Loved Elegance* or *The Nymphs, The Man Who Loved Tragedy, Philousa* (or perhaps *The Girl Who Was Kissing Someone*), *The Phrygian, The Exile, Choregis* (or perhaps *The Female Choregos*), *The Liar.* W. Geoffrey Arnott offers an exhaustive study of Alexis' career and the fragments of his plays in *Alexis: The Fragments* (Cambridge, 1996).

Amipsias: Victorious at least once at the City Dionysia (*IG* II² 2325. 62; just after Phrynichus Comicus and just before Plato Comicus), first no later than 414, when *Revellers* took the prize, and probably at least once at the Lenaia near the end of the century (*IG* II² 2325. 133). Aristophanes alludes rudely to him (as well as to Phrynichus Comicus and Lycis) at *Ra.* 12–15 for his allegedly unamusing use of comic porters. Thirty-nine fragments (over half merely glosses of odd words) of his comedies survive, along with seven titles: *Cottabus-Players, The Glutton, Connus* (City Dionysia 423; second), *Revellers* (City Dionysia 414; first), *Seducers, Sappho,* and *The Sling.* Piero Totaro offers a detailed study of Amipsias' career and the fragments of his plays in *Tessere,*133–94.

Amphis: Pollux i. 233 (citing fr. 38. 1) and vii. 17 seems to refer to Amphis as a 'Middle Comic' poet, and his repeated references to the philosopher Plato (frr. 6 = **F7**; 13 = **F9**) place him in the early to mid-fourth century. His name is not Athenian, and he was probably from the island of Andros (thus Kirchner). Forty-nine fragments of his comedies survive, along with twenty-six titles: *Athamas, Acco, The Female Oiler, Alcmaeon, The Vine-Dresser, Amphicrates, The Bath-House, Women in Power, Crazy about Women, The Ring, Dexidemides, The Dithyramb, Seven Against Thebes, Day-Labourers, The Oaf, The Plasterer, The Female Barber, Dice-Players, The Girl from Leucas, Odysseus, Ouranos, Pan, The Vagabond Acrobat, Sappho, Men Who Loved Their Brothers,* and *The Man Who Loved His Comrades.*

Anaxandrides: Victorious ten times (test. 1. 3), first in 376, according to the Marmor Parium (*FGrHist* 239 A 70 = test. 3). Inscriptional evidence shows that three of his victories came at the Lenaia (*IG* II² 2325. 142), so the other seven must have been at the City Dionysia, including in 375 (*IG* II² 2318. 241), when he also took third at the Lenaia (*IG Urb. Rom.* 218. 5). A substantial fragment of his complete competitive record survives in *IG Urb. Rom.* 218. He wrote sixty-five plays (test. 1. 3), and his career continued into the early 340s (*IG Urb. Rom.* 218. 8; fourth at the City Dionysia in 349 with either *Rustics* or *Anchises*). He was probably from the city of Camirus on Rhodes (test. 1. 1; 2. 9), although the *Suda* (test. 1. 2–3) reports that 'according to some authorities' he was from Colophon. The *Suda* (test. 1. 3–4) also reports that Anaxandrides was 'the first to introduce love-affairs and rapes of girls' (sc. to the comic stage). Eighty-two fragments (including two *dubia*) of his comedies survive, along with forty-one titles: *Rustics, Anchises, Aeschra* (or perhaps *The Ugly Woman*), *The Girl from Ambracia* (probably second, near the end of his career), *The Rival in Love* (fifth), *Achilleus, The Madness of Old Men, Twins, The Birth of Dionysus* (probably second), *Helen, Erechtheus* (City Dionysia 368; third), *Pious Men, Painters or Geographers* (or *The Geographer*), *Heracles, Thessalians, The Treasure, Theseus, Io* (City Dionysia 374; fourth), *The Ritual-Basket-Bearer, Cercius* or *Cercion, The Female Cithara-Player, Hunters, The Comic Tragedy, Women from Locris, Lycurgus, The Ma[dwoman]* (364; probably second), *Melilot, Nereus, Nereids, Odysseus* (City Dionysia between 373 and 358; fourth), *The Expert in Hoplite Fighting, Pandarus, Cities, Protesilaus, The Girl from Samos, Satyrias, Sosippus, Tereus* (not victorious), *Outrageous Behaviour, The Drug-Prophet,* and *The Libation-Vessel-Bearer.*

Anaxilas: Assumed to be a 'Middle Comic' poet, although there is no specific ancient evidence to this effect. Forty-three fragments of his comedies survive, along with at least twenty titles: *The Rustic, Antido[, The Pipe-Player, Botrylion, Glaucus, Manliness, Thrasyleon, Calypso, Circe, The Lyremaker* or *The Perfumemaker, Cooks, The Recluse, Neottis, Nereus, The Bird-Keepers, Wealthy Men* or *Wealthy Women, Hyacinthus* or *Hyacinthus the Pimp, The Graces, The Goldsmith,* and *Seasons.*

Anaxippus: The *Suda* (test. 1) calls him a 'New Comic' poet and places his *floruit* 'in the time of Antigonus and Demetrius Poliocetes', near the end of the fourth century. Eight fragments of his comedies survive, along with five titles: *The Man Who Tried To Hide His Face, The Claimant at Law, The Thunder-Bolt* or *The Man Who Was Struck by a Thunder-Bolt, The Citharode,* and *The Well.*

Antiphanes: Victorious eight times at the Lenaia, first probably in the late 360s or early 350s (*IG* II² 2325. 146; just after Ephippus); the *Suda* (test. 1. 4) reports that he took the prize a total of thirteen times, so his other five victories must have been at the City Dionysia. The *Suda* (test. 1. 3–4) also reports that he was born in the 93rd Olympiad (i.e. between 408 and 404), and says that some authorities claimed that he had written 365 plays, while others set the number at 280. An anonymous essay on comedy (test. 2. 3–4, 8) sets the number of preserved plays at 260, and claims that he staged his first comedy in the 98th Olympian (i.e. between 388 and 384), when according to the *Suda* (test. 1. 3) he would have been about 20 years old; the *Suda* adds that he lived to be 75 (test. 1. 5). That Antiphanes was not an Athenian by birth, but was later granted citizenship, seems to have been generally accepted, although where he was from originally was disputed (test. 1. 2 Kios, Smyrna, Rhodes; test. 2. 4 Thessalian Larissa). His son Stephanus produced some of his plays and was a comic poet in his own right (test. 1. 4; 2. 7–8). 327 fragments (including ten *dubia*) of Antiphanes' comedies survive, along with 138 titles: *The Rustic, Sisters, Adonis, Athamas, Egyptians, Aeolus, The Seamstress, The Girl Who Was Hit by a Javelin, The Female Oiler, The Fisher-Woman, Alcestis, The Man Who Was Trying to Get Home Safe, Andromeda, The Birth of Mankind* or *The Birth of the Gods* (restored), *Antaeus, Anteia, The Female Rival in Love, The Man Who Was Trying to Starve to Death, Vanished Money, Arcas, The Girl Who Was Kidnapped, Archestrate, The Archon, Asclepius, Profligates, The Pipe-Player, The Pipe-Girl* or *Twin Girls, The Man Who Was in Love with Himself, The Sex-Maniac, The Birth of Aphrodite, Bacchants, The Girl from Boeotia, The Bumblebee* (or *The Bumble-Cup*), *Bousiris, Boutalion, The Man from Byzantium, The Marriage* or *The Wedding Feast, Ganymede, Glaucus, Gorgythus, Deucalion, Twins, Men Who Were Twice as Big, The Man Who Recovered a Runaway, Men Who Were Unlucky in Love, Hard to Sell, The Girl from Dodona, The Girl Who Couldn't Talk, The Man from Epidaurus, The Heiress, Euthydicus, Fair Sailing, The Girl from Ephesus, The Man from Zacynthus, The Painter, The Charioteer, Thamyras, Men from Thoricus* or *The Man Who Was Digging a Trench, The Doctor, Knights, Caineus, Carians, The Female Dirge-Singer, The Gardener, The Cithara-Player, The Citharode, Cleophanes, The Fuller, The Man from Mt Cnoithideus* or *Pot-Belly, The Girl from Corinth, The Statuette-Maker, The Female Barber, Dice-Players, Cyclops, The Beggar's-Bag, Lampas, Lampon, Little Leptinus, The Man from Leucas, Leonides, Lemnian Women, The Lydian, Lycon, Malthake, Melanion, Meleager, Melitta, The Metic, Medea, The Mendicant Priest of Cybele, Metrophon, Midon, Minos, The Enemy of Rascals, Monuments, Seducers, The Miller, The Female Initiate, Young Men, Neottis, The Strong Man, Oenomaus* or *Pelops, The Bird-Diviner, Women Who Looked Like Each Other* or *Men Who Looked Like Each Other, Men Who Shared a Father, Omphale, Men Who Shared a Name, Orpheus, The Pederast, The Parasite, The Girl Who Was Secretly Given in Marriage, Proverbs* or *The Man Who Quoted Proverbs, Wealthy Men, Poetry, The Man from Pontos, The Shepherd, The Puzzle, Step-Children, Sappho, Hard Times, The Scythian* or *The Scythians* or *The Bulls, The Soldier* or *Tycho, Timon, The Wounded Man, The Tritagonist, The Etruscan, The Water-Pitcher, Sleep, Phaon, The Man Who Loved His Comrades, Philiscus, The Man Who Loved*

Thebes, Philoctetes, The Man Who Loved His Mother, The Man Who Loved His Father, Philotis, The Man From the Deme Phrearrhioi, and *Chrysis.*

Archedicus: According to the *Suda* (test. 2), one of Archedicus' plays (fr. 4) contained an attack on Demosthenes' nephew Demochares (d. 275), placing him in the late fourth or early third century. Four fragments of his comedies survive, along with two titles: *The Man Who Was Quite Mistaken* and *The Treasure.*

Aristophanes: Probably victorious at least once at the City Dionysia, with *Babylonians* in 426 (*IG* II² 2325. 58), and at least three times at the Lenaia, with *Acharnians* in 425, *Knights* in 424, and *Frogs* in 405. His career began in 427, with *Banqueters* (see **D2** with introductory n.), and he died in the early 380s. Aristophanes was regarded as one of the three great masters of Athenian 'Old Comedy' (along with Cratinus and Eupolis), and his plays continued to be read and commented on well into the Roman period. His sons Araros, Philippus, and Nicostratus were also comic poets: Araros is said to have been heavily involved in the production of *Wealth* II in 388 (test. 1. 54–6) and to have been responsible for the posthumous performances of *Aeolosicon* II and *Cocalus* (*Cocalus* test. iii), with which he seems to have taken the prize at the City Dionysia in 387 (*IG* II² 2318. 196), while Philippus was twice victorious at the Lenaia (*IG* II² 2325. 140) and apparently produced some of Eubulus' comedies (Eub. test. 4). (Aristophanes' third son is sometimes said to have been called not Nicostratus but Philetaerus, and a man by that name appears in the catalogue of Lenaia victors with two victories, the first probably in the late 370s, at *IG* II² 2325. 143 (just after Anaxandrides and just before Eubulus).) Eleven of Aristophanes' comedies survive complete: (in chronological order) *Acharnians* (Lenaia 425; first), *Knights* (Lenaia 424; first), *Clouds* II (a revised version of the lost original; see below), *Wasps* (Lenaia 422; second), *Peace* I (City Dionysia 421; second), *Birds* (City Dionysia 414; second), *Lysistrata* (Lenaia 411), *Women Celebrating the Thesmophoria* (City Dionysia 411), *Frogs* (Lenaia 405; first); *Assemblywomen* (391?), and *Wealth* II (388). In addition, we have 976 fragments (including fifty-two *dubia*) of the other comedies, as well as thirty-four titles: *Aeolosicon* I and II (posthumous performance), *Amphiaraus* (Lenaia 414) *Anagyrus, Babylonians* (City Dionysia 426; first), *Farmers, Old Age, Gerytades, Daedalus, Banqueters* (427; second), *Danaids, Dionysus Shipwrecked, Dramas or The Centaur, Dramas or Niobus, Peace* II, *Heroes, Women Celebrating the Thesmophoria* II, *Cocalus* (posthumous performance), *Lemnian Women, Clouds* I (City Dionysia 423; last), *Islands, Odomantian Ambassadors* (?; restored), *Merchantships, Storks, Wealth* I (408), *Poetry, Polyidus, The Proagon, Women Occupying Tents, Frying-Pan Men, Telemessians, Triphales, Phoenician Women,* and *Seasons.*

Aristophon: Probably victorious at least once at the Lenaia, around 350 (*IG* II² 2325. 151; just after Alexis). Fifteen fragments of his comedies survive, along with eight titles: *Babias*, *Twin Girls (or Twins) or The Pan of Coals*, *The Doctor*, *Callonides*, *Perithous*, *Plato*, *The Pythagorean*, and *Philonides*.

Bato: According to Plutarch (test. 3), Bato attacked the Stoic philosopher Cleanthes of Assos (d. 232) in one of his plays, and Arcesilaus of Pitane, who was head of the Academy from *c.*268–242/1, barred him from the school until Cleanthes himself interceded. Bato is thus to be dated to the middle of the third century. Eight fragments of his comedies survive, along with four titles: *The Aetolian*, *The Murderer*, *Benefactors*, and *The Partner in Deception*.

Callias Comicus: Victorious at least once at the City Dionysia, in 446 (*IG* II² 2318. 76–8), and most likely a second time later (*IG* II² 2325. 53, recording two victories; restored just after Crates and just before Teleclides); he competed repeatedly between 440 and 431 (*IG Urb. Rom.* 216. 1–6, a fragment of his complete competitive record). According to the *Suda* (test. 1), his father Lysimachus was a ropemaker. Forty fragments, most very scanty and none longer than two lines, of his comedies survive, along with eight titles: *The Egyptian*, *Atalantas*, *Frogs*, *Iron Mortars* or *Iron Entrails* (restored) (probably Lenaia, between 436 and 432; fourth), *Cyclopes* (434, a year he staged a play at the other festival as well, taking fifth; third), *Men in Shackles*, *Satyrs* (probably Lenaia 437; fourth), and *Men of Leisure*. Olimpia Imperio offers a detailed study of Callias' career and the fragments of his comedies in *Tessere*, 195–256.

Clearchus Comicus: Victorious at least once at the Lenaia, probably in the early to mid-330s (*IG* II² 2325. 154; just after Dionysius). Five fragments of his comedies survive, along with three titles: *The Citharode*, *Corinthians*, and *Pandrosus*.

Crates: Victorious three times at the City Dionysia, first probably in the late 450s or very early 440s (*IG* II² 2325. 52; just before Callias and Teleclides); a scholium on Ar. *Eq.* 537 (test. 3. 2) reports that he was originally one of Cratinus' actors. Aristophanes at *Eq.* 537–40 (424 BC) refers to him as an important representative of the previous generation, and according to Aristotle in the *Poetics* (test. 5), the influence of the Sicilian comic poets made him the first Athenian comic poet to abandon the 'iambic' style and produce plays with a connected storyline. The *Suda* (test. 1. 1) reports that his brother was an epic poet named Epilycus (otherwise unknown). Sixty fragments (including four *dubia*) of Crates' comedies survive, along with ten titles: *Neighbours*, *Heroes*, *Wild Beasts*, *Lamia*, *Metics*, *Games*, *Men in Shackles*, *Orators*, *Samians*, and *Daring Deeds*. Whether he is to be identified with Crates II, another comic poet to whom the *Suda* (test. 1) assigns three titles,

The Treasure, Birds, and *The Man Who Loved Money,* the first and last of which seem more appropriate for 'Middle Comedy', is unclear.

Cratinus: Victorious six times at the City Dionysia, first probably in the mid- to late 450s (*IG* II² 2325. 50), and three times at the Lenaia, first probably in the early 430s (*IG* II² 2325. 121; just before Pherecrates and Hermippus). According to the *Suda* (test. 1. 2–3), he wrote twenty-one comedies. He was still competing in 423, when his *Wineflask* took the prize at the City Dionysia (see **B1–B12** n.); he died shortly thereafter, at a very advanced age (test. 3). Cratinus was regarded as one of the three great masters of Athenian 'Old Comedy' (the others being Aristophanes and Eupolis), although his poetry is several times described as relatively graceless, harsh, and crudely abusive (test. 17; 19); his plays continued to be read and studied in the Hellenistic and Roman periods. That he was related to the fourth-century comic poet Cratinus Junior is a reasonable hypothesis but cannot be proven. Of his comedies 514 fragments (including ten *dubia*) survive, along with twenty-nine titles: *Archilochuses, Cowherds, Bousiris, Women from Delos, Dramatic Productions, Dionysalexandros, Dionysuses, Runaway Women, Men on Fire* (probably an alternative title for *Idaeans*) *Eumenides, Euneidans, Women from Thrace, Idaeans, Cleoboulinas, Spartans, Soft Men, Nemesis, Laws, Odysseuses, Men Who See Everything, Gods of Wealth, The Meeting at Pylae, The Wineflask* (City Dionysia 423; first), *Satyrs* (Lenaia 424; second), *Men from Seriphus, Trophonius, The Storm-Tossed* (Lenaia 425; second), *Cheirons,* and *Seasons.*

Crobylus: Assumed to be a 'Middle Comic' poet, although there is no specific ancient evidence to this effect. Eleven fragments of his comedies survive, along with three titles: *The Man Who Tried to Hang Himself, The Woman Who Was Trying to Leave Her Husband* or *The Woman Who Left Her Husband,* and *Falsely Supposititious.*

Damoxenus: Victorious once at the City Dionysia, probably in the mid-270s (*IG* II² 2325. 75; just after Philemo and just before Phoenicides). Three fragments of his comedies survive, along with two titles: *The Man Who Felt Sorry for Himself* and *Foster-Brothers.*

Dionysius Comicus: Victorious at least once at the Lenaia, probably in the early 330s (*IG* II² 2325. 153; just before Clearchus). According to Athenaeus (test. 1), he was from the city of Sinope on the southern coast of the Black Sea. Ten fragments of his comedies survive, along with four titles: *The Man Who Was Hit by a Javelin, The Law-Giver, Men Who Shared a Name,* and *The Woman Who Was Saving Someone* or *The Female Saviour.*

Diphilus: Victorious three times at the Lenaia, first probably in the late 310s (*IG* II² 2325. 163; just before Philippides). Like Dionysius Comicus a generation or so earlier, he came from the city of Sinope on the southern coast of the Black Sea (test. 1. 3; 2. 2–3; 3. 3–4). An anonymous essay on comedy (test. 1. 4) reports that he wrote 100 plays. Of his comedies 137 fragments (including two *dubia* and two *spuria*) survive, along with 59 titles: *Ignorance, Brothers, The Taker of Cities* (revised as *The Eunuch or The Soldier*), *The Female Oiler, Amastris, Anagyris* or *The Man Who Had No Money, The Men Who Were Trying to Get Home Safe* or *The Man Who Was Trying to Get Home Safe, The Greedy Man, The Chariot-Acrobat, The Woman Who Was Trying to Leave Her Husband* or *The Woman Who Left Her Husband, The Bath-House, The Boeotian, The Marriage, Danaids, The Woman Who Was Quite Mistaken, Summoners, Hecate, Olive-Grove Guards, Men Who Were Being Treated with Hellebore, The Merchant, Men Who Sacrifice to the Dead* or *Sacrifices to the Dead, The Man Who Made a Legal Claim, The Heiress, The Female Guardian, The Painter, Cheats* or *Worshippers* (conjectural), *Heracles, The Hero, The Treasure, Theseus, The Citharode, Men Drawing Lots, The Girl from Leucas, Lemnian Women, The Madman, Misanthropes* or *The Men Who Loved People* (conjectural), *The Little Monument, Pederasts, The Concubine, The Man Who Was Paralysed, The Parasite, The Daughters of Pelias, The Beggar's-Pouch, The Brick-Carrier, The Busybody, Pyrrha, Sappho, The Sicilian, Men Who Were Dying Together, Foster-Brothers, Synoris, The Man Who Was Being Slaughtered, The Raft, Telesias, The Grandmother, Tithraustes, The Man Who Loved His Brother* or *Men Who Loved Their Brothers, The Well,* and *The Goldsmith.*

Ephippus: Victorious at least once at the Lenaia, probably in the late 360s or early 350s (*IG* II² 2325. 145; just after Eubulus). Twenty-eight fragments of his comedies survive, along with twelve titles: *Artemis, Bousiris, Geryones, Merchandise, Ephebes, Circe, Cydon, The Shipwreck Victim, Men Who Looked Like One Another* or *Spitbearers, The Peltast, Sappho,* and *Philyra.*

Epicharmus: A Sicilian (Doric) poet active in Syracuse in the 480s and 470s and perhaps earlier; discussed at length in the Introduction, pp. 6–11. The titles suggest that his plays were mythological or 'ethical' in character, and had little or no explicit political content. No Epicharmean lyric has been preserved, and there is no solid evidence for a chorus. According to Aristotle in the *Poetics* (test. 5), the Sicilian poets exercised an important influence on early Athenian comedy and in particular on Crates (first victorious in the late 450s or very early 440s). By the fourth century, Epicharmus had come to be identified as the author of a collection of didactic treatises written in trochaic tetrameter catalectic and known today as the *Pseudepicharmeia*; see **A18–A19** with nn. Of Epicharmus' comedies 239 authentic fragments survive, along with at least forty-seven titles: *The Rustic, Alcyoneus, Amycus, Antanor, Robberies, Atalantas, Bacchants, Bousiris, Earth and Sea, The Old Woman,*

Dexamenus, Dictyes, Dionysuses, another Dionysus play, *Hope or Wealth, The Festival, The Victor* I and II, *The Wedding Of Hebe, Heracles in Search of the Belt, Heracles at Pholus' House,* perhaps another Heracles play, *Sacred Envoys, Cyclops, Revellers or Hephaestus, Male and Female Logos, The Megarian Woman, Medea, The Months, Muses, Islands, Odysseus the Deserter, Odysseus Shipwrecked,* perhaps another Odysseus play, *The Sausage, Periallus, Persians, The Monkey, Citizens, Pyrrha and Promatheus* or *Deucalion* or *Leucarion, Sirens, Sciron, The Sphinx, The Thirties, Trojans, The Man Who Liked Lying Down, Philoctetes, Dancers,* and *Cookpots.*

Epicrates: Described by Athenaeus (test. 2) as a 'Middle Comic' poet. Eleven fragments (including one *dubium*) of his comedies survive, along with six titles: *Amazons, Antilais, Difficult to Sell, The Merchant, The Crossroads or The Frills-Seller,* and *The Chorus.*

Eubulus: Victorious six times at the Lenaia, first probably in the late 370s or 360s (*IG* II² 2325. 144; just before Ephippus). According to the *Suda* (test. 1), which dates him to the 101st Olympiad (i.e. 376/2) and identifies him as 'on the border between the Middle and the Old Comedy', he produced 104 comedies. An obscure notice in a *scholium* on Plato (test. 4) appears to suggest that some of his plays were staged by Aristophanes' son Philippus. Of his comedies 150 fragments (including three *dubia*) of his comedies survive, along with fifty-eight titles: *Ancylion, Anchises, Amaltheia, Men Who Were Trying to Get Home Safe, Antiope, The Impotents, Auge, Bellerophon, Ganymede, Glaucus, Daedalus, Danae, Deucalion, Dionysius, Dolon, Peace, Europa, Echo, Ixion, Ion, Basket-Bearers, Campylion, The Man Who Was Glued to the Spot, Cercopes, Clepsydra, The Lark, Dice-Players, Spartans or Leda, Medea, The Mill-Girl, Mysians, Nannion, Nausicaa, Neottis, Xuthus, Odysseus or Men Who See Everything, Oedipus, Oenimaus or Pelops, Olbia, Orthannes, Pamphilus, The All-Night Festival, Parmeniscus, The Pentathlete, Plangon, The Pimp, Procris, Prosousia or Cycnus, Semele or Dionysus, The Shoemaker, Female Garland-Vendors, Sphinx-Carion, Titans, Wet-Nurses* or *The Wet-Nurse, Phoenix, The Graces, Chrysilla,* and *The Harp-Girl.* Richard L. Hunter offers a careful study of Eupolis' career and the fragments of his plays in *Eubulus: The Fragments* (Cambridge, 1983).

Euphanes: Victorious at least once at the Lenaia, in the mid- to late 350s (*IG* II² 2325. 149; just before Alexis). Two fragments of his comedies survive, along with two titles: *Muses* and *The Pan of Coals.*

Eupolis: Victorious four times at the City Dionysia (cf. test. 1. 2–3; *IG* II² 2325. 59; just after Pherecrates, Hermippus, and Aristophanes), first some-time between 425 (the year after Aristophanes' initial victory at the festival) and 421, when his *Flatterers* took the prize (test. 13. c), and three times at the

Lenaia, first in 426 (*IG* II² 2325. 126). Eupolis began competing in 429 (test. 2a. 6) and was thus an almost exact contemporary of Aristophanes, although he died earlier, in 411 or thereabout (cf. *IG* I³ 1190. 52 (a casualty-list)). He was regarded as one of the three great masters of Athenian 'Old Comedy' (along with Cratinus and Aristophanes), and his writing is said (test. 24) to have been particularly gracious and charming; his plays continued to be read and commented on into the Roman period. Of Eupolis' comedies 494 fragments (including five *dubia*) survive, along with seventeen titles: *Nanny-Goats*, *Draft-Dodgers (or Men-Women)*, *Autolycus* I (420) and II, *Dyers*, *Demes*, *Helots*, *Flatterers* (City Dionysia 421; first), *Spartans*, *Marikas* (Lenaia 421), *New Moons* (Lenaia 425; third), *Cities*, *Men from the Deme Prospalta*, *Taxiarchs*, *Vigilantes*, *Friends*, and *The Golden Race*. Ian C. Storey provides a full-length treatment of Eupolis' career and plays (including a translation of all the fragments) in *Eupolis: Poet of Old Comedy* (Oxford, 2003).

Hegesippus Comicus: Fragment 2 refers to Epicurus (341–270), placing Hegesippus most likely in the third century. Three fragments (including one *dubium*) of his comedies survive, along with two titles: *Brothers* and *The Men Who Were Fond of Their Comrades*.

Heniochus: Described by the *Suda* (test. 1. 1) as a 'Middle Comic' poet. Five fragments of his comedies survive, along with eight titles: *Gorgons*, *Twice Deceived*, *The Heiress*, *Thorycion*, *Polyeuctus*, *The Busybody*, *Trochilus*, and *The Man Who Was Fond of His Comrades*.

Hermippus: Victorious at least once at the City Dionysia, in 435 (*IG* II² 2318, a new fragment published by Capps, *Hesperia*, 12 (1943), 1–3; *IG* II² 2325. 57; just after Pherecrates and just before Aristophanes), and four times at the Lenaia, first probably in the mid- to late 430s (*IG* II² 2325. 123; just after Cratinus and Pherecrates). His brother Myrtilus was also a comic poet (victorious once at the Lenaia, in 427 (*IG* II² 2325. 125)). Of Hermippus' comedies ninety-four fragments survive, along with ten titles: *Agamemnon*, *The Birth of Athena*, *Female Bread-Sellers*, *Demesmen*, *Europa*, *Gods*, *Cercopes*, *Fates*, *Soldiers* or *Female Soldiers*, and *Porters*.

Lysippus: Victorious with *Catachenai* at an unidentified festival in 409 (*IG Urb. Rom.* 216. 7–9, which also notes that only this play and *Bacchants* were preserved, sc. in the Library at Alexandria). Capps proposed restoring Lysippus' name above line 56 of *IG* II² 2325 (a victor at the City Dionysia in the 430s, immediately before Pherecrates); he might be better placed in line 70 (around 400; just after Theopompus and Cephisodorus). Ten fragments of his comedies survive, along with three titles: in addition to those above, *The Thyrsus-Keeper*.

Menander: Victorious at least once and no more than four times at the Lenaia (*IG* II² 2325. 160; just before Philemon), first supposedly with his earliest play, *Anger*, in the late 320s (test. 49), although this date may represent ancient scholarly confusion of his first performance and his first victory. *The Difficult Man*, at any rate, took the prize at the Lenaia in 316 (test. 50), while the Marmor Parium (*FGrHist* 239 B 14 = test. 48) reports that Menander was first victorious in 315, presumably referring to the City Dionysia, where he took the prize at least four and perhaps as many as seven times (test. 46, giving an overall lifetime total of eight victories). He is said to have been a student of Theophrastus (test. 8) and to have received professional training from Alexis (test. 3. 5–6), and to have written 108 plays (test. 1. 4; 3. 7–8; 46; 63). He died in the late 290s (test. 2; 21), and thus had a relatively short career. But his plays continued to be staged, read, and studied until late Roman times. Substantial portions of a number of Menander's comedies (indicated with an asterisk below, and accessible in Arnott's three-volume Loeb edition) have been preserved on fragmentary papyri, along with over 900 other fragments and 100 titles: *Brothers* I and II, *Men of Halae*, *The Fisherman* or *The Fishermen*, *The Girl Who Was Dedicated to a God*, *The Girl from Andros*, *The Hermaphrodite* or *The Cretan*, *Cousins*, *The Suspicious Man*, *The Arrhephoros or The Pipe-Girl* (or *The Pipe-Girls*), *The Shield**, *The Man Who Felt Sorry for Himself*, *The Masochist*, *The Sex-Maniac*, *Achaeans or Peloponnesians*, *The Girl from Boeotia*, *The Farmer**, *Glycera*, *The Ring*, *Dardanus*, *The Superstitious Man*, *The Bridesmaid*, *Twin Girls*, *Twice a Swindler**, *The Difficult Man* or *The Misanthrope**, *The Dagger**, *The Girl Who Was on Fire*, *The Man Who Was Being Summoned*, *The Heiress* I and II, *Men at Arbitration**, *The Eunuch*, *The Ephesian*, *The Charioteer*, *The Hero**, *Thais*, *The Girl Who Was Possessed by a God**, *The Girl from Thessaly*, *The Treasure*, *Thrasyleon*, *The Doorman*, *The Priestess*, *Men from Imbros*, *The Horse-Groom*, *The Sacred-Basket-Bearer*, *The Female Dirge-Singer*, *The Carthaginian**, *The Liar*, *The Headdress*, *The Cithara-Player**, *The Girl from Cnidus*, *The Flatterer**, *The Cretan*, *Steersmen*, *Women Being Treated with Hemlock**, *The Girl from Leucas**, *Locrians*, *Drunkenness*, *The Girl from Messene*, *The Girl from Melos*, *The Mendicant Priest of Rhea*, *The Misogynist*, *The Man Who Was Hated* or *Thrasonides**, *The Ship-Owner*, *Nemesis*, *The Lawmaker*, *The Recruiter of Mercenaries*, *The Girl from Olynthus*, *Compatriots*, *Anger*, *The Child*, *The Concubine*, *The Deposit*, *The Girl Whose Hair Was Cut Short**, *The Girl from Perinthus**, *The Necklace*, *The Man Who Was Married Previously*, *The Man Who Summoned Someone in Advance*, *The Men Who Were Being Sold*, *The Girl Who Was Beaten with a Stick*, *The Girl from Samos**, *The Sicyonian* or *Sicyonians**, *Soldiers*, *Women Sharing Lunch**, *The Girl Who Cooperated in Love*, *Fellow-Ephebes*, *The Wet-Nurse*, *Trophonius*, *The Pitcher*, *Hymnis*, *The Supposititious Child* or *The Rustic*, *Phanion*, *The*

Phantom*, *Men Who Loved Their Brothers*, *The Chalceia Festival*, *Chalcis*, *The Widow*, *The Good Woman*, *The Fake Heracles*, and *The Coward*. A. W. Gomme and F. H. Sandbach, *Menander: A Commentary* (Oxford, 1973), concentrate on the substantially preserved plays, but include a brief final section on some of the larger book-fragments (pp. 690–721).

Metagenes: Victorious twice at the Lenaia, first probably around 410 (*IG* II² 2325. 128; just after Poliochus and just before Theopompus). Twenty fragments of his comedies survive, along with four titles: *Breezes or the Dunce*, *Thuriopersians* (never staged), *Homer or Athletes* or *Sophists*, and *The Man Who Loved Sacrifices*. Matteo Pelegrino offers a detailed study of Metagenes' career and the fragments of his comedies in *Tessere*, 291–339.

Nicophon: Victorious at least once at the City Dionysia, probably in the mid- to late 400s (*IG* II² 2325. 67; just before Theopompus), and at least once at the Lenaia, around the same time (*IG* II² 2325. 131; just after Theopompus and Polyzelus). Thirty mostly insubstantial fragments of his comedies survive, along with six titles: *Adonis* (388, at the same festival as Aristophanes' extant *Wealth*), *The Birth of Aphrodite*, *Men Who Live from Hand to Mouth*, *The Man Who Comes up from Hades*, *Pandora*, and *Sirens* (never staged).

Nicostratus Comicus: One of Aristophanes' sons (Ar. test. 1. 56; 3. 14–15), along with Philippus and Araros, both of whom were also comic poets. Athenaeus (13.587d) refers to Nicostratus as belonging to 'Middle Comedy'. Forty fragments of his comedies (including one *dubium*) survive, along with twenty-three titles: *Habra*, *The Female Rival in Love*, *Antyllus*, *The Man Who Was Driven Away*, *Kings*, *The Slanderer*, *Hecate*, *Hesiod*, *The Hierophant*, *The Couch*, *Spartans*, *The Cook*, *The Winemaker*, *The Fowler*, *Pandrosus*, *The Woman Who Swam Alongside*, *Countrymen*, *Wealth*, *The Orator*, *Syrus*, *The Loan-Shark*, *Falsely Tattooed*, and *The Bustard* (title corrupt and problematic).

Pherecrates: Victorious at least once at the City Dionysia, first probably in the mid-440s (*IG* II² 2325. 56; the fourth entry after Teleclides and three poets whose names have been lost, and just before Hermippus), and twice at the Lenaia, first probably in the mid- to late 430s (*IG* II² 2325. 122; just after Cratinus and just before Hermippus). According to an anonymous essay on tragedy, he wrote eighteen plays, suggesting that one or more of the surviving titles must be eliminated somehow (i.e. by assigning the play to another author who wrote a comedy by the same name, and assuming an ancient scholarly error, or by identifying e.g. *The Human Heracles* and *The Fake Heracles* as a single play with multiple titles). Of his comedies 288 fragments (including six *dubia*) survive, along with eighteen titles: *Good Men*, *Savages*, *The Human Heracles*, *Deserters*, *Hags*, *The Slave Teacher*, *The Forgetful Man or The Sea*, *The Kitchen or The All-Night Festival*, *Corianno*, *Good-for-Nothings*,

Jewelry, Miners, Ant-Men, Persians, Petale, Tyranny, Cheiron, and *The Fake Heracles.*

Philemo: Victorious at least once at the City Dionysia, in 327 (Marm. Par. *FGrH* 239 B 7), and three times at the Lenaia, first probably around the mid-310s (*IG* II² 2325. 161; just after Menander). According to the *Suda* (test. 1. 1) and an anonymous essay on comedy (test. 2. 5), he was originally from Syracuse; Strabo (test. 3), on the other hand, claims that he came from Soli in Cilicia. The anonymous essay (test. 2. 6–7), supported by Diodorus Siculus (test. 4; cf. test. 1. 3), reports that ninety-seven of his plays were preserved. He is repeatedly said to have lived to an advanced age (e.g. test. 1. 4; 4; 5. 2–6), and his career must have continued well into the third century. His son Philemo Junior was also a comic poet and was victorious six times at the City Dionysia (*IG* II² 2325. 74). Of Philemo's comedies 198 fragments (including four *dubia*) survive, along with sixty-one titles: *The Rustic, The Mendicant Priest, Brothers, The Aetolian, Men Who Were Revealing Themselves, The Woman Who Tried to Recover Her Youth, The Murderer, The Man Who Tried to Starve to Death, Apollo?, The Man Who Was Kidnapped* or *The Girl Who Was Kidnapped, The Pipe-Player, The Babylonian, The Marriage, The Ring, The Dagger, The Merchant, The Man Who Was Moving Out, The Man Who Tried to Make a Legal Claim, Euripus, Piggy-Back Riders, The Ephebe, Heroes, Thebans, The Treasure, The Doorman, The Doctor, The Liar, Partners, The Girl from Corinth, The Stonecarver, The Man Who Was in Pursuit or Brothlet, The Metic, The Seducer, Myrmidons, The Initiate, Neaira, Portion-Holders, The Bastard, Night, The Pancratiast, The Little Child, Children, Palamedes?, The Public Festival, The Man Who Tried to Sneak In, Drunk and Disorderly, The Man Who Waxed His Legs, Half a Chiton, The Beggar-Woman or The Girl from Rhodes, Pyrrhus, The Fire-Bearer, The Carnelian, The Sicilian, The Soldier, Men Who Were Dying Together, The Fellow-Ephebe, The Supposititious Child, The Phantom, Philosophers, Standing Guard,* and *The Widow.*

Philippides: Victorious at least once at the City Dionysia, in 311 with *The Initiate* (*IG* II² 2323a. 41), and at least twice at the Lenaia, first probably in the late 310s or 300s (*IG* II² 2325. 164; just after Diphilus); the *Suda* (test. 1) calls him a 'New Comic' poet and reports that he wrote forty-five comedies. According to Plutarch (test. 2), Philippides was a friend of King Lysimachus (d. 281); a long honorary inscription dating to 283/2 (*IG* II² 657 = test. 3) describes his benefactions to the Athenian people and attests to his wealth and political influence. Forty-one fragments of his comedies survive, along with sixteen titles: *Women Celebrating the Adonia, Amphiaraus, The Woman Who Tried to Recover Her Youth, Vanished Money, The Pipes, The Woman Who Was Tortured, The Cupmaker* (conjectural), *Lakiadai, The Go-Between, The*

Initiate (City Dionysia 311; first), *The Woman Who Tried to Sail Off with Others*, *Men Who Loved Their Brothers*, *The Man Who Loved Athens*, *The Man Who Loved Money*, *The Man Who Loved Office*, and *The Man Who Loved Euripides*.

Philyllius: Victorious at least once at the City Dionysia, probably in the late 410s (*IG* II² 2325. 64; just after Plato Comicus), and once at the Lenaia, early in the fourth century (*IG* II² 2325. 136; just after Theopompus and Polyzelus). Thirty-three mostly insubstantial fragments of his comedies survive, along with ten titles: *Aegeus*, *Anteia*, *Atalanta*, *Auge*, *The Twelfth Day*, *Helen*, *Heracles*, *Washing-Women or Nausicaa*, *Cities*, and *The Well-Digger*.

Phoenicides: Victorious twice at the City Dionysia, first probably in the mid- to late 270s (*IG* II² 2325. 76; just after Damoxenus); he also took fifth at the Lenaia in 285 with *Men Who Tried to Get Home Safe* (*IG* II² 2319. 56), and fourth in 284 with *The Poet* (*IG* II² 2319. 65). Hesychius (test. 2) claims that he was from Megara. Five fragments of his comedies survive, along with five titles: *Men Who Tried to Get Home Safe*, *Pipe-Girls*, *The Girl Who Was Hated*, *The Poet*, and the *Phylarch*.

Phrynichus Comicus: Victorious at least once at the City Dionysia (*IG* II² 2325. 61), probably in the early 410s and certainly before 414, when Amipsias (whose name comes next on the list) took the prize with *Revellers*, and twice at the Lenaia, first in 428 (*IG* II² 2325. 124; just after Hermippus and just before Myrtilus and Eupolis). Ninety-three fragments (including seven *dubia*) of his comedies survive, along with ten titles: *Epialtes* or *Ephialtes*, *Connus*, *Cronus*, *Revellers*, *The Recluse* (City Dionysia 414; 3rd), *Muses* (Lenaia 405; second), *Initiates*, *Female Grass-Cutters*, *Satyrs*, and *Tragic Actors or Freedmen*.

Plato Comicus: Victorious at least once at the City Dionysia, probably in the late 410s (*IG* II² 2325. 63; just after Amipsias and just before Philyllius). His career is said by one source (test. 6) to have begun in the 88th Olympiad (427–424; cf. **E19**; **E24**), and if he was victorious at the Lenaia, his initial victory probably came earlier in his career and his name has been lost in the final portion of Section III col. I of *IG* II² 2325. Of Plato's comedies fragments (including nine *dubia* and two *spuria*) survive, along with thirty-one titles: *Adonis*, *Women Coming from a Sacrifice*, *Griffins*, *Daedalus*, *Greece or Islands*, *Festivals*, *Europa*, *Zeus Abused*, *Io*, *Cleophon* (Lenaia 405; third), *Laius*, *Spartans or Poets*, *Morons*, *Menelaus*, *Metics*, *Ants*, *Victories*, *The Long Night*, *Wool-Carders or Cercopes*, *The Little Child*, *Peisander*, *In Terrible Pain*, *The Poet*, *Ambassadors*, *Staff-Bearers*, *Equipment*, *Sophists*, *The Alliance*, *The Rabble*, *Hyperbolus*, and *Phaon*.

Poliochus: Victorious once at the Lenaia, probably in the late 410s (*IG* II² 2325. 127; just before Metagenes and Theopompus). Two fragments of his comedies survive, along with one title, *The Whoremonger*.

Posidippus Comicus: Victorious four times at the City Dionysia, first probably around 290 (*IG* II² 2325. 71). The *Suda* (test. 1) says that he staged a play (presumably his first) three years after Menander's death, i.e. sometime in the early 280s, and Athenaeus (14.652c–d = test. 5) mentions a letter to him from the comic poet, anecdotist, and bon-vivant Lynceus of Samos, whose *floruit* is in the first half of the fourth century. He was from the Macedonian city of Cassandreia (test. 1; 2; 12). According to the *Suda*, he wrote thirty plays. Forty-five fragments of his comedies survive, along with eighteen titles: *The Man Who Tried to Recover His Sight*, *The Girl Who Was Locked Out*, *Arsinoe*, *The Celt*, *Demesmen*, *The King's Man*, *The Hermaphrodite*, *The Girl from Ephesus*, *The Bell*, *Women from Locris*, *Men Who Tried to Change*, *Myrmex*, *Men Who Looked Like One Another*, *The Child*, *The Pimp*, *Foster-Brothers*, *The Man Who Loved His Father*, and *Dancing Women*.

Sophron: A Syracusan (Doric) mime-writer dated by the *Suda* (test. 1. 2) to the mid-480s to mid-460s; discussed in the Introduction, pp. 11–12. Sophron's mimes were in prose (e.g. test. 1. 3; 3. 2), although according to some authorities it had a rhythmic character and he is occasionally treated as a poet (test. 19 with K–A ad loc.). Diogenes Laertius reports that the mimes were brought to Athens by Plato (test. 6), and they were certainly known to Aristotle (test. 2–3). Sophron's work was conventionally divided into 'Female' and 'Male Mimes' (test. 1. 3). One hundred and seventy-one mostly very brief fragments of the mimes survive, along with ten titles: ('Female Mimes') *Seamstresses*, *Women Who Say That They Will Drive out the Goddess*, *Women Viewing the Isthmian Games*, *The Bridesmaid*, *The Mother-in-Law*, ('Male Mimes') *The Messenger*, *The Fisherman and the Farmer*, *The Tuna-Fisher*, *Scaring Children*, and *Promythius* (sic). A detailed discussion and commentary on the fragments, accompanied by a facing translation, is offered by J. H. Hordern, *Sophron's Mimes* (Oxford, 2004).

Strato Comicus: Identified by the *Suda* (test. 1) as a 'Middle Comic' poet. Only one fragment of his comedies survives, from *Phoenicides*.

Strattis: Described by Athenaeus (test. 3) as a little later than Callias Comicus, although his *Anthroporestes* dates to after 408 (fr. 1, alluding to the performance of Euripides' *Orestes*) and his *Atalantos or Atalanta* (or *Atalantas*) is said to have been staged 'much later' than Aristophanes' *Frogs* in 405 (*Atal.* test. ii). Geissler proposed restoring his name at *IG* II² 2325. 138 (a poet victorious once at the Lenaia two years after Philyllius' victory). Ninety-one fragments (including one *dubium*) of Strattis' comedies survive, along with nineteen titles: in addition to those above, *Good Men, Vanished Money, Zopyrus on Fire, Iphigeron* (perhaps to be attributed instead to Apollophanes), *Callippides, Cinesias, Lemnomeda, Macedonians or Pausanias, Medea, Myrmidons, Men from the Deme Potamos, Pytisus(?), Troilus, Philoctetes, Phoenician Women, Chrysippus,* and *Men Who Keep Cool.*

Susarion: Identified by various ancient sources (e.g. test. 1. 2; 2. 2–3; 3; 4. 2–4; 5. 2) as the 'inventor' of comedy; the Marmor Parium (*FGrHist* 239 A 39 = test. 1) places him between 582/1 and 561/0 BC and associates him with the Attic deme Icarion (cf. test. 2. 3). The one supposed fragment of his poetry is a forgery (**I1** with introductory n.).

Teleclides: Victorious three times at the City Dionysia, first probably in the mid-440s (*IG* II² 2325. 54; after Callias), and five times at the Lenaia, first on the second occasion the contest was held, sometime in the mid- to late 440s (*IG* II² 2325. 119); he must thus have been one of the dominant poets of his generation. Portions of his complete competition record (largely unrevealing) survive in *IG Urb. Rom.* 215. Seventy-three mostly very tiny fragments of his comedies survive, along with five titles (and a few letters from two others): *Amphictyonies, Honest Men, Hesiods, Prytaneis,* and *Tough Men.*

Theognetus: Fragment 2 mentions the entertainer Pantaleon, who according to Athenaeus (14.616a) was referred to posthumously by the Stoic philosopher Chrysippus of Soli (*c.*280–207), placing Theognetus most probably sometime in the third century. Two fragments of his comedies survive, along with three titles: *The Centaur, The Phantom or The Man Who Loved Money,* and *The Man Who Loved His Master.*

Theopompus Comicus: Victorious at least once at the City Dionysia, probably in the late 400s (*IG* II² 2325. 68; just after Nicophon), and twice at the Lenaia, first in the late 410s (*IG* II² 2325. 129; just after Metagenes); the *Suda* (test. 1) calls him an 'Old Comic' poet and a contemporary of Aristophanes, and reports that he staged twenty-one plays. Of his comedies 108 fragments (including 11 *dubia*) survive, along with twenty titles: *Admetus, Althaea, Aphrodite, Batyle, Peace, The Hedonist, Theseus, Callaeschrus, Bar-Maids, The Mede, Nemea, Odysseus* (or *Odysseuses*), *The Children, Pamphile, Pantaleon, Penelope, Sirens, Female Soldiers, Teisamenus,* and *Phineus.*

Timocles: Victorious once at the Lenaia, probably in the mid- to late 320s (*IG* II² 2325. 158); the traditions associated with him have been confused by an ancient belief that there were two poets named Timocles (test. 1), as well as by the existence of a homonymous tragic poet (*TrGF* 86). Forty-two fragments of his comedies survive, along with twenty-seven titles: *Egyptians,*

The Bath-House, The Ring, Delos, Demosatyrs, Women Celebrating the Dionysia, Dionysus, Dracontion, The Letter, The Spiteful Man, Heroes, Icarian Satyrs, Men from Caunus, The Centaur or Dexamenus, Conisalus, Forgetfulness, Men from Marathon, Neaira, Orestautocleides, The Busybody, The Man from Pontus, Porphyra, The Boxer, Sappho, Conspiratorial Things (corrupt), *The Man Who Loved Jury-Duty,* and *The Fake Bandits.*

Xenarchus: Assumed to be a 'Middle Comic' poet, although there is no specific ancient evidence to that effect. Fourteen fragments of his comedies survive, along with eight titles: *Boutalion, Twins, The Pentathlete, Porphyra, Priapus, Scythians, The Soldier,* and *Sleep.*

Translations of the Fragments

A1. Epicharmus fr. 18, from *Bousiris* (VI/V)

If you saw him eating, first of all, you'd die. His throat emits a roar; his jaw rattles; his molars resound; his canine teeth squeak; he snorts loudly; and he wiggles his ears.

A2. Epicharmus fr. 48, from *The Wedding of Hebe* (VI/V)

Poseidon himself has come bringing wonderful [corrupt] sea breams and parrot wrasses in Phoenician merchant-ships. The gods aren't permitted to throw even their shit away!

A3. Epicharmus fr. 40, from *The Wedding of Hebe* (VI/V)

He brings shellfish of every sort: limpets, *aspedoi*, *krabuzoi*, *kikibaloi*, sea-squirts, scallops, barnacles, purple shellfish, tightly closed oysters, which are difficult to pry open but easily gobbled down; mussels, *anaritai*, whelks, and sword-shells, which are sweet eating but sharp to be impaled upon; and the cylindrical razor-shells. Also the black conch, which [corrupt] for children of fishermen; and others that live on land, both conchs and sand-dwellers, which have a bad reputation and are inexpensive, and which all human beings refer to as *androphuktides*, whereas we gods call them white conchs.

A4. Epicharmus fr. 51, from *The Wedding of Hebe* (VI/V)

and a swordfish and a *chromis*, which according to Ananius is the best fish there is in the spring, whereas the *anthias* is best in winter.

A5. Epicharmus fr. 50, from *The Wedding of Hebe* (VI/V)

There are lobsters, *kolubdainai*, and the one that has little feet but large hands, whose name is crayfish.

A6. Epicharmus fr. 97, from *Odysseus the Deserter* (VI/V)

(A.) . . . this wandering statement . . . [obscure] as if encountering . . . (Odysseus) . . . I could have done this very easily, as opposed to what . . . (A.) But I see—why are you whining, wretch?—here are the Achaeans, close at hand! . . . (Odysseus) . . . so that I be utterly miserable. (A.) But you *are* quite a miserable person! . . . (Odysseus) because I wouldn't hurry back like this; being beaten is unpleasant. . . . I'll go there; and I'll sit down and say that these things are easy even for people more clever than me. (A.) You seem to us altogether fitly and reasonably to call down curses, if one is willing to think about it. (Odysseus) . . . if only I were . . . from the place where they ordered me . . . to prefer bad things to good . . . and to accomplish my dangerous mission and get divine glory . . . after going to the city and getting good, clear information, to bring back a report about the situation there to the bright Achaeans and the beloved son of Atreus, and get away unscathed myself.

A7. Epicharmus fr. 99, from *Odysseus the Deserter* (VI/V)

And when I was keeping my neighbours' pig safe for the Eleusinia festival, I lost it by some god's will, not my own. As a result, he said I was engaged in barter with the Achaeans, and swore I was betraying the pig.

A8. Epicharmus fr. 100, from *Odysseus the Deserter* (VI/V)

Peace-and-Quiet is a lovely lady, and lives near Self-Control.

A9. Epicharmus fr. 70, from *Cyclops* (VI/V)

Yes, by Poseidon, it's much more concave than a mortar!

A10. Epicharmus fr. 71, from *Cyclops* (VI/V)

Sausages are a delicious thing, by Zeus, as is the haunch!

A11. Epicharmus fr. 72, from *Cyclops* (VI/V)

Pour (some wine) into the cup and bring it (to me)!

A12. Epicharmus fr. 135, from an unidentified play (VI/V)

The very first thing that happened in the battle that took place against Cronus, they say, was that Pallas perished (at the hands of the goddess born) from the head of Zeus. And in order to be frightening, she immediately threw his skin around herself; which is why everyone then referred to her as 'Pallas'.

A13. Epicharmus fr. 32, from *Hope or Wealth* (VI/V)

Dining with whoever's willing—he only needs to issue an invitation!—as well as with whoever's unwilling—and then there's no need for an invitation. When I'm there, I'm on my best behaviour, and I generate a lot of laughs, and praise the man who's hosting the party. And if someone wants to quarrel with him, I attack the fellow and get similar grief back. Then, after I've eaten and drunk a lot, I leave. No slave accompanies me carrying a lamp; I make my way alone, slipping and sliding in the darkness. If I meet the night-patrol, I credit the gods with having done me a favour, if all they want to do is whip me. When I come home, in terrible shape, I sleep with no bedding. At first I don't notice, so long as the unmixed wine envelops my mind.

A14. Epicharmus fr. 147, from an unidentified play (VI/V)

(A.) What's this? (B.) A tripod, obviously. (A.) Then why does it have four feet? It's not a tripod; I'd say it's a tetrapod! (B.) It's called a tripod; but it's got four feet. (A.) If it ever had two feet, you're thinking of Oedipus' riddle!

A15. Epicharmus fr. 146, from an unidentified play (VI/V)

(A.) † A sacrifice leads to a feast, and a feast leads to drinking. (B.) Sounds good to me, at least! (A.) But drinking leads to wandering the streets drunk; wandering the streets drunk leads to acting like a pig; acting like a pig leads to a lawsuit; <a lawsuit leads to being found guilty;> and being found guilty leads to shackles, stocks, and a fine.

A16. Epicharmus fr. 214, from an unidentified play (VI/V)

The mind sees and the mind hears; everything else is deaf and blind.

A17. Epicharmus fr. 213, from an unidentified play (VI/V)

He was formed, and was dissolved, and went back again to where he came from, earth to earth, but the spirit upward. What part of this is difficult to understand? Nothing.

A18. [Epicharmus] fr. 244, from *Practical Maxims* (V)

In here there are many things of all sorts, which a person could use with a friend or with an enemy; when he's speaking in court or in the Assembly; with a low-born man, a well-born man, a foreigner, someone quarrelsome, a drunk, or a craftsman. And if someone has some other trouble, pointed responses are in here for these as well. There are also wise sayings in here; and if someone were to put his confidence in them, he would be a cleverer and generally better man. There is no need at all to speak at length; (what is needed) is to apply just one of these lines, whichever is useful, to the matter. For I used to be accused of being pointlessly clever, as well as long-winded and unable to express my maxims concisely. Because these things were said about me, I am composing this device, so that someone can say: 'Epicharmus was a wise man. He said many clever things of all sorts, expressing them in a single line, providing proof that he himself was concise . . .' . . . everyone who learns these things will appear wise . . . will never any word . . . any of these things will cause grief to the man who . . . who does to/by them . . . very learned . . . I will also say . . . to those . . . bad things to these . . . For different people enjoy different things, not the same things . . . all these things it is necessary so that . . . and then to say (them) at the right time . . . concise . . .

A19. [Epicharmus] fr. 269, from *Practical Maxims*

Marrying is like throwing a triple six or three ones by chance. For if you get a woman with orderly manners who's not inclined to make you miserable in other ways, you'll have good luck in your marriage. But if you get one who likes to leave the house and is a chatterer and extravagant, it's not a wife you'll have, but a life-long, well-dressed misfortune.

A20. Sophron fr. 4. a, from *Women Who Say That They Will Drive out the Goddess* (V)

(A.) Set the table down right there. Take a lump of salt in your hand and place a laurel garland on your head. Go over to the hearth, now, and sit down. You—give me the hatchet! Bring the puppy from over there. And where's the bitumen? (B.) Here it is. (A.) Hold the torch and the frankincense. Alright now—all the doors need to be open wide, please! You—look over here, and put out the torch at once! Keep quiet, now, while I spar with her. Lady, you've been presented with a dinner and faultless guest-gifts . . . and [corrupt] . . .

A21. Sophron fr. 3, from *Women Who Say That They Will Drive out the Goddess* (V)

A threefold sacrifice of healing drugs has been buried beneath (it) in a cup.

A22. Eupolis fr. 261, from *Men from the Deme Prospalta* (V)

(A.) The whatchamacallit, do you hear? (B.) Heracles! This joke of yours is vulgar, Megarian, and extremely forced † bright light you see the children †

B1. Cratinus fr. 193, from *The Wineflask* (423 BC)

But I want to return to the story. Previously, when he was paying attention to another woman, he behaved badly † to another. † But now that he's old, he seems to me . . . † never of him previously †

B2. Cratinus fr. 194, from *The Wineflask* (423 BC)

Previously I was his wife, but now no longer.

B3. Cratinus fr. *195, from *The Wineflask* (423 BC)

But now, if he spies a barely adolescent little Mendaean wine, he follows it and dogs its tracks and says: 'Damn! how soft and white it is! Is it strong enough for three?'

B4. Cratinus fr. 199, from *The Wineflask* (423 BC)

How, how could someone put a stop to his drinking, his excessive drinking? I know—I'll crush his pitchers, and smash his wine-buckets and all the other vessels he uses for drinking to bits; he won't even own a vinegar-dish that holds wine any longer!

B5. Cratinus fr. 197, from *The Wineflask* (423 BC)

You are aware, perhaps, of the preparation . . .

B6. Cratinus fr. 208, from *The Wineflask* (423 BC)

You keep babbling. Add him to the list! Cleisthenes will be amusing in a dramatic interlude shooting dice † at the height of his beauty †.

B7. Cratinus fr. 209, from *The Wineflask* (423 BC)

Snuff Hyperbolus out and list him in the lamp-market!

B8. Cratinus fr. 211, from *The Wineflask* (423 BC)

Impoverished citizens, understand my (words)!

B9. Cratinus fr. 210, from *The Wineflask* (423 BC)

No matter what they do, they can't get ship-sheds or reed fencing.

B10. Cratinus fr. 200, from *The Wineflask* (423 BC)

But I do indeed recognize the depravity of my folly.

B11. Cratinus fr. *203, from *The Wineflask* (423 BC)

If you drink water, you couldn't produce anything clever.

B12. Cratinus fr. 198, from *The Wineflask* (423 BC)

Lord Apollo, what a flow of words! The streams are gurgling; his mouth has a dozen springs and there's an Ilisus in his throat. What more could I say? Unless someone plugs his mouth, he's going to flood everything here with his poetry.

B13. Cratinus, *Dionysalexandros* test. i

. . . judgement, Hermes goes away, and they make some remarks to the spectators about the poets; and after Dionysus appears, they make fun of him and jeer him. After Hera offers him unshakable royal power, Athena offers him courage in war, and Aphrodite offers that he be the best-looking and most sexually attractive man there is, he judges her the winner. After this, he sails to Sparta and takes Helen away, and returns to Ida; shortly thereafter he hears that the Achaeans are laying the country waste and looking for Alexandros. He hides Helen as quickly as he can in a basket, changes his own appearance to make himself look like a ram, and waits for what will happen next. After Alexandros appears and catches them, he orders (his men) to take them both to the ships to turn them over to the Achaeans. But when Helen is reluctant, he pities her and detains her to be his wife; but he sends Dionysus off to be surrendered. The satyrs follow along, encouraging (him) and saying that they will not abandon him. Pericles is made fun of quite persuasively in the play via innuendo for having brought the war on the Athenians.

B14. Cratinus fr. 42, from *Dionysalexandros* (430 BC?)

You want doorposts and painted porticoes.

B15. Cratinus fr. 43, from *Dionysalexandros* (430 BC?)

No, (I want) to walk through greenish cow-manure and sheep-shit.

B16. Cratinus fr. 327, perhaps from *Dionysalexandros* (430 BC?)

She offers you a tongue full of ever-flowing lovely words to wield in the Assembly; you'll win every debate with it.

B17. Cratinus fr. 41, from *Dionysalexandros* (430 BC?)

The minute you heard her words you began to gnash your front teeth.

B18. Cratinus fr. 40, from *Dionysalexandros* (430 BC?)

(A.) What sort of clothing was he wearing? Tell me this! (B.) He had a thyrsus, a multi-coloured *himation*, and a drinking-cup.

B19. Cratinus fr. 45, from *Dionysalexandros* (430 BC?)

The fool goes around saying 'Baa! baa!' like a sheep.

B20. Cratinus fr. 47, from *Dionysalexandros* (430 BC?)

For you're not, in fact, the first hungry person to go to dinner uninvited.

B21. Phrynichus Comicus fr. 19, from *The Recluse* (414 BC)

My name is Recluse. I live a life like Timon's, with no wife or slave, easily angered and unapproachable, never laughing or speaking to anyone, keeping my own counsel.

B22. Aristophanes fr. 372, from *Women from Lemnos* (late 410s BC or after)

(This is) Lemnos, which produces fine, soft fava beans.

B23. Aristophanes fr. 373, from *Women from Lemnos* (late 410s BC or after)

The king here was Hypsipyle's father Thoas, the slowest of human beings at running.

B24. Philyllius fr. 7, from *Heracles* (V/IV)

So, do you want me to tell you who I am? I'm the so-called Meal-Day of the Foretasters.

B25. Aristophanes fr. 403, from *Islands* (V/IV)

(A.) What do you mean? Where are they? (B.) Here they are—coming down the exact entrance-way you're looking towards.

B26. Aristophanes fr. 410, from *Islands* (V/IV)

How stooped towards the ground and gloomy-looking she is, as she goes along!

B27. Eupolis fr. 245, from *Cities* (late 420s BC?)

(A.) This is Tenos. (B.) You've got a lot of scorpions—and informers too!

B28. Eupolis fr. 246, from *Cities* (late 420s BC?)

This is Chios, a lovely city; she sends you warships and troops whenever they're needed, and in other respects she's nice and obedient, like a horse that needs no goad.

B29. Eupolis fr. 247, from *Cities* (late 420s BC?)

(A.) Where's the last one? (B.) This is Cyzicus, who's full of large coins. (B.) Well, when I myself was doing guard-duty once in this city, I screwed a woman for a nickel, as well as a boy and an old man. You could sweep its cunt clean all day long.

B30. Eupolis fr. 13, from *Nanny-Goats* (420s BC?)

We feed on brush of every sort, consuming the soft shoots of fir, prickly-oak, and strawberry tree, and also foliage in addition to the shoots; and tree-medick, fragrant sage, and leafy yew; wild olive, lentisk, manna-ash, white poplar, holm oak, oak, ivy, heather, *promalon*, buckthorn, Jerusalem sage, asphodel, rock-rose, Valonia oak, thyme, savory.

B31. Aristophanes fr. *322, probably from *Heroes* (410s BC?)

Wherefore, gentlemen, be on guard and show respect to the heroes, since we are the stewards of bad things and good, and we keep a close watch on evildoers such as thieves and muggers, and give them diseases: to have an enlarged spleen or a cough, or to suffer from dropsy, or to have a runny nose, mange, or gout, or to go crazy, or to have eruptions on one's skin, swollen glands, a chill, or a fever. . . . we give to thieves . . .

B32. Crates fr. 16, from *Wild Beasts* (V)

(A.) So no one's going to own a male or female slave, and an old man's going to do all his work himself? (B.) Certainly not—because I'll make everything capable of moving itself. (A.) How will this help them? (B.) All his household equipment will come of its own accord, whenever someone shouts 'Table! Set yourself beside me! And get yourself ready with no help! Knead, my little grain-sack! Pour some wine, ladle! Where's the cup? Go wash yourself! Get up on the table, barley-cake! The cookpot should already have been pouring out the beets. Fish! Get over here!' 'But I'm not roasted on the other side yet.' 'Then turn yourself over, baste yourself, and sprinkle on some salt!'

B33. Teleclides fr. 1, from *Amphictyonies* (V)

Well, I'll describe the sort of life I furnished mortals with in the old days. Peace, first of all, was as readily available as washing-water. And the earth didn't produce fear or sicknesses; everything they needed was there spontaneously. For every torrent-gully flowed with wine, and barley-cakes fought with loaves of bread around people's mouths, begging them to gulp down the whitest ones, if they would be so kind. The fish would come home, roast themselves, and serve themselves on the tables. A river of broth flowed next to their couches, rolling along warm chunks of meat. There were streams of little sauces for anyone who wanted some of this food, so there was no reason to begrudge a man soaking his mouthful until it was soft and gulping it down. There were [corrupt] sprinkled with seasonings in little dishes. Roast thrushes accompanied by milk-cakes flew into their mouths, and there was an uproar as the unbaked cakes jostled one another around their jaws. The children used to play knucklebones with slices of sow's womb and meat-trimmings. People were fat back then and as big as the Giants.

B34. Pherecrates fr. 137, from *Persians* (V)

What need will we have any longer for your ploughs, yokemakers, sickle-makers, or smiths, or for sowing or staking? Rivers of black broth, gushing abundantly with rich sprinkle-bread and cakes of the finest barley, will flow spontaneously through the crossroads from Wealth's springs so we can draw from them. Zeus will rain *kapnias* wine, dumping it over the roof-tiles like a bathman. Streams of grape-clusters will pour down from the roofs, accompanied by cakes stuffed full of cheese, as well as by hot pea-soup and lily-porridge-cakes. The trees in the mountains will shed not leaves but roasted kid-meat sausages, soft baby squid, and stewed thrushes.

B35. Aristophanes fr. 581, from *Seasons* (410s BC?)

(A.) In mid-winter you'll see cucumbers, grape-clusters, summer fruit generally, garlands of violets— (B.) Also a blinding dust-storm, I expect! (A.) The same man will sell thrushes, pears, honeycomb, olives, beestings, after-birth pudding, swallow-figs, cicadas, still-born kids; and you'd see harvest-baskets pouring out a mix of figs and myrtle-berries as thick as snow. (B.) So they'll sow gourds along with their turnips, with the result that no one knows any longer what time of year it is? (A.) Isn't this the greatest possible good, if a person can buy whatever he wants throughout the year? (B.) To the contrary—this is the greatest possible evil! Because if this weren't the case, they wouldn't desire things or spend money. *I* would lend them this for a little while and then take it away. (A.) I too do this for the other cities, with the exception of Athens; but *they* have these advantages, because they respect the gods. (B.) A lot of good they've got from showing you respect, according to you! (A.) What do you mean? (B.) You've turned their city into Egypt instead of Athens.

B36. Plato Comicus fr. 96, from *Wool-Carders or Cercopes* (V/IV)

Greetings, assembly of ancient-born spectators, clever in every way!

B37. Cratinus fr. 360, from an unidentified play (V)

Greetings, crowd that laughs loudly for no reason, very best judge of our cleverness—on the days that follow festivals! Your mother, the noise produced by the bleachers, bore you as a lucky child.

B38. Plato Comicus fr. 99, from *The Little Child* (V/IV)

Were I not under terrible pressure, gentlemen, to turn in this direction, I wouldn't have proceeded to a speech like this.

B39. Metagenes fr. 15, from *The Man Who Loved Sacrifices* (late 400s BC?)

I vary my plot interlude by interlude, in order to feast the audience with many novel appetizers.

B40. Lysippus fr. 4, from *Bacchants* (V)

not raising the nap on or sulphuring other people's ideas

B41. Cratinus fr. 342, from an unidentified play, perhaps *The Wineflask* (423 BC)

'Who are you?' some subtle spectator might ask, a bit of a quibbler, a pursuer of little sayings, a Euripidaristophanizer.

B42. Eupolis fr. 89, from *Dyers* (410s BC?)

† and that man † I collaborated with the bald guy on *Knights* and presented it to him as a gift.

B43. Pherecrates fr. 102, from *Small Change* (V)

But I say to the judges who are currently judging not to violate your oath or judge unfairly; otherwise, by the god of friendship, Pherecrates will make another speech about you that's far more slanderous than this one!

B44. Eupolis fr. 392, from an unidentified play (V)

But listen, spectators, and understand my words; for right at the beginning I'm going to defend myself to you (a line or more is missing) . . . what got into your heads, that you claim that foreigners are clever poets. Whereas if someone from right here, who's no less brilliant, applies himself to poetry, he seems to be utterly crazy, and he's insane and drifting away from his senses, according to you. But take my advice: totally change your ways, and don't be resentful when one of us young men enjoys the art of music.

B45. Eupolis fr. 172, from *Flatterers* (421 BC)

We'll tell you about the way of life flatterers enjoy; so listen to how we're elegant men in every respect. First of all, we have a slave attendant—generally belonging to someone else—and a little [corrupt] of him. And I have these two lovely outer robes, and I change one of them for the other and regularly go off to the marketplace. When I spy someone there who's a fool but rich, I'm all over him immediately. No matter what the rich guy says, I heap praise on it and pretend I'm stunned with pleasure at his words. Then we go off in various directions to dinner, pursuing someone else's barley-cake. The flatterer must immediately say many clever things there, or he's kicked out. I know this happened to the tattooed Acestor; he made an insolent joke, and the slave took him outside, wearing a criminal's collar, and turned him over to Oineus.

B46. Cratinus fr. 255, from *Cheirons* (late 440s–before 429 BC)

We barely completed these things over two years.

C1. Adespota comica fr. 1062, from an unidentified play

'Why then should *I* care about *your* affairs?', one of you might say. And *I'll* quote the Sophoclean line: 'I have suffered terrible things'. Old Cronus gulps down and gobbles up all my children, and he doesn't turn even one of them over to me. Instead, *he* gives me the finger, takes whatever *I* give birth to off to Megara, and sells and eats it; because he's afraid of the oracle in the same way . . . a dog. For Apollo once loaned Cronus a drachma and didn't get it back. He was angry about this and no longer loaned him anything valuable, or any household items, by Zeus, or any money. Instead, he prophesied that Cronus would be expelled from his kingship by a child. So since he's afraid of this, he swallows down all his children.

C2. Heniochus fr. 5, from an unidentified play (IV)

I'll tell you their names one by one in a moment; but they're all cities of various sorts, which have been acting foolishly for a long time now. Perhaps one of you might interrupt to ask what the setting here is now. He'll learn this from me. This entire area round about is Olympia; and as for the stage-building over there, imagine that you're seeing an embassy-tent. Alright! What are the cities doing here, then? They came to make manumission sacrifices at a time when they were just about free of their tribute payments. And then, after that sacrifice was made, Ms Irresolution ruined them by making them her guests day after day, holding them spellbound for a long time now. Two women are always with them and keep them upset: Democracy is the name of one of them, and the other one's name is Aristocracy. As a result of their influence, the cities have repeatedly got drunk and behaved badly.

C3. Eubulus fr. 89, from *Procris* (IV)

(A.) Spread a soft bed for the dog! Put one of our Milesian wool blankets under him, and a saffron-dyed robe over him! (B.) Apollo! (A.) Then moisten his wheat-pudding with goose milk! (B.) Heracles! (A.) And anoint his feet with the Megalleian perfume!

C4. Anaxilas fr. 12, from *Circe* (IV)

She'll turn some of you into mountain-ranging, mud-trodding pigs, some into wildcats, others into savage wolves or lions.

C5. Anaxilas fr. 13, from *Circe* (IV)

For it's a terrible thing, my friend, to have a pig's snout and need to scratch!

C6. Antiphanes fr. 131, from *Cyclops* (IV)

I'll furnish us with the following mainland items: a cow from my herd, a mud-treading he-goat, a heavenly she-goat, a castrated ram, a castrated boar, an uncastrated pig, a hog, a hare, kids, fresh cheese, dry cheese, chopped cheese, grated cheese, sliced cheese, cottage cheese.

C7. Epicrates fr. 5, from *Difficult to Sell* (IV)

For what's more unpleasant than being summoned 'Slave! slave!' to where they're drinking, and to serve some beardless little boy at that? And to bring the pisspot, and see half-eaten milk-cakes and bird-meat lying there, none of which a slave's allowed to eat, even if it's left over—according to the women.

But what makes me crazy is that if one of us eats any of this food, they call him an impudent glutton.

C8. Antiphanes fr. 75, from *Ganymede* (IV)

(A.) Alas! You're asking much too complicated questions. (Laomedon) Alright, I'll say it clearly. If you know anything about the kidnapping of my child, you need to speak quickly before you're hung up. (A.) Are you posing this to me as a riddle to solve, master, (when you ask) if I know anything about the kidnapping of your child? Or (if not), what's the point of what you said? (Laomedon) Someone hurry up and bring me out a strap! (A.) Alright—maybe I didn't figure it out. So are you punishing me for this? Don't! You should have been passing a cup of saltwater around. (Laomedon) Do you know, then, how you have to drink it? (A.) Me? I certainly do. (Laomedon) How? (A.) I have to get a guarantee from you! (Laomedon) No; you have to put your hands behind your back and drain it without taking a breath.

C9. Dionysius Comicus fr. 3, from *Men Who Shared a Name* (IV)

Come on now, Dromo! If you have any subtlety, cleverness, or elegance in you, show it to your teacher; I'm asking for a demonstration of your technique. I'm leading you into enemy territory; boldly lay it waste! Suppose they count the chunks of meat as they hand them over, and keep an eye on you; make them tender and stew them intensely, and confuse the count in the way I'm describing for you! Suppose there's a big fish; its guts belong to you! And if you filch a slice of the meat, that's yours too—as long as we're inside the house. Once we're outside, it's mine! As for the offal and the other parts that go along with them, which by their nature can't be counted or checked and have the rank and station of trimmings, tomorrow they can make us both happy. By all means give the dealer in plunder a share, so you can get through the door with less worry. Why do I need to make a long speech to someone who knows what I'm thinking? You're my pupil, and I'm your teacher. Remember my advice, and come along here with me.

C10. Antiphanes fr. 180, from *The Parasite* (IV)

(A.) After this will come another one, large, noble, as big as the table— (B.) What are you talking about? (A) A spawn of Carystus, born of earth, bubbling— (B.) Say what you mean! Spit it out! (A.) I'm referring to a casserole-dish (*kakkabos*); you might perhaps call it a *lopas*. (B.) Do you think

I care about the name, about whether people like to call it a *kakkabos* or a *sittubos*? All I know is, you're talking about a pot!

C11. Aristophon fr. 5, from *The Doctor* (IV)

I want to tell him the sort of person I am. If someone's giving a feast, I'm the first one there, and as a result my nickname's been Meat-Broth for a long time now. If one of the drunks has to be grabbed about the waist and hoisted off the ground, you can figure I look like an Argive wrestler. If we need to attack a house, I'm a ram. If we need to go up on a ladder; I'm Capaneus. As for standing up to blows, I'm an anvil; for forming fists, I'm Telamon; for making passes at handsome boys, I'm smoke.

C12. Crobylus fr. 8, from an unidentified play (IV)

(A.) For dealing with these really hot items, I've got fingers that resemble Mount Ida, of course; and I take great pleasure in giving my oesophagus a steam-bath with little slices of fish. (B.) You're a kiln, not a human being!

C13. Antiphanes fr. 200, from *The Soldier or Tycho* (IV)

(A.) Tell me—you say you spent a lot of time on Cyprus? (B.) Yes, the whole war. (A.) Where, precisely? Tell me! (B.) In Paphos, where you could see something extraordinarily luxurious, as well as incredible. (A.) What? (B.) When the king was having dinner, he was fanned by pigeons—and pigeons only! (A.) How? I'm going to ignore everything else and ask you this. (B.) How? He anointed himself with perfume that was imported from Syria and scented with the type of fruit, they say, that pigeons often eat. The pigeons were there, flying around, because of its smell; they could have roosted on his head, except that slaves sitting beside him kept shooing them off. But they stayed just a bit away from him, not too far in either direction; and they fanned up the air enough to make the cloud of scent just the same size as he was and not too strong.

C14. Philemon fr. 95, from an unidentified play (IV/III)

The one whose attention no one has ever escaped when he's doing something bad or good—that's who I am, the Air, whom you might also call Zeus. I'm everywhere, which is something only a god is capable of: in Athens, in Patras, in Sicily, in every city and every house, in all of you. There's nowhere that Air isn't present; and since he's present everywhere, he has no choice but to know everything.

C15. Adespota comica fr. 1084, from an unidentified play

(A.) Has anyone in the city suffered more terribly than me? No, by Demeter and Sky. I've been married for four months; my father convinced me to do it. Since my wedding night—Lady Night, I call on you as an honest witness to the story I'm telling!—I've never slept apart from my wife for a single night ... never ... been ... after the wedding feast ... I felt a just love. And ... For I was enchanted by her straightforward manner and her honest way of life, and I grew fond of her, and she cared for me as well. Why are you bringing me all these things and showing them to me one by one, given that my heart aches when I see them? Put ... where even now ... (B.) So that there can be ... before ... (at least a dozen lines are missing) ... (A.) ... of my wife ... (B.) Of your mother ... she gave it to your wife ... And ... sealed ... her ring ... (A.) Open it up, so that we can see if anything useful's preserved in it. (B.) Ah! (A.) What is it? (B.) Half of an old, torn robe, nearly eaten up by moths. (A.) Nothing else? (B.) Also necklaces and a single ankle-bracelet. (A.) Give them to me; and shine the lamp on them as you do. Didn't you see inscribed ... ? Hey! Open the top! (B.) Letters ... you poor thing ... I saw letters. (A.) What's the point? ... A child's tokens are inside it, and my mother was safeguarding them. Put them back where they were; I'll seal them up. There's no advantage at the moment, by Zeus, in prying into obscure matters. It's not our business; let's consider the trouble we have sufficient. If I ever get myself together ... I'll open it up again ... nothing ...

C16. Menander fr. 296, from *The Necklace* (IV/III)

(Laches) The lovely heiress is probably going to sleep happily now. She's accomplished a great and notorious deed: she drove the girl who was bothering her out of the house, just like she wanted, so that everyone could stare at Crobyle's face and she could be widely recognized as my wife—and queen. As for how she looks—she's a donkey among monkeys, as the saying goes. I'd rather not mention the night that led to so many troubles. Alas, that I married Crobyle, even if she brought a dowry of ten talents, with her nose as long as your forearm! So how can her insolence be endured? It can't, by Olympian Zeus and Athena; there's no way. A little slave-girl, who did her work and had it done before the order was complete! Let her be expelled! [corrupt]

C17. Menander fr. 297, from *The Necklace* (IV/III)

(Laches) I'm married to an heiress ogre. Haven't I told you about this? (B.) No. (Laches) We have a mistress over our house, our fields, and † everything in place of her †. (B.) Apollo! How difficult that is! (Laches) As difficult as it can be. She makes trouble for everyone, not just me—for my son in particular, and my daughter. (B.) You're describing an impossible situation. (Laches) I'm well aware of that.

C18. Adespota comica fr. 1063. 1–34, from an unidentified play

(A.) . . . having put my confidence. (Megas) Run along; don't worry about anything . . . is inside. So get yourself going, get yourself going now, and be serious about it! Be a man now, Megas! Don't leave Moschion in the lurch! I want to, by the gods, I want to. But I unexpectedly fell into a wave of troubles, and I'm in distress; I've been worried for a long time now that Fortune's verdict may go against me. You're a coward, by Athena, you're a coward! I see what's going on. *You're* trying to avoid trouble, and you're blaming Fortune. People at sea—do you see my point?—are often confronted with difficulties of every sort: a storm, wind, water, a huge wave, lightning, hail, thunder, seasickness, thunderheads, darkness. But all the same, each of them stays hopeful and doesn't despair of the future. One fellow lays hold of the brails . . . looks; another prays to the Samothracian deities, asking them to help the pilot; pulls in the sheets . . . (three lines that contain only scattered letters follow) . . . to all nobly eagerness . . . For I see my master here . . . with him. I'll quickly go inside and wait for the right moment to reveal myself to them. (B.) I've been treated more outrageously, Laches, than anyone else ever has been; and you've done this by sending me here. (Laches) Don't talk this way! (B.) By Heracles, how else would I feel? I said repeatedly to you there: 'What are you sending me for—' (Laches) Yes indeed. (B.) 'bringing your son news about his marriage and intending to offer him your daughter? But if he doesn't listen to me, how am I going to force him to marry her, if you're not there?' . . . hearing word of the matters . . . his mother . . . was persuaded to say to me . . .

D1. Hermippus fr. 63, from *Porters* (late 430s/early 420s BC)

Tell me now, Muses whose home is on Olympus, about all the good things Dionysus brings here for men with his black ship during the time he is a captain on the wine-dark sea. From Cyrene there is silphium stalk and cowhides; from the Hellespont mackerel and every kind of salt-fish; from

Thessaly barley meal and sides of beef. And from Sitalces there is mange for the Spartans, and from Perdiccas a huge number of ships full of lies. Syracuse supplying us with hogs and cheese . . . (a line or more is missing) . . . And as for the Corcyreans—may Poseidon destroy them in their hollow ships, for their heart is divided! That's where all these items are from. From Egypt comes hanging gear, that is, sails and papyrus ropes; and from Syria comes frankincense. Beautiful Crete furnishes cypress wood for the gods, while Libya has vast amounts of ivory for sale, and Rhodes offers raisins and dried figs that bring sweet dreams. He brings pears and goodly apples from Euboea, slaves from Phrygia, and mercenaries from Arcadia. Pagasae supplies us with servants and men with tattoos, and hazelnuts and shining almonds are provided by the Paphlagonians; for these are the accessories of a feast. Sidon again offers dates and wheat, Carthage blankets and embroidered pillows.

D2. Aristophanes fr. 233, from *Banqueters* (427 BC)

(A.) Tell me about these Homeric terms: What do they refer to as *korumba*? . . . What do they refer to as 'strengthless heads'? (B.) No—let your son and my brother tell us: What do they refer to as *iduoi*? . . . What does *opuein* mean?

D3. Strato Comicus fr. 1, from *Phoenicides* (IV)

I've taken a male Sphinx into my house, not a cook! For, by the gods, I don't understand a single word he says. He's here with a full supply of strange vocabulary. The minute he entered the house, he immediately looked me in the eye and asked in a loud voice: 'How many *meropes* ("people") have you invited to dinner? Tell me!' 'I've invited the Meropes to dinner? You're crazy; do you think I know these Meropes?' 'Isn't a single *daitumôn* ("guest") going to be present?' 'Philinus is going to come, and Moschion, and Niceratus, and so-and-so, and so-and-so.' I went through them, name by name; I didn't have a single Daitumôn among them. He got irritated, as if he was being treated badly because I hadn't invited Daitumôn. Very strange. 'Aren't you sacrificing an earthbreaker?' 'No, I'm not,' I said. 'A bull with a wide forehead?' 'I'm not sacrificing a bull, you miserable creature.' 'Are you making a sacrifice of *mêla* ("sheep", but also "apples")?' 'No, by Zeus, I'm not.' '*Mêla* are sheep.' 'Apples are sheep? I don't know anything about any of this, cook,' I said, 'and I don't want to. I'm quite unsophisticated; so talk to me very simply.' 'Bring the *oulochutes* here!' 'What's that?' 'Barley.' 'Why then, you idiot, do you talk in riddles?' 'Is any *pêgos* available?' '*Pêgos*? Suck me! Will you say what you want to say to me more clearly?' 'You're an ignoramus, old man,' he says. 'Bring me salt; that's what *pêgos* is. Let me see it.' A basin was there. He made the sacrifice and said countless words of the sort no one, by Earth, could have understood: *mistulla, moires, diptucha, obeloi*. The result was that you would have had to get Philetas' books to understand everything he said. But now I took a different tack and began to beg him to talk a bit like a human being. Persuasion herself would never have convinced him if she were standing right there next to him. I suspect the bastard's been the slave of some sort of rhapsode ever since he was a boy, and has got stuffed full of Homeric vocabulary.

D4. Eubulus fr. 118, from an unidentified play (IV)

Does Homer anywhere describe any of his Achaeans as eating fish? And as for pieces of meat, all they did was roast them, since he hasn't represented any of them as doing any stewing, not even a little. And none of them laid eyes on a prostitute, and they jerked off for ten years. The expedition turned out badly for them: after seizing a single city, they left having been fucked a lot harder up the arse than the city they captured then.

D5. Timocles fr. 6, from *Women Celebrating the Dionysia* (IV)

My good sir, listen and see if what I say makes sense to you. Man is a creature doomed to trouble by his very nature, and life brings many griefs with it. He therefore invented these distractions from anxious thoughts; because after the mind forgets its own affairs and is entranced by someone else's suffering, it goes away happy as well as educated. First consider, if you please, how the tragedians benefit everyone. After one fellow, who's a pauper, realizes that Telephus was poorer than he is, he immediately puts up with his poverty more easily. The man who suffers from madness thinks of Alcmaeon. Someone has an eye infection; Phineus' sons are *blind*. Someone's child has died; Niobe's lifted his spirits. Someone's crippled; he sees Philoctetes. An old man's down on his luck; he learns about Oineus. For when a person considers all the misfortunes greater than his own that have happened to other people, he complains less about his own troubles.

D6. Antiphanes fr. 189, from *Poetry* (IV)

Tragedy's an altogether enviable type of poetry! The plots, first of all, are familiar to the audience before anyone even speaks a word, so all the poet has to do is offer a reminder. † says † 'Oedipus', they know everything else:

his father's Laius; his mother's Jocasta; who his daughters and sons are; what's going to happen to him; what he's done. If someone says 'Alcmaeon', on the other hand, he's as good as mentioned all his children, plus the fact that he went crazy and killed his mother, and that Adrastus is going to get annoyed immediately and come home and go off again. Then, when they've run out of anything to say and have totally collapsed from exhaustion in their dramas, they raise the theatrical crane like a white flag—and the audience is satisfied! But we don't have these advantages, and we have to invent everything: new names . . .; and then what happened previously, the current situation, the conclusion, and the introduction. If some Chremes or Pheidon leaves out even one of these items, he's hissed off the stage. But Peleus and Teucrus can do anything.

D7. Timocles fr. 27, from *Orestautocleides* (IV)

Old women are sleeping around the miserable fellow: Nannion, Plangon, Lyca, Gnathaena, Phryne, Pythionice, Myrrhine, Chrysis, Conalis, Hierocleia, Lopadion.

D8. Cratinus fr. 17, from *Cowherds* (V)

who didn't give Sophocles a chorus when he requested one, but gave one to the son of Cleomachus, whom *I* wouldn't have thought deserved to serve as my trainer even for the Adonia!

D9. Phrynichus Comicus fr. 32, from *Muses* (405 BC)

Blessed Sophocles, who lived a long life and died a fortunate and clever man; he wrote many fine tragedies and died easily, after suffering no misery.

D10. Antiphanes fr. 228, from an unidentified play (IV)

Tell me—what's the point of life? I say it's drinking. Look at the trees along torrent streams that stay moist all day and all night; how large and beautiful they grow! But those that resist are destroyed root and branch.

D11. Eubulus fr. 26, from *Dionysius* (IV)

Euripides is responsible for 'I saved you as so many know' and 'Maiden, if I save you, will you show me gratitude?' And they collect my *sigmas* and mock my troubles—as if they were themselves great poets!

D12. Diphilus fr. 74, from *Synoris* (IV/III)

(A.) You've come out very well as far as this throw goes. (B.) You're funny. Raise the bet a drachma. (A.) It's been lying there for a long time. (B.) If only I could throw a Euripides! (A.) Euripides would never save a woman; don't you see how hostile he is to them in his tragedies? But he liked parasites. As he says: 'For if any rich man fails to support at least three people who don't contribute to the dinner expenses, might he perish and never return to his fatherland!' (B.) Where are these verses from, by the gods? (A.) What do you care? It's not the play we're considering; it's the attitude.

D13. Eupolis fr. 148, from *Helots* (early 420s BC?)

Singing the works of Stesichorus, Alcman, and Simonides is old-fashioned; but Gnesippus can be heard. He invented night-time songs for adulterers holding harps to use to summon women out to them.

D14. Pherecrates fr. 155, from *Cheiron* (V)

(Music) No, I'm quite willing to discuss it; for your heart gets pleasure from listening, and mine from speaking. Melanippides was the beginning of my troubles. He was the first of them to get hold of me, and he loosened me up and made me a dozen strings more supple. But all the same, he was actually decent to me—in comparison to my current troubles. The damned Athenian Cinesias destroyed me so completely, by putting dissonant modulations into his strophes, that the right-hand parts of his dithyrambic poetry seem left-handed, as if you were seeing a reflection in a shield. But all the same, I could actually put up with him. Whereas Phrynis introduced a kind of private whirlwind and completely destroyed me, by bending and twisting me; he had twelve tunings in five strings. But the fact is that he too was decent to me; because even if he made a mistake, he made it good again. But Timotheus, my dear, has buried me and ground me down to nothing in a completely shameful way. (Justice) What's Timotheus like? (Music) He's a Milesian redhead. He's given me trouble—he's outdone all the others I'm discussing—by dragging me through perverse anthills. And if he meets me somewhere, when I'm walking alone, he strips me and undoes me with a dozen strings . . . (a line or more is missing) . . . discordant and unholy treble notes and musical sounds; and he fills me to the brim with caterpillars, just like what happens to cabbages.

E1. Nicostratus Comicus fr. 30, from an unidentified play (IV)

Don't you realize that the right of free speech is poverty's armour? If a man loses it, he's abandoned the shield that guards his life.

E2. Amphis fr. 17, from *Day-Labourers* (IV)

Then isn't isolation as good as gold? The fundamental source of a good life for human beings is a piece of land; it's the only thing capable of concealing poverty. Whereas the city is a theatre full of patent bad luck.

E3. Antiphanes fr. 202, from *The Soldier or Tycho* (IV)

Any human being who thinks that anything he owns is his for life is very much mistaken. Either a special levy snatches away everything he's accumulated; or he gets involved in a lawsuit and is ruined; or he serves as a general and is fined; or he's selected as a *chorêgos*, and provides golden clothing for his chorus but is reduced to rags himself; or he hangs himself while serving as a trierarch; or he's captured as he's sailing somewhere; or his slaves cut him to bits when he's walking along the street or fast asleep. Nothing is certain, except what a man spends on enjoying himself on a day-by-day basis. Even that's not completely secure, because someone could come up and steal the table while it's sitting in front of him. So when you've got a mouthful past your teeth and swallowed down, you can consider that the one possession you've got firm control of.

E4. Eupolis fr. 384, from an unidentified play (V)

Indeed, although many possibilities present themselves, I don't know what to say; that's how extraordinarily upset I am when I consider the state in your time. For we old men didn't run it like this in the past. In our day the city's generals, first of all, were drawn from the most important families and were pre-eminently wealthy and from the best backgrounds; we prayed to them like gods—in fact they *were* gods. As a result, our state was secure. But now our forces are led any which way, since we select scum as generals.

E5. Eupolis fr. 219, from *Marikas* (Lenaia 421 BC)

We now have as generals men you previously wouldn't have chosen to be wine-inspectors. Oh city, city! You're more lucky than sensible.

E6. Eupolis fr. 262, from *Men from the Deme Prospalta* (probably 429 BC)

His mother was some Thracian ribbon-vendor.

E7. Antiphanes fr. 194, from *Sappho* (mid-360s?)

(Sappho) It is feminine and keeps its children safe beneath the folds of its garment. And although they are mute, they raise a resounding cry through the sea-surge and the whole mainland to whichever mortals they wish, and even those who are not there can hear them, although their perception is deaf . . . (a line or more is missing) . . . (B.) Yes—because the thing you're referring to is a city, and the children it nourishes inside itself are the politicians. They shout and bring the overseas revenues from Asia and Thrace here. And while they're splitting the money up among themselves and constantly abusing one another, the people sit nearby, hearing and seeing nothing. (Sappho) . . . For how, old sir, could a politician have no voice? (B.) If he's convicted three times of making an illegal proposal . . . And yet I thought I'd figured out exactly what you said. But tell me (the answer). (Sappho) The feminine object is a writing tablet, and the children she carries around inside herself are the letters. Although they're mute, they speak to anyone they want who's far away. And if someone else happens to be standing nearby, he won't hear the man who's reading.

E8. Diphilus fr. 101, from an unidentified play (IV/III)

A courtesan's oath is just like a politician's; they each swear to suit the person they're talking to.

E9. Plato Comicus fr. 202, from an unidentified play (V/IV)

For if one son-of-a-bitch dies, two politicians grow back. Because we don't have an Iolaus in our city who'll cauterize their heads. You've let someone bugger you; that's why you'll be a politician!

E10. Eupolis fr. 102, from *Demes* (412 BC?)

(A.) This fellow was the best man there was at speaking. Whenever he came forward, he caught the other politicians from ten feet back when he spoke, just like good runners do. (B.) You're describing someone fast! (A.) And on top of his speed, a sort of persuasiveness used to sit on his lips. That's how enthralling he was; he was the only politician who left his stinger in his audience.

E11. Teleclides fr. 45, from an unidentified play (late 440s/early 430s?)

and the cities' tribute payments; and the cities themselves, so that he could bind some and destroy others; and walls of stone, so that he could build them here, and on the other hand knock them down instead over there; treaties, power, might, peace, and wealth and good fortune.

E12. Cratinus fr. 258, from *Cheirons* (late 440s–429 BC)

And Political Division and first-born Time had sex and gave birth to the greatest tyrant, whom the gods refer to as Head-gatherer.

E13. Cratinus fr. *259, probably from *Cheirons* (late 440s–429 BC)

And as his Hera, Buggery bears Aspasia the shameless concubine.

E14. Hermippus fr. *47, probably from *Fates* (430 BC?)

King of the satyrs, why in the world are you unwilling to weigh a spear in your hand, but instead offer bold speeches about the war, although Teles' spirit is in you? And if a little hand-knife used for chopping is rubbed on a hard whetstone, you gnash your teeth, upset by shining Cleon.

E15. Adespota comica fr. 957, from an unidentified play

Phormio promised to set up three silver tripods, and then he dedicated one— made of lead.

E16. Adespota comica fr. 461, from an unidentified play (424–422 BC)

Cleon's a Prometheus—after the fact.

E17. Eupolis fr. 331, from an unidentified play (424–422 BC)

For you were the first, Cleon, to address us with the word 'Rejoice!', despite causing the city much grief.

E18. Eupolis fr. 316, from *The Golden Race* (429–422 BC)

O fairest of all the cities Cleon watches over, how fortunate you were before, and now you'll be even more so! . . . (a line or more is missing) . . . First of all, everyone ought to have had an equal right of free speech . . . (a line or more is missing) . . . For how would anyone not be happy to associate with a city like this one, where someone so thin and ugly can . . .

E19. Plato Comicus fr. 115, from *In Terrible Pain* (429–422 BC)

I who, first of all, waged war on Cleon.

E20. Aristophanes fr. 102, from *Farmers* (late 420s BC)

(A.) I want to be a farmer. (B.) So who's stopping you? (A.) You are; since I'm offering you 1,000 drachmas, if you release me from my offices. (B.) We accept them; because that makes 2,000, when added to what we got from Nicias.

E21. Phrynichus Comicus fr. 62, from an unidentified play (late 420s–413 BC)

For I'm well aware that he was a good citizen, and he didn't walk around looking frightened, like Nicias does.

E22. Teleclides fr. 44, from an unidentified play (probably mid-410s BC; before 413)

Didn't Charicles offer you a mina to keep you from telling that he was the first child born to his mother, from her purse? And Nicias son of Niceratus offered four minas; but as for why he offered them, I'm not going to say, although I know quite well. Because the fellow's a friend, and I think he has some sense.

E23. Eupolis fr. 193, from *Marikas* (Lenaia 421 BC)

(Marikas) How recently have you been with Nicias? (B.) I haven't seen him, except just now, when he was standing in the marketplace. (Marikas) The fellow admits that he's seen Nicias! And yet what could he have been up to, when he saw him, unless he was engaged in treachery? (Chorus of Poor Men) Did you hear, age-mates, that Nicias has been caught red-handed? (Chorus of Rich Men) Would you convict an outstanding man on the testimony of some bum, you lunatics?

E24. Plato Comicus fr. 183, from *Hyperbolus* (late 420s/early 410s BC; before 417)

For he didn't speak Attic, dear Fates, but whenever he needed to say *diêitômên*, he'd say *dêitômên*; and whenever he needed to say *oligon*, he'd say *olion*.

E25. Plato Comicus fr. 203, from an unidentified play (after 417 BC)

But what's happened to him is what his behaviour deserves, although it's too good for him and his tattoos. Ostraca weren't invented for people like this.

E26. Pherecrates fr. 164, from an unidentified play (V)

For although Alcibiades isn't a man, so it seems, he's now every woman's man.

E27. Adespota comica fr. 123, from an unidentified play (415–412 BC)

The dainty Alcibiades, O Earth and gods, with whom Sparta wants to have an affair.

E28. Phrynichus Comicus fr. 61, from an unidentified play (after 415 BC)

(A.) My dear Hermes, be *careful*, so you don't fall and knock a piece off yourself, and give an opportunity for slander to another Diocleides who wants to cause some trouble. (Hermes) I'll be careful; I don't want to offer a reward for information to the murderous foreigner Teucrus.

E29. Plato Comicus fr. 201, from an unidentified play (early 380s?)

(The People) Grab my hand, grab it, as fast as you can! I'm about to elect Agyrrhius general! . . . (a line or more is missing) . . . Mantias is standing beside my speakers'-stand . . . (a line or more is missing) . . . It's nourishing the foul-smelling Cephalus, who's a despicable disease.

E30. Eubulus fr. 106. 1–9, from *Sphinx-Carion* (IV)

(A.) It is something that lacks a tongue but speaks; the female shares a name with the male; it safeguards many winds; is hairy but at other times hairless; says things that make no sense to the sensible; and extracts one law from another. It is one and many; and if someone wounds it, it remains unwounded. What is it? Why are you puzzled? (B.) It's Callistratus! (A.) No— it's an arsehole. You're always talking nonsense. An arsehole's both tongueless and capable of speech; there's one name for the many of them; when wounded, it's unwounded; it's hairy and hairless. What more do you want? It's a guardian of many winds.

E31. Timocles fr. 4, from *Delos* (*c.*324 BC)

(A.) Demosthenes has 50 talents. (B.) He's a lucky fellow, if he's not offering anyone else a share. (A.) Moerocles has also got a lot of gold pieces. (B.) The fellow doing the giving is a fool; but the one doing the getting is lucky! (A.) Demon's also got something, and Callistratus too. (B.) They were poor, so I forgive them. (A.) Hypereides, who's clever at composing speeches, also got something. (B.) He'll make our fishmongers rich, because he's a glutton— enough of one to make the seagulls look like Syrians!

E32. Philippides fr. 25, from an unidentified play (*c.*300 BC)

The man who trimmed the year down to a single month; who took over the Acropolis as an inn, and introduced his courtesans to the Virgin; whose fault it was that the frost burned the grapevines; because of whose impiety the sacred robe was ripped down the middle; who converted divine honours into human ones—these things ruin a people, not comedy.

F1. Eupolis fr. 386, from an unidentified play (V)

And I also hate Socrates the impoverished chatterer, who's thought about everything else; but as for where he could get something to gobble down, he's paid no attention to this.

F2. Eupolis fr. 395, from an unidentified play (V)

After Socrates got the cup that was passed from left to right, as he was singing a passage of Stesichorus to the accompaniment of the lyre, he stole the wine-jug.

F3. Callias Comicus fr. 15, from *Men in Shackles* (V)

(A.) Why are you so haughty and so proud? (B.) Because I can be! For Socrates is responsible.

F4. Amipsias fr. *9, perhaps from *Connus* (City Dionysia 423 BC)

Socrates, best of a few men and most foolish of many, have you too come to us? You're quite tough! Where would you get yourself a heavy wool cloak from? . . . (a line or more is missing) . . . This problem originated as an insult to the shoemakers . . . (a line or more is missing) . . . Even though he's hungry, this fellow never ventured to be a flatterer.

F5. Teleclides fr. 41, from an unidentified play (V)

Mnesilochus is the one who's roasting a new play for Euripides; and Socrates is feeding wood to the fire.

F6. Epicrates fr. 10, from an unidentified play (IV)

(A.) What about Plato and Speusippus and Menedemus? What's occupying their time nowadays? What deep thoughts, what sort of speculation is under investigation at their establishment? Give me an insightful account of these matters, if you've come with any knowledge of them, by Earth! (B.) I know enough to give you a clear report about this. For during the Panathenaic festival, I saw a herd of young men in the exercise grounds of the Academy, and I listened to unspeakably strange discussions. They were producing definitions having to do with natural history, and trying to distinguish between animals, trees, and vegetables; and in the course of these discussions they attempted to determine which category the gourd belongs to. (A.) What definition did they settle on? And what category did they put the plant into? Reveal this, if you have any information! (B.) At first they all stood silent and gazed at the ground for a long time, thinking the matter through. Then suddenly, while the other boys were still staring at the ground and considering the question, one of them said that it was a round vegetable; another a type of grass; and a third a tree. And a Sicilian doctor, when he heard this, farted on them for talking nonsense. (A.) I imagine they got terribly angry and shouted that they were being mocked? Because during conversations of this sort † it's appropriate to do something like that. (B.) The young men paid no attention. But Plato was there, and very gently and with no sign of excitement he ordered them once again to try to determine what category it belonged to. And they began drawing distinctions.

F7. Amphis fr. 6, from *Amphicrates* (IV)

(A.) As for what benefit it is you're going to get from her, I know less about this, master, than I do about Plato's 'Good'. (B.) Pay attention!

F8. Theopompus Comicus fr. 16, from *The Hedonist* (V/IV)

For one thing isn't one, and two are scarcely one, according to Plato.

F9. Amphis fr. 13, from *Dexidemides* (IV)

Plato, how true it is that all you know is how to scowl, haughtily raising your eyebrows like a snail!

F10. Alexis fr. 223, from *Men from Tarentum* (IV)

(A.) Because the Pythagoreans, according to what we hear, don't eat fish or anything else that's alive; and they're the only people who don't drink wine. (B.) But Epicharides eats dogs, even though he's a Pythagorean. (A.) After he kills them, I imagine; because then it's not alive anymore. . . . (a line or more is missing) . . . (A.) Pythagorean terms, over-subtle arguments, and finely chiselled thoughts provide their nourishment, but what they have on a daily basis is the following: one loaf of high-quality bread for both of them, and a cup of water. That's it. (B.) You're talking about a prison diet! Do all these wise men live like this and endure such misery? (A.) No; these people have a luxurious existence compared with others. Don't you realize that Melanippides is a disciple, and Phaon, Phyromachus, and Phanus? And that once every four days they get a single cup of barley-groats for dinner?

F11. Aristophon fr. 10, from *The Pythagorean* (IV)

As for going hungry and eating nothing, consider yourself to be looking at Tithymallus or Philippides. When it comes to drinking water, I'm a frog; when it comes to enjoying bulbs and vegetables, a caterpillar; as regards not bathing, dirt; as for spending the winter in the open air, a blackbird; for putting up with stifling heat and talking at midday, a cicada; for not using olive oil or even giving it a glance, a dustcloud; for walking around without shoes just before dawn, a crane; for not even sleeping a little, a bat.

F12. Aristophon fr. 12, from *The Pythagorean* (IV)

(A.) He said he went down to the abode of those below and saw each of them, and the Pythagoreans were very different from the other dead. Because Pluto only eats with them, he said, on account of their piety. (B.) You're talking about a tolerant god, if he enjoys spending time with people who are covered with dirt! . . . (a line or more is missing) . . . (A.) They eat both . . . and vegetables, and they drink water to go with them. (B.) But none of the younger men would put up with their fleas and cheap robes or their refusal to wash.

F13. Eubulus fr. 137, from an unidentified play (IV)

You of the unwashed feet, who make your beds on the ground and whose roof is the open sky, unholy gullets, who dine on other people's goods, O snatchers of casserole-dishes full of white belly-steaks!

F14. Menander fr. 114, from *Twin Girls* (IV/III)

For you'll walk around with me wearing a cheap robe, as the wife of Crates the Cynic once did . . . (a line or more is missing) . . . And he disposed of his daughter, as he himself said, by giving her away on thirty days' approval.

F15. Menander fr. 193, from *The Horse-Groom* (IV/III)

(A.) There was a certain Monimus, Philo, who was a wise person but a bit less well known. (Philo) The one with the beggar's pouch? (A.) No—with *three* pouches! But that fellow said something quite different, by Zeus, from 'Know yourself' and those other famous phrases, and superior to them, filthy beggar though he was. Because he said that everything generally taken to be true is nonsense.

F16. Theognetus fr. 1, from *The Phantom or The Man Who Loved Money* (III)

You'll be the death of me, sir, with these arguments! You're stuffed full of little speeches from the Stoa Poikile, and they've made you sick. 'Wealth doesn't really belong to a person, whereas wisdom is our own; it's frost versus ice. No one ever lost his wisdom after he got it.' Miserable me—what a philosopher the gods forced me to share a house with! You learned your letters backwards, fool! Your books turned your life upside-down! You've offered your philosophical babbling to earth and heaven—and they're completely uninterested in what you have to say.

F17. Hegesippus Comicus fr. 2, from *Men Who Were Fond of Their Comrades* (III)

When someone demanded that the wise Epicurus tell him what the Good is, this thing they're constantly seeking, he said it was pleasure. Well said, best and wisest! There's no greater good than chewing; the Good is an attribute of pleasure.

F18. Bato fr. 3, from *The Murderer* (III)

When a man can lie down with a beautiful woman in his arms, and have two little pots of Lesbian wine—this is 'the thoughtful man', this is 'the Good'. Epicurus used to say what I'm saying now. If everyone lived the way I do, no one would be odd or an adulterer.

F19. Alexis fr. 25, from *The Instructor in Profligacy* (IV/III)

Why do you say these things, mixing up the Lyceum, the Academy, and the gates of the Odeion, the sophists' babbling? None of these things is good. Let's drink! Let's really drink, Sicon, Sicon! Let's enjoy ourselves as long as we can nourish our souls! Have a wild time, Manes! Nothing gives more pleasure than the belly. It alone is your father and your mother too, whereas personal distinctions, by which I mean ambassadorships and generalships, have the sound of empty boasts equivalent to dreams. A divinity will bring about your death at the fated moment. All you'll have is what you eat and drink; everything else—Pericles, Codrus, Cimon—is dust.

G1. Poliochus fr. 2, from an unidentified play (V)

A small, swarthy barley-cake kneaded full of bran was what each of us had twice a day, and a few figs. Sometimes we roasted a mushroom; and if there was a bit of rain, we caught a snail. And there were wild vegetables and a bruised olive, and a little dubious wine to drink.

G2. Antiphanes fr. 174, from *Omphale* (IV)

For how could any decent person ever leave this house, when he sees these white-bodied loaves filling the kitchen and moving constantly in and out of it, and when he sees their form changed by the baking-shells, a creation of an Attic hand, put on display by Thearion for his demesmen?

G3. Alexis fr. 140, from *Linus* (IV/III)

(Linus) Yes, go over and pick any papyrus roll you like out of there, and then read it— (Heracles) Absolutely! (Linus) examining them quietly, and at your leisure, on the basis of the labels. Orpheus is in there, Hesiod, tragedies,

Epicharmus, Homer, Choerilus, prose treatises of every type. This way you'll show me what subject you're naturally inclined to. (Heracles) I'm picking this one! (Linus) First show me what it is. (Heracles) It's a cookbook, according to the label. (Linus) It's obvious you're quite a philosopher, since you've passed by works like these and chosen Simus' trade! (Heracles) Who's Simus? (Linus) A very clever person. He's now turned to tragedy; he's far and away the best cook among the actors, according to the people who employ him, and the best author among the cooks . . . (a line or more is missing) . . . (Linus) This guy can't stop eating! (Heracles) Say what you want; I'm hungry, that's for sure!

G4. Plato Comicus fr. 189, from *Phaon* (391 BC)

(A.) Here in this deserted spot I want to go through this book privately. (B.) Tell me, please, what's this? (A.) A new cookbook by Philoxenus. (B.) Give me a sample of it! (A.) Alright, listen. 'I shall begin with hyacinth bulb and conclude with tuna.' (B.) With tuna? Well, it's [corrupt] much better to be posted here in the rear then! (A.) 'Subdue the hyacinth bulbs with hot ash; drench them with sauce; and eat as many as you can. Because this makes a man's body stand up straight. So much for that; I move on to the children of the sea.' . . . (a line or more is missing) . . . 'Nor is a casserole-dish bad; but a frying pan is better, I think.' . . . (a line or more is missing) . . . 'As for the perch, the speckle-fish, the dentex, and the shark, do not cut them up, lest vengeance from the gods breathe down upon you. But roast and serve them whole; for this is much better. † If you get hold of the tentacle † of an octopus at the right season, a stewed one is far better than a roasted one—provided it is bigger. But if there are two roasted ones, I say to hell with the stewed one. The mullet refuses to be of assistance to the male muscle; for it is devoted to virgin Artemis and hates hard-ons. The scorpion-fish, on the other hand—' (B.) Will, I hope, sneak up and sting you in the arse!

G5. Ephippus fr. 15, from *Men Who Looked Like One Another or Spitbearers* (IV)

(A.) But do the shopping without spending too much money; anything's acceptable. (B.) Give me my orders, master. (A.) Don't be extravagant; keep it simple and buy whatever's available, for appearances' sake. Squid and cuttle-fish are enough; if a crayfish is for sale, one or two will be enough for our table. Sometimes eels come from Thebes; buy some of them. A little rooster, a little ringdove, a little partridge—things like that. If a hare appears, bring it home. (B.) How stingy you are! (A.) But you're too extravagant. In any case, we've got meat. (B.) Did someone send it? (A.) No; the lady of the house made a sacrifice. Tomorrow we'll dine on Corone's little calf.

G6. Alexis fr. 16, from *The Man Who Had a Cataract* (IV/III)

Whenever I see the generals with their eyebrows raised, I think they're behaving terribly, although I'm not too surprised that men who've been awarded high honours by the city are a bit more proud than other people. But when I see the damned fishsellers staring down at the ground, with their eyebrows over their heads, it makes me choke. If you ask 'How much are you selling the two gray mullets for?', he says 'Ten obols.' 'Ouch! Would you take eight?' 'If you buy the other one too.' 'My good sir, take the money and don't fool around.' 'That's the price; run along!' Isn't this more bitter than gall itself?

G7. Posidippus fr. 1, from *The Man Who Tried to Recover His Sight* (III)

In the course of hiring a cook, I've heard all the abusive remarks the cooks made against each of their competitors—how one fellow doesn't have a discriminating nose, when it comes to fish; as for another, that his mouth's no good; as for a third, that he's ruined his tastebuds, so that he prefers overly heavy seasonings, or uses too much salt or vinegar, or nibbles the food, or burns things, or can't stand the smoke or the fire. I've gone from the fire to the butchers' knives! But this one here made his way through the knives and the fire.

G8. Alexis fr. 24, from *Asclepiocleides* (IV/III)

I myself learned to cook so beautifully in Sicily that I sometimes make the dinner-guests gnaw on the casserole-dishes, they like the food so much.

G9. Anaxippus fr. 6, from *The Citharode* (IV/III)

Bring me a soup-ladle! And fetch twelve skewers, a meat-hook, a mortar, a small cheese-grater, an axe-handle, three bowls, a flaying-knife, and four cleavers! Fetch the little cauldron, the one from the spice-market, first, you bastard! Are you running behind again? And the contest-axe!

G10. Antiphanes fr. 221, from *Philotis* (IV)

(A.) So then, as for the *glaukidion*, I'm ordering you to stew it in brine, like other times. (B.) What about the little sea-bass? (A.) Roast it whole. (B.) The thresher shark? (A.) Stew it in a sauce. (B.) The eel? (A.) Salt, marjoram, and water. (B.) The conger eel? (A.) The same. (B.) The ray? (A.) Green herbs. (B.) There's a tuna steak. (A.) Roast it. (B.) The kid-meat? (A.) Roasted. (B.) The other meat? (A.) The opposite. (B.) The spleen? (A.) Let's have it stuffed. (B.) The jejunum? (A.) This guy's going to be the death of me!

G11. Philemo fr. 82, from *The Soldier* (IV/III)

What a desire came over me to come and tell earth and sky how I prepared the food! By Athena, it's nice to be successful at everything! I've served the fish just as tender as he was when I got him, not dosed with cheese or buried in herbs. But just as he was when he was alive, that's how he was roasted; that's how soft and gentle a fire I furnished the fish when I roasted him. And I won't be believed . . . (a line or more is missing) . . . It was just like when a bird snatches something too big to swallow at a gulp. It runs around in a circle trying to hold onto it and does its best to swallow it down, and the other birds chase it. It was the same thing. The first of them to understand the pleasure the casserole-dish offered jumped up and began to run away in a circle, holding it; and the others were hot on his heels. I had occasion to raise a cry of joy; because some of them snatched something, some got nothing, others got it all. But I was given muck-eating river-fish! If I'd got a parrot wrasse just now, or an Attic *glaukiskos*, O Zeus the Saviour, or an Argive boar-fish, or a conger eel, which Poseidon takes to heaven for the gods, from beloved Sicyon, those who ate it would all have become gods. I've invented immortality; whenever people who are now dead get just a whiff, I bring them back to life.

G12. Archedicus fr. 2, from *The Treasure* (IV/III)

First of all, while the fish is lying there uncooked, the guests appear. 'Pour water over my hands!' 'Take the fish and get out of here!' I put the casserole-dish on the fire and sprinkled the coals thoroughly with oil, and produce a flame. While the vegetables and pungent side-dishes are keeping my employer happy, I deliver the fish stewed with the juices still in it, along with a perfect brine sauce, which every free man could dip his food into. At the cost of a cup of oil I've saved myself perhaps fifty dinner parties.

G13. Eubulus fr. 63, from *Spartans or Leda* (IV)

And in addition to these items, you'll have a tuna steak, chunks of pork, and kid-meat sausages and boar's liver and rams' testicles and ox-meat wieners and sheeps' heads and kid's jejunum and hare's stomach and wurst and franks and a lung and bangers.

G14. Eubulus fr. 72, from *Oedipus* (IV)

The first man to discover dining on someone else's food was well disposed to average people, it seems. But if anyone invites a friend or a foreigner to dinner and then assesses him part of the cost, let him go into exile and remove nothing from his house!

G15. Alexis fr. 259, from *The Exile* (IV/III)

Chaerephon's always coming up with some new trick and getting his dinners without contributing any money. The minute the sun comes up, he goes and stands in the place where the cooks rent their pots and pans. If he sees something being rented for a feast, he asks the cook who the host is; and if he finds the door open, he's the first one in.

G16. Alexis fr. 263, from an unidentified play (IV/III)

No one noticed that I was where he wanted the business to take place. Water was poured over my hands. A slave came carrying the table, on which lay not just cheese or different types of olives or side-dishes supplying us with more steam and bullshit than anything else. Instead, a casserole-dish was set beside us that exuded the sumptuous smell of the Seasons and represented the circle of the whole sky. Everything good that's up there was in it: fish and kids; and a scorpion-fish ran between them; and hard-boiled eggs cut in half suggested the stars. We set our hands to work. The other fellow was busy talking to me and nodding his head; so the whole enterprise devolved to me. To sum up, I didn't stop digging at the dish until I'd made it look like a sieve.

G17. Euphanes fr. 1, from *Muses* (IV)

When Phoenicides saw a boiling hot casserole-dish full of Nereus' children among the crowd of young men, he restrained his hands, although they were stirred with passion. 'Who claims he is terrifying when it comes to eating from a common pot? Who (claims he is) terrifying when it comes to snatching hot food from the midst? Where is Corydos, Phyromachus, or mighty Neilus? Let him confront us—and I wouldn't be surprised if he gets nothing!'

G18. Alexis fr. 15, from *The Man Who Had a Cataract* (IV/III)

(A.) Unless [corrupt] every item individually, you wouldn't get a penny out of me. (B.) Fair enough. (A.) Bring me an abacus and some counting pebbles! Go ahead! (B.) There's raw saltfish for five bronze-pieces. (A.) Next item! (B.) Mussels for seven bronze pieces. (A.) No sacrilege so far. Next item! (B.) An obol for the sea-urchins. (A.) You're still clean. (B.) Wasn't what came after that the cabbage you kept shouting for? (A.) Yeah—it was good. (B.) I paid two obols for it. (A.) Then why did we shout for it? (B.) The cube saltfish cost three obols. (A.) Didn't he charge anything for [corrupt]? (B.) My dear sir, you don't know how matters are in the marketplace; the crickets have consumed the vegetables. (A.) Is that why you charged double for the saltfish? (B.) That's the saltfish-dealer; go ask him about it. Conger eel for ten obols. (A.) That's not much. Next item! (B.) I purchased the roast fish for a drachma. (A.) Damn! It dropped like a fever, then [corrupt]. (B.) Add on the wine I bought when you were drunk: three measures, at ten obols per measure.

H1. Plato Comicus fr. 71, from *Spartans or Poets* (V/IV)

(A.) Have the men finished dinner yet? (B.) Almost all of them. (A.) Good work! Why don't you run and bring the tables out? I'm coming to pour the washing-water. (B.) And I'm coming to sweep up. (A.) Then, after I pour the libations, I'll bring them the *cottabus*-equipment. The slave-girl should already have had her pipes ready at hand and be practising her playing. I'm going now to pour Egyptian perfume for them, and then the type scented with iris root. After that I'll bring each guest a garland and give it to him. Someone should mix a fresh bowl of wine. (B.) It's been mixed, in fact. (A.) After you put the frankincense on the (brazier) [corrupt] . . . (a number of lines are missing) . . . The libation's already taken place, and they're well into their drinking; a traditional song's been sung, and the *cottabus*-equipment has been removed from the room. A little girl holding pipes is playing a Carian song for the guests; I saw another one holding a lyre, and then she began to sing an Ionian song along with it.

H2. Nicostratus Comicus fr. 27, from *Falsely Tattooed* (IV)

And you get the second table ready! Put all kinds of dainties on it, and get perfume, garlands, incense, and a pipe-girl!

H3. Clearchus Comicus fr. 4, from *Pandrosus* (IV)

(A.) Take some water over your hands. (B.) No, no; it's fine. (A.) Take it, my good sir; there's no harm done. Slave-girl! Put some nuts and dainties on the table!

H4. Ephippus fr. 8, from *Ephebes* (IV)

Wheat-pudding came in after this, and Egyptian perfume; someone opened a transport-jar of Phoenician wine; wafer-bread came, dainties, a honey-cake, a milk-cake, a massive supply of eggs. We were nibbling on all these items. So we were vigorously chewing the food we had; for we were in fact also feeding some fellow-chewers.

H5. Diphilus fr. 70, from *Sappho* (IV/III)

Archilochus, take this after-washing cup full of Zeus the Saviour, the Good Divinity!

H6. Antiphanes fr. 172. 1–4, from *Women Who Looked Like One Another* or *Men Who Looked Like One Another* (IV)

They dined this way—I want to give a summary account of what happened in the meantime—and a Thericleian cup dedicated to Zeus the Saviour came, full of the luxurious, nobly born drop from Lesbos, and foaming. Each man took it in his right hand.

H7. Philyllius fr. 23, from an unidentified play (V/IV)

I'll furnish Lesbian, mellow Chian, Thasian, Bibline, and Mendaean, so no one gets a hangover.

H8. Hermippus fr. *77, perhaps from *Porters* (late 430s/early 420s BC)

† Mendaean they piss even † the gods themselves in their soft bedclothes. As for Magnesia's pleasant gift and Thasian, over which drifts a scent of apples, I rank this far and away the best of all wines except faultless, painless Chian. But there is one particular wine, which they refer to as 'mellow'; when casks of it are tapped, out of its mouth comes the divine scent of violets, of roses, of hyacinth. It fills the whole high-roofed house, a mix of ambrosia and nectar. *This* is what nectar is; *this* is what I need to give my friends to drink at a large meal—whereas my enemies can have Peparethan!

H9. Alexis fr. 9, from *Aesop* (IV/III)

(A.) This is something ingenious you have in Athens, Solon, and cleverly conceived. (Solon) What specifically? (A.) You don't drink unmixed wine at your parties. (Solon) Yes—because it's not easy to do so; they sell it in the wagons already mixed, not to make a profit, but looking out for the buyers, so they have healthy heads after they drink all night. This, you see, is the Greek style of drinking: to use cups of a modest size, and have a bit of banter and pleasant conversation with one another. The other style amounts to bathing, not drinking—that is, drinking from a wine-cooling vessel or buckets. (A.) Actually, it amounts to death!

H10. Pherecrates fr. 76, from *Corianno* (V)

(A.) It's undrinkable, Glyce. (Glyce) Did she pour something watery into your cup? (A.) Actually, it's *entirely* water. (Glyce) What did you do? What mixture did you pour in her cup, you nasty creature? (B.) Two parts water, Mummy— (Glyce) And how much wine? (B.) Four parts. (Glyce) Damn you to hell! You ought to be pouring wine for frogs!

H11. Anaxandrides fr. 1, from *Rustics* (IV)

(A.) What style are you prepared to drink in now? Tell me! (B.) What style are we prepared to drink in? Whatever style you'd like. (A.) I suppose, father, that you want us to proceed counterclockwise and speak in honour of the man who's drinking? (B.) Proceed counterclockwise and speak? Apollo! Like over a corpse?

H12. Alexis fr. 21, from *The Man Who Was Mutilated* (IV/III)

For Chaireas wasn't a symposiarch but a public executioner, proposing twenty cups as toasts.

H13. Antiphanes fr. 57, from *The Birth of Aphrodite* (IV)

(A.) I'm talking about *this*, don't you understand? The 'lampstand' is the *cottabus*-equipment. Pay attention! Eggs . . . five as a prize. (B.) For what? This is ridiculous. How are you going to play *cottabus*? (A.) I'll teach you. To the extent that someone throws his cottabus onto the disk and makes it fall— (B.) The disk? What disk? (A.) This little thing set on top. (B.) Are you talking about the little platter? (A.) That's the disk;—this fellow wins. (B.) How's anyone going to know this? (A.) If he just touches it, it'll fall onto the *manês*, and there'll be an enormous clatter. (B.) By the gods—does the *cottabus* also have a Manes to serve it? . . . (one or more lines are missing from the text) . . . Take the cup and show me how. (A.) You need to curl your fingers like a crab's claws, as if you were playing the pipes; pour in a little wine, not too much; and then let it go! (B.) How? (A.) Look here! Like this. (B.) Poseidon! How remarkably high it went! (A.) You can do the same thing. (B.) I wouldn't reach there if I was using a sling. (A.) Alright—time to practise!

H14. Plato Comicus fr. 46, from *Zeus Abused* (V/IV)

(A.) . . . to play *cottabus*, until I get dinner ready for the two of you inside. (Heracles) I'm quite willing; I'm sure to win. (A.) But you have to play in a mortar. (Heracles) Bring the mortar! Bring water! Set cups beside us! Let's play for kisses. (A.) I'm not letting you play in such an unrefined way. As the *cottabus*-prizes for the two of you I'm setting these platform shoes here that she's wearing, and also your cup. (Heracles) Damn! This contest that's coming up is bigger than the one at the Isthmus!

H15. Antiphanes fr. 85, from *Men Who Were Twice as Big* (IV)

(A.) What'll be in it, then, for the gods? (B.) Nothing, unless someone mixes some wine. (A.) Hold on. Take hold of the cup; and then don't recite one of these old-fashioned pieces, the Telamon or the Paean or the Harmodius.

H16. Aristophanes fr. 444, from *Storks* (390s BC?)

One fellow was singing the story of Admetus while holding a laurel bough; but the other was trying to force him to sing the Harmodius song.

H17. Philemo fr. 45, from *The Seducer* (IV/III)

(A.) There should have been a pipe-girl there, Parmenon, or a *nablas*. (Parmenon) What's a *nablas*? (A.) You don't know, you lunatic? (Parmenon) No, by Zeus, I don't. (A.) What do you mean? You're not familiar with a *nablas*? In that case, you don't know about anything good. Are you also unacquainted with *sambukê*-girls?

H18. Eubulus fr. *93, probably from *Semele or Dionysus* (IV)

For I mix up only three bowls of wine for sensible people. One is dedicated to good health, and they drink it first. The second is dedicated to love and pleasure, the third to sleep; wise guests finish it up and go home. The fourth bowl no longer belongs to me but to abuse. The fifth belongs to shouting; the sixth to wandering drunk through the streets; the seventh to black eyes; the eighth to the bailiff; the ninth to an ugly black humour; and the tenth to madness extreme enough to make people throw stones . . . (a line or more is missing) . . . Because a great deal of wine poured into one little jar easily knocks drunks' legs out from under them.

H19. Alexis fr. 160, from *Odysseus Weaving* (IV/III)

(A.) For extended socializing and many parties on a daily basis tend to produce mockery; and mockery causes far more grief than pleasure. Because that's how verbal abuse begins; and as soon as you say something, you immediately hear it back. Next comes name-calling; and then you see people punching each other and acting like drunken boors. (B.) Yes; these things naturally happen this way. What need was there for a seer?

H20. Pherecrates fr. 162, from *Cheiron* (V)

If you invite a friend to a large meal, don't be upset when you see him there; for a bad man behaves like this. But enjoy yourself, entirely at your ease, and make him happy . . . (a line or more is missing) . . . If one of us invites someone to dinner when he's making a sacrifice, we're upset if the fellow comes, and we give him dirty looks while he's there, and want him to leave as soon as possible. Then he somehow recognizes this and puts on his shoes; but then one of the other guests says 'Are you leaving already? Why don't you drink a bit? Take off his shoes!' And the man who's making the sacrifice gets upset at the one who's detaining the other, and immediately quotes the elegiac lines: 'And neither hold back anyone who is unwilling to remain with us, nor wake the man who is asleep, Simonides.' Don't we say things like this over our wine, when we have a friend to dinner?

I1. [Susarion] fr. 1, an ancient forgery (date uncertain)

Listen people! Susarion son of Philinus, a Tripodiscan from Megara, says the following: Women are trouble. But all the same, demesmen, one can't have a household without trouble. For both marrying and not marrying are trouble.

I2. Eubulus fr. 115, from *Chrysilla* (IV)

Damn the bastard, whoever he was, who was the second man to marry. I won't say anything bad about the first one; because he had no experience, I think, of this trouble. But the second fellow had heard what sort of trouble a woman is . . . (one or more verses are missing) . . . Oh much-honoured Zeus! Then am I ever going to say anything bad about women? By Zeus, may I die if I do; they're the best possessions there are. If Medea was a bad woman, Penelope was something great. Someone will say Clytaemestra was bad; I counter her with the good Alcestis. Perhaps someone will speak badly of Phaedra; but, by Zeus, there's the good— Who was there? Who? Alas, miserable me—I quickly ran out of good women, whereas I still have many bad ones to mention.

I3. Menander fr. 236, from *The Misogynist* (IV/III)

(Simylus) I'm not feeling good about the business. (B.) Yes—because you've got it the wrong way around. You see the difficulties in it and the things that are going to cause you grief, but you're not looking at the positive aspects. You couldn't find a single good thing, Simylus, that doesn't also have some bad attached to it. An expensive wife is annoying, and she doesn't let her husband live the way he wants. But here's one good thing that comes from her: children. And when her spouse gets sick, she takes care of him; when he has bad luck, she stays by his side; and when he dies, she buries him and wraps him properly. Consider these things, whenever some day-to-day matter makes you unhappy; this way you'll put up with the whole business. But if you constantly focus on what's making you unhappy, and don't balance it against the anticipated benefits, you'll always be miserable.

I4. Menander fr. 804, from an unidentified play (IV/III)

This is how we all ought to get married, by Zeus the Saviour, so that we come out ahead. We shouldn't enquire into things that are completely useless—who the grandfather of the woman one's marrying was, and who her grandmother was—but not enquire or look into the character of the bride with whom one's going to live. And we shouldn't take the dowry to a money-changer's table, so that a tester can determine if the silver's any good—money that won't remain inside the house for five months—but make no test of the woman who's going to be constantly sitting inside the house for her entire life, and get at random someone thoughtless, hot-tempered, difficult, or perhaps talkative. I'll parade my own daughter around the whole city. You who want to marry her, talk to her! See in advance what size trouble you're going to get; for a woman's necessarily an evil thing, and the man's lucky who gets the least substantial evil.

I5. Menander fr. 815, from an unidentified play (IV/III)

You're overstepping the married woman's boundaries, wife, I mean the courtyard door; for the courtyard door's considered the outer limit of the house for a free woman. Chasing someone and running out into the street still barking at him—that's what a dog does, Rhode!

I6. Plato Comicus fr. 188, from *Phaon* (391 BC)

Alright, ladies. You know I've been praying for a long time for your foolishness to turn into wine; for your mind doesn't appear to me to be in the wineshop, as the saying goes. If you want to see Phaon, you have to make numerous preliminary sacrifices of the following sort first: first of all, a preliminary offering is made to me, the Rearer of Children, consisting of an uncastrated cake, a pregnant wheat-paste cake, sixteen perfect thrushes in honey-sauce, and twelve moon-shaped pieces of hare-meat. As for the rest now † these thing very cheap †. Pay attention! Three half-measures of hyacinth bulbs for Orthannês, and a little platter of myrtle berries plucked by hand for Conisalus and his two attendants; because the deities dislike the smell of lamps. † four [corrupt] † for the Hounds and the Huntsmen; a drachma for Lordôn; three obols for Cybdasus; a hide and sacrificial barley-cakes for the hero Celês. This is what you have to spend. If you were to bring these items, you'd get in. Otherwise, you can long in vain to be fucked.

I7. Alexis fr. 103, from *Isostasion* (IV/III)

Everything else, first of all, is secondary to them in comparison with making a profit and plundering the people close to them, and they stitch together plots against everyone. And whenever they get rich, they take new courtesans, novices at the craft, into their houses. They immediately reshape them, so they don't act or look the same any longer. A girl happens to be short; cork's attached to the soles of her shoes. She's tall; she wears a thin-soled shoe and puts her head down on her shoulder when she goes outside; this reduces her height. She's got no arse; her mistress discreetly puts a pad on her, so that people who see her comment loudly on what a fine rear end she has. She's fat; they have some of the chest-pieces that belong to the comic actors, and by attaching these at a right angle, they use them like poles to separate her clothing from her belly. A girl has blond eyebrows; they draw them in with soot. It happens that her skin's dark; her mistress covers her with white lead. A girl's skin is too white; she rubs rouge on herself. She has an attractive feature; it's put on display naked. She has nice teeth; she has to laugh, like it or not, so that everyone who's there can see what a lovely mouth she has. And if she doesn't like laughing, she'll remain inside all day with a thin piece of myrtle wood, like what the butchers always have when they sell goats' heads, stuck upright between her lips. So eventually she grins, like it or not.

I8. Xenarchus fr. 4, from *The Pentathlete* (IV)

The young men are behaving terribly, terribly, unbearably, in our city. For (they live in a place) where there are very good-looking girls in the brothels, whom you can see basking in the sun with their breasts bare, half-dressed and lined up one after another in a column. A man can select whichever one he likes—thin, fat, round, tall, withered up, young, old, middle-aged, ancient—without setting up a ladder and entering the house secretly, or coming in through a peep-hole beneath the roof, or being carried in craftily in a heap of bran. For they're the aggressors and they drag customers in, calling the old men 'daddykins' and the younger ones 'sweet brother'. And you can (have sex with) any of them with no fear and cheaply, during the day, in the evening, any way you want. Whereas the women you can't see, and can't see clearly when you do see them, but always trembling and frightened [fearful, having your life in your hand] . . . (one or more lines are missing) . . . How in the world, Cypris, mistress of the sea, can they fuck them, when they recall Draco's laws as they're moving in time with their partners?

I9. Timocles fr. 24, from *Men from Marathon* (IV)

What an enormous difference between spending the night with a free girl and with a prostitute! Damn! The firmness of her flesh! Her colour and breath! Ye gods! The fact that everything's not too ready for you, and you have to struggle a little, and get slapped and punched by her soft hands. That's nice, by Zeus the greatest!

I10. Epicrates fr. 8, from *The Chorus* (IV)

The damned go-between took me in completely, swearing 'By the Maid, by Artemis, by Pherrephatta' that the girl was 'a heifer, a virgin, an unbroken filly'. In fact she was an utter mouse-nest.

I11. Phoenicides fr. 4, from an unidentified play (III)

By Aphrodite, I'd rather not put up with working as a courtesan any longer, Pythia; to hell with it! Don't talk to me about it. I failed; it's not for me; I want to put an end to it. As soon as I took up the trade, I had a lover who was a soldier. He was constantly talking about his battles and showing off his scars as he talked. But he didn't produce any income. He claimed he was getting a grant of some sort from the king, and he was always talking about it. And because of this grant I'm describing, the bastard was granted me as a gift for a year. I got rid of him and got someone else, a doctor. He brought quite a few people into the house and performed surgery or cauterized them. He was a beggar and an executioner, and he seemed worse than the other one to me; the first told a tall tale, whereas the second produced corpses. Fate linked me with a third lover, a philosopher, who had a beard, an inexpensive robe, and an argument to make. I got into obvious trouble; indeed, I fell right into it. Because he used to give me nothing [corrupt] he said that money's no good. 'Alright, it's bad—so give it to me, throw it to me!' He didn't listen.

I12. Epicrates fr. 3, from *Antilais* (IV)

Lais herself's a lazy drunk, who's intent only on eating and drinking every day. I think the same thing's happened to her as happens to the eagles. When they're young, they eat sheep and goats and hares they catch in the mountains, snatching them up into the air because they're so strong. But when they eventually grow old, then they perch on top of the temples, terribly hungry; and then this is regarded as a marvel. Lais as well would be properly considered a marvel now; because when she was a young nestling, she was driven wild by the largest coins, and you would have got an audience with Pharnabazus sooner than with her. But since she's now running the long-distance race in years and is losing her figure, seeing her's easier than spitting. She goes out everywhere to drink and accepts any coin of any size; and she has sex with anyone of any age. She's grown so tame, my dear friends, that she now takes money from a man's hand.

J1. Eupolis fr. 327, from an unidentified play (V)

where the books are sold . . . (a line or more is missing) . . . I went around to the garlic market, the onion market, and the frankincense market, straight toward the spice market, and around the cheap-goods market.

J2. Nicophon fr. 10, from *Men Who Live from Hand to Mouth* (V/IV)

small-fry-sellers,   charcoal-sellers,   dried-fig-sellers,   leather-robe-sellers, barley-groat-sellers, spoon-sellers, book-sellers, sieve-sellers, oil-and-honey-cake-sellers, seed-sellers.

J3. Nicophon fr. 6, from *Men Who Live from Hand to Mouth* (V/IV)

I have loaves of bread, barley-cake, wheat gruel, barley-groats, barley loaves, spit-bread, honey-cake, pour-cakes, barley gruel, unbaked cakes, another type of barley-cake, fried cakes.

J4. Menander fr. 150, from *The Ephesian* (IV/III)

Now I think, by the gods, that I see myself in the 'circles', naked, running in a circle, and being sold.

J5. Aristophanes fr. 680, from an unidentified play (V/IV)

He got a basket and is collecting dung.

J6. Antiphanes fr. 123, from *The Man from Mt Cnoethideus or Potbelly* (IV)

They're making odd announcements in the fishmarket, where someone just now was calling out loudly, claiming to have sprats sweeter than honey. If that's the case, nothing's stopping the honey-vendors for their part from saying or shouting that they're selling honey more rotten than sprats.

J7. Amphis fr. 30, from *The Vagabond Acrobat* (IV)

It's a million times easier to go to the generals and be thought to deserve an audience and get an answer to your questions than when you go to the damned fishmongers in the marketplace. As for them, if someone picks up one of the fish lying there and asks about it, he first stares silently at the ground, like Telephus—and rightly so; for they're all murderers, to put it simply—and beats an octopus, as if he wasn't paying any attention and hadn't heard. The other fellow gets angry . . . and then, without pronouncing his words completely, but taking off a syllable, '(Th)at'd be (f)our (ob)ols'. 'The spet?' '(Ei)ght (ob)ols.' Anyone who buys fish has to listen to this sort of thing.

J8. Alexis fr. 78, from *The Heiress* (IV/III)

If a pauper buys lots of fish, and has plenty of money for this but not enough for other things, this fellow's stripping everyone who crosses his path at night of their robes. So whenever someone has his clothes taken, let him keep watch in the fishmarket as soon as the sun's up; and let him arrest the first poor young man he sees buying eels from Micion, and take him off to jail.

J9. Diphilus fr. 87, from an unidentified play (IV/III)

There's no occupation more awful than being a pimp. I'm willing to walk the streets selling roses, radishes, lupine-beans, olive pomace, absolutely anything rather than keep whores.

J10. Eubulus fr. 80, from *Pamphilus* (IV)

And *I*—for a big new wineshop happened in fact to be directly opposite the house—I kept an eye out there for the girl's nurse; and I told the bartender to mix me a pitcher of wine that cost an obol, and to set the biggest drinking-cup he had beside me ... (a line or more is missing) ... 'The cup's been empty for a long time now! How dry it is!' ... (a line or more is missing) ... As soon as she took hold of a remarkably big [corrupt], really big, she's made it disappear; and she immediately drained the drinking-cup.

J11. Nicostratus Comicus fr. 22, from *Countrymen* (IV)

For no matter whether the neighbourhood bartender sells someone wine, a torch, or vinegar, the bastard gives him water and sends him away.

J12. Damoxenus fr. 3, from an unidentified play (III)

One particular young man was playing ball, perhaps 17 years old and from Cos—the island evidently produces gods! Whenever he cast a glance at us sitting there, as he was receiving the ball or passing it to someone else, we all immediately starting shouting. How graceful he looked, and how he handled and held himself, whatever he said or did! He's as beautiful as they come, gentlemen! I've never heard or seen anything so lovely before. I would've suffered an even greater injury, if I'd stayed longer; as it is, I'm not entirely in my right mind.

J13. Anaxandrides fr. 35, from *Odysseus* (IV)

For I'm well aware you always mock one another. If someone's handsome, you call him 'Sacred Marriage'; if he's a midget, you call him 'Drop'. Someone emerges from his house glistening . . . ; this fellow's 'Pussy'. Democles walks around covered with oil; he's been dubbed 'Meat-broth'. Someone likes to be dry or dirty; he's proclaimed 'Dust-cloud'. A flatterer follows behind a man; he's nicknamed 'Dinghy'. Someone generally goes around having had no dinner; he's 'Fasting Mullet'. If someone stares at handsome boys, he's 'The New Theatre-maker'; if he steals a shepherd's lamb as a joke, he's called 'Atreus'; if it's a ram, he's 'Phrixus'; if it's a sheepskin, he's 'Jason'.

J14. Phrynichus Comicus fr. 3, from *Epialtes* or *Ephialtes* (V)

The most difficult job we have today is to protect ourselves from them. They have a kind of sting in their fingers, a hostile bloom of youth. They always speak pleasantly to everyone as they circulate through the marketplace; but when they're in their seats, they rip long scratches there into the people they speak to pleasantly, and they all put their heads together and laugh.

J15. Plato Comicus fr. 168, from *The Alliance* (V/IV)

For they compared them to these children who regularly draw a line in the street, divide into two groups, and stand, some of them on one side of the line, the rest on the other. And one stands between the two groups and drops a potsherd for them; if the light side lands facing up, one group has to run away quickly, and the others have to chase them.

J16. Strattis fr. 48, from *Phoenician Women* (V/IV)

if the sun obeys children when they say 'Come out, dear sun!'

J17. Plato Comicus fr. 98, from *The Little Child* (V/IV)

Bring me this! Get the basket over here and show it to me! Where's the knife in it?

J18. Adespota comica fr. *142 (undated)

Who's such a fool and so utterly credulous that he expects that, when thigh-bones stripped of flesh and a gall bladder—things even *hungry* dogs don't regard as edible—are burning, the gods are all happy and accept this as a portion of honour?

J19. Eupolis fr. 88, from *Dyers* (410s BC?)

you who play the drum well, produce notes on the strings of exotic harps, wiggle your arse, and stretch your legs high in the air.

J20. Pherecrates fr. 43, from *The Slave Teacher* (V)

(A.) I had become a *kitharos*-fish and was doing my shopping like that. (B.) The *kitharos* is a good omen and is clearly connected with Apollo. (A.) What disturbs me, my good woman, is that they say 'There's some trouble in a *kitharos*'.

J21. Philemo fr. 101, from an unidentified play (IV/III)

Whenever I see someone keeping an eye out for who sneezed or who said something, or watching to see who's approaching, I sell the fellow immediately in the marketplace. Each of us walks, speaks, and sneezes for himself, not for the rest of the city. However things happen, that's how they are.

J22. Menander fr. 106, from *The Superstitious Man* (IV/III)

(A.) I hope something good happens to me, much-honoured gods! As I was putting on my shoes, I broke the strap on the right one. (B.) As you might expect, you babbler—because it was rotten! You're a cheapskate who doesn't want to buy new shoes.

Greek Index

General Index

Academy 239, 240, 254
Acarnan 173
Acestor 115
Achilleus 171
Admetus 315
Adonis and Adonia 177
Adrastus 174; *see also* Seven Against Thebes
Aêr 141
Aeschylus 27, 46, 175–6, 205, 237; *Eu.* 175; *Supp.* 351: 346
Aesop 307
Agathon 182, 185
Agora, places individual commodities sold in 358; *see also* occupations
Agrius 172
Agyrrhius 220
Ajax 314
Alcibiades 213, 214, 219, 374
Alcimus (of Sicily) 11 n. 24; *FGrHist* 560 F 6: 9–10
Alcman 181
Alcmeon 171, 173, 174; *see also* Seven Against Thebes
Alexander the Great 222–3
Alexis 11 n. 24, 25, 388, 402–3, 412
Amaltheia 131
ambassadors 255
Amipsias 22, 382, 403; *Connus* 17, 236
Ammonius 28
Amphiaraus 171; *see also* Seven Against Thebes
Amphis 403
Amphoterus 173
Ananias fr. 5. 1: 46
Anaxagoras 237
Anaxandrides 25, 386, 388, 403–4
Anaxilas 404
Anaxilaus, tyrant of Rhegium 8
Anaxippus 25, 404
Andromachus 219; *see also* Herms, affair of
Anthesteria 159
Antiphanes 25, 388, 404–6
Antisthenes 248
Apatouria 94
Aphareus 386
aphrodisiacs, *see* food
Aphrodite 89, 139, 177, 311, 336; Pandemos 168; *see also* Bruzzone, Rachel

Apollo 87, 126, 172, 314, 375; temple at Delphi 251
Apollodorus of Athens 9, 11, 25, 28, 61, 64
Apollodorus of Gela 389
Araros 388, 406
Arcadia 162
Archedicus 406
Archestratus of Gela 11 n. 24, 46, 268; fr. 13. 4: 270; fr. 16. 3–4: 270
Archilochus 17, 303–4; fr. 109: 85
archons 18, 176–7
Argonauts, and Harpies 171; and Hypsipyle and the Lemnian women 93; and Idaia 171; and Jason 93, 138, 171, 371; and Phineus 171
Aristarchus of Samothrace 28
Aristides 'the Just' 205, 217
Aristogeiton 315
Aristomenes 21
Aristophanes 385, 386, 387, 388, 406, 411, 413; re-performance of plays 1, 21–2, 25, 26, 28, 29, 81, 111, 113; *Eq.* 526–36: 17
Aristophanes of Byzantium 23, 28, 134
Aristophon 407
Aristotle 6, 7, 27, 416; *Po.* 1447^{b}10–11: 11; 1448^{a}28–34: 2; 1448^{a}31–2: 67; 1448^{a}33–4: 12, 383; 1449^{a}4–5: 11–12 2; 1449^{a}10–11: 3; 1449^{a}11–12: 4; 1449^{a}38–^{b}5: 2; 1449^{b}2, 4–5: 2; 1449^{b}5–9: 2, 8, 10, 17, 24; 1451^{b}25–6: 173; *Rh.* 1394^{b}11–25: 10
Aristoxenus of Selinous 12 n. 29
Aristoxenus of Taras or Tarentum 11 n. 24
Artemis 172, 271; Orthia sanctuary 5, 6
Aspasia 87–8, 208
Atargatis 224
Athena 42, 54, 89–90, 225; control of aegis 54
Athenaeus of Naucratis 29
Athens 159, 168; autochthony of inhabitants 107; imports into 158; use of mercenaries 162; use of nicknames 369–71; use of slaves 162, 200; voting in assembly 220; women in Theatre 169
athletics, bathing and oiling 370; boxing 174; *palaestra* / wrestling school 367; *pankration* 174; wrestling 137, 317
Atreus 371